MEREDITH: THE CRITICAL HERITAGE

THE CRITICAL HERITAGE SERIES

GENERAL EDITOR: B. C. SOUTHAM, M.A., B.LITT. (OXON)
Formerly Department of English, Westfield College, University of London

For list of books in the series see back endpaper.

MEREDITH

THE CRITICAL HERITAGE

Edited by

IOAN WILLIAMS

Lecturer in English Literature
University of Warwick

BARNES & NOBLE, Inc.
NEW YORK
PUBLISHERS & BOOKSELLERS SINCE 1873

First published 1971
by Routledge & Kegan Paul Limited
Broadway House, 68–74 Carter Lane
London, EC4V 5EL

© *Ioan Williams, 1971*

First published in the United States, 1971
by Barnes & Noble, Inc.

ISBN 389 04106 8

Printed in Great Britain

General Editor's Preface

The reception given to a writer by his contemporaries and near-contemporaries is evidence of considerable value to the student of literature. On one side we learn a great deal about the state of criticism at large and in particular about the development of critical attitudes towards a single writer; at the same time, through private comments in letters, journals or marginalia, we gain an insight upon the tastes and literary thought of individual readers of the period. Evidence of this kind helps us to understand the writer's historical situation, the nature of his immediate reading-public, and his response to these pressures.

The separate volumes in the *Critical Heritage Series* present a record of this early criticism. Clearly, for many of the highly productive and lengthily reviewed nineteenth- and twentieth-century writers, there exists an enormous body of material; and in these cases the volume editors have made a selection of the most important views, significant for their intrinsic critical worth or for their representative quality—perhaps even registering incomprehension!

For earlier writers, notably pre-eighteenth century, the materials are much scarcer and the historical period has been extended, sometimes far beyond the writer's lifetime, in order to show the inception and growth of critical views which were initially slow to appear.

In each volume the documents are headed by an Introduction, discussing the material assembled and relating the early stages of the author's reception to what we have come to identify as the critical tradition. The volumes will make available much material which would otherwise be difficult of access and it is hoped that the modern reader will be thereby helped towards an informed understanding of the ways in which literature has been read and judged.

B. C. S.

Contents

MEREDITH

The Ordeal of Richard Feverel (1859)

MEREDITH

MEREDITH

The Ordeal of Richard Feverel (1859)

MEREDITH

The Ordeal of Richard Feverel (1859)

MEREDITH

The Ordeal of Richard Feverel (1859)

17 Unsigned review, *Leader*, 2 July 1859 — 61
18 Unsigned review, *Critic*, 2 July 1859 — 63
19 G. E. JEWSBURY, *Athenaeum*, 9 July 1859 — 67
20 Unsigned review, *Spectator*, 9 July 1859 — 69
21 Unsigned review, *Saturday Review*, 9 July 1859 — 71
22 Unsigned review, *Illustrated London News*, 13 August 1859 — 76
23 SAMUEL LUCAS, *The Times*, 14 October 1859 — 77
24 Unsigned review, *Westminster Review*, October 1859 — 84

Evan Harrington (1861)

25 Unsigned review, *Spectator*, 19 January 1861 — 86
26 Unsigned review, *Saturday Review*, 19 January 1861 — 87

Modern Love and Other Poems (1862)

27 R. H. HUTTON, *Spectator*, 24 May 1862 — 92
28 A. C. SWINBURNE, reply to Hutton, *Spectator*, 7 June 1862 — 97
29 J. W. MARSTON, *Athenaeum*, 31 May 1862 — 100
30 Unsigned review, *Saturday Review*, 24 October 1863 — 103

Sandra Belloni (1864)

31 RICHARD GARNETT, *Reader*, 23 April 1864 — 108
32 G. E. JEWSBURY, *Athenaeum*, 30 April 1864 — 111
33 MRS HARDMAN, *Saturday Review*, 28 May 1864 — 114
34 Unsigned review, *Westminster Review*, July 1864 — 119
35 Unsigned review, *Examiner*, 23 July 1864 — 121
36 JUSTIN M'CARTHY, an early appreciation, 1864 — 124

Rhoda Fleming (1865)

37 J. C. JEAFFRESON, *Athenaeum*, 14 October 1865 — 136
38 Unsigned review, *Saturday Review*, 14 October 1865 — 139
39 Unsigned review, *Westminster Review*, January 1866 — 144

Vittoria (1867)

40 Unsigned review, *Saturday Review*, 2 February 1867 — 147
41 G. E. JEWSBURY, *Athenaeum*, 23 February 1867 — 152

viii

The Adventures of Harry Richmond (1871)

Beauchamp's Career (1876)

The Egoist (1879)

Poems and Lyrics of the Joy of Earth (1883)

CONTENTS

The Empty Purse (1892)

Lord Ormont and His Aminta (1894)

The Amazing Marriage (1895)

Odes in Contribution to the Song of French History (1898)

Note on the Text and Acknowledgments

This collection contains reviews of most of Meredith's publications and a selection of articles and comments about his work which were made during his lifetime. The documents are presented in chronological order, except that the sequence is interrupted so as to keep reviews of each volume under one heading and to relate closely connected items (e.g. Nos. 27 and 28). Quotations from Meredith's works have been for the most part replaced by references: in the case of poems, to the lines concerned; in the case of novels, to the chapter. Where material relating to Meredith has been omitted the omission is indicated by a row of dots within square brackets. When a passage is reprinted from a longer article or book its origin is indicated in the title and/or the head-note. All documents are reprinted as they occur, except for minor alterations for standardization of titles. Errors of sense and significant errors of spelling have been retained. Footnotes followed by an asterisk belong to the original.

I am grateful to the management of the *New Statesman* and the *Spectator* for enabling me to identify some of the authors of articles in *Athenaeum* and *Spectator*. I should also like to thank Mr Harold Beaver and Mrs J. Rawson, of the University of Warwick, and Dr V. J. Daniel of St Hugh's College, Oxford, for their help with various points of information.

I should like to acknowledge the following permissions to reprint copyright material. Associated Book Publishers Ltd (W. L. Courtney, 'George Meredith's Novels' and A. Symons, 'A Note on George Meredith'); Clarendon Press, Oxford (*Letters of George Meredith*, ed. C. L. Cline, 1970); Field Fisher & Co. (George Moore, *Confessions of a Young Man*); Hodder & Stoughton Ltd (James Moffatt, 'Meredith in Perspective'); *New Statesman and Nation* (S. P. Sherman, 'Meredith's Historical Importance', A. Symons, review of *A Reading of Life*, O. Seaman, review of *Odes*); Sir Arthur Conan Doyle Estates (Sir Arthur Conan Doyle, 'Mr. Stevenson's Methods in Fiction').

Introduction

There are certain features of Meredith's work which made him a difficult author for his contemporaries: his dynamic conception of character; his metaphoric style; his rejection of convention; his oblique narrative methods; and his attempt to create a fictional structure which would permit the full development of his subject. Meredith's work is not only difficult, however; it is also liable to charges of affectation, obscurity, structural weakness, and a lack of proportion. It has always been hard for individual critics to distinguish between his successful experiments and his lapses from good taste; different critics have chosen the same passages as examples of both. Consequently, his reputation has been more than usually liable to fluctuate, and it cannot be said that there has ever been a clear general agreement about his permanent place in letters. Even now, so long after his experiments have ceased to shock, critics are often without the understanding of his aims and methods needed to distinguish between the superlatively good and the annoyingly bad. Meredith's work is a trial for the reader which has brought out the best in only a few and which has left the field of criticism—littered with examples of bitterness and exaggeration.

The history of Meredith's reception involves more than one dramatic change of public taste. From the publication of his first volume of *Poems* in 1851 to *The Ordeal of Richard Feverel* in 1859, Meredith enjoyed a fair and encouraging reception. After *Richard Feverel*, from 1860 to 1875, while he tried to reconcile his artistic purpose with the demands of the reading public, his work met with an inadequate and disheartening response. During these years, as the author of *Modern Love* (1862), *Sandra Belloni* (1864), *Rhoda Fleming* (1865), *Vittoria* (1867), and *Harry Richmond* (1870), Meredith steadily gained reputation among a younger generation of readers, but failed to make an impact on the public at large or to obtain from the critical Press the degree of respect and understanding to which he was entitled. By 1874 he had given up the attempt to reach a wide public and had retired behind a mask of indifference. Ironically, it was at this point that his popularity began. From 1875 to 1885 there was a dramatic improvement in his position.

New writers studied his work with an enthusiasm which was all the keener because they could accuse their predecessors of neglecting it. Young men, like W. E. Henley, R. L. Stevenson, James Thomson, Arthur Symons, Richard Le Gallienne, welcomed Meredith as the opponent of mid-Victorian attitudes and the apostle of modernism. They came to his novels with a sense of excitement and discovery and succeeded in imparting something of their feeling to a wider audience. Meredith could never have been a popular writer as Dickens was, or even as Thackeray and George Eliot were, but by 1885, with the publication of *Diana of the Crossways*, he had reached a public as wide as he could ever have expected. That year also saw the publication of the first volumes of his collected works and marks the beginning of another phase of his reputation. From 1885 to the end of the century his position was established as the leading English writer. His seventieth and eightieth birthdays (1898 and 1908) brought acknowledgments from all over the world. In his later years he became the subject of thousands of articles and books; he was offered several honorary degrees and granted the Order of Merit. When he died the once-neglected novelist was generally considered to have been the last of the giants, a great teacher, a writer of heroic merits and heroic defects, whose death marked the end of an epoch. His reputation stood at this point until the end of the First World War. Then people began to speak of his work as dated, his philosophy barren, his literary achievement minor. His late recognition and rise to fame meant that the inevitable reaction was delayed. The change in taste and sensibility which followed the First World War accentuated the natural decline in his popularity, and from this last phase of under-estimation he has not yet been recovered.

THE EARLY PHASE (1851–9)

Meredith's first volume of poems did not escape censure for shallowness, inequality, and lack of proportion, but reviewers were generous with their praise. The *Leader*'s reviewer found no depth of insight, but praised the elegance and charm of the poems (No. 1). William Rossetti discerned 'engaging human companionship and openness', marred by some disproportion (No. 4). Charles Kingsley condemned the same fault, but discovered health and sweetness (No. 5). *The Shaving of Shagpat* (1856) met with a similar reception. The *Spectator* critic raised a charge of cleverness against it, which was later to be used with devastating effect on the reading public.[1] George Eliot and G. H.

Lewes were more sympathetic. The former thought that interest lagged towards the end of the story but called it 'a work of genius, and of poetical genius' (No. 7). Lewes used the same phrase, called the language 'simple, picturesque, pregnant', and added in compliment that Meredith's name had now become known as 'the name of a man of genius—of one who can create' (No. 8). Naturally enough, the reaction to *Farina* (1857) was less favourable, because it lacked certain of the qualities which had made its predecessor popular. Writers in the *Spectator* (No. 12) and *Critic* (No. 14), thought it an improvement on *The Shaving of Shagpat*, the *Athenaeum* reviewer said that it was full of 'riotous and abundant fancy' (No. 16), but the *Saturday Review* foreshadowed more recent judgments in calling it relatively flat and dull (No. 13). Meredith himself described it as 'an original and entertaining book' (No. 15).

Up to 1859 Meredith was considered an intelligent and able writer who was steadily increasing his reputation. One or two critics even took him to task for misapplying his talents, warning him: 'The problems of our times, and the wants of the men around us, are such as to demand all our best energies.'[2] *The Ordeal of Richard Feverel* satisfied demands that the author of poems and fantasies should show his substantial qualities in a serious novel, set in the times around him (No. 8), and in doing so it put an end to his honeymoon with the critics. *Richard Feverel* transformed Meredith into a painfully original and earnest novelist whose work enforced the most serious consideration. The reaction of the critics was by no means entirely favourable, partly because as it was first published the novel contained evidence of confused purpose which successive revisions only partly removed. As it appeared in 1859 *Richard Feverel* deserved Samuel Lucas's description as 'extremely weak in the development of its main purpose' (No. 23). Early readers found it difficult to decide whether the author meant to attack all systems, to attack the particular system of Sir Austin, or merely to enforce a moral about the sowing of wild oats. The fully developed and original statement within the novel could not clearly emerge. Even so, the book was well received. The seduction scene and Meredith's boldness in treating delicate subjects earned him some hostile criticism and lost him the circulating-library sale which would have brought financial success, but taken as a whole the reviewers honestly tried and in large measure succeeded in giving the novel the consideration which it merited. No other novel by the same author was to receive so favourable a treatment for many years.

THE MIDDLE YEARS (1860-75)

The period between 1860 and 1875 was the most productive of Meredith's life, although he had to work as editor, publisher's reader, war correspondent, ghost writer, reviewer, and hack. Even in spite of his sustained efforts, he was often embarrassed for money, and had to abandon the publication of poetry and finance several of his novels himself. Yet he kept up an attempt to reconcile his higher interests with those of the reading public which had so enthusiastically responded to some of his contemporaries. Each of his novels between *Evan Harrington* and *Harry Richmond* was the result of a new attempt to achieve popularity. The wider public, however, was busy with Mrs Wood and Miss Braddon and was deaf to his appeal, while reviewers were sparing in their appreciation of an effort which should have put Meredith at the forefront of contemporary English letters.

In 1860 Meredith's situation was promising. As the author of *Richard Feverel*, with *Evan Harrington* appearing serially in *Once a Week* in opposition to Wilkie Collins's *Woman in White*, he had a good deal of public attention. *Evan Harrington*, however, was not very well received. Reviews were scarcer than for *Richard Feverel* and reviewers showed little sense of Meredith's distinctive aims and qualities. The *Spectator* critic approved the change in tone and subject-matter from *Richard Feverel* and found that the author's vein of humour was clearing as he grew older (No. 25). The *Saturday* reviewer praised the novel's freshness, said that the characterization of Louisa was excellent and approved the tone (No. 26). A short notice in the *Examiner* described the story as 'cleverly told in vigorous and pointed English'.[3] Unlike the other novels of this period, *Evan Harrington* went into a second edition within five years, but after *Richard Feverel* it was clearly an anticlimax.

Meredith's next volumes brought him once more into full public attention, but not with effects which were calculated to improve his general popularity. *Modern Love and Poems of the English Roadside* (1862) attracted vigorous comment. One of the most favourable reviews was contributed to the *Morning Post* by Commander Maxse, to whom the book was dedicated, but even Maxse censured the obscurity of Meredith's manner.[4] The *Saturday Review* compared Meredith with Browning and said that his main talent lay in the 'racy and vigorous style' of the 'Roadside' poems. To this critic the 'Ode to the Spirit of Earth in Autumn' was a 'ranting rhapsody', and he agreed with writers in the *Spectator* and *Athenaeum* in censuring the author for his choice of subject in 'Modern Love'—'a mistake so grave as utterly to disqualify the chooser from achieving any great and worthy result in art' (No. 30). Meredith spoke of this reviewer as having 'gently whipped' him. The *Spectator* review (No. 27) caused him pain which he remembered until the end of his life. Swinburne's famous reply to the *Spectator* (No. 28) took a stand against crude moralistic criticism of literature, but left untouched the real basis of defence against the charges of meretricious sensationalism which the *Spectator* critic urged. The final effect of the reviews on the public could not have been pleasant. Meredith's name was strongly associated with indecency and obscurity. And there was no other edition of 'Modern Love' until 1892.

Meredith's next publication, like *Evan Harrington*, was designed to procure him a degree of popular success, but even before it was published he became doubtful about its chances. *Sandra Belloni* was published at his own expense and does not seem to have brought him much return, though reviews were neither scarce nor hostile. In the *Saturday Review* Mrs Hardman expressed doubts about the novel's 'exact drift' and the benefit to be derived from 'profound analysis of the characters of young women' (No. 33). Richard Garnett, in the *Reader*, detected an excess of artifice (No. 31). G. E. Jewsbury thought that it would be an improvement if Meredith wrote more simply (No. 32). On the whole, however, critics were sympathetic and understood what he was trying to do. The *Examiner* gave a clear exposition of the subject (No. 35), and the *Westminster Review* even prophesied Meredith's future popularity, explaining the lack of contemporary appreciation by his 'subtlety of expression', the dramatic quality of his talent, and his insistence on the development of character, ending with an earnest recommendation of the novel as a serious study of modern society (No. 34).

Meredith thought that the failure of *Sandra Belloni* to make a popular appeal resulted from its lack of external action, its open ending, and its obtrusive didactic commentary. His next two novels, *Vittoria* and *Rhoda Fleming*, a 'Plain story', were planned to give excitement and more straightforward narrative interest. In both cases he was disappointed with the response of the critics and the public at large. Reviewers found *Rhoda Fleming* an unattractive novel, though they were not without appreciation of its seriousness of purpose. The *Saturday* reviewer showed an understanding of Meredith's art, pointing out his tendency to distance himself from the action and to use oblique methods of narration, and suggested that his chief defect was weakness of construction (No. 38). The *Morning Post*'s critic wrote with sympathy, though he thought that readers would find the story difficult to follow. The *Westminster Review* followed the *Spectator*'s example and accused Meredith of over-cleverness (No. 39), and in the *Athenaeum* J. C. Jeaffreson observed a 'factitious sprightliness and ponderous gaiety' (No. 37).

Though *Vittoria* had the advantage of an exotic background and a subject involving exciting external action, it made less impact on the public than its predecessors. G. E. Jewsbury spoke for many readers when she protested against its complexity: 'How are human beings with limited faculties to understand all the distracting threads of this unmerciful novel?' (No. 41). A writer in the *Saturday Review* (No. 40) discerned originality and conscientious labour, skilfully applied, but thought it was overstrained, weakly constructed, and lacking in 'due repose'. In a private letter Swinburne expressed the growing concern of more sympathetic readers who mistrusted the direction of Meredith's development:

How very noble is most of Meredith's *Vittoria*; but of late he has been falling or tripping rather here and there into his old trick of over-refining. Art must dispense with hair-splitting; and he can so well afford to leave it. . . . Nothing can be more truly and tragically great than the operatic scene or the 'Duel in the Pass'; indeed the whole figure of Angelo is (as the French say) 'epically' noble. Such a painter has no right to put us before or behind the scenes with riddles and contortions in place of clear narrative and large drawing.[5]

Vittoria, Meredith told Swinburne, passed 'to the limbo where the rest of my works repose', and 'the illustrious Hutton of the *Spectator* laughs insanely at my futile effort to produce an impression on his public.'[6] Before long he moved on to *The Adventures of Harry Richmond*, still thinking 'by drumming to make the public hear at last'.[7] By reflecting the adventures of Richmond Roy in his son's account of his own development he thought to reconcile the interests of the public with his own and make 'a spanking bid for popularity',[8] though he was aware of the danger he ran in developing the subject with subtlety. The novel certainly came closer than anything else he wrote to satisfying the demand for romance, excitement, adventure, and humour, but it fell as flat as its predecessors, sales were slow, and the critics unenthusiastic.

The best review of *Harry Richmond* appeared in the *Spectator*. The writer thought that the novel was below the first-rate, lacking 'movement, stream, current, narrative flow', outlined the author's faults of affectation, obscurity and weakness of construction, and criticized the characterization of Janet Ilchester. But the final effect of his review is one of appreciation for Meredith's high qualities (No. 44). In the *Athenaeum* A. J. Butler was moderate in his praise (No. 42). The *Westminster* reviewer was mildly approving (No. 45). The *Examiner* critic complained petulantly about what he considered the excessive praise that Meredith had been receiving, calling him a 'prophet to a few' (No. 43). To this reviewer Meredith's 'gospel' was that women's hearts are only toys to play with 'or coin to profit by' (No. 43). Mrs Oliphant, who was later to comment in similar vein about *The Egoist* (No. 64), found *Harry Richmond* an 'odd but very clever book' (No. 47).

Meredith's position during the period which ended in the middle 1870s was outlined by Justin M'Carthy in his *Reminiscences*:

> The truth is, that just then George Meredith was not known to the general public at all. He had a small circle of enthusiastic admirers scattered here and there among English readers—wherever you happened to go you were sure to meet some one of these, and when you did meet one of them, you met with a man or woman to whom the reality of George Meredith's genius was an obvious and a positive fact.[9]

M'Carthy claimed to be among the very first of these admirers who directed public attention to Meredith's work. In his article in the *Westminster Review*, July 1864 (No. 36), he offered an assessment of Meredith's qualities and defects. He condemned the ending of *Richard Feverel* and was cool towards *Sandra Belloni* as a whole because he could not sympathize with any of the characters; he also suggested that Meredith's compositions lacked the 'fusing heat' of emotion and that he was without the narrative skills of Victor Hugo or Wilkie Collins. But the character of Emilia, M'Carthy thought, proved that Meredith possessed the 'essential qualities of a great novelist'. His article was a landmark in the criticism of Meredith's work. Though he was aware of defects, M'Carthy had an enthusiastic appreciation which was not seen again for several years.

Meredith was never, as M'Carthy said, without any following at all, but the persistent lack of interest in his achievement and development as a writer shown by the critics as well as the public at large eventually made him withdraw into himself. Over the years between 1859 and

1875 his attitude to English readers and critics hardened into contempt. Criticism in England, he wrote to James Thomson, 'gets no farther than the half-surfeited boy in the tuck shop, he likes this bun, he hates that tart'.[10] As successive novels failed to attract a fitting response, he began to assume a cynical indifference and to comment bitterly on reviewers as 'Sunday parsons, the children of pay, slaves of the multitude, leaders of the blind'.[11] 'Have you ever met a Reviewer'? he asked Augustus Jessop. 'It is curious how small this thing that stings can be.'[12] Eventually he gave up the attempt to reconcile his artistic vision with public taste. Ironically, this happened just as his work began to meet with enthusiastic approval and public response.

AN APPROACH TO FAME (1875–85)

Beauchamp's Career (1876), Meredith informed a correspondent, was not likely to be popular. But the critical response to this novel was unprecedentedly enthusiastic and marked a turning-point in Meredith's own career. After 1876 his work received respectful attention. Increasingly he came to be regarded as the leading figure in English literature and an established master of prose. Through the later 1860s and early 1870s appreciation for his work had been growing among a younger generation, to whom he brought an exciting challenge. Sir W. Robertson Nicoll, born in the year when Meredith's first volume was published (1851), told the story of his own growing enthusiasm for the scarcely known author in *A Bookman's Letters* (1913). According to Nicoll, a story was current that five young men met and resolved that Meredith should be boomed: 'These were Grant Allen, and Saintsbury, and Minto, and Henley, and another unnamed. The result of the gathering was that Meredith *was* boomed.'[13] The story may be apocryphal, but similar incidents could well have happened, and the list of young men determined to praise Meredith could be lengthened indefinitely with names of writers and critics like William Sharp, R. L. Stevenson, James Thomson and George Gissing. The effects of their work were seen in the quickly spreading influence of Meredith's name. The way in which his reputation developed during this period is illustrated by Mrs Humphrey Ward's account of how she came to appreciate the novelist she was later to call the foremost among English writers:

Of his work and his genius I began to be aware, when *Beauchamp's Career*—a much truncated version—was coming out in the *Fortnightly* in 1874. I had heard him and his work discussed in the Lincoln circle, where both the Pattisons were quite alive to Meredith's quality; but I was at the time and for long afterwards, under the spell of French limpidity and clarity, and the Meredithean manner repelled me. About the same time, when I was no more than three or four and twenty, I remember a visit to Cambridge, when we spent a week-end at the Bull Inn, and were the guests by day of Frederick Myers and some of his Trinity and King's friends. Those two days of endless talk in beautiful College rooms with men like Frederick Myers, Edmund Gurney, Mr Gerald Balfour, Mr George Prothero, and others, left a deep mark on me. . . . And among the subjects which rose and fell in that warm electric atmosphere, was the emergence of a new and commanding genius in George Meredith. The place in literature which some of these brilliant men were already giving to *Richard Feverel*, which had been published some fifteen years earlier, struck me greatly; but if I was honest with myself, my enthusiasm was much more qualified than theirs. It was not until *Diana of the Crossways* came out . . . that the Meredithean power began to grip me. . . .[14]

With the appearance of *Beauchamp's Career* Meredith's reputation was assured; with *The Egoist* it was confirmed; and with *Diana of the Crossways* it spread beyond the circle of enthusiastic admirers to affect, if not the widest novel-reading public, the whole number of those who pretended to culture or education.

From W. C. Carr, writing in the *Saturday Review* (No. 53), *Beauchamp's Career* received one of the most thoughtful appreciations that could have been given to a contemporary novel. Carr identified Meredith's dual interest in the personal and social aspects of his subject and showed their relationship, pointing out the fitness of the novel's form and style. At the other extreme, Alexander Shand and Dr Littledale thought that Meredith would have done better to have continued in the manner of *Farina* (Nos. 50 and 51). Other writers, in the *Athenaeum* (No. 48), *Examiner* (No. 49), and *Canadian Monthly* (No. 52), considered Meredith's lack of popularity, attributing it to his difficulty, circuitous style, and oblique narrative methods. In the *Secularist* James Thomson was enthusiastic (No. 54). Starting from a comparison between Meredith and Browning in respect of their relationship with the public, he described the characteristics of Meredith's fiction with overwhelming enthusiasm. His was a less measured praise than the reader of Meredith was used to hear.

The appearance of *The Egoist* (1879) was the occasion for an equally enthusiastic review, but in the meantime Thomson had used the pages of *Cope's Tobacco Plant* to introduce *Richard Feverel* to readers who were still unaware of its existence. Here Thomson again compared Meredith and Browning:

> He may be termed, accurately enough for a brief indication, the ROBERT BROWNING of our novelists; and his day is bound to come as Browning's at length has come. The flaccid and feeble folk, who want literature and art that can be inhaled as idly as the perfume of a flower, must naturally shrink from two such earnestly strenuous spirits, swifter than eagles, stronger than lions. . . . But men who have lived and observed and pondered, who love intellect and genius and genuine passion, who have eyes and ears ever open to the mysterious miracles of nature and art . . . will find a royal treasure house of delight and instruction and suggestion in the works of George Meredith.[15]

In his review of *The Egoist* (No. 62), Thomson surveys contemporary criticism of Meredith's work. In his diary, referring to the *Athenaeum's* review of *The Egoist*, he called it: 'The first critique of any of George Meredith's books I had ever come across, in which the writer showed thorough knowledge of his works and anything like an adequate appreciation of his wonderful genius.' A week later he wrote: 'cordial praise from *Athenaeum, Pall Mall Gazette, Spectator, Examiner*. At length! Encouragement. A man of wonderful genius and a splendid writer may hope to obtain something like recognition after working hard for thirty years, dating from his majority.'[16] These expressions are too vivid to be accurate, but they contain a good deal of truth. As S. M. Ellis put it: 'With the publication of *The Egoist* Meredith took possession of his kingdom.'[17] There were still hostile voices, but the general tone was changed to one of respect and admiration.

In her review of *The Egoist* Mrs Oliphant wrote with a sharpness which reflected the sudden growth of his popularity. Other critics were more moderate. The *Examiner* critic thought the prelude appalling and said that Meredith was 'a great deal too clever', but discovered among the characters the most subtle analyses that had appeared since Balzac. Similarly, the criticisms of the *New Quarterly Magazine* appeared in a generally approving context. Meanwhile, W. E. Henley and James Thomson were doing their best to push the novel into public notice. Thomson, who thought it the critic's duty to make an audience for the novelist, went so far as to assert that Meredith's dialogue was 'the best of our age': 'It is so spontaneous, unexpected, involuntary, diversified by the moods, the blood, the nerves, the ever-varying circumstances and relations of the interlocutors' (No. 62). Henley, more objective, charged Meredith with affectation, obscurity, and artificiality, but at the same time praised him most liberally (Nos. 57, 59, and 61).

To most of the reviewers who welcomed *The Egoist*, *The Tragic Comedians* (1881) was a disappointment. The novel sold well, perhaps because of its political interest, but was poorly and sparsely reviewed. Joseph Jacobs in the *Athenaeum* concentrated on the relation between Meredith's fiction and the heroine's autobiography and found it difficult, he said, to judge the novel because of its dependence on the factual source.[18] A writer in *Truth* thought that Meredith's characteristic faults were more pronounced in *The Tragic Comedians* than elsewhere:

His morbid vivacity of style, his anxious brilliance, his restless wordiness, his unscrupulous and unconquerable passion for self display, are more apparent, I think, in the *Tragic Comedians*, than in anything (in prose) of his I have read.[19]

The *Daily News* was more enthusiastic:

He has in a wonderful way, and with a command of brilliant language all his own, analyzed and commented on an episode of life as strange, as mystifying, and as interesting, as is to be found in the repertory of the world's dramas. The personages are few and the action brief. Fateful, however, and tragic is the story as an old Greek play.[20]

The *Westminster Review*, in the shortest of notices, remarked nothing but the author's affectation.[21]

Readers and critics were unanimous in finding Meredith's next novel more attractive. Like *The Tragic Comedians*, *Diana of the Crossways* had a story based on fact, involving a notorious scandal in high life; but it also had a pronounced love-interest and a relatively straightforward plot. Henley called it an ordinary novel written by a genius and said that it atoned for *The Tragic Comedians*. The *Spectator* was characteristically impervious to Meredith's design and called the novel an 'apologia for witty and beautiful ladies who love to skate on thin ice' (No. 74). Several reviewers observed the discrepancy between Diana's actions and the narrator's assessment of her character, but all with due allowance for the brilliance of the portrayal and the novel's 'excitement, romance, realistic force'. Arthur Symons defended even Meredith's affectation on the grounds of its suitability for the realization of a 'rarely revealed nature' of the heroine (No. 75).

THE FIRST COLLECTED EDITION

By 1885 many critics and reviewers had begun to wonder why so many of Meredith's works were out of print. Early editions of all his books before *Diana of the Crossways* were attracting high prices in book sales while readers like Symons lamented that even the very latest novel would soon be unavailable. Eventually in 1885, Chapman and Hall, in conjunction with Roberts Bros of Boston ventured to begin to issue the first collected edition.

Many writers in literary journals and newspapers took the occasion to observe the value of Meredith's work, the length of his apprenticeship, and the late but enthusiastic reception of his novels by a wide public. The *Saturday Review*, unusual in its understanding of Meredith's aims and methods, was typical of many in the respectful tone of its re-marks and the fair-mindedness of its conclusion: 'There ought to be curiosity and mental activity enough in the English speaking and English reading world to give Mr Meredith a fame and a recognition corre-sponding to his deserts.'[22] W. L. Courtney was less enthusiastic (No. 77), finding in Meredith's work a 'desperate cleverness', 'which is always isolated, repellent, obstructive'. Some of Meredith's gifts, Courtney thought, could not be rated too highly, but he possessed a deficiency of creative and a superfluity of critical faculty which prevented him from being among the greatest artists in fiction. The tone of this article from an unsympathetic writer is one of the many indications that Meredith, in 1885, had at last arrived.

THE LAST PHASE

The free availability of Meredith's novels after 1885, the enthusiasm of influential writers, did much to spread his name among a wide audience. A factor of equal importance was the length of time since he had begun to write. By the 1880s the British public was beginning to catch up with Meredith, so that ideas which had earned him the mistrust of earlier generations were now recognized as foreshadowing exciting modern attitudes. His continuing fertility and restless mental activity enabled him to adapt his art to the circumstances of the day and gave it an air of modernity greater than it actually possessed. The author of *One of Our Conquerors*, though he was sixty-three years old and had been formed in an earlier period, was a present element in the con-temporary scene.

The influence of non-literary factors in the consideration of Meredith's work was reflected in one of the earliest articles exclusively devoted to it. Arabella Shore's thoughtful and intelligent literary appreciation in the *British Quarterly* (No. 55) was motivated by her interest in Meredith as an opponent of repressive social and moral codes, as an advocate of women's rights. Towards the end of the century there were many readers who took a similarly non-literary interest in the novelist and poet, as the representative of modernism and the proponent of a creed even more suitable than Browning's for adaptation to the conditions of ordinary living. Even while the public disliked the direction his work was taking, he remained the foremost intellectual of the day. By 1900, however, his work seemed more advanced than it actually was; and by 1914 his kind of intellectualism had begun to appear facile and academic.

From the 1880s, as Meredith came to be considered the established leader of English letters, he drew the fire of iconoclastic writers like George Moore. At the same time, as the apostle of modernism and the leader of an *élite* he attracted the praise of Oscar Wilde and Arthur Symons, who made his work serve strange purposes (see below, Nos. 84 and 115). The praise of disciples was sometimes indiscreet. R. L. Stevenson, for example, acknowledged his great debt to Meredith in terms which gave wide offence. He told an American reporter:

I am a true blue Meredith person. I think George Meredith out and away the greatest force in English letters, and I don't know whether it can be considered a very encouraging thing that he has now become popular or whether we should think it a discouraging thing that he should have written so long without any encouragement whatever. It is enough, for instance, to disgust a man with the whole trade of letters, that such a book as *Rhoda Fleming* should have fallen flat; it is the strongest thing in English letters since Shakespeare died, and if Shakespeare could have read it he would have jumped up and cried, 'Here's a fellow!' No other living writer of English fiction can be compared to Meredith. He is the first, and the others—are not he. . . . I serve under Meredith's colours always.[23]

Similarly, J. M. Barrie, in the *Contemporary Review*, asserted that Meredith was 'the greatest wit this country has produced' and 'one of the outstanding men of letters, since the Elizabethan age'.[24]

These statements irritated more conservative writers, like William Watson, who struck back decisively in the name of common sense (No. 85). Watson thought that popularity was a necessary condition of quality in fiction. In his article Dickens, Thackeray, George Eliot and Shakespeare were brought forward to prove that difficult material need not cause obscurity or affectation. Watson subjected the statements of Stevenson and Barrie to fair and rigorous examination. His position was similar to that of many later critics—that Meredith, though an able writer, was not a good novelist, but, like many of his conservative colleagues before and since, he used a tone which was unnecessarily sharp.

A counterblast to Watson's attack was delivered by Richard Le Gallienne (No. 87), an enthusiastic student of Meredith who was soon to become the author of the first book-length study of his work. Le Gallienne took Watson as the type of the Philistine. Despite some affectation, Le Gallienne was moderate in his assertions, urging as his strongest argument that Meredith's difficulty stemmed from the nature of his purpose. After a survey of the confusingly diverse statements of the critics, he concluded: 'Whatever else is to be proven, one thing is certain, that George Meredith is a centre of power, of whatever nature, in whatever degree.'

The debate over the novelist's merits was intensified by the publication of his next novel. The audience which had welcomed *Diana of the Crossways* was stunned by *One of Our Conquerors* (1891), at once among the most original and eccentric of novels, and, Meredith himself confessed, a 'trying piece of work'.[25] The 'darkness' of the critics, however, was not as great as he later asserted, though there was no lack of sharp criticism.[26] The *Spectator* characteristically said that Meredith lacked the qualities of even a good second-rate novelist, concluding: 'So affectedly grotesque a style would ruin even a good novel, and to describe *One of Our Conquerors* as a good novel is impossible' (No. 92). The *Saturday Review* found the the author's 'usual faults' of 'incoherence, prolixity, straining after epigram, seeking after the uncommon, lack of firmness of character-drawing and allusiveness' (No. 91). *The Times* thought that there was an underlying fine conception, but that it had been spoiled in execution (No. 90). On the other hand, critics in the *Anti-Jacobin* and *Athenaeum* (Nos. 88 and 89) were prepared to accept Meredith's demands. Lionel Johnson set aside the common argument that the years in the wilderness had spoiled Meredith, and suggested that close attention would make the 'whole greatness of the design evident' (No. 93). Johnson's appreciation was an unusually intelligent apprehension of Meredith's purpose and achievement.

Critics were less dogmatic about *Lord Ormont and His Aminta* (1895).

Some who had been unable to accept *One of Our Conquerors* welcomed this novel. A writer in the *Literary World*, for example, who thought that the Meredith cult had taken a hard knock with the publication of *One of Our Conquerors*, placed *Lord Ormont* among the best of his novels (No. 104). Another writer, in the *Cosmopolitan* (No. 103), declared that it contained the 'essentials of romantic sanity and health'. One or two critics were harsh. In the *Pall Mall Gazette* a reviewer said that, although the swimming incident provided one great scene, the novel as a whole was a 'tirade', in which 'the jaded reader gets not an instant's respite' (No. 99). The *Spectator* critic was also unsympathetic, and accused Meredith of being unable to attain organic integrity (No. 100), and Henry James, from his special standpoint, denounced Meredith's handling of the subject (No. 102). Lionel Johnson found grounds for appreciation again, pointing out that the novel, though typical in 'tone, intention, spirit, theme', was untypical in execution and yet contained some qualities which were uniquely Meredith's own (No. 97).

Meredith's position was not materially affected by the publication of his last novel, *The Amazing Marriage* (1896). In the *Spectator* James Ashcroft Noble reaffirmed the journal's view that Meredith was no more than a second-rate writer with a few good things (No. 113). W. E. Garrett Fisher thought the style of the novel beyond all praise (No. 112), while Edmund Gosse thought it 'deplorably clever and distressing' (No. 106) and Alice Meynell emphasized the book's painfulness (No. 108). Several critics objected to the character of Carinthia, one in a pointed and memorable phrase: 'Life had to bore holes with a pickaxe to let understanding into her' (No. 111).

While these last novels were being published, writers were making serious attempts to analyse the character of Meredith's work and to assess the importance of his long career, and on the whole these critics of his later years showed understanding and appreciation.[27] Many who were willing to criticize the novelist's affectation or obscurity respected his ability to vitalize an abstract subject and to inform the elements of character 'with the very essence of humanity' (No. 95). Others, like William Barry, found his genius the 'very head and front' of his offence:

Sooner than ride round in the trodden sawdust, Mr Meredith leaps the barrier and declines the customary feats of horsemanship. There shall be no story because he cannot invent a new one. He slurs over the moving incidents, slackens his pace when he should be running full tilt, narrates instead of painting a scene, and balks the primitive instinct which longs for picturesque and exciting action. No wonder that he is dry beyond any writer of novels known to us—dry and exasperating; tediously brilliant; witty and wise out of season; filling our eyes with diamond dust which is as blinding as sand or steam. . . .[28]

H. M. Cecil, in the *Free Review* (No. 105), anticipated later criticism in accusing Meredith of contriving the actions of his characters, or failing to provide them with a realized context and being unable to give his novels a proper vertebrate structure. He also repeated Socialist charges that Meredith's fictional world was entirely artificial and that his characters were drawn from the higher reaches of society.[29] J. M. Robertson, in the *Yellow Book* (No. 114), attacked Meredith on literary grounds, though he was keenly aware of his ability and agreed with Cecil in thinking that his faults were produced by isolation. Like G. S. Street, Robertson and Cecil treated Meredith as a classic; their measured assertions and analyses indicated the extent to which he was already regarded as the representative of a past generation.

THE LATER POETRY

The increased leisure and financial security which Meredith attained after his middle years renewed his willingness to be known as a poet. Between 1862 and 1883 he published no volume of verse, and even after that date he had to publish his poems at his own risk. Partly in resentment at what he called the refusal of the English public to accept him as a poet, he prevented copies from being sent out for review. Even so, the later volumes were not inadequately reviewed, though many critics were obliged to conclude that increasing age had a more serious effect on the author's verse than on his prose. *Poems and Lyrics of the Joy of Earth* (1883) was sympathetically received by Mark Pattison, Alice Meynell, and Walter Kerr, all of whom found freshness and originality in the volume. *Ballads and Poems of Tragic Life* (1887) obtained less favour. In a review which seriously annoyed the poet, W. E. Henley pointed out that, with very fine qualities and occasional successes, Meredith's verse was unequal and at times uninspired (No. 79). The *Westminster Review* fell back on the figure of the wheat and the tares (No. 80). By this time most writers were agreed that Meredith's verse deserved high respect for the quality of thought, the evident ability and flashes of genius, but that it was not of the highest order. The increase in ruggedness and tortuousness as Meredith grew older brought continual protest. As one sympathetic critic remarked, the fools who rejected the poet in his earlier years were no longer of any importance; what mattered now was his inability to communicate with the new audience which he had gained (No. 94). Gradually the idea became current that Meredith has lost his ability to distinguish between effective metaphor and hopeless eccentricity of statement. What doubts remained after *The Empty Purse* (1892) were dispelled by *Odes in Contribution to the Song of French History* (1898). Reviewers were unanimous in preferring 'France, December 1870', written over twenty years before the other three poems which comprised the volume. Francis Thompson, declaring himself amazed at the power and flagrancies, the anarchy and turbulence of the volume, called it an 'unlawful wonder' (No. 116). The *Saturday* reviewer wrote with 'bewilderment and acute distress', pointing out the lack of proportion which marred the later poems (No. 177). The *Athenaeum* critic remarked that outside 'France, December 1870' there were sometimes touches reminiscent of Lewis Carroll (No. 119). More than one writer drew attention to the line, 'The friable and the grumous, dizzards both'. The reviewers of *A Reading of Life* (1901), had nothing new to add. The views of many readers were summarized by the reviewer of *Selected Poems* (1897):

We would not seem ungracious: the Poems leave untouched our feeling of high respect for their author; they display an intensely poetical nature; a mind daring, original, and profound, and a marvellous command of language. But we feel, on laying the book down, what Meredith himself says in the beautiful poem, 'The Lark Ascending'. . . . That is just what these beautiful writings lack. The poet must interpret: it is not enough for him to analyze or lecture; and so, though they reveal a personality that is massive, and a genius that is magnificent, these verses remain just outside the fold.[30]

MEREDITH'S ATTITUDE TO CRITICISM IN LATER YEARS

Meredith might fairly have complained about the unfairness or stupidity of individual critics at any time in his career, but he preferred to assume an attitude of contempt. His early sensitivity and willingness to respond to intelligent criticism ended with his attempt to reconcile his aims with the interests of the public at large. He retained a sharp eye for the comments of reviewers and critics, and was not above taking offence, but persisted in declaring his alienation from the British public. Thus, he told an interviewer towards the end of his life:

The press has often treated me as a clown or a harlequin—yes, really! and with such little respect that my fellow-citizens can scarcely put up with me. Do not cry out! Certainly at this late hour they accord me a little glory: my name is celebrated, but no-one reads my books. As for Englishmen, I put them to flight because I bore them. With regard to foreigners I am but an illustrious unknown. Think! all my poems were, until 1896, published at my own expense! Really it is so! No-one has bought by books—my novels or my poems. And now, book-collectors snatch up my first editions, which are sold for twenty or twenty-five guineas.[31]

On these grounds he discouraged Walter Jerrold and G. M. Trevelyan from writing about his work and pretended indifference to the republication of his poetry. Probably this pose was as much the result of embarrassment about praise as of sensitivity to hostile criticism. In familar conversation he showed that he was far from indifferent. Robertson Nicoll reported:

Once I heard him talk much about criticism. He laid great stress on the fact that he had never replied to a critic. Of this he seemed to be very proud. He owned that he had felt the temptation on more occasions than one. He spoke of the sick feeling with which he had read Hutton's reviews of *Modern Love* in the *Spectator*. There was compensation, however, in Swinburne's noble reply. He was distinctly hurt about some remarks about *One of Our Conquerors*. . . .[32]

Meredith's sensitivity, however, was never great enough to make him turn aside from his pursuit of originality or idiosyncrasy. He possessed artistic integrity; but he also had a peculiar reserve, heightened by his isolation from audience and critics. Individual reviews hurt or pleased him, but critics never influenced him to modify his style or technique. He was aware of defects in his work, but regarded them as inevitable; he asked his readers to appreciate his virtues until he became tired of their exclusive concentration on his vices; and then he retired into himself.

MEREDITH'S RECEPTION IN AMERICA

It was part of Meredith's affectation in later years to exaggerate the quickness and enthusiasm of the American response to his work. The *Literary Digest* reported in the year of his death:

America would have been glad to welcome Meredith to her shores, and he is said to have regretted that he never came. 'They have always liked me better in

America,' he remarked recently to an American visitor. 'They don't care about me in England.'[33]

The basis of his impression of American enthusiasm seems to have been the relatively high financial returns which he received after the publication of the first collected edition of his novels. He wrote in 1888:

Yesterday I had a startler myself, in the shape of a Draft on Barings from the publishers of my works in Boston, U.S.A. by way of Royalty. Honour to that Republic! I had heard of large sales over there, and a man of experience wrote, through the publishers, to tell me it is nothing to what it will be. But I confess the touch of American money has impressed me with concrete ideas of fame.—I have not been writing much. I must soon be doing, or the trick will quit me. Without placing myself high—or anywhere,—I am, I moan to think, disdainful of an English public, and am beset by the devils of satire when I look on it.[34]

Yet the impression that he had been more quickly received in America was certainly an illusion. E. J. Bailey has remarked: 'In the first fifteen years of Meredith's literary career . . . there was not apparently a single work referring to Meredith in any American periodical.'[35] Until 1885 very few of his works had been published in America at all. *Evan Harrington* appeared there in 1860, but the only public response was a short notice in *Harper's New Monthly Magazine*: '. . . a spirited novel, illustrative of the distinction of rank in English society, and remarkable for the vivacity of its narrative and the dramatic raciness of its dialogue.'[36] After *Evan Harrington* came *The Egoist* (1879) and *The Tragic Comedians* (1881). Then in 1885 came two editions of *Diana of the Crossways* from two different publishers and the beginning of the first collected edition. According to W. M. Fullerton, it was only then that the American public began to awaken to Meredith at all. In a note appended to Le Gallienne's *George Meredith* (1890) he wrote:

I remember so well when the name of Meredith first became in America a name to conjure with and most clearly of all I remember the surprised awakening for some of us when we realised for how long this man had been writing, and that we had known nothing of him. . . .
  Before the appearance of the first uniform edition . . . George Meredith was scarcely known at all in America. I recall Professor Crosswell of Harvard once saying to me that he had just been reading a very remarkable book, the work of a great mind, naming one of the novels of Meredith, and his asking me if I knew anything about the book. . . . For a long time even the great libraries were without a volume by Meredith except a small poorly-printed Bowdlerised edition of *Diana* which did scarcely any service whatever in making him known

in America. And then the first uniform one-volume edition appeared from Roberts Brothers in Boston, and the triumphal progress began.[37]

According to Fullerton, one of the most influential factors in making Meredith's work more widely known was an article by Meredith's friend, Flora Shaw, who described for her American audience a visit to Boxhill and outlined the novelist's opinions about life and literature.[38] More critical was an article by G. P. Baker, which was stimulated by Shaw's essay, in which he treated Meredith's works not as 'mere novels', but as 'immensely expanded statements of a philosophical theory of their author's' (No. 81). Baker anticipated a change in taste which would bring about the conditions demanded in the opening chapter of *Diana*.

A year later George Parsons Lathrop published a thoughtful but rather eccentric consideration of Meredith's work in the *Atlantic Monthly*. Lathrop made some errors of fact and of sense: the lesson of *Sandra Belloni* and *Vittoria*, he remarked, 'seems to be For freedom and country everything must be sacrificed, even the love and hopes of all individual patriots'. *The Egoist*, moreover, he asserted, 'is Meredith's worst novel, an inflated, obese, elephantine comedy, which is not comic'. Finally, the fact that *Diana of the Crossways* involved a report of a divorce case gave him grounds for accusing Meredith of titillating the impure appetites of readers by introducing scandal. On the whole, however, Lathrop's comments were well considered—diffuseness, lameness of movement, and lack of proportion—and his conclusion was eminently sensible: 'Meredith is simply Meredith and we must take him as he is.'[39]

Another article in the *Atlantic Monthly*, eleven years later, subjected Meredith's whole work to careful scrutiny—again with rather uneven results. Paul Elmer More, reviewing the Scribner 'Boxhill' edition of the novels, found 'the same lack of graceful ease, the same laboured ingenuity in his narration and character-drawing' as in his style. More thought that Meredith's method of characterization put him in the same category as the naturalists and made him liable to the charge of presenting only a partial and false view of human character. He discerned the characteristics of Meredith's technique, but he attributed the novelist's attempt to realize his characters in visual and physiological terms to a desire to underplay the element of volition. Accordingly, More saw Clara Middleton's fate not as the final victory over passion and egoism, but the 'final succumbing in marriage with a character of placid but undeveloped strength'.[40]

Among the most perceptive of nineteenth-century American studies was the work of Stuart P. Sherman, published in the *Nation* to mark the novelist's death (No. 123). Beginning with a sketch of the development of Meredith's reputation, Sherman went on to analyse his achievement; 'He desired to represent men and women dramatically, revealing the secret springs of their characters in their speeches and acts. But for fatally long periods in many of his novels he would allow them neither to speak nor to act.' Sherman carefully assessed Meredith's contribution to literature and thought, suggesting that his future reputation would be based on his work as a constructive thinker rather than as an artist, though he had solved the problem of contemporary literature fifty years before it existed. Sherman also sketched out Meredith's relationship to his contemporaries, including those who had achieved a larger measure of artistic success, none of whom, he thought, 'fused within himself so many and so diverse powers'. The tone of balanced and objective appreciation which is struck here is not atypical of late nineteenth-century American criticism of Meredith. Beginning a little later than the English, American critics have on the whole fewer errors of commission to lament before the end of the century and fewer of omission since.

MEREDITH'S REPUTATION ON THE CONTINENT

Outside England and America, Meredith's work found an earlier reception in France than in Italy and Germany. In spite of Meredith's own interest in Germany, little attention was paid to him there before 1910, though an authorized translation of his works began to appear in 1904 and one or two articles came out before his death. German criticism after 1910 has been selected, translated, and edited by G. B. Petter in his rather confusing book, *George Meredith and His German Critics* (1939). According to Petter, German students have atoned for their delay in appreciating Meredith by the frequency of their later efforts. In Italy *Richard Feverel* was translated as early as 1873, *Diana of the Crossways* in 1906 and articles on Meredith were published in *Nuova Antologia* in 1906 and 1909.

In France there were few translations. *Sandra Belloni* appeared as early as 1866, but nothing else came out until Henri Davray's translation of the *Essay on the Idea of Comedy* in 1898. This was followed by *The Egoist* (1904) and *The Tragic Comedians* (1901). Criticism in France was also slow to start, and it was not until the present century that Meredith's work received very much attention. Emile de Forgues' short note on *Vittoria* in 1867 remained the only sign of critical interest in France until Marcel Schwob's *Spicilège* and Madame Daudet's *Notes sur Londres* (1896). Between 1898 and 1909, however, a number of essays were published by Henri Davray, Emile Legouis, Firmin Roz, and P. Heriot, so that by the year of Meredith's death French critics had made a substantial contribution towards the study of his work. Constantin Photiades, in 1910, published his *George Meredith: sa Vie—son Imagination*, which contains some useful notes of the novelist's conversation. Then in 1923 René Galland's two scholarly studies appeared: *George Meredith: les cinquante premières années* and *George Meredith and British Criticism*. Within two years Galland's books were followed by a critical study by Lucien Wolff (1924) and a chapter by Ramon Fernandez in his *Messages* (1926) which contains a striking description of Meredith's dynamic technique of character presentation.

MEREDITH'S REPUTATION IN THE TWENTIETH CENTURY

Sixty years ago Meredith's work was an unavoidable fashion, its appreciation part of the literary orthodoxy which had grown slowly over preceding decades. Book-length studies of his work, bibliographies, and comments on the critical history began to appear long before his death and continued in a steady flow until 1914. In the post-war period, however, his reputation underwent a decline from which it has not yet recovered. Since the end of the war writers have frequently contrasted the height of Meredith's fame at the turn of the century with the lack of contemporary esteem for his works. In 1928, for example, Virginia Woolf wrote: 'Twenty years ago the reputation of George Meredith was at its height. His novels had won their way to celebrity through all sorts of difficulties, and their fame was the brighter and the more singular for what it had subdued.'[41] A year later Sencourt observed that Meredith was read neither by the wider public nor by those who followed the literary fashion,[42] and twenty years after that Edward Sackville West found occasion to remark that 'Mention of his name in instructed company at any time since the First German War has produced an instant reaction of impatience or disgust'.[43] The situation has not changed greatly since 1949. Meredith's work still remains, for the most part, without readers and his critics often fall short of what he deserves. The high point of criticism was reached in 1910 with Percy Lubbock's review article (No. 125). Since then Meredith has not received attention proportionate to the quality of his work or the degree of his historical importance. Critics less rigorous than Lubbock have been too often content with applying critical formulae and repeating the platitudes of their predecessors.

Meredith's continuance in the desert to which all the great Victorian writers were at one time or another banished is probably to be attributed to two main factors: that he has not yet been out of favour for more than a generation, and that his work conflicts with what has been the dominant mode of criticism since the 1920s. Influential writers like F. R. Leavis and E. M. Forster reacted against Meredith in their youth, and the resulting derogatory or dismissive statements remain prominently on record to discourage readers who have not yet had an opportunity to incur a familiarity with his novels or his poetry.[44] And comparison with George Eliot, whose popularity had begun to fade before Meredith achieved his greatest fame, suggests that an important factor in his continued unpopularity is his refusal to provide a certain type of 'felt' life or realized context of life. A period which gives as much attention to *Middlemarch* and *Anna Karenina* as that recently past is likely to admire Meredith only after an effort of adjustment greater than most readers would wish to make. Meanwhile, whether he is read or not, he remains, as Le Gallienne called him, 'a centre of energy', a figure of immense importance in his period, a writer as vigorous as and more versatile than his contemporaries, an artist with a unique capacity to present an impression of unified intellect and passion, and, as Virginia Woolf observed, one whose work 'must inevitably be disputed and discussed'.[45]

NOTES

1. *Spectator*, xxviii, 29 December 1875.
2. *Eclectic Review*, May 1858.
3. *Examiner*, 23 March 1861.
4. *Morning Post*, 20 June 1862.
5. Letter to F. C. Waugh, October 1866.
6. 2 March 1867; *Letters* (1970), ed. C. L. Cline, I, 354.

7. Letter to William Hardman, September 1870; *Letters* (1970), I, 426.
8. Letter to Augustus Jessop, 18 May 1864; *Letters* (1970), 255. The phrase is actually used with reference to an early version of the novel.
9. J. M'Carthy, *Reminiscences* (1899), 375.
10. Letter to James Thomson, 27 November 1879; *Letters* (1970), II, 588.
11. Letter to James Thomson, 4 July 1879; *Letters* (1970), II, 576.
12. Letter to Augustus Jessop, 18 May 1864; *Letters* (1970), I, 255.
13. W. Robertson Nicoll, *A Bookman's Letters* (1913), 6.
14. Mrs Humphrey Ward, *A Writer's Recollections* (1918).
15. James Thomson, 'An Old New Book', *Cope's Tobacco Plant*, May 1879. The occasion of this article was the publication of the revised edition of *Richard Feverel* (1878).
16. Quoted from H. S. Salt, *The Life of James Thomson* (1889), 140–1.
17. S. M. Ellis, *George Meredith* (1919), 306.
18. *Athenaeum*, No. 2776, 8 January 1881.
19. *Truth*, ix, 20 January 1881.
20. *Daily News*, 27 January 1881.
21. *Westminster Review*, lx, April 1881.
22. *Saturday Review*, lxii, 24 July 1886.
23. R. L. Stevenson to a reporter; see *Pall Mall Gazette*, xlviii, 8 August 1888, 'An Evening with Mr R. L. Stevenson', originally in *Daily Examiner*, San Francisco.
24. J. M. Barrie, *Contemporary Review*, liv, October 1888.
25. Letter to J. H. Hutchinson, 15 October 1906; *Letters* (1970), III, 1573.
26. Meredith told Photiades that the reviewers of *One of Our Conquerors* 'groped blindly in their own great darkness'; *George Meredith* (1913), trans. A. Price (1923), 9.
27. The writer of an article on 'Mr Meredith's Novels' in *Edinburgh Review*, clxxi, January 1885, was an exception. He thought that the moral of *Lord Ormont* was that it was advisable and excusable to seduce your benefactor's wife.
28. William Barry, *Quarterly Review*, clxxiii, October 1891, 'English Realism and Romance'.
29. Interesting information as to how Meredith appeared to the Fabians is given in an exchange of letters in the *Star*, 1, 10, 14, 15, 16, 17 September 1891. There is also G. B. Shaw's letter to S. M. Ellis (*George Meredith* (1919), 247), which described how Meredith appeared outdated to Shaw long before the end of the century.
30. *Pall Mall Gazette*, xlv, 13 October 1897.
31. *George Meredith* (1910), trans A. Price (1923).
32. *A Bookman's Letters* (1913), 10.
33. *Literary Digest*, xxviii, 29 May 1909.
34. Letter to George Stevenson, 15 January 1888; *Letters* (1970), II, 902–3.

35. E. J. Bailey, 'Meredith in America: a Comment and a Bibliography', *Studies in Language and Literature in Celebration of the Seventieth Birthday of James Morgan Hart* (1910), 44.
36. *Harper's New Monthly Magazine*, xxii, January 1861.
37. Richard Le Gallienne, *George Meredith* (1890), Appendix.
38. *New Princeton Review*, iii, April 1887.
39. G. P. Lathrop, *Atlantic Monthly*, lxi, February 1888.
40. P. E. More, *Atlantic Monthly*, lxxxiv, October 1899.
41. Virginia Woolf, 'The Novels of George Meredith', January 1928; *Collected Essays* (1966), i.224.
42. B. de Sencourt, *The Life of George Meredith* (1929), 314.
43. *Inclinations* (1949), 33.
44. E. M. Forster, *Aspects of the Novel* (1927) (1962 ed.), 96–100, and F. R. Leavis, *The Great Tradition* (1948), 33; *New Bearings in English Poetry* (1932) (revised ed., 1950), 25. Leavis's brief comment in the latter book could have come from R. H. Hutton.
45. Virginia Woolf, 'The Novels of George Meredith', January 1928; *Collected Essays* (1966), I.232.

LIST OF GEORGE MEREDITH'S PUBLICATIONS

1851 *Poems*
1856 *The Shaving of Shagpat*
1857 *Farina*
1859 *The Ordeal of Richard Feverel*
1860 *Evan Harrington, Once a Week,* 11 February–13 October
1862 *Modern Love and Poems of the English Roadside*
1864 *Emilia in England* (later renamed *Sandra Belloni*)
1865 *Rhoda Fleming*
1866 *Vittoria, Fortnightly Review,* 15 January–1 December
1870 *The Adventures of Harry Richmond, Cornhill Magazine,* September 1870–November 1871
1874 *Beauchamp's Career, Fortnightly Review,* August 1874–December 1875
1879 *The Egoist, Glasgow Weekly Herald,* 21 June 1879–10 January 1880
1880 *The Tragic Comedians, Fortnightly Review,* October 1880–February 1881
1883 *Poems and Lyrics of the Joy of Earth*
1884 *Diana of the Crossways, Fortnightly Review,* June–December
1887 *Ballads and Poems of Tragic Life*
1888 *A Reading of Earth*
1890 *One of Our Conquerors, Fortnightly Review, Australasian,* and *Sun* (New York), October 1890–May 1891
1892 *Poems. The Empty Purse*
1893 *Lord Ormont and His Aminta, Pall Mall Magazine,* December 1893–August 1894
1895 *The Amazing Marriage, Scribner's Magazine,* January–December 1895
1898 *Odes in Contribution to the Song of French History, Cosmopolis,* March, April, May 1898. When published in volume form, the three odes, 'The Revolution', 'Napoleon' and 'Alsace-Lorraine', were accompanied by the earlier 'France, December 1870' from the *Fortnightly Review,* January 1871
1901 *A Reading of Life, with Other Poems*

POEMS

1851

---

1. Unsigned review, *Leader*

ii, 5 July 1851

The *Leader* was a Radical newspaper which ran between 1850 and 1860, to which Meredith seems to have contributed regularly; it was edited by G. H. Lewes (see below, No. 8, headnote).

Among the many volumes of ambitious verse which the inconsiderate 'request of friends' annually usher into public oblivion, there are generally two or three to 'repay' the reader, if not the publisher—volumes with glimpses of 'the enchanted gardens'—verse writers who have something more than the 'accomplishment of verse,' Mr Meredith's volume is one of these. Amidst pages of indifferent writing, carelessness, and commonplace, are mingled pages bright with fancy, and musical with emotion. A nice perception of nature, aided by a delicacy of expression, gives to these poems a certain charm not to be resisted; and, although they betray no depth of insight nor of feeling, although they are neither thoughtful nor impassioned, yet they rise from out the mass of verses by a certain elegance and felicity of expression which distinguish them. Read this and judge:

[Quotes 'South-West Wind in the Woodland', ll. 1-98.]

The versification of these poems is frequently careless and unmusical to a degree that nothing can excuse; and in general we complain of a want of that care and thought which a true poet would bestow upon his trifles. There is something piquant and alluring in the opening of a pastoral we are about to quote; but the rugged verse and commonplace conclusion make us regret it was not a fragment ending where our extract ends:

[Quotes 'Love in the Valley', st. 1-4.]

Deckar, in one of his chaotic plays, uses the quaint but truthful simile, 'untameable as flies';[1] the same observation of Nature is implied in Mr Meredith's—

> Then Winter, *he who tamed the fly!*

But the verse is rather quaint than poetic, inasmuch as it is throwing Winter into insignificance to select fly-taming as *the* characteristic of its power. We noticed other examples of this same tendency; but the whole volume is too obviously a collection of trifles to demand close criticism. We notice it because the workmanship of these trifles is elegant and fanciful.

2. Unsigned review, *Spectator*

xxiv, 22 August 1851

Meredith's relations with the *Spectator* is a subject in itself. This review, and No. 12, below, was perhaps by *Spectator's* first Editor, Stephen Rintoul (1787–1858), who had no prejudice against the young novelist. In 1861, however, the journal was acquired by R. H. Hutton and Meredith Townsend. From then on literary reviews were the responsibility of Hutton (1826–97), whose inclination to the moralistic interpretation of literature prevented him from treating Meredith's work objectively. Hutton was a very intelligent and important critic, respected by Arnold, Clough, F. D. Maurice, Browning, and Newman, and there is no doubt that his opposition did much to damage Meredith's reputation.

This volume possesses considerable poetical feeling and poetical faculty, but displays more of promise than performance. Mr Meredith has the

[1] Thomas Dekker, *The Honest Whore* (1604), part I, scene xiii.

characteristics of young or unstudied writers. His subjects are often too limited or common, and an attempt to impart attraction by treatment does not always succeed, the result being a curious quaintness rather than novelty. With the power of independent judgment and observation, Mr Meredith falls too much into the ruts of a school, and, without very closely imitating any writer in particular, frequently reminds the reader of Tennyson or Keats, with occasional touches of the Brownings; though this manner is so common among poetical aspirants, that it may be as much a literary fashion as an individual imitation. Mr Meredith has occasionally, too, a sensuous warmth of image and expression, which, though not passing propriety, might as well be tempered. With the exception of want of breadth and novelty in the subjects, these things, though they may injure the style or lower the class, can hardly be said to impair the interest of the poems. Mr Meredith's greatest fault is overdoing: he rarely knows when he has said enough: besides continually overlaying his ideas by expansion, he introduces similes not always the aptest, and in addition to making them more prominent than the principal idea, runs them on till they become a new subject. This fault would detract from the interest of any composition; but it admits of an easy remedy. If Mr. Meredith intends to cultivate poetry, this over-exuberance must be steadily repressed. For example, 'The Sleeping City' consists of twenty-nine stanzas, fourteen of which are devoted to the Eastern Princess in the city whose inhabitants were turned to stone; a mere illustrative image being nearly as long as the incident itself. It may seem that there is something of the spirit of Sterne's stop-watch in this; but, to borrow a remark from Sir Fretful Plagiary, 'the watch on these occasions, you know, is the critic.'[1]

The poems are mostly of the kind called occasional; consisting of everyday incidents, or themes suggested by some object common to every observation. These are occasionally varied by classical subjects running into a short tale—as the metamorphosis of Daphne, or the shipwreck of Idomeneus. In most of them there is poetical imagery, feeling, and diction; the last if not altogether original yet unhacknied, with frequent felicity of idea or phraseology, though sometimes of an odd kind. Description is perhaps Mr Meredith's strongest point; but he has also looked upon society and the questions which now agitate it. This glance may not have produced absolute originality, but it has saved him from the commonplaces of poetasters. The following stanzas are from a poem called 'The Olive Branch'—the name of a vessel thus

---

[1] *Tristram Shandy* (1760–7), III. xii, and R. B. Sheridan, *The Critic* (1779), i. i.

christened because a dove dropped an olive sprig upon it at the moment of launching.

[Quotes 'The Olive Branch', st. 15–20.]

3. J. A. Heraud, *Athenaeum*

No. 1243, 23 August 1851

John Abraham Heraud (1799–1887) wrote regularly for the *Athenaeum* between 1843 and 1868. He also wrote for the *Quarterly* and *Fraser's* and published several epic poems, including *The Descent into Hell* (1830) and *The Judgement of the Flood* (1834).

From the mass of volumes of verse which load our table, we select one that deserves a somewhat better introduction to our readers than could be given under our accustomed title of 'Poetry of the Million'.

It would seem that the class of 'singers' is on the increase. The Singer is distinguished from the Poet much in the same manner as aptitude is from genius. The poet is a fully developed spirit, uniting to a wide experience a philosophical judgment and the qualifications of an artist in verse. The 'singer' simply requires an instinct for song and a desire to use the gift on exciting occasions. The form is accordingly, for the most part, lyrical, and the matter frequently personal. The turn of a phrase, a delicate cadence, some grace of diction or tenderness of sentiment will suffice as a distinguishing merit, and establish the claim of the minor minstrel, whose themes are generally as fugitive as his flight is brief.

Mr Meredith is to a certain extent a writer of the class indicated—but he may even claim to be something more. His small volume contains some essays with an epic ambition in their aim not unlike the classic imitations of Tennyson. 'Daphne', 'Antigone', and 'The Shipwreck of Idomeneus' are the titles and themes of such attempts. These are not without poetic fervour. They show a fair acquaintance with Greek models, and a power of verbal combination of considerable 'mark and likelihood'. Occasional negligences betray his want of mastery. Thus, in the lyrical poems, some of which might almost be called beautiful, we meet at times with stanzas that are quite prosaic in feeling and in diction. Many of the pieces, too, are set exercises—such as the leading poem of the series, entitled 'The Olive Branch'. This is the name of a ship—and the moral is this:

[Quotes 'The Olive Branch', st. 29–30.]

This mere theme-writing is the fault of the volume, and betrays the young writer. But his 'juvenilia', if such they be, are of positive merit—and of more promise. Take the following tricksy ditty:

[Quotes 'Song', 'Love within the lover's breast'.]

This, in fact, is merely pretty—yet it has a smack of Herrick in it. The example is not a sound one—and we counsel Mr Meredith not to let the spell of the old erotic poet lead him into paths where the master himself found more weeds than flowers—and whose flowers, even as culled and bound by Herrick, look pale beside those that grow in the atmosphere of nobler thought.

As a quaint example of Mr Meredith's poems, take the following:

[Quotes 'Will o' the Wisp'.]

It is not always, however, that the author is so elaborate in his verbal and rhythmical displays. One more example must suffice our readers, to enable them to determine on Mr Meredith's chance to keep his permanent station *without* the poetical playgrounds of 'The Million'.

[Quotes 'The Death of Winter'.]

It will be said, no doubt, that these are small beauties—and even as such are chargeable with affectation. We fear that the objections must be allowed—and in an older writer they would have determined our verdict in a harsher sense. But where the 'prentice-hand' is so manifest as in this volume, we accept the signs of care and intention which it exhibits as indications of an artistic tendency in the 'singer', and to a certain extent as pledges that one day he may become a poet.

4. W. M. Rossetti, *Critic*

x, 5 November 1851; signed 'W.M.R.'

William Michael Rossetti (1829–1919), younger brother of Dante Gabriel and Christina, was twenty-one when he wrote this article. Later Meredith became intimate with the Rossettis and for a time in 1863 rented a room in Dante Gabriel's house in Cheyne Walk.

The full poet is a thoroughly balanced compound of perception and intellect. By the first faculty he sees vividly, and feels to the inmost; by the second, he understands deeply and largely, and applies with a subtle searching breadth. The power of expression is a correlative of both; but it belongs more immediately to the first. Though TENNYSON had not been the author *in posse* of *In Memoriam*, he might equally have produced such perfect word-painting as we find in *Mariana*; but a want of that perception which constitutes the essence of the latter would have made the former more faint from first to last.

Of the perceptive poet we have had no other such complete example as KEATS. It is the delight in what he sees, the sympathy with what he narrates, that endows him with his marvellous power of expression. To him everything was an opportunity. Yet, he saw nature and emotion as rather suggestive than typical; as exciting the thoughts outwards, not leading them inwards. His poems have but little of the unconscious simile (to be found so largely in those of TENNYSON for instance), the implication in description of an inner essence and ulterior meaning. KEATS portrays his object with keen exquisite picturing, but which aims only at the phenomenal fact; or else he makes use of the simile direct. His enthusiasm was less an inner fire than a visible lambent halo. He saw loveliness in nature, or found it the incentive to lovely thoughts. He rested in the effect. 'A thing of beauty is a joy for ever.'

Mr MEREDITH seems to us a kind of limited KEATS. He is scarcely a perceptive, but rather a seeing or sensuous poet. He does not love nature in a wide sense as KEATS did; but nature delights and appeals closely to him. In proportion, however, as his sympathies are less vivid, excitable, and diffusive, he concentrates them the more. He appropriates a section of nature, as it were; and the love which he bears to it partakes more of affection. Viewing Mr MEREDITH as a Keatsian, and allowing for (what we need not stop to assert), the entire superiority of the dead poet—we think it is in this point that the most essential phase of difference will be found between the two: and it is one which, were the resemblance in other respects more marked and more unmixed than it is, would suffice to divide Mr MEREDITH from the imitating class. The love of KEATS for nature was not an *affectionate* love: it was minute, searching, and ardent; but hardly personal. He does not lose himself in nature, but contemplates her and utters her forth to the delight of all ages.[1] Indeed, if we read his record aright, he was not, either in thought or in feeling, a strongly affectionate man; and the passion which ate into him at the last was a mania and infatuation, raging like disease, a symptom and a part of it. It is otherwise with Mr MEREDITH. In his best moments he seems to sing, because it comes naturally to him, and silence would be restraint, not through exuberance or inspiration, but in simple contentedness, or throbbing of heart. There is an amiable and engaging quality in the poems of Mr MEREDITH, a human companionship and openness, which make the reader feel his friend.

But, perhaps, it is chiefly in the impressions of love that our new poet's likeness and unlikeness at once to the author of *Endymion* and *Lamia* are to be recognized. We are told that women felt pique at KEATS for treating them in his verses scarcely otherwise than flowers or perfumes; as beautifiers and the object of tender and pleasurable emotion—a charm of life. They missed the language of individual love, dignified, and equal. Nor was the quarrel without a cause: but the reader will probably, at the first reading of the very charming, melodious, and rhythmical poem which we proceed to quote, think us unfair in trying to fasten it on Mr MEREDITH:

[Quotes 'Love in the Valley'.]

Surely, it may be said, there is passion enough here, and of a sufficiently personal kind. True, indeed: this is not a devotion which sins through lukewarmth, and roams uncertain of an object. It will not fail to obtain an answer, through dubiousness of quest: and if it shocks at all, it shocks the delicacy, not the *amour-propre*. But its characteristics are, in

---

[1] We hope it is superfluous to explain that, in what is here said of Keats, we seek only to discriminate, not to depreciate; and that we love and reverence him as one of the most glorious of poets.

fact, the same as those at which exception was taken in the case of KEATS. The flame burns here, which there only played, darting its thin quick tongue from point to point: but the difference is of concentration only. The impressionable is changed for the strongly impressed—the influence being similar. Here again the love, like our poet's love of nature, has the distinct tone of *affection*. It is purely and unaffectedly sensuous, and in its utterance as genuine a thing as can be. We hear a clear voice of nature, with no falsetto notes at all; as spontaneous and intelligible as the wooing of a bird, and equally a matter of course.

The main quality of Mr MEREDITH's poems is warmth—warmth of emotion, and, to a certain extent, of imagination, like the rich mantling blush on a beautiful face, or a breath glowing upon your cheek. That he is young will be as unmistakably apparent to the reader as to ourself; on which score various shortcomings and crudities, not less than some excess of this attribute, claim indulgence. The 'Rape of Aurora' for example, is certainly too highly-coloured; 'Daphne' objectionably spun out, even if but in regard to length; and 'Angelic Love' other than angelic. The following, against which this plea cannot be urged, is a graceful and fitting companion to 'Love in the Valley'.

[Quote 'Song', 'Under boughs of breathing May'.]

Our last quotation displays Mr MEREDITH in one of his more exclusively descriptive pieces. But we may observe that, here too, the emotion is what most distinctly impresses itself, while the description proper, though not wanting in precision and minuteness, looms somewhat faintly:

[Quotes 'Song', 'The daisy now is out upon the green'.]

We have assigned Mr MEREDITH to the Keatsian school, believing that he pertains to it in virtue of the more intrinsic qualities of his mind, and of a simple enjoying nature; and as being beyond doubt of the perceptive class in poetry. In mere style, however, he attaches himself rather to the poets of the day: the pieces in which a particular bias is most evident being in a Tennysonian mould—as the 'Olive Branch', and the 'Shipwreck of Idomeneus'—while some of his smaller lyrics smack of HERRICK. He has a good ear for melody, and considerable command of rhythm; but he seems sometimes to hanker unduly after novelty of metre, attaining it, if there be no other means to his hand, by some change in length or interruption of rhyme which has a dragging and inconsequent effect. That his volume is young is not its fault: nor are we by any means sure that is its misfortune. Some jingle-pieces there are, indeed—mere commonplace and current convention, which mature judgment would exclude: but the best are those whose spirit is the spirit of youth, and which are the fullest of it. We do not expect ever quite to enrol Mr MEREDITH among the demigods or heroes; and we hesitate, for the reason just given, to say that we count on greater things from him; but we shall not cease to look for his renewed appearance with hope, and to hail it with extreme pleasure, so long as he may continue to produce poems equal to the best in this first volume.

5. Charles Kingsley, *Fraser's Magazine*

xliv, December 1851

Charles Kingsley (1819–75) was already an established author when he wrote this appreciative review. The passage reprinted is part of a general review article and the reference in the first line is to Thomas Lovell Beddoes (1803–49), whose *Poems, Posthumous and Collected* (1851) Kingsley had just been discussing.

Quite antipodal to the poems of Mr Beddoes, and yet, in our eyes, fresh proofs of the truth of those rules which we have tried to sketch, are the poems of Mr George Meredith. This, we understand, is his first appearance in print; if it be so, there is very high promise in the unambitious little volume which he has sent forth as his first-fruits. It is something, to have written already some of the most delicious little love-poems which we have seen born in England in the last few years, reminding us by their richness and quaintness of tone of Herrick; yet with a depth of thought and feeling which Herrick never reached. Health and sweetness are two qualities which run through all these poems. They are often overloaded—often somewhat clumsy and ill-expressed—often wanting polish and finish; but they are all genuine, all melodiously conceived, if not always melodiously executed. One often wishes, in reading the volume, that Mr Meredith had been thinking now and then of Moore instead of Keats, and had kept for revision a great deal which he has published; yet now and then form, as well as matter, is nearly perfect. For instance:

[Quotes two songs, 'The Moon is alone in the sky', and 'I cannot lose thee for a day'.]

In Mr Meredith's Pastorals, too, there is a great deal of sweet wholesome writing, more like real pastorals than those of any young poet whom we have had for many a year. Let these suffice as specimens:

[Quotes 'Pastorals', vll, ll 38–48.]

Careless as hexameters; but honest landscape-painting; and only he who begins honestly ends greatly.

[Quotes 'Love in the Valley', st. 1–3.]

What gives us here hope for the future, as well as enjoyment on the spot, is, that these have evidently not been put together, but have grown of themselves; and the one idea has risen before his mind, and shaped itself into a song; not perfect in form, perhaps, but as far as it goes, healthful, and consistent, and living, through every branch and spray of detail. And this is the reason why Mr. Meredith has so soon acquired an instinctive melody, which Mr Beddoes, as we saw, never could. To such a man, any light which he can gain from æsthetic science will be altogether useful. The living seed of a poem being in him, and certain to grow and develope somehow, the whole gardener's art may be successfully brought to bear on perfecting it. For this is the use of æsthetic science—to supply, not the bricklayer's trowel, but the hoe, which increases the fertility of the soil, and the pruning-knife, which lops off excrescences. For Mr Meredith—with real kindness we say it, for the sake of those love-poems—has much to learn, and, as it seems to us, a spirit which can learn it; but still it must be learnt. One charming poem—for instance, 'Daphne'—is all spoilt, for want of that same pruning-knife. We put aside the question whether a ballad form is suitable, not to the subject—for to that, as a case of purely objective action, it is suitable—but to his half-Elegiac, thoughtful handling of it. Yet we recommend him to consider whether his way of looking at the Apollo and Daphne myth be not so far identical with Mr Tennyson's idea of 'Paris and Œnone', as to require a similar Idyllic form, to give the thoughtful element its fair weight. If you treat external action merely (and in as far as you do so, you will really reproduce those old sensuous myths) you may keep the ballad form, and heap verse on verse as rapidly as you will; but if you introduce any subjective thought, after the fashion of the Roman and later Greek writers, to explain the myth, and give it a spiritual, or even merely allegoric meaning, you must, as they did, slacken the pace of your verse. Let Ovid's *Fasti* and *Epistles* be your examples, at least in form, and write slowly enough to allow the reader to think as he goes on. The neglect of this rule spoilt the two best poems in *Reverberations*, 'Balder', and 'Thor', which, whatever were the faults of the rest of the book, were true and noble poems;[1] and the neglect of it spoils 'Apollo and Daphne'. Mr Meredith is trying all through to mean more than the form which he has chosen allows him. That form gives free scope to a prodigality of objective description, of which Keats need not have been ashamed; but if he had more carefully studied the old models of that form—from the simple Scotch ballads to Shakespeare's 'Venus and Adonis'—a ballad and not an idyl—he would have avoided Keats' fault of too-muchness, into which he has fallen. Half the poem would bear cutting out; even half of those most fresh and living stanzas, where the whole woodland springs into life to stop Daphne's flight—where

[Quotes 'Daphne', st. 84 and 86.]

Every stanza is a picture in itself, but there are too many of them; and therefore we lose the story in the profusion of its accidentals. There is a truly Correggiesque tone of feeling and drawing all through this poem, which is very pleasant to us. But we pray Mr Meredith to go to the National Gallery, and there look steadily and long, with all the analytic insight he can, at the 'Venus and Mercury', or the 'Agony in the Garden'; or go to the Egyptian Hall, and there feast, not only his eyes and heart, but his intellect and spirit also, with Lord Ward's duplicate of the 'Magdalen'[2]—the grandest Protestant sermon on 'free justification by faith' ever yet preached; and there see how Correggio can dare to indulge in his exquisite lusciousness of form, colour, and chiaro-'scuro, without his pictures ever becoming tawdry or over-wrought—namely, by the severe scientific unity and harmonious graduation of parts which he so carefully preserves, which make his pictures single glorious rainbows of precious stone—that Magdalen one living emerald—instead of being, like the jewelled hawk in the

---

[1] *Reverberations* (1849) was by W. M. W. Call.
[2] Kingsley is refering to the current exhibition of Lord Ward's collection of paintings in the Egyptian Hall, Piccadilly. The building was erected in 1812 by William Bullock, originally to house his museum of natural history.

Great Exhibition, every separate atom of it beautiful, yet as a whole utterly hideous.

One or two more little quarrels we have with Mr Meredith—and yet they are but *amantium iræ*, after all. First, concerning certain Keatist words—such as languorous, and innumerous, and such like, which are very melodious, but do not, unfortunately, belong to this our English tongue, their places being occupied already by old and established words; as Mr Tennyson has conquered this fault in himself, Mr Meredith must do the same. Next, concerning certain ambitious metres, sound and sweet, but not thoroughly worked out, as they should have been. Mr Meredith must always keep in mind that the species of poetry which he has chosen is one which admits of nothing less than perfection. We may excuse the roughness of Mrs Browning's utterance, for the sake of the grandeur and earnestness of her purpose; she may be reasonably supposed to have been more engrossed with the matter than with the manner. But it is not so with the idyllist and lyrist. He is not driven to speak by a prophetic impulse; he sings of pure will, and therefore he must sing perfectly, and take a hint from that microcosm, the hunting-field; wherein if the hounds are running hard, it is no shame to any man to smash a gate instead of clearing it, and jump into a brook instead of over it. Forward he must get, by fair means if possible, if not, by foul. But if, like the idyllist, any gentleman 'larks' his horse over supererogatory leaps at the coverside, he is not allowed to knock all four hoofs against the top bar; but public opinion (who, donkey as she is, is a very shrewd old donkey, nevertheless, and clearly understands the difference between thistles and barley) requires him to 'come up in good form, measure his distance exactly, take off neatly, clear it cleverly, and *come well into the next field*'. . . . And even so should idyllists with their metres.

THE SHAVING OF SHAGPAT

1856

---

6. Unsigned review, *Critic*

xv, 1 January 1856

This short notice is part of a general review article. The Owen Meredith referred to was the pseudonym of Edward Robert Bulwer Lytton (1831–91), poet and dramatist, the son of Edward Bulwer Lytton, novelist and politician. To mistake George for the better-known Owen was common, and this is the first of several warnings from the reviewers to readers.

It is necessary to premise that George Meredith, the author of *The Shaving of Shagpat*, is *not* Owen Meredith, the poet who, under that name, thinly disguises his relationship to Sir E. L. Bulwer Lytton. It is an Eastern tale, told in imitation of the Eastern style, and therefore, like all such imitations, a mistake. It is a good story spoilt by the adoption of a bad medium for telling it. This is the reason. An Englishman cannot think Eastern thoughts; the Western mind is cast in a very different mould. Hence there is a manifest discrepancy between the ideas and their dress. They are not in keeping; the drapery does not sit naturally upon the foreign figure; all is stiff and constrained. The Briton is seen palpably under the turban. So it has ever been, and so it must ever be. Mr George Meredith's skill in making a story, and humour in relating it, does not compensate for the imperfections of an impossible imitation. If he would write an English story in the English manner, laying his scenes among places familiar to him, and making his personages of those whom he has met in the actual world about him, he would, we believe, be entirely successful, for he has a playful fancy, much invention, and a pleasant manner of telling a tale, which would be sure to win and keep the attention of an audience. As a mere *brochure* for Christmas, this volume may be accepted; but the author designed something more than a book for the season, which has failed only because he has attempted that in which nobody has ever yet succeeded. Even burlesque comedy cannot be endured through so many pages.

7. George Eliot, *Leader*

vii, 5 January 1856

Like G. H. Lewes (see below, No. 8), George Eliot probably got to know Meredith through his contributions to the *Leader*. Later Meredith took over the 'Belles Lettres' section of the *Westminster Review*, which had been written previously by Eliot. She disliked the tone of Meredith's reviews, which she called 'flippant and journalistic', and wrote to John Chapman, Editor of the *Westminster*, urging that he replace Meredith. In their early years the two novelists must have been familiar. Later, however, they showed little awareness of each other's work.

No art of religious symbolism has a deeper root in nature than that of turning with reverence towards the East. For almost all our good things —our most precious vegetables, our noblest animals, our loveliest flowers, our arts, our religious and philosophical ideas, our very nursery tales and romances, have travelled to us from the East. In an historical as well as in a physical sense, the East is the Land of the Morning. Perhaps the simple reason of this may be, that when the earth first began to move on her axis her Asiatic side was towards the sun—her Eastern cheek first blushed under his rays. And so this priority of sunshine, like the first move in chess, gave the East the precedence though not the pre-eminence in all things; just as the garden slope that fronts the morning sun yields the earliest seedlings, though those seedlings may attain a hardier and more luxuriant growth by being transplanted. But we leave this question to wiser heads—

'Felix qui potuit rerum cognoscere causas.'[1]

[1] Virgil, *Georgics*, ii. 490: 'Happy he who can discern the causes of things.'

40

(Excuse the novelty of the quotation.) We have not carried our reader's thoughts to the East that we may discuss the reason why we owe it so many good things, but that we may introduce him to a new pleasure, due, at least indirectly, to that elder region of the earth. We mean *The Shaving of Shagpat* which is indeed an original fiction just produced in this western island, but which is so intensely Oriental in its conception and execution, that the author has done wisely to guard against the supposition of its being a translation, by prefixing the statement that it is derived from no Eastern source, but is altogether his own.

The Shaving of Shagpat, is a work of genius, and of poetical genius. It has none of the tameness which belongs to mere imitations manufactured with servile effort or thrown off with simious facility. It is no patchwork of borrowed incidents. Mr Meredith has not simply imitated Arabian fictions, he has been inspired by them; he has used Oriental forms, but only as an Oriental genius would have used them who had been 'to the manner born'. Goëthe, when he wrote an immortal work under the inspiration of Oriental studies, very properly called it *West-östliche*—West-Eastern—because it was thoroughly Western in spirit, though Eastern in its forms.[1] But this double epithet would not give a true idea of Mr Meredith's work, for we do not remember that throughout our reading we were once struck by an incongruity between the thought and the form, once startled by the intrusion of the chill north into the land of the desert and the palm. Perhaps more lynx-eyed critics, and more learned Orientalists, than we, may detect discrepancies to which we are blind, but our experience will at least indicate what is likely to be the average impression. In one particular, indeed, Mr Meredith differs widely from his models, but that difference is a high merit: it lies in the exquisite delicacy of his love incidents and love scenes. In every other characteristic—in exuberance of imagery, in picturesque wildness of incident, in significant humour, in aphoristic wisdom, *The Shaving of Shagpat* is a new *Arabian Night*. To two thirds of the reading world this is sufficient recommendation.

According to Oriental custom the main story of the book—*The Shaving of Shagpat*—forms the setting to several minor tales, which are told, on pretexts more or less plausible, by the various *dramatis personæ*. We will not forestall the reader's pleasure by telling him who Shagpat was, or what were the wondrous adventures through which Shibli Bagarag, the wandering barber, became Master of the Event and the destroyer of illusions, by shaving from Shagpat the mysterious identical

---

[1] Goethe's *West-östlicher Divan* was published in 1819.

which had held men in subjection to him. There is plenty of deep meaning in the tale for those who cannot be satisfied without deep meanings, but there is no didactic thrusting forward of moral lessons, and our imagination is never chilled by a sense of allegorical intention predominating over poetic creation. Nothing can be more vivid and concrete than the narrative and description, nothing fresher and more vigorous than the imagery. Are we reading how horsemen pursued their journey? We are told that they 'flourished their lances with cries, and jerked their heels into the flanks of their steeds, and stretched forward till their beards were mixed with the tossing manes, and the dust rose after them crimson in the sun'. Is it a maiden's eyes we are to see? They are 'dark, under a low arch of darker lashes, like stars on the skirts of storm'. Sometimes the images are exquisitely poetical, as when Bhanavar looks forth 'on the stars that were above the purple heights and the *blushes of inner heaven that streamed up the sky*'; sometimes ingenious and pithy: for example 'she clenched her hands an instant with that feeling which knocketh a nail in the coffin of a desire not dead'. Indeed, one of the rarest charms of the book is the constant alteration of passion and wild imaginativeness with humour and pithy, practical sense. Mr Meredith is very happy in his imitation of the lyrical fragments which the Eastern tale-tellers weave into their narrative, either for the sake of giving emphasis to their sententiousness, or for the sake of giving a more intense utterance to passion, a loftier tone to description. We will quote a specimen of the latter kind from the story of *Bhanavar the Beautiful*. This story is the brightest gem among the minor tales, and perhaps in the whole book. It is admirably constructed and thoroughly poetic in its outline and texture. . . .

8. G. H. Lewes, *Saturday Review*

i, 19 January 1856

Lewes, as Editor of *Leader*, must have known Meredith when he wrote this article. Their acquaintance was a lasting one. Meredith consulted Lewes about *Evan Harrington* and published *Vittoria* in the *Fortnightly Review* under his editorship.

Little did we imagine that a work of genius was announced under the incomprehensible title which has, for many weeks past, met our eye among the advertisements of new books. *The Shaving of Shagpat*! what could it mean? 'An Arabian Entertainment!' what might that be? It is very seldom that an announcement which piques curiosity is followed by a work which satisfies the curiosity; but in *The Shaving of Shagpat* a quaint title ushers in an original and charming book, the work of a poet and of a storyteller worthy to rank with the rare storytellers of the East, who have produced, in the *Arabian Nights*, the *Iliad* of romance.

The *Shaving of Shagpat* is an imitation of the Oriental stories; not by any means a servile imitation, but the sort of imitation which naturally springs from kindred power. It is more Eastern than Goethe's *West-östliche Divan*, less directly imitative than Rückert's Oriental poems.[1] Mr Meredith has thoroughly caught the spirit of Arabian romance, and pleasantly tinges his style with the colour and imagery of Arabian eloquence. But although his inventions are as oriental as 'Sinbad' or 'Ali-baba', he assures us in the Preface that they are inventions of his own, and not derived from Eastern sources. It needs such an assertion to convince the reader that he is not listening to the veritable fictions of the East. Both the humour and the poetry seem to issue from the same abundant and delightful source that gave us the *Arabian Nights;* and to produce such a work, which shall not be a rifaccimento, but which shall read like an original, requires very peculiar powers in the writer. Nothing would be easier than to write a tale of enchantment after the Arabian model; but only to rare minds is it given to write a tale

[1] Frederick Rückert (1788–1866), German poet and dramatist.

43

which shall increase the treasures of fiction, while strictly adhering to the old forms.

The Shaving of Shagpat is a collection of stories, connected together by the tale which gives its title to the book. Shibli Bagarag, the Persian Barber, has had great things predicted of him by the readers of planets. These predictions unsettle him, and send him wandering in quest of greatness. He is to become Master of the Event, and to live in the memories of men. That Event is nothing less than the shaving of Shagpat, the clothier who gives his name to the city of Shagpat, and who, arrogant in hairiness, is much revered by men. To shave a clothier, be he never so hairy, will not seem a difficult task, nor the event a great Event. But, O rash reader! the task is more perilous than it seems to thee—the Event more portentous. Hair has become sacred in the cities of Shagpat and Oolb: and barbers an abomination. Thwacks, not sequins, await Figaro. Poor Shibli Bagarag, in the innocence and pride of his art, offers to shave the King, and his reward is fifty thwacks; and ''tis certain, that at every thwack, the thong took an airing before it descended upon him'. Nevertheless, thwacked and reviled though he be, Shibli Bagarag loses not heart. His mind is fixed on becoming Master of the Event. Shave the hairy Shagpat he will; and shave him he does. But *how* he does it, by what magic through what perilous enterprizes, baffling malignant genii with potent spells, now nearly losing the prize just as it is within his grasp, and now by timely aid recovering himself—these, and all the marvellous stories which he hears the while—must be sought in the volume itself. We will not blunt the edge of curiosity by even hinting what we know. If any reader, from the age of ten to the age of eighty, resists the fascination of the stories, it is a proof that he has no imagination.

Although written in prose, liberally sprinkled with verses, after the Eastern manner, the work is a poem throughout. In every page we are aware of the poet. Not that he gives us that detestable hybrid vulgarly called 'poetical prose', with its dissonances of fragmentary metre, and its fine writing which noodles call 'beautiful language'. The prose is prose—not broken-up verse; the language is simple, picturesque, pregnant—not ornate inanities addressed to the ear. A random specimen or two will show what we mean:

O my father, there is all in this youth, the nephew of the barber, that's desirable for the undertaking; and *his feet will be on a level with the task we propose for him—he is the height of man above it.*

Again:

Thereupon he exulted, and his mind strutted through the future of his days, and down the ladder of all time, exacting homage from men, his brethren.

Again:

At the hour indicated, Khipil stood before Shahpesh again. He was pale, saddened; his tongue drooped like the tongue of a heavy bell, that when it soundeth giveth forth mournful sounds only: he had also the look of one battered with many beatings.

There are characteristic specimens—not the best that could have been quoted, but the fairest representatives of the whole. The imagery is brief—generally conveyed in half a sentence—as where the shell closes on the lovers, 'writing darkness on their very eyeballs'; or where the astonishment of the Vizier is expressed thus, 'He made a point of his eyebrows'; and the sun is said 'to shoot a current of gold over leagues of sea'.

The style, although Oriental in its figurativeness, is European in its concision; we miss the luxuriant redundancy of Oriental expression, and are grateful for its absence. In revising the work for another edition, Mr Meredith will do well to look with a little more severity on certain expressions, and get rid of such verbs as 'to verse', 'to lute', and 'to bosom', which are not English, and are not needed. While suggesting alterations, we would further suggest another trifle, which is that he substitute *lion* for *panther* in the passage where Ruark falls upon his foes and smites them to the earth. Any Arab would tell Mr Meredith that the panther, terrible as it is in force and ferocity when in a death-struggle, is timorous as a cat, and never attacks men except in self-defence. To compare the onslaught of a warrior to that of a panther springing on a troop of men, is therefore a false image.

These are very small faults, yet they are all we have espied in a book the charm of which has surpassed that of any Eastern work we ever read since the Arabian Tales; and George Meredith, hitherto known to us as a writer of graceful, but not very remarkable verse, now becomes the name of a man of genius—of one who can *create*.

9. Unsigned review, *Idler*

March 1856

If a patriotic publisher were now to bring out, for the first time a three-volumed story entitled *The Arabian Night's Entertainments*, we must confess that we should find a certain difficulty in reviewing it. What could a conscientious critic say of such a collection of stories? How could he fill the required two columns? Of course, we know that many critics would go off into a digression on Dickens or Bulwer; that many more would state, in two lines, that 'This book is a collection of Eastern stories, containing much that is readable, at the same time being picturesque. The following extract,' etc. The same difficulty exists with regard to Mr George Meredith's *Shaving of Shagpat*. It is a collection of Eastern stories, interspersed with quotations from 'the poet', and altogether reminds us very favourably of the stories which saved a lady's head during the term of a thousand and one nights. We can best describe its qualities in the words of Mr Puff, 'characters strongly drawn—highly coloured—hand of a master—fund of genuine humour —mine of invention—neat dialogue—attic salt'.[1] But what does the title mean? asks the impatient reader. Simply this, Shagpat was a clothier with hair of an extraordinary length, in which some magic spell existed. Shibli Bagarag, a barber, attempted several times to shave him; but was repulsed by Shagpat, and met with many beatings from many viziers. A certain hair on Shagpat's head, called the Identical, had in it the magical power, and when Shagpat was lulled in sleep by an opiate, and Shibli Bagarag attempted to shave him, the Identical sprang up, and hurled the barber to the other side of the chamber. Finally, Shagpat is shaved in a somewhat incomprehensible manner, reminding us of the conclusion of a pantomime. Such is the basis of Mr Meredith's book, and on this basis sundry stories are erected, dealing in magic, beauty, and the other elements of an Eastern tale. We have to thank Mr Meredith for a very pleasant and very original volume.

[1] R. B. Sheridan, *The Critic* (1779), i. 2.

10. George Eliot, *Westminster Review*

xvii, April 1856

This is George Eliot's second review of *The Shaving of Shagpat*; (see above, No. 7). The review is part of a general review in the 'Belles Lettres' section of the *Westminster* and is preceded immediately by a discussion of sculpture.

We turn from the art which most of us must leave our homes to get even a glimpse of, to that which has at least the advantage of visiting us at our own firesides—the art of the romancer and the novelist; and the first work of fiction that presents itself as worth notice is the *Shaving of Shagpat*, an admirable imitation of Oriental tale-telling, which has given us far more pleasure than we remember to have had even in younger days from reading *Vathek*—the object of Byron's enthusiastic praise. Of course, the great mass of fictions are imitations more or less slavish and mechanical—imitations of Scott, of Balzac, of Dickens, of Currer Bell,[1] and the rest of the real 'makers'; every great master has his school of followers, from the kindred genius down to the feeble copyist. The *Shaving of Shagpat* is distinguished from the common run of fictions, not in being an imitation, but in the fact that its model has been chosen from no incidental prompting, from no wish to suit the popular mood, but from genuine love and mental affinity. Perhaps we ought to say that it is less an imitation of the *Arabian Nights* than a similar creation inspired by a thorough and admiring study. No doubt, if a critical lens were to be applied, there would be found plenty of indications that the writer was born in Western Europe, and in the nineteenth century, and that his Oriental imagery is got by hearsay; but to people more bent on enjoying what they read than on proving their acumen, the *Shaving of Shagpat* will be the thousand and *second* night which they perhaps longed for in their childhood. The author is alive to every element in his models: he reproduces their humour and practical sense as well as their wild

---

[1] Currer Bell was the pseudonym of Charlotte Brontë.

imaginativeness. Shibli Bagarag, the barber, carries a great destiny within him: he is to shave Shagpat the clothier, and thus to become Master of the Event. The city of Shagpat, unlike the city of London, regards shaving, and not the beard, as the innovation; and Shagpat is a 'miracle of hairiness, black with hair as he had been muzzled with it, and his head, as it were, a berry in a huge bush by reason of it,' and when the countenance of Shagpat waxed fiery it was as 'a flame kindled by travellers at night in a bramble bush, and he ruffled and heaved, and was as when dense jungle-growths are stirred violently by the near approach of a wild animal'. Moreover, among the myriad hairs of Shagpat is the mysterious 'Identical', which somehow holds the super-stition of men in bondage, so that they bow to it without knowing why—the most obstinate of all bowing, as we are aware. Hence, he who will shave Shagpat, and deliver men from worshipping his hairy mightiness, will deserve to be called Master of the Event; and the story of all the adventures through which Shibli Bagarag went before he achieved this great work—the thwackings he endured, the wondrous scenes he beheld, and the dangers he braved to possess himself of the magic horse Garaveen, the Lily of the Enchanted Lea, and other indispensable things, with his hair-breadth escapes from spiteful genii— all this forms the main action of the book. Other tales are introduced, serving as pleasant landing-places on the way. The best of these is the story of Khipil the Builder, a humorous apologue, which will please readers who are unable to enjoy the wilder imaginativeness of Oriental fiction; but lovers of the poetical will prefer the story of Bhanavar the Beautiful. We confess to having felt rather a languishing interest towards the end of the work; the details of the action became too complicated, and our imagination was rather wearied in following them. But where is the writer, whose wing is as strong at the end of his flight as at the beginning? Even Shakespeare flags under the artificial necessities of a denouement.

11. Unsigned review, *New Quarterly Review*

v, April 1856

This passage is part of a general review article. Illustrative quotations have been omitted.

We turn with pleasure, however, to the *Shaving of Shagpat*. We do not know that it is likely to become popular. But of this we are certain, that should it have the good fortune to meet with the attention it deserves, no degrading place will be assigned to the narrative of the adventures of 'Shibli Bagarag, nephew to the renowned Baba Mustapha, chief barber to the court of Persia,' and of the manner in which he fulfilled that which had been ordained, namely, the shaving of 'Shagpat, the son of Shimpoor, the son of Shoolpi, the son of Shullum'. It is a book destined to be classical, for whether designed to be an allegory (a supposition not entertained by us) or a story written in imitation of Eastern fiction, we have in every line proof of a gorgeous imagination, literary skill of a high order, and considerable dramatic power. We may add to this list of qualifications those of quiet irony, humour, pathos, and an energy of imitation, unflagging from beginning to end. [. . .]

We cannot do justice to Mr Meredith's creation. We can only repeat, that if read it will be admired. It is remote from those facts that usually occupy the mind of man. But should it attract notice equal to its literary merit, the *Shaving of Shagpat* will be remembered and studied as a classical production, side by side with *Vathek, Nourjahad,* and *Anastasius*.[1] In another edition we would suggest the elimination of some portion of the poetical interpolations, as unequal to the prose and interrupting the narrative. A smaller number would not injure the Eastern style.

[1] *Vathek* (1786) was by William Beckford, *Nourjahad* (1767) by Mrs Frances Sheridan, and *Anastasius* (1819) by Thomas Hope.

FARINA

1857

---

12. Unsigned review, *Spectator*

xxx, 22 August 1857

Washington Irving undoubtedly did some mischief to literature when he introduced the style of grave yet facetious grotesque, mingling as it often did an under-current of reality with obvious burlesque. Even in the hands of the master, the subject would run away with him: sentiments, even incidents, were introduced without much purpose; the style sometimes enlarged into verbiage; the quaint manner occasionally dropt into mannerism. These faults, which were rare in the original, became prominent in his imitators. It is so easy to invent scenes that spring from nothing, and lead to nothing; to produce fine sentiments and rich imagery, also apropos of nothing; or to expand into flatness some idea *intended* to be jocular. Hence, tales with a mixture of diableries, grave fun, and burlesque, have often turned out very dull affairs, at least to many people, for 'de gustibus' applies to fiction as to other things.

Mr Meredith's *Farina, a Legend of Cologne*, is a great improvement upon *The Shaving of Shagpat;* though there is enough of forced quaintness, 'passages that lead to nothing', and facetiousness that is only pleasantry to those who can bring themselves to relish it. The larger portion of the story, however, consists of scenes with action, persons, and purpose, that possess interest in themselves, and contribute their quota to the whole; the quaint mode of representation giving character to the narrative.

It is possible that some notion of accounting for the origin of eau de Cologne may have prompted Mr Meredith; for the hero and lover Farina is a student of chemistry, accused by his rivals of pursuing the black art. Nothing, however, is made of this idea beyond enabling the

Emperor of Germany to enter Cologne by aid of Farina, when monarch and courtiers had been driven back by the stench from a hole down which the Devil had made his escape. The tale is one of love and rivalry, planned to illustrate grotesquely the manners and superstitions of the middle ages in Germany. Margarita Gottlieb, the White Rose of Germany, is the daughter of a very rich and worthy citizen of Cologne, who is sufficiently eminent to rank the Emperor among his borrowers. Margarita is sought by the principal youth of the city, who form themselves into a White Rose club, for praising and defending the lady; which last, however, they do not effect when they are wanted. There are scenes designed to exhibit quaint burgher characters and customs; others to expose, as we imagine, the weakness even of saintly men when brought face to face with Satan and his flatteries. The interest of the story turns upon the love difficulties of Farina and Margarita, for the lady is carried off by a brutal robber baron, hight Werner, to his castle; old Gottlieb is opposed to the match. However, Margarita is rescued by Farina, aided by the Water-lady and an English soldier of fortune; and the Emperor manages the old burgher, out of gratitude for overcoming the Devil through Farina's means.

Guy Goshawk, the English adventurer, is the most busy personage in the tale, and the most interesting; albeit he is somewhat conventional in his bluff bearing, frank hostility, fair fighting, and liking for good living. Here he is in his first rescue of Margarita. Werner's band riding into Cologne have seen her at the window; and one robber makes a bet with another that he will have a kiss in twenty minutes. Time has been lost in preliminaries with Gottlieb, and the high-spirited maiden, persuading her father to withdraw, comes forward herself.

[Quotes 'The Wager', from '"Cologne! broad day!"' to 'agreement from the troop'.]

13. Unsigned review, *Saturday Review*

iii, 29 August 1857

The *Shaving of Shagpat* was so clever, and contained such an amusing and humorous imitation of Oriental story-telling, that it was natural to look forward with considerable interest to the appearance of another tale by the same author. Mr Meredith has now given us *Farina, a Legend of Cologne*. We must confess that we are disappointed. The subject does not seem to us worth handling, and the comic part is more grotesque than piquant. There is much art displayed in the management of the different points of the story, and a neatness and finish in the turns of language and the contrivance of situations. There is also some pretty word-painting of Rhine scenery and cathedral and city effects. But the whole seems to us flat and dull. We feel throughout as if the good chapter must be the next, until we get to the end of the book, and find that our chances are over. It is true that the dulness is that of a clever man. There is never anything petty or vulgar, and every page contains a sentence or two which no one but a practised writer could have written. Still, no subordinate merits can redeem the original faults of a trifling subject and a walk of comedy that is necessarily barren. We cannot, therefore, help regretting that Mr Meredith was not content to rest his reputation on the *Shaving of Shagpat*.

The name of *Farina* points at once to the nature of the legend which Mr Meredith has undertaken to tell and expand into a volume. There is a rich citizen of Cologne, with a pretty daughter, to protect, worship, and fight for whom is established 'The White Rose Club'. But Gretchen smiles on none of the amorous swashbucklers, and turns an eye of favour only on Farina, a youth suspected of sorcery because he is always distilling subtle odours and potions. Baron Werner, of Werner's Eck, one of the ruffian lords of the Rhine, sees this beauty, and determines to carry her off. He succeeds in doing so; but Farina vows to rescue her, and calls to his aid a stalwart Englishman, rejoicing in the name of Goshawk, whose acquaintance he has recently made in a street row got up by the White Rose Club and the followers of Werner. Before, however, he can attend to the calls of love, Farina has to attend to those of business, for a monk whom he considers himself bound to obey summons him

52

to take part in an expedition to the top of the Drachenfels. This monk, afterwards known as St Gregory, climbs the mountain in order to have a personal conflict with the devil. Farina witnesses the conflict, and sees the vanquished demon spread his wings and make for the city of Cologne. Gretchen is rescued, but when she and her friends return to Cologne they find the city in the utmost dismay and confusion. For Satan, although vanquished on the Drachenfels, has his revenge, and having disappeared downwards in the midst of the city, has left behind him a poisonous stench, which kills man and beast. The Emperor himself is lying outside the city and cannot enter. A youth claims an audience with him, and informs him that he has succeeded in distilling a wonderful scent, which will baffle the wiles of the devil. His majesty tries Farina's Eau de Cologne, and, finding it perfectly efficacious, enters the city in triumph, and rewards the inventor with the hand of his mistress.

We sympathize with Mr Albert Smith when he declares, in his admirable ascent of the Rhine, that there really is nothing in the Rhine legends—that they are great bores, and had better be forgotten.[1] A long story about the devil making a smell, and a Farina inventing Eau de Cologne to take the smell away, seems to us very poor fun. There is nothing to be got out of such an incident. The monk talks about it in appropriate monkish phraseology, but the subject is as dreary as ever. 'Sathanas', we read, 'fights not, my son, with his fore-claws. 'Tis with his tail he fights, O Farina. Listen, my son: he entered to his kingdom below through Cologne, even under the stones of the Cathedral Square, and the stench of him abominably remaineth, challenging the nostrils of holy and unholy alike.' Happy is the man who can laugh at this—it seems to us about as lively as the funny column of a county paper. Nothing can nowadays be more *triste*, tedious, and dispiriting, than the comic stories about the great enemy of mankind which diverted, and perhaps instructed, the ecclesiastical gossips of the middle ages. Yet, like all persons and things which have once become part of the stock of storytellers, this source of mingled terror and amusement is occasionally had recourse to by uninventive narrators, long after the old feeling has passed away which made the early stories endurable. There is much to be added to the history of the Devil, since Defoe wrote it.[2] There was the use made of him by the romancists of

---

[1] Untraced; but perhaps a reference to the beginning of Albert Richard Smith's *The Story of Mont Blanc* (1853).
[2] Defoe's book was published in 1726.

last century, who brought him in as a *diabolus ex machinâ*, to give sudden and fearful turns to horrible plots. There was the graceful mode of alluding to and speaking of him, employed by Walter Scott and others, who had, as a matter of business, to tell a modern generation old stories in which his intervention made a part, and who spoke of him without any affectation or pretence. Then came the ludicro-serious attempt of Mr Kingsley to write the devil up, and introduce him as a sort of walking gentleman in the ordinary English novel.[1] And now we have Mr. Meredith polishing him off with dapper little turns and flourishes.

We also feel inclined to quarrel with Mr Meredith's word-painting. Certainly Mr Ruskin has a great deal to answer for, as no one now can describe simply and temperately, but must keep up to the Ruskin level, and put on his colours thick and bright. Mr Meredith weighs us down with the precious stones which he heaps on us whenever he has got any common object of nature to describe. We open the volume, and find in one page that a lover who is disappointed is 'of the fallen, and of the fallen would he remain, but that tears lighten him, and through the tears stream jewelled shafts, dropt down to him from the sky, precious ladders inlaid with amethyst, sapphire, blended jasper, beryl, rose-ruby, ether of heaven flushed with softened bloom of the insufferable Presences'. In the next page we hear of a certain courtyard, that it was of 'lush deep emerald grass, softly mixed with grey in the moon's light, and showing like jasper'. Again, we turn the page, and read that the hero looked at Werner's Eck by night, and saw among other things, that 'behind lay scattered some faint-twinkling stars on sapphire fields, and a stain of yellow light was in a breach of one wall'. Now these jewels come cheap on paper, and can, of course, be had in any quantity; but do they really look well, and produce the fine effect for which they are intended? We confess they seem to us a mere trick of the trade, and do not produce any other impression than that of something rich, which would be arrived at by an enumeration of any other articles of a high market value. Certainly, they are better than phrases which mean nothing. By throwing ourselves on the kindness of Messrs Hunt and Roskell, we might be enabled to appreciate the appearance of a ladder of beryl;[2] but no human assistance could teach us what is meant by 'softened bloom of the insufferable Presences'. We wish Mr Meredith would not insist on giving us so much for our money. We should

[1] Perhaps a reference to *Westward Ho!* (1855), ch. xiii.
[2] Hunt and Roskell occupied a jeweller's shop at 156 New Bond Street.

prefer a chaster article; and we can only hope that an author who has so many excellent qualities will when he next comes before the public, choose a better subject, and cut down by one-half his estimate of what is due to himself and his readers in the way of fine language.

14. Unsigned notice, *Critic*

xvi, 1 September 1857

Farina is by the author of *The Shaving of Shagpat*, a comical allegory published about twelve months ago, and which obtained a good deal of popularity. The success of it probably prompted him to produce another facetious story, laying the scene of this one at Cologne in the middle ages—the lives of Farina and Margarita Gottlieb, the daughter of a wealthy citizen, forming the groundwork of a plot which enables Mr Meredith to introduce the citizens of the times and the Rhine robbers, and an English traveller, one Guy Goshawk, and to depict them truth-fully enough perhaps, but with an exaggeration of their oddities such as George Cruikshank would have produced them with his pencil—like, yet unlike. The author has a taste for the grotesque, and is skilful in the drawing of it, so as to avoid the danger of falling into the absurd, which is just one step beyond it. *Farina* is an improvement upon the former work, and cannot fail to amuse the most sober-minded reader.

15. Meredith, *Westminster Review*

xii, October 1857

This unsigned review has been traditionally attributed to George Eliot. By October 1857, however, the reviews in the 'Belles Lettres' section of the *Westminster* were being written by Meredith himself. For this reason the quotations are reproduced.

The Author of *Farina* has exposed himself to a somewhat trying ordeal. Last year he treated us to a delightful volume of well-sustained Oriental extravagance, and we remember our friend Shibli Bagarag too well to be easily satisfied with any hero less astonishing. It was refreshing to leave the actual and the probable for a time, and follow Mr Meredith's lead into the bright world of imagination. The hope of such another enchanted holiday prepared us to welcome his new tale with all due honour and cordiality. It was with something like disappointment, therefore, that we found ourselves brought down to the vulgar limits of time and place, and our appetite for the marvellous entirely spoilt by scenes which challenge prosaic considerations of historical truth and the fitness of things. The title *Farina: a Legend of Cologne*, will naturally carry the reader's mind to those ungainly-shaped bottles, with which the British tourist is sure to return laden from the city of evil smells. Mr Meredith is pleased to bestow a high antiquity on the famous distillation, and his hero, doubtless the first of all the Jean Marie's, is invested with the dubious honours of a dealer in the black art, on account of his suspicious collection of bottles and vases, pipes, and cylinders. But when the Devil is beaten in single combat on the Drachenfels, and returns from whence he came, entering to his kingdom under the Cathedral Square, and leaving behind him a most abominable stench, Farina's perfumed water does good service. The Kaiser, six times driven back by the offence to his nostrils, is enabled to enter the good city of Cologne, and then and there reward the restorer of a pure atmosphere with the hand of his long-loved bride. For the rest, the story is sufficiently slight. We have the blonde and bewitching heroine,

Margarita, and her troop of lovers, who prove their devotion by such strenuous interchange of blows in her honour, that there is not one of them who is not black and blue; and we have *the* lover, Farina, tender and true, brave as Siegfried, and worshipping his 'Frankinne' with such fanatical homage, as 'Conrad the Pious' might have sung. Margarita's father Gottlieb Groschen, the rich Cologne citizen, is a characteristic specimen of the prosperous mediæval Rhinelander, and we cannot give our readers a more favourable specimen of Mr Meredith's style than by introducing the father and daughter, engaged in receiving that nuisance of the middle—as of all ages—morning visitors:

A clatter in the Cathedral Square brought Gottlieb on his legs to the window. It was a company of horsemen sparkling in harness. One trumpeter rode on the side of the troop, and in front a standard-bearer, matted down the chest with ochre beard, displayed aloft to the good citizens of Cologne, three brown hawks, with birds in their beaks, on an azure star-dotted field. 'Holy Cross!' exclaimed Gottlieb, low in his throat, 'the arms of Werner! Where got he money to mount his men? Why, this is daring all Cologne in our very teeth! 'Fend that he visit me now! Ruin smokes in that ruffian's track. I've felt hot and cold by turns all day.' The horsemen came jingling carelessly along the street in scattered twos and threes, laughing together, and singling out the maidens at the gable-shadowed window [*sic*] with hawking eyes. They were in truth ferocious-looking fellows. Leather, steel, and dust, clad them from head to foot; big and black as bears; wolf-eyed, fox-nosed. They glistened bravely in the falling beams of the sun, and Margarita thrust her fair braided yellow head a little forward over her father's shoulder, to catch the whole length of the grim cavalcade. One of the troop was not long in discerning the young beauty.

They come to the door with a 'thundering smack', and one is perforce admitted:

Margarita heard 'wafted in a thunder of oaths,' ''Tis the maiden we want; let's salute her and begone! or cap your skull with something thicker than you've on it now, if you want a whole one, happy father!' 'Gottlieb von Groschen I am,' answered her father, 'and the Kaiser—' ''Sas fond of a pretty girl as we are! Down with her, and no more drivelling! It's only for a moment, old Measure and Scales!' 'I tell you, rascals, I know your master, and if you're not punished for this, may I die a beggar!' exclaimed Gottlieb, jumping with rage. 'May you die as rich as an abbot! And so you will, if you don't bring her down, for I've sworn to see her; there's the end of it, man!'

Fearing violence to her father, Margarita comes down; her brutal admirer explains:

MEREDITH

'I'm no ninny, and not to be diddled; I'll talk to the young lady!—Silence out there! all's going proper;' this to his comrades through the door. 'So, my beautiful maiden! thus it stands:—We saw you at the window, looking like a fresh rose with a gold crown on.' . . . 'Schwartz Thier!' says Henker Rothhals to me, 'I'll wager you odds you don't have a kiss of that fine girl within twenty minutes counting from the hand smack!' 'Done,' was my word, and we clapped our fists together. Now, you see, that's straightforward!'

How Margarita escapes this indignity, how she becomes the captive of the terrible Werner himself, and how she is rescued, we have not space to tell; much clever and vigorous description is to be found in the narrative, and Mr Meredith has been very successful in setting before us a vivid picture of the coarse, rough manners, the fierce, war-like habits, and the deep-seated superstition of the 'good old times' of chivalry. The character of the jovial Squire Guy the Goshawk, is especially well done. As a whole, we think *Farina* lacks completeness, and the ghostly element is not well worked in. The combat between Saint Gregory and the Devil is made ludicrous by its circumstantiality. It was not as a jeering satirist that the old monkish legends set forth Sathanas, and there is a clumsiness in the whole affair which accords ill with the boldness and skill displayed in other portions of the tale. We must also protest against Father Gregory's use of the nominative case 'ye' instead of the accusative 'you', monk though he be, and privileged doubtless to speak bad grammar at will; nor can we admire many passages, in which the Author has sacrificed euphony, and almost sense, to novelty and force of expression. With these blemishes, *Farina* is both an original and an entertaining book, and will be read with pleasure by all who prefer a lively, spirited story to those dull analyses of dull experiences in which the present school of fiction abounds.

16. H. F. Chorley, *Athenaeum*

No. 1570, 28 November 1857

Henry Fothergill Chorley (1808–72), was a critic, a student of music and a dramatist. His review begins with a description of Cologne which has been omitted.

We fancied, from the title of his legend, that the lively Author of *The Shaving of Shagpat* was about to introduce us into that exquisite flower-garden from which these 'blessings flow'—that he intended to tell us under what configuration of planets, in what month of the sun's year, blossom and bud, and leaf and stem, were to be gathered—and to name the craftsman who made the first alembic, in which the mixture thereof was distilled—but, though his tale has 'Farina' on its label, let none tap it (to use Horace Walpole's favourite verb) expecting anything fragrant, or soft, or gentle. Wild it is, on the contrary, and impudent and fierce—full of a riotous, abundant fancy, such as we have not fallen in with of late. It is a masque of ravishers in steel—of robber knights, who sat on their towers looking up and down the gorges of the Eifel to see what manner of prey might be coming—of water-woman more terribly fascinating than Loreley—of monks nearly as sharp in dealing with the Great *Too-well-known* as St Dunstan himself. It has also a brave and tender deliverer and a heroine proper for a romance of Cologne. We cannot better afford a specimen of our romancer's manner than by giving a glimpse of the said heroine, in the attitude of the *Lady of Shalott*—only with a partner over her web:

[Quotes 'The Tapestry Work', from 'Now Margarita was ambitious' to 'gazing into the street'.]

We will not pretend to say what the maiden saw in the street, and what came of the sight. Those who love a real, lively, audacious piece of extravagance by way of a change from well-meant tales of reformatory schools, or of the strong-minded woman, whose 'pride of sex' makes her propose to the gentleman as to the weaker vessel—those who may be tired of Transatlantic namby-pamby, and of Parisian *quarter-worldliness*—those who do not object to goblins at Christmas-time, nor to Paladins seven or seventy feet high, who ride rides outdoing the ride in Mr Browning's capital ballad—will enjoy *Farina*, as a full-blooded specimen of the nonsense of Genius. Readers of the class of *Mr Burchell*[1] need not trouble themselves to cut the leaves of the legend.

[1] Presumably Goldsmith's character in *The Vicar of Wakefield*, who says: 'English poetry is nothing at present but a combination of luxuriant images, without plot or connexion...' See *Collected Work...*, ed. A. Friedman (1966), IV, 46.

THE ORDEAL OF RICHARD FEVEREL

1859

This novel in its first published form contained a good deal of material which was later excised in successive revisions (1878 and 1896). Early reviews often quoted passages which were later dropped, and such passages are reprinted here in full.

17. Unsigned review, *Leader*

x, 2 July 1859

The Ordeal of Richard Feverel can be designated less as a novel than as a philosophical criticism upon the various methods of educating children. Education is perhaps one of the most difficult sciences in the world; not because it is difficult to bring out the minds of the young, but because it is so difficult to discover whether or not you are leading it in the right direction. And, moreover, it carries with it so grave a responsibility that no one who is not certain of his capabilities to instruct and enlighten, ought to take upon himself the task of leading forth the bud with the flower.

The ordeal of Richard Feverel is the story of a mistaken system of education. Deserted—when his child is in its infancy—by a wife of whom he was dotingly fond, Sir Austin Feverel forms unto himself a system of education for his only son, which he supposes will enable him to escape from the vices and temptations of the world. Not even from his earliest infancy does 'the system' work well; when he is a child he is wild, wilful, wayward, unapproachable; when he is fourteen he is almost transported in consequence of his desire for deadly revenge. Feeling insulted by his father's request to strip before the doctor, in order that he may be examined as to any ailment which may affect his future prospects, he sallied forth upon a hunting expedition with one of

61

his friends. Shooting a partridge [*sic*] belonging to a neighbouring farmer, he is horsewhipped by this injured worthy, and—wailed [*sic*] and breathing deadly enmity—he departs to meditate upon future vengeance. He falls unluckily enough upon a man who is out of work, and for 'a consideration' this unfortunate is persuaded to set fire to one of Farmer Blaize's hayricks—Farmer Blaize being the enemy. In the course of the evening, therefore, the farmer's hay goes 'to blazes'; and the boys, unconscious that Sir Austin sees them and overhears their conversation, stand flattening their noses against the window-panes, enjoying the fun. Ultimately, of course, the boy is detected—has to beg pardon, and the affair is cleared up, although poor Tom Bakewell stands a very good chance of being transported for life. At length, after many minor episodes, the lad marries at nineteen a heroine of eighteen; and after a three months' honeymoon subsides into a careless, reckless, man about town. He has married without his father's consent, and leaving his spouse in the Isle of Wight, he comes up to London to obtain his father's forgiveness. The 'system' now begins to work. Somehow or another his father has some crotchetty idea that he ought to be left to himself for some time, and accordingly, for about nine months, Mr Richard Feverel is left to his own resources in the great metropolis, awaiting in anxious suspense his father's coming. In his London experiences he meets with certain bland and easy gentlewomen, who bestow their favours upon the first handsome man they meet, and falls in love, as he supposes, with one of them. The result of this is that he disgraces himself—is ashamed to go home to his wife—rambles about with his *inamorata*; and at length, upon learning that a man has desired to seduce his wife, returns home to say good-bye, and fights a duel. His wife dies of brain fever, and he is left to the reader's imagination.

The story, although it continues throughout to be wild, fantastic, and in some degree enervating, is not without its moral or its purpose. But we doubt if young people will read it. Although it begins hopefully, it ends too disastrously. Through the mist of morbidity and gloom which pervades the commencement we seem to recognize 'a good time coming'; but when we come to the end we are unnecessarily and wofully disappointed. George Meredith can write well and conceive grandly, but he has yet to learn to correct, or at any rate to conceal, his eccentricities.

18. Unsigned review, *Critic*

xix, 2 July 1859

The idea upon which Mr George Meredith's novel is based is not particularly new. From that royal Egyptian experimentalist referred to by Herodotus who secluded an infant from all communion with human beings, for the purpose of ascertaining what is the natural and consequently original language,[1] down to the present time, the notion of endeavouring to submit nature to crucial experiments has occurred to many writers. More than one novelist, in more than one language, has even hit upon the same idea as Mr Meredith, and has carried it out with different success. That idea is to make a father bring up his son upon some preconceived system of Procrustean rigidity, and who finds his speculations overturned and his conclusions evaded by those passions which are inseparable from human nature, but which he has omitted from the postulates of his problem. The idea of Sir Austin Absworthy Bearne Feverel is misogynism—he is a hater and a contemner of woman. He is one who expects that Woman will be the last animal civilised by Man. He has written a book in which he develops this and similar ideas, and resolves to prove his theory by educating his infant son according to it. Him will he so hedge round with scientific principles that Youth shall escape its own corruptness, and he shall be advanced 'to a certain moral fortitude ere the Apple-disease is spontaneously developed'. What the worthy baronet meant by the Apple-disease is faintly shadowed forth by the reception which the confession of his intention met with among certain of his female acquaintance—being a misogynist we cannot call them friends:

> Mrs Blewins said the idea was very original.
> 'A gigantic task!' said Mrs Cashentire.
> 'It's more than ye'll do though, take my word for it,' said the M'Murphy; and the Hon. Mrs Breakyeline vowed, 'She liked a man to be a man.' She was evidently not the uncorrupted Eve.

So it is upon this principle that the education of young Richard Feverel proceeds. The adventures of his early years are very various, and

[1] Herodotus, ii.2.

MEREDITH

are related with something of Shandean humour, and, indeed, the whole book forcibly reminds us in various ways of Sterne's remarkable work. There are personages surrounding the Baronet and his son who are full of quaint humour and sententious reflection, and who serve very well to give a body to the story. There is his brother Algernon, a Guardsman; and his nephew Adrian Harley, a modern melancholy Jacques, a youth who is full of wise saws and modern instances, and who unites the wisdom of Epicurus to that of Seneca. These, by the various parts which they play in the education of the youth and by the scenes in which they take part, make up about the only excuse that can be urged for expanding so slender a story into the proportion of three volumes.

To make a long story short, the young Richard from his very earliest years exhibits unmistakable evidence of being possessed by at least his full share of original sin. In vain is 'The System' brought to bear upon him—in vain do the watchful eyes of the Baronet spy at the first buddings of the mental weed-crop; young Hopeful will run astray, and that to such purpose, that, in revenge for a horse-whipping, he is guilty of arson before he attains his fourteenth year. With qualities so precocious, what wonder if his father's woman-hating principles are speedily set at nought? Long ere he attains years of discretion he is over head and ears in love with the beautiful and innocent Lucy Desborough, the niece of a neighbouring farmer. Here is a pretty pickle! Not only a complete refutation of the system, but a *mesalliance* into the bargain! The Baronet, however, has his remedy. Richard must marry a young lady who has also been brought up upon a system—this time a gymnastic one. In his development of this system, Mr. Meredith somewhat travels into the burlesque:

Sir Austin turned to Mrs Caroline, and inquired anxiously if the child took much medicine. 'The smallest occasional doses,' Mrs Caroline remarked, to an accompaniment of interjectory eyebrows and chins from all her younger daughters, and a reserved demure aspect of the elder ones. 'I do not like much medicine for children,' said the Baronet, a little snappishly. 'Only the smallest occasional doses?' Mrs Caroline repeated, making her voice small, and the doses sound sweet. 'My son has had little or nothing,' said the Baronet. The young ladies looked on the father of that son with interest. 'Will you come and see our gymnasium?' Mrs Caroline asked quickly. 'It is,' she added, rising with heroic effort, 'not to be compared to our country one. But it is of excellent use, and all my girls exercise in it, when in town, once a day, without intermission. My principle is, that girls require a development of their frames

64

as well as boys; and the more muscle they have, the better women they make. I used it constantly till disappointment and sorrow broke the habit.'—'On my honour, madam,' said the enraptured Baronet, 'you are the only sensible woman I have met,' and he offered his arm to conduct the strenuous invalid. Daughters and little dogs trooped to the gymnasium, which was fitted up in the court below, and contained swing-poles, and stride-poles, and newly invented instruments for bringing out special virtues: an instrument for the lungs, an instrument for the liver, one for the arms and thighs, one for the wrists; the whole for the promotion of the Christian accomplishments. Owing, probably, to the exhaustion consequent on their previous exercises of the morning, the young ladies, excepting Carola, looked fatigued, and pale, and anything but well-braced; and for the same reason, doubtless, when the younger ones were requested by their mother to exhibit the use of the several instruments, each of them wearily took hold of the depending strap of leather, and wearily pulled it, like mariners oaring in the deep sea—oaring to a haven they have no faith in. 'I sometimes hear them,' said their mamma, 'while I am reclining above, singing in chorus. "Row, brothers, row," is one of their songs. It sound[s] pretty and cheerful.' The Baronet was too much wrapped up in the enlightenment of her principle to notice the despondency of their countenances.

Needless to say, however, that youth has *its* way, and Sir Austin has not his. His son steals a march and runs away with Lucy. And here begins the more serious part of the story. After a brief honeymoon, Richard, urged by Adrian Harley, the family diplomatist, and by his wife herself (who thinks she sees the policy of it), leaves his pretty bride in the Isle of Wight, and returns to attempt a reconciliation with his father, who will have none of him for a time, his dignity being offended; and so Richard remains for some time exposed to the temptation of London. Here he falls in with a dangerous woman, a temptress and an enchantress, *and his education having unfitted him for combating the wiles of such women*, this promising youth, fresh from the side of a pure and beautiful wife, falls—falls miserably—to a rouged, champagne-drinking Paphian. The scenes which relate to this catastrophe are dwelt upon by Mr Meredith with too much minuteness; and, indeed, in many parts of his book he betrays a fondness for gloating over what had better be only hinted at, which is far from being in good taste.

After the fall comes remorse, and Richard Feverel is sufficiently ashamed of himself to avoid his innocent wife. She, by the good offices of friends, becomes reconciled to Sir Austin whilst he is away. The woman with whom he has sinned becomes in all respects his perdition. Happening to hear that the nobleman whom she had deserted on his account, had been paying attentions to his wife, he forthwith challenges him; and, after an interview with his wife, he meets him upon the field, and receives a severe wound. This kills poor Lucy; but the last chapter leaves us in hopes that he, the sinner, may survive.

It is impossible to deny that this work has a great deal of vigour about it; but whether that vigour be applied to a proper purpose is another question. With the broad principle that a worldly education is best for a worldly career we agree; but that scarcely required *The Ordeal of Richard Feverel* for its proof. Mr Meredith is a man who has evidently thought much and deeply; but there are many passages in his book which lead us to believe that his mind is none of the purest. To some extent, therefore, he disproves his own lesson, that much knowledge of the world is good for the purity of the soul. His work is certainly meat for strong men rather than food for babes. Perhaps the greatest objection to be urged against this certainly very clever book is the tendency which its author exhibits to run into balderdash. The incidents upon which the following scene is based may perhaps be natural love; yet it must be confessed that the language chosen for their expression is decidedly hyperbolical:

[Quotes xix, from 'The tide of colour' to end.]

In his attempts to be humorous, though certainly sometimes successful (as in the grave scraps of conversation of the wise youth Adrian Harley), Mr Meredith is equally apt to run into extremes. We do not believe, for example, that any butler ever existed of whose pedantry the following can be taken for a fair specimen:

'Pardon me, Mr Adrian,' Berry doubled his elbow to explain. 'Pardon me, sir. Acting recipient of special injunctions, I was not a free agent.' Adrian tacitly acknowledged the choiceness of the phraseology, and asked if he had seen Benson. 'I have enjoyed an interview with Mr Benson, sir.'—'I dare say you did enjoy it, Berry!' Berry protested: 'On my honour, sir! From the plenitude of health and spirits, I regarded Mr Benson with profound—a— profound—' a word fine enough for his emotion seemed wanting. 'Mr Richard have shattered his ganglions, sir,'—'His what?' Adrian asked. Berry corrected the casual error: 'I should say, his idioshincrazy, sir.'—'Accentuate the fourth, not the fifth, syllable, Berry.'—'Exactly, sir. His idihoshincrazy. I may have my own retrospections against Mr Benson; but, hem! as homo,'—and Berry ventured a familiar smile as he joined Adrian on classical ground; 'as homo, sir I am concerned.'

The same tendency to exaggeration displays itself constantly. We doubt whether there are many young ladies in the habit of using

Rotten-row who are desirious of 'riding their ponies stride-ways', nor that ladies of fashion smoke privately to such an extent as to inspire their daughters with an ambition to do likewise.

To sum up, we are of opinion that this work has great merits and great defects, and we believe that these are very evenly balanced.

19. G. E. Jewsbury, *Athenaeum*

No. 1654, 9 July 1859

Geraldine Endor Jewsbury (1812–80), was considered a substantial novelist in her own day. She contributed regularly to the *Athenaeum* and reviewed other novels of Meredith (see below, nos 32 and 41).

This *Ordeal* is about as painful a book as any reader ever felt himself inexorably compelled to read through, in spite of his own protests to the contrary—for read it, and read it through, he must, if he once begins it, for the sole purpose of knowing what comes of it all. The book is very clever, with a fresh, vigorous vitality in the style; but it is *not* true to real life or human nature; only true to an abstract and entirely arbitrary idea. If such a man as Sir Austen ever started from his own fixed idea—if he could so abstract himself from all the friction of counteracting motives and the contradictions which are the main elements in human nature—if he could so hold to his purpose that, even where most thwarted, his instinct is not to take things as they are and deal with them accordingly, but to try to turn them back into the philosophical groove from which they have perversely strayed—if a human being were a trailing plant to be trained over a wonderful and elaborate lattice-work of systems and ordinances—then might all that happens in this book have come to pass, and the reader would have read it with the feeling that no probability was being outraged; he would feel that, however painful, it was a natural combination of those mysterious powers—'fixed fate, foreknowledge, and free-will'—which was at work, and not an entirely arbitrary and improbable assumption of the question before it was asked. The reader feels that none of the characters are real, live human beings; but then they are all so like life, their conversation is so bright and spirited, that it affects the reader like a painful reality to see such cruelty and blindness and blundering, such child's play with the most sacred mysteries of life, even though he is quite aware of the fiction that lies at the root of this 'seeming show'. The story of *The Ordeal of Richard Feverel* is brief enough as regards its facts. Sir Austen Feverel is a baronet who has been bitterly wronged in life; a faithless wife and a treacherous friend round the story of his griefs. Being very proud, very sensitive, with a great leaven of insane philosophy, he resolves that his only son shall be brought up on a system of art and nature which shall train him to be superior to the strokes of fate, and to be, moreover, all that the most perfect human being was ever intended by nature to be, both in mind and body. This 'system' he follows rigidly, with blind despotism, and though a good man, full of generous and noble instincts, this 'system' makes him cruel, hard, relentless, in all that relates to its requisitions. His son grows up to be a very fine young man, but his father cannot recognize where the 'system' which had worked well on the youth should give way to common sense when he grows to the age of a reasonable, rational, responsible human being. The progress of the theory, and the confusion worked by counteracting and contrary facts, make a tolerably perplexed and entangled piece of work. The misery, sin, and sorrow that ensue because Sir Austin will lean to his own understanding, and keep up his system like an immutable destiny that must be worked out—and how the accident of base men, and vain, weak, domineering women, concur to strengthen all that is wrong and perverse—and how the only blame-less creature, the one thoroughly good, gentle, unselfish being, who would have retrieved and redeemed all—the one good angel thrown into the strife—is the one who falls the victim, and in death, although she could not do it in life, brings all the long ordeal to a solution, leaving the actors, not to grief and tears, the tumult of a grief with hope in it, but to cold despair and the silence of eternal regret, making a sort of modern adaptation of the old Greek tragedy, which is what we suppose the author intended. The only comfort the reader can find on closing the book is—that it is not true. We hope the author will use his great ability to produce something pleasanter next time.

20. Unsigned review, *Spectator*

xxxii, 9 July 1859

Of the novels mentioned in the first paragraph, Bulwer Lytton's *The Caxtons* was published in 1849 and Thomas Love Peacock's *Headlong Hall* in 1816.

The Ordeal of Richard Feverel is, like *The Caxtons*, a Shandean novel of contemporary English life, but freer and less mechanical in its Shandyism. While Sir Bulwer Lytton is related to Sterne rather as a plagiarist than as an imitator, Mr Meredith remodels the elementary ideas he borrows, and his novel bears some such generic resemblance to its prototype as subsists between *Vanity Fair* and *Tom Jones*. A likeness in certain points may also be traced between it and the works of the author of *Headlong Hall*, which themselves are offshoots of the great Shandy stock.

Sir Austin Feverel, the high-souled and tender-hearted Tory Baronet, who valued his enormous hereditary wealth chiefly as an accessory and an evidence to the chivalric Norman and royal Welsh blood along with which it had descended to him, was in most respects a very different person from Mr Shandy senior, the retired Turkey merchant. There was this, however, in common between the respective heads of the two houses, that each had an only son to train, and each had peculiar and transcendental views as to the manner in which that work was to be wrought out to the most brilliant results. How Mr Shandy's mind got its twist we are not told; it was the shock of a terrible calamity that gave a fatal obliquity to Sir Austin's judgment and turned him into an obstinate builder-up of lopsided systems. The wife and the friend in whom he had garnered up his soul united in betraying him. Thenceforth he had nothing left him to do in the world but to love and guard his infant son, and to elaborate a science of humanity on which his education should be founded. The first principles of that science were laid down in 'The Pilgrim's scrip', a book of original aphorisms chiefly relating to women, 'whom the writer seldom extolled, and appeared with all conscience to rank as creatures still doing service to the Serpent: bound to their instincts, and happily subordinate in public affairs, though but too powerful in their own walk'. He regarded them as necessary evils; he could be civil, courteous, chivalrous towards them; but he held it to be his chief duty to keep his son aloof from their wiles until his thirtieth year, by which time 'the system' would have sufficiently fortified him to encounter the perils of matrimony. Du reste, Sir Austin entertained sound physiological views; his discipline was excellent in many of its details, and he showed great sagacity in its administration, so that everything went on as well as heart could wish until young Richard attained his fourteenth birthday. Then came the first hitch in the working of the system. The youth who for sixteen years longer was to have been as soft wax in his provident father's hands, showed that he had a will of his own, and to such purpose that he set fire to a farmer's ricks in revenge for a horsewhipping. Atonement was made for this misdeed, but symptoms still more alarming broke out as 'the blossoming season' approached, and they developed themselves at such a rate that the 'scientific humanist' deemed it necessary so far to modify his plans as to betroth his son at eighteen and marry him at twenty-five. But nature and chance will defeat the best laid schemes of mortal man, however profound his science. While the Baronet is travelling in quest of a maiden worthy to match with his noble boy, things are happening at home which his system had not provided for. At five o'clock on a summer morning the dreaming youth is afloat on the river, and forgetting to pull, lets his boat glide with the stream.

[Quotes xiv from 'Above green-flashing plunges' to end and xv to 'depth of its lightest look'.]

Up to this point of the story its pleasant course has run in comedy, farce, or idyl, such as that we have just quoted; but soon its current grows dark and troubled. We will not deprive our readers of a pleasure by prematurely revealing the sequel, but we break no secrets in bidding them imagine how Sir Austin would behave on hearing of his son's treason against the system, and what sort of consequences were likely to follow from his obstinate determination to make the laws of nature bend to his own abstract theories. Excellent man that he is, and wise in many things, it is his folly to imagine that he can take the place of Providence towards his son, and this folly becomes his punishment. With him all is conscience and a tender heart, but as he himself remarked of some one else, his conscience is a coxcomb. He is a gentleman well worth knowing; and those who make his acquaintance will have at the same time the pleasure of reading a moving and suggestive story, in which there is more of vigorous thought, imagination, wit, humour, and pathos, than would suffice to make the fortune of a score of average novels.

It may be asked, if it was the author's purpose to exemplify the evil consequences of making false theories predominate in the education and government of the young, why did he choose so extreme and exceptional a case for the illustration of his principle? What practical lesson for the guidance of ordinary mortals can be deduced from the errors of so very eccentric a person as Sir Austin Peverel? [*sic*] The objection is more specious than valid, for Sir Austin is not purely and simply a monomaniac. Make due allowance for the irony and comic exaggeration with which his ways and doings are set forth, and it will be found that these are not so abnormal as at first sight they may appear to be. The doctrines he holds on the mutual relations of father and son are such as are more or less vaguely entertained by multitudes of well-meaning blunderers of the present day; the only difference is that in Sir Austin's mind they exist in peculiar clearness and force, and he acts upon them with peculiar consistency.

21. Unsigned review, *Saturday Review*

viii, 9 July 1859

There is much thought embodied in this book, and the author has worked hard to give his thoughts expression. What he has to say, he has taken the trouble to make part of his plot. The young authors of ordinary novels generally adopt the convenient habit of permitting their more reflective characters to indulge in philosophical digressions, or else the story is boldly interrupted, and the author honestly takes up his little parable in a direct address to the reader. A bargain is avowedly offered. If we will eat so much flour, we shall have so many plums—if we will let the writer have his sermonizing out, we shall have a plot, a heroine, and many comic phrases. We will not say that the teaching is in vain, for the philosophy is almost exclusively conceived for the edification, and published for the pleasure, of the author; and if he is made good and happy by it, who will grudge him his ewe lamb? But in point of art, it is a much higher feat when a novelist trusts to the action of his plot, to the circumstances in which he places his characters, and the course they are supposed to take, in order to produce the impression he desires. The great superiority of this method is that the teacher supplies not only doctrine but illustration; and the difficulty of contriving imaginary circumstances which shall really illustrate his doctrine is so great that he deserves great credit if he achieves moderate success. The merit of Mr Meredith's book appears to us to be, that he has tried to work his subject out to what he thinks its legitimate conclusions, and that there is originality and boldness in the steps he takes to bring about the desired result. The book is full of faults, affectations, and ambitious failures; but it is distinguished from the ordinary novel of the day by having something in it.

The Ordeal of Richard Feverel is stated on its title-page to be a History of Father and Son. The Father is a philosopher, who tries to make the world square with his philosophy, and to bring up his Son to the highest limit of human perfection by shaping all the circumstances of his youth. The system breaks down—the fortunate youth is miserable—the circumstances turn out the worst in which the boy could have been placed. The philosopher is beaten by the attractions which the outer-world, and especially the outer-world of women, will always offer to the most ingenuous and virtuous. The boy, who is kept in entire seclusion, manages to meet a farmer's niece by moonlight, and to marry her before he is twenty. When he is married, and his father is playing off the batteries of a most philosophical anger so as to drive him to the exact stage and kind of repentance most desirable, the fascinations of the unsystematic world again triumph over the system, and the young husband is carried away by the trickeries and arts of a much naughtier woman than the young wife from whom his father contrives for a time to separate him. This, then, is the thesis which Mr Meredith has been at such great pains to prove against its adversaries. Nature will beat a system. Fathers cannot so contrive the circumstances under which their sons will have to fight the battle of life that temptation shall be powerless. The doctrine is unquestionably true, but we confess it seems also to us to be a truism. We do not see that this moral has any bearing on human life which it can have been worth so much trouble and thought to illustrate. For, if we accept the tale literally, we know at once that the whole thing is entirely imaginary. No real fathers try to bring up their sons on a rigid system that aims at producing virtue by wholly excluding temptation. If there are any who make this attempt, they must be very few, and far too exceptional for the teaching of the book to have any general value. And if we set down the extremity to which the system of the elder Feverel is carried as an artistic exaggeration designed merely to produce a strong impression, and suppose that the meaning of the author is merely that systems of education should not be too rigid, this novel fails to throw any light on the question what is meant by a system being too rigid. What ought a father to do?—that is the problem. It is no gain to know that he ought not to try to shut up his son in a seclusion where the very separation from the other sex in which the safety of the youth is supposed to lie sets his imagination on fire. Let us take for granted what no one will seriously dispute. The difficulty is what the anxious parent should do—how much should he interfere, how much should he desire a certain kind of experience for the boy, how far is sense to be purchased at the expense of innocence.

We venture to guess that Mr Meredith took up the subject not because he had any particularly definite lesson to instil, but simply because the problems which are suggested by the subject of a youth's education with regard to the other sex happen to interest him. Richard Feverel, the patient in the educational experiment, has a foil provided for him in the person of the son of his father's attorney, who appears at intervals in the book as humble companion and odd man. This young gentleman runs the usual course of gentish profligacy, and is acquiring a knowledge of town while his friend is detained by the parental system in the country. But in process of time he is touched and overpowered by the sweetness, beauty, and innocence of Richard's wife—viewing her not with passion or admiration, but with a mere emotion of what the author terms dog-like affection. This young fool is too brutish and insignificant a person to permit us to consider him as really meant as a contrast to the hero, or we might suppose Mr Meredith an advocate of the 'wild oats' theory which he elsewhere takes occasion to discuss and reject. Then, through the character of the minor personages of the tale there runs a strong vein of amativeness. Even the philosopher himself makes or accepts a sort of half-love, which is provoked and tendered by a female admirer, and all the men and women in the book are open to flirtations more or less proper. Perhaps there is a sort of truth in thus representing the world, but what, for the

73

purposes of the tale, do we gain by knowing it? Mr Meredith plays, in fact, with his subject, and delights in viewing it in different aspects. Now he shows that strictness fails—now that laxity fails—now that the whole world is full of temptations. We are not helped by this, and we regret that Mr Meredith should have written a didactic novel to teach us so little. A novel need not be didactic; but if it is, it ought to point in some appreciable direction. In the most famous of didactic novels, for instance, there is a lesson on the very subject handled by Mr Meredith, which if not an indisputably true lesson, is at least a lesson. In *Wilhelm Meister* the author invites us to observe that a wise man can extract out of the perplexities caused by the relations of the sexes food for his own self-culture. The doctrine of self-culture has not been accepted in England; but at least, if a man believes in it, he may be excused for submitting it to the reading public through the medium of fiction. But the mere trifling with a moral question does not seem to us either within the proper sphere of romance or a good use of the human intellect. Mr Meredith does not follow the usual habit of novelists, and devote a mere passing remark to the deepest enigmas; yet, on the other hand, he does not appear to have deemed it a part of his duty not only to think long over his subject, but to wait until he had arrived at some sort of result before he began to communicate his thoughts.

In boldness of one kind, Mr Meredith's novel far outstrips any English work of fiction that has been published in recent years. He does not allow any conventional notions of impropriety to stand between him and the description of the scenes he thinks necessary to carry out his main purpose. In the third volume, his object is to show the strength of the temptations to which men are exposed when their worldly position or the advantages they can command are such as to induce those most expert in wickedness to bring all their machinery to bear on the work of ruin. There is much that is repulsive in the strange scenes which show how the lady appointed to overcome the hero coils him in her net, but no one can hesitate to say that it is the repulsiveness of a horrible truth. There is nothing shadowy, vague, or mock-moral about this portraiture of immorality. The author knows what he means and what he is talking about, and he puts it on paper. We do not object to this. It is quite right that there should be men's novels, if only it is understood at the outset they are only meant for men. There is every difference between Mr Meredith's tale and such a story as *Out of the Depths*.[1] The latter was not written for men, but for the general public;

[1] *Out of the Depths; the Story of a Woman's Life* (1859) was by Henry Gladwyn Jebb.

whereas *The Ordeal of Richard Feverel* is entirely a man's book. There is great danger in literature altogether shrinking from the topics usually handled among men, for men thus get an impression that all the representations of life given in fiction are hypocritical and superficial. And if a writer has to deal with such a subject as the arts by which a thorough-paced London intriguer gets a well-meaning man into her power, these arts must be represented as they are, or the effect ascribed to them will be absurd. But although Mr Meredith is perfectly justified, if he pleases, in touching on such matters in a novel intended for men—and although we allow that an English writer who writes frankly when engaged in such a task, and who yet never loses hold of the main principles of English morality, is doing a service by preventing French novels being the only exponents of the deeper abysses of life—yet any one who undertakes the work places himself under a great responsibility. He ought to show that he has an object in view which will justify his presenting the public with what is at least dangerous and disgusting; and here it is that the weakness of moral purpose in the story tells to a serious degree. To show that an absurd and imaginary system of education breaks down under very powerful temptations, is much too useless an end to warrant the introduction of some of the most unflinching sketches of immorality that the pen of a modern Englishman has ventured to draw.

The minor characters of a tale are too important as indications of the promise of an author to be passed over when we are estimating the strength and weakness of the first novel of any considerable importance which Mr Meredith has published. The reader must not be deterred by the poor wit and stilted affectations with which the story opens, nor suppose that all the minor characters are like the shadowy tribe introduced at the beginning. There are one or two really clever, natural, and well-drawn characters among the subordinate personages of the tale. There is a farmer who gives the hero a thrashing, and a nurse who comforts him in adversity; and, whether their appearance in the book is due to the memory or the invention of the author, they do him great credit. Other of the minor characters are overlaid with the affectations of the author, who is still in the imitative stage, and, in point of style, sits at the feet of Mr Charles Reade. There are weary bits of landscape-painting at the beginnings of chapters, and it is seldom that any portion of the book can be called entertaining. But still, after all that can be said against it has been said, there remains this great plea on the other side—that it is a book out of the common way, and that the author thinks after his fashion, and is not afraid. If *The Ordeal of Richard Feverel* is all that Mr Meredith can do, it is a failure; but it gives us hopes that it may prove the prelude to a work that will place Mr Meredith high in the list of living novelists.

22. Unsigned review, *Illustrated London News*

XXV, 13 August 1859

Mr George Meredith has attracted the attention of the reading public in a satisfactory sense more than once before the production of his latest work, *The Ordeal of Richard Feverel*, and his reputation will not be qualified by his newest essay in the walks of fiction. To begin with a quiet censure, it may be stated that there is a touch of Bulwer Lytton both in the groundwork of the story and in much of the sententious moralizing, which is scarcely to be considered accidental. There is even a characteristic resemblance in the father of the hero, Sir Austin Feverel, to the progenitor of Pisistratus Caxton,[1] which is not toned down sufficiently to prevent recognition, even though there be the patent and essential difference between the philosophic, rustic gentleman and student, and the wealthy baronet, whose domestic sorrows have driven him to the resource of writing a book of aphorisms which he calls 'The Pilgrim's Scrip'. The story is founded on the notion of a father, as abstract in his notions and theories as the composer of 'The Pilgrim's Scrip' must necessarily be, endeavouring to educate and marry a son on philosophic principles, and to keep him as a thing apart from the world. Of course the system is one continuous failure, beginning in infancy, running through boyhood with ingenious perversity, and ending with the grand mistake of all in the marriage of the son in early manhood with the niece of a coarse farmer, one of the tenants of Sir Austin, but whose natural and inborn tendency to be an exact lady, and a thorough loving and trusting woman, is traced to the fact that her father had good blood in his veins, and, being a lieutenant in the Navy, was a gentleman by profession. Of the temptations of Richard Feverel, of his fall into the perilous regions of the 'demi-monde' (which, by-the-by, is sketched with a breadth and boldness of hand which makes one admire

[1] Pisistratus was the hero of Lytton's *The Caxtons* (1849) and *My Novel* (1853).

as much the courage as the skill of Mr Meredith); of the sufferings, sorrows, and death of his child-wife, but not until she had been gathered to the hearts and arms of everyone of her husband's friends and relatives, while a mystical and fanciful theory of remorse on his part keeps him away from the realization of a happiness beyond what he would have dreamt of—we can say that they are delineated with a vigour, an earnestness, and a sustained variety which render the story just one of those the merits of which people are accustomed to describe by the statement that they have read it through without a check. The episodical incidents and characters are well drawn, and the latter admirably grouped around the principal personages of the tale; and, with the one drawback we have alluded to above, the merits of the book and the place it ought to take in its class are undeniable.

23. Samuel Lucas, *The Times*

Friday, 14 October 1859

Samuel Lucas (1818–88), as well as critic for *The Times*, was Editor of *Once a week*. When Lucas wrote this article he had already agreed to serialize *Evan Harrington* in that periodical. Later Meredith appealed to him for advice and submitted himself to Lucas's corrections.

The writer of an extraordinary novel must expect a more than ordinarily strict criticism. It is a compliment to him and a duty to the public. A compliment to him, because, notwithstanding his offences, he is treated with the attention due to a superior artist. A duty to the public, because, notwithstanding his effectiveness, it is requisite, for the sake of heedless or incompetent readers, to indicate, if we can, his artistic deficiencies. But there is unusual difficulty in performing a critic's duty upon this occasion. Mr Meredith is an original writer, and his book is a powerful book, penetrative in its depth of insight, and rich in its variety of experience. But it is also very oracular and obscure in parts, and, as we conceive, extremely weak in the development of its main purpose. On the other hand it is so crystalline and brilliant in its principal passages, there is such purity mingled with its laxness, such sound and firm truth in the midst of its fantastic subtleties, that we hesitate whether to approve or condemn; and we have a difficulty even in forming a judgment on such strange contrarieties.

Let us premise that Mr Meredith belongs to a class of fictionists who are more rare than welcome—more honoured than popular. There are two classes of novelists (apart from the simious tribe, who are mere meaningless imitators), and Mr Meredith is of the *humourist* class, which draws its presentment of mankind in a large degree from its inner consciousness, while the other class paints life phenomenally, as the majority would see it. The distinction hardly holds, in an absolute sense, as separating rigidly the one class from the other; but it is a distinction which applies more or less in every instance in which a fictionist is entitled to be characterised at all. The humourist draws more from his humour than from obvious facts—from his models of thought than from the manners of his time. He spins his web, like the spider, out of his own bowels, instead of gathering his materials here and there and building them up like the ant. The opposite class, among whom are the Shakespeares and Scotts, are more expansive in their conceptions, and, concurrently, more dependent on externals for their means. The humourist—take even Rabelais for example—is subjective, self-searching, self-evolved and sustained; he is a stronger solvent of his secret pabulum, whatever that may be, and he hangs on the gauzy films of his own imagination. His task is obviously more arduous, for he relies so much on himself; and his success is proportionate to the power which is in him. But his success is not a popular success, for it is personal and distinctive; nor can he be tried by popular tests which are the devices of the average mind. Now Mr Meredith belongs to the latter class more exclusively than most novelists, and his characters are more entirely symbols and shadows of his thought than ordinary everyday denizens of the world about him. It would be unfair to try him by the standard relations of novels to life; for, as a humourist, he conceives humourists, and includes them in a world of his own shaping.

But it *is* fair and appropriate to try if his world holds together on its own principles, and, with this view, to question the plan and object of its creation. We are not certain that we fully understand its object in the present case, and this may be our fault. Is it, however, *really* our fault, or Mr Meredith's, that we are not able to render his meaning with confidence? It is not *his* fault that we should have to suggest the point as a question, and should fall back with some misgiving on our vague apprehensions?

As we conceive, the purport of Mr Meredith's book is to explode the system of an offended humourist—one Sir Austin Feverel, a despiser of women, into whose disparagement of the gentler sex there enters a large measure of pique and of personal resentment, occasioned by the treachery and desertion of his wife. Having a son—one Richard Feverel —on his hands to educate, and for whom he entertains strong affection, nevertheless he gratifies his wrath at his wife by subjecting this boy to the ordeal of an educational system which is to render him forcibly a pattern of moral excellence. He deceives himself into believing that he acts as he does out of regard to his son; for his pique leavens his theory, and eventually becomes its Nemesis. There is a vagueness, or rather a confusion in Sir Austin's motives, which his system partakes, for its tendency and appliances are by no means transparent. Its gist, as applied to Sir Austin's educational crotchet, is this: 'That a golden age, or something near it, might yet be established on our sphere, when fathers accepted their solemn responsibility, and studied human nature with a scientific eye, knowing what a high science it is to live; and that, by hedging round the youth from corruptness, and at the same time promoting his animal health, by helping him to grow, as he would, like a tree of Eden; by advancing him to a certain moral fortitude ere the Apple Disease was spontaneously developed, there would be seen something approaching to a perfect man, as the Baronet trusted to make this one son of his, after a recipe of his own.' The Apple Disease, as it is quaintly termed, is the mutual affection of the sexes, supposed to have been generated in Paradise, as a consequence of our corrupted nature, and from this affection it is the endeavour of Sir Austin to preserve his son as long as possible, by training him on a Spartan nurture, with all the advantages of science. His design is only half approved by the relatives whom he hospitably houses, and who, according to their various temperaments and views, oppose or acquiesce in his design. His sister, Mrs Doria, who has a daughter Clare, whom she destines for Richard, and who has 'the far sight, the deep determination, the resolute perseverance of her sex, where a daughter is to be provided for, and a man overthrown', fixes herself at Raynham, Sir Austin's residence, with the deliberate intent to watch the system, and sap it. But Richard is saved from becoming the shuttlecock of these contending influences by his indifference to his cousin Clare, who is, nevertheless, tenderly attached to him. He grows up with partial and dubious help from the system, a brave, strong-willed, high-minded boy, given to feats and pranks of unusual audacity, but with no premature symptoms of the Apple Disease, until Sir Austin shuts up the safety-valve of poetry to which he had become addicted, and precipitates a crisis:

[Quotes xiv, 'When nature has made us' to end.]

The damsel is the niece of a neighbouring farmer, and the interview proceeds to its denouement thus naturally in the manner of Ferdinand and Miranda, through a passage replete with freshness and vigour of no common order:

[Quotes xv, 'Richard, with his eyes' to 'she may not be his for ever'.]

As the above description augurs, the System is likely to succeed through the boy's luck in finding a pure and charming object for his first affections. But his father is bent on looking out a suitable bride for his son, according to *his* notions of the requisites of a mate worthy of his pure-blood barb. And though in the meantime the Fairy Prince has himself discovered the Princess, the envious fates keep Cinderella out of the father's sight, until the latter hears of the spontaneous attachment through a cynical relative, and determines to break off what he considers the boy's foolish liaison. Thereupon Richard is summoned to town and kept out of the way of his betrothed till she can be secluded from his search by arrangement with her parents. When he is allowed to return to Raynham, Lucy has disappeared, and the thwarted passion of the boy throws him into a brain fever. The scientific humanist beholds his son prostrate, 'forgetful even of love—a drowned weed borne onward by the tide of the hours'; and prays over him without remorse, supporting his anxiety by his unbounded faith in the physical energy he attributes to the System.

This providential stroke had saved the youth from Heaven knew what! 'Mark!' said the baronet to Lady Blandish, 'when he recovers, he will not care for her.'

The lady had accompanied him to the Bellingham Inn on first hearing of Richard's seizure.

'Oh! what an iron man you can be,' she exclaimed, smothering her intuitions. She was for giving the boy his bauble; promising it him, at least, if he would only get well and be the bright flower of promise he once was.

'Can you look on him,' she pleaded, 'can you look on him, and persevere?' It was a hard sight for this man who loved his son so deeply. The youth lay in his strange bed, straight and motionless, with fever on his cheeks, and altered eyes.

'See what you do to us!' said the baronet, sorrowfully eyeing the bed.

'But if you lose him?' Lady Blandish whispered.

Sir Austin walked away from her, and probed the depths of his love. 'The stroke will not be dealt by me,' he said.

His patient serenity was a wonder to all who knew him. Indeed, to have doubted and faltered now was to have subverted the glorious fabric just on the verge of completion. He believed that his son's pure strength was fitted to cope with any natural evil; that such was God's law. To him Richard's passion was an ill, incident to the ripeness of his years and his perfect innocence, and this crisis the struggle of the poison passing out of him—not to be deplored. He was so confident that he did not even send for Dr Bairam. Old Dr Clifford, of Lobourne, was the medical attendant, who, with head-shaking and gathering of lips, and reminiscences of ancient arguments, guaranteed to do all that leech could do in the matter. The old doctor did admit that Richard's constitution was admirable, and answered to his prescriptions like a piano to the musician. 'But,' he said, at a family consultation, for Sir Austen had told him how it stood with the young man, 'drugs are not much in cases of this sort. Change! That's what's wanted, and as soon as may be. Distraction! He ought to see the world, and know what he's made of. It's no use my talking, I know,' added the doctor.

'On the contrary,' said Sir Austin, 'I am quite of your persuasion. And the world he shall see—now.'

. . .

When the young experiment again knew the hours that rolled him onward, he was in his own room at Raynham. Nothing had changed: only a strong fist had knocked him down and stunned him, and he opened his eyes to a gray world. He had forgotten what he lived for. He was weak, and thin, and with a pale memory of things. His functions were the same, everything surrounding him was the same; he look[ed] upon the old blue hills, the far-lying fallows, the river, and the woods; he knew them, but they seemed to have lost recollection of him. Nor could he find in familiar human faces the secret intimacy of heretofore. They were the same faces; they nodded and smiled to him. What was lost he could not tell. Something had been knocked out of him. He was sensible of his father's sweetness of manner, and he was grieved that he could not reply to it, for every sense of shame and reproach had strangely gone. He felt very useless. In place of the fiery love for one, he now bore about a cold charity to all.

Thus in the heart of the young man died the spring primrose, and while it died another heart was pushing forth the primrose of autumn.

But the baronet and Richard himself are deceived as to his state, as the event proves when the deception is exploded by a recurrence of

81

opportunity, on Richard's appearance in town. Again he meets Lucy, and rushing to his goal, in defiance of the System, he instantly carries her off, and with the assistance of some minor agents succeeds in marrying her. This stage of the hero's ordeal, while Lucy is secluded preparatory to her nuptials, is told with charming freshness and grace, and we conceive that here the author is most adroit and felicitous. But then comes the faulty remnant, which spoils an effective story by inconsequential proceedings on the part of both father and son. The father declines to receive his son's bride, and, without withdrawing his countenance, keeps out of the way of explanations, apparently aiming at some further probation of his pupil; and the son, by misrepresentation of the fitting mode of propitiation, is induced to abandon his wife for a long interval, and to mortify his affections to do homage to his father. Worse than this, in an artistic sense, he is untrue to his own nature and to the passion which is represented as occupying him intensely; for in the interval he is tempted by an enchantress of the *Demi-monde*; and without a thought of love, in a paroxysm of sublime pity, he falls. Justly does Mr Meredith exclaim at the conclusion of his brilliant incantation scene—'Was ever hero in this fashion won?' for the winning of the hero under such circumstances revolts our notions of consistency and drags us from the sphere of harmonious art into the chaos of caprice. It is a small compensation that these inconsistencies are the framework of powerful scenes, for they tend to no test of the System, *pro* or *con.*, and they hurry us forward to a *dénoûement* still more unsatisfactory. Thus, long after the baronet has been reconciled to his daughter-in-law, Richard is kept from returning to his wife by remorse. When he does return, recalled by the knowledge that in the meantime he has become a father, and his wife receives him with a tenderness reviving hope and confidence, a duel succeeds in which he is wounded, and the wife who had borne up against the agony of desertion; in possession of her child and anticipating a reunion with her husband, dies of cerebral excitement. Mr Meredith thereupon turns round and accuses the System of murdering his heroine; but for this unnecessary sacrifice of an innocent victim, unnecessary because at this stage in reference to the System it proves nothing, we take the liberty of accusing Mr Meredith himself. His Lucy is exquisitely painted, her conduct throughout is admirable, she is the pure gentle sufferer in the contest of father and son, and when the author owed her compensation, and just as we are expecting him to render it, she is hurried off the scene by a catastrophe in defiance of poetical justice. This is neither the ancient nor the true method. The poet who has to expiate the sins of a race may provide an innocent victim in deference to Nemesis, but even he rescues his Iphigenia at the critical moment, or, if he immolates his Antigone, it is to find the means of punishing her persecutor. Mr Meredith's, on the contrary, is the pure wantonness of authorship, a barbarity like that for which Mr Charles Dickens is so often answerable —that of smothering innocents out of pure sentimentalism; and if he does not, like Mr Dickens, linger on the agonies of his victims, he deserves equally to be haunted by the ghost of his most beautiful creation.

Nor, as we said, does the world which Mr. Meredith has brought together as a test of the System otherwise answer its purpose. The System is not responsible for Richard's temptation and neglect of his wife; for Richard's nature, as depicted, should at least have prevented this. He is represented as completely under the dominion of his instincts, yet he yields to contrary influences in the very conjuncture where instinct would have proved strongest and most certainly invincible. Nor is it the System which retains him in London; but Mr Meredith, who accomplishes the result at the expense of congruity and probability. The System is arraigned, but it is never tried fairly, its merits or demerits are unsolved to the last. It is not the System, but the luck of discovering a Lucy which makes Richard up to a certain point a satisfactory result. It is not the System, but Richard's inconsistency which undoes this result, and it is pure accident which at the last precipitates the catastrophe. The System is tried, but it can neither be acquitted or condemned on this evidence, and the verdict to be taken on Mr Meredith's thesis is simply 'not proven'.

At the same time let us fairly acknowledge the striking merits of this imperfect book. Every touch in the picture of Clare is consistent and harmonious. In Lady Blandish, Sir Austin's semi-platonic friend, there are traits of feminine nature which evince deep penetration. Good old Mrs Berry, the deserted wife, who promotes the union of the young couple, is a more arbitrary delineation, but touched with infinite humour. According to her own account of herself, she is 'a widow and not a widow, and haven't got a name for what she is in any dixonary. "I've looked, my dear, and"—she spread out her arms—"Johnson haven't got a name for me."' Excellent is her advice to Lucy, 'Mind me and mark me; don't neglect your cookery. Kissing don't last, cookery do.' By attention to this useful advice Lucy succeeds very naturally in conciliating the favour of Adrian Harley, the man of the world, Sir

Austin's nephew and cool counseller in ordinary. Adrian's character is thus skilfully elaborated, under the designation of the Wise Youth: [Quotes from 'Adrian had an instinct for the majorities' to 'a piece of blank paper'.]

Thus Mr Meredith shoots at Adrian with the bow of Apollo, but the Wise Youth and the 'Pilgrim's Scrip,' an imaginary work of the baronet's, are none the less the chorus to his tragedy, and as obtrusive as any chorus of the Athenian stage.

One other word remains—this book has been charged with impurity, and tabooed, as we hear, in some quarters by the over-fastidious. It certainly touches a delicate theme, and includes some equivocal situations, but of impurity, in the sense of any corrupting tendency, we see not a trace, and we will not endorse the imputation. It is a novel, in short, which may be read by men and women with perfect impunity if they have no corrupt imaginations of their own to pervert the pure purpose of the author.

24. Unsigned review, *Westminster Review*

xvi, October 1859

This review from the 'Belles Lettres' section of the *Westminster* deals with several books other than *Richard Feverel*. The novel referred to in the opening passage is Charles Kingsley's edition (1859) of Henry Brooke's *The Fool of Quality* (1760-72), which belongs to the genre of exemplary stories which Meredith was poking fun at in his own novel.

To turn from this book to *The Ordeal of Richard Feverell*, is to exchange the atmosphere of the eighteenth for that of the nineteenth century. The subject of both works is the same, the careful development of a young man by an old one; but how different the treatment, how wide asunder the results! The very conception of the problem differs in them, and is as opposite as instruction and education, as light and darkness; and yet we of the nineteenth century cannot avoid loving our darkness in conflict with a better light more than such poor conceptions of the light as are offered us in the *Fool of Quality*. It is strange that so short a time should have brought about such a change in the modes of thought on a subject treated of and profoundly felt from all time. The political is the smallest of those revolutions which have intervened between the dates of the two publications.

Are our notions of morality different from those of our grandfathers? Was human life with them so simple as shown us in the *Fool of Quality*? Did men then stalk about with conceptions as impersonal as the skeleton of the Decalogue? Did flesh and blood, young passion and mature thought, find room within that narrow circle? Were all conflicts external and none deep-seated in the mind? Were good and evil such simple alternative as there represented? We cannot remember two books which, read immediately after one another, will give a clearer insight into the modes of thought of their respective periods. *The Ordeal of Richard Feverell* is the history of a father and son; the former, disappointed in, and forsaken by his wife soon after the birth of his son, devotes himself, with all the resources that high position and great wealth put at his command, to the education of that son. A scientific Humanist, he proposes to stand between the object of his affections and every ill that can befall him from the world or from himself, and the result—with every exertion and self-denial on the father's part, in spite of the deepest love and profoundest calculation—is to leave his noble-minded son, at the close of the narrative, afflicted with the heaviest sorrows and the bitterest remorse that the human heart can suffer and survive. How can this be? it will be said. We reply, take *The Ordeal of Richard Feverell* and see; the framework of the story is so simple that it will not bear extracting from the book without injustice to its author and great detriment to its perusal; but if anyone is attracted by profound observation, humour, passion, and tenderness, let him procure this book and a quiet day for its enjoyment. The characters are numerous and well-defined; among them will be found representatives of almost every prevailing conception of life; but, true to its time, the book offers no solution of any of the difficulties it lays open to us; the nineteenth century struggles through it with but faint glimpses of its goal.

The *Shaving of Shagpat* had already shown us that any work of Mr Meredith's might be expected to abound in poetical images, rich language, and facile invention; but the present work rises far above the limited circle of an Arabian tale, and shows its author to be as observant of his contemporaries as deep read in Oriental fiction.

85

EVAN HARRINGTON

1861

25. Unsigned review, *Spectator*

xxxiv, 19 January 1861

Mr George Meredith, who must not be confounded with the poet who takes the name of Owen Meredith, is a writer of uncommon ability. *The Shaving of Shagpat, Farina,* and *The Ordeal of Richard Feverel,* all show talent and culture not of the ordinary kind. *Evan Harrington* is as clever as any of those former works, and without some of their faults. As a story, it is interesting, and will carry the usual style of novel reader on swimmingly to the end in spite of much allusive matter above his comprehension, which may be marked in every chapter. This cannot be said truly of its predecessors. They were written by the author to please himself, without much regard to talking over the heads of his hearers. There was a good deal of youthful display of eccentricity about them quite as much as of genuine originality. The best sort of originality in fictitious writing is almost always unconsciously attractive and alluring, not surprising or startling. Mr Meredith's vein of humour in literary composition is clearing and fining down as he grows older. We surmise from *Evan Harrington* that he is still young. His charm to an intelligent reader is that he thinks and speaks of what he has seen and known, for himself—he is not conscious of imitating anyone, even in *The Ordeal of Richard Feverel,* which had the misfortune to bear a superficial resemblance to Sterne. *Evan Harrington* has no imitative trick about it, conscious or unconscious; it is a good story on a subject not yet hackneyed. The hero is the son of a tailor in a country town—which tailor has a soul above buttons, and is every inch a man—and a gentleman as far as mind, appearance, and manners go. Old Harrington's wife is also a handsome and a ladylike woman. She shows her sense of gentility and good-breeding in attending to the shop which her

86

much-admired husband neglects. We are very sorry to say, Evan's father dies in the first chapter—a chapter, be it observed, of remarkable cleverness, putting the reader au fait of all necessary knowledge without stepping a sentence out of the high-comedy scene enacted by the neighbours who are discussing Mr Harrington's character after his death. The grocer and the butcher, and Kilne, the publican, all have a kind word for the splendid fellow who was a tailor, and yet rode, and hunted, and dressed, and dined, with the best in the country occasionally, and was really so much of a man as not to be ashamed of not being a gentleman. There was a story current which gave him the nickname of Marquis. It is thus told by Kilne, who had it from Harrington himself—

[Quotes i, from '"Kilne," said he' to 'Marquises to match him'.]

26. Unsigned review, *Saturday Review*

xi, 19 January 1861

Who would have thought that a really good novel could have been written on so very unpromising a subject as the history of a tailor who was mistaken for a gentleman? *Evan Harrington* is a surprisingly good novel; for we are almost incredulous of our own admiration until the story has fairly carried us away with it, and then we own that there can be no doubt about its power to interest us. At first, it seems like trifling with readers that a novelist should take for his theme a subject so exactly appropriate to a farce. We resign ourselves to a pleasant writer, and say that if Mr Meredith chooses to write such a book we like to read it, but that it is a pity he is not working a more promising field. When we have finished, we look back as on a story new in conception, new in the study of character, fresh, odd, a little extravagant, but noble and original. Hackneyed novel readers must own that here they have the luxury of a novelty offered them. The tailor is a gentleman by education, in thought, and in every act. Half against his will he is taken for a member of a well-known family bearing the same name, and he is welcomed to the house of a baronet, and to the heart of the baronet's daughter. The young people love each other, and the tailor wins the lady in the character of a gentleman. Rose's maid kindly informs him how her young mistress shuddered when she repeated to herself the awful word 'snip', which some malignant who suspected the truth had suggested with respect to her lover. But whenever honesty distinctly bids him to own he is a tailor, he does so; and after he has been led by passion to avow his love he summons up all his courage, and tells Rose that he is the snip she detests. She is all frankness, loyalty, and enthusiasm, vows she will never desert him, goes straight to her father and mother and avows to them that a tailor is to be their son-in-law. It is hard to fancy the situation in real life, but no one can say that it is impossible; and directly we have become familiarized with the thought, an author who seizes on it has a vast range of feeling to work upon in order to win our attention. Mr Meredith has made the discovery that if the farcical side of life is taken seriously, it is full of fine tragedy and comedy. This may almost be called a discovery, for even if every one would have previously acknowledged its truth, no one had made a romance out of his perception of it. A shy honest man is contrasted and coupled with a frank, dashing, honest girl, and they are separated by tailordom. There is no end to the struggles of passion and principle that this opening may not lead to. Very judiciously, Mr Meredith makes the tailor's love triumphant early in the story. He is not kept low too long. He is soon ennobled by the love bestowed on him by a heroine who deserves to be a heroine. The mental difficulties and social struggles of a couple advanced thus far give much more room for subtle delineation and for high-strung feeling than if the tailor were only emancipated at the end of the story from his goose and cabbage. *Evan Harrington* has the great merit of increasing as it goes on in interest. The tailor becomes nobler and better. The heroine passes through her little troubles in a way that makes us sometimes pity her and sometimes admire her. The story has, of course, it defects. It pays the penalty of originality. Tailordom in the clouds is a novelty; but we have a little too much of tailordom in the clouds. A novelty must in these latter days of writing be something special, singular, and probably minute. If the writer passes into the general current of life, he has been anticipated. This tailor-gentleman is something out of the way, and all society is made to sweep rather exclusively round the one central figure of an ambiguous snip. This is the inevitable drawback the author has had to pay for the choice of his subject, and in spite of the drawback his choice has turned out wonderfully successful.

There are three things which a writer who wants to produce a good novel must hit upon. He brings with him, we will suppose, a fine style and an abundance of philosophical remarks, which he can pour over any subject; but in the subject he selects he must offer us, first, a good plot; secondly, one or more striking, new, and fully-described chief characters; and thirdly, a good group of those minor personages who are the Gibeonites of the leading performers, and draw water and hew wood as they are wanted. Mr Meredith has got a new plot, and a good hero and heroine, who are, as it were, part of the plot; for the whole story turns on the feelings of a particular sort of tailor and a particular sort of tailor's betrothed. And he has also got a prominent character to help the plot on, and to put the hero and heroine in and out of their troubles; and this prominent character is so well drawn as to raise Mr Meredith to a very considerable height in the list of novel writers. This person is a sister of the tailor, and by a skilful manoeuvre she has managed to marry a penniless Portuguese Count. The one dream of the Countess's life is to marry her brother to an heiress, and her greatest personal ambition is to conceal for ever that she is the daughter and sister of a tailor. She goes with the tailor-hero to the Baronet's house, and there spins her plots, brings all the men to her feet, quarrels with the women, and so manages by a mixture of flattery, courting, lies, and threats, that even old acquaintances who knew her in her unfledged days dare not say to each other that this magnificent and fascinating Countess de Saldar de Sancorvo is the tailor's daughter they once flirted with. The one inherent fault of the book naturally casts its shade over the Countess. All this struggle to avoid the exposure of tailordom is petty and monotonous in itself, and is only raised by the noble traits of character it awakens in Rose and her snip. The Countess is amusing from the first, but the amusement she provides us with is that of a good farce, until she begins to borrow a dignity from the elevation of the persons whose fortunes she affects. But if we take her as she is meant to be—if we once accept this horror of tailordom as capable of awakening profound emotions—she is admirable. There are touches in her portrait that are masterly. She mixes up with her detestably mean stratagems a strange recognition of the claims of Providence which is irresistibly comic; and the affectation of foreign habits, manners, and opinions which she puts before her as a shield and an attraction is so natural that it seems as if we must have been reading about a real person. If any one wants to gain a notion of the trouble and contrivance it takes to write a good novel, let him ask himself how far he would be capable of devising a series of stratagems by which a foreigneering Countess should bring together or separate a tailor and a young lady.

The minor characters belong to a lower walk of art. They are not bad or good. Many men and women could have struck them off; and not a few of them are familiar friends in the world of farces. The rapid young gentleman, shunning care, quoting scraps of poetry, and finally marrying a lady's-maid; the eccentric bachelor, as whimsical as he is rich; the drawling, offensive, hard lordling, have long been 'household words' on the comic stage. It is indeed very difficult to draw a minor character with sufficient distinctness, unless by giving it certain very marked peculiarities. These may be the peculiarities of a class, and then we have the usual pert lady's-maid, roguish valet, eccentric uncle, and so forth. Or the peculiarities may be merely the accidental signs of an individual, and then we have Mr Carker with his teeth, and persons of a similar stamp. Mr Meredith tries hard to keep his minor characters out of these fixed and unnatural forms, and he succeeds so far that the characters he chooses to assign them tell upon the action of the story, and do not merely grow beside it. There is also a mode of constructing minor characters, which Mr Meredith adopts with some success. It is that of making them studies of moral development under peculiar circumstances. Thus, for example, there is a second young lady in love with the tailor. She is a sickly fright, diseased in body and mind. But she fixes her affections on the tailor, and is ready to die when he will not have her. The truth which she has more particularly the honour of illustrating is that a young lady so formed in body and soul would be especially captivated with the externals of a lover. She adores the build, the look, the hair, and eyes of the tailor, and is indifferent to his loyalty and generosity. She thus acts as a foil, and brings to light the more elevated tastes of the heroine. We are quite ready to allow, as we read the story of this poor creature's sorrows, that Mr Meredith may very likely be right, and that Juliana loves the sort of qualities in a man which a sickly fright would be likely to love. When we have once acknowledged this, we cannot avoid seeing that, although she is not very pleasant to read about, she lends at once plausibility and interest to the story.

It is very difficult to measure the kind of praise which such a book as *Evan Harrington* ought to receive; and yet criticism ought to be able to offer some scale by which praise is to be regulated. Readers naturally ask themselves what is the merit that is really meant to be attributed to a book which they are advised to read. We cannot fix the position of every good book, but still we may approximate to doing so. Every now and then there is published a work, like *Esmond*, or *Adam Bede*, or *Martin Chuzzlewit*, which is clearly first-rate, which becomes at once part of English literature, and helps to form the thought and style of a generation. On the other hand, there are every season published not only heaps of trashy stories, but a fair supply of readable, meritorious, creditable novels. Further, there are every year, or almost every year, published four or five really good novels, powerful in their way, new, or rather new, capable of making an impression and of suggesting thought. Such works do not generally raise an expectation that they will be handed down to any very late date; but as they pass away, we feel that they are some of the best things that we reject and let float at once down the stream. Some of them may survive, for the judgment of contemporaries has often been reversed, and another generation may think even more of them than we do. But usually the contemporaries are right, and in the abundance of romances it is best they should be forgotten after they have given delight for a short time. To this class *Evan Harrington* seems to us to belong. It is not a great work, but it is a remarkable one, and deserves a front place in the literature that is ranked as avowedly not destined to endure.

MODERN LOVE AND OTHER POEMS

1862

27. R. H. Hutton, *Spectator*

xxxv, 24 May 1862

For R. H. Hutton see above, No. 2, headnote.

Clever bold men with any literary capacity are always tempted to write verse, as they can say so much under its artistic cover which in common prose they could not say at all. It is a false impulse, however, for unless the form of verse is really that in which it is most natural for them to write, the effect of adopting it is to make the sharp hits which would be natural in prose, look out of place—lugged in by head and shoulders—and the audacity exceedingly repellent. This is certainly the effect upon us of this volume of verse. Mr George Meredith is a clever man, without literary genius, taste, or judgment, and apparently aims at that sort of union of point, passion, and pictorial audacity which Byron attained in 'Don Juan'. There is, however, no kind of harmonious concord between his ideas and his expressions; when he is *smart*, as he is habitually, the form of versification makes the smartness look still more vulgar, and the jocularity jar far more than it would in prose. On the whole the effect of the book on us is that of clever, meretricious, turbid pictures, by a man of some vigour, jaunty manners, quick observation, and some pictorial skill, who likes writing about naked human passions, but does not bring either original imaginative power or true sentiment to the task. The chief composition in the book, absurdly called 'Modern Love', is a series of sonnets intended to versify the leading conception of Goethe's 'elective affinities'. Mr Meredith effects this with occasional vigour, but without any vestige of original thought or purpose which could excuse so unpleasant a subject, and intersperses it, moreover, with sardonic grins that have all the effect of an intentional affectation of cynicism. This is not quite always the case, however, or we should soon throw the book contemptuously aside; for the jocularities are intolerably feeble and vulgar. The best, or one of the best sonnets, describes the concealed tragedy of social life when the hero (if he is to be so called) with his wife and the lady for whom he has since formed a passion are walking on the terrace before dinner with a brilliant party:

[Quotes 'Modern Love', xxxvii.]

There is considerable vividness in this description, especially of the 'grey seniors' who 'question Time in irritable coughings', but the intended poetry is meretricious; no one who feels truly can help feeling that to speak of 'the low, rosed moon' as 'the face of Music mute', is a snatch at the glitter and varnish of apparent, not real poetry. There is no analogy, subtle or otherwise, between the round simplicity of the moon's face and the spirit of music, which always involves the unity of melodious variety. A true poet has said,

> Slow, slow, fall
> With indecisive motion eddying down,
> The white-winged flakes, *calm as the sleep of sound,*
> Dim as a dream;[1]

and this is beautiful, for it really translates the language of hearing into the language of sight. But to speak of the moon as 'face of Music mute', appeals to no subtle analogy at all, and is a mere unmeaning eulogium on that admirable planet. Such a criticism is doubtless small —but in these minute touches lies the true distinction between a poet and one

> Who hides with ornament his want of Art[2]

Mr George Meredith has a sense of what is graphic, but he never makes an excursion beyond that into what he intends for poetry without falling into some trick of false ornamentation. For one more example we will take the most reflective of these sonnets, in which Mr Meredith is teaching us how to learn from Nature not to attach irretrievably to any mortal thing. The idea is forcibly expressed till it is intended to rise into a sort of tragic climax at the end, when it soars

[1] Untraced.
[2] A. Pope, *Essay on Criticism* (1711), 296.

MEREDITH

into an absurd parody of Tennysonian metaphor that is a perfect
specimen of the foolish-sublime:

[Quotes 'Modern Love', xiii.]

What is the 'forever of a kiss'? Is Mr Meredith trying to distinguish
between 'the transient' and 'the permanent' in kisses, 'das reine seyn'
and 'reine nichts' as the German sages say,[1] and to single out the permanent element, that which expresses 'the infinite'. If this rash suggestion
be at all near the mark, we are still painfully in the dark as to the force
of the word 'renewed'. If the 'renewed forever of a kiss' in any way
refers to the renewal of this infinite element, as ordinary people would
suppose—why is *this* the moment when we are exhorted to '*lose
calmly love's great bliss*'? If it be a leave-taking the force of the word
'renewed' on this particular crisis is hid from us. And what are we to
say of the last line? Surely the 'sound' of a kiss is not the true poetic and
permanent element therein? If there is a 'forever'—an eternal element—
in these expressive symbolic actions at all, we submit that it is not in the
sound—that on the contrary the sound is an accidental and rather
unfortunate adjunct and accident in them. And what can Mr Meredith
mean to suggest by speaking of them as sounding through a 'listless
hurricane of hair'? That which is heard through a hurricane—though
we will not rashly answer for a 'listless' hurricane, hurricanes usually
appearing to us quite too much in earnest—is usually a thunderclap
and nothing less—and if Mr Meredith really means to be sentimental
about a kiss that in any way resembles a thunderclap, we fear few will fall
into his mood. Probably the 'listless hurricane of hair' was meant as a
gorgeous metaphor addressed to the eye and not to the ear—the hair
being a non-conductor of sound, softening or smothering the loud
report alluded to, and resembling a 'listless hurricane', only in the
tumultuous tangle of agitated locks, expressive of the *abandon* of great
grief. But turn it how you will we fear this meretricious piece of fine
writing turns out to mean that some very loud sound has been heard
in spite of great obstacles—which sound and which obstacles are
supposed to heighten the anguish of renunciation. We fear there was
something of a 'listless hurricane' of ideas in the author's mind when he
extemporized this very noble language.

This, it will be said, is verbal criticism; but that is not so. No clever
man who prizes grandiloquent ornament above modest meaning
is guilty of a mere verbal negligence, for this goes to the heart of the

[1] That is, 'the pure being' and 'the pure nothing'.

94

matter. Mr Meredith, too (though, so far as we understand the intended drift of his 'Modern Love', we can accuse it of nothing worse than meddling causelessly, and somewhat pruriently, with a deep and painful subject, on which he has no convictions to express), sometimes treats serious themes with a flippant levity that is exceedingly vulgar and unpleasant, and perhaps even unjust to himself:

[Quotes 'Modern Love', xxv.]

This is wretched jocularity, as pointless as it is coarse, and though it is certainly the worst sonnet in the series, after reading the whole through several times, there seems to us no more purpose, poetic or moral, to be got out of the series, than out of this single sonnet—the general drift being that there is a good deal of tragic misunderstanding, leading to desperate unfaithfulness in the marriage of proud minds who might have been very happy if they had so chosen—a common-place which is illustrated with a freedom that mistakes itself for courage, and is simply bad and prurient taste. The thing has no kind of right to the title 'Modern Love': 'Modern Lust' would be certainly a more accurate though not a true title, there is something of real love, but more of the other embodied in the sonnets.

In the verses which do not hinge on this sort of subject, there is the same confusion between a 'fast' taste and what Mr Meredith mistakes for courageous realism—poetic pre-Raphaelitism. For instance, Mr Meredith has, in some verses on a scene in the Alps, given us a vision of the spirit of Beauty, whom he proposes in a vehement kind of half-and-half enthusiasm, one half sentiment the other half beer, to introduce to a London cabman. The poem is long and rambling, but we extract such verses as bear upon this great idea. The poet is speaking at first—as we gather—of the spirit of poetic beauty:

[Quotes 'By the Rosanna' (original version), st. 9–10, 13–14, 16, 19–20, 25–6.]

This is not intellectual courage, nor buoyancy of spirit, nor anything but a spasmodic ostentation of fast writing. There are moods in which a man of high animal spirits is apt to think that any nonsense which amuses himself in an irrational moment is good enough to amuse the world; and because Mr George Meredith was amused for the moment with the incongruity of fancying a greasy-coated cabman with his arm round Calliope, and with his own poor pun on that person's 'driving the world', he thought it, we suppose, a mark of intellectual pluck to print it. It really is only noisy vulgarity, which, in so clever a man—for he is clever and graphic in his way—is exceedingly unworthy. There is a deep vein of muddy sentiment in most men, but they should let the mud settle, and not boast of it to the world. Mr Meredith evidently thinks mud picturesque, as, indeed, it may be, but all picturesqueness is not poetry. One gains a graphic picture of a good deal of interior mental mud without verse to help us. Mr Meredith thinks we do not get enough, and the solution given here is sometimes a very thick one indeed. The best thing in the book is 'Juggling Jerry', which is not vulgar nor tawdry, as so much of the volume is.

'London by Lamplight' touches a subject on which many other pens are also employed—the condition of the poor of large towns, and the extent of prostitution: but it is real, important, and too instant to be stale.

[Quotes 'London by Lamplight', st. 1–9.]

Many passages of rare and some of quaint description will be found in the volume. We take one that exhibits the peculiarity by which Mr Meredith attempts to invest common subjects with a novelty they would not otherwise possess.

[Quotes 'The Death of Winter'.]

28. A. C. Swinburne, a reply to R. H. Hutton, *Spectator*

xxxv, 7 June 1862

The early friendship and mutual sympathy of Swinburne and Meredith was followed by a period of estrangement during their middle years, though they were reconciled when they were old. During the early 1860s they were intimate, admiring each other greatly. Swinburne appears as Tracy Runningbrook in *Sandra Belloni* (1864). This letter is Swinburne's most enthusiastic comment on Meredith's work. Later he criticized *Vittoria* and *Beauchamp's Career* and told a friend: 'Browning was born with a stammer, but I fear Meredith has cultivated his stammer' (*A Bookman's Letters*, W. Robertson Nicoll, 1913, 15. See also Introduction).

Sir

I cannot resist asking the favour of admission for my protest against the article on Mr Meredith's last volume of poems in the *Spectator* of May 24th. That I personally have for the writings, whether verse or prose, or Mr Meredith a most sincere and deep admiration is no doubt a matter of infinitely small moment. I wish only, in default of a better, to appeal seriously on general grounds against this sort of criticism as applied to one of the leaders of English literature. To any fair attack Mr Meredith's books of course lie as much open as another man's; indeed, standing where he does, the very eminence of his post makes him perhaps more liable than a man of less well-earned fame to the periodical slings and arrows of publicity. Against such criticism no one would have a right to appeal, whether for his own work or for another's. But the writer of the article in question blinks at stating the fact that he is dealing with no unfledged pretender. Any work of a man who has won his spurs, and fought his way to a foremost place among the men of his time, must claim at least a grave consideration and respect. It would hardly be less absurd, in remarking on a poem by Mr Meredith, to omit all reference to his previous work, and treat the present book as if its author had never tried his hand at such writing before, than to criticize the *Légende des Siècles*,[1] or (coming to a nearer instance) the *Idylls of the King*, without taking into account the relative position of the great English or the greater French poet. On such a tone of criticism as this any one who may chance to see or hear of it has a right to comment.

But even if the case were different, and the author were now at his starting-point, such a review of such a book is surely out of date. Praise or blame should be thoughtful, serious, careful, when applied to a work of such subtle strength, such depth of delicate power, such passionate and various beauty, as the leading poem of Mr Meredith's volume: in some points, as it seems to me (and in this opinion I know that I have weightier judgments than my own to back me) a poem above the aim and beyond the reach of any but its author. Mr Meredith is one of the three or four poets now alive whose work, perfect or imperfect, is always as noble in design as it is often faultless in result. The present critic falls foul of him for dealing with 'a deep and painful subject on which he has no conviction to express'. There are pulpits enough for all preachers in prose; the business of verse-writing is hardly to express convictions; and if some poetry, not without merit of its kind, has at times dealt in dogmatic morality, it is all the worse and all the weaker for that. As to subject, it is too much to expect that all schools of poetry are to be for ever subordinate to the one just now so much in request with us, whose scope of sight is bounded by the nursery walls; that all Muses are to bow down before her who babbles, with lips yet warm from their pristine pap, after the dangling delights of a child's coral; and jingles with flaccid fingers one knows not whether a jester's or a baby's bells. We have not too many writers capable of duly handling a subject worth the serious interest of men. As to execution, take almost any sonnet at random out of the series, and let any man qualified to judge for himself of metre, choice of expression, and splendid language, decide on its claims. And, after all, the test will be unfair, except as regards metrical or pictorial merit; every section of this great progressive poem being connected with the

---

[1] *La Légende des Siècles* was an epic poem by Victor Hugo, published in three series (1859, 1877, and 1883).

other by links of the finest and most studied workmanship. Take, for example, that noble sonnet, beginning

> We saw the swallows gathering in the skies,

a more perfect piece of writing no man alive has ever turned out; witness these three lines, the grandest perhaps of the book:

> And in the largeness of the evening earth,
> Our spirit grew as we walked side by side;
> *The hour became her husband, and my bride;*

but in transcription it must lose the colour and effect given it by its place in the series; the grave and tender beauty, which makes it at once a bridge and a resting-place between the admirable poems of passion it falls among. As specimens of pure power, and depth of imagination at once intricate and vigorous, take the two sonnets on a false passing reunion of wife and husband; the sonnet on the rose; that other beginning:

> I am not of those miserable males
> Who sniff at vice, and daring not to snap,
> Do therefore hope for heaven.

And, again, that earlier one:

> All other joys of life he strove to warm.

Of the shorter poems which give character to the book I have not space to speak here; and as the critic has omitted noticing the most valuable and important (such as the 'Beggar's Soliloquy', and the 'Old Chartist', equal to Béranger for completeness of effect and exquisite justice of style, but noticeable for a thorough dramatic insight, which Béranger missed through his personal passions and partialities), there is no present need to go into the matter.[1] I ask you to admit this protest simply out of justice to the book in hand, believing as I do that it expresses the deliberate unbiassed opinion of a sufficient number of readers to warrant the insertion of it, and leaving to your consideration rather their claims to a fair hearing than those of the book's author to a revised judgment. A poet of Mr Meredith's rank can no more be profited by the advocacy of his admirers than injured by the rash or partial attack of his critics.

[1] Pierre-Jean Béranger (1780–1857), popular lyric poet and political satirist.

29. J. W. Marston, *Athenaeum*

No. 1805, 31 May 1862

John Westland Marston (1819–90) was a dramatist, critic and journalist and a poet of some reputation.

The story of 'Modern Love' is rather hinted at than told. There is nothing of orderly statement and little of clear and connected suggestion. These sonnets resemble scattered leaves from the diary of a stranger. The allusions, the comments, the interjections, all refer to certain particulars which are not directly related, and have to be painfully deduced. We are not sure that, after great labour, we have arrived at Mr Meredith's drift; but we are quite sure that, if we have, we do not care for it. So far as we have groped our way, the tale seems that of a man who is jealous of his wife. It appears that she is still faithful to the bonds of wedlock, though not to those of love. The phases of the husband's torture are elaborately set forth—often with spasmodic indistinctness, but now and then with real force and imagination. A May-day recalls the Spring when she yet loved him. At a village festival he sardonically contrasts his refined misery with the coarse happiness of the revellers. At dinner the wedded pair play host and hostess, and mask their wretchedness with smiles. Here is a recollection of past joy, which appeals to the heart through ear and eye, like an echo from a ruin:

[Quotes 'Modern Love', xvi.]

Few of the sonnets, however, are so intelligible as the foregoing. The abrupt and obscure style which too often prevails may be learnt from the next example. Yet, whoever has patience to spell out its meaning, may catch a fine image in the closing lines:

[Quotes 'Modern Love', v.]

It would seem—but we still write under correction—that the husband strives to console himself by the stimulant of a new passion. We infer that the expedient is a double failure. Yielding no relief to the conscientious husband, it revives, through jealousy, the all-but-dead affection of his wife. But her contrition apparently comes too late, for we think she takes poison. Still, this is a mere conjecture, from a dark hint or two, which the reader can interpret for himself:

> About the middle of the night her call
> Was heard, and he came wondering to the bed.
> *'Now kiss me, dear! it may be, now!'* she said.
> *Lethe had pass'd those lips, and he knew all.*

We have already intimated that 'Modern Love' contains passages of true beauty and feeling; but they are like the casual glimpses of a fair landscape in some noxious clime, where the mists only break to gather again more densely. Besides, the best gifts of expression would be wasted on a theme so morbid as the present. It is true that poetic genius has often revealed to us the diseases of our nature; but they have been only a portion of the exhibition. The causes which produced them, and the results in which they were expiated or subdued, have also been given. The bane has shown the virtue of the antidote. In 'Modern Love' we have disease, and nothing else.

With a sense of relief we turn to the more wholesome poems in the volume. 'Grandfather Bridgeman' is a pathetic story, told with fair effect and with some success in the delineation of character. In his portrait of the farmer, however, Mr Meredith does not always discriminate between the homely and the coarse. The poem is disfigured, too, by abrupt transitions, and, at times, by a vagueness of style inexcusable in one who can write to the point when he pleases. 'The Old Chartist', again, is well drawn upon the whole; but the lesson which he derives from a water-rat, though correct, is not sufficiently obvious. A moral of this kind should not have to be reasoned out, but, like that of a fable, should seize the reader at once. Of Mr Meredith's character-pieces the best is 'Juggling Jerry'. Jerry is a conjuror struck with mortal sickness: he pitches his tent on a familiar spot, where his old horse has been used to graze, and where the gorse blooms from which he has often hung his kettle. In this scene he recalls to his wife the story of their lives, and strives to comfort her in the closing hours of their union. The pathos and humour of this conception enhance each other, while the poor juggler's love of nature is true in itself and expressed in the graphic idioms that befit the speaker. The lyric of 'Cassandra' embodies a fine conception of the dying prophetess, and is free from the blemishes of caprice and obscurity. We cannot say as much for 'Phantasy', which is founded on the poetical superstition of The Willis. 'Phantasy' is written with spirit, and contains some striking though grotesque pictures. We grant that the subject admits of fantastic treatment; but freedom is here pushed into license. In poetry, even humour should not be prosaic and coarse; but Mr Meredith's is both. His dancing Phantom has nothing of the supernatural charm that belonged to her in the original legend, which, by the way, formed some years since the groundwork of a *ballet* for Taglioni. The *danseuse* might have taught a lesson to the poet. She raised the invention of the *maître de ballet* into poetry; Mr Meredith takes a poetical conception and degrades it into that of a ballet-girl:

> A darling of pink and spangles;
> One fair foot level with her face,
> And the hearts of men at her ankles.

This whim of thrusting bald realities into poetry reaches its climax in the lines headed 'By the Rosanna'. The poem opens with a life-like description of the 'torrent river', and the dash of its waters is caught happily in the verse. The grandeur of nature, however, only suggests to Mr Meredith London by gaslight; and, for the Naiad who should haunt the solitude, he invokes the 'Season-Beauty', who, in this case, seems to be an inveterate jilt. After other profound questions touching the lady, he demands:

> What say you, if, in this retreat,
> While she poises tiptoe on yon granite slab, man,
> I introduce her, shy and sweet,
> To a short-neck'd, many-caped, London cabman?

Of course there is a philosophy running through this doggrel, and we subscribe to the writer's doctrine when he says:

> If Sentiment won't wed with Fact,
> Poor Sentiment soon needs perfuming.

—Still, the 'fact', however plain, must have a poetic life in it. Of course there may be such life in a cabman; but to find it we must see the man's nature, not merely the 'short neck' and 'many capes' which represent him here. Mr Meredith's forced transitions from the ideal to the prosaic are merely an outrage upon taste. The versatility at which he aims is admirable when shown within the limits of Art, but worthless as easy when it transgresses them.

The absurdities of this volume are the more to be lamented because, in spite of them, it displays some fine qualities. There is an Autumnal Ode, for instance, which, though not free from the author's besetting vagueness, has noble passages. The wild evening finds its faithful mirror and the wind its own turbulent chant in the lines that follow:

[Quotes 'Ode to the Spirit of Earth in Autumn', ll. 28–46.]

Few readers, we think, will deny the poetic feeling and the truth of observation which our extract reveals. But if these gifts are to produce a lasting result, Mr Meredith must add to them a healthier purpose, a purer taste and a clearer style.

30. Unsigned review, *Saturday Review*

xvi, 24 October 1863

We are in the present day overrun by clever writers of fiction, and of that species of verse which is spun from the same kind of intellectual web that produces fiction. But the names of English novelists and versifiers now living who may be said to unite real originality of thought and aim with conspicuous cleverness in workmanship are almost few enough to be counted on the fingers. Among these few Mr George Meredith unquestionably holds a place. His novel of *Evan Harrington*, which appeared three or four years ago, contained some of the most purely original conceptions that have been attempted by any writer of novels of character for a long time past. The same may be said of the volume of poems which he has, like Professor Kingsley, Miss Muloch [*sic*], Mr Farrar, and half a score more, as in duty bound, composed and published.[1] He is in the habit of genuinely drawing from his own resources of observation and reflection, and his strong thought and quaint expression remind us, here and there—though at a considerable interval—of Robert Browning. In skill of phrase and rhyme he is quite as happy as his greater contemporary, and often less obscure.

[1] Dinah Maria Mulock (1826–87), later Mrs Craik, was famous as the author of *John Halifax, Gentleman* (1857). Frederick William Farrar (1831–1903), novelist and theological writer, was author of *Eric, or Little by Little* (1858).

The poem of 'The Old Chartist' is, for instance, a capital piece of writing, with an obvious and simple design. An ancient shoemaker, who in early life has had the misfortune to cross the water on account of misbehaviour on a Chartist platform, returns to his native town at the expiration of his time, and is converted to common sense by seeing a water-rat scrubbing his face contentedly by a brookside. The fresh-hearted old vagabond is made to soliloquize thus:

[Quotes 'The Old Chartist', st. 1–2.]

He presently espies the water-rat going through his morning's washing, and the train of natural thought and feeling set in motion by that sight is exceedingly well described. The first wonder is the apparent incongruity of cleanliness with the antecedents and present position of a rat:

> His seat is on a mud-bank, and his trade
> Is dirt . . . and yet
> The fellow's all as anxious as a maid
> To show a decent dress, and dry the wet.

In the eye of nature, however, there seems to be nothing incongruous:

[Quotes 'The Old Chartist', st. 9.]

This simple spectacle introduces into the breast of the old grumbler the thin end of the wedge of self-knowledge. He has been picking holes in his superiors' coats and denouncing the wrong, while he ought to have been *doing* the right. He will henceforward be wiser, and live the life of the rat, 'pleasing himself and his Creator'. He will go quietly home, mend the gentry's boots, comfort his old wife—who, while detesting his ways and his views, had faithfully stood by him with the consoling tea-can in the dock—and on some future Sunday he will bring his fine daughter, with her smug draper-husband, to see the model democrat of the mud-bank. The 'Old Chartist' is certainly a good piece of writing of its kind, and 'Juggling Jerry', the 'Beggar's Soliloquy', and 'Grandfather Bridgeman', are nearly, if not quite, up to the same standard.

It is in the direction of this racy and vigorous style of composition that Mr George Meredith's real *forte* lies, though he would hardly be inclined to subscribe to that opinion. Few people who have aimed at fine writing find it easy or pleasant to believe that their strength lies, after all, on something which, from the fine writer's point of view, seems to be very far below. However, a perusal of Mr George Meredith's more ambitious productions, and especially of 'Modern Love'—

the composition which he has thought worthy of giving a name to his collection—leads one reluctantly to the conclusion that he has entirely mistaken his powers, and has utterly marred what might have been a rare and successful volume. It was bad enough to quit the 'English Roadside' for a ranting rhapsody like the 'Ode to the Spirit of Earth in Autumn', which we should conjecture to have been written at a very early age, when Shelley was less perfectly understood than ardently and blindly adored. The lines which follow, and which are supposed to indicate the rising of a violent southwester, are among the milder and less uproarious passages of the ode:

[Quotes 'Ode to the Spirit of Earth in Autumn', ll. 36–46.]

The first line reminds one of the old illustration to the fable, where the traveller, wrapped in a cloak, is plodding along beneath the influence of two round faces, one representing the north wind and the other the sun. The single voice issuing from the 'out-puff'd cheeks' is made to boom 'a chorus' to the preluding shrieks, the nature of which last we should conceive that it must be equally difficult to imagine and to describe. The 'yellow realm of stiffen'd Day' no doubt sounds as if something like it might have occurred in *In Memoriam;* but we venture to assert that no parallel passage to the line is to be found in that poem, any more than to the 'thunderingly streaming' appearance which was remarked in the south-west wind's mantle. There is a passage in the otherwise excellent poem called 'Grandfather Bridgeman' which is congenial to these extracts, and seems too good of its sort to be omitted. It is not often that metaphor is confused with more completeness than in this description of a summer morning:

> The day was a van-bird of summer; the robin still piped, but the blue,
> A warm and dreamy *palace* with voices of larks ringing thro',
> Looked down as if *wistfully eyeing* the blossoms that fell *from its lap.*

It is, as we have said, bad enough that a writer of real ability and skill should allow himself to associate this kind of fustian with poems of worth and merit. But Mr George's Meredith's descent from his 'roadside' style of thought and composition to his lyrical mood is, we regret to say, only trifling compared with the change which he undergoes when he indulges in an elaborate analysis of a loathsome series of phenomena which he is pleased to call 'modern love'. The poem called 'Modern Love' is of considerable length, and has clearly had a large share of labour bestowed on its preparation. The mere composition

is sometimes very graceful, and always exceedingly ingenious. The few
short passages quoted below appear to us to contain real beauty:

> With slow foot
> The low, rosed moon, the face of Music mute,
> Begins among her silent bars to climb.

> How many a thing which we cast to the ground,
> When others pick it up becomes a gem!
> We grasp at all the wealth it is to them;
> And by reflected light its worth is found.
> Yet for us still 'tis nothing! and that zeal
> Of false appreciation quickly fades.

> The golden foot of May is on the flowers,
> And friendly shadows dance upon her brow.

> Wavering pale before me there,
> Her tears fall still as oak-leaves after frost.

But no word-painting or clever analysis can atone for a choice of
subject which we cannot help regarding as involving a grave moral
mistake—a mistake so grave as utterly to disqualify the chooser from
achieving any great and worthy result in art. The whole of this poem
is occupied in portraying the miseries of married life as it exists in our
modern society. The writer's apology for his choice would probably
be the same that he has put into the mouth of one of his characters:

> These things are life;
> And life, they say, is worthy of the Muse.

A more flimsy sophism could hardly be devised. The Muse is
undoubtedly concerned with all forms of life, but these things are
decay, and deformity, and death. So far from a condition of doubt and
uncertainty on the general tone of matrimonial morality being in any
sense an interesting or attractive thing, it is one of the most disastrous
calamities that can befall a nation. To write of the rotten places of our
social system as if they were fitting subjects for the Muse is just as
reasonable as it would be to compose a sonnet to the gout or an ode to
the small-pox. Besides, the subject is old and outworn, exhausted by
far abler hands than those of Mr George Meredith. With the great
literary error of *Don Juan* before his eyes, it was scarcely worth his
while to commit the sickly little peccadillo of 'Modern Love'. It was no
doubt his conviction, derived from French authorities, that there is a

species of nineteenth-century infidelity, more recondite, more interesting, more intellectual, forsooth, than those which have gone before, and that this novelty was not undeserving of a bard. If he should be at any time desirous of taking the measure of his work, it would not be an uninstructive process to read over the poem of 'Guinevere' in *Idylls of the King*, and then to peruse some half-dozen of his own cantos. The contrast might disabuse him of the notion that he has succeeded in producing, under the title of 'Modern Love', anything worthy of the name of art. If he could regard his clever performance as others see it, he might perhaps agree with us in thinking that his utmost achievement has been to throw the thin veil of Coan drapery over a set of grinning skeletons.

SANDRA BELLONI

1864

On its first appearance this novel was entitled *Emilia in England* and was only changed to *Sandra Belloni* when it was included in the collected edition of 1886. I have used the later title throughout, but kept the earlier one for contemporary references.

---

31. Richard Garnett, *Reader*

iii, 23 April 1864; signed 'G'

Richard Garnett (1835–1906), Keeper of Printed Books in the British Museum, produced several books himself, including *Relics of Shelley* (1862) and *Twilight of the Gods* (1888).

The announcement of a new work by Mr George Meredith is necessarily one to provoke much curiosity and expectation, since even a moderate approximation to the end he has been wont to propose to himself implies unusual ability of an unusual description. Mr Meredith belongs to that select band of humorists who mainly rely for effect upon the pungency and piquancy of their diction, whether uttered in their own character or placed in the mouths of their *dramatis personæ*. Few writers indeed could dispose of resources adequate to so sustained a display of intellectual pyrotechnics as that which has now lasted Mr Meredith through nine volumes. It is comparatively easy to devise humorous situations; but this is farce. Mr Meredith's works are the best modern representatives of the genteel comedy of a hundred and fifty years since. Incident and character are not neglected; but both are subordinate to dialogue. The personages have their prototypes in nature, but are still somewhat idealized: they are like and not like people we have seen. They are rather types of character than individuals.

Maskwell in Congreve's comedy, for example, is a really scientific combination of the chief traits of a designing villain; but we may perceive at once that these have been ingeniously put together in the study, not copied from the living model. It is a significant circumstance that all Congreve's plays were composed at an age when Mr Meredith had hardly begun to write. The latter's experience of life is consequently much wider, and there is that in the genius of his time which causes him to be more solicitous about the truth of things. Nevertheless, next to the intellectual brilliancy of his writings, their most salient feature is their artificial aspect. A principle of intelligent selection seems to have presided over their genesis and development. The story is carefully chosen for the sake of some favourite idea snugly bedded in the centre of it—a Psyche-germ, swathed in a rich cocoon of illustration. The personages are all selected with a similar view, and their sayings and doings meted out with the nicest accuracy. The style again is highly *recherché*, spiced with epigram, and elaborated even to obscurity. It might easily be surmised that Mr Meredith experienced considerable difficulty in arraying his thoughts in their appropriate garment of speech, and that the frequent harshness of his exposition was the evidence of a victory won by a vigorous growth over an unkindly soil. Thus rich, original, strained and artificial, the general effect of one of Mr Meredith's novels is very much that of a fine landscape seen through tinted glass—a pleasing variety, so long as there are plain windows in the house. To read Mr Meredith in his turn is to season the feast of literature with an exquisite condiment: to read nobody but Mr Meredith would be like making a dinner of salt—Attic, of course.

Emilia in England is fully equal to the author's former works in humour and power, and only less remarkable in so far as it is less original. The plot is a variation on the theme of *Evan Harrington*. The comedy of that admirable novel turned on the struggle of three sisters, upheaved into a higher than their natural sphere, with the demon of Tailordom; their frantic efforts to entomb the monstrous corpse of their plebeian origin beneath the hugest available heaps of acted and spoken lies; the vigorous resistance of that ghastly being to this method of disposing of him, and his victorious assertion of his right to walk the earth. The more serious interest arose from the entanglement of their straightforward brother in their web of imposition, not without the participation of the mischievous deity of Love. In *Emilia* we have three sisters again—the Misses Pole—Pole, Polar, and North Pole, or as the profane have entitled them, Pole, Polony, and Maypole. The situation is fundamentally the same, but so far varied that the ladies have no chance of concealing their mercantile origin, of which, indeed, to do them justice, they are not ashamed. They simply wish to get higher, and, by way of justifying their ambition to themselves, have set up a fancied code of feelings supposed to be proper to the highest circles, to which, by way of demonstrating their fitness for the same, they make it the study of their lives to conform.

[Quotes i from 'They went on perpetually mounting' to 'their own test of intrinsic value'.]

That is, they lived by a conventional rule, just as the baronet in Mr Meredith's first novel brought up his son upon system. Mr Meredith appears to entertain a special detestation for anything cut and dried, and the gist of his present work is a sarcastic but quiet exposure of the evil these ladies wrought against their better nature. The following passage will give some idea of what these worshippers of Fine Shades are called upon to endure:

[Quotes xvi from 'At breakfast in the morning' to 'hostile to its influences'.]

Emilia Belloni, the heroine, is an entire contrast to the Miss Poles. She is in most respects a repetition of Rose Jocelyn in *Evan Harrington*—a pattern of pure nature, perfect guilelessness, absolute unreserve, and entire surrender to self-oblivious passion. She combines the unembarrassed purity of an antique statue with the fire of a painting of the modern school. She is most pathetic in her confiding simplicity—in her frankness perfectly irresistible. This complete self-abandonment is powerfully contrasted with Wilfrid Pole's merely sentimental feeling for the beautiful stranger, and paralleled with Merthyr Powys's devotion to the cause of Emilia's country. Here are the materials of an excellent drama; and, though the interest of the book does not mainly depend upon the incidents, there are sufficient to prevent it from flagging to any great extent. The chief obstacles to its success will probably be found in the peculiarity of the style, the quaintness (so pleasant to those who have once learned to relish it) of Mr Meredith's habits of thought, and the idealisation of the characters. There is a soul of truth in them all; but sometimes rather grotesquely incarnated. A hostile criticism might enlarge on their unlikeness to ordinary mortals. The reply must be that they are meant to embody certain types of thought and feeling, and consequently rather made to order than sketched from the life. This employment of Mr Meredith's talents is perfectly legitimate, especially after the proofs he has given of his ability to reproduce actual character with unimpaired effect. Observation alone could have furnished material for such vivid delineations as those of Mrs Chump, in whose vicinity sentiment is barely possible, and Mr Pericles, Greek millionaire, musical bear, and beneficent ogre. Perhaps the scenes where he appears are the richest in a work scintillating throughout with wit and humour, nor yet devoid of patches of tender moonlight, like this last appearance of Emilia in England:

[Quotes lviii, from 'A sharp breath of air' to 'Emilia's voice was in the air'.]

32. G. E. Jewsbury, *Athenaeum*

No. 1905, 30 April 1864

For Geraldine Jewsbury see above, No. 19, headnote.

Emilia in England is a charming story, and we recommend our readers to get it for themselves. It keeps up all the promise of *The Ordeal of Richard Feverel*, and is not so painful in its interest as that novel, which we consider a great addition to the comfort of a work of fiction. Our sensibilities are fatigued by the strong sensation novels we have daily to encounter: even as the music of Verdi is said to wear out the voices of robust singers. We are grateful for a little legitimate interest that does not drive on the edge of a knife between perdition and a happy issue out of difficulties. The Emilia of the work before us is the daughter of an eccentric old musician, an Italian refugee, who is not only a man of musical genius, but also given to gin-and-water: a predilection which keeps his wife and daughter in constant difficulties. Emilia's history, told by herself, has a humour and pathos which keeps the reader between laughing and crying. The simplicity is charming with which the poverty and privations of the bare, naked details of their pinched and painful life are mixed up with the glorious possession of musical genius, which flashes up and 'transforms the real to a dream', making that beautiful which was not so. This little episode is the gem of the book. Emilia's plaintive but matter-of-fact remembrance of the 'large potatoes' which her father flings away in his wrath, contrasts quaintly with the description of her father breaking his violin, which affects the reader like the killing of a living creature. The character of Emilia herself is a fine study of the nature and development of a true artist. It must, we should imagine, be drawn from life. Emilia, with her straight-forward simplicity—her child-like indifference about the future, except as a vague golden dream, where ways and means are entirely super-seded or unthought of—is charming; only her utter ignorance of the ways of the world and her entire indifference to appearances make her an *enfant terrible* for those worthy Misses Pole who undertake to produce her in society. However, her unconsciousness of all evil, and the straightforward intrepidity with which she does exactly what she intends, carry her through snares and pitfalls which make the reader tremble, but which she neither perceives nor understands, and which she escapes as though led by an angel. We have seldom met in fiction with a character which we have felt to be so fascinating. The contrast between Emilia and the other personages in the book is cleverly brought out. They are not bad people by any means; but, with one exception, they are flawed by insincerity and worldly motives. Their wisdom turns to foolishness, and they betray their weakness in contact with her perfect and unconscious nature. The plot is very slight. Emilia, a young girl, with a genius for music, and a voice that is a wonder of melody, is adopted by a pretentious family of the name of Pole, partly from good-nature and partly out of vanity. They are the daughters of an uneducated rich merchant, and they want to be more refined and more fastidious, and, above all, they want to become leaders of good society; they are very tiresome, and are made too much of, for they have no geniality; they are as dry as sand; and the reader feels no interest in their elaborate sayings and doings. They are, however, kind to Emilia, and their brother falls in love with her. She is attached to him with all her heart, and in a most embarrassing, matter-of-fact fashion. The young man, without actually intending any harm, allows himself to be entangled in a flirtation with a fine lady, which becomes serious. Like many other men, he tries to go two ways at once, which never answers. Emilia's grief and despair are as true to her nature as the rest of her character; her love is strength, not weakness. The reader will be dreadfully sorry for her, none the less so because her suffering is predestined by the very nature of the man to whom she has become attached, and whom she has made into a hero. There is a Mr Pericles, a Greek, who is very well sketched. He is a selfish, heathen Greek, with no religion except the love of music; he is a new character in fiction; his desire to make Emilia into a voice and nothing else, is amusing. There is a Mrs Chump, a vulgar Irishwoman; she talks a great deal too much, wearies the reader, and is a great clog on the pleasure of reading the book. There are several other minor characters that are cleverly drawn; but the interest centres in Emilia. The Poles, her friends, fall into trouble; the father becomes embarrassed in business, and makes away with Mr Chump's fortune. Emilia, out of gratitude for their kindness, works on Mr Pericles, and, by proposing to give up a prospect of marriage with a man who deserves to be her husband, and to go to Italy and study at the Conservatoire in Milan for three years, she induces him to refrain from ruining the Poles. The story leaves off; it does not conclude: Emilia goes to Milan; and we hope she will come back to England to ascend the throne which Grisi[1] has left vacant. We have a right to expect that the author will continue the history of Emilia in a future work. We entreat him, in conclusion, not to waste labour and space in elaborating characters which are not interesting, in right of either their sayings or their doings. The style of *Emilia in England* is brilliant, but it becomes fatiguing after a while; it resembles flint and steel struck together—the succession of sharp blows eliciting sparks. It would be a great improvement if the author could conceal his art, and write more simply.

[1] Giulia Grisi (1811–69), celebrated singer, at the height of her fame between 1834 and 1849.

33. Mrs Hardman, *Saturday Review*

xvii, 28 May 1864

This review was by the wife of Meredith's close friend, William Hardman (1828–90), who appears as Blackburn Tuckham in *Beauchamp's Career*. An account of Hardman's friendship with Meredith is given in *A Mid-Victorian Pepys. The Letters and Memoirs of William Hardman*, ed. S. M. Ellis (1923–5).

If a novel is bound to be amusing, and to make a man read on until, as Sydney Smith said, he forgets to dress for dinner, either this is not a novel or it is a failure.[1] It is not in the least amusing, and it might easily inspire a sense of pleasure when the dinner hour came, and it was time to leave off reading it. But it is, in its way, very well worth reading, and has more in it than most novels that delight the reader. The fashion of the day is to put all thoughts into the shape of fiction, and to devote a large portion of thought to the analysis of contemporary English society, and of the individuals who fall under its leading types. Therefore, when a thoughtful man has a special point in this analysis to take, he writes a tale to illustrate it. The question is, which shall be the bread and which the sack—shall it be principally analysis, or principally adventure and love-making? The market, we believe, says the latter; but authors are quite at liberty to ignore the market, and choose the former with Mr Meredith. The special point which has engaged his attention is the growth of sentimentalism of a spurious nicety and priggishness, of a sham grandeur of aspiration mixed with very commonplace aims at social success, which is, he considers, a marked and inevitable feature of advancing civilization. Just as improved agriculture produces fat pigs and very streaky bacon, so, he says, a society increasing in wealth and in the arts of comfort produces this sort of sickly sentimentalism. To the persons that display it in an eminent degree, two classes of characters stand in such a contrast as novelists find

[1] *Edinburgh Review* (1826), xliii, February, 395; see also *The Wit and Wisdom of the Reverend Sydney Smith* (1860), 7.

convenient. In the first place, there are straightforward, open, untutored characters, or the direct opposite; and, secondly, there are neutral characters, partly operated on by the sentimentalism and the social ambition of the main subjects of analysis, and partly impelled by a wavering admiration of the more passionate and direct specimens. This is the play of characters which Mr Meredith has chosen to illustrate, and those whom such a subject can interest will find it handled with subtlety and ingenuity in *Emilia in England*. They will also be cheered in their studies by coming upon many passages written in excellent English, upon some poetical and some playful touches, and upon many wayside observations full of oddity, picturesqueness, or truth.

The machinery is tolerably simple. There are three Miss Poles, who represent the sickly striving sentimentalism. They have a brother, who is the neutral character; and they have a young musical *protégée*, who is Italian, passionately fervid and transparently childish. The Miss Poles are the daughters of a retired alderman, and want to have a choicer set than their birth has entitled them to. They chiefly reckon for their promotion on the extreme delicacy, refinement, and loftiness of their manners and characters, on their tact and turn for manœuvring, and on their determination to stick by each other. Emilia is a young girl with a wonderful voice, whom they find singing in a wood, and whom they invite to their house, in order that the possession of a social wonder may give them celebrity. Wilfred, their brother, makes love to Emilia, and she returns his passion with an ardour far surpassing what he feels, as his respect for society, his subjection to his sisters, and an inborn weakness of character make him continually uneasy under Emilia's love, and lead in the end to their being delighted to give each other up. There is not the faintest attempt made at any character or situation being natural. The whole set of people seem to live in a kind of cloudland, and to behave as no English families ever behaved or thought of behaving. But that is immaterial, for all the story, and all the persons in it, are only vehicles for the analysis of character. Of the Miss Poles, we are told at the outset that 'they supposed that they enjoyed exclusive possession of the Nice Feelings, and exclusively comprehended the Fine Shades'. They lived in a world of their own, in which they were supreme. Even when they had secured the acquaintance of the great lady of the district, and had admired her manners and knowledge of society, they 'allowed themselves to bow to her with the greater humility, owing to the secret sense they nursed of overtopping her still in that ineffable Something which they alone possessed'. And Mr Meredith offers it as a general observation, that persons who nourish the nice feelings, and are intimate with the fine shades, carry with them their own test of intrinsic value. It is the union of this internal sublimity with the utmost attention to the small things of life and the minutest usages of society that Mr Meredith has set himself to paint. When the sisters first saw Emilia, after they had been venting their enthusiasm and exclaiming that her voice was divine, they discovered that each of the three had noticed that Emilia's bootlace was loose, and that, while admiring her performance, they had each been silently speculating as to the indications of character and condition which this vagrant article might be taken to give. We are perfectly aware that it has now become a sort of profession for educated and able men to study the minuter shades of thought and feeling to which young women are subject, and therefore Mr Meredith is quite justified in setting himself seriously to solve this important problem. Given three young women with a union of sentimentalism and worldliness, what will be the impression produced on them by meeting with another young woman whose voice is magnificent but whose bootlace is unfastened? Very likely Mr Meredith's answer is right, and they would think more of the bootlace than of the voice.

Mr Meredith does not like the sentimentalism he describes, though he maintains that all civilization depends on sentimentalism. So he makes the sentimentalism of the Miss Poles give way under the trials of real life. The agencies that undermine the sentimentalism of young women are apparently two. In the first place there is misfortune; in the next place there is love-making. The Miss Poles have their fine shades and nice feelings roughly dealt with by hearing that their father is seized with paralysis. The sick-room is too stern a reality for sentimentalism. They are further reduced to common sense, or at least are led in that direction, by their father during his illness disclosing to them that he is ruined, and must marry a certain Mrs Chump because he is her trustee and has spent her money. Undoubtedly it would be difficult for even the most sentimental of young ladies to believe that this is the sort of marriage that is made in heaven. But this is all very plain sailing, and reflects little credit on an analyser of character. Any one could see that sentimental and aspiring young women would be brought down a little by learning that their father was paralytic, ruined, and obliged to marry a woman he had cheated. But it requires a much more ingenious and subtle artist to show how sentimentalism gives way under the pressure of love-making. The Miss Poles are all described as liking to love in an uncertain hazy way, disguising their emotions even from themselves, and utterly puzzling their lovers. A novelist can always say that his heroines are pretty, and a pretty face will make some men do anything, or otherwise it is hard to understand why any one should be supposed to go through so great a bore as making love to such girls as these sisters are described. However, they are in a novel, and girls in a novel can have as many lovers as the novelist chooses. The second sister, Cornelia, is the most lofty, moony, and super-subtle of the three, and she loves an organist, who is a moody sort of creature, but who is highly educated, wears a tail-coat, and ultimately turns out to be a baronet. They meet in woods, and exchange books and so forth, and one day the organist wants things to make a little more progress. But the lady is far too much in cloudland for that, and wants nothing more than an everlasting reign of sentiment. Now comes the play of nice feelings and the opportunity for intricate analysis. The organist remarks, 'You have not to be told that I desire your happiness above all earthly things.' The lady, on this, begins to study his clothes, and sees him to be tolerably dressed. 'For cynicism, the younger brother of sentiment, and inheritor of the family property, is always on the watch to deal fatal blows through such vital parts as the hat, or the "h's", or indeed any sign of inferior estate.' But as the gentleman's get-up gives no opening for cynicism to intrude, the lady is obliged to make a reply, which if diplomatic is not discouraging, and to answer, 'You know how I love this neighbourhood.' They then go on in a complicated play and counterplay of feelings, and at last 'they who had never kissed as lovers kissed under the plea of friendship'. The chapter is headed 'The Pitfall of Sentiment', and the pitfall appears to be that young men who have flirted sufficiently long with vague, dreamy, sentimental girls, will at last bring them to the realities of life by kissing them. The same conclusion ends the flirting in a wood of another of the sisters, as to whom and her admirer we read that 'Edward was unaware that Adela was mastering him talking common sense in the tone of sentiment. He, on the contrary, talked sentiment in the tone of common sense, and, of course, he was beaten.' This is so abstruse that we are as glad as the young lady could have been to get to the plain unanalytical kiss which occurs in the next page.

Emilia is woman without civilization, the untutored delightful savage, loving frantically and openly where she does love, and saying straight out without the slightest disguise whatever she feels and thinks. When the sisters first see her in the wood, they ask her whether the place does not inspire her, to which she replies simply that she does not come into the wood for inspiration, but because the women at the farm where she lodges will not let her sing in the house. When a great admirer of music thinks of sending her to Italy, and asks her how much money she has, she candidly replies that she has 4*l*. 19*s*. in her pocket. When she tells her lover who she is, she appeals at once to a standard which she is unaware is not the standard of society or of a young cavalry officer, and tells him, 'My father is one of the most wonderful men in the whole world—he is one of the first violins at the Italian Opera, and own nephew to Andronizetti.' When she and Wilfred make love, all the ardour and emotion come from her. When he is away from her, he even asks himself whether he loves her, and soon comes 'to shudder to think that he has virtually almost engaged himself to the girl'. Not that he gives her up at once, for their love scenes grow warmer and warmer for some time. Only it is she always that is in earnest. As the tale goes on, she loses her illusions, the disenchantment being greatly aided by Wilfred determining to take service in the Austrian army. She even begins to like another man who is of the direct and honest sort, and who goes out to fight for Italy. The end sees her on the point of setting out for Italy to study art for three years, but with an understanding that, if her new lover can wait three years, he may then be rewarded with the affection and domestic companionship of a woman with a superb and perfected voice. When we have got thus far, and have fairly seen Emilia out of England, we lay aside her history with a puzzled feeling, sensible that there has been much to admire in what we have read, but doubtful what is the exact drift of the whole, and perhaps not altogether persuaded by this example as to the great value of all this profound analysis of the characters of young women. What appears to be the concluding lesson of the work may be very true, and few would be inclined to deny that 'travelling to love by the way of sentiment, attaining to the passion bit by bit, does full surely take from us the strength of our nature, as if (which is probable) at every step we paid fee to move forward'. But whether it is worth while to express this in a novel which is wholly devoted to enforcing it, is difficult to say.

34. Unsigned review, *Westminster Review*

xxvi, July 1864

A new novel by the author of the *Ordeal of Richard Feverell* [*sic*] is a thing looked forward to with eager expectation by what at present is a strangely restricted circle of readers. We shall be much surprised if the publication of *Emilia in England* does not greatly extend that circle. It is one of the drawbacks of a decided originality, that the general public are some time before they catch the unaccustomed note. How many years did Mr Thackeray charm a few appreciative readers before *Vanity Fair* threw a new light upon all that had gone before it? We are not prepared to say that Emilia will prove Mr Meredith's *Vanity Fair*, but we feel the full assurance that the fates have such a turning-point in store for him in his literary career. His originality is not his only disadvantage with the great bulk of those who take up a novel in search of mere amusement, for in his pages they come across a subtlety of expression, and a delicate indication of modes of thought and feeling, which demand an amount of attention not willingly given, except to those authors who have so fully gained the public ear that inattention becomes a reproach to their readers. There is still another of Mr Meredith's merits which, from the same causes, for a time limits the number of his admirers; we mean the essentially dramatic character of his talent, and the artistic manner in which he makes his very numerous actors grow under the reader's eye, and develope in the course of the narrative, the personal peculiarities they are intended to play. In his pages you find no ready-made type whose conduct can beforehand be predicated, whatever the circumstances in which it is placed. Like human beings, they must be considered in their past history and present temptations. This makes anything but easy reading; in return, however, those who care for real art, have living persons before them, and not nicknames, which at once suggest the whole compass of action which can be expected from their possessor. Again, the peculiar tone in which Mr Meredith criticizes the features of modern society, is at first calculated to ingratiate him with no conceivable section of that society. He runs a violent tilt against no prevailing vice, by exaggerating its odiousness, and conciliating those who can suppose themselves free from it. The weaknesses of a highly conventional condition of life at which the chief doctrines of the present novel are levelled, are shown to be at the same time compatible with many excellences, and even in the charming ideal of natural feeling which his heroine presents, as their antithesis, the seeds of possible depravation are allowed to show themselves with a truth that requires a wholesome taste for their full appreciation. The hazards of natural passion are not withdrawn from view, that the illusions and deceptions of sentimentalism may shine with an exclusive light; upright sincerity and open straightforwardness are invested with no immunity from the natural consequences of the conflicts they must endure, but are warmly advocated on their inherent merits. Though full of interest as a story, *Emilia in England* is essentially analytic in its treatment, and will be adequately relished only by those to whose capacity of thought it so strongly appeals.

Evidently the result of long reflection, it requires something of the frame of mind in its readers which has presided at its construction. The central figure of the half-Italian girl whose truth and simplicity are made the touchstone of all she comes in contact with, is one of the most charming in the whole range of modern fiction; the history of her girlish love is told with that mastery of the language of passion in which none approach Mr Meredith, and told without shrinking on one side, or possibility of offence on the other. It is impossible here to give any sketch of the plot, the characters are too numerous, and none can be omitted in any adequate attempt to convey the total impression of the work, to those who have not read it. Indeed, the wealth of imagination and thought which is lavished upon this large company is something wonderful; each individual is a true person, and their number, though in some sort necessitated by the ground-plan of the action, must have called for an amount of patient elaboration that but few will properly recognize. The three sisters, who at first take up the friendless heroine, are masterpieces of delicate ironical handling, but the irony is of that kindly sort which admits of liking and esteem in spite of its shafts. Their brother lover—Emilia's half-hearted lover—is a manly fellow when he has any other adversary than his own heart, which, after all, masters him in spite of every effort of his own, though too late for his happiness. But we sin against our limits, and must break off with an earnest recommendation to all those who can appreciate the lay sermon of a novel, which treats the phenomenon of modern society with a conscientious study, to take up *Emilia in England*, but to do so in no hurry. It cannot be read off and thrown aside, rather will it repay renewed acquaintance, and charm more on second perusal than on the first.

35. Unsigned review, *Examiner*

No. 2947, 23 July 1864

This is one of the twelve or eighteen novels published in the course of a year, that a private gentleman who desires to see the better class of the fictions of the day fairly represented among his books, may be content to buy. For Mr George Meredith still proves himself an author with originality of wit, and he writes the clear, accurate English, individual yet unaffected, which is the hall-mark of a book by a true member of the guild of letters.

The story is, indeed, itself levelled against affectation. With all its prevailing shrewdness of tone and occasionally caustic humour, the main interest of the book is sentimental; it is the rightful King Sentiment carrying war into the borders of the usurping King Sentimentality. The beautiful Emilia, with a rare gift of music in her voice and in her soul, is the daughter of an impetuous Italian violinist, and of his care-worn English wife, sordidly trained except for the touch of true fire in her father's music, and the artist nature which she has inherited from him. Absolutely and most simply natural and truthful, with a wholesome appetite for her dinner, she is open as unclouded day, and, as the world goes, naive to eccentricity. With that character, the thread of her life crosses threads with the life of the family of a City of London Merchant who is not so substantial as he seems, and whose three daughters have little in them of the refined sentiment for which they desire to be esteemed. Such are the warp and woof that constitute the main texture of Mr George Meredith's story, but the tale has plenty of plot, and other threads go to the making of the pattern. The young ladies of the merchant's household, Arabella, Cornelia, and Adela Pole, are brought amusingly into the presence of the raw material of which they are fashioned, in their father's old sweetheart, Mrs Chump. Those persons in the tale who mount the Hippogriff come in the end even to tragic grief, and Emilia finds her way safely, through many illusions raised upon her way, across the wild sea of false sentiment into the haven of a true man's deep and quiet love. As for the Hippogriff, says Mr Meredith in a passage that may be taken for expression of the moral of his story—'Souls harmonious to Nature, of whom there are few, do not mount this animal. Those who have true passion are not at the mercy of Hippogriff—otherwise *Surexcited Sentiment*. You will mark in them constantly a reverence for the laws of their being, and a natural obedience to common sense. They are subject to storm, as is everything earthly, and they need no lesson of devotion; but they never move to an object in madness.'

In his own writing Mr Meredith is, as we have said, unaffected and original. He rises on occasion to expressions of true passion, and in his level passages, he never sinks into commonplace. But his genius has a flavour that appeals, in some slight degree, to a taste not yet fully acquired by the reader who has seldom strayed beyond the bounds of English literature. The influence of Jean Paul Richter, or of German writers of his school, upon an English mind, is felt in many a passage of true sentiment and humour that blends practical English reason with a tint, as it were, of German fancy. But there is imitation of no man, Englishman or German. Mr Meredith gives us ripe fruit of his own mind, that simply shows, like a good tree, which way the sun shone when its fruit was ripening. Jean Paul might have written those interpolations of the philosopher who, with his reference to Hippogriff-riding, occasionally steps in with a comment on the action of Emilia's story.

[Quotes xliv, from 'He distinguishes being on the Hippogriff' to 'that which belonged to her'.]

When Emilia's sentimentalist lover, Wilfrid Pole, has one evening upset a pot-boy in his frenzied rush after Emilia, and, on his way to the house where he will see her, attempts with horrible result to cover the smell of the bad beer by saturating his breast with 'Alderman's Bouquet', the same philosopher observes 'that Wilfrid, thus setting a perfume to contend with a stench, instead of waiting for time, change of raiment, and the broad, lusty airs of heaven to blow him fresh again, symbolizes the vice of Sentimentalism, and what it is always doing'.

Wilfrid's sister Cornelia, trained into a life of petty affectations, brings, for want of natural straightforwardness, her true love to a tragic end; and her sentimentalizing lover, riding furiously upon Hippogriff, sums up his own case by sending an unnecessary pistol bullet through his brain.

Sir Purcell had not been told of her tribulations, and he had not expressed any doubt of her truth; but sentimentalists can read one another with peculiar accuracy through their bewitching gauzes. She read his unwritten doubt, and therefore expected her unwritten misery to be read. So it is when you play at Life! When you will not go straight, you get into this twisting maze.

Whatever it may be in real life (and we have some inkling of what it is there) assuredly it would make fierce havoc with the plots of novels, if people ever said or did in them, at critical turns of life, what it would be commonly natural for them to say or do.

Here is a glance at the young ladies of the Pole family. The Poles of Brookfield hope to take a leading position in their district, but so do the Tinleys of Bloxholme, and

[Quotes i, from 'The Tinleys had winged a dreadful shaft' to 'in a magnifying mirror'.]

And here is Emilia in fearless confidence with Cornet Wilfrid Pole, who is beginning to be enamoured in his way; and in her way, yet ignorant of mankind, so too is she. She has had her harp broken in a country fray between two rival clubs when, at the wish of a rustic friend, she had consented to do so unconventional a thing as go and sing to a boothful of bumpkins after their club dinner. Wilfrid has found her and fought a way for her out of the scuffle. Now he is seeing her home through a wood.

[Quotes xii, from 'A pillar of dim silver rain' to 'almost bashfully, and with new feelings'.]

The fact that in Emilia's wholesome mind this love dies out for want of its fit sustenance, and is replaced by a new plant that slowly grows and strengthens under the right influences, is an essential part that contains much of the spirit of the story. There is no health in endless brooding over a misplaced affection. If it be misplaced, it must want that by which it should be sustained, and the fiction of its everlasting life under such circumstances is at best an obstinate and amiable self-deception, a sickness of mind. Soul as well as body must be fed, and with wholesome meat too, not on tipsy cake and kisses.

36. Justin M'Carthy, an early appreciation

1864

Justin M'Carthy (1830–1912) was historian and critic and student of his own period. Among his works were *Modern Leaders* (1872) and *A History of Our Own Times* (1879–80). For his *Reminiscences* (1899), see above, Introduction. The article from which this passage is produced was originally published in the *Westminster Review*, xxvi, July 1864, under the title of 'Novels with a Purpose', and reprinted in M'Carthy's *Con Amore* (1868).

Mr George Meredith is a novelist of the philosophic school. He is one of the boldest and the ablest of his class in our day. No man we know of has more resolutely gone into literature with a total disregard of popularity. His *Shaving of Shagpat* produced something like a sensation, but he has not sought after sensations of any kind. Men without a tithe of his intellect have found a far wider celebrity. He is, indeed, but little known to the novel-reading public in general, and the announcement that a new novel has issued from his hands does not, we suspect, create any particular excitement among Mr Mudie's ordinary subscribers.[1] The public for whom one of Miss Braddon's novels must appear in a second edition the very day after its first publication, and for whom a third edition follows the second before the week is well out, is not likely to be fascinated much by a philosophical author with whom thought is everything and incident nothing.[2] Mr Meredith's

[1] Charles Edward Mudie (1818–90), founder of the most famous of the Victorian lending libraries in 1842, quickly came to dominate the market. An order for three hundred copies of *Richard Feverel* was withdrawn after complaints from readers.
[2] Mary Elizabeth Braddon (1837–1915). later Mrs Maxwell, became known as the author of *Lady Audley's Secret* (1862).

novels are not bought at a railway station to beguile a journey, or carried in the hand down to the seaside to while away the tedium of a semi-fashionable autumnal holiday. They are not amusing. A man or woman must be really in earnest to care much about them at all; and the grand requisite of the popular novel of our day undoubtedly is that it shall require no thought or trouble of any kind. But those who read steadily through Meredith's books will find themselves well rewarded for their pains, if they have brains and culture enough in themselves to appreciate brains and culture in their author. Perhaps not a large proportion of the novel-reading public have now any distinct recollection of *The Ordeal of Richard Feverel*. It was published in 1859, and we doubt not that the tramp of the Napoleonic legions and the cannon of Solferino and Magenta somewhat disturbed and deafened at that time the ears of the reading community; and, indeed, we hardly know whether the English world has since had time to settle down into the temper which a philosophical novel requires. *The Ordeal of Richard Feverel* is a novel of the thoughtful, deep, half-cynical, wholly earnest kind which has so often striven, perhaps not with signal success, to arrest the attention of a public only craving for easy entertainment. It is somewhat in the style of Sterne; a good deal more in the style of one who, acknowledging himself a follower of Sterne, had a warmer heart, a purer soul, and a richer, quainter fancy than the British sentimentalist, we mean Jean Paul Richter. Mr Meredith is often strikingly like Richter in style, with, almost as a matter of necessity, a considerable dash of the Carlylese phraseology. Here and there, indeed, something of unmistakable and pure Carlyle flashes in. Life, as seen in certain worldly and cynical eyes, is for instance described as 'a Supreme Ironic procession with Laughter of Gods in the background', and many such sentences occur here and there which read as if they were fairly plucked out of *Sartor Resartus* or *The French Revolution*. But the general character of the book is that of a sort of British Richter—Richter adapted to the ordinary course of English life, describing British schoolboys and aristocrats, and ladies of fashion, and ladies only too much in fashion, and country farmers, and Pimlico lodging-house keepers, and used-up, worthless men about town. There is nothing of imitation about all this, nor is any particular passage to be easily pointed out which seems to have been too palpably tinged with the *Titan* and *Hesperus* dyes.[1] But the mind of the author appears to be, within its range, quite akin to that of Richter, and the affinities of fancy and feeling

[1] *Titan* was published between 1800 and 1803, *Hesperus* in 1795.

have no doubt been strengthened by close and loving study. *The Ordeal of Richard Feverel* is full of passages which are rich in quaint poetic beauty; full of keen, pungent, epigrammatic sayings; of sharp, shrewd reflections, revealing much insight into the realities of human nature; of the warm glow of an ardent, manly heart, and of a tender, graceful, genial blending of love and pity. Utterly unlike in its plan and its personages, the book somehow reminds one frequently of Richter's *Flegeljahre*;[1] only that with George Meredith the ways and weaknesses and virtues of the two brothers seem fused into the one form of Richard Feverel. It is essentially a book with a purpose. Richard Feverel is the only son of a man of high rank and noble nature, who, disappointed in his domestic life, and left alone with his child, turns philosopher, and resolves to bring up the boy upon a grand, supreme system, which shall defy all the temptations and dangers of the world, the flesh, and the devil. It is to be a moral and physical education combined, and all the resources of science and wealth (love appears to have been hardly considered in the matter) are to be exhausted to produce this perfect *homunculus*, this human wonder-flower. Of course the system fails, not extravagantly, or grotesquely, or farcically, or more, indeed, than any other system for the nurture of any other *homunculus* must almost of necessity fail. The *homunculus* cannot be kept in the glass bottle. Richard Feverel turns out on the whole a truthful and honourable man, but he is not much nearer to absolute truth and honour than most of the rest of us, and his life is neither happy nor perfect. He marries merely for love and not at all for science, and he is not much more true, it must be avowed, to the one guide than to the other. He whom high moral principle was to have ruled supremely, is little better than the mere slave of impulse. All the good christening gifts which the fairy Science gave are more or less counteracted in their operation by the one malign spell cast by the fairy Passion whom the wise parent would fain not have bidden to the ceremony at all. This is in a few words a sort of bald argument or bare outline of a brilliant, fanciful, and withal, earnest and thoughtful book. It is not a very pleasant book. The mere quaintnesses and fantastic eccentricities of the style, although modest and sober when compared with those in which Richter revels, are quite enough to warn the commonplace novel reader at the very beginning that these paths are rather thorny and tangled for his easy lounging walk. But apart from merely superficial objections, the story, with all its beauty, tenderness, and boldness, leaves a melancholy, and what is

[1] *Flegeljahre* appeared in 1804-5.

perhaps worse, an unsatisfactory impression behind it. People in general do not now, we think, read Rousseau's *Emile*; but those who are familiar with that masterpiece of a dead philosophy will probably agree with us as to the profoundly unsatisfactory and disheartening impression which its catastrophe leaves on the mind. Was it for this, the reader is inclined to ask, that science and love did their utmost to make one path smooth, one human existence bright, and noble, and happy? Was Emile from his birth upward trained to the suppression of every selfish thought, to the scorn of all ignoble purpose, to an absolute devotion for truth, courage, purity, and benevolence, only that he might be deceived in his dearest affections, and that the crowning act of his existence might be an abnegation of self which we can scarcely even regard with admiration? The author had a right to shape his moral and deal with his creations as he would, yet we feel pained and shocked that he should have deemed it right to act thus harshly towards the beloved offspring of his system. Something of this surprise and disappointment fills the mind when we have reached the close of Richard Feverel's ordeal, and find that he has left his brightest hopes and dearest affections dead and buried behind him. The book closes with a sharp snap or crash; we feel as if something were suddenly wrenched away with pain and surprise; a darkness falls down upon the mind. Artistically we cannot help regarding this as a defect, although of course it is strictly in keeping with a recognition of the possibilities and even the daily chances of life; but the course of the story does not lead us to expect anything of the kind, while its whole construction does lead us to expect a harmonious and dramatic conclusion. If Lady Castlewood in *Esmond* were to die suddenly of an unexpected fever; if Romola were to be killed off, like the wicked personage in one of Massinger's plays, by a flash of lightning, no one could say that either of these catastrophes was out of the common range of human probabilities. But a work of fiction, whether novel or drama, requires harmony, coherence, or sequence; and, although talent can assert its power over us in defiance of this law, yet it assuredly forfeits some of its legitimate influence when it fails to acknowledge it. We cannot at all see why poor little Lucy, Richard Feverel's gentle, innocent, loving wife, should be sacrificed in order that the ordeal of her husband should be made the more severe. In human nature, is such an ordeal really purifying and strengthening? Is heavy, unexpected, and, it must be added, really unmerited calamity calculated to make the sufferer brave, and strong, and faithful? Truly we doubt it. And we doubt still more whether the ardent, impulsive, fitful sort of being Mr Meredith has painted as his hero, would become any the better for having so fantastic and remorseless a penalty attached by fate to his father's system and his own single transgression. A novelist is free to write a book with a purpose if he likes, but having done so, he must submit to be judged according to the nature of his purpose and clearness with which he has developed it. In this respect we read *Richard Feverel* fascinated, we lay it down dissatisfied. What of the sowing of wild oats, whereof the novelist has so much to say, of which he has so many remarks that are fanciful and humorous, and so many that are sound and shrewd? Are they to be sown or not, these wild oats? Richard Feverel does not sow his in time, but he scatters just one little handful rather late in season, and it produces such a ghastly and Cadmean crop, that all the early flowers and fruits of his life are choked and blighted. We do not feel that we are brought any nearer by the experience of Richard Feverel to the solution of that great social question about the sowing of the human wild oats. The author approaches it boldly enough, and sometimes alludes to it in words which may perhaps have caused startled hands occasionally to cover very modest eyes. But even those who, like ourselves, think the business of art as well as the business of life, sometimes requires a little putting away of formulas and suppression of scruples, do not find that we derive much more of distinct and wholesome counsel from Richard Feverel, than we might have had from the most decorous and maidenly of the John Halifax school.[1] Roderick Random is one type of young man. We acknowledge him truthful, plain, and vigorous enough, but he cannot do much to help us on with the work of human improvement; for while he frankly acknowledges all his errors, he clearly does not think that there was the slightest need to avoid them, or desire that his sons, in their spring-time, should be any wiser than their sire. John Halifax is another type of young man—such a type as one may find among the saints whom young ladies of High Church tendencies are fond of painting and of contemplating. But ordinary life benefits little from the example of John Halifax. It is of no use bidding us poor creatures of clay to be like the illuminated saints, with dovelike eyes always looking piety, and gentle hands folded in perpetual devotion. That is the clever young lady's type of what masculine humanity ought to be; and a very admirable type it would be, well deserving of strenuous imitation, if men could by any process be so re-moulded as to have the souls and impulses of good young women instead of their own

[1] By Dinah Maria Mulock; see above, No. 30, n. 1.

more rugged and passionate natures. Then there is the Arthur Pendennis type—picture the most elaborate, faithful, perfect known to our day, inspired by the very light of genius itself, the whole soul, spirit, and character of the English young man of Victoria's reign put into the form of a novelist's hero. But Pendennis's author declined to approach the wild oats question; frankly acknowledged in so many words, that he had duly considered the matter, and preferred to omit it altogether, believing that the age had grown too wicked to bear an honest argument of it, and refusing to set it out in any plain and plausible way for the use of boarding-schools and genteel society. The world, it seems to us, lost something thereby. No man of our time could have touched this pregnant question so delicately, yet so effectively, as Thackeray could; for, with a perception of man's ordinary nature which nothing could elude, he had at once a gentle, pitying sense of human weakness, and a high and noble standard of human duty. Richard Feverel does attempt frankly and boldly to approach the wild oats question; but having borne the risk and odium of approaching it, he suddenly shrinks back from it again, and, on the whole, we do not feel that we have learned much more than Miss Muloch could have taught us—that all men, and all women too, ought to be perfect, if they could only contrive to reach that blest condition. This much may be said in disparagement of the book, regarding it as a novel with a purpose; but as a mere novel of character, it would not be easy to speak too highly of the talents which it indicates. Some of the men drawn by Mr Meredith are sketched with a hand so light, and yet so firm, that a sense of their reality impresses itself imperceptibly, and yet indelibly, on the mind. The women, perhaps, are less happy, and the author often sacrifices to that odd freak of modern taste which requires perfect ignorance as well as innocence in womanhood. He gives, for example, a heroine, so in-effably unconscious of the world's ways, that in the absence of her husband she spends her evenings tête à tête, and in the twilight, with a renowned London profligate of fashion, and never once suspects that he devotes himself to her society with any other motive than a dis-interested desire to improve her knowledge of history. Indeed Mr Meredith's women are, on the whole, much open to the objection so commonly urged in disparagement of Thackeray's female characters—they are pretty, loving, innocent, and silly; or they are clever, selfish, and bad. They know nothing at all; have, in fact, a perfectly Eden-like and Fayaway kind of innocence, difficult, we should think, to be retained up to years of discretion in this modern world of ours; or they know rather too much, and are a good deal too fond of hinting at their knowledge. Their innocence rather too much reminds one of the *fausse Agnes* style of thing, and leaves the suspicious mind in a sort of doubt whether it is dealing with hypocritical affection or with down-right idiotcy.

Mr Meredith's habit is to seize one or two central figures, and to lavish upon the development of their natures the fulness of his artistic power; all other forms and objects are merely thrown in as accessories, as furniture, as a mere background. Carelessness, haste, frequent vagueness, sudden bursts of caricature, are naturally the common phenomena of this artistic condition. In the novel which has issued from his pen within the last few weeks, that which we may call the psychical interest is even more engrossingly developed than in *Richard Feverel. Emilia in London* [sic] is the unfolding of one human nature, the examination of one human heart. It is not an amusing, we can hardly even call it an agreeable story. There is something melancholy and occasionally harsh about its prevailing tone. Though it closes hopefully, its general effect is rather disheartening. Yet *Emilia in London* [sic] is in its general structure perhaps an improvement on *Richard Feverel*. It is more of a novel and less of a philosophic essay. The style has fewer eccen-tricities in it, and there are indeed scarcely any of the fits and starts which disturb the reader of *Richard Feverel*. Its supreme merit consists in the fact that it has added to fiction one thoroughly original and perfectly natural human character. The story is simple in its outline. A girl, the daughter of an Italian living in London, is blessed with a wonderful voice and a passionate love for music. Italy and music are the organic passions of her existence; but there grows up over these a new and still more consuming passion. She falls in love with a young cavalry-officer—a man not without brains and not without heart, but still much below her in truthfulness and depth of nature. He is divided between her and the world; and at last she sees that the heart she seeks is not in him, and she has strength to put him away. Emilia is stricken down, but not wholly crushed. She has received a fearful wound, but not a mortal blow. She suffers cruelly, but she survives. This is in few words the argument of the story. Emilia's own character is the life and the beauty of it. She is genius without culture; goodness without rule; love without worldly restraint. Her passion for music, for Italy, and for Wilfrid, is blended with consummate skill. We remember no character in modern literature that so faithfully pictures the nature which is filled with a genius for music. Not even Consuelo, in George Sand's novel,[1] is so perfect an impersonation. The musical and the poetic are not represented in life by the same sort of human nature; but in books there is hardly any distinction ever drawn. The novelist commonly acts as if there were but one kind of artist nature, and as if the sole difference between painter, poet, and musician were contained in the different modes wherein the genius of each expresses itself. In life every one must be to some degree conscious how entirely unreal is this assumption. The most gifted musician often disappoints in intellectual companionship all but musicians. Intellect, and strangely enough the more poetic phase of intellect, seems often wanting in the singer whose whole soul is filled with music. Mr Meredith has expressed his sense of this peculiarity in the admirably drawn character of Emilia. In everything, save that which regards song alone, her intellectual nature is commonplace and prosaic. Passion lifts her to heights which are in themselves essentially poetic and dramatic; and a pure, truthful simplicity keeps her always above the vulgarities of existence. That which would vulgarize others is dignified by her; but still she has nothing whatever in her honest childlike heart which reminds one of the Sappho or the Corinna; or even of the stage singer whom ordinary romancists have sometimes painted. There is nothing ideal about her, and she walks the earth with the tread of a mere woman. After the somewhat too theatrically arranged incident which introduces her to the reader, we never again quit the beaten highway of modern prosaic life. In her moments of exaltation and her deep sufferings, her artist's passion, and her fervent woman's love, this singular, simple child of genius is affined by nature to the plainest and least romantic creature who ever cooked a husband's dinner. If there seems anything strange and fantastic in the character of Emilia, it is only because simple reality seems so often strange and fantastic when boldly introduced to supplant some long-established conventionality of fiction.

Emilia is not by any means the only original and yet faithful character in this remarkable book. Mr Pericles, the Greek millionaire, with his passion for music, and for the discovery of prima donnas, his cold selfish heart, his coarse nature, and his thin varnish of French polish, is drawn with a bold and masterly hand. We do not remember anything like Mr Pericles in a novel before; but we have seen him and heard him talk in real life many times. Mr Pole, the British merchant, and the three Miss Poles, are realities; and Mr Merthyr Powys is a manly, gallant being, whom England's sympathies with Italian struggles have

[1] *Consuelo* was published in 1842–3.

made real in many forms for our generation. Perhaps beyond these few
figures all becomes hazy; although there are some well-painted scenes
occasionally even where these are not. But the art which sets a whole
group of people before us full of individual life, to be remembered
separately and distinctly always, has not yet been attained by the author
of these volumes. Even where the three Miss Poles are concerned, it
takes a long time before the reader has the idiosyncrasies of each firmly
fixed in his mind; and he often finds himself turning back to the first
chapter to ascertain which of the three he has just been meeting, as
people reading a play have to refer to the *dramatis personæ*, to refresh
their memories about the identities of Diego and Pedro and Lorenzo
and the rest. The title of the book and the manner of its conclusion
alike lead us to expect that we are yet to hear more of the career of
Emilia. We have read only of her life in England; and may look with
interest and hope for further tidings of her—for she is the one only
personage in the book who inspires the reader with a genuine interest.
Herein lies one heavy defect; such a defect, indeed, that if Mr Meredith
deserves censure for having permitted it to exist, he may claim
admiration for having in any manner succeeded in surmounting it.
Except for Merthyr Powys, who is but slightly sketched, there is no
creature, man or woman, in the book (after the heroine, of course)
capable of filling the mind, even for a moment, with interest or
affection. It is not that the people are more selfish, more full of defects,
than any ordinary group of people taken from life at random, but they
do not interest us as the most commonplace beings in Thackeray's or
even in Trollope's pages always do. If they have marked peculiarities,
we do not seem to care to observe them. If they have no marked
peculiarities, we allow them to glide away from our memory altogether,
without the slightest effort to retain them. Affection for any of them
seems out of the question, even where one feels convinced that people
having such and such qualities in real life could scarcely fail to win our
affection. Even Sir Purcel Barrett, the disinherited owner of an empty
title, fails to awaken anything like real interest; although his melancholy, morbid condition of mind, in the gloomy haunted border-land
between sanity and madness, is analysed with much skill. His sudden
tragic end is but a mere surprise and shock. It produces bewilderment,
but hardly any other sensation. In truth, most of Mr Meredith's
secondary characters are not realities: they are walking types, embodied
aphorisms; conceits, or fancies, or crotchets of the author put into
human shape, as the magician turns a broomstick or a distaff into the

semblance of a human creature, and draped, according to the author's whim, in pantaloons or petticoats. Their conversation is often unintelligible; a mere interchange of verbal subtleties and quiddities. The author seems indeed to have deliberately chosen in some instances to render his meaning, and the meaning of what his personages do and say, an absolute mystery. The result is that he rarely reaches, still more rarely commands, the feelings of the reader, although he almost always engages the intellect. Only where he has to deal with Emilia herself does he abandon himself to the mere impulses of his artistic genius. That he can put aside the critic at all, may well give us hope for his greater success hereafter. Aphorisms, however epigrammatic and brilliant, reflections upon life, however quaint, fanciful, and truthful, can at best be but the ornaments of a work of fiction. The character of Emilia is to us the first completely satisfactory evidence that Mr Meredith really has in him the essential qualities of a great novelist. This alone makes his latest work a sign of progress since the days of *Richard Feverel*.

What then on the whole is the fair judgment to be passed on the works of Mr Meredith? They reveal to us undoubtedly the operations of a mind endowed with great and genuine power; of a quick sensitive feeling nature; of a rich and sometimes a prodigal fancy; of an intellect highly cultured, and matured by much observation. Still the books are hardly to be called successful in themselves. They exhibit a combination of faculties entirely above the ordinary range, they are distinguished by a freedom from the commonplace rare indeed in our days; and they have the power to set the reader thinking more often and more deeply than even the productions of greater intellects can always do. But the intellectual man predominates in them; and therefore they are not great works of fiction. The fusing heat of emotion which melts the substances of a novel into one harmonious and fluent whole is wanting. The glow of absolute genius is never felt. The moment of projection never arrives; the several substances never combine into the golden mass; they remain cold, solid, and individual to the last. The reader is never carried away by the story; he never loses sight of the narrator; he never for a moment feels as if he were moving among the people of the novel, sharing their trials and their joys. Mr Meredith falls into the common error of intellectual men who go about to construct a story upon purely intellectual principles. It is not enough to draw men and women with vigorous and lifelike touches. Mr Meredith has done this in many instances with entire success. Emilia is a character wholly new to literature, and painted with

consummate skill. Adrian, the Wise Youth of *Richard Feverel*, is such a
picture as Bulwer in his brightest days might have been proud to own.
It is not enough to have a keen observance of the shades of human feeling; it is not enough to write eloquently, epigrammatically, and
pathetically; to have a racy faculty of humour; even to have deep
feeling and the capacity to express it in words and scenes. All these
faculties, or most of them, are essential to the entire success of a novelist.
But besides all these, there is something else needed. There are the
ingredients; but there must likewise be the capacity to combine and
fuse them into one harmonious whole. There must be in fact the story-
teller's essential faculty—the capacity to tell a story. Whatever the gifts
a man lavishes over his work, the first thing we must demand of him, if
he is to be a novelist, is the power of holding firmly the attention and
interest of his readers. Whether he writes for a purpose or without it,
this faculty is equally essential. It may not be the highest quality, but it
is the most indispensable. Whatever poetic inspiration a man may have,
it is obvious that if he have no ear for rhythm or music he cannot be a
poet. So of the novelist, he must be a story-teller first of all. Now Mr
Meredith has not as yet developed in himself the faculty of the story-
teller. It is quite possible that he may yet prove it to be among his gifts,
but his novels thus far do not sufficiently display it. Men of faculties far
inferior to him have this gift to a degree incomparably higher. Some
men have it, and having scarcely anything else, take a high place and
exercise a wide influence by virtue of that faculty alone. The best story-
teller our age has seen is a man to whom the phrase 'inspired idiot'
would seem very fairly to apply—we mean the inexhaustible author of
The Count of Monte Cristo.[1] In our own literature Mr Wilkie Collins is
undoubtedly an admirable story-teller. He is not to be compared for a
moment with Mr Meredith in intellect, and fancy, and true perception
of human feeling; but he is a good story-teller, and his books are read
everywhere, while Mr Meredith's novels only extort the half-reluctant
admiration of some rare groups of intellectual readers. No doubt one
reason is that Mr Meredith always seems to write with a purpose. He is
always apparently meditating on some phase of human life, some
tendency of human nature, some melancholy confusion or misdirection
of human effort; and his whole soul is not in the work itself, but in
something behind it, and of which it only faintly shadows out the reality
and the meaning. He is too much of a thinking man: he needs the spirit
which abandons itself wholly to the work, becomes lost in it, and has

[1] Published in 1844–5 by Dumas *père*.

for the time no *arrière pensée*, indeed no individual existence apart from it. The critical faculty is too strong in him, and therefore, even when he begins to grow earnest, he forthwith sets about to analyse this very earnestness, and it naturally vanishes in the effort. 'I have never thought about thinking', says Goethe. Mr Meredith seems almost always to think about thinking. He is like one who, half waking in the morning out of some vivid and fascinating dream, endeavours, instead of allowing the beautiful images still to float perceptible but unquestioned across his sensations, to seize them distinctly, to master their meaning, to individualize their outlines, and then finds them fading away, to be followed only by cold, grey reality. If one will be a dreamer, let him abandon himself to his dreams. In the land of fiction, feeling and fancy must guide; intellect must be content to follow. Mr Meredith does not want the feeling or the fancy, he only gives them the wrong place in his combinations. He must endeavour to keep the critic and the philosopher a little more in the background, and let the poet or the story-teller take the leading part. It was Virgil and not Aristotle who conducted Dante to the places where he saw the marvellous sights, and found the materials for the wonderful story. Mr Meredith has much of a poet's nature, and only needs the courage to trust it more fully. Among his poetic qualities is one peculiarly rare in our day; so rare, indeed, that most of our writers seem to have lost it altogether—that which appreciates and idealizes as woman's highest charm, her womanhood. He can therefore describe the growth of young and passionate love as few in our day can or will do. The lover of our English romance today is a creature without sex. The hero adores the heroine because of her virtues, or her gifts, or her modesty, or her truth, or her physical beauty; but the element of her womanhood is almost entirely eliminated from his sensations. Either humanity is supposed to have lost the sentiment, or it is ashamed of it. The late Nathaniel Hawthorne was one of the very few authors of our day who endeavoured to restore the love of woman to its old, poetic, human, sensuous, yet unselfish nature. Mr Meredith has striven in the same direction, and the very effort in itself proves a mind which is capable of perceiving and expressing some of the realities which are most truly poetic, and of rendering to them their reality and their idealism at once. Some of the early love-scenes in *Richard Feverel* are themselves sufficient to justify the most serious regret that one endowed with so much of the poet's sympathies and the romancist's vivid power, should too often be induced to sink the story-teller in the critic, the poet in the social philosopher. . . .

RHODA FLEMING

1865

---

37. J. C. Jeaffreson, *Athenaeum*

No. 1981, 14 October 1865

John Cordy Jeaffreson (1831–91), was a novelist, biographer and miscellaneous writer. Among his works were *Novels and Novelists from Elizabeth to Victoria* (1858) and *Victoria, Queen and Empress* (1893).

Were *Rhoda Fleming* slightly better or a good deal worse, the critic would have no difficulty in passing judgment upon it; but as it is, we are at a loss how to do justice to its undeniable merits without misleading the reader to think it an interesting novel. First, let full tribute be rendered to its acceptable qualities, amongst which may be mentioned an abundance of unaffected humour, two or three excellent pictures of rural life, much vigorous writing, and occasional manifestations of genuine poetic insight into human nature. Admirable for truthfulness of outline, detail, tone, are some of the rural characters of the old-world yeoman-life of Kent and Hampshire, from which the materials of the story are principally drawn. For instance, the bovine stolidity and honest dullness of Farmer Fleming, and the racy bluntness of Jonathan Eccles, are illustrated with exquisite art. Something might be said in praise of every person, stick, flower, stone of Queen Anne's Farm, and of the Hampshire yeoman's homestead. Some of the scenes, moreover, are highly dramatic. The interview between Rhoda Fleming and Robert Eccles, for instance—when, throwing off the air and tone of a quiet young farmer, Robert startles the girl by revealing at the same time the devilry and heroism of his nature—is a piece of writing which inclines us to credit the author with capabilities of which he has previously given no indication. Good again, but in a very different way, is the humour which sets forth how Farmer Fleming's credulity and childish fancy cause him to believe that his brother-in-law is a miserly millionnaire, whilst in fact the imagined possessor of fabulous wealth is merely a bank-porter in the City, who adds to the narrow income of his official salary by acting the part of usurer to the more thriftless clerks of his employer's bank.

But notwithstanding its irregular strength and many good points, *Rhoda Fleming* does not long retain the high opinion which its opening chapters create. Anxious to amuse, Mr Meredith is morbidly afraid of being thought prosy; and in places he is betrayed by his eagerness and dread into exhibitions of factitious sprightliness and ponderous gaiety. Wishing to shine, he commits the fault that he most desires to avoid; and by striving to put his thoughts in piquant language, he at times renders it no easy task for the reader to catch his meaning. Setting forth the forlorn plight of a young man who is kept waiting for dinner at a club to which a friend has invited him, Mr Meredith says, 'Algernon waited dinnerless *until the healthy-going minutes distended and swelled monstrous and horrible as viper-bitten bodies, and the venerable Signior, Time, became of unhealthy hue*'. It is not till the reader has perused this passage several times, and has studied it by the light of the context, that he sees its true significance. Surely Mr Meredith had better have simply said, 'Algernon waited dinnerless for a couple of hours'. In like manner, when he draws attention to a letter written by a young man under the influence of a very beautiful and apparently unprincipled woman, he says, 'The value of the letter lies in the exhibition it presents of a rather markworthy young man, who has passed through the hands of a— (what I must call her; and in doing so, I ask pardon of all the Jack Cades of letters, who, in the absence of a grammatical king and a government, sit as lords upon the English tongue)—a crucible-woman'. What is a 'crucible-woman'? Who are 'the Jack Cades of letters'? Such passages as these are all the more noticeable because the author, who thus through straining after 'point' falls into rigmarole, can, when it pleases him to do so, write with purity, force, and terseness.

Mr Meredith's chief defect seems to be one for which there are but slender hopes of remedy. He lacks the story-teller's special power of holding the attention by an easy flow of thoughts, until some over-powering interest has been roused as to the course of the narrative. To define this faculty would be difficult—to enumerate the various tricks and artifices by which it achieves its object would be more easy;

but the best and simplest way to appreciate its special force is to examine some of the works of fiction in which it is conspicuous by its absence. Every season produces two or three loosely-written and thoroughly foolish novels, which through the agency of this faculty are pleasant, notwithstanding their literary deficiencies, and readable in spite of their folly; and every season produces the same number of tales in which humour, wit, learning exert themselves in vain because they are unaided by the story-teller's special talent. Through want of this quality, *Rhoda Fleming* is a failure. In the opening chapters—where he introduces us to the bright flower-beds and drowsy tranquillity of Queen Anne's Farm, to ambitious Mrs Fleming and her two lovely daughters, who like their mother look upwards in life—the author commands our sympathy and gratitude; but as soon as Mrs Fleming is buried with suitable pomp, and the beautiful Miss Dahlia Fleming is sent to London, we begin to feel the want of that which nowhere appears in the book—the romance-writer's peculiar art. And when this want has once made itself felt, it is felt more strongly with every turn of a fresh leaf. Instead of seeming to cover and surround him, the story seems to be slipping through the reader's fingers; and it is not without labour that Dahlia is traced through sin to shame, through shame to brain-fever in a London hospital, and onwards to a condition of angelic penitence. All that concerns Dahlia's sacrifice of womanly honour is the least satisfactory part of the book—her fall being a case of sin and suffering wrought through woman's heedlessness and passion rather than man's design, and her seducer having for his palliation the excuse of the boy who, on being charged with plucking his master's fruit, pleaded that the pear fell into his open hand. Whilst Dahlia makes acquaintance with wicked pleasure and consequent humiliation in London, Rhoda remains by her father's side—comforting the rugged yeoman, and bravely maintaining her belief in the goodness of her fallen sister; and at the conclusion of the tale, when Dahlia, repenting of her past misbehaviour, and declining to marry her remorseful seducer, devotes her life to pious labour, Rhoda gives her hand to Robert Eccles. The reader is led to hope that Robert does not relapse into his old habits of intemperance, and that Rhoda is an exemplary wife to the man who first told her his love when disgrace had newly fallen on her home.

38. Unsigned review, *Saturday Review*

xx, 14 October 1865

It is a great comfort to those who admire manly thinking and good English to find that Mr Meredith has, for a time at least, abandoned the over-subtle and unfruitful speculations upon character and society which made his last novel a peculiarly conspicuous instance of both originality and labour failing to redeem the prime mistake of an ill-chosen theme. There are so few writers who combine creative power with that faculty of a large and liberal observation of life which alone can make their creations real or worth studying, that one grudges anything like waste of a kind of ability so uncommon. Mr Meredith no doubt takes a high place among novelists of this rank. In all his books he introduces us to fresh and vigorously drawn characters. He never resorts to the 'common form' of fiction. The mass of novels are like a very select circle in society; night after night, though the names and dresses and scenes are slightly changed, the reader meets exactly the same set of people, and they all talk in exactly the same fashion, and do the same sort of things. It is something for which to be grateful to find a writer who has the power, and takes the trouble, to exhibit new characters; and to exhibit them, moreover, as doing and feeling what they would do and feel in the ordinary human way, not as if they were visibly playing at being characters in a novel. Besides this, Mr Meredith has the excellent negative quality of abstaining from superfluous and unprovoked padding. He does not deny himself frequent asides—though they are rarer in *Rhoda Fleming* than in his previous books—but then these asides are not digressions on things in general. They spring easily from the action of the story, and we are not sent clean out of our track and then back into it again by two violent jolts. Of course, in escaping from the vices or feebleness of ordinary fiction, it was not to be expected that Mr Meredith should altogether avoid the invention of one or two vices of his own. He is occasionally obscure in his reflections, carrying his reader too hastily forward over stony places and up steep ascents of argument, and landing him breathless he scarce knows where. A plain man has a desire, perhaps a weak one, to see the path by which he has been transported into unfamiliar regions, but Mr Meredith inconsiderately argues in seven-league boots. The fault is the natural result of one of his chief excellences. He has such a complete and personal intimacy with the people of his story, he realizes so vividly to himself their characteristics and the effects of the situation upon them, as to forget that the reader of a novel knows nothing about the personages who act in it beyond what the author chooses to tell them. We require to have a very great deal told us about a man whose character we are asked to understand, when we only know him through the imperfectly conducting medium of print. The same vividness of conception on the part of the author may perhaps account for the oblique way in which the incidents of the story are revealed. We seem to be too often introduced to the effect before getting any insight into the cause. The author has fully pictured the incident to his own mind, and then hastens to consider its consequences upon the character whom it concerns, the reader meanwhile rather wondering what it is all about, and what has happened. One or two things are scarcely made clear at all. What Mrs Lovell and Major Waring had done in India, and what was the secret of the blood-stained handkerchief, are things only divulged to us very dimly, and left vague even to the very end. Obviously it is not pleasant to see the play through a film.

But these passing obscurities may well be forgotten in the vigorous and impressive painting of the more prominent figures, as well as in the admirable manliness with which Mr Meredith has treated a situation that is commonly made the occasion either of sermonizing or of sentimentalism. The author declines to win popularity by either of these favourite and infallible devices. A girl who has been seduced is not, to him, a person whom, as an artist, it is his business either to preach over or to cry over. It may be the duty of the parson to moralize about the falling away; and, on the other hand, a great many people like to have the woman who has committed this particular offence against society written about in a tone of mingled pity and pruriency, a mixture of snivelling and sniffing. With all this the artist has nothing to do. It is not his part to pass sentence for sins against society, nor to surround the sinner with all manner of artificial saintly crowns and heavenly haloes. To him the woman who sacrifices herself for passion is what she is, and no more. Much of her worth may survive, or she may be as unworthy after a fall as she was before. One must look at her with 'rightful manliness'—without 'those false sensations, peculiar to men, concerning the soiled purity of women, the lost innocence, the brand of shame upon her, which are commonly the foul sentimentalism of such as can be too eager in the chase of corruption when occasion suits, and are another side of pruriency, not absolutely foreign to the best of us in our youth'. 'The young man who can look upon them we call fallen women with a noble eye is to my mind he that is most nobly begotten of the race, and likeliest to be the sire of a noble line'. In the same way, the stern sister is drawn without a touch of exaggeration in the direction either of sympathy or caricature. Rhoda's conviction that her sister in spite of all appearances is married, and her anger with anybody who ventures to hold the more probable opinion, are brought out with remarkable truth. In the days of their youth she and her sister had accidental occasion to ponder much on the harshness with which the village had treated a luckless girl who had returned to it with a blemished name. 'They could not fathom the meaning of their father's unkindness, coarseness, and indignation. Why and why? they asked one another blankly. The Scriptures were harsh in one part, but was the teaching to continue so after the atonement?' Then, in years after, when Dahlia's name became spotted, 'the old and deep grievance in her heart as to what men thought of women and as to the harshness of men' was strongly stirred up. Her intense faith in her sister, and her resolute facing of the suspicions to which men's mean natures prompted them, furnish the key to the first half of her action in the story. This faith, indeed, is the only quality which keeps Rhoda from being too absolutely cold and passionless to be either truthfully drawn or interesting. When the fatal fact is forced upon her, and a chance of marriage is offered to her sister, the instinct which their Hebrew religious teaching implants in most English girls of strong nature impels her remorselessly to drive the fallen creature to the only step which can set her erect again before the world, though permanent wretchedness should be the clear result. She knows that 'it is a good and precious thing to do right', and this is the one item of belief and knowledge to which she holds fast. And even when she finds that she has thus inflicted a curse upon her sister, 'she had still a feeling of the harsh joy peculiar to those who have exercised command with a conscious righteousness upon wilful, sinful, and errant spirits, and have thwarted the wrong-doer'. But—by an excellent touch by which the author shows the thoroughness and pliancy of his conception—she tries in vain to console herself in reflecting that the doom had been righteously executed when the unhappy Dahlia is before her. 'Away from the tragic figure in the room, she might have thought so, but the horror in the eyes and voice of this awakened Sacrifice struck away the support of theoretic justification. Great pity for the poor enmeshed life, helpless there, and in woman's worst peril—looking either to madness or to death for an escape—drowned her reason in a heavy cloud of tears'.

The weaker sort of novelist generally prides himself amazingly on what he deems the consistency of his characters. That is, he first casts them in a mould, rigidly and unchangeably formed, and they move to and fro on the scene like figures of iron propelled in one inevitable direction by interior clockwork. But Mr Meredith is wholly free from this barren and enfeebling notion. Rhoda is stern, earnest, of the Hebrew or Puritanic complexion. But she is incredulous of her sister's sin for all that. Even when it is proved, she has no hard reproaches for the sinner. And a confidence in what her creed and custom have taught her to look on as the righteous course does not shut her heart up against sympathy with the creature upon whom the righteous course—as is too often its wont—has brought unutterable wretchedness. This flexibility of a distinctly drawn character before changing circumstances is an effect which our novelists rarely attempt. Mr Meredith in all his books is particularly fond of tracing these variations. He places his personages in a number of given situations, and seems as it were to watch, almost for his own diversion, the development of character which ensues. The reader is persuaded that the growth of the hero or heroine's nature is spontaneous, though under the influence of surrounding things; and this, in its own way, is a very distinct triumph of art. In the character of Edward Blancove the author produces the same effect of movement, but, as it appears to us, with less success. The pivots on which the movement turns are less intelligible and less natural. Witty, selfish, half-cynical, to begin with, he is somehow overwhelmed by a moral revolution which leaves him devoted, and, indeed, on one occasion absolutely pious. The reader may complain that nothing through the first volume and a half furnishes even a hint that at bottom Edward has the smallest richness of nature, and that nothing has happened to produce so sudden a development of fine qualities. The ambitious and highly-cultivated *young* man is, we know, apt to react against the impulses both of ambition and of intellectual fastidiousness, and, when in the mood, to sacrifice prospects and everything else to a yearning for simplicity and a kind of virtuousness. But it is hard to see why inability to fathom the depths of Mrs Lovell's character should make Edward write to Dahlia: 'And I, who have sinned against my innocent darling, will ask her to pray with me that our future may be one, so

142

that I may make good to her what she has suffered, and to the God whom we worship the offence I have committed'.

Mr Meredith's exclusive devotion to play of character would seem to lie at the root of what is his chief defect—weakness of construction. His situations hang too loosely together. Provided he can make his characters grow and move, provided he can throw a sufficient variety of light and colour over them, he is comparatively indifferent to the close coherence of his incidents, or to anything like a compact and finished story. There is unquestionably something exceedingly poor in the popular craving for a minute final account of what becomes of everybody who has figured to go through a muster-roll of all his characters at the end of the third volume, sending all the bad people into misery, and rewarding all the good people by happy lives ever after. This makes the whole thing so plainly and horribly artificial that we cannot expect a writer who claims a place among artists to institute this sort of parade. Still, Mr Meredith leaves us a little too abruptly. It seems as if he had got as much amusement for himself as he wished out of the movements of his characters, and then had ceased to take interest in what might become of them. The reader may be pardoned for feeling rather less like an Epicurean god. Mr Meredith has the art of drawing men and women so like flesh and blood that we naturally have at least a human interest in their fate.

There are in *Rhoda Fleming* some admirably fresh and vigorous sketches of country life and nature. The father of Rhoda is an excellent specimen of the sturdy British yeoman, whose ideas are very few and very simple, but obstinate and deep-rooted in proportion. He is overwhelmingly grateful, and even respectful, to the man who marries his daughter, though he knows him to be a villain; and he insists on her joining her husband, though her joining him means certain and enduring misery. All this makes us dreadfully angry, but it is uncommonly true to rural nature. The scene at the Pilot Inn, too, is exquisitely humorous and truthful. So are the minor characters of Mrs Sumfit and Master Gammon, the two old farm-servants. The latter is really inimitable. Dahlia is lying ill up-stairs:

[Quotes xlvii, from 'Nevertheless, the sight of Master Gammon' to 'appeared to meditate'.]

Algernon Blancove is a capital study of the minor rank. 'This youth is one of great Nature's tom-fools, an elegant young gentleman out-wardly, of the very large class who are simply the engines of their appetites, and to the philosophic eye still run wild in woods'. However, 'the most worthless creature is most serviceable for examination, when the microscope is applied to them [it?],[1] as a simple study of human mechanism'. This sentence may be said to be the secret of Mr Meredith's workmanship. It is essentially microscopic, and those who have a sufficiently strong taste for art to relish such studies will find *Rhoda Fleming* very well worth reading. Besides this, the story itself is eminently interesting—almost too interesting, in fact, to leave us tranquil enough for the appreciation of the more substantial part.

39. Unsigned review, *Westminster Review*

xxix, January 1866

Everything that Mr Meredith writes is sure to be clever. Over-cleverness, indeed, is his fault; and over-cleverness has the same effect on a book that over-dressiness has on a human being. In his present novel this fault is very conspicuous. His heroine, Farmer William, John, Master Gammon, and the scenes in which they are placed evidently owe their inspiration to a study of George Eliot. And Mr Meredith, throughout the three volumes, is constantly attempting to give us those homely descriptions of farm life, those rustic sayings, which stamp such an individuality upon all that George Eliot writes. But his power is here weak, and his cleverness only makes his weakness more apparent. He never reaches George Eliot's incisiveness; he never gains that concentrated force by which in one or two words she reveals a character. Thus, he makes his rustics talk about London, but he never reaches such a description as we once heard from the lips of a Wiltshire shepherd, 'Danged if the streets there been't fifteen hurdles athwert'. He describes horsy rustics, but he never puts such a sentence into their mouths as we once heard in Yorkshire, that county *aptum equis*, from a horse-dealer on seeing a lion in a show, 'Please, sir, has that 'ere lion been clipped'? He is constantly hitting all round the nail, but never hits it, or,

---

[1] The square brackets belong to the original text.

if he does, hits it on one side. George Eliot with one stroke drives home. We feel that what her characters say is precisely what they did say, and nothing else, and that you can substitute nothing better. This we do not feel with Mr Meredith; and this is precisely the gulf that yawns between genius and mere cleverness. But Mr Meredith is over-clever. Thus, he introduces us to a Hampshire farmer who fattens sheep upon melons. When we read this we feel as if we do when we read, in the Song of Solomon, 'take us the foxes, the little foxes, that spoil the vines'.[1] The facts are probably true in both cases, but they do not come under our observation, and therefore do not strike us as natural. George Eliot would most probably have made her farmer interested in a peculiar breed of Hampshire pigs, and so maintained a local colouring. A writer like Bulwer Lytton, who is essentially a clever man without a spark of genius, would have inevitably fallen into some mistake similar to Mr Meredith's. Mr Disraeli would doubtless have indulged in the mysteries of a 'cross' between a Southdown and a Cotswold. We are not for a moment impugning Mr Meredith's facts. The lion, we all know, in Africa, refreshes himself on the water melon, and we have no doubt that the 'Cotswold lion', as a Cotswold ram is commonly called in Gloucestershire, would, if he had the opportunity, do the same. We are simply pointing out the effects of over-cleverness. Mr Meredith must not be confounded with the writers of the Cockney school. He takes pains; as a rule, too, avoids all slang, and has a real love for Nature. Yet every now and then we come upon passages, the absurdity of which we know not whether to ascribe to carelessness or a mere straining after fine things. Thus, to take only a few examples, we read, 'The days at a well-ordered country house, where a divining lady rules, speed to the measure of a waltz, in harmonious circles, dropping like crystals into the gulf of Time, and appearing to write nothing in his book' (vol. i. p. 271). Whatever the philosophers may think of space, Mr Meredith is determined that time shall not be a mere mental phenomenon. Here the days first waltz, then crystallize themselves, after which we are hardly surprised that they can't write. And then, what is a 'divining lady' at a country house, a spiritualist, or what? So, too, Mr Meredith talks of a 'skimming cab' (vol. ii., p. 207). This is one of those things that are too good to believe in, or, if they exist, should be kept on purpose for the hero or the heroine; and not, as in this case, for the two villains of the story. So, too, he paints for us a lady with 'soft blue eyes, out of which a thousand needles flew' (vol. ii., p. 61). That needles have eyes

[1] ii. 15.

145

everyone knows, but this will be the first time, we suspect, that anyone will have heard of the converse. Still the book is very clever. Its great fault, to our mind, is a want of sincerity, and this would vitiate far greater cleverness than even Mr Meredith possesses. . . .

VITTORIA

1867

40. Unsigned review, *Saturday Review*

xxiii, 2 February 1867

It is a somewhat difficult task to give a fair review of a book in which there is apparently a wide disproportion between the expenditure of ability and the result obtained. In the not uncommon case where the popularity of an author exceeds what would seem to be his due, the critic cannot but feel a certain diffidence; he may be demolishing a windbag, but, on the other hand, he may be merely giving another example of the occasional inferiority of the cultivated to the popular judgment. Contemporary reviews of Keats and Wordsworth still unpleasantly shake the general belief in critical infallibility. In the reverse case the task is less invidious. A compliment thrown away can at any rate do no harm; but there is still an unpleasant sensation that there must be some undiscovered flaw in the criticism. It is the exception for a writer to display much ability in any direction without obtaining a fair amount of recognition, and it is therefore incumbent upon anyone who asserts the existence of talent which has failed of due appreciation to point out the circumstances to which the failure is due. This is a short statement of the duty we have to discharge to Mr Meredith. There can be no mistake either as to his abilities, or as to his failure in obtaining a corresponding place in popular esteem. In *Vittoria*, which is just published from the *Fortnightly Review*, he has shown as much power of thought and style as would fit out a dozen writers of sensation novels. There is scarcely a page in which there is not evidence of originality, and, what is much rarer, of conscientious labour, often skilfully applied. The conversations, instead of being the slipshod collections of says-he's and says-she's with which most novelists eke out their narrow materials, are only too pointed and vigorous for the interlocutors. Almost every character stands out distinctly and forcibly; some show great originality of conception. The descriptions, again, of natural scenery are really picturesque and compact, instead of being diluted verbiage spun out at random. Yet, with all these merits, and we might conscientiously speak of others, we fear that Mr Meredith's novel has the unmistakable fault of being hard to read. It is often so clever as to be on the verge of genius, but somehow we don't get on with it. It is a succession of brilliancies which are never fused into a brilliant whole; and it is cram full of smart sayings which have an awkward way of just stopping short of the intelligible. We have, in short, that unpleasant sensation which is sometimes produced by talk of a very clever man who wants to be a little cleverer still—who overstrains himself in the effort to be exceedingly smart, and ends by talking something which neither he nor his company quite understand, which simple persons assume to be wonderful because if is not quite intelligible, and which nobody finds to be genuinely entertaining.

The first thing which strikes the reader, in considering this phenomenon, is the curious nature of Mr Meredith's style. It gives us the impression of prose striving to be poetry. It has the compressions, the odd turns, and sometimes almost the rhythm of poetry, though it never quite gets its feet off the ground. To quote a few sentences almost at random, a man is described as 'flashing a white fist and thumping the long projection of his knee with a wolfish aspect'. With an imperceptible change this might be a fragment of blank verse. A woman lifted over a precipice 'felt the saving hold of her feet plucked from her, with all the sinking horror, and bit her underlip, as if keeping in the scream with bare stitches'. Then we are told that 'the pale spiked dialogue broke, not to be revived'; we hear of a 'spirit writhing in the serpent coil of fiery blushes'; or are informed concerning a gentleman who had good reasons for feeling that the hours passed slowly, that 'the face of time had been imaged like the withering masque of a corpse to him'. These sentences may perhaps read, in their detached shape, something like the ordinary fine writing of inferior novelists; but in fact they are genuine attempts to express something forcibly, and seem to be natural in Mr Meredith. The only fault we find with them is that they imply an effort to put more into a quiet prose sentence than it can contain, with the natural result of making it cramped and uncomfortable. A similar defect may be traced in Mr Meredith's dialogues. As we have said, they are never trivial or commonplace. His characters do not talk, as Mr Trollope's so often contrive to do, down half a page in asking for a cup of tea or a railway-ticket. But their smart sayings are so full of epigram and hidden allusion and indirect satire that we often feel a little oppressed by their wisdom, and venture to doubt whether Mr Meredith quite understands it himself. Here is a bit of the 'pale spiked dialogue'. Someone mentions, with a hidden sarcasm, that bullfinches should be fed on grapes before singing. Another replies:

'To make them exhibit the results, you withdraw the benefit suddenly, of course?'
'We imitate the general run of Fortune's gifts as much as we can,' said Merthyr.
'That is the training for little shrill parrots; we have none in Italy,' Laura sighed, mock dolefully; 'I fear the system would fail among us.'
'It certainly would not build Como villas,' said Lena.
Laura cast sharp eyes on her pretty face.
'It is adapted for caged voices that are required to chirrup to tickle the ears of boors.'

We fully admit that this sarcasm is so refined as to be almost beyond us. If we had room for the context, our readers might be quicker; meanwhile we can only mention that it has some reference to an Italian cantatrice who is present. The defect in this writing is obvious; it is laborious, and yet the labour has not been carried far enough. A little less effort might have left it easy; a little more might possibly make it at once polished and intelligible. It is a great mistake, in blacking boots, to leave off just before they begin to shine, for then all the previous labour is thrown away; in literature it seems to be not merely thrown away, but actually prejudicial. The truth seems to be that Mr Meredith has one of those restless minds which have an ever exaggerated fear of becoming a bore. There is no due repose in his writing; and yet, though he is always bristling with point, he has hardly enough patience to obtain a thoroughly satisfactory result.

When we come to his plot and his characters, a similar weakness appears even more decidedly. The plot is by far the weakest part of the book. We have studied it with due attention, but must confess ourselves baffled. The main design is indeed evident enough. Vittoria is a noble Italian woman with a marvellous voice. She is to give a signal at the opera for the rising in Milan during the troubles of 1849. The signal rather misses fire, owing to a bewildering complication of plots and counterplots, and Vittoria is herself suspected; she is, however, loved by a young noble who has joined the conspiracy; and, after a variety of troubles during Charles Albert's struggle against Austria, she marries him. He throws himself into Brescia previously to its bombardment, and shortly after the battle of Novara is captured by an Austrian detachment and shot. Before this point is reached there has been a whirl of Italian patriots, spies, and conspirators, of Austrian officers and duchesses, and of English tourists, working out all kinds of complicated schemes, which absolutely makes the brain giddy. To determine who is wanting to do what, at any given moment, is as difficult an intellectual employment as hunting out a railway puzzle in Bradshaw[1] or solving a chess problem. The relations of every one to his or her neighbour depend upon so many delicate strings that we should be quite content to take Mr Meredith's own account of their purposes. But here he unfortunately fails us; he has evidently studied his own plot so carefully that it probably seems as plain to him as the chess problem would to Mr Morphy.[2] He can work it, so to speak, without seeing the board; whereas we should require a careful study before we could call to mind the relative action of the pieces. And thus he makes demands upon the attention of his readers of which he is probably not aware. Indeed, he is so familiar with the incidents that he sometimes forgets to make them plain, even when he is relating them. Thus an important scene is described as follows—Rinaldo, we should say, being a conspirator, and presumably an assassin, in Austrian hands, and the woman an Italian acquaintance:

Then a procession walked some paces on. The woman followed. She fell prostrate at the feet of Count Karl (the Austrian commander). He listened to her and nodded. Rinaldo stood alone with bandaged eyes. The woman advanced to him; she put her mouth on his ear; there she hung. Vittoria heard a single shot. Rinaldo lay stretched upon the ground, and the woman stood over him.

We confess that, after reading this account carefully, we could not make out what had happened. And our perplexity was not quite dispelled until the end of the next volume, in spite of one intermediate explanation. It then turned out that the woman, who was a great admirer of Rinaldo, had shot him by leave of Count Karl, to save him from the shame of execution; and, further, that this benevolent action had been imposed upon her by her husband, who was a great conspirator,

[1] George Bradshaw (1801–53) established his famous Railway Guide in 1839.
[2] Paul Charles Morphy (1837–84), American lawyer and chess-player.

as a punishment for having previously disobeyed him in helping Rinaldo to escape. Now this is a dramatic incident, and one which, in the hands of many writers, would have led up to absurd sensational writing. That would doubtless have been objectionable, but it is as unreasonable in a different way to tell the story so that we don't quite know whether it has happened or not.

The difficulty thus produced in following Mr Meredith is aggravated in still another way. The characters, as we have said, are really very clever, and some perhaps deserve a stronger epithet. But we must really object to the eccentric way in which they make their exits and their entrances. Some of them are formally introduced to us in the good old-fashioned way, and we feel that it is our own fault if we do not afterwards succeed in identifying them. But others drop in, as it were, accidentally, and the reader is expected to be perfectly familiar with their tastes and peculiarities. Some of them, it seems, have appeared in a former novel of Mr Meredith's, but that is no justification for spoiling one which should be complete in itself. As we have, we must confess, the misfortune of not being familiar with *Emilia Wyndham*, [*sic*] we cannot explain the evident affection with which the author regards certain subordinate actors in the story. Their previous history may be a sufficient justification to Mr Meredith himself, but it is an artistic fault when the first and second conspirators and all the mere walking gentlemen are portrayed with as much care as the hero and heroine. It adds to the distracting effect of the plot, of which we never know very well what is the main thread and what is merely incidental, that we are in equal ignorance as to the relative importance of the characters. The interest is too much dispersed already by the nature of the story, and this system tends rather to increase the dispersion. With all this fault-finding, however, we must add that the characters are, in our opinion, the strongest point of Mr Meredith's very clever, though rather unreadable, performance, and that if two or three of them were extracted from the labyrinth in which they are placed, and set to turn some simple machinery, they would make a far more interesting story.

We must conclude by one more very obvious though unfavourable piece of criticism; which is, that a writer imposes a great additional burden upon himself when he takes for the scene of his story a country and time with which most of his readers are little familiar, and as to which—to state a far more important objection—his own mind can scarcely be saturated with knowledge up to the proper point. The greater triumphs of fiction are certainly won on ground with which both writer and readers are thoroughly familiar, and it wants no great philosophy to see the reason. Mr Meredith, already so incomprehensible to the vulgar, can scarcely afford to carry extra weight without absolute necessity.

41. G. E. Jewsbury, *Athenaeum*

No. 2052, 23 February 1867

For Geraldine Jewsbury see above, No. 19, headnote. The name 'Wilfrid' is misspelt throughout this article.

Vittoria is the continuation of a work by the same author, published some years ago, called *Emilia in England*. The same characters are introduced; but, with the exception of Emilia herself, who is again the heroine, under the name of Vittoria, the leading personages of the former novel are mere accessories to the present story. Wilfred Pole, who was Emilia's lover, and who did not behave very chivalrously, is, as Wilfred Pierson, a lieutenant in the Austrian service, a useful subordinate in the drama. The present novel is the whole drama of the Italian rising in 1848, carried along from its outbreak until the fatal battle of Novara. The work evinces knowledge on the part of the author of Italian life as well as of Italian revolutionary politics. All the documents, letters, intentions, and counter-intentions, of the centres and head-centres of the revolution, seem to have been laid at the author's disposal, and he, to judge by the result in his book, must have made a good use of them. The seething and surging of the revolutionary movement are well caught; but the reader is lost in the maze of events, and confused by the movements hither and thither of the excited actors, both Austrian and Italian. There are dramas within dramas; hopes and fears, loves and hatreds, private and political; the movements of armies; 'trumpets, alarums, excursions and retreats', battles, single combats, not a few duels—to say nothing of the histories, tales and reports told by one person to others with the vehemence of intense personality. The personages of the drama, or rather panorama, get incidentally involved in events, which are life or death to the parties concerned, but which have only a slight bearing on the fortunes of the story. Such is Wilfred Pierson's night adventure, when he is forced to enter a house to assist the Austrian lover of an Italian lady to escape from the men who have surrounded the house to kill him as he comes out. No mortal memory can keep in mind the Lauras, the Amalias, the Leckensteins, the Violettas, the Austrians pure and simple, the Austrianized Italians, the prudent Italians, the patriots, the conspirators. Opera politics and intrigues are super-added; for is there not a Signora Irma de Karski, a rival *prima donna*, who hates Vittoria as a woman and a singer! How are human beings with limited faculties to understand all the distracting threads of this unmerciful novel? But, then, by way of compensation, each episode has its own interest, and the most insignificant personage has the stamp of being a genuine human being, and not a lay figure. One of the best and most individual portraits is that of Barto Rizzo, the conspirator. He is the type of the man who cares for his own way, and who will sacrifice a cause to his own prejudices; yet he is honest and energetic, if untractable and perverse, and doing more mischief than good. Luighi [*sic*], the spy, is also an excellent sketch of a supple Italian, with a turn for roguery, and yet capable of honesty when his heart is touched. The first scene between Luighi [*sic*] and Barto Rizzo is a comedy containing the germs of a tragedy, which is worked out to the sorrowful end. Vittoria has been chosen to make her *début* at La Scala, in an opera written by her lover, Count Carlo Ammiani, which is full of revolutionary meaning, but so veiled that it has passed the Censorship; but in the end she is to sing a patriotic song, not set down in the libretto, which is to be the signal for the insurrection in Milan. There are signals all over the country, by which the rising is to be simultaneous. All is arranged, and all is going well, when Vittoria recognizes some English visitors, her old English friends, and their brother Wilfred, now an Austrian officer. In her desire to save them from the terror and confusion of the outbreak, she writes a letter of warning to Wilfred, not unlike the famous one sent in the Guy Fawkes conspiracy, and which, according to popular tradition, led to the discovery of the plot. This comes to the knowledge of Barto Rizzo, who takes his own measures to secure the letter, and having read it, he denounces Vittoria as a traitress. The rising is put off; the whole plan is thrown into confusion —some wishing to go on, others to draw back. Signor Antonio Pericles, the Greek fanatic for music, whom the readers of *Emilia in England* have met before, institutes a small plot of his own, to have her carried off to an Austrian fortress, where she will be kept safe and out of mischief. There is much complication about this little plot, and it has fibres which extend far and wide, and eventually it has serious results. The Austrian authorities are on the alert, the city is in a ferment. Vittoria appears, carries the house by storm, sings the patriotic song, and, rousing the people to madness, she has to be smuggled out of the city, for the Austrians dare not seize her; but the insurrection that had been planned for that night has collapsed. Vittoria wanders about in the most perplexing manner, finding herself in Turin with Charles Albert, following his army, helping the wounded on the field of battle, carried off once more by the amusing Signor Pericles, whose distraction at the carelessness with which she risks the loss of her voice is a comic relief. She meets her lover, and has an interview with him on a battle-field. Then she is spirited away again—Barto Rizzo doing mischief all the time, and other enemies and false friends working at cross-purposes. There is an excellent and spirited account of the campaign—the brief success, the bright hopes, the final failure. Carlo and Vittoria are married, live together a few happy months, and then in another unsuccessful conspiracy Carlo falls—a victim to the insane suspicion of Barto Rizzo. Wilfred Pierson, who has done good service as a patient ass, marries the Austrian lady to whom he was betrothed. Vittoria lives like a heroine, and brings up her young son to be a hero, and the curtain drops on the end of the first Italian deliverance in 1858. The book is well and carefully written, though the affectations of style and speech are many and various. There is an air of effort, which gives a sense of fatigue to the reader, greater even than the marches and counter-marches, the journeys, flights and returns; but the book is a piece of good and honest hard work. For such as care to hear about the state of Italy and the Italians in the last years of Austrian rule, *Vittoria* will be a book they can read.

THE ADVENTURES OF
HARRY RICHMOND

1871

42. A. J. Butler, *Athenaeum*

No. 2297, 4 November 1871

Arthur John Butler (1844–1910), a translator, historian and critic, gave much of his attention to Dante.

Anyone who has turned over the leaves of the *Cornhill Magazine* during the past two years or so, dipping, after the fashion of magazine-readers, into a page here and a page there, must have been struck with a story the thread of which was much harder to follow than is usually the case with serially-published novels. Gipsies and German princes were perhaps the principal figures left on the mind of a chance reader; but there were also an irascible squire, an eccentric merchant skipper, and a youth who was as perplexing as anyone, for his name seemed at one time to be Richmond, at another Roy. Now that *The Adventures of Harry Richmond* has appeared in a collected form, the connection of these curious figures has become a little more distinct, and the whole story has taken as coherent shape as any story of Mr Meredith's is likely to do. His method of narrating in short *staccato* sentences, with an immense number of full stops, joined to his habit of constantly changing his scene, and only favouring his readers with the slightest possible intimation that a person who three lines back was in Hampshire is now in the heart of Germany, or *vice versa*, renders his novels by no means easy reading, if we would understand what is going on, and keep up with the progress of events. He is also fond of exercising his reader's ingenuity by giving only the very slightest hint at the real causes of some of the most important events. In the present book, for instance, we are left almost to our own resources to understand why Harry Richmond is set upon by four gipsies at night and beaten almost to death—an incident upon which hangs in great measure the result of the story. We understand that there is a mistake; but we do not know who was the intended victim, and what his offence: we can only say, that although we have an idea, we are by no means sure that it is a right one. Not but what we are inclined to think that Mr Meredith is right in departing so far from the ordinary practice of novelists as to leave his mysteries unsolved, or at least not solved in that crude way which is prevalent, and which only gives us the same satisfaction that we gain from reading a book of riddles, and turning to the end to look at the answers. In the same way we never know exactly what was the parentage of Harry Richmond's father. He believes himself to be the legitimate son of a royal personage; his friends believe him to be the son, but illegitimate; but we have no intimation as to the truth of either theory, nor whether, if untrue, Mr Richmond (or Roy, as he prefers to call himself) is a conscious swindler or a monomaniac. The author perhaps rather suggests the former; we incline to the latter and more charitable view.

Such being Mr Meredith's characteristics, it is not to be wondered at if we decline to give any sketch of the plot of this curious book. It is quite worth reading; but it is itself a sketch in three volumes, in spite of the extraordinary minuteness of description. Though we know nothing ourselves about the gipsies (it is our loss), we feel certain that the girl Kiomi must be drawn from life. She is a wonderful creature, with her strange fierceness and affection; and we feel that Mr Meredith has done us almost a personal wrong in bringing her to harm, which, moreover, from all we have ever heard of her race, seems an unnecessary stretch of probability. As to the other prominent characters, we must say that, while the most part of them are of a class almost as strange to us as gipsies, and we suspect in some cases more imaginary, they are admirably consistent with themselves; and, given the circumstances, which are perhaps hardly probable, would almost certainly have acted as they are made to do. Mr Meredith uses to the full the novelist's privilege of bringing his characters together. We are apt in real life to think 'that the world is very round', so constantly do we find out connections between people whose only point of contact we believed to be their common relation to ourselves; but this is nothing to the boldness with which our novelists, and Mr Meredith among them, bring the very ends of the earth, or at least the earth of their story, together for their own purposes. This, perhaps, is one of the points of distinction between the novelist proper and the romancer: the novelist shapes his story by the exigencies of facts, the romancer shapes his facts by the exigencies of his story. Both are good in their way; and if our definition may pass, we will say that *The Adventures of Harry Richmond* is a good romance.

We have already noticed the odd construction of sentences peculiar to Mr Meredith; but beyond this we have not much fault to find with his style. He uses odd forms sometimes, such as 'gloriful' and 'modestest'; and we are glad that he has given us an opportunity of raising our testimony against the use of 'supposititious' as a synonym for 'supposed', which it is not, although thanks to the daily papers it is in a fair way to become so. However, Mr Meredith is so little an offender in this way, that we need say no more, beyond advising our reader to order *The Adventures of Harry Richmond*.

43. Unsigned review, *Examiner*

No. 3328, 11 November 1871

Mr Meredith writes cleverly, but his cleverness has been turned to very bad account in this latest and, apparently, most ambitious of his novels. It is in the form of an autobiography, tracing the history of the hero from his birth till he is about thirty years old; and it is, doubtless, intended to teach us many grand lessons about hereditary weaknesses in particular, and all sorts of political and social matters in general. Towards this end Mr Meredith sets at defiance all ordinary rules of composition, and indulges in the wildest vagaries of plot-making; but the net result of his efforts is a work so enigmatical, and with such constant affectation of wit, that it is very irksome reading, and so disappointing in the end that the reader who has plodded through the three volumes is likely to vow that he will never take up another of Mr Meredith's novels. In saying this, we believe we are speaking heresy. Mr Meredith is a prophet to a few, and his habit of jerking out common-

places as if they were wisdom is likely to be fascinating to some young
ladies. It is a poor habit, however, and it seems to have worn itself
nearly threadbare in *The Adventures of Harry Richmond.*
'Is it any waste of time to write of love?' says Harry Richmond. 'The
trials of life are in it, but in a narrower ring and a fierier. You may learn
to know yourself through love, as you do after years of life, whether
you are fit to lift them that are about you, or whether you are but a
cheat, and a load upon the backs of your fellows. The impure perishes,
the inefficient languishes, the moderate comes to its autumn of decay—
these are of the kinds which aim at satisfaction, to die of it soon or late.
The love that survives has strangled craving; it lives because it lives to
nourish and succour like the heavens. But to strangle craving is indeed
to go through a death before you reach your immortality'. Those
sentences are a fair sample of the meaningless sententiousness with
which Mr Meredith writes; and they are put into the mouth of an
utterly selfish man who, after keeping at arm's length, during many
years, a young lady whom he is only disposed to marry in case another
love affair, in which he is engaged, should prove hopeless, at last comes
back to her with a lying assurance that he has loved her all along, and
attempts to induce her then to take him instead of another man, to
whom, after waiting many years for the other, she has betrothed
herself. It may be a good thing to write down the sentimentalism that
abounds in novels. But it is certainly a bad thing to encourage the
view in favour with many fashionable gentlemen that love-making is a
lordly pastime for the superior sex, only culpable when it leads to
actual seduction or adultery, and that women's hearts are only toys to
play with or coin to profit by; and this is the gospel that Mr Meredith
preaches.

Harry Richmond's history would have made the thread of a good
novel, had it been told simply and without praise. He is the son of an
unprincipled adventurer, who is 'the son of an actress and somebody',
and who accordingly spends everybody's money that he can get hold
of in carrying on a lawsuit for recognition of his claims upon royalty,
and is meanwhile living as much like a prince as he can, when he is not
in a debtor's prison. Harry Richmond has, in Squire Beltham, a rich
grandfather by his mother's side, and the blunt, honest squire's character
is not ill drawn, though the drawing is a rough and exaggerated sketch,
not a finished portrait. The squire wishes to make him his heir on
condition of his renouncing his father, and in the hope, though this is
not an absolute condition, that he will marry his cousin Janet. Harry's

father plays at higher game. He maintains an underhand connection with his son, squanders his money, and schemes for his marriage with a German princess. Thus, after an account of Harry's childish and schoolboy life, which is perhaps the best portion of the book, the complications of the story are brought about. Mr Meredith has some power in constructing his puppets. All the leading figures in the novel are sharply cut, and many of the minor characters are fairly elaborated and individualized; but they are only puppets. They speak and act unnaturally, and if, taken one by one, some of them are tolerable, their combined action is as preposterous as that of the puppets in a Punch-and-Judy show. Mr Meredith describes English life, not as it is, but as it pleases him to represent it, and his description is alike unpleasant and unprofitable. This is the more to be regretted, because he throws out hints and collects rough material enough to stock two or three good novels with proper handling.

44. R. H. Hutton, *Spectator*

xlv, 20 January 1872

For R. H. Hutton see above, No. 2.

This book shows originality, wealth of conception, genius, and not a little detailed knowledge of the world; the outline of the tale is bold and flowing, and the individual figures are painted with considerable, though unequal skill; some of the scenes are full of force of a very unusual kind, and some are touched with a real delicacy and tenderness; and yet it would be far truer to say that it has the stuff for half-a-dozen first-rate novels in it, than that it is a first-rate novel itself. It wants, in the first instance, movement, stream, current, narrative-flow, and secondly, something of ease and simplicity of style. We are late in reviewing it, but, to say the truth, it is a novel which invites delay rather than prompts rapidity. In spite of its animation and its fullness of life, it is very slow reading, for more than one reason. There is an allusiveness and occasionally also an affectation of affluent expressiveness about the manner of the author which are provoking, and induce one to throw the book aside for a time from vexation at its assumption. But this is not the principal reason for the manifold retardations with which the reader meets. These are mainly due to the diminishing instead of the increasing interest of the tale as it proceeds, and the want of clear relation between the different parts of it. The enormous expansion of the social finesse in the least interesting part, and, perhaps above all, the little sympathy we have with the hero of the autobiography who is the connecting-thread of the whole, and who, instead of making us feel eager about his future, is always giving us a foretaste of something uncomfortable and embarrassing, destroy our interest in the development. Nor is that strong disposition to postpone the next chapter, which is due to the hero's uncomfortable complexities of inconsistent obligation, in any way overcome by the strength of the sympathy one is made to feel for either of the two young ladies between whom he is so good as to divide his affection with perplexing equality. One of them (Ottilia), indeed, is a beautiful picture, full of clear intellectual grace and tender intensity; but then she is a German princess, and so much is made of her position and of the disastrous character of the mésalliance she is willing to enter into, that she stands almost aloof from the story, and you hardly know whether she herself does not wish for some imperious call of duty to break off the engagement; certainly there is no glimpse given us, during the long period of her lover's absence, of any feeling in her which tends to make the reader eager for a happy solution of the difficulties of the situation. She descends from the clouds, as it were, whenever the hero is in some worse than usual trouble, to shed her benign affection over him; but the condescension is made so much of, and her retirement behind the veil of the royal caste is so complete while it lasts, that one cannot catch the smallest possible impatience for the issue from the picture of her gracious tenderness and her deep but perfectly self-restrained and almost self-condemned devotedness; rather do we feel disposed to shrink the more from the issue, feeling a distinct prevision of its uncomfortable character. As for the other young lady (Janet Ilchester), we never know her well enough to feel much interest in the development of what, in her too, presents itself, with less intelligible reason, as a curiously self-contained and sedate affection. There seems to be a real want of consistency too between the rather repulsive picture of her as a child, a picture which makes her somewhat sly and very selfish, and the picture of her perfect courage and indomitable resolution as a woman; we do not say that the two pictures might not be reconciled, but only that they *are* not—that the graduated shades between them are not supplied, and that her love for the hero is so very imperfectly painted, that it is hardly possible to feel any sympathy with her till within a very few pages of the close. Thus Harry Richmond, the hero himself, being radically uninteresting, and his career full of moral awkwardnesses of that particular kind which slightly repel instead of exciting the wistful interest of the reader, and as the story of neither of the heroines with whom he falls in love supplies in any degree the predominant fascination in which he himself is so deficient, we are left to the extraordinary cleverness of the conceptions of the tale itself to supply the want of current in the plot—a very poor substitute, if only on this account, that these conceptions are full of complexity and finesse which rather exhaust the attention when made the principal interests, instead of the mere by-play, of a narrative otherwise full of forward movement and vivid interest.

The main intention of the story is to sketch the influence of the hollow conceit of great descent on the mind of the hero's father, Roy Richmond (supposed to be the son of a Royal Duke who had married privately without acknowledging his marriage), a man full of tact and resource and social ambition (of the poorer kind)—a charlatan, in fact, of a large and skilful and loveable sort, with every gift except those which would make him ashamed of playing the actor all his life, and especially of playing the actor all his life for so trivial a prize as the reluctant recognition of his birth by society and the Government; and especially to sketch this unreal kind of genius for social magnificence, in direct contrast to the solid earthly character of a rich, positive, passionate, swearing old English squire—the hero's grandfather, Squire Beltham, whose daughter Mr Roy Richmond has married against the Squire's will. Between these contrasted personages, father and grandfather, an internecine war for the leading influence over the hero's body and soul goes on from the first page to the last of the book. We cannot say that so far as the stage of these contending influences is laid in the mind of young Harry Richmond we care very much for the issue—at least, after the stage of boyhood is past, a period during which the picture of the struggle is drawn with great power and effect. But the contrast between the airy, grandiose, strategic genius of the hare-brained, but half-loveable charlatan and castle-builder, with his magnificent belief in his own destiny, his really grand play of fancy, and his almost disinterested dreams of a great career for his son, and the coarse, warm-hearted, violent, narrow, successful old English squire, 'acred up to his lips, consolled up to his chin', and distinguished in his class by the real lucidity of his business mind, and therefore possessed with a double intensity of loathing for the hollow, scheming, and visionary pretensions of his son-in-law, is drawn from beginning to end with marvellous power. The two scenes in which their first and last battles are fought at the very opening of the first volume and towards the close of the third are scenes of strange vigour; and if connected together by a plot half as good as are several of the links in it, they would have been remembered amongst some of the best things in English literature. But, as we have intimated, young Harry Richmond, after he has passed the boyhood stage, is not drawn with any real power, while the vast detail in which his father's faculty for social intrigue and the construction of a grand plot is developed, though full of cleverness, becomes utterly wearisome before the close. If a little of the minuteness of study spent upon this no doubt very original, but still exhaustible conception, had been devoted to Janet Ilchester, the story might have been vastly improved, both by subtraction and by addition—by taking away from the superfluity of an over-developed idea, and by remedying the deficiency of a figure very imperfectly conceived and drawn. Neither Mr Richmond nor Squire Beltham—unquestionably the great figures of the piece—can be fairly illustrated by any extract we have space to give; but the mode in which the would-be royal charlatan first acquired his ascendancy over his son's mind is so finely painted, and that, too, within limits possible to a newspaper, that we will illustrate it by giving the young man's recollections of his father's method of exciting in him as a child intense interest in the grander episodes of English literature and history:

[Quotes ii, from 'He was never away on the Sunday' to 'display of foresight on my father's part'.]

That is full of a humour that one regards as almost too great to be compatible with a mind so inflated with grandiose dreams as that of the would-be royal adventurer; but it is one of the most delicate feats of ability in the book to make us feel how much of true humour and nobility there is combined with Mr Roy Richmond's theatrical, pageant-loving character, and rather ignoble aims. It is impossible to think of him without his charlatanerie, and yet it is impossible to think of him as not possessing qualities both intellectual and emotional too good for his charlatan schemes—and this, notwithstanding that he himself never seems to have the shadow of a distrust of his own aims from the beginning to the close of his ambitious career. So completely is the man a quasi-royal adventurer, a patron who needs very substantial help, a Grand Seigneur who has to depend for his hopes on more solidly established Grands Seigneurs, a man whose every gift, whose elasticity, whose willingness to stoop in order to soar the better in future, are manufactured, as it were, to suit his dreams and hopes, that we are hardly able from the beginning to the end to conceive of any intellectual or moral nature in the man independently of the part he is acting. That he loves his son thoroughly, and the woman who renounced him for her sister's sake, is clear; that he can see the absurd side of other people's littlenesses is clear also; but that he could have any intellectual conviction, or moral conviction, or political conviction outside of the exigencies of his part in life, seems almost impossible. It need hardly be observed that the conception of such a character is very original, and that the insanity in which the author makes it terminate, when the bubble bursts, is most truly as well as finely conceived. Had but our author spared us half the detail!

Besides the great charlatan and the great English squire, there is much in the story to show the author's talent. There are even delicate touches here and there—like that which represents the Princess Ottilia as recurring to the imperfect English of her childhood's first acquaintance with Harry Richmond, when she asks him, after his declaration of love, whether he can be patient, and adds, with tender humour, in the precise form of her former childish stiffness, 'It is my question'; and again, like that which makes the poor old pretender to royal blood recall, when all his schemes are in ruins, his promise to his old housekeeper that she should have a memorial erected to her by his hand, and mutter to himself, 'Waddy shall have her monument'. These delicacies of delineation are not very common in the book, but the few there are are touches of real genius. Nor must we forget, in enumerating the finer elements of the book, the exquisite episode of the child's runaway adventure with the gipsy girl Kiomi—a picture almost as faithful and as full of colour and humour as any to be found in modern literature.

On the other hand, as we have said, the book has great faults. There is a great exuberance of dull, protracted, social intrigue, and a terrible flatness about the hero himself. But worst of all is the want of simplicity of style and the frequently false and disagreeable turns given to expression, as when the child remembers of his schoolmaster's daughter to whom he had been talking of her young lover, 'she laughed and *mouthed me over* with laughing kisses'; or again, when he is falling in love with the Princess Ottilia, and in answer to a remark of hers he is moved to declare his passion, but does not, a state of feeling which he thus expresses—'*Something moved my soul to lift wings*, but the passion sank'. There are plenty of illustrations of this love of affectation in the style, and still more of an apparently affected obscurity of manner, which tend to spoil a novel containing the evidence of really great powers.

45. Unsigned review, *Westminster Review*

xli, January 1872

Mr Meredith has long since won a recognised position in literature. Whatever he writes, and he has written much, is distinctively marked by real genius. He possesses in no ordinary degree insight into character, humour and wit, descriptive power, and lastly real poetical feeling. He has made for himself a unique position. He holds in literature a place by himself. We know no one with whom to compare him for the purposes of criticism. In his latest novel, *The Adventures of Harry Richmond*, which has been the delight of so many readers of the *Cornhill Magazine*, this circumstance is more than usually apparent. Criticism in Mr Meredith's case is always difficult. But in *Harry Richmond* the difficulty is doubled. The work is one by itself. It is, in truth, not a novel, but a romance. Mr Meredith does with the reader what he pleases—transports him into a world of his own, and dazzles him with creations of his own teeming fancy. Whilst we are reading, we are fascinated and spell-bound. It is not until we have closed the book, and the spell has lost some of its charm, that we feel ourselves to be critically inclined. Criticism, especially of the cold-blooded kind, would, we fear, make short work of Mr Meredith's pleasant extravagance. For our own part we are more disposed to call attention to the gay fancies and the wealth of poetry which the author has so freely scattered over his pages.

46. Unsigned notice, *Vanity Fair*

vii, 23 March 1872

Mr Meredith is perhaps one of the most original writers of the day, and though possibly he may not be appreciated by everyone, still even his enemies must allow his singular power and energy. In its own way, *The Ordeal of Richard Feverel* was one of the most remarkable novels of its time, and this last, though not approaching it in conception or force, is full of interest, though we cannot help saying that it is rather annoying to be left at the end scarcely any wiser than we were at the beginning. None of the mysteries with which this curious book abounds are elucidated; we never find out who Harry Richmond's father really was, and the way in which Harry's engagement with the Princess Ottilia is broken off is very vague and shadowy.

We do not propose attempting any sketch of the plot, for the whole book is so well worth reading, and so complicated in its surroundings, that we can only beg our readers to order a copy for themselves. We think we cannot be far wrong when we say that they cannot fail to be interested.

47. Margaret Oliphant, *Blackwood's Edinburgh Magazine*

cxi, June 1872

Margaret Oliphant (1828–97), historian of Blackwood's publishing house and regular contributor to the magazine, was a novelist herself of no inconsiderable stature. Her review of *The Egoist* was very harsh; see below, No. 64.

The first part of this book, treating of the boyish adventures of its hero and his friends, is charming, full of easy power and delightful absurdity. The baby portion is a perfect childish idyl, and nothing can be finer than the picture of Harry's extraordinary and captivating father as he appears to his child. But the luxuriance of unrestrained imagination runs riot to such an extent that it is very difficult to trace out the meaning of the latter part, or not to believe that all the personages have gone mad together. The imbroglio of German princes and princesses, the daring deeds of that Minerva-Diana who in English is called Janet, and the ineffable absurdities of Harry's father, who thinks himself a royal duke, and behaves as such, run all to seed at the end, and produce such a thicket of incidents and emotions, as it is very difficult for the reader to force his way through. But this thicket is everywhere bright with strange bits of description, with gleams of insight and quaint clever sayings, such as afford a pleasant clue to the reader, by means of which he can guide himself out and in of the labyrinth. It is not a novel in the legitimate three-volume sense of the word, but it is a very odd and very clever book. . . .

BEAUCHAMP'S CAREER

1876

48. A. J. Butler, *Athenaeum*

No. 2514, 1 January 1876

For A. J. Butler see above, No. 42, headnote.

It is not probable that Mr Meredith will ever be a popular author. In the first place, it is no easy matter to read one of his books. We do not mean that his language is obscure; but his extraordinary reticence, so to speak—his refusal to allow himself an author's right of knowing what his characters do when they are, as one may say, out of his sight— makes it necessary for the reader to be on the alert for the slightest allusions and indications, if he would not altogether miss the thread of the story. Then he is anti-sensational to the last degree, and seldom or never allows any violent action to take place on the scene before the eyes of his readers. Thus, in the present story there occur a duel, a horse-whipping, and a violent death, in each of which one or other of the principal persons is more or less closely concerned; but we see no more of them than we do of the slaughter of Medea's children or the suicide of Jocasta. Indeed, we get a less detailed account than a Greek dramatist would have given us, for Mr Meredith does not even employ a 'Messenger', but our knowledge of the facts is gained from scattered fragments of conversation. In more respects than one, however, he seems to us to have a share of the spirit of the fathers of tragedy. There is a truly Sophoclean irony about the perfectly pitiless way in which he allows his characters to play their little drama; never, after the fashion of so many novelists, expressing the least approval or reprobation of them, never letting the reader suppose that he has any sympathy for one more than another, utterly regardless of 'poetical justice', and careless of satisfactory endings: to use his own words, when speaking of the one detestable person in the story, 'The secret of his art would seem to be to show the automatic human creature at loggerheads with a necessity that winks at remarkable pretentions, while condemning it perpetually to doll-like action'. We do not mean to say that Mr Meredith never lets us see which of his characters he personally likes or dislikes, or rather the different degrees in which he likes them; for, except the one referred to above, Cecil Baskelett, 'captain in England's grand reserve force, her Horse Guards, of the Blue division', we doubt if he can be said to dislike any; but the point is, that he has reached that high stage of the novelist's art where his own predilections have no more influence on the fortunes of his characters than Mr Freeman's, say, on the result of the battle of Bouvines.[1] Of course, a story written on these principles is delightful to the attentive reader or student of mankind. He is not let all at once into the secrets of the heart of every personage, but is left to discover their characters by means of study, every whit as close as is required in real life. The result of this is that they become to him living people, and when he lays down the book it is with a strange feeling, as though he were suddenly being parted from a number of real acquaintances. This is helped by another characteristic of Mr Meredith's style, arising from that dramatic turn of mind which we have noticed. He ends his story once and for all. The curtain drops on such of the characters as happen to be on the stage at the moment: there is none of the ordinary lifting and re-lifting it to show us what becomes of one and another. Beachamp's career is over, just when, to ordinary eyes, it might be thought to be beginning; and nobody's career else matters to the story-teller. In fact, in mathematical phrase, the rest are only functions of the variable Beauchamp; and when that vanishes, they vanish too. That is as it should be, a glance at all the greatest works of fiction will suffice to show; but few novelists have the courage to refrain from an epilogue in one form or another. Mr Meredith's way is undoubtedly, however, the more impressive. Richard Feverell gazing on the fact of his dead wife, Dr Shrapnel and Lord Romfrey looking at the insignificant bit of mud-bank life remaining in this world in the place of Beauchamp—the boy, that is, to save whom Commander Beauchamp has laid down his life in much the same fashion as the midshipman Nevil Beauchamp took up his pen to challenge the French colonels—these are

[1] Edward Augustus Freeman (1823–92), historian, author of *History of the Norman Conquest* (1867–79) and *History of Sicily* (1891–2). The Battle of Bouvines was fought in 1214, when Philip of France defeated John of England.

pictures that stay long by one, and which would be uselessly blurred by any reference to the subsequent history of survivors. We are half sorry now that we have told our readers how Beauchamp's career ended. For ourselves, we must own that we were perfectly unprepared for this termination to the gallant enthusiasms of the sailor-politician, just when it seemed that he had learnt to recognize the great fact that existing institutions possess sufficient inertia to make them important elements in calculating the political rate of progress. His is a finer character than that of Richard Feverell, who, having less of the active temperament, is caught in the very snare out of which Beauchamp, at the cost of much struggling, 'fighting it out', as his Mentor the Radical Doctor bade him, 'within him,' manages to break. If our readers want to know what we mean, let them read both books. They will have plenty of time, for Mr Meredith is not one of those who think a story every four or five months the least that a novelist must produce for an expectant public. There is no doubt that the four or five years, or more, which he appears to allow for the due elaboration of his stories, are fully as well occupied as the same period of their lives; and undoubtedly he has his result to show. It would be ridiculous to give an outline of the events of *Beauchamp's Career*, as indeed any reader who has read what we will have said will understand: the interest of the book does not depend upon action alone. We can extract, however, a few of the little pithy sayings, in which, to our mind, Mr Meredith has but one rival among modern novelists. Of Mr Romfrey, afterwards Lord Romfrey, Nevil's uncle, we are told, 'It was the quality of this gentleman to foresee most human events, and his capacity to stifle astonishment when they trifled with his prognostics'. Miss Halkett, clever girl though she is, would hardly, we think, have met the metaphors of a male politician with, 'I know you would not talk down to me, but the use of imagery makes me feel that I am addressed as a primitive intelligence'. If there is a fault in Mr Meredith's portraitures, it is that the level of ability to talk well is pitched rather too high throughout. When Captain Baskelett 'baits' Dr Shrapnel, his fluent nonsense is too clever for what he is meant to be—the average officer in the 'Blues'. But Mr Meredith, in his own person, may say what he likes. For instance, 'The judge pronouncing sentence of condemnation on the criminal is proverbially a sorrowfully minded man; and still more would he be so, had he to undertake the part of executioner as well. This is equivalent to saying that the simple pleasures are no longer with us; it must be a personal enemy now to give us any pleasure in chastising and slaying'. One more instance we will give of Mr Meredith's peculiar humour, and one having the merit of being generally applicable. 'Sound sleep,' he says, 'like hearty dining, endows men with a sense of rectitude, and sunlight following the former, as a pleasant spell of conversational ease, or sweet music the latter, smiles a celestial approval of the performance.' But from beginning to end the book is full of suggestive sentences and happy phrases. Mr Meredith's style also seems to us much improved since we reviewed *Harry Richmond* four years ago. It is still somewhat fluctuating, reminding us now of Thackeray, now of Bulwer, once or twice even of Victor Hugo, but more often than not, and when it is best, it is the author's own. *Richard Feverell* [sic] placed him high among English novelists, but *Beauchamp's Career* has, we think, distinctly raised him; and we do not see any reason why he should not eventually reach a point where, in the opinion at least of those who regard novels as works of art, and not merely collections of anecdotes, he would have scarcely a rival among the writers of fiction of our generation . . .

49. Review, *Examiner*

No. 3545, 8 January 1876; signed 'G.B.S.'

It is tolerably easy to understand why Mr George Meredith's books are *caviare* to the general multitude. They not only call for mental exercise in a greater degree than perhaps any other novels published, but their author is always so terribly in earnest. He cannot, under any circumstances, be a comfort to Mr Mudie's ordinary reader, for Mr Meredith has an unpleasant way of suggesting that society at present exists under somewhat imperfect conditions, and that for these imperfect conditions the individual is largely responsible, because of his apathy and selfishness. It is, therefore, perhaps, scarcely to be wondered at that the bulk of novel readers, who only read to be amused, or to 'kill time', as the phrase is, should be evilly disposed towards this brilliant writer who takes a keen pleasure in wielding his rapier, and hitting society deftly under the fifth rib. He is one of the most prominent moralists in fiction; but unfortunately for himself he is to some extent in prose what Mr Browning is in poetry—the cherished favourite of the few rather than the widely read of the many.

If any words of ours could extend his audience, we should gladly utter them in the case of *Beauchamp's Career*, for whatever its faults may be, it is unquestionably one of the best novels of the season. While it was running through the pages of the *Fortnightly Review* it was impossible to form a general estimate of its merits from a trenchant chapter or two here and there, but now that we have had an opportunity of reading it through consecutively and uninterruptedly, we have no hesitation in bearing testimony to its cleverness and power. Mr Meredith has written no book since *The Ordeal of Richard Feverel*, in which is to be found so much epigrammatic writing, or which contains so many interesting individual studies. And this we say while we are not blind to the fact that to enjoy this latest novel thoroughly the closest attention is required, while even then the reader will run the risk of being occasionally perplexed. Still, the consumers of novels are in the habit of being surfeited with *bonbons* in the present day, and a writer who is professedly not a dealer in sweetmeats is a welcome exception. We are overwhelmed with novels of mere incident, the author being used by the reader merely for the sake of the entertainment or the excitement he can be made to afford. Such authors are like the 'little systems' of the poet. 'They have their day and cease to be.'[1] They also have their reward. Mr Meredith is a writer of a different stamp; he writes from other motives, and writes other things.

Nevil Beauchamp was a cadet of the noble house of Romfrey, and very early showed a chivalric spirit, accompanied by opinions, social and political, which terribly exercised his uncle, the Hon. Everard Romfrey, who was filled with the pride of ancestry. Beauchamp's character is delineated by Mr Meredith in two or three lines. 'Beauchampism, as one confronting him calls it, may be said to stand for nearly everything which is the obverse of Byronism, and rarely woos your sympathy, shuns the statuesque, pathetic, or any kind of posturing. His faith is in working and fighting.' He rushes off to the Crimea, behaves gloriously, becomes acquainted with the son of one Comte de Croisnel, and is finally found lying in Venice, on the conclusion of the war, suffering from an attack of fever. Impressionable to a degree, young Nevil falls desperately in love with Renée, sister of Roland de Croisnel, whose life he had saved. She is betrothed to a French Marquis

[1] *In Memoriam*, Prologue, 17–18.

double her age, notwithstanding Nevil's entreaties, and the fact that she loves the young Englishman. We here pause to notice the beautiful descriptions of scenery given in this chapter, where the friends are represented as at sea under the Alps. The poetry of the time and the place have nearly conquered Renée, but the Fates interpose. She fulfils her destiny, and Nevil returns to England. He becomes acquainted with Dr Shrapnel, a Radical of a very pronounced type, imbibes his opinions, and issues his address on the most advanced principles to the electors of Bevisham. He is opposed by his cousin, one Captain Baskelett, brought down by his uncle Mr Romfrey for that purpose, and the latter carries the day. Beauchamp endeavours to indoctrinate Cecilia Halkett, a young lady whom he had known from his youth, with his extreme views, but while she is proof against these she is not proof against love. Beauchamp does not discover this, or is too engrossed in his mission to humanity to give way to love a second time. He makes every kind of useless but heroic sacrifice for his ideas, and wounds all the aristocratic connections he possesses, and who pride themselves upon their blood and their Toryism. Dr Shrapnel has made one thorough convert to his principles—one who gives his life and substance for the cause he has at heart. It is impossible to follow all the intricacies of the plot of the book. All the incidents, in truth, are but valuable for the development of a really noble character. It is fitting, we feel, after reading of such a life that it should end heroically in saving the lives of those shipwrecked at sea. Beauchamp is one in advance of his age, even of this present year of grace, and while taken by itself his career was magnificent. He was of little avail in overturning the abuses of society; he thought of humanity, while humanity thinks of the individual.

Even while we are not sure that we thoroughly comprehend all the purpose of this novel, it is impossible not to be struck with its merits. There is intellectual wealth enough in it to set up half-a-dozen writers of fiction. The characters of Beauchamp, Mr Romfrey, Dr Shrapnel, and Renée, are wonderfully real and life-like. We can fancy many readers saying that *Beauchamp's Career* wants a key, but it will amply repay anyone all his trouble in endeavouring to find it.

50. A. I. Shand, *The Times*

8 January 1876

Alexander Innes Shand (1832–1907), a journalist and writer of sporting sketches, also left a volume of memoirs in which he refers to Meredith (*Days of the Past*, (1905), 183–4).

No one can say that Mr George Meredith is wanting in knowledge of men and life. If he had the knack of stooping to the tastes of his readers, he would take a place among the very foremost of our novel writers. His books are over-charged with brilliancy of thought, and overdone with epigram and sarcasm and dry shrewd humour. It is often very difficult to follow his meaning in the coruscations of his roving fancy. Unfortunately, the redundancy of those original ideas that rise simultaneously in rapid succession are a positive snare to him. He not only writes high over the head of the average reader, but he credits him with his own quickness of apprehension, and, glancing from point to point, indulges recklessly in elision. Each separate sentence becomes more or less of a study, though the spirit of it may be well worth extracting for those who have the necessary brains and patience. Mr Meredith pounces on phrases and epithets that are out of the common, and then, by his unfamiliar application of them, lays a constant strain on the attention. We are sometimes inclined to suspect that he is mocking our dullness to his own serious injury. In *Beauchamp's Career*, he seems to have gone further in that direction than in any of his previous writings, and when we think of the popularity he ought so easily to have attained, we regret that he did not persevere in his earlier and more simple manner. His *Legend of Cologne*, slight as it was, was well-nigh perfect in its way.

Beauchamp, a man of high connections, small means, great expectations, and that subtle personal fascination which proves irresistible with women, elects deliberately to head a crusade against all the most cherished prejudices and ideas of his caste. Entirely dependent on a Tory country gentleman of the old school, he broaches the broadest

Radical and Socialist doctrines in season and out of season. He gets returned to Parliament in the Radical interest; he sits at the feet of a political teacher held in holy abhorrence by his dearest friends; he goes the length of stumping the county in the most subversive of company. If he can run himself into a dilemma that threatens him with ruin he is certain to do it, and when once he has fairly 'put his foot in it', no power of persuasion will tempt him to draw back. Impracticable as he is, his career would have been cut short prematurely had he had to do with men of commonplace feelings and animosities. Happily for him, the character of his uncle is as original as his own, while the older man is amenable to the female influence which the seductive Beauchamp can always command. This uncle quarrels with him, but never casts him off, and nothing is better in its way than the eccentric scene where the enthusiast who plays fast and loose with his prospects calmly reiterates his possible demands for money on the man he has been crossing in every way. Hesitating like Captain Macheath between a couple of rival beauties, French and English, he never loses his hold upon either, although each can tax him with infidelity to the other. In the end he falsifies our most plausible speculations as to his selection by throwing himself at the feet of a third lady, who has more of intellectual sympathy than love for him. He might never have wrung from her an actual consent to their union, had he not taken her to sea with himself and her uncle in a yacht placed at his disposal by the heiress he has been sighing for half through the book, and who would have asked nothing better than to be pressed into marriage with him; and at last he hesitates about taking possession of the prize that has fixed his fancy, because he considers anything but a civil ceremony superstitious, and feels that, out of deference to her female prejudices, he must ask the benediction of a priest. How far Mr Meredith subscribes to the daring creed of his hero we do not venture to say, but the point of the story is that Beauchamp's career is so far successful, thanks to the dogged honesty of his convictions, and the steadfastness of his conduct. Were his life to be written from a slightly different point of view, his convictions would be characterized as subversive crotchets, and his conduct denounced as erratic to insanity. He makes no allowances for the feelings of himself or other people in going straight towards his end; he is utterly wanting in judgment or tact, and has anything but a lively sense of gratitude. For a woman he once adored he makes such sacrifices as he refuses to the uncle who has brought him up, and who furnishes him with the means of making a fool of himself; and ninety-nine uncles out of a hundred would have cut him out of their wills on half the provocation. Yet Beauchamp floats over everything where other men would be swamped; he retains the regard of the best men and the affection of the best women in the story—a rival who has no special tie to him prevails on a grand-aunt not to disinherit him; the poorer classes worship him for his democratic opinions with a gratitude little common to their class; and a seasonable illness brings about a general reconciliation scene, which his uncle the earl celebrates by an act of self-abasement that Beauchamp had set his heart upon, but which is barely conceivable. It is true that this fortunate demagogue is drowned just as his eccentricities and extravagance have proved their own reward, but his melancholy fate only hallows his memory, and Tory earl and Radical doctor mingle their tears over his watery grave. We are aware that a bald outline of the plot does great injustice to the novel. Spite of its defects, beauties of many kinds are scattered broadcast over it, and those who have patience to pick out the gems will be well rewarded. But if Mr Meredith will imitate his hero in taking his own way in the face of tastes and opinions, he can scarcely expect his hero's good luck in having everything his own way after all.

51. R. F. Littledale, *Academy*

15 January 1876

Richard Littledale (1833–90) was an Anglican controversialist.

When Mr George Meredith produced the *Shaving of Shagpat*, now many years ago, the fertility of invention in that clever book made its readers cheerfully condone its defects of local colour, which betrayed the author's unfamiliarity with the Arab East. It was such as to forecast, as time would decide, either a series of sparkling romances, or a devotion to the stage for the production of spectacular extravaganzas such as Mr Planché used to write and Mdme Vestris get up in the old Lyceum days.[1] Neither anticipation has been realized, and of the comparatively

[1] Lucian Matthews (1797–1856) acted and sang under the name of Madame Vestris. James Robinson (1796–1880), collaborated with her when she managed the Olympic Theatre from 1831.

few books which Mr Meredith wrote after his initial success, the only one whose memory he cares to preserve on his title-page is one which, though written with a certain *verve*, had rather too much of the Shandean flavour, too long kept, to leave a very pleasant taste in the mouth. The first few pages of *Beauchamp's Career*, reminding one of Sallust's moralising at the beginning of his *Catiline*, show that Mr Meredith has passed from the influences of the Rabelaisian humour of Swift and Sterne to the very diverse type of Mr Carlyle, and thus by derivation to the genius who chiefly affected even his style, Jean Paul Richter. He has been almost too lavish of material in this new story, which contains quite half as much again as the ordinary three-volume novel, and thus, perhaps, overdoes the very justifiable reaction from the thin textures which are more commonly offered. This fault was exemplified markedly about sixty years ago in the *Two Emilys*, one of those *Canterbury Tales* of the Misses Lee, another of which served Lord Byron as the groundwork of his *Werner*.[1] This story is so crowded with incident—and very well managed incident too—that although it occupies less than half of one of the two volumes of Bentley's reprint in the 'Standard Novels',[2] yet it produces on the reader the effect of an exceptionally long narrative, and causes some fatigue from that one cause. And so, a little less lavishness would have improved *Beauchamp's Career* as a story to be read at once, though no doubt helping materially to keep up its interest when issued by instalments. But the kind of story Mr Meredith has undertaken to write belongs to a school equally removed from Sterne and from Carlyle, for it bears more resemblance to Mr Hannay's novels than to any others with which we can compare it; yet though written with much pains, considerable cleverness, and occasional sparkle, it exhibits too much effort, and has little of the ease and paradoxical quaintness of *Singleton Fontenoy* and *Eustace Conyers*, from whose politics it is also amusingly divergent.[3] There is not much plot, but, as already observed, there is a good deal of incident, and some of the social types are cleverly sketched, though, in the electioneering scenes, Mr Meredith has been surpassed by more than one predecessor. The end of the book will dissatisfy most readers, and as there is no

[1] Harriet (1757–1851) and Sophia (1750–1824) collaborated in several volumes of fiction. Their *Canterbury Tales* came out in five volumes from 1797 to 1805.

[2] Bentley's 'Standard Novels' series began as Colburne and Bentley's Standard Novels in 1831 with Cooper's *The Pilot*. There were three series from 1855 to 1860, and altogether 158 novels.

[3] James Hannay (1827–73), critic and novelist, published *Singleton Fontenoy, R.N.*, in 1850 as his fifth novel, and *Eustace Conyers* in 1855 as his seventh and last.

sufficient artistic reason to make it necessary, it might be cut out and recast in any future edition, just as Lord Lytton dealt, on further consideration, with his *Lucretia*. But we rise from perusal with the conviction that it is not as a novelist that Mr Meredith can look for a permanent name in literature. As critic or essayist there is probably a career open to him.

52. Unsigned review, *Canadian Monthly*

ix, April 1876

The most remarkable novel which has been running through any English serial of late, is the one which has lately been concluded in the *Fortnightly Review*, *Beauchamp's Career*, by George Meredith. Its author is far less read and less heard of than he deserves to be—probably because his works are of a class beyond the appreciation of the average novel-reader, who cares only for highly wrought plot and sensational incidents; and partly, also, because his circuitous and somewhat recondite style, strong and vivid as it is, resembles that of Browning too much to be palatable to the man who takes up a work of fiction for relaxation only, and does not care to be confronted with social problems or literary enigmas at every turn. But Mr Meredith is obviously too 'terribly in earnest' to care for spreading sail to catch a breath of popular applause. He writes to depict life as he sees it, its inconsistencies and ironies, and more especially its evils and its needs. *Beauchamp's Career* will probably be far less widely read than *The Boudoir Cabal*,[1] but any true lover of literature will rank it as far superior to that clever satire as *Romola* or *Middlemarch*, is to a novel of Rhoda Broughton's.[2] The atmosphere of the story is not—like that of *The Boudoir Cabal*—one of petty intrigue and political chicanery, with hardly anything to relieve the disgust excited by the pictures of the hollow rottenness of metro-

[1] *The Boudoir Cabal* (1875) was by Eustace C. G. Murray.
[2] Rhoda Broughton (1840–1920) produced twenty-six volumes of fiction between 1867 and 1920.

politan society. In *Beauchamp's Career*, we are in the midst of ordinary, healthy English life—out-door and in-door—but chiefly country life, with the pure air of the downs or the bracing sea-breezes blowing freely about us, and good, honest English characters to study, honest and sturdy even in their thoroughly English prejudices.

Nevil Beauchamp, though pertaining by class to the aristocracy is, by nature, of the stuff of which honest Radicals are made—warm, generous and chivalrous in all his impulses, boiling over with indignation at the sight of a wrong, and with impatience to redress it—an impatience which often fails to discriminate, and baffles its own ends by injudicious rashness—and withal as inflexibly obstinate as his Tory uncle, Everard Romfrey, himself, who does all he can to bring back his 'crack-brained' nephew, as he calls him, to ordinary class prejudices and 'common sense'. His Tory cousin, at a later period, thus descants upon Beauchamp's peculiarities: 'Lydiard tells me he has a very sound idea of the value of money, and has actually made money by cattle-breeding; but he has flung ten thousand pounds on a single building outside the town, and he'll have to endow it to support it—a club to educate Radicals. The fact is, he wants to jam the business of two or three centuries into a lifetime. Beauchamp's no Radical. He hasn't forgiven the Countess of Romfrey for marrying above her rank. He may be a bit of a Republican, but really, in this country, Republicans are fighting with the shadow of an old hat and a cock-horse.'

Nevil is in the naval service, 'fought to the skeleton in our last big war', and contracted a warm friendship in the Crimea with a young French officer, the Comte de Croisnel. Returning to Venice with De Croisnel, invalided by a wound, he meets the object of the *grande passion* of his life—the sister of his friend—the fascinating Renée de Croisnel—decidedly the most feminine and interesting female character in the book. The reader can never quite get over the regret that their romantic intercourse, amid the enchanting scenery of the Gulf of Venice, did not arrive at its natural conclusion on account of the previous betrothal of Renée to an old French marquis, whom she was marrying to please her father, and whom she persisted in marrying from a mistaken idea of duty—although her affection was irrevocably given to Beauchamp. This perversion of right the author allows to occur twice over in the book, without protest on his part, notwithstanding that, in this case, the step works out its natural evil results. Wifely happiness and wifely duty, in the true sense of the word, are of course impossible to the woman who has given her hand to one and her heart to another; and half of the unhappy complications of Beauchamp's subsequent career are to be traced to the ineffaceable first love which is ever and anon springing up with renewed life at the most inopportune moments.

Renée, as a French marquise, goes to live at her husband's chateau of Tourdestelle, and Beauchamp returns to England, throws himself heart and soul into politics, and comes under the influence of an earnest ultra-radical, an old gentleman of Utopian ideas, Carlylean style, and inextinguishable zeal, Dr Shrapnel by name, under whose tutelage he soon develops into a Radical of the most advanced type. As Dr Shrapnel afterwards observed, 'You, Beauchamp, when I first met you, you were for England, England! for a breadth of the palm of my hand comparatively—the round of a copper penny, no wider! And from that you jumped at a bound to the round of this earth; you were for humanity. Ay, we sailed our planet among the icy spheres, and were at blood-heat for its destiny, you and I.' Dr Shrapnel is the most original and powerful study of character in the book, probably because the type is especially congenial to the author's genius and peculiar form of expression.

Nevil, of course, looks towards a political career, and runs for the family borough, in which, had he not been a Radical, he would have had no difficulty in succeeding. But his uncle and his other friends, after vainly endeavouring to change his views, bring in a Tory candidate of their own. Beauchamp has no chance. Any prospects which he might have had are effectually shot out by an inopportune and apparently useless summons to visit Renée at Tourdestelle, and by vague rumours about the 'French Marquise', which become associated with his name. These also embarrass his relations with the daughter of his old Tory friend, Colonel Halkett—the beautiful and aristocratic Cecilia, who begins by trying to win back her old playmate to the path of Toryism and peace, and ends by finding her own Toryism disturbed and her heart won by the handsome, impracticable young sailor. There is a long conflict between Beauchamp's old love for Renée and the new and more auspicious affection which Cecilia's rare though somewhat cold attractions have awakened, which is warmly encouraged by his uncle, in the hope that the alliance may steady his nephew's erratic tendencies. An inexcusable personal indignity, however, inflicted by his uncle on poor old Dr Shrapnel, diverts the current of Beauchamp's thoughts from love-making, and absorbs them in the determination to win a reluctant apology from his haughty uncle, and he loses the golden opportunity which would have won the beautiful heiress for his wife. A sudden impulsive appearance of Renée in London—although Nevil acts nobly in the matter—still further mars his prospects in this direction, and is the real cause at last of his irrevocable loss of Cecilia, whose conduct in the end is certainly disappointing. It would appear as if the author had determined to run counter to all ordinary conceptions and traditions, when he makes his heroine, after a long and devoted attachment to one man, and at the very time having a half-platonic inclination to marry another, suddenly, at a moment's notice, accept a *third*, towards whom she had seemed utterly indifferent; while the hero, who has so long oscillated between his affection for her and his old love for Renée, as suddenly offers himself to a girl of whom we have heard but little before, and who, in her turn, had had her mind occupied by another. To be sure, she had just nursed Beauchamp through a nearly fatal attack of typhoid fever—caught by visiting a poor man who had ruined himself by voting for him—and it was not unnatural that his heart should be caught on the rebound from his unsuccessful wooing. But Cecilia's conduct, while not impossible, appears so unaccountable as rather to interfere with our interest in, and realization of, the story. We are told that though she felt she had accepted a man from whom she strongly desired to be free, though conscious of still loving Beauchamp so devotedly that the news of his illness and danger distracts her, and sends her to assist in nursing him, she has yet 'such a high conception of duty' that 'not the less did she retain her cold resolution to marry to please her father and fulfil her pledge'. As a characteristic example of the author's intricacy and peculiarity of style, we give the following rather mystical analysis of Cecilia's feelings of regret for Beauchamp after accepting his rival:

[Quotes, from 'Cecilia had said to herself' to 'St Francis of Assisi excepted'.]

This may be a very clever analysis of a young woman's thoughts at such a time, but we do not think such a description of them would ever have been recognized by the subject of them, and are inclined to think them rather a part of the 'inner consciousness' of the author than of his heroine. The *sang-froid* of Cecilia's *fiancé* as to her devotion to Beauchamp, of which he was quite aware, and his determination to hold her to a loveless engagement, are also somewhat improbable, as is the philosophical matter-of-course way in which Lord Romfrey takes *his* wife's absolute adoration of her friend and *protégé*, Beauchamp, for whom, throughout the story, she displays the devoted, disinterested, untiring affection of which some women are capable. Her feat in securing the wished-for apology from the proud Lord Romfrey is one of the most remarkable things in the book—so dexterously and, on the whole, naturally is it brought about. And though we are provoked for the time at the improbabilities in the *dénouement*, yet so vivid is the author's presentation of the new and unexpected relations, that, in view of Beauchamp's complete matrimonial happiness, we almost forget our displeasure and disappointment in Cecilia, and are inclined to think Nevil's marriage with 'dowerless Jenny' the best thing that could have happened to him. And we forgive Lord Romfrey, too, for all his hardness and even cruelty, and are more sorry than we could have believed for his disappointment in the death of his child.

Nothing in the story is more powerful, more nobly touching, than its close. It was inevitable that Beauchamp's 'career' should end with the story, and we recognize, even amid the pain we feel at the sudden and unexpected catastrophe, that a more fitting close it could not have had. Beauchamp had fought bravely for his country; he had, as Dr Shrapnel said, 'jumped at a bound to the round of this earth', and been 'for humanity'; but he dies neither for his country nor for 'humanity,' but to save an eight-year-old urchin, whose life was of no particular consequence to anyone but his mother, a fisherman's wife. By such apparently needless and meaningless casualties are often the noblest lives and purposes cut short; yet it was not a meaningless end to a chivalrous and unselfish life. The catastrophe is told in a page, briefly—as it were reluctantly—without any highly-wrought pathetic description, such as we have in the previous illness of the hero. The pathos is rather that of a *seen* tragedy than of a *told* one—abrupt and stunning as would be the reality itself. But no elaborate description or multiplication of words could leave the impression produced by the closing picture— Lord Romfrey and Dr Shrapnel, natural antagonists and opposite as the poles, bowed together in a common affection and a common inexpressible grief, as they blankly stare at 'the insignificant bit of mudbank life remaining in the world in place of him', and say, in looks, not words, 'This is what we have in exchange for Beauchamp!'

53. J. C. Carr, *Saturday Review*

xli, 13 May 1876

Joseph William Comyns Carr (1849–1916), a dramatist and critic, also edited the *English Illustrated Magazine*.

In *Beauchamp's Career* Mr Meredith has ventured upon a bold experiment. He has striven to combine the study of individual character with the expression and discussion of modern ideas, and, in place of the precise portraiture of contemporary manners which serves the ordinary novelist by way of background, he has here given us a complex network of social and political problems in which the chief figures of the story are caught and entangled. Indeed all the characters, from the highest to the lowest, are made in their different degrees to feel the intellectual pressure of their time. They are compelled to live and breathe in an atmosphere that is heavily charged with the strong and conflicting currents of modern thought, and by the skill of the artist they are made to absorb into themselves some of the elements of this conflict, and to express its progress and development in their own persons. Mr Meredith is not, however, to be confounded with the novelist with a purpose. His outlook is too wide and his understanding of character too deep to permit him to use men and women as puppets summoned merely to enforce and expound a particular creed, nor is the author in his own behalf disposed to suggest any sure and ready solution of the many problems he loves to present. What he attempts is merely to bring individual character into sharp and close relation with the dominant influences of a chosen period. He forces the actors of his drama, not only to wear the appropriate costume of the time, but to bear its intellectual burdens, and he does not permit them even for a moment to indulge the placid indifference which in actual life is enjoyed by so vast a proportion of the human race. The value of such an experiment must of course in a large measure depend upon the fitness of its author to conduct it with effect, and in the present instance this, we think, has been attained, though in a peculiar way. For it so happens that the peculiar characteristics of Mr Meredith's style perfectly accord with the conditions of the chosen scheme of art. Like the invention of a Japanese artist, his mode of workmanship reflects the singularity as well as the beauty of actual nature. It is attuned to the discords no less than to the harmonies of a present world, and, just as the changes of common existence are cynical in their abrupt transitions from high to low, so also are the changes of Mr Meredith's style. The imagination which is one moment charged with a poetic intensity of feeling trips in the next upon a trivial fact, and retreats in discordant laughter, and the eloquence that seems strong enough to be sustained drops suddenly and almost unawares into mere shrewd speculation. Looking further we may perceive that these peculiarities of style answer to deeper intellectual tendencies. Mr Meredith is never content with the mere artist's enjoyment of the permanent truths of character. His powers have often been proved strong enough for the highest order of work in this kind, and in *Beauchamp's Career* the imaginative insight is as keen and deep as ever; but here, as before, the work of the artist is constantly interrupted by the invasion of an active and restless intellect which seeks material for argument and speculation, arresting the deeper study of character by a brilliant statement of some of the unsettled problems of the time.

It is the special merit of the plan of *Beauchamp's Career* that it affords scope for the expression of both these tendencies. In the social and political aspects of the story the author finds ample opportunity for the play of sarcasm and argument, while in the portraits of Beauchamp himself, of Cecilia Halkett, or of Lord Romfrey, he proves that his control of the higher artistic gift has lost nothing in strength or certainty. But what is most remarkable in the book, considered as a whole, is the skill with which the writer has brought the two elements of his work into combination. The political and social portions of the novel do not stand apart as mere independent episodes in the progress of the story. There is a Parliamentary election, but its description is not dragged into the legend for the mere sake of picturesque or humorous effect, nor is the novelist often tempted to desert the main business of the plot for the discussion of social theories. The means by which he has escaped these defects are at once simple and successful. He has perceived that character may be developed by the agency of political conflict as well and as truly as by any other sort of circumstance, and he has accordingly forced the different persons of the story into political agitation. Love plays a certain part in the progress of the plot, but it is love complicated with politics. The women as well as the men, and the trivial as well as the more serious characters, are all made to circle round a set of political circumstances. Politics are made the test by which individual character is tried and its special qualities distinguished, and in the skill with which each actor is made to express and reveal his whole nature in the presence of these political ideas lies the artistic triumph of the book.

Nevil Beauchamp, the central figure in the story, may be taken as an example of the success of Mr Meredith's method. Almost from the beginning of the novel he is represented as entirely absorbed by political ideas; but the type of character developed under the pressure of these ideas has an independent existence, easily separable from the special means chosen for its expression. The same type which is here made the champion and exponent of radical principles might with equal truth have been presented in the service of religious fanaticism, and it is of course to the praise of Mr Meredith's powers as an artist that he has been able to endow his creation with so much vitality that we can realize the man apart from the special conditions of his growth. We can almost pardon the author's elaboration of the political parts of his work in consideration of the result, and we can feel that a piece of human portraiture of this depth and value was well worth having, whatever the means chosen for the painting of it. Nevil Beauchamp is represented as a man of aristocratic traditions who descends with enthusiasm into the popular arena. With the temper and ambition of a martyr, he is prepared for any sacrifice, either for himself or for his caste, and he never ceases to be indignantly surprised with others who are not equally conscious of their guilt, or equally anxious for chastisement. The secret of a character like this lies in the fact that the desire for sacrifice generally precedes the occasion of it, and, as a consequence, the result is often insignificant and sometimes ludicrous. For it is only by a radical defect of intellectual perception, nearly always accompanied and symbolized by entire absence of humour, that this kind of character can support itself with enthusiasm. Nevil Beauchamp is a type of the class who believe that all evil is curable, and who insist on regarding the permanent characteristics of humanity as moral deformities for which each individual is to be made morally responsible. To such minds contact with the world and experience of practical life do not bring increased knowledge, but only beget fiercer rebellion, and life often ends as it began in a sacrifice that is logical but ineffective. Mr Meredith has worked out this character with entire mastery and skill, and with astonishing sympathy. Beginning with the youth whose generous instincts are still unpledged to any social theories, and upon whose intellect no excessive demands have yet been made, he traces the gradual ascendency of the social reformer, and marks with inflinching accuracy the sacrifice of proportion and the loss of force as the young man's enthusiasm passes under the control of an intellect too weak for its guidance. The passages of life at Venice and the love-making with Renée mark the transition from the one phase to the other. At first the lover stands confessed, fascinating us as he fascinates his companion by the splendid directness and sincerity of his impulses. We acknowledge the powerful presence of a gallant youth who has a right to woo and to win; but in a little while the spirit of the reformer is aroused, and the force of the individual passion is impoverished by the touch of calculating philanthropy. He begins to argue the social wrong of Renée's pre-arranged marriage with the aged French Marquis, and strives in the most natural manner to rest his own claims to the lady upon the claims of humanity. But this plan of summoning argument to the aid of impulse, though a very natural device for any lover in distress, has a special significance in the case of Nevil Beauchamp. It marks the beginning of a mental conflict which finally throws the character off its balance under pretence of asserting the control of reason. From this moment Nevil's intellect, which is weak, assumes command over his impulses, which are strong, and the passionate lover developes by an entirely natural process into the fanatical politician. Nothing in the book is finer, either in conception or execution, than the description of the night in Venice which closes this first stage in the hero's career. Mr Meredith has a method of conducting dialogue which is admirably suggestive of the dramatic intensity of critical moments in the lives of his characters. He can reject the trivial realities of the scene without destroying its truth of colour, and so powerfully compresses the sequence of events that speech has no choice but to flash out the inner-most meaning of the speaker.

The subsequent events in the life of Beauchamp, though they sometimes carry the reader too far into the realm of speculative politics, are of essential service in completing the portrait thus effectively sketched in. It is very natural, for example, that Beauchamp, on his return to England, should fall under the influence of the Radical Dr Shrapnel, that in consequence he should find himself in sharp conflict with his own people, and that his next essay in love should be perpetually thwarted by separation of political ideas. And Mr Meredith has been no less sympathetic in showing the constant courage and nobility of his hero than relentless in marking his feeble mental steerage. Beauchamp continues as he had begun, always ready for sacrifice, and indifferent to ridicule, often blundering, but always with a certain dash and distinction which no intellectual shipwreck can destroy. Once only in the course of a career which is made pathetic by its failures, and once more at its close, the real personality of the man reasserts itself and breaks away from its bondage of theories. Renée, the old love, with whom he had never thought of discussing politics, summons him to her side. She is married now, and he is in the midst of a contested election, but the summons is magical. He leaves his politics with the sudden alacrity of a soldier called into action, and, although the quick insight of the Frenchwoman perceives a change in her hero, he recovers in her presence something of the force and fascination of the earlier time. Here again Mr Meredith has been peculiarly fortunate in his work. The rapidity of his method, the abrupt and pregnant statement of what is essential to expound the intellectual and passionate movement of the scene, is admirably adapted to paint the sudden meeting of old lovers who must as suddenly part again. But perhaps the stroke of strongest and truest art is that by which the author closes the career of his hero. It is in the logic of such a character that the measured results of its labours should be often insignificant and its courage always unfailing, and in the manner of Beauchamp's death both these truths are sufficiently expressed. He is drowned in trying to save another's life, but this other is not the heroine, nor indeed any character with a place in the story, but a nameless little urchin who had fallen out of a boat in Southampton Water. Beauchamp did not need a life's political conflict to teach him brave or generous instincts; but these instincts were from the first the better and truer part of him, and it is therefore right that they should survive his intellectual troubles and flash out again at the last.

We have only briefly touched upon the central figure in the story, leaving the reader to find out for himself the details of the picture, and to study without interference the subordinate figures who fill the scene. Of these Cecilia Halkett seems the most, and Lydiard the least, successful. It is true that the latter is only a slight sketch, but Mr Meredith has himself shown in the case of Lord Palmet that the slightest sketch can be endowed with vitality. Among the characters whose portraiture is more decisive Tuckham is perhaps the most unsatisfactory figure and his union with Cecilia Halkett is scarcely made credible to us. But these minor failures scarcely trouble the general progress of the story, nor do they hinder the expression of Beauchamp's personality. All the characters with whom he is brought closely into contact, Cecilia Halkett, Renée, Earl Romfrey, and Dr Shrapnel are living creatures, upon whose portraiture the author has spent scarcely less care than upon that of the hero himself. Wider objections which might be brought against the novel depend, as we have already hinted, not upon imperfect skill, but upon defects inherent in the scheme, and which partly correspond with fixed characteristics in the author's method. The combined study of the permanent truths of character, and of the shifting and unsettled problems of political and social life, necessarily imports a discord which no skill can wholly conceal; but where the writer by the nature of his own genius is constantly tempted to this twofold labour it is better that he should choose, as Mr Meredith has chosen in *Beauchamp's Career*, a theme which provides in itself the material necessary for the exercise both of his creative and critical faculties.

54. James Thomson, *Secularist*

i, 3 June 1876

James Thomson (1834–82), author of *City of Dreadful Night* (1880), was one of Meredith's earliest partisans. His essays from *Cope's Tobacco Plant* (ed. W. Lewis), were separately published in 1880 and his essays on Meredith were privately printed in 1910. He began to correspond with Meredith in 1877 and met him two years later. Meredith had a high opinion of his work. See also Introduction.

Mr Meredith stands among our living novelists much as Robert Browning until of late years stood among our living poets, quite unappreciated by the general public, ranked with the very highest by a select few. One exception must be made to this comparison, an exception decidedly in favour of the novelists and novel-readers; for whereas

Tennyson, the public's greatest poet, is immeasurably inferior to Browning in depth and scope and power and subtlety of intellect, George Eliot, the public's greatest novelist, is equal in all these qualities, save perhaps the last, to her unplaced rival, while having the advantage in most deservedly popular qualities, and the clear disadvantage in but one, the faculty of describing vigorous or agonistic action. The thoughtful few have succeeded in so far imposing their judgment of Browning upon the thoughtless many, that these and their periodical organs now treat him with great respect, and try hard to assume the appearance of understanding and enjoying him, though doubtless their awkward admiration is more genuine in the old sense of wonder or astonishment than in the modern of esteem or love. But the thoughtful few are still far from succeeding to this extent in the case of George Meredith. Even literary men are unfamiliar with him. For having in some freak of fun or irony specified only two of his other books, and these among the earliest, on his title-page; leaving etcs. to represent *Farina, Evan Harrington, the Adventures of Harry Richmond, Modern Love and other Poems*, with his masterpieces, *Emilia in England* and its sequel *Vittoria*; he has reaped the satisfaction of learning that many of his well-informed reviewers manifestly know nothing of these obscure writings. For the rest, the causes of his unpopularity are obvious enough, and he himself, as he more than once lets us know, is thoroughly aware of them. Thus he interjects in the present work (iii. 218-9):

[Quotes from 'We will make no mystery' to 'to my own voice more than is good'.]

Not only does he appeal to the conscience residing in thoughtfulness; he makes heavy and frequent demands on the active imagination— monstrous attempts at extortion which both the languid and the sentimental novel-reader bitterly resent, and which indeed if they grew common with authors (luckily there is not the slightest fear of that!) would soon plunge the circulating libraries into bankruptcy. The late Charles Dickens, who coincided at all points with the vulgar taste as exactly as the two triangles of the fourth proposition of the first book of *Euclid* with one another, carried to perfection the Low-Dutch or exhaustive style of description, which may be termed artistic painting reduced to artful padding, minutely cataloguing all the details, with some exaggeration or distortion, humorous or pathetic, of each to make them more memorable; so that every item can be checked and verified as in an auctioneer's inventory, which is satisfactory to a business-like people. George Eliot with incomparably higher art paints rich and solid pictures that fill the eye and dwell in the mind. But George Meredith seldom does this, either in the realm of Nature or in that of Humanity, though the achievement is well within his power, as none of our readers can doubt who studied, being fit to study, those magnificent selections from his *Vittoria* in the SECULARIST (No. 10, March 4) entitled 'Portrait of Mazzini' and 'Mazzini and Italy'. He loves to suggest by flying touches rather than slowly elaborate. To those who are quick to follow his suggestions he gives in a few winged words the very spirit of a scene, the inmost secret of a mood or passion, as no other living writer I am acquainted with can. His name and various passages in his works reveal Welsh blood, more swift and fiery and imaginative than the English. And he says in the *Emilia*, with fair pride of race:'All subtle feelings are discerned by Welsh eyes when untroubled by any mental agitation. Brother and sister were Welsh, and I may observe that there is human nature and Welsh nature'. If his personages are not portrayed at full length, they are clear and living in his mind's eye, as we discern by the exquisitely appropriate gesture or attitude or look in vivid moments: and they are characterised by an image or a phrase, as when we are told that the profile of Beauchamp 'suggested an arrow-head in the up-flight'; and Renée: 'her features had the soft irregularities which run to rarities of beauty, as the ripple rocks the light; mouth, eyes, brows, nostrils, and bloomy cheeks played into one another liquidly; thought flew, tongue followed, and the flash of meaning quivered over them like night-lightning. Or oftener, to speak truth, tongue flew, thought followed: her age was but newly seventeen, and she was French'. And as with the outward so with the interior nature of his personages. Marvellous flashes of insight reveal some of their profoundest secrets, detect the mainsprings and trace the movements of their most complex workings, and from such data you must complete the characters, as from certain leading points a mathematician defines a curve. So with his conversations. The speeches do not follow one another mechanically adjusted like a smooth pavement for easy walking: they leap and break, resilient and resurgent, like running foam-crested sea-waves, impelled and repelled and crossed by under-currents and great tides and broad breezes; in their restless agitations you must divine the immense life abounding beneath and around and above them; and the Mudie novice accustomed to saunter the level pavements, finds that the heaving and falling are sea-sickness to a queasy stomach. Moreover he delights in the elaborate analysis of abstruse problems, whose solutions when reached are scarcely less difficult to ordinary apprehension than are the problems themselves; discriminating countless shades where the common eye sees but one gloom or glare, pursuing countless distinct movements where the common eye sees only a whirling perplexity. As if all these heavy disqualifications were not enough, as if he were not sufficiently offensive in being original, he dares to be wayward and wilful, not theatrically or overweeningly like Charles Reade, but freakishly and humoristically, to the open-eyed disgust of our prim public. Lastly, his plots are too carelessly spun to catch our summer flies, showing here great gaps and there a pendent entanglement; while his catastrophes are wont to outrage that most facile justice of romance which condemns all rogues to poverty and wretchedness and rewards the virtuous with wealth and long life and flourishing large families.

In exposing his defects for the many, I have discovered some of his finest qualities for the thoughtful and imaginative few, and need now only summarize. He has a wonderful eye for form and colour, especially the latter; a masterly perception of character, a most subtle sense for spiritual mysteries. His dialogue is full of life and reality, flexible and rich in the genuine unexpected, marked with the keenest distinctions, more like the bright-witted French than the slow and clumsy English. He can use brogue and *baragouinage* with rare accuracy and humorous effect; witness the Irish Mrs Chump and the Greek Pericles in *Emilia*. Though he seldom gives way to it, he is great in the fiery record of fiery action; thus the duel in the Stelvio Pass, in *Vittoria*, has been scarcely equalled by any living novelist save by Charles Reade in that heroic fight with the pirates in *Hard Cash*. He has this sure mark of lofty genius, that he always rises with his theme, growing more strenuous, more self-contained, more magistral, as the demands on his thought and imagination increase. His style is very various and flexible, flowing freely in whatever measures the subject and the mood may dictate. At its best it is so beautiful in simplest Saxon, so majestic in rhythm, so noble with noble imagery, so pregnant with meaning, so vital and intense, that it must be ranked among the supreme achievements of our literature. A dear friend said well when reading *Vittoria*: Here truly are words that if you pricked them would bleed. For integral grandeur and originality of conception, and for perfectness of execution, the heroine of his *Emilia* appears to me the sovereign character of our modern fiction: in her he has discovered a new great nature, whom he has endowed with a new great language. In fine, I am aware of no other living English writer so gloriously gifted and so little known and appreciated except GARTH WILKINSON.[1]

These general remarks, a poor tribute of gratitude for many hours of exquisite delight, which I could not refrain from tendering when opportunity offered, have left me but scant space for special notice of George Meredith's last work; which, like the *Vittoria*, first appeared in the *Fortnightly*. Nevil Beauchamp is a gallant young naval officer, well-born and well-bred, who after service in the Crimea, on the west coast of Africa and elsewhere, comes home a radical reformer. He has been greatly influenced by the works of Carlyle, and now experiences the personal influence of a Carlylesque Dr Shrapnel, one of the best and kindest of men, hated and feared by all Whig and Tory respectabilities as a firebrand of revolution and anarchy. Beauchamp fights an election for a very corrupt constituency (Bevisham, which appears to mean Southampton), is beaten, and takes to lecturing and writing for the people. His political career may have been partly suggested by that of Admiral Maxse, to whom, being then captain, George Meredith 'affectionately inscribed' his volume of Poems fourteen years back. Beauchamp, a fascinating enthusiast, with spiritual affinities to Shelley, is not so absorbed in politics as to be free from the grand passion; and the story of his loves in their ravelling and unravelling is the artistic glory of the book, where it must be read at full length to be appreciated. The SECULARIST must concern itself rather with the political and social sketches and discussions, which are full of keen wit and independent thought. I regret that there is space only for some brief extracts. . . .

[1] James John Garth Wilkinson (1812–99), as well as a Swedenborgian poet, was a scientific writer and translator.

55. Arabella Shore, *an early appreciation*

Arabella Shore (*fl.* 1855–98), published several novels and a volume of *War Lyrics* (1855) in collaboration with her sister, Louisa Catherine. The article from which this passage is taken is the first substantial attempt at an intelligent appreciation of Meredith's work outside the framework of the review. It was published in *British Quarterly Review*, lxix, April 1879.

We have no fear for Mr Meredith's future fame: it would not even much surprise us to see him spring to a sudden present popularity. It needs but that some great critic should pronounce that sentence, which sooner or later excelling work must extort from criticism, to place him, even in popular recognition, among the few great writers of the time. In the meanwhile he remains for the private delight of those who can discover genius for themselves—a choice, if a somewhat isolated, ground, and much such as has been attained in poetry by Mr Browning, who, though acknowledged as a first-rate poet, and studied by true poetry-lovers, has never become the favourite of those who read for amusement.

If we search for reasons why so brilliant a fiction writer should not command universal success, the most obvious of these is that his stories are weighted with so much subtle and profound thought working its way through such concentrated and sometimes quaint phraseology, that the popular reader is liable to an exertion of which the popular reader is most apt to be impatient—that of pausing to study the meaning. In this and other respects he resembles the German, Jean Paul Richter, whose pages, a flowery, thorny tangle of ideas and characters, a jungle as it were, difficult and delightful alike, cannot certainly be galloped over by the breathless reader as in a steeplechase.

Another reason why he is not always easy to follow, may be that he sometimes indulges in indirect expression of his meaning, and in not so much presenting before us as implying or suggesting the links of his narrative. But this is only occasional, and then the meaning is always worth making out; and the indirect expressions embody so much wit, or sense, or fancy, that we love the work the more for the trouble it has given us.

To analyze Mr Meredith as a writer a little more closely—he is made up of philosopher, poet, and humourist, these characters being intrinsically, almost perplexingly, mingled in him. As a philosopher, he stands outside his creations and the world he places them in, and notes with tranquil, impartial, never unkindly, sarcasm all the weak points of classes and individuals. He does not in general deal in pathos, though often one sharp touch will betray what he knows of the deepest depths of suffering. But he prefers always the attitude of the calm observer and critic of the various tragic or comic, or, as he mostly makes them, tragi-comic, situations of human life. In favour of this his chosen mood he mostly fixes on incidents which do not involve final despair so much as stages of struggle, perplexity, and distress; although as little is he addicted to giving us a close of perfect satisfaction. Entangled social and personal relations are his *forte*, for he studies the laws which underlie their phenomena and produce their various combinations. As was once said of Mr Browning, he 'takes little account of the stock passions'. That is, he does not care to exhibit characters and actions merely in their elementary form. He traces their development from various causes, he shows them rooted in exceptional conditions, or conflict with other motives and circumstances, and finally analyzes the outcome of all this with a great delicacy of insight and touch, while never losing sight of general laws and the resultant phenomena.

We have said that Mr Meredith is a poet, and it needs not to refer to the glowing and vigorous verse which he has written to satisfy ourselves that the very essence of the poetical inspiration is in him. It breathes through single phrases and through whole passages of beautiful nature-picturing, and in the imagery which accompanies his analyses of mental conditions, and especially the conditions of feeling. But this imagery is not the imagery of what we must call the sentimental (chiefly feminine) novel writing of the present day, limited, that is, to the purely emotional kind, with fancy relations between the immediate atmospheric conditions and the subjective moods of the moment. There is a backbone of strength through all his play of fancy, for it is all strictly in aid of that searching analysis which forms the groundwork of the whole. This combination of poetic perception with philosophic thought, so conspicuous in George Eliot also, is essential to creative intellect of the highest order, though the thinking need not be gone through before the reader's eyes.

To say a word on Mr Meredith's humour, it may be defined as the Philosophy of the Comic. It is very peculiar, almost unique; in style it is marked by a certain laborious conscientiousness, a painstaking gravity which seems to be carefully searching for the exact words that may fit his meaning, and produces at last a sense of the most appropriate absurdity. The grotesque may sometimes be carried a little too far; but on the whole Mr Meredith's own phrase of 'thoughtful laughter' will well express the sensations that his pleasantry excites.

Mr Meredith has published seven complete novels, besides three or four clever, humorous little extravaganzas, these latter most comically realistic or strangely shot through with fantastic idealism. Of the novels, the first and probably best known is the *Ordeal of Richard Feverel*, of which a republication has recently appeared, a work loaded to excess with thought and youthful imagination, that seems to throw over its pages a shine as of the morning. It has also, perhaps, the most fire of passion and force of pathos of all Mr Meredith's works, and in one of the personages, Sir Austen Feverel, [*sic*] the paternal System-monger, the analysis of character is as fine and subtle as anything he has written. Still there is a crudeness of handling, situations too violent, and humour, to our taste at least, unpleasingly broad. The work, in fact, is so clearly youthful, alike in its promise and its faults, that we prefer to pass it over, and single out for detailed criticism two only, *Emilia in England* and *Beauchamp's Career*, two of the latest, and, while quite as original in conception and treatment as the others, the most carefully worked and entirely successful, as we consider, of all. In *Emilia*, as story and treatment, the faults are too obvious to need pointing out, but it is brilliant with genius which promises art: in *Beauchamp* we gladly recognize a maturity, a mellowing, a beautiful finish, which sets it as a crown upon all his other works. In almost all these others, certain errors of taste, chiefly connected with the comic element, occur to mar our enjoyment: here the fault is, we think, wholly absent.

The object of *Emilia in England* is to paint a being accidentally evolved and developed, under no conventional constraint, of absolute naturalness, and with the addition of one splendid faculty. There is another object, too, which we trace more confusedly, in the history of the Pole family—a picture of artificial and sentimental refinement, with small root of reality in it, pretensions which prove unequal to any strain, which wreck the one in whom they represented something true, and frankly subside in the others into meanness and vulgarity. Perhaps, next to the heroine, the most distinctive figure is that of the delightfully odious Mr Pericles, the great millionaire, the Greek merchant, the musical virtuoso, selfish, determined, unscrupulous, and not wholly repellent only because he is so irresistibly humorous. Such characters do not give us the idea that he is designedly creating humorous figures, or casting about for subjects for laughter, but as if he had actually known them, and was reproducing with grave fidelity their strong and quaint traits, so that we know them too. But by far the happiest of his creations is Emilia herself. She is at once vividly real, and singularly difficult to define. We feel only a strong and constant attraction, as if we were always watching some object of curious study, wondering with pleasant perplexity what she will do next. She has at once transparent sincerity, intensity, and childlike objectiveness; she does not theorize about herself; she exerts no command, no deliberate fascination; she seems simply to cling to others, to need them and their love; and is as successful as if she were the most finished coquette in drawing hearts after her. Perhaps with all her truthfulness and devoted passion she is a kind of artless coquette. She has that need which a great French writer has signalized as the woman's ruling characteristic, the need that the men about her should be interested in her, as if she instinctively knew that personal magnetism is all the power that woman can hope for—and she has it. Poor, obscure, a foreigner, of lowly birth and ignoble surroundings, absolutely devoid of culture, with nothing but her divine voice, her wondrous eyes, and her ardent simplicity, she makes for herself a sphere and a destiny. Her nature has the purity of fire, whose life and movement reject all taint, but it has too the sudden rash impulses hurrying her into perils that might be ruin, were it not for the good star that seems always pledged to protect her. So all at last goes well with the generous, impassioned creature; and the grateful self-devotion which makes her bind herself to three years' subjection in order to pay her benefactor's debts, and the patriotic feeling which gradually takes hold of her heart as the first ill-fated passion is burnt out, give the stamp of nobleness to her character.

That germ of a new element indicated at the close of this story is fully developed in the novel which is meant as its sequel, *Vittoria*. Here we have her career as a patriotic singer in Italy, devoted to her country's cause, and closely linked with the men who champion it. There is nothing in the undeveloped Emilia which might not mature into the grave and lofty Vittoria: that strenuousness which is one of her vital attributes, though appearing at first fitfully amongst the unorganized conditions of her life, is all concentrated in the double-stranded passion for her country and her lover. Yet it must be owned that Mr Meredith has drawn with more vivid strokes the little witch of the first story than the stately sibyl of the second.

The main object of *Beauchamp's Career* is, no doubt like that of *Emilia in England*, to paint one marked individuality; but, from the conditions in which he has placed it, *Beauchamp's Career* may fairly be called a political novel. The young aristocratic Radical, fiercely *aux prises* with all the social and political forces of his class, is for ever throwing himself into the boiling surges of political agitation, and stirring up the problems that lie seething in the deeps around us. These problems Mr Meredith fearlessly lays hold of, and sets before us as seen and interpreted by various minds, but does not effect to solve them himself. He could not perhaps have done so without committing himself to that objectionable thing, a novel with a purpose. Yet these vital matters are so touched on as to make us feel that he regards them as great realities, not as mere art-properties; that he must have felt them as a man before handling them as an artist; and we here and there find glimpses of opinions which tell us that he has sought at least within himself for their solution.

One reason perhaps why the great principles and causes involved in the controversies of the present time are thus left undecided, and still in conflict, is because such a view of the subject suits best with the career of the hero, which concludes nothing. He is a fine crusading nature, doomed to be one of the noble failures of a world not yet ripe for the root-and-branch changes he would force upon it. He fails also because he can see but one object at a time, and that isolated from all the other objects that modify it, and from all the facts that would suggest the best mode of attaining it. He has will, resolution, self-devotion, sharp perception, passionate eloquence, but he has not insight. He is described by one of the onlookers as the '*ingénu*, or peculiarly heavenly messenger, who pretends that he ought never to have any harm done him, although he carries a lighted match'. It must be owned that he has, too, some moral deficiencies that partly account for his failure in 'winning souls'. He can never accommodate his means or modify his action; and courtesy, consideration, fairness and patience even towards women, disappear when he sees himself obstructed in his course, or when, as must often happen to such uncalculating natures, he finds himself at variance with himself. These defects stand very much in his way in the two love affairs which with sailor-like illogicalness he is pursuing at one and the same time, and which are further damaged by a half-hearted irresolution much less sailor-like; though luckily these faults do not greatly hinder him with the third, which follows immediately on the heels of the two others. One is vexed to find that this seemingly fiery lover has never really made up his mind about any of the 'objects', and fixes upon the last apparently because she is the only one left him.

The story, then, is the history of Beauchamp's loves and politics: round these are grouped his party friends and enemies, his antagonistic kindred, his female friends, sympathizing, compassionately disapproving, loving. The incident which colours the whole story, producing by a natural series of consequences all the difficulties and leading to the conclusion, springs out of Beauchamp's candidature for Bevisham, and his consequent close alliance with the leading Radical there. An outrageous injury inflicted on the latter estranges his devoted follower from all his own relations and friends, cuts short his love-suit, embitters his nature, and throws into a ferment the society of which he forms a part. All these various results are traced with skill; and many and sometimes entangled as the threads of the story are, we follow them with unflagging interest till the whole skein is reeled off. We cannot pretend to be quite contented with the solutions of the respective love struggles which we have been studying so long. But Mr Meredith seems more penetrated with the bathos of human life than with its occasions of climax, and is apt to prefer even a fiasco to a triumphant success. The last chapters, full of beauty as they are, are in other respects not quite satisfactory: the conclusion seems to be hurried over, and we suspect that the author had planned a different one, more led up to by the preceding scenes. We think that the story would have been better arranged if the beginning, dwelling on Beauchamp's boyhood, had been abridged in favour of a fuller working out of the end—the more so as this beginning does not promise the interest which is awakened as soon as the hero becomes man and lover.

But it is only when we have closed the book, and the spell is dissolved, that we become conscious of these objections. It is indeed no easy matter to criticize *Beauchamp's Career* aright. It keeps us *thinking* the whole way, and when we have come to the end we feel that we have learnt so much, or rather had so much suggested to us, we have had to trace so many roots of human action laid bare, and have been dazzled with so much splendour of language, have had to keep hold of so many threads and possess ourselves of so many enigmatically-stated truths, that we feel at once the difficulty and yet the necessity of trying to summarize our impressions and define the charm that has so constrained us. Perhaps one chief element of that charm is in the variety and lifelikeness of the characters which surround Beauchamp, in various relations; and though Mr Meredith's personages a little too much resemble their author in the intellectual subtlety of their ideas and the terse epigrammatic quaintness of their speech, they have yet a rare dramatic truthfulness. Such are his uncle, Lord Romfrey (perhaps the best drawn character in the book), 'the splendid old man', 'in mind a mediæval baron, in politics a crotchety unintelligible Whig', 'to whom the game laws are the corner-stone of law and of a man's right to hold his own', with his interest in birds, and beasts, and herbs, 'what ninnies call nature in books', who, stormed by his nephew's impetuous indignation, only 'takes a chair, saying, with the utmost placidity, "Windy talk, that"'; Rosamond Culling, who interests more than she attracts us, with her 'habit of wringing an unanimous verdict from a jury of temporary impressions'; Dr Shrapnel, who is made to lay a strong hold on our affections, as he did on Beauchamp's, who 'stooped from his height to speak, or rather swing the stiff upper half of his body down to his hearer's level and back again, like a ship's mast on a billowy sea'; the warmhearted, bigoted, testy old Tory gentleman, Colonel Halkett; and Blackburn Tuckham, 'an exuberant Tory, who was the reverse of the cavalier': but we must give the description of him.

[Quotes xxvi, from 'Mr Tuckham had a round head' to 'will come back a Liberal.']

As for the three fair creatures who are the objects of Beauchamp's polytheistic worship, and who are all subtly and tenderly delineated, we have Renée, with the pathos of her destiny, her French grace, and the 'wild sweetness of her eyes', the story of whose relations with Beauchamp during that idyllic Venetian episode is like a long lyrical sigh of love and sorrow; Cecilia, the very flower of high-born, high-bred English girlhood, the lily of maidens, with its golden heart where the possibilities of passion lie enfolded, who 'sees suitors come and go, as from a watch-tower in the skies'; and Jenny, 'whose eyes Beauchamp had seen weighing and balancing questions more than he quite liked', the embodiment of delicate feminine intellect, complete at all points, young, gentle, firm, and wise.

We will not further anticipate the course of the story, but must just notice what we think perhaps the raciest and most lifelike picture in the whole, that of the electoral canvass, of which the characters and humours

—especially the 'general piety' of Mr Oggler, and the melancholy fanaticism of that 'young monster of unreason', Colpendike [sic] the shoe-maker—are admirably hit off.

We must wind up our notice of this particular work with a few words on the author's style, shown, as we think, here in its maturity. But it would need almost his own powers to do justice to the splendour and strangeness of it, joined with an exactness of expression, such as can proceed only from clearness of idea and a perfect sense of the value of words—that sense which almost in itself constitutes genius. This style of his is so unique, that it calls for a word or two more, as, though thoroughly native to the writer, it is evidently very carefully wrought. There is a marked absence of the obvious seductive cadences, the easy pathetic tricks which express the receptive and gently emotional, rather than the creative and passionate mind. Not even the wild music of passion does he freely indulge in, and for all the rant that simulates it he has an utter abhorrence. His ordinary style, especially that of his vivid dialogue, is terse, abrupt, full of force, point, and colour, in brief, strong sentences, like the waves of a short chopping sea. But in his most reflective and most touching passages he has that grave sustained tone which seems to dominate the situation, using its restrained pathos, its musical suggestions, and its deep inquiring murmur, according to a law of his own.

We must attempt to give some idea of our author's peculiar style of thought and language, as far as three or four of the briefest and slightest touches can avail:

[.   .   .   .

In this, and in his other novels, as indeed in most novels of any thought, we find frequent suggestions on that most fruitful of subjects—the social relation of the sexes. His allusions are either light playful glances, or suggestive hints, absolutely impartial in their tone, and as little committing him to any fixed view on the subject as do the many-sided lights in which he has set the more general problems of which we have spoken. We shall here touch only on the ideas that may be gathered from this work as to his view of that now much debated question, the position of women in the social system, as fixed by nature or defined by conventional law. Whatever are Mr Meredith's opinions as to the natural mental tendencies of women, we were hardly prepared to find the woman of high intelligence and culture, lovingly trained in an atmosphere of generous Liberalism, retrograde into what the hero and

we imagine the author would regard as the prejudices of more commonplace women. We can hardly suppose that a writer of such fine insight
and catholic comprehension gives in his adhesion to that metaphysical
theory of some modern philosophers, which asserts a mysterious,
invariable, ineradicable instinct of sex and temperament, leading women
to one particular type of intellectual, moral, and political ideas.*[1] Perhaps
we may take comfort in the argument—whether intended or not—
against this theory, supplied by another woman's intellectual growth,
her power of taking in new ideas, and candidly admitting their force.
Granting that all this development is first wakened by a strong personal
interest—a case which, whether in man or woman, is in early youth
almost the rule—yet opposed as it is to all the influences of her position
and bringing up, to the thousand prejudices of hearth and home and
castle and convention, and coupled, even before her 'conversion', with
an independence of judgment which could not always be hoodwinked
by father or lover, we may fairly, we think, check the conclusion from
the former instance with what may be drawn from this.

The picture of this clear and ripening intellect, framed in so fair a
form, suggests the hope that Mr Meredith is no friend to that 'hard and
fast line' which would deny to women, and to women only, all those
potentialities of growth and that requisite previous enlargement of
traditional limits and removal of obstructions which have in all else
become the law.

For Beauchamp himself, it may be observed that, with characteristic
inconsistency, he tries to convert Cecilia by force of reasoning, while
still finding it 'impossible to believe that women thought'. A false and
lowering estimate of half the human race is not uncommon in young
men, whose knowledge of women has been gathered mainly from
tradition or unwise experience. Such an estimate is apt, in after years,
to harden into a contemptuous uncompromising determination to
'keep things just as they are', or to justify itself by the metaphysical
theory above alluded to. In either case society is the worse, and justice
missed in legislative decisions which these ideas underlie. No definition
of woman's nature can be sound that does not take into account, and is
not limited by, the conditions under which social laws have placed her.

We have scarcely done justice in our preceding remarks to the
delicate charm, at once a subtly sympathetic insight and a generous

[1] We are not, be it remembered, speaking of those Conservative tendencies as right or
wrong, but only mooting the theory that makes them a characteristic of sex, independent
of reason or influence.*

truthfulness, with which Mr Meredith has pourtrayed the best feminine types among those that come to view on the social surface. He has so pourtrayed them that we can believe him to have, kept to himself, an ideal of something rarer still, of what woman might be, perhaps will be, of what possibly some women even now are. Half-faces of this ideal appear in his works, ranging from the exquisite intellectual German princess, Ottilia, in the *Adventures of Harry Richmond*, to the untrained child of nature, Emilia. The former indeed is but a charming suggestion; but even as she is, placed in this present generation of young men, she would appear to have been found by them

> too wise, too good
> For human nature's daily food.[1]

Yet may we not hope from Mr Meredith some day a fuller exposition of that 'perfect woman' who we are sure is no stranger to his conceptions?

To conclude. To all those questions that arise out of that great organization of humanity that we call civilized society there is an answer in the eternal moral code, to which we can but approximately attain, but which all who think and write on these matters are bound to study and set forth as well as they can. This work is nobly done by reproducing the noblest examples of those who live to find it. May not we trust that he who has seen so well and thrown with so bold a hand on the canvas the different lights in which the most serious problems present themselves to different minds, may, by some clear illuminating ray cast from his own in some future work, aid in the great task of social regeneration.

[1] W. Wordsworth, 'She was a Phantom of delight'.

THE EGOIST

1879

56. Unsigned review, *Examiner*

No. 3744, 1 November 1879

When the critic, weary of wading through wastes of three volumes, receives another batch of novels for review, the first impulse is to cry out in despair over the new mass of twaddle which will have to be read and digested. The result is, of course, that the books are successively opened and their titles scanned with something of a jaundiced eye. One hopes for something fresh and bright, but one hardly dares to expect it. Yet this frame of mind is not necessarily one which implies hasty judgment and condemnation. On the contrary, the wish for a good story is often father to the thought, and a tale which opens fairly well is assumed to be clever throughout, and read with friendly interest till its ineffable weariness at last destroys the illusion. With *The Egoist*, Mr George Meredith's latest work, the case is exactly the reverse. Nothing could be more appalling than the prelude, with its imitation of Carlyle, paradoxes meant for philosophy, and its obscure passages intended for deep wisdom. Obscurity, we can assure Mr Meredith, is not necessarily interesting. And want of intelligibility disfigures, unfortunately, more than the mere prelude of *The Egoist*. The author will probably say that the reader's stupidity is in fault; but we submit that novelists do not write only for persons who are preternaturally acute in filling up elisions and elucidating *variorum* readings. The average intelligence will be frequently puzzled as to what the speakers mean; the jerky pauses with which their conversation is interrupted may be true to nature, for in social converse expression and gesture help towards comprehension, but in a novel, where the mind has to grasp the meaning without any outward aid, it is necessary for the various characters to express themselves more distinctly than they would in real life. And, strange to say,

all the people in the book, with perhaps the sole exception of the ladies
Eleanor and Isabel, are thus given to enigmatic and elliptical utterances.
It is pleasant, indeed, to turn from the gush or slanginess of the modern
heroine to the pregnant and picturesque, though obscure, conversation
of Lætitia Dale and Clara Middleton; but the latter is scarcely natural,
and the continual strain on the reader's mind becomes singularly
fatiguing. Frequently failing to discover, at a first reading what someone means, it becomes necessary to go through the passage twice, or
even thrice. Now useful as this careful re-perusal may be in a work on
mathematics or philosophy, it should scarcely be necessary in a novel;
the less, as when the meaning is at last approximated to, it turns out not
to have been worth all the trouble. As we are now pointing out the
faults of *The Egoist* (reserving its more numerous and more important
excellencies to the last, as children keep the tit-bits to finish up with),
we cannot pass without notice its early chapters, in which pseudo-
Carlyleism is carried to an incredible extent, and Mrs Mountstuart's
silly expression, 'he has a leg', is harped on like clothes in *Sartor Resartus*.
In intimate connection with, and sequence of, the elliptical style of
dialogue, is the fact that the conversations are generally stilted. They
must necessarily be so, since everyone talks with *sous-entendus* and in
riddles. Dr Middleton, who is represented to us as a learned man, and
is supposed to be pedantic, is often not more so than Colonel De Craye,
the lively Irishman; and the exchange of epigrams over dinner and
luncheon, although brilliant and sharp, is utterly unlike the real dis-
jointed talk of even the wittiest society. It may be gathered from the
above that Mr Meredith is a great deal too clever. It is much better that
he should be too clever than, like the majority of novelists, too dull;
but yet the result is that the book will very likely not please the general
public. Very much more attention is required to understand it than will
suffice to grasp a good heavy book of 'useful knowledge'; and the
general public does not like to have philosophy and acute remarks on
men and things presented to it under the garb of a novel. Occasionally,
one might almost fancy that the author had attempted a sequel to the
New Republic, for here and there, particularly after he has overcome
the reminiscences of the Chelsea philospher which cramp him in the
beginning, he develops a wonderful facility for epigrams.[1]

It is not our intention to summarize the plot of this singular and
powerful work. There is, in fact, not much plot to summarize, and we

[1] *The New Republic* (1877), a brilliant satire on Ruskin, Jowett, Arnold, Pater, and
others, somewhat in the manner of Peacock, was by W. H. Mallock.

hold this statement to be almost the highest praise we can award. For when a book is of absorbing interest without a single startling incident, without a murder, without even an elopement (except a very minor one mentioned in the first chapter), and deprived of the adventitious aids of railway accidents, shipwrecks, or other *dii ex machina*, we may be sure that there is much nature and much thought in it. Were there not it must infallibly be dull, and *The Egoist* is never dull. It is the story of a man who possesses every advantage under the sun—who is young, healthy, rich, good-looking, a perfect gentleman, and (as we are told a little too often) 'anything but obtuse'. But he is an egoist—an egoist of a type which now that Mr Meredith has discovered it for us we feel to be anything but uncommon. Self is the pivot on which everything must move, and he is gracious, kind, even generous, not with a selfish motive exactly, but impelled by the necessity of being able to say to himself that he is gracious, kind, and generous. This character is admirably developed, and the development is so gradual and so natural that we would not spoil it by attempting to trace its course. Any summary of one of the most subtle analyses which have appeared in a work of fiction since Balzac's *Cousin Pons* and *Cousin Bette* would necessarily be bald and insufficient, if it did not appear positively repulsive. So far from Sir Willoughby Patterne (in whose surname a pun on his qualities is clearly intended) being repulsive, we are, on the contrary, frequently forced to pity him, for his egoism is so blind that he fails to see what every reader can see, and yet it is so natural that his blindness is felt to be inevitable. And towards the conclusion of the work we have not only pity, but almost sympathy, with the unfortunate man whom neither fortune, nor talents, nor good looks, nor wealth, could save from being twice jilted, and who bears his misfortune with a stoic diplomacy as admirable as it is the inevitable outcome of his character. The clever passages in which this character is elucidated are numerous, and if we were to attempt quotation, we might never finish. As an illustration, however, of Mr Meredith's power, we give the following.

Sir Willoughby having heard of a gallant exploit performed by an obscure cousin, a lieutenant in the Marines, in a distant colony, imagines him to be a young and sprightly officer, sends him a cheque, and invites him to the Hall:

[Quotes i, from 'Young Willoughby made a kind of shockhead', with omissions to 'and had a face of crimson'.]

Although we are not actually told as much, there can be no doubt that this little incident settles Sir Willoughby's chances with Miss Durham, who breaks the engagement. Further on, when, after some years, he is once more engaged, Miss Middleton is discussing with Sir Willoughby the future of the lieutenant's son, Crossjay, whom he spoils, and says:

[Quotes viii, from ' "Mr Whitford has chosen the only method"' to ' "It was the point in dispute"'.]

Now in this little passage Sir Willoughby is represented as doing a distinctly kind thing—undertaking, that is, the future of his little cousin. But the way he does it, and the manner in which he makes a dependant of the boy by doing it, at once makes the action repulsive to his betrothed. And scenes like these, following naturally from the ordinary life of a country home, gradually occasion the feelings of repulsion with which she regards him, and bring on, not the catastrophe, for there is none, but the conclusion, which we will not betray.

We have already mentioned that clever remarks abound. The deep study devoted to the character of the Egoist comes out in the hero's considerations about allowing a girl with whom he has flirted on and off for years, and who is supposed to nourish a secret but deep attachment for him, to marry elsewhere: 'Marriage has been known to have such an effect on the most faithful of women that a great passion fades to naught in their volatile bosoms when they have taken a husband. We see in women especially the triumph of the animal over the spiritual'. And Mrs Mountstuart is occasionally particularly good; she says that 'men won't learn without groaning that they are simply weapons taken up to be put down when done with'.

But the book is so full of passages worth quoting and worth thinking over that we feel we are doing Mr George Meredith an injustice by cutting out a few of his 'happy thoughts', which, to appreciate, must be read in the context. They will then afford as much food for merriment as for more serious consideration, and must needs attract the attention to a much greater extent than the involved plots or unnatural surprises which characterize most of our modern novels. Our only fear is that the book may be over the heads of the majority of readers.

57. W. E. Henley, *Athenaeum*

No. 2714, 1 November 1879

William Ernest Henley (1849–1903), poet, essayist, editor, collaborated with R. L. Stevenson in several plays. Henley was perhaps Meredith's most indefatigable partisan, wrote on *The Egoist* wherever he could (*Pall Mall Gazette*, *Academy*, *Teacher*), and continued to advertise his work widely, though he had serious reservations about Meredith's style and technique. Meredith wrote to Stevenson on 4 June 1878: 'Should you be in communication with Mr Henley, I beg you will convey to him my sense of the honour he does me by giving so much attention to my work. I, who have worked for so many years not supposing that anyone paid much heed to me, find it extraordinary. His praise is high indeed, but happily he fetches me a good lusty clout o' the head now and again, by which I am surprisingly well braced and my balance is restored. Otherwise praise like that might operate as the strong waters do upon the lonely savage unused to such a rapture'. Later, however, Henley's criticism caused Meredith annoyance. See below, No. 79, headnote, and Introduction.

Those who have read Mr Meredith's novels with insight and attention are aware that they have some of the highest qualities to be found in contemporary fiction. If their author has a great capacity for unsatisfactory writing, he has capacities not less great for writing that is satisfactory in the highest degree. He has the tragic instinct and endowment, and he has the comic as well; he is an ardent student of character and life; he has wit of the swiftest, most comprehensive, and most luminous order, and humour that can be fantastic or ironical or human at his pleasure; he has passion and he has imagination; he has considered sex—the great subject, the leaven of imaginative art—with notable audacity and insight. He is as capable of handling a vice or an emotion as he is of managing an affectation. He can be trivial, or grotesque, or satirical, or splendid; and whether his *milieu* be romantic or actual, whether his personages be heroic or sordid, he goes about his task with the same assurance and intelligence. In his best work he takes rank with the world's novelists. He is a companion for Balzac and Richardson, an intimate for Fielding and Cervantes. His figures fall into their place beside the greatest of their kind; and when you think of Lucy Feverel and Mrs Berry, of Evan Harrington's Countess Saldanha [sic] and the Lady Charlotte of *Emilia in England*, of the old Regency dandy in *Harry Richmond* and the Sir Everard Romfrey of *Beauchamp's Career*, of Renée and Cecilia, of Emilia and Rhoda Fleming, of Rose Jocelyn and Lady Blandish and Ripton Thompson, they have in the mind's eye a value scarce inferior to that of Clarissa and Lovelace, of Bath and Western and Booth, of Andrew Fairservice and Elspeth Mucklebackit, of Hulot and Philippe Bridau, of Vautrin and Madame Marneffe and Balthasar Claës. In the world of man's creation his people are citizens to match the noblest; they are of the aristocrats of the imagination, the peers in their own right of the society of romance. But, for all that, their state is lonely and forlorn. It seems a reproach upon the intelligence of novel-reading mankind that so small a section of the public recognize their true eminence.

Happily, and unhappily, their author is even more to blame for this neglect than his public. Mr Meredith is one of the worst and least attractive of great writers as well as one of the best and most fascinating. He is a sun that has broken out into spots innumerable. The better half of his genius is always suffering eclipse from the worse half. He writes with the pen of a great artist in his left hand, and the razor of a spiritual suicide in his right; for, like certain others of his age and temper, he is the owner and the victim of a monstrous cleverness which will neither be suppressed nor admonished, and will not permit him to do things as an honest, simple person of genius would. As Shakespeare, in Johnson's phrase, lost the world for a quibble, and was content to lose it, so does Mr Meredith discrown himself of the sovereignty of contemporary romance to put on the cap and bells of the professional wit. He is not content to be plain Jupiter; his lightnings are less to him than the fireworks he delights in; and his pages so teem with fine sayings, and magniloquent epigrams, and gorgeous images, and fantastic locutions, that the mind would welcome dulness as a glad relief. He is tediously amusing; he is brilliant to the point of being obscure; his helpfulness is so extravagant as to worry and confound. This is the secret of his un-popularity. His stories are not often good stories and are seldom well told; his ingenuity and intelligence are always misleading him into treating mere episodes as solemnly and elaborately as a main incident; he is ever ready to discuss, to ramble, to theorize, to dogmatize, to indulge himself in a little irony, or a little reflection, or a little artistic misdemeanour of some sort. But other novelists have done these things before him, and have been none the less popular, and are actually none the less readable. None, however, has pushed the foppery of style and intellect to such a point as Mr Meredith. Not unfrequently he writes page after page of English as ripe and sound and unaffected as heart could wish; and you can but impute to wantonness and recklessness the splendid impertinences that ensue elsewhere. To read him at the rate of two or three chapters a day is to have a sincere and hearty admiration for him, and a devout anxiety to forget his defects and make much of his merits. But they are few who can read a novel on such terms as these; and to read Mr Meredith straight off is to have an indigestion of epigram, and to be incapable of distinguishing good from bad, the author of the parting between Richard and Lucy Feverel—which appears to us to be the high-water mark of novelistic passion and emotion—from the creator of Mr Raikes and Dr Shrapnel, who are two of the most flagrant unrealities ever perpetrated in the name of fiction by an artist of genius.

It is greatly to be hoped that *The Egoist* will be read and studied as it deserves, for it is as good in its way as *Richard Feverel* itself. It is described by Mr Meredith as a comedy in chapters; and those who do not know what comedy is had better procure them a Molière at once and read, ere they attempt *The Egoist*. Just as Molière, in the figures of Alceste and Tartuffe, has summarized and embodied all that we need to know of indignant honesty and the false fervour of sanctimonious animalism, so in the person of Sir Willoughby Patterne has Mr Meredith succeeded in quintessentializing the qualities of egoism, as the egoist appears in his relations with women and in his conception and exercise of the passion of love. Between the means of the two authors there is not, nor can be, any sort of comparison. Molière is brief, exquisite, lucid; classic in his union of ease and strength, of purity and sufficiency, of austerity and charm. In *The Egoist* Mr Meredith is even more artificial and affected than is his wont; he bristles with allusions, he teems with hints and side-hits and false alarms, he glitters with phrases, he riots in intellectual points and philosophical fancies; and though his style has never yet become him so well, his cleverness is yet so reckless and indomitable as to be almost as fatiguing here as elsewhere. But in their matter the great Frenchman and he have not much to envy each other. Sir Willoughby Patterne is a 'document on humanity' of the highest value; and to him who would know of egoism and the egoist the study of Sir Willoughby is indispensable. There is something in him of us all. He is a compendium of the Personal in man; and if in him the abstract Egoist have not taken on his final shape and become classic and typical, it is not that Mr Meredith has forgotten anything in his composition, but rather that there are certain defects of form, certain structural faults and weaknesses, which prevent one from accepting as conclusive the aspect of the mass of him. But the Molière of the future (supposing such a product to be possible) has but to pick and choose with discretion to find in Mr Meredith the stuff for a worthy companion figure to Tartuffe, Alceste, and Célimène.

Comedy [says Mr Meredith] is a game played to throw reflections upon social life, and it deals with human nature in the drawing-room of civilized men and women. . . . Credulity is not wooed through the impressionable senses, nor have we recourse to the small circular glow of the watchmaker's eye to raise in bright relief minutest grains of evidence for the routing of incredulity. The comic spirit conceives a definite situation for a number of characters, and rejects all accessories in the exclusive pursuit of them and their speech.

These three sentences are the first in *The Egoist*, and they explain Mr Meredith's idea of the Comic and the apparent method of his book. It is, however, by no means certain that the book is a proof that he has put his theory altogether into practice. That is not so clear. The plot of *The Egoist* is comic, and some of its personages are comic also; and both plot and personages are comic in the best and highest sense. But has Meredith rejected 'all accessories in the exclusive pursuit' of his characters and their speech? Has he verily refrained from having recourse 'to the small circular glow of the watchmaker's eye' to rout the incredulity of himself and the public? Unluckily there is much that is superfluous in *The Egoist*; its personages are scarcely all comic personages; much of their speech—though all of it is representative—is too trivial to be typical, and so to take rank as comic speech. Mr Meredith's personality, in fine, has proved too irrepressible to allow him to consummate his effort by giving to it the fine finish he has taught us to expect in a work of perfect comic art; and though his matter is unexceptionable, he has not been able so to fuse and shape it as to produce the effect he foresaw and intended. There is infinitely too much of statement and reflection, of aphorism and analysis, of epigram and fantasy, of humours germane and yet not called for; so that in the end the impression produced is not the impersonal impression that was to be desired, and the literary egoism of the author of Sir Willoughby Patterne appears to overshadow the amorous egoism of Sir Willoughby himself, and to become the predominating fact of the book.

To object thus much to Mr Meredith's work we have had to judge him by the highest possible standard. His book is so strikingly original, so astonishingly able, that it is a hard matter to keep ourselves from condoning what seem to us its vices in favour of its virtues. Its minor personages are one and all of rare significance and value; its dialogue is surprisingly sustained and apt; there are pages in it of analysis and deduction that open up new views and fresh vistas on human character and the human mind; there are chapters of an imaginative truth so vivid and intense as to be discomforting. Mr Meredith has not succeeded in doing exactly what he wished to do; perhaps it would be fairer to say that he has succeeded in his intent, and succeeded for himself alone. But all this to the contrary, there is no question but *The Egoist* is a piece of imaginative work as solid and rich as any that the century has seen, and that it is, with *Richard Feverel*, not only one of its author's masterpieces, but one of the strongest and most individual productions of modern literature.

58. R. H. Hutton, *Spectator*

lii, 1 November 1879

For R. H. Hutton, see above, No. 2, headnote.

We have been amused, impressed, bored, and filled with admiration and disappointment by Mr George Meredith's new story. Of Sir Willoughby Patterne, the typical egoist and the hero of the comedy, Mrs Mountstuart Jenkinson observed at his coming of age, 'You see he has a leg'. The word is mystic, and of various interpretation; it characterizes him from that time forth. Mrs Mountstuart, we may remark, is a fatal coiner of epithets. She hits off all her acquaintance with a good-natured, but appalling accuracy, and thereby saves Mr Meredith the necessity of too often blushing at his own cleverness. He naïvely admires her wit as much as we do. She describes Vernon Whitford, Sir Willoughby's cousin and destined rival, as 'Phœbus Apollo turned fasting friar'. Laetitia Dale, the egoist's first lady-love, and Constantia Durham, his second, are similarly given in a phrase; the former has 'a romantic tale on her eyelashes'; the latter is a 'racing cutter'. We are the more grateful to Mrs Mountstuart for these and other luminous hints concerning the people with whom we are brought in contact, because after Mr Meredith has done his best, he does not succeed in teaching us much more about them. We get plenty of elaboration, but little further practical insight. To return to young Sir Willoughby, the god of himself and the county; after jilting Laetitia, who is poor, he engages himself to Constantia, who is healthy and wealthy, as well as handsome. But she jilts him (though he will not allow himself to regard the matter in that light), and he goes abroad for three years; meets Laetitia, on his return, in a lonely lane, looks in her eyes, 'found the man he sought there, squeezed him passionately, and let her go, saying— "It was decreed that we should meet"'. She accordingly hopes for a time again, tremulously, but subsides once more, on learning that he has started fresh game in the person of one Clara Middleton, whom Mrs Mountstuart presently pronounces to be 'a dainty rogue in porcelain'. Clara is the heroine, and is much described.

She is the daughter of the rich and learned scholar, Dr Middleton, a strong figure, with a grand head and rolling voice; when angered, he is like 'a Dictionary bitten'; but at all times, a humorous and refreshing personage. The engagement between Clara and Willoughby is somewhat hurriedly formed; she is young and ignorant of the world, and, to her, love was 'one of the distant blessings of the mighty world, lying somewhere in the world's forests, across wild seas, veiled, encompassed with beautiful perils, a throbbing secrecy, but too remote to quicken her bosom's throbs'. She begins to learn her own mind later, and has fits of gravity and misgiving, and in her reveries sings to herself, 'above her darker-flowing thoughts, like the reed warbler on the branch beside the night-stream'. When her lover came to embrace her, she took the salute with apparent insensibility, but a moment later she blushed crimson, 'divinely feminine in reflective bashfulness'. However, circumstance and civilization unite to make a coward of her; modern women are 'like Prussians, who must both march and think in step'. After many doubts and hesitations, plans made and defeated, plots and palpitations, she is at length despairingly emboldened to request Sir Willoughby to release her from her engagement. He is at first incredulous of the serious intention of the 'profane request', but on her timed reiteration, treats it as a maiden folly—a fear of unworthiness of her great destiny—on which point he chivalrously reassures her, and will hear no more of the matter. Hereupon intrigues begin, and very ingeniously are they conducted. Prominent among the intriguers, though by no will of his own, is Crossjay, a delightfully boyish boy, who, with Dr Middleton, are the most nearly human creatures in the book. Vernon Whitford, this boy's tutor for the Navy, is employed through two and a half volumes chiefly in hunting over the country after him to fetch him back to his lessons, Crossjay's predilection being for birds' eggs, ponds, earth, hedges, and rainstorms. When found, he has to be pulled out of the ground, rank of the soil, like a root. In the end, he is mainly essential in running the unhappy egoist to earth; and is then made one of the many millstones which are hung round the baronet's humiliated neck, previous to plunging him into the matrimonial sea.

We shall not, however, follow the story to its conclusion, which is very cleverly wrought out, a necessity being upon us to say something of the writing and the writer. Mr Meredith's reputation is high, and there is no doubt about his ability. Now, it is conceivable, but not inevitable, that a man of ability should be able to write a good novel, or even comedy in narrative; and there are few more agreeable sensations for a reviewer than to open a virgin volume with the assurance that he will find it full of good literature—as good ten years hence as now. It was with an assurance, or at least with an anticipation, of this sort that we applied our paper-knife to the *Egoist*. The first effect was vigorous, and not unpromising. The writer has an individuality: he is a humourist. He makes us think of him a great deal, not by directly introducing himself to us, as Thackeray does, but after the same fashion that we are led to think of Carlyle while reading his *French Revolution*. In fact, Mr Meredith often calls up an image of a handsome, witty, polished juvenile cousin of Carlyle, in eighteenth-century costume, with neat, powdered wig, lace ruffles, knee-breeches, and silk stockings, of keen and curious vision, but too courteous to be profound or stirring, who regards the world as a foolish piece of protoplasm, chiefly valuable as stuff out of which to cut epigrams and apt similes. His thought moves in images, sometimes felicitous, but as often grotesque or obscure. An inability to fall into conventional modes of expression is characteristic of humourists, but then the unconventionality should throw fresh light

upon the subject-matter, should explain it, not disorganize it merely.
Mr Meredith's eccentricity is like that of a 'left-handed' snail-shell;
he must curl the wrong way, or the genius of his eccentricity is lost.
The humourist, being a person, and generally the most conspicuous
person in his book, he should be careful always to be captivating, otherwise his reader is liable to reject all he brings in rejecting him. Mr Meredith is frequently captivating, but he does no know when to stop. We
are compelled to question whether he is humorously affected, or only
affectedly humorous. He is a sort of modern hermetic philosopher of
drawing-rooms; there is too often more novelty in his way of saying a
thing than in the thing he says; and although Mr Meredith is ordinarily
very circumspect, this is a fault which is quite as apt to mislead the
writer as the reader. It is occasionally best and wisest to be straightforward and simple; there are times when wit will not do the work of
strength. Such times are perilous to Mr Meredith. Once more, he does
not know when, or he is unable, to stop; and we find him lavishing
much delicate fancy and brisk ingenuity upon matters in themselves
unimportant; as if a man were to spend his life carving out of a perish-
able melon-rind, a work of art that he might just as easily have wrought
in everlasting ivory. The links in his chain of argument are elaborated
in such cunning open-work of verbal filagree, that the argument is no
longer a chain, but a curiosity; it must be supported, it will support
nothing. Again, his subtlety in the matter of adverbs and adjectives—
the latter especially—is astonishing; but qualification is not invariably
insight, and we are driven to ask whether the writer, who knows so
well what a thing looks like, knows equally well what it is? He can
always say a good thing, when he gives his mind to it; but now and
then he is absent-minded, and then he is prone to parody himself; his
pen, left to its own devices, and still conscious whom it belongs to,
perpetrates an empty quip, that has the form, but not the substance, of
its owner. Upon the whole, as we turn page after page, our expectations
are continually whetted, because of the difficulty of believing that so
much promising material shall not fulfil its promise; but we are constrained to say, at the end, that it does not. The story, such as it is,
would be better plainly dressed; its clothes are too good for it. Perhaps
no story would be good enough for such clothes. And there is, after all,
only a certain amount of gold to be got out of the human mine; what
is the use of exciting our cupidity beyond the possibility of its gratification? Shakespeare dug pretty deep, but he did not go about his
work in nearly so promising a manner as does Mr Meredith.

Nevertheless, Mr Meredith has a great deal of the artist in him; and very likely he is aware of his own limitations, and does what he can to fortify his position. He opens with an artful 'prelude', in which he defines the comedy, as distinguished from the novel proper. The comedy is spirit and essence, unclogged by the novel's dull, interminable realism of detail. The truth is, of course, that Mr Meredith has no genius for detail. M. Emile Zola has, and could doubtless write as convincing an essay in favour of his view as Mr Meredith has done in favour of his. Mr Meredith knows many clever tricks of narrative. For example, he will reproduce, at an interval of several pages or chapters, a particular, marked phrase of conceit, which, carrying the mind back to the previous utterance of it, causes all that lies between to appear parenthetical, and thus gives an appearance of rapidity and homogeneity to the whole. Again, in the midst of much logical incoherence, he will observe a thread of humorous coherency, like a juggler who pretends to make a mistake with what we afterwards discover to have been his best skill. In his moralizing moments he does not proffer you the naked truth, but gives you the conventional lie, robed in the ridiculous splendour of a monkey on a hand-organ, thus revealing its ugliness better than actual revelation could do. Of dialogue he is prodigal; but it is not characteristic dialogue, or rather it is characteristic of nobody but Mr Meredith. The speeches chime with the context, but not with the people who are made to utter them. Precious human nature is pulled out of shape, in order that the author may not lose the credit of his own epigrams; and sometimes the ear catches in these utterances the fatal lilt of blank verse. But his people are altogether Mr Meredith's weak point; he can see them, he can 'hit them off', but he cannot enter into them and sympathize with them as individualities. What they are made to say and think is what they really might have said and thought—presented through the refracting medium of the thoughts and sayings of Mr Meredith. The analysis both of Sir Willoughby and of Clara Middleton is exhaustive, and we feel that much of it is correct, but it does not enable us once to catch a genuine glimpse of either of them. The traits are all there, but not the distinct persons; to make adaptation of one of Mr Meredith's own sayings, he describes his characters admirably, piecemeal; when it comes to the putting of them together, he does it coldly. After closing the book, we feel, in the retrospect, that the style is the most memorable thing about it. It is like a wayward wind blowing against the current of the story, and raising little humorous waves and eddies which both look pretty, and prevent our getting a clear view of what lies underneath. The whole work (to use another simile, for which Mr Meredith must excuse us, since a prolonged and not unprofitable indulgence in his society is answerable for it) reminds us of one of those picture-puzzles that are given to children, to find out the figure or the significance which is hidden from the first view. The result of our inspection of Mr Meredith's puzzle resolves itself into the single word—'Clever'.

59. W. E. Henley, *Pall Mall Gazette*

xxx, 3 November 1879

For W. E. Henley, see above, No. 57, headnote. The *Pall Mall Gazette* was a Conservative journal begun in 1865 under the editorship of Meredith's close friend, Frederick Greenwood (1830–1909).

The author of *Richard Feverel* and *Harry Richmond* is a man of genius, who so far has succeeded in hiding his own merits from the common eye. It is not everybody who can appreciate justly and temperately either his books or himself. People who read him do so but to criticize. Some there are who will not have him on any terms; others admire him exceedingly and yet admit that they read him with vexation. At its best his work is of the first order; at its worst, it is brilliant, but tedious. One of the very few moderns who have the double gift of tragedy and comedy, he is one of the wittiest men of his generation and an original humorist to boot; he has a poet's imagination and he is a quick observer; he has studied human nature and human life, and he is a master of his native tongue. But with all this he fails of acknowledged pre-eminence in his art. And the reason appears to be that he writes for himself alone. Extremely clever, he seems to prefer his cleverness to his genius. He is usually so bent on giving full play to his intellectual activity as to seem to ignore the novelist's main function and to do his best to misuse the novelist's best gifts. He fatigues and bewilders where, if he so willed

MEREDITH

it, he could more easily attract and explain. You cannot see what he would do for the sparks he beats out in the doing. He so riots in dazzling quip and quiddities as to be sometimes almost unintelligible and often antipathetic. He invites us to listen to a story, and proceeds to fling out ideas and phrases that never cease to startle attention; he volunteers a statue, and presents a gift so hung about with chains of carved cherry-stones as to be almost unrecognizable through its finery. It is no wonder that he should have been called 'a kind of Foppington-Fielding', or that one should think of him as of a Molière who somehow prefers to be Marivaux. It is no wonder that, with qualities as bright and vigorous as have ever been devoted to the novelistic art, he should be the least read of great contemporary writers. Of course it is a good thing to be the author of *Rhoda Fleming* and *Beauchamp's Career*, of *Richard Feverel* and *Evan Harrington*, of *Vittoria* and *Harry Richmond* and *Emilia*; for with all their faults these books are so many works of genius, and works of genius are not common. But it would have been a better thing so to have written them as to have made them intelligible to the world at large. Such masterpieces of dramatic portraiture as Mrs Berry and Sir Everard Romfrey, as Mr Pericles and the Countess Saldanha [*sic*]; as Emilia Belloni and Lucy Feverel, as Ripton Thompson and Cecilia Halkett, and the rest of their 'co-mates and brothers in exile', are far too good, whether as works of art or as studies in humanity, to have no other abiding place than the galleries of the curious. It is to be hoped that a happier fate than theirs attends their kindred in *The Egoist*. To say nothing of Sir Willoughby Patterne himself, it would be a real loss to letters and a reproach on the reading public if such admirable por-traitures as Clara Middleton and Letitia Dale [*sic*], as Vernon Whitford.

Mr Meredith's new book is one of the most striking works of our time; and in it he has attempted the performance of a feat in art. His object in *The Egoist* appears to have been the production of a novel that should have to life and actuality the same relation as the *Misanthrope* and *Tartuffe*, and in this he has to a certain extent succeeded. To expect to find in *The Egoist* a picture of contemporary manners and existence would be to expose oneself to the risk of disappointment. The conventionality that informs it is as obvious and as artificial as that of Molière himself. In real life people no more talk in Mr Meredith's vein than they do in that of Philinte and Célimène; they no more com-port themselves like Clara and Sir Willoughby than they do like Orgon and like Tartuffe. But then Mr Meredith is not at all intent upon painting the real. His intention is not naturalistic, it is comic; his work is not a novel nor even a romance, it is a comedy in chapters. He has tried not to report but to summarize, not to expand but to condense, to be not representative but typical, to pursue not individuals but qualities. He has had to reflect rather than to observe, to abstract more than to embody; and his work in some sort is an appeal to the public of to-day to care no more for that 'conscientious transcription of all the visible' and 'repetition of all the audible' which it is fast coming to regard as the chief function of art and the chief business of the artist. But it is also something more. Successful or unsuccessful, *The Egoist* appears to us to be the first specimen of a new *genre* in literature; and it has yet to be proved that, as Fielding denied the authority of any 'pitiful critic' whatsoever to question his authority over a style of which he was the inventor,[1] Mr Meredith may not with good reason refuse to have any argument with those who find his work imperfect. He has made his own rules, and may fairly assert himself to be the best judge of how far he has or has not abided by them. For this reason, if for no other, it may without difficulty be conceded that Mr Meredith's peculiar style is nowhere so appropriate as it is in *The Egoist*; that it is less questionable here than elsewhere for him to indulge in those sallies of elaborate and freakish humour that distinguish his writing generally; that he may cram his pages with reflections and be as witty as he pleases, so long as his wit and reflections are germane to the issue he has in view. What, however, we have a right to expect in return for this consideration is that he should so far subdue his own effective personality as to put out of peril the illusions he has raised and that it is his readers' wish to maintain. This he has failed to do; and his book is not the absolute success it might have been. It is of extraordinary merit, but it seems hardly to have fulfilled its intention. Even as regards its principal figure, it must be considered as containing rather the materials for a great comic type than the type itself.

'Comedy', says Mr Meredith in his prelude, 'is a game played to throw reflections upon social life, and it deals with human nature in the drawing-room of civilized men and women'. Those who would inquire further into the properties and function of comedy will do well ere they attempt *The Egoist* to read an old essay of Mr Meredith's, in which the uses of comedy are defined and directions are given by which the comic may be recognized. Thus fortified they may proceed to deal with *The Egoist*, and consider for themselves how far Mr Meredith's theory is borne out by his practice. If they read the book as it deserves

[1] Cf. *Tom Jones*, II, i, and v, i.

—and there is not a sentence in it but is worth attention—they will find that, whatever its pretensions as a piece of pure comedy, it contains an abundance of fine wit and humour, remarkable insight into human motive and human character, an infinity of brilliant dramatic speech, a great many passages of reflection and analysis of very high order, and several characters that are among the best of Mr Meredith's creations. The egoist is an egoist in love, and the story is that of his defeat by a true and natural woman. Egoism, as personified in Sir Willoughby Patterne, is confronted with unselfishness, as figured in Vernon Whitford and in Clara Middleton, and is at last reduced to beg for mercy at the hands of one of its victims, Letitia Dale [sic]. That is the situation. Of the way in which Mr Meredith has treated it the public will judge for themselves. The work is so complete and elaborate as to be indescribable in the compass of a newspaper article. It must speak for itself. It will do so to some purpose.

60. Unsigned review, *Saturday Review*

xlviii, 15 November 1879

To a rightly constituted mind there is something almost awful about the position which Mr Meredith occupies among contemporary novelists. He has written some half-dozen books which are the delight of all who know them, and that is probably more than can be said for any, save one or two, of living authors; yet the public at large care so little for him that no one, as far as we know, has yet thought it worth while to ascertain the aspect of his study or his favourite food for breakfast; and, if we are not misinformed, many people believe him to be identical with the Viceroy of India.[1] He is at least to be envied in this, that the intelligent appreciation of a few has not, as in so many other cases, exposed him to the unreasoning, and therefore impertinent, adulation of the many. He has founded no school, he has inspired no enthusiasts. Hereby his readers profit; for we could name more than

[1] That is, Edward Bulwer Lytton; see above, No. 6, headnote.

one writer of fiction, among the most eminent, who, in order to keep abreast with the eulogies of an undiscerning clique, have gradually succeeded in depriving their work of all but money value. Mr Meredith's rate of production perhaps contributes to the same result. When a writer allows some three or four years to elapse between the publication of any two of his works, he leaves time enough for half-a-dozen 'swarmeries' to run their course, and succeeds in becoming himself almost forgotten. 'Cunctando restituit rem';[1] he puts average novel-readers back in the position which they occupy towards new writers whose reputation is still to make.

The faithful few, however, do not so soon forget anyone who, while he has amused them, has also made them think; and thus we fain would hope that the announcement of a new novel by George Meredith is not entirely without significance. It does not, indeed, promise that gentle stimulus to the imagination, that 'purging of the passions', almost unalloyed by intellectual effort, which we are accustomed to associate with the name of a novel, and to think of in connection with armchairs, pipes, and slippers; still less the feast of wines on the lees, very doubtfully refined, which some novelists, chiefly ladies, have led us to expect from them. It is a solid organism which requires three years' gestation; and *The Egoist* is perhaps the most solid work, even to the verge of toughness, which Mr Meredith has ever produced. For this reason we can imagine that it will be even less popular than others of his stories. It is purely a study of character; incident counts for very little in it. There are no exciting episodes as there were in *Beauchamp's Career*, no broad humour as in *Harry Richmond*. If the first few chapters may be regarded as a prologue, the action of the story proper, which begins with the introduction of Clara Middleton, occupies but a few days, and takes place amid the uneventful surroundings of an English country house. The characters are such as we might expect to find there. Sir Willoughby Patterne would probably strike us, if we met him in ordinary society, as a good specimen of the 'landed aristocracy', with rather more cultivation than is always found among the members of that interesting class. He has, however, as we gather from various indications, missed one important branch of education. A story is told of an eminent lawyer who was proposing the health of an equally distinguished member of the same profession. 'My learned friend', he said, in the course of his eulogy, 'when he was a boy, observed to his father, with that perspicacity which has always marked his character, "Papa, I think I

[1] Ennius, quoted by Cicero, *De Officiis*, I, xxiv, 84: 'by delaying restored the state'.

ought to go to a public school". "And why ought you to go to a public school, my boy?" said his father. "Because I should get my—certain portion of the frame—kicked", replied my learned friend, "and it would do me good to get it kicked". I need hardly say that my learned friend never did go to a public school'. Such was also the unlucky fate of Sir Willoughby Patterne. Now, if the kicking be not physically administered in youth, it is almost certain to be morally administered in mature age, and to be proportionately more painful. Of this truth the poor baronet has an instinctive consciousness, which reveals itself in a kind of morbid shrinking from what he calls 'the world'. His declaration against this monster puzzles his betrothed at first; without being frivolous, she has the healthy sympathy for the human race which is characteristic of the girl of eighteen. Women, moreover, do not require to go to a public school. Presently, however, it gives her the first inkling of the real character of this accomplished and generous gentleman. He is, in truth, thoroughly selfish, an 'egoist', as Mr Meredith, adopting current slang, writes the word which used to be 'egotist'. Possibly there may be a shade of difference in the connotation. It is not so much that Sir Willoughby loves the world less, as that he loves himself more; a feeling which is not improbably at the root of a good deal of what gets the credit of being self-effacement.

But the selfish man is not content to live absolutely alone; he must have a world, but it must be a world of his own choosing, ready to admire and approve. Sir Willoughby has two maiden aunts, who perform this function admirably; but maiden aunts do not suffice to a man of spirit. There is also a young lady of the neighbourhood, one Lætitia Dale, who has written poetry in his honour, and is well educated and handsome; but he is sure enough of her. A wife would be a capture from the ranks of the enemy; one of the world brought over to his worship. He has had one bad time of it already with that world. A young lady to whom he was engaged had the bad taste to prefer a mere captain of horse, and jilted the baronet on the eve of their marriage; and the world, as represented by two gossiping old ladies, talked terribly. His second *fiancée*, as we have said, reads his character only too clearly, and struggles to be released before it is too late. At this point the 'comedy' proper begins. A timely exhibition of some wonderful port secures Clara's father to the cause of his prospective son-in-law, and he refuses to listen to her entreaties to leave Patterne Hall, when the state of her affections has become perfectly clear to her. The moves and counter-moves of the two parties to this curious game are traced with inimitable skill. The author's handling of his puppets is most dexterous, and he even succeeds in importing to the reader a portion of his own Olympian indifference. Sir Willoughby has not an amiable trait in his character, and yet we find it impossible to hate him as we hate far less unamiable people in far less clever stories. We could not rejoice if he were to break his neck or be detected in a forgery. It is clear indeed that he must be beaten in the end, otherwise the story would be rather a tragedy than a comedy; but our interest is centred not upon the retribution itself, but upon the way in which it is to come about. The Nemesis comes as usual from an unexpected quarter; it would spoil the reader's pleasure if we were to indicate it further.

The rough outline we have given obviously admits of being filled in with plenty of details, and there is room for a good deal of byplay. Besides Sir Willoughby and his betrothed, the chief players in the game are his cousin Vernon Whitford, a scholar with a story, who at the present time is acting as a kind of secretary to the baronet; the afore-named Lætitia Dale; and, least in size but not in importance, a boy, Crossjay Patterne, son to a distant kinsman, a gallant but unpresentable elderly captain of Marines. He is the one thoroughly delightful personage in the book, and serves by a natural irony of fate to precipitate the issue which the cunningly devised schemes of his elders have only succeeded in confusing. The chorus, so to speak, is composed of elderly ladies. The leader is Mrs Mountstuart Jenkinson, widow of an Indian official, with a knack of smart sayings—a kind of good-natured Mrs Cadwallader—and she is supported by Lady Busshe, the spiteful gossip, and Lady Culmer, her ally; the two maiden aunts serving as a foil to these. Sir Willoughby's friend and prospective 'best man', Colonel De Craye, is introduced chiefly in order to complicate the cross-purposes which render the latter part of the story exceedingly amusing. On the stage we can imagine it most effective; perhaps, for reading, the strain on the reader's intellect required in order to keep all the tangled threads in view at once is almost too great to be pleasant. Add to this that, owing to Mr Meredith's habit of omitting in most cases the usual indication of the speaker, it is not always easy to see whose blunder one is contemplating; and, when there are some four or five people each under a misunderstanding as to the meaning of all the others, this becomes perplexing. Another source of difficulty is one common to all Mr Meredith's novels, and arises from his method of letting the reader know no more about the people than he can see for himself. When they are not actually before us, they are as completely gone as in real life, and we have no opportunity, as we should have in real life, of questioning them as to their thoughts and doings while they were away. The only author who has adopted this method, so far as we know, is M. Flaubert, and he only in one story, the clever, but rather unsatisfactory, *L'Education Sentimentale*, which always reads as if it had been constructed by the process of writing it in *feuilletons* and then suppressing every alternate one.

Though, as we have said, the broad fun of *Harry Richmond* and some parts of *Richard Feverel* is lacking here, there are plenty of touches of Mr Meredith's quaint humour. The description of a luncheon, just when everybody feels that a crisis is impending, as 'a meal of an assembly of mutes and plates that struck the ear like the well-known sound of a collection of offerings in church after an impressive exhortation from the pulpit', while 'a sally of Colonel De Craye's met the reception given to a charity-boy's muffled burst of animal spirits in the silence of the sacred edifice', is very characteristic. So also is the dialogue between Dr Middleton and the maiden aunts when the Doctor, who is, after all, not wholly the slave of old port, is beginning in his turn to appreciate the character of the man to whom he has promised his daughter:

[Quotes xliv, from ' "This," Dr Middleton said to the spinster aunts' to 'expect to be a little looked up to'.]

Those who persevere to the end of the book will find their reward. They have been fairly warned that there will be some hard reading to accomplish. There must be no skipping; the book must be read, not page by page like the ordinary novel, but line by line. We doubt whether *The Egoist* will much widen Mr Meredith's public; but the only regret that it will cause to those who know him will arise from the thought that it will be so long before they meet him again.

61. W. E. Henley, *Academy*

vi, 22 November 1879

For W. E. Henley, see above, No. 57, headnote.

In *The Egoist* the author of *Harry Richmond* and *The Ordeal of Richard Feverel* has produced a piece of literature unique of its kind. He has nothing to learn of comedy in the abstract; he proved that long ago in the brilliant fragment on the comic spirit and its uses read by him at the Royal Institution. But it is a far cry from a proper understanding of comedy to an artistic exemplification of its function and capacities, and they are very few who have attempted the journey with success. Mr Meredith is indisputably of their number. His book is fairly described as a Comedy in Chapters, for it has the same intention and the same relation to actuality and human life as the master-works of Molière. It is an epitome in narrative of a certain well-thumbed chapter treating of the egoist in love, the egoist as he appears and is in his relations with woman; and in the figure of its hero, Sir Willoughby Patterne, Mr Meredith has summed up enough of human nature to make it typical and heroic. Of course Sir Willoughby's story is as conventionally told as Alceste's own. Its personages are not human beings, but compendiums of humanity; their language is not that of life and society pure and simple, but that of life and society as seen and heard through the medium of comedy; the atmosphere they breathe is as artificially rare as that of Orgon's parlour. To live with them you must leave the world behind, and content yourself with essences and abstractions instead of substances and concrete things; and you must forget that such vulgar methods as realism and naturalism ever were. Thus prepared, you will find *The Egoist*, as far as its matter is concerned, a veritable guide to self-knowledge and a treatise on the species of wonderful value and comprehensiveness. As to its manner, that is a very different thing. I can well believe that there are many who will read *The Egoist* with impatience and regret, and many more who will not read it at all. To prepare oneself for its consideration with the

Imposteur and *L'Ecole des Femmes* is a mistake. Mr Meredith's style, it seems to me, has always been his weak point. Like Shakespere, he is a man of genius, who is a clever man as well; and he seems to prefer his cleverness to his genius. It is not enough for him to write a book that is merely great; his book must also be brilliant and personal, or it is no book to him. It may be that in *The Egoist* his reckless individuality is less ill seen than in *Beauchamp* or *Emilia*; it may be that, as the inventor of a Literary *genre*, he may insist on being criticized according to his own canons. Certain it is that in his Comedy in Chapters he has asserted himself more vigorously, if that were possible, than in any other of his works. It is a wilful hurly-burly of wit, wisdom, fancy, freakishness, irony, analysis, humour, and affectation; and you catch yourself wishing, as you might over Shakespere, that Mr Meredith were merely a great artist, and not so diabolically ingenious and sympathetic and well informed and intellectual as he is. Speaking for myself, I have read *The Egoist* with great and ever-increasing interest and admiration. To me it is certainly one of the ablest books of modern years. It is full of passion and insight, of wit and force, of truth and eloquence and nature. Its characters, from Sir Willoughby downwards, are brilliantly right and sound; it has throughout the perfect good breeding of high comedy; there is not a sentence in it, whether of dialogue or analysis or reflection, but is in some sort matter for applause. All the same, I cannot but believe that its peculiarities of form are such as must stand inevitably in the way of its success. I cannot but believe that, with all its astonishing merits, it will present itself to its warmest admirers as a failure in art, as art has hitherto been understood and practised. Mr Meredith has written for himself, and it is odds but the multitude will decline to listen to him. Nor, so far as I can see, is the multitude alone to blame.

62. James Thomson, *Cope's Tobacco Plant*

January 1880; signed 'Sigvat'

For James Thomson, see above, No. 54, headnote.

When the *Tobacco Plant* ventured to assert and prophesy of George Meredith (May, 1879; article, 'An Old New Book'): 'He may be termed, accurately enough for a brief indication, the Robert Browning of our novelists; and his day is bound to come, as Browning's at length has come'; the writer little thought that day would come so soon. He knew that his author had been labouring nobly for about thirty years amidst general neglect, producing magnificent works immediately consigned to 'that oblivion of oblivion which has never had any remembrance'; and he had read in a paper calling itself Literary a review of that same Old New Book, *The Ordeal of Richard Feverel*, treating it as quite a new book, condemning it to the pillory, and pelting it there with such rotten eggs as these: 'It would even be unjust to compare such writings [*sic.*] with the scavengers and dust collectors of ordinary life. The latter are necessary to the cleanliness and health of the community, while the literary refuse and rubbish, &c. . . . a long series of paltry dialogue, of a surprisingly fervent nature. . . . When the author moralizes, he does not halt for words, but chucks them in anyhow, dragging along with him a string of vapid nonsense'.

With the appearance of *The Egoist* has come the dawning of Mr Meredith's day, after a night so long and dreary and dense; during which, while working on undaunted, he must have had sore need of Schopenhauer's consolation: 'The number of the years that elapse between the appearance of a book and its acknowledgment gives the measure of time that the author is in advance of his age. The entire neglect which my work has experienced proves that either I was unworthy of my age, or my age of me'.[1] The first clear light that I saw was reflected from the *Athenæum* (Nov. 1, 1879), in almost the

---

[1] Arthur Schopenhauer (1788–1860), in his essays and his *The World as Will and Idea* (1819), frequently expresses similar sentiments. The exact reference is untraced.

first critique I had seen evincing the critic's familiarity (a familiarity breeding the very opposite of contempt) with all the writer's works. Here are a few rays: 'He has considered sex—the great subject, the leaven of imaginative art—with notable audacity and insight. In his best work he ranks with the world's novelists. He is a companion for Balzac and Richardson, an intimate for Fielding and Cervantes. . . . In the world of man's creation his people are citizens to match the noblest; they are of the aristocracy of the imagination . . . there is no question but *The Egoist* is a piece of imaginative work as solid and rich as any that the century has seen [I would except a very few others, among them two or three of Meredith's own, which are greater simply because their main theme is greater], and that it is not only one of its author's masterpieces, but one of the strongest and most individual performances of modern literature'. This was cheering for a most devout admirer who had been watching through a quarter of a century for the dayspring, confounded by its prodigious delay. Other hills and hillocks caught the new radiance, kindling rapidly as the beacon-fires that announced the fall of Troy, or those others that signalled the approach of the Armada. Thus the *Pall Mall*: 'One of the most striking works of our time. . . . Of extraordinary merit. . . . The work is so complete and elaborate as to be indescribable in the compass of a newspaper article'. Similarly, the *Spectator, Examiner, Daily News,* and I know not how many more. The last-named reflects: 'It will be extremely interesting to see how the English public will take Mr George Meredith's last publication. *The critics Mr Meredith has had always with him. But the critics cannot make a public,* and hence the uncertainty and amusement of watching the *honest English mind* over this last highly seasoned dish which Mr Meredith has placed before it. Will the plain palates relish the exquisite savours of so delicate a wit? Will they appreciate the subtle essences he has cunningly distilled into the dish?' I have italicized the words from which I dissent. Firstly, if by critics the writer means public critics, as surely every reader must understand him to mean, I ask in amaze, When and where have they shown their appreciation of Mr Meredith? I know of but one high class or popular review or magazine which has called attention to his works as a whole—the *British Quarterly,* and that not until last April. And where in the high class and literary weeklies are to be found anything like adequate appreciations of his previous books? Where, in the whole range of our periodical literature throughout the last twenty years, can one discover the tributes justly due to the magnificent genius and insight and energy, the wit and humour and passion of the 1859 *Richard Feverel*, the *Modern Love, and other Poems*, the *Emilia in England*, the *Vittoria*, the *Harry Richmond*, the *Beauchamp's Career*? Why, even of this last, issued in three volumes in 1876, when the author had been twenty-five years before the public, I can find no notice in the 'Contemporary Literature' department of the *Westminster Review*, though I find a whole separate article on Ouida's novels; in the *Athenæum* it is only noticed as one of a batch of six 'Novels of the Week'; in the *Academy* also as one of a batch of six 'New Novels', the critic, no less a man than Dr Littledale, expressing himself thus: 'Though written with much pains, considerable cleverness, and occasional sparkle, it exhibits too much effort. . . . we rise from perusal with the conviction that it is not as a novelist that Mr Meredith can look for a permanent name in literature. As critic or essayist there is probably a career open to him'. Against these I am happy to cite *Cope's Tabacco Plant* (which had not put forth its precious leafage when the earlier books appealed to the dear deaf stupid public), uttering wisdom at its 'Smoke Room Table' (June, 1876) in this wise: 'We have the story of Nevil Beauchamp's love and love-perplexities told as none but George Meredith could tell it, with marvellous subtleties of insight and expression, and framed in scenes such as only he can suggest in a few swift words, instinct with spirit and luminous with beauty'. And again: 'We can cordially commend it and all his works to the meditative smoker, who grudgeth not several slow whiffs over a knotty point when the knot is really worth untying for the sake of that which it involves'. Those knots, which neither the clumsy public nor the practised critics could untie, *Cope*, smoking, unravelled right deftly; and Nicotina, who is Wisdom, is justified of her children. Truly, if the critics have always been devoted to Mr Meredith, it has been with a most secret devotion, never exposed to the vulgar eye; a devotion wonderfully like that of Balzac's discreet Napoleonists after Waterloo and the Restoration, proved unostentatiously by the capital Ns and golden bees embroidered on their braces! (In *La Femme de Trente Ans*, if I remember rightly.) Secondly, the critics *can* make a public, and always *do* make a public if they set themselves to the work; and they do it with the greater ease because the English mind is *not* honest, any more than it is intelligent. The English mind follows the fashion; purchases what is cried up, irrespective of its real value; applauds what is applauded, without knowing the reason why; puts Shakespeare and Milton conspicuous on its bookshelves, disposes the most pious gilt-edged volumes on its drawing-room table, while really only enjoying its paper or its novel of the day. Thus the critics can make a public—that is, a demand—for any book, to the profit of the author; and, if the book be good, to the profit of the community also; for some of the volumes bought for mere fashion's sake must meet eyes that will read them for true love's sake.

Turning now to *The Egoist*, it may, I think, be safely affirmed that Mr Meredith's genius has never shown itself more keen and alert and brilliant, more thoroughly master of all the materials requisite for the work in hand; and that his style has never been more swift and flexible and subtle for piercing to the inmost heart of his personages, through the triple armour of conventionality and deception and self-deception. As the work is a Comedy, it abounds in dialogue; and I have long deemed Mr Meredith's dialogue not only the best of our age, but unsurpassed, if equalled, in our whole literature: it is so spontaneous, unexpected, involuntary, diversified by the moods, the blood, the nerves, the ever-varying circumstances and relations of the interlocutors; differing thus in kind from the dialogue of ordinary novels and plays just as the actual interview between any two or more persons differs from the suppositious interviews which each has mapped out before-hand.

Even were there room here, I should not attempt a summary of the plot: and as for extracts, the whole book is a precious extract, 'distilled thought in distilled words'; the studious reader has in Meredith, as in Browning, the delight—so rare in this age of infinite empty scribbling and interminable chronicling of the smallest of small beer—to find every sentence full-charged, 'every rift loaded with ore', and with ore rich in metal. I must confine myself to merely indicating the chief characters, and giving one or two flying glimpses of quality. The central personage. Sir Willoughby Patterne, the Egoist, who with characteristic unconsciousness furnishes his own title, is, I presume, one of the most thoroughly studied and exhibited types in the whole range of literature. We get him by heart in all his stages and phases, from the highest to the lowest, from the surface to the centre; from his lordly magnificence and despotic bountifulness as the idol of his little world, to his most abject crouching and slinking through the sloughs of falsehood in evasion of the scorn or mockery of that very world he detests and despises. For there are tragic situations and passions here as in most great comedy; as the author well remarks at one point: 'Jealousy had invaded him [Sir W.]. He had boasted himself above the humiliating visitation. If that had been the case, we should not have needed to trouble ourselves much about him. A run or two with the pack of imps [the invisible hounds of the hunting Comic Muse] would have satisfied us'. Then there is Lætitia Dale, 'with a romantic tale on her eyelashes'; poetical, thoughtful, from girlhood the too humble adorer of the Egoist, who graciously permits her unsoliciting worship. After many years of hope deferred and patient suffering, she is an old woman of thirty, with her eyes at length sorely opening or opened; 'she is coming three parts out of her shell, and wearing it as a hood for convenience'. There is Clara Middleton, 'dainty rogue in porcelain', the second betrothed of the Egoist, whose first betrothed, 'the racing cutter', ran away and married another just before the appointed day. Clara is 19 to Sir W.'s 33, and her desperate struggles to get free from the engagement occupy a large portion of the book. There is Vernon Whitford, 'the lean long-walker and scholar, Phœbus Apollo turned fasting friar'; who, drenched in a storm, 'looked lean as a fork with the wind whistling through the prongs'. He is Sir W.'s poor cousin and secretary; high-minded, austere, reticent; young, but with a sad past somewhat like that of George Warrington in *Pendennis*. But in the end he burns out gloriously transfigured. He says of Clara, 'She gives you an idea of the Mountain Echo'. There is Horace de Craye, colonel in the Guards, handsome, ready-witted, Norman-Irishman, who says and does most excellent things, and plays an active part in the intrigue. There is Dr Corney, also Irish, and a little more so, who drives Vernon demented by his eulogy of Clara: 'I'll not call her perfection, for that's a post, afraid to move. But she's a dancing sprig of the tree next it. Poetry's wanted to speak of her. I'm Irish and inflammable, I suppose, but I never looked on a girl to make a man comprehend the entire holy meaning of the word rapturous, like that one. . . . But you're a Grecian, friend Vernon. Now, couldn't you think her just the whiff of an idea of a daughter of a peccadillo goddess'? (Compare the delicate gradations of the Irishry, in part intentional, in diction and thought of the aristocratic guardsman and the jolly doctor, with the Cork brogue broad enough to hang your hat on of Mrs Chump in *Emilia in England*.) There is Crossjay, with whom Vernon charges himself, son of a very poor relative of Sir W., Capt. Patterne of the Marines; 'a rosy-cheeked, round-bodied rogue of a boy of twelve, with the sprights of twelve boys in him, who fell upon meats and puddings, and defeated them, with a captivating simplicity in his confession that he had never had enough to eat in his life. . . . Subsequently he told his host and hostess that he had two sisters above

MEREDITH

his own age, and three brothers and two sisters younger than he: "All
hungry"! said the boy. His pathos was most comical'. Crossjay is 'real
grit', and is of first-rate importance in the plot. There is Mrs Mountstuart Jenkinson, the rich widow, kindly, but with a prompt, keen
tongue, responsible for the character-definitions above quoted: 'Her
word sprang out of her. She looked at you, and forth it came; and it
stuck to you, as nothing laboured or literary could have done'. While
grand phrases are mouthing round about Sir W. on the festival of his
majority, she says, 'You see he has a leg'. There are two maiden aunts,
mere amiable echoes and shadows of their idol the Egoist; and two
titled ladies of the county, representatives of the inquisitive and tattling
world. Lastly, there is the Rev. Dr Middleton, the widowed father of
Clara, a scholar with an independent fortune, whose strength and weakness is love of good living. He is of the family of Drs Folliott and Oppi-
mian [sic], with whom you may have excellent converse in the *Crotchet
Castle* and *Gryll Grange* of the humorous and caustic T. L. Peacock;
but he develops robust individual characteristics. He pronounces upon
another: 'He is a fine scholar, but crotchety, like all men who cannot
take their Port'. *He can* take his Port; and Port can take him (not
overtake him, mind), as Sir W. discovers, and uses it with splendid
effect on the doctor, with terrible recoil upon poor Clara. The richest
chapter for jolly humour (I speak not of the subtle and recondite
humour) in the whole work is the second of Vol. II, 'An Aged and a
Great Wine': the gradual mellowing, within the limits of clerical
decorum, of the doctor under the influence of this, administered by the
astute and patient designing Egoist, is unsurpassable. I must quote a
little, to gain for this scanty notice the benediction, 'All's well that
ends well':—

[Quotes xx, from ' "I am going down to my inner cellar" ' to 'He was
melted', with omissions.]

Wherewith I commend the good reader to a book which he will find
as well worth sipping slowly, in long-lingering relish of its consummate
fragrance and flavour and cordial potency, as the Rev. doctor found
that noble nonagenarian Port; Senatorial Port! deep-sea deep!

63. Unsigned review, *New Quarterly Magazine*

N.S., iii, January 1880

No summary can do justice to the cleverness of Mr Meredith's characters. The Egoist lives for himself; but the views he takes of that self and
the duties of his position are so lofty as to be ideal. Called by Providence
to be the greatest magnate in his county, it is not for him to frustrate
the intentions of fate by seeking the society of those who are his equals,
or possibly his superiors. A baronet, he mistrusts the peerage. London
he feels to be destructive of all individuality, but at Patterne Hall his
talents have room to do themselves justice. There he is in his element,
worshipped by the country-side in general, and by Lætitia Dale, the
daughter of a half-pay officer, in particular. From childhood she has
known him, and taken him for her hero; nor was he ever slow to return
an appreciation so sympathetic. She alone makes him feel the full
measure of his powers; in a way, she inspires as well as worships [—] a
combination irresistibly flattering. If her charms were of a more
conspicuous order, he would marry her; but she is not queenly enough
to be mistress of Patterne Hall. Her function in life is to be his counsellor
and friend, perhaps, as she is penniless, the governess of his children.
In short, he keeps up a standing flirtation with her, ringing the changes
of his conversation on three eternal topics—love, friendship and duty.
She, poor soul, resigns herself; now and again she cannot prevent
the unquenchable spark of hope from blazing up, but it is herself and
not him she blames for this. Meanwhile, Sir Willoughby finds other
ladies more presentable, but less satisfactory. As a young man he had
been jilted most unaccountably. Clara Middleton, the choice of his
mature years, is incapable of such conduct; and yet he finds in her, too,
a strange grain of perversity. Mr Meredith conceives an egoism which
passes muster in every relation of life, except the all-important one.
As a lover Sir Willoughby is charming till accepted; and then somehow
he appears a trifle unsympathetic. Gradually the girl finds out that it is

MEREDITH

impossible for him to understand any single thought of hers. He either
ignores her words, or blandly twists them to an echo of his own sentiments. In desperation she implores him to release her. He replies that
with her he has no fears of the future. Nevertheless he has many doubts
which he confides to Lætitia Dale. Clara's rebellion at last becomes so
open that the neighbours begin to give marks of significant curiosity.
Sir Willoughby, whose tortures are now crowned by jealousy,
would let her go if only he could find some master-stroke to save his
self-esteem. To be known as a twice-jilted man is more than he can
bear. At last he resolves to punish the ungrateful girl by casting her off
in favour of Lætitia, and so to emerge faithless from the difficulty, but
not a victim. To his amazement Lætitia refuses him; and next day,
when, as a last resource, he resumes his claim upon Clara, he finds that
the secret has leaked out. The neighbourhood comes swarming in to
learn the truth about his rumoured change of mistress. He has to face
them, knowing in his heart he is a thrice-jilted man. The book ends
with a fine stroke of dramatic justice. Lætitia Dale at length agrees to
marry him, but before doing so tells him the true story of her life. The
better part of her is dead; it died gradually with her illusions. She
believed in him once: she knows him now. He has made her an egoist,
and she can marry without love.

While Lætitia Dale's history exposes the cruel side of egoism, Clara
Middleton brings to light the ridiculousness of it. An admirable contrast
to Lætitia, she makes a delightful heroine. With her sense of fun, and
healthy instincts of liberty and enjoyment, she is more than a match for
twenty egoists. The distress Sir Willoughby causes her is nothing to
the agonies she makes him undergo. Mr Meredith, though he has
created these two charming pictures of womanhood, does not allow
himself to be diverted from his main object—the pursuit of egoism.
Indeed, he hunts down the quarry somewhat too ruthlessly for the
patience of the readers, who are kept in suspense as to the fate of the
heroines, while Sir Willoughby is made to dance for their amusement
on the red-hot plates of perplexity. But though the author has made a
mistake in fixing the reader's sympathies elsewhere than on his central
personage, he atones for it by the completeness with which he carries
out his representation. In another point Mr Meredith's treatment
slightly fails. His determination to exhibit Sir Willoughby as the type
of self-love makes him forget to put the reader in a position to understand the feelings of the personages in the story towards its hero. They
regard him as a paragon; the reader, who possesses the key to his

character and knows him to be a wretch, is puzzled by their want of perception. Mr Meredith, it is true, furnishes a sort of explanation of this difficulty through the mouthpiece of one of his characters, who has guessed the truth. 'The miracle is,' he moralizes, 'that the world won't see. But the world is a piggy-wiggy world for the wealthy fellow who fills a trough for it, and that Sir Willoughby has always very sagaciously done'. None the less, the fact remains, that the qualities which hid the egoism from the superficial eyes of the world are not dwelt on, or are mentioned with a touch of irony which prevents their producing the desired effect. In short, the situation which exists at the opening of the novel requires a certain effort of the imagination before it can be fully realized; but there is hardly a work of fiction which does not make some such call upon the reader's forbearance.

Mr Meredith's style is a cross between Mr Carlyle's and Mr Browning's, if such a compound be imaginable. It is a nut confessedly hard to crack. He is so artificial as to seem to have lost the power of using straightforward language. The simplest statement becomes an epigram under his hands; his epithets contain the pith of elaborate metaphors; his metaphors are like the bursting of rockets, which light up new aspects of familiar scenes in a flash of fantastic light. The objections to such a method of composition are obvious. It is perhaps enough to say that it is apt to be unintelligible. We venture to quote, somewhat invidiously, the only passage which fairly baffles all comprehension:—

Who, [says the notable humorist, in allusion to this book (of Egoism)], who can studiously travel through sheets of leaves, now capable of a stretch from the Lizard to the last few pulmonary strips and shreds of leagues, dancing on their toes for cold—explorers tell us—and catching breath by good luck, like dogs at bones about a table, on the edge of the Pole? Inordinate, unvaried length, sheer longinquity, staggers the heart, ages the very heart of us at a view. And how if we manage finally to print one of our pages on the crow-scalp of the solitary outside?

Some effort is obviously required to enjoy an author capable of producing such a passage as the above. Yet the reader of good courage cannot fail to find himself richly compensated for his pains. If he read carefully, he will find not only that every sentence has a meaning, but also a definite purpose. He will admire the effect produced by a number of minute touches. As he enters into the spirit of the author, he will enjoy a sense of surprise in discovering for himself the treasures of wit and imagination wrapped up in the hard sentences. So far as popularity is concerned, Mr Meredith's manner may be said to be his only enemy; but no one who takes the trouble to enjoy this admirable book can say that style is his weak point.

In literature, however, popularity may be taken to mean that an author is admired on trust by the crowd of readers who are incapable of real appreciation. Mr Meredith has never enjoyed fame of this sort, though his reputation has always stood high with a small audience; but *The Egoist* is so unmistakably good, that we should not wonder if it were elevated to a position of embarrassing honour, on a pinnacle confronting even those occupied by *Middlemarch* and *Daniel Deronda*. We mention these names to indicate the standard by which the book should be judged, and not for the sake of instituting comparisons, which, except in the case of an imitator and his model, are always misleading. The originality of *The Egoist* cannot fail to surprise the reader. Mr Meredith has made a sort of discovery in the art of novel-writing, and he seems to have wished to denote this fact by his subordinate title 'A Comedy in Chapters', as well as by the elaborate disquisition upon comedy which forms the introduction. Roughly paraphrased, his theories amount to this: Modern society has exhausted the freshness and wonder of the world, and suffers in consequence from monotony. As the bloom of youth wears off, men find themselves utterly bored, and long for some point of view which will restore their interest in people and things they know only too thoroughly. This disease—*la maladie du siècle*, about which the French are so mysteriously emphatic —it must be observed, is a real and not an imaginary illness. Brisk people who deride it as the result of dyspepsia, fail to perceive that they are able to laugh, not because their digestions are good, but because they have discovered the point of view that suits them, either that of sport, or business, or family. For those who cannot thus escape, art is the specific, since to seek help from science in this predicament is as if 'tired pedestrians should mount the engine-box of headlong trains'. Of all forms of this remedy comedy is the best, not only showing us how to regard the world, but supplying the tonic that makes the spectacle exhilarating; it cures as well as demonstrates. In opposition to the spirit of comedy Mr Meredith places that of analysis and realism, which can find nothing in human nature without the help of 'the circular glow of the watchmaker's eye to raise in bright relief minutest trains of evidence'. Analysis only aggravates the disease by exhibiting to the patient elaborate spider's webs spun from his own inside. The one method looks at men from their own point of view; the other, that of comedy, regards them from an abstract station of its own, and concentrates in a single type the result of years of observation.

Thus far Mr Meredith is only following the lead of Molière. The 'Egoist' is a type in the same way as 'Harpagon', but with an important difference. Molière exhibited certain qualities in the broadest form they could be made to assume, without regarding the modifications under which they must have been more or less disguised in real life. Such a representation of character suffers from a want of light or shade, a fault Mr Meredith avoids. Instead of taking egoism in a rudimentary stage, while still capable of infinite shades of variation in every direction, he presents the vice in its most complex and highly developed aspect. In savage societies egoism is a virtue, being nothing but the instinct of self-defence. As civilization advances, it becomes a frankly brutal vice, subordinating every consideration to its desires. It is in this, their obtrusive phase, that Molière delighted to paint qualities. Mr Meredith prefers a more subtle manifestation of his subject. Sir Willoughby Patterne, the Egoist, is the descendant of many generations of egoists, all of whom in turn have contributed their quota to the formation of his character. To such a pitch of refinement has self-love attained in him, that, so far from adopting his pleasures as his rule in life, the fatuous wretch conceives himself to be a model of devotion to duty. His egoism is like colour-blindness; it is impossible to convince him that the world is not what he sees it to be. Conceived in this spirit, the egoistical hero has all the interest of a distinct individuality, without ceasing to be a type. We pay Mr Meredith a high compliment when we say he enables the reader to understand what is meant by Comedy, in the best and fullest sense of the word.

64. Margaret Oliphant, *Blackwood's Edinburgh Magazine*

cxxviii, September 1880

For Margaret Oliphant, see above, No. 47, headnote.

The author of *The Egoist* holds an exceptional position in literature. He is not a favourite with the multitude, but if that is any compensation, he is a favourite with people who are supposed to know much better than the multitude. His works come before us rarely; but when they do come, there is a little tremor of expectation in the air. The critics pull themselves up, the demigods of the newspapers are all on the alert. It is understood that here is something which, though in all probability caviare to the general, it will be a creditable thing, and a point in a man's favour to admire. Like Mr Rossetti's pictures, there is a certain ignorance, a certain want of capacity involved in the absence of appreciation. Not to know Mr Meredith is to argue yourself unknown; and *The Egoist* has been regarded with a great deal of respectful admiration. It is a book which sets out with very high pretensions, and claims to represent to us the leading qualities of the human race in an exceptionally clear and animated way. It is 'a comedy in narrative', challenging comparison with the masterpieces in that different branch of art; and even among these masterpieces, a certain selection must be made to justify the comparison, for the unity of its sentiment indicates such comedies as the *Avare* and the *Misanthrope*, rather than the livelier works of mingled interest with which (not to speak of Shakespeare) Goldsmith and Sheridan have furnished us. This, it will be seen, is rather an appalling ordeal for a book in three large volumes, with scarcely an incident from beginning to end, all turning upon the question who is to marry Sir Willoughby Patterne, and occupied with the exhibition of that gentleman's character to the world. Mr Meredith informs us in his prelude, which ought to have been called the prologue, that in order to elucidate the Book of Earth, the lore of human self-estimation and wisdom, Art is the specific.

[Quotes 'Prelude', from 'The chief consideration for us' to 'in one comic sitting'.]

After this prelude and promise the author goes on, as we have said, to three huge volumes, made up of a thousand conversations, torrents of words in half lines, continued, and continued, and continued, till every sentiment contained in them is beaten to death in extremest extenuation, and the reader's head aches, and his very bones are weary. The first volume is fine, the second tedious, the third beyond all expression wearisome. Sir Willoughby Patterne is an egotist of the sublimest type. How he makes everybody and everything subservient to him, keeping in hand a mild and gentle worshipper who lives close by, and is always ready to burn incense to him, while he engages himself to marry, one after the other, two younger, richer, more beautiful heroines; how he pets and applauds a humble hero in the Marines, who has glorified the name of Patterne in a far-off war, but says 'not at home' when that hero appears in the shape of an elderly and shabby lieutenant; how he permits his poor cousin to take the expenses of that lieutenant's boy, and himself administers half-crowns and crowns, but will take no responsibility for the little dependant; how he disgusts the beautiful young heroine who has hastily pledged herself to accept him, so that she struggles through two long volumes in her attempts to get free from him before the eyes of his worshippers, till one by one they fall away, and even the romantic and poetical Letitia [*sic*] has her eyes opened; how at last he is cast upon the compassion of this first love, a poor diminished creature, found out on all sides; and how even Letitia [*sic*] refuses, and will only consent to have him on the most unrelenting and continued pressure. This is the story. If it had been made a comedy of, in three moderate Acts, instead of three large volumes, it might have been, with the amount of power expended, a fine one. But to tell us of an art which 'condenses whole sections into a sentence', and volumes in a character, and afterwards to serve up this slender story in about a thousand pages of long-winded talk, is the most curious and barefaced contradiction. We do not think we ever found ourselves astray in such a tangle of conversation in all our experience: true, the action of a comedy is conducted by conversation, but not, ye gods! in such bucketsful. To have the lively successions, the rapid movement, the clear-cut lines of a good comedy suggested to us, and

MEREDITH

then to read, and read, and read, till the brain refuses further comprehension, and only a spectrum of broken lines of print remains upon its blurred surface, is cruel. For a week or two after we complete the book we find ourselves haunted with that shadow of conversations, thus—

[Quotes xxii, from 'She will not be bridesmaid' to ' "Do I wish that" '?]

But this is an easy specimen. It is like silly verse without the rhyme; the talk in which each speaker occupies a line and a half is more painful still. Even now, at a happy distance from our first reading, we have but to think of the book, and lo! the air is marked all over with those adumbrations, with all manner of jerks and dashes, and notes of interrogation added on.

At the same time, we cannot but allow that the entire self-absorption of Sir Willoughby Patterne has a certain sublimity in it. If there was but half of it, and still better if there was but a third part, it would be powerful. A man who is his own law, and who never deviates from one magnificent principle of self-reference, can scarcely be without a certain force. The incident of the lieutenant's visit referred to above, will be as good a specimen as any of the manner of man. Sir Willoughby, on hearing of the marine's gallantry, had sent him a present and a complimentary letter, being intent on taking for himself and his name all the credit possible. He went so far as to invite the unknown cousin to Patterne Hall. But one day, while he is walking on the stately terrace with his betrothed and various other fine people, he sees in the distance 'a thickset man' advancing to the door of the hall.

[Quotes i, from 'His brief sketch of the creature' to 'lady did not reply'.]

This is Sir Willoughby at the sublime point; but by-and-by, when he quotes page upon page in a wordy attempt to convince his second betrothed lady (Miss Durham having saved herself abruptly by a runaway match) that the release she asks is impossible, all the grandeur of his attitude is lost, and the merest stupidity of unreason takes hold upon the self-seeker. Even his pride does not take fire. It is roused by the revolting idea that anyone should wish to be free from him, but only into exasperating attempts to ignore the lady's meaning, or endless adjurations on the subject of fidelity. As for Clara Middleton, his *fiancée*, she is almost equally wearisome in the perpetual twitter and flutter of her wings, as she struggles for the release which he will not give: she half runs away, then returns again, and talks, talks—in the

238

library, in the laboratory, to half-a-dozen confidants, to her father, and to Sir Willoughby himself, protesting that she will not marry him, but never venturing to break the bond for herself. The first effort for freedom is made in the first volume; but it is not till the very end of the third, and after arguments and discussions innumerable, that the bond is broken and Clara is allowed to go free. All the devices of the man who will not acknowledge to himself that he is not the idol of all his world, to save his own pride, fatigue us hugely before we are done with them. Mr Meredith has fallen into the reverse error from that of those novelists who blacken all their secondary characters in order to have an intense white light of perfection upon their hero or heroine. All the people surrounding Patterne House and all the guests in it, and even the two meek aunts, Eleanor and Isabella, see through the hero and all his little motives, and the centre of self in which he lives and moves, before we are done with him. His dependants are not taken in by his profound self-worship. He is 'jilted' twice. Letitia Dale [sic], who began by worshipping, accepts his hand, only, so to speak, by force, declaring that she does not and cannot love him. This seems to us as little true to nature as the existence of one black swan among a multitude of crows. The Egoist who takes nobody in is a most feeble specimen of his kind. In a general way, even the worst specimens impose more or less upon their surroundings, and it is very rare indeed where there is not one out-and-out believer to keep the self-worshipper in countenance. But Sir Willoughby has not a creature left to stand by him. The stupidest of his retainers sees through him—even his old aunts. Mr Meredith, indeed, partly justifies this by promising us, in his high-flown prelude, the pathos without which he says 'no ship can now set sail'. 'The Egoist surely inspires pity', he says. But the universal abandonment of the hero is too much. A man who makes so ineffable a fool of himself, so disgusts everybody, and exposes himself to be kicked all round by every humiliating toe that chooses to point itself at him, is by far too poor a creature to be raised to the eminence of a pattern egoist. He is in reality, after the first volume, a very poor counterfeit, not worthy in any way of his *rôle*.

And it is hard to have to repeat to a writer of such reputation as Mr Meredith, and one who is the favourite of the clever, the pet of the superior classes, *goûté* above all by those who confer fame—what it is so common to say to all the poor little novelists (chiefly female) who are rated in the newspapers about the devices to which they are driven to furnish forth their third volume—but unpleasant as the duty is, we must fulfil it. Had the author of *The Egoist* been superior, as he ought to be, to that tradition, his book would have been infinitely better. Had he confined it to one volume, it might have been a remarkable work. As it is, it will do no more than hang in that limbo to which the praise of a coterie, unsupported by the world, consigns the ablest writer when he chooses to put forth such a windy and pretentious assertion of superiority to nature and exclusive knowledge of art. Weakness may be pardonable, but weakness combined with pretention is beyond all pity. Mr Meredith's fault, however, is perhaps less weakness than perversity and self-opinion. He likes, it is evident, to hear his own voice—as indeed, for that matter, most of us do. If 'the water were roasted out of him', according to the formula of the great humorist whom he quotes in his prelude, there might be found to exist a certain solid germ of life and genius; but so long as he chooses to deluge this in a weak, washy, everlasting flood of talk, which it is evident he supposes to be brilliant, and quaint, and full of expression, but which, in reality, is only cranky, obscure, and hieroglyphical, he will do that genius nothing but injustice.

POEMS AND LYRICS OF THE JOY OF EARTH

1883

65. Unsigned review, *St. James's Gazette*

vi, 25 June 1883

St. James's Gazette was a Conservative journal begun in May 1880 under the editorship of Frederick Greenwood. (See above, No. 59, headnote.)

Whosoever knows them knows that Mr Meredith's novels are marked by great and rare qualities; but he makes so constant, so urgent a demand on the imagination, his thought is so subtle and penetrating, and his modes of expression are sometimes so dark with excess of light that he does not succeed very well with the 'ordinary reader'. And he is as brilliantly and carelessly exacting in his poetry as in his prose. In the present volume there are passages which will not be easily mastered even by those who are most eager to get at the heart of them; and there are not a dozen poems in the book the full meaning of which can be immediately apprehended. But true literature is something more than matter for amusement; and Mr Meredith's poems, like his novels, amply reward the study they demand. They are the work of a man of genius, who looks at the world steadily and independently, and who possesses the secret of helping and consoling his readers while he spurs them to the exercise of their better faculties.

A deeply pessimistic note has been the chief characteristic of much of the poetry that has appeared lately in England, and in most other countries; and even in these 'poems and lyrics of the joy of earth' there are touches of sadness. All the same it is clear that Mr Meredith is one of those poets who ask no more of the world than it is capable of giving, and who find in it inexhaustible sources of happiness. Although there is much that is new in his manner of treating his themes, there is nothing new in the themes themselves. They are the pleasures that spring from appreciation of the forms, colours, voices, and processes of nature: from love, from the wise government of passion, from the pursuit of worthy social ends. Such pleasures are familiar enough; but one of the functions of the poet is to reveal the meanings that may lie hidden in familiar things; and Mr Meredith's teaching is that if men cannot find their ideal in the circumstances which they are actually placed, they may miss it altogether. In this respect he resembles Goethe, who, with all his love of 'culture', is still the most persuasive modern teacher who has undertaken to disclose the significance of the common facts of life. It is not merely in his aims that Mr Meredith reminds us of Goethe: some qualities of the work of the two poets are also akin. Both produce the same impression of perfect sincerity; writing only of what they have seen, and felt, and know. Mr Meredith shares, too, Goethe's art of giving an appearance of distinction even to the humblest subjects: while both poets are in a certain sense 'realists', they irradiate the real world with the light of their own fancy and emotion.

Mr Meredith's novels revealed long ago the remarkable force and insight with which he is able to depict the passion of love. His heroes and heroines are not far removed above the level of humanity, nor are their adventures strange. Yet in the story of their affections Mr Meredith finds means to produce the effects of the noblest kind of romance. In poetry Mr Meredith exhibits in still larger measure this striking characteristic. Both in *Richard Feverel* and in *Vittoria* he sometimes almost strains the resources of the language to give form to what cannot be adequately expressed in prose. But passion is never too ardent for one who is a master of poetic methods; and in Mr Meredith's love poems there is a warmth and a glow unsurpassed by any contemporary writer. Of the sights and sounds of nature he hardly writes as a mere observer. It is rather as if he shared the life of the outer world, in which he finds nothing too small for his sympathies. Most imaginative writers interpret the spirit of nature by systematic description; but this method is too tedious for Mr Meredith's eager temper. What he has seen he reproduces by a few bold and rapid strokes; and he is so happy in his choice of epithets that those he selects almost invariably suggest a complete and vivid picture.

Mr Meredith does not deal directly with subjects which belong rather to philosophy than to poetry, but in nearly all his poems there are hints and indications of deep reflection. And he is as fresh and stimulating in the presentation of ideas as in the expression of feeling. Carlyle himself was not more impressed by the conception that man forms part of a system which is controlled by unalterable laws; but Mr Meredith differs from Carlyle in thinking less of the conditions in which the order of the universe works disaster than of those which bring good to men. And men interest him even more than nature; he has a profound and curious knowledge of the forms of evil which spring from 'egoism'; but his perception of these things does not lead him to indulge in Carlyle's scorn. He has a poet's faith in the reality of 'progress'; by which he means chiefly the slow evolution of a social sentiment which may in the end be strong enough, without depriving passion of any of its attractive qualities, to bring it into accord with reason. Mr Meredith holds with the Positivists that the individual owes to the race a debt which the utmost labour in its service cannot fully pay; and to this idea, which is essentially a poetic one, he gives a lustre it does not possess even in the brilliant rhetoric of Mr Frederick Harrison.[1]

When we pass from the general characteristics of Mr Meredith's poetry to particular poems, it is not difficult to select the one in which he exhibits most completely the resources of his genius. The most beautiful thing in this book is 'Love in the Valley', a poem of which there is a sketch in a volume 'now extinct'. Mr Meredith describes the measure as 'trochaic, variable in short syllables according to stress of the accent'. Without seeming to praise it extravagantly, it would be hard to do justice either to the diction of this exquisite poem or to the variety and beauty of its images. Pure genius and nothing less is at work in every stanza of this most finished and yet most spontaneous piece of verse; which, if its author had done nothing else, would have secured for him an enduring place among English poets. The natural scenes depicted in the poem are sketched swiftly, but with such brightness and precision that we see them as distinctly as we see the radiant figure that moves among them—a figure gathering primroses on the hill 'with her fair companions', tending the flowers in her garden, tilting the milk-pitcher for thirsty boys at play, laughing, singing, and at last made serious by the approach of one who becomes 'the light and living of her eyes'.

---

[1] Frederick Harrison (1831–1923), critic and student of philosophy, was the leading exponent of Positivism in England, and from 1880 to 1905 President of the English Positivist Committee.

In 'The Day of the Daughter of Hades' there are elements of deep pathos; for Skiageneia is permitted to enjoy only a glimpse of the earth, and Callistes, worn by love for her, 'withers rathe, dry to his prime'. But in the incidents of her 'holiday of delight' Mr Meredith describes with splendid effect the influences which may give worth to human life; and there are lines of extraordinary energy and beauty in the passage in which we are told of the coming of 'the god of implacable brow' to bear his daughter back to the nether world. The story of Melampus, who in reward for his kindness to a brood of snakes was endowed with the capacity of reading the secrets of nature, is one of the most suggestive creations of Greek fancy; and Mr Meredith makes it the subject of a poem in which he finely shows to how many facts otherwise inexplicable we may find the key in sympathy. In another poem he celebrates the years in which Phœbus served in the fields of Admetus; and it may, perhaps, be read as an allegoric representation of the power of the poetic spirit to dignify the associations of daily toil. Few poets would have courage to attempt a new study of the lark's flight and song; but Mr Meredith's 'The Lark Ascending' must be read with admiration, even after Shelley's famous ode.

66. Unsigned review, *Pall Mall Gazette*

xxxviii, 29 June 1883

When this article was written the *Pall Mall Gazette* was being edited by Meredith's close friend, John Morley (1838–1923), later Viscount Morley of Blackburn, a Radical politician, journalist and author.

The greatest poets of the world are popular by a kind of sublime commonplace. They transform the common motives and passions of man's life into a higher meaning, without losing their natural simplicity and obviousness. But this gift belongs only to a few, nor is it always equally present even to those who have it. Perhaps no wrong is done to others if we say that it is constant in Homer and Shakspeare alone. Many poets touch it at their best, but are not sure of it; Wordsworth is a striking example of great success mixed with great failure. Others, again, are popular by artistic commonplace, if we may so call the expression of ideas of average quality, taking the standard from the audience to whom they are addressed, in a pleasing and appropriate form. Longfellow furnishes an almost perfect type of this kind of popularity. Great skill and equability of execution are needed to redeem it from sinking into vulgarity; and failures (quite compatible, however, with temporary success) are many. There are yet other poets who, having their own ideas and their own forms of imagination, and not being Homer or Shakspeare, cannot express themselves in a universal form. And these, though true and it may be great poets, never become popular at all. Thus Milton is classical, but not popular. Ask an educated Englishman at random what was the great vision of the guarded mount, and he shall stare and gasp. Yet *Lycidas* is beyond all rational question one of the most perfect of English poems. This quality, or rather absence of the popular quality, has many diverse roots and forms. It may be a stately elaboration of scholarship, as with Milton, or it may be, as with Shelley, a lyrical exquisiteness that lives in an air of its own, which the reader must learn to breathe. Or it may be that the poet's mind has peculiar lines of working, and will not run in the brain-ruts of our accustomed traffic. Such is Mr Browning's case to a great extent; though often he cuts the knot in masterful fashion, breaking out upon us as it were and dragging us his own way by sheer force of intellect. And in these cases the difficulty is greatest. For what is required for understanding the poet is not merely scholarship, nor attuning oneself to a certain mood, but a subtler intellectual sympathy, which nature may happen to provide, but otherwise must be compassed with more or less effort. And the requisite effort being different in every reader, and widely different views being held on the whole matter of the function of poetry, opinions are pretty sure to differ whether the effort is worth undertaking.

Mr George Meredith, whose new volume of lyrics is the text of these reflections, is of the poets who all but formally renounce popularity. The reader who is content with Longfellow and becomes restive at Mr Browning will find Mr Meredith intolerably difficult. But the lover of poetry will study his poems and come back to them, for they have true fire and invention, and admirable workmanship, and moreover (no light thing to say nowadays) there is never a false or unhealthy note in them. Why, then, is Mr Meredith's verse difficult? for we must admit the difficulty. We think it is so for much the same reasons as his prose. It is not that single words or phrases, as a rule, are obscure, or that violent constructions abound. But there is a constant presence of something slightly unexpected, an accumulation of unfamiliar shapes and sequences. We are dazzled by a succession of shifting lights, coming from points a little off the usual range of sight. The hardest ascent for the mountaineer is not that where the most difficult places have to be climbed, but that on which there are no easy places. And something of this kind is the effect of Mr Meredith's work. Those who can really study poetry will nevertheless find their reward.

The title of the volume is not further explained than by the general tone which runs through the poems, but that explains enough. Mr Meredith restores an old aim of the poet, now in some danger of being forgotten, that of celebrating the good which man has in that he simply lives and shares in the seasons. The chief poem in the book, and to our mind the finest, 'The Day of the Daughter of Hades', sets forth this idea by way of a myth—a myth which, we believe, is new, and certainly is beautiful. Skiageneia, the daughter of Hades and Persephone, visits the upper earth by stealth, when her parents go up for the meeting of Persephone with Demeter:

> Our Lady of the Sheaves
> And the Lily of Hades, the sweet
> Of Enna—

and Callistes, a mortal youth, saluting the maiden of the underworld as a kind of divine vision, leads her through field and wood, delighting in the richness of summer, the corn, olive, and vine. From the hill they look down over pastures and lake and sea; she is glad to talk of the country gods, of the nymphs and of Pan; but she cares not for cities and war, and will not hear of the slain of Troy, whom she knows all too well. Still further they mount, and she sings in her new joy:

[Quotes 'The Day of the Daughter of Hades', st. viii, ll. 35–53; 68–9.]

But Hades has lost his child, and comes up in darkness and storm to carry her home. The description, full of power and truth to nature, is too continuous to be quoted piecemeal.

Altogether the poem is of strong and fine temper, and a notable addition to a kind of serious lyric in which few have excelled. Another classical poem, 'Phœbus with Admetus', is remarkable for the invention of the metre, which is new and, when once the rhythm is grasped, very musical. For the illustration of this we must tear the last stanza from its context:—

[Quotes 'Phœbus with Admetus', st. viii.]

Another metrical experiment is 'Melampus', which in another form shows the true poet as above all things a student of nature. For absolute beauty of verse, however, both these must yield to 'Love in a Valley', a series of stanzas meant—if we may judge from a slight typographic indication—to be read as a *liederkreis* rather than as a continued poem. Almost at random, in the difficulty of choosing, we take these two:

[Quotes 'Love in the Valley', st. ii and xxv.]

The 'primrose mountain' is an example of a difficulty not uncommon in Mr Meredith's work: he expects much knowledge and observation of his reader. To many this will probably be unintelligible. But the fact is that the colour of young beech-leaves against an illuminated sky is that of the primrose, without a shade's difference; and whoever has noted this will understand Mr Meredith at once. As to the substance, 'Love in a Valley' is that rare thing in poetry, a love-poem of wholly direct and simple motive, which is neither trivial, conceited, nor cloying. 'The Lark Ascending' is not new in metre, and can neither be analyzed nor quoted from. But it is a true and almost perfect lyric, and the reader who is deeply pleased by it may know that the heart of English poetry is open to him.

We started with a kind of warning: have we not belied it? After all we have said, we think it not superfluous. The first poem in the volume, 'The Woods of Westermain', should be read last; otherwise many a reader may be scared by its fleeting fancies and abrupt transitions, or by the spectres and 'scaly dragon-fowl' that haunt its lines: yet to come to fields

> Where old-eyed oxen chew
> Speculation with the cud

is worth some adventure and perplexity. Also there is a certain 'Ballad of Fair Ladies in Revolt', which needs more than one reading to grasp its drift as a whole. The volume is closed with a small collection of sonnets, not all of them connected with the general idea that pervades the rest of the poems. One of the most perfect in execution is 'The Star

Sirius', with which we may leave off. The classicism of 'godly night' is daring, but justifiable and effective:

[Quotes 'The Star Sirius'.]

67. Mark Pattison, *Academy*

xxiv, 21 July 1883

Mark Pattison (1813–84), scholar, essayist and critic, was Rector of Lincoln College, Oxford, from 1861. He contributed to *Essays and Reviews* (1860). According to Mrs Humphrey Ward (*A Writer's Recollections*, 1918), Pattison and his wife were enthusiastic about Meredith in 1874.

This is one of the most remarkable, perhaps the most remarkable, of the volumes of verse which have been put out during the last few years. But, indeed, the name of the author is a sufficient guarantee that so it would be; Mr George Meredith is known to be little given to offering his readers that which is common.

Mr Meredith is well known, by name, to the widest circle of readers —the novel-readers. By name, because his name is a label warning them not to touch. They know that in volumes which carry that mark they will not find the comfortable conventionalities and paste diamonds which make up their ideal of 'life'. Worse than this, Mr Meredith's prose requires attention—an impertinent requirement on the part of a novelist. Everybody knows that we go to a novel in order that we may occupy a vacant mind without giving attention.

To a higher, and vastly smaller, circle of readers, Mr Meredith's stories—*The Ordeal of Richard Feverel, Emilia in England, Vittoria, The Egoist*—are known as creations, singular without being eccentric, but whose singularity is marked by an imaginative presentment rather than by any special attraction of the characters and events presented. There is an atmosphere of poetry about the doings of his personages which gives us a happy fairy-land sensation, even when, as is often the case, we do not much care for the doings themselves. The circle (a select one) of the readers of these novels, know that Mr Meredith is a poet—in prose. Perhaps some of them may not know that he is a poet in the more usual acception of the term. Two little ventures of the usual 'minor poetry' class, some thirty or more years back, had the inevitable fate of such volumes, came into the hands of but few, and were soon forgotten even by them. As Mr Meredith does not include these poems in the list of his works which he has allowed to be given on the fly-leaf of the present volume, perhaps he is now unwilling to own them, and desires to have them regarded as 'juvenilia'. Any comparison of the present George Meredith with the George Meredith who had not yet stamped his quality upon *The Shavings* [*sic*] *of Shagpat* would be waste of labour. Yet I could almost fancy that more than one of the pieces in the new volume are developments of germs deposited in the earlier epoch of thought.

What is true of a whole poetic career is also true of any volume of collected pieces composed at long intervals. No one, not even a critic, is always at his best. But in poetry we may go further, and say that the best of any poet is so rare and costly that it is indeed 'paucorum [*sic*] horarum'. Take, *e.g.*, the six volumes of Wordsworth's *Poetical Works*, and count the pieces—nay, rather, the lines—in which Wordsworth is at Wordsworth's best. We may strike out everything written after 1809, the most of it being not only below Wordsworth, but absolutely unworthy of him. All that is instinct with vital power in Wordsworth might be contained in a volume of much less compass than Mr Matthew Arnold's *Selections*. A few sheets of letterpress would give us all that can live of Wordsworth—all except the Wordsworthian 'Self'; and to distil this essence we must have the whole of the nine books of the *Excursion* and the whole of the fourteen books of the *Prelude*.

It is, therefore, no disparagement to say of the poems in the present volume that they are unequal in poetic merit. They all have the Meredithian quality, but in varying degrees of perfection. They are all out of the same vineyard, but of different vintages. To come to details. 'Love in the Valley', *e.g.*, does not rise in general conception and design above the average level of the 'minor poet' as we know him. For this reason it will probably be one of the most popular. It has also the ordinary fault of the modern English poetry—diffuseness, the beating out of a small particle of metal into too thin foil. Yet 'Love in

the Valley' is redeemed from commonness by single strokes which are
not within the reach of everyday, as well as by a vigour of language
which is Mr Meredith's own property among all his competitors. Take
this stanza, descriptive of morning light:—

[Quotes 'Love in the Valley', st. vii.]

I do not defend 'bloomy' here said of dew. Mr Meredith might have
learned the meaning of 'bloomy' from Milton, who uses it properly
of the spray bursting into leaf in an English April. To apply 'bloomy' to
dew is too like that deplacement of epithet which is one of the tricks
by which the modern school of poets seeks to supply a spurious
originality.

'The Day of the Daughter of Hades' is also liable to the charge of
diffuseness. And it has the more serious fault of being a versified treatment of a legend provided by the Greek mythology. Because the Greek
mythology is the most poetical known to us, it is natural to conceive
that it must be good 'material' for a poem. It was still possible in
Milton's day, it was just possible for Gray to vivify a classical myth. Even
Gray only appeals to 'Delphi's steep', &c., incidentally; he does not
insist on the classic theme. In the time in which we live, classical
personages are too remote from the imaginative sphere of all but a
score or two of Greek scholars to be helps to illusion. The nineteenth-
century poetical reader knows nothing of Grecian Sicily. It is super-
adding another difficulty, which is superfluous, to one which is inherent
in the nature of the case. We have to make a separate effort to get
together the Greek imagery, in addition to the effort which all poetry
demands of passing beyond the stereotype forms of every-day life to
the spirit within them. Skiageneia, the daughter of Hades, is a thoroughly Burne Jones maiden, tall as a poplar, with a 'throat' and a wan
smile, with 'redness that streamed through her limbs in a flitting glow'.

The piece which gives its character to the volume, and raises the
whole above the average of the reproductions of Rossetti with which
we are familiar, is the first, which is entitled 'The Woods of Westermain'. This piece seizes the imagination with a power which the vague
and rather featureless 'Daughter of Hades' does not possess. Many poets
have signalled the romance that lies in forest depths, 'the calling shapes
and beckoning shadows'. No poetical forest has surpassed in wealth of
suggestion 'the woods of Westermain'. In these woods is no wizardry;
no supernatural agents are at work. But if you enter them with a
poet's eye and a poet's sensibility you may see and hear that natural

magic which surpasses all the fictitious tales of sorcerers, witches, wood gods, of Fauns and Dryads. The poem teaches, not didactically—for nothing is farther from its form or its thought than the inculcation of doctrine—how what we see depends upon what we are; how transcendent influences are only to be approached through the real—the[n] transmuted by the soul of the seer:

> Even as dewlight off the rose
> In the mid a jewel sows.
> Look you with the soul you see't.

The doctrine is old enough; the psychology of religion and that of poetry agree in it. Keats's Endymion, baffled in the search of the ideal, learns to find it in the real. In 'the woods of Westermain'—ordinary woods, peopled only by the squirrel and the snake, the green woodpecker and the night-jar—you may read the whole history of the origin and development of things, from the time 'when mind was mud', 'earth a slimy spine, Heaven a space for winging tons'. It is wholly in your own power what you shall make of earth. As you choose to look, she is either a dust-filled tomb or radiant with the blush of morning. Gaze under, and the soul is rich past computing. You must not only look, you must put off yourself, sink your individuality, you must let her 'two-sexed meanings melt through you, wed the thought'. Your rich reward will not only be in the power of understanding, but in a quickening joy, the 'joy of earth' showered upon you without stint.

> Drink the sense the notes infuse
> You a larger self will find;
> Sweetest fellowship ensues
> With the creatures of your kind.

In contrast with the pessimistic tone and despairing notes of the modern school, Mr Meredith offers 'a song of gladness', and smiles with Shakspere at a generation 'ranked in gloomy noddings over life'.

Such seems to be the drift of this remarkable lyric, remarkable rather for its expression than for its contents. Unfortunately, Mr Meredith's healthy wisdom is veiled in the obscurity of a peculiar language which makes even his general drift doubtful, and the meaning of many score lines absolute darkness. Some writers, whom it is a fashion to admire, are obscure by twisting plain things into words that are not plain. They make platitudes into verbal puzzles. Mr Meredith's obscurity proceeds from a better motive. He knows that poetry can only suggest, and destroys itself if it affirms. And as the moods he desires to suggest are remote from common experience, so also must the suggestive imagery be. Even the English language is inadequate to his requirements, and he tries to eke it out by daring compounds. The same resource tried long ago by Aeschylus was found to degenerate into bombast in a language which lends itself more readily to compounds than ours does. In Mr Meredith's lines these compounds have seldom the merit of being happily formed or of condensing expression. If we allow that their use originated in the poverty of the existing language, the habit of employing them constantly and upon all occasions grows up from their trouble-saving convenience. They are stopgaps, and fill the place when the sense cannot be moulded into words proper without an expenditure of time which no modern writer will give. That the habit has settled itself upon Mr Meredith's pen the following sample, taken from a very few pages, will show. We have—poppy-droop; bronze-orange; swan-wave; shore-bubble; rock-sourced; lost-to-light; instant-glancing; iron-resounding; spear-fitted; fool-flushed; ripple-feathered; dew-delighted; fountain-showers; stripe-shadowed; treasure-armful; circle-windsails; bully-drawlers; and so on without stint or limit. How many in the above collection, gathered at random, can be said to recommend themselves by their own elegance, or to be indispensable to the sense required, which most do but feebly express?

That I may not take an ungracious leave of a volume in which may be found so much to interest, I give a specimen of the sonnets, of which there are some twenty-three in the volume.

[Quotes 'Earth's Secret'.]

68. Alice Meynell, *Merry England*

i, August 1883

Alice Meynell (1847–1922), poet, journalist and essayist, formed friendships easily with elderly men of letters. She attracted the attention of Meredith in the early 1890s, received a presentation copy of *The Amazing Marriage* and began a friendship with him which caused Coventry Patmore—another admirer—some concern. Meredith reviewed her essays in *National Review*, August 1896.

Mr George Meredith has produced a volume—*Poems and Lyrics of the Joy of the Earth*—in which we hear the individual note, the separate voice, which is the first thing we listen for when a poet begins to sing. So long as the voice is personal and singular it does not need that the tune should be new. And Mr Meredith's subjects are for the most part as familiar as showers and moonrise and the careering of the wind, and as fresh. There is no freshness so perfect as that of the familiarity of Nature; and with regard to the character of the note, too, it is clear that if all the poets were natural their voices would all be distinct as their faces. And Mr Meredith is fresh because he takes the natural initiative which is a man's natural right; it is unnatural to belong to a school, unnatural to use and abuse the vocabulary which others have set in vogue. After the individuality of the note comes its quality—beautiful or not beautiful. Mr Meredith's note is at times excessively beautiful, always interesting, and always significant.

There are no disheartening shortcomings or boundaries in these large and vigorous poems. If every poet must have one of two demerits —faults or limitations—Mr Meredith is to be congratulated on having faults, and not limitations. To our mind the possession of faults is preferable to that of limitations. At times he frees his reader's thought, sets him above the poverties of time and place, and asks him, as Virgil asked Dante in an eternal world, '*Che pensi*'? 'What thinkest thou'?

---

¹ *Inferno*, v, iii.

Among the loveliest and most suggestive lines are those on 'The Day of the Daughter of Hades', in which the ever wonderful tale of Ceres and her child is told with a mysterious passionateness:

[Quotes iii, ll. 27–37.]

This is masterly imagery and purely magical poetry. It recalls that other exquisite image of the cloud-moon and the water-moon, by which Rossetti expressed the weeping together of the mother and daughter in 'Rose Mary'. But Rossetti's thought was more penetrating in its emotion; Mr Meredith's is more liberal and glorious.

Of the sonnets, the following on 'Appreciation' is admirable for lucidity as well as for power of feeling and grace of metaphor:

[Quotes 'Appreciation'.]

We have said that this is one of the more fortunate poets who have faults. The principal of these in his case is obscurity, seldom if ever unconquerable by a little application, but sometimes profound at the first glance. Again, Mr Meredith has a way, which many must find distasteful, of overworking a simile too precisely and insistently. This is an instance:

> 'Spiral' the memorable lady terms
> Our minds' ascent: our world's advance presents
> That figure on a flat; the way of worms.

By-the-way, who is the lady quoted? Will any of our readers tell us? The saying sounds like one of George Eliot's, though we do not remember it in her writings. With regard to metrical form, it is to be noted that Mr Meredith uses quantity in a manner unusual in English or any modern verse. Those of his poems in which this peculiarity occurs should be read in time as music is sung. Negroes would recite them to perfection. He evidently doubts his white readers' comprehension of the rhythm intended, for he gives a guide to the scansion. This is a specimen of lines in which quantity plays this important part:—

> Lovely are the curves of the white owl sweeping
> Wavy in the dusk lit by one large star.

This is indeed *tempo marcato*; and we cannot but think the insistent rhythm is undignified. To thresh to, to march to, to rock or dance a baby to, quantitative verse is all very well; but accent is sufficient for poetry which is read in repose.

69. W. P. Ker, *Contemporary Review*

xliv, September 1883

William Paton Ker (1855–1923), scholar and critic, was the author of several books which remain current: *Epic and Romance* (1897) and *The Dark Ages* (1904).

Mr George Meredith's *Poems and Lyrics of the Joy of Earth* have very little in them that is conventional or old-fashioned. Their general theme is an old one, it is true, but it is dealt with in a manner that is far from being common-place. The characteristic mark of the poems is the confidence with which they insist that the Earth and Man are not hackneyed or uninteresting subjects. Not all the prose pages that have ever been spoken or written concerning the unity and variety of Nature, concerning the destiny of man, can depress the spirit of a poet who chooses to forget the prose phrases. These *Poems and Lyrics of the Joy of Earth* have a fire in them which is dangerous to obstructions and commonplaces. They tear away comfortable theories that put a veil on the mystery of Nature. They are Protestant and destructive; the poet claims in them his right to disregard what he has not verified, his independence of tradition. He will have none of the superstition that the former glory has passed away from the earth. The earth is beautiful and terrible to any one who will claim his birthright as a son of the earth, and no nation or time has any special grace in this matter. It was once fashionable to say, with the *enfants du siècle*, that 'we have come too late into a world too old'. That saying came from prejudice and cowardice, and the poets who give up that prejudice have their reward. They find the way into 'that new world which is the old', a world whose beauty is none the less eternal because poets and prosaists have spent centuries in making phrases about it.

There is nothing half-hearted or dispirited in Mr Meredith's poems. They do not apologize in any way for their existence. They speak out because they have something to say, because the poet is quite sure of his object. The way in which the mythologies are used is an example of the unhesitating spirit of the poems. 'Phœbus with Admetus', 'Melampus', and 'The Day of the Daughter of Hades', are poems taken from Greek legends. None of them show any misgiving about the expediency of repeating old stories. They are not repetitions of old stories; they are not antiquarian poems about Greek gods and heroes—they are poems about the earth and its life. 'The Day of the Daughter of Hades', tells how the Sicilian youth Callistes met the daughter of Hades and Proserpine, when she had risen for one day to the upper air to see the living things on the Sicilian earth, and to sing about them—not to learn the art of war, or the constitutional history of the Sicilian cities. The dignity of this story, its effectiveness and beauty, come from the real contrast between the majesty of the life of earth and the unrest of the life of man. This idea is no fiction of the poets, and it is this that gives life to the shadowy figure risen from the under world. 'The Woods of Westermain' and 'Earth and Man', are the most difficult poems in the book, perhaps because they have received no help from mythology. They are closely akin in their subject—the progress of man in knowledge, hindered by 'his distempered devil of self', which stands between him and the secret of the life of Earth and Man. 'Love in the Valley' is more easily comprehensible. The variety of images in it, the clearness with which it reflects all the aspects of the fortunate valley, give it a character of its own among pastorals.

DIANA OF THE CROSSWAYS

1885

70. W. E. Henley, *Athenaeum*

No. 2994, 14 March 1885

For W. E. Henley see above, No. 57, headnote.

In *Diana of the Crossways* Mr Meredith has atoned for the faults of *The Tragic Comedians*. Opinions differ, and there are those, we believe, to whom Alvan and Clotilde von Rüdiger—'acrobats of the affections', as they have been called—are pleasant companions, and the story of those feats in 'the gymnastics of sentimentalism' in which they lived to shine is the prettiest reading to be found. Others, not so fortunate, or, to be plain, more honestly obtuse, persist in finding that story tedious, and the bewildering appearances it deals with not human beings—not of the stock of Rose Jocelyn and Sir Everard Romfrey, of Dahlia Fleming and Lucy Feverel and Richmond Roy—but creatures of gossamer and rainbow, phantasms of spiritual romance, abstractions of remote, dispiriting points in sexual philosophy. Opinions differ, as we have said; and it is probable that even as they varied over Clotilde and Dr Alvan, so will they vary over Diana Merion and Percy Dacier. To our thinking, *Diana of the Crossways* is one of the best of all Mr Meredith's books. It has no touch of the tremendous spiritual tragedy which forms the subject of *Rhoda Fleming*—in some ways the greatest of its author's achievements; nor, on the other hand, is its essence so peculiar and rare as that spirit of comedy whose expression in Sir Willoughby Patterne sets *The Egoist* on a pinnacle apart among novels, and marks the writer for one of the breed of Shakspeare and Molière. It keeps a mean between the two extremes; it has affinities with both, and copies neither. It is a study of character, and it is also a study of emotion; it is a picture of fact and the world, and it is touched with generous romance;

it is rich in kindly comedy, and it abounds in natural passion; it sets forth a selection of many human elements, and is joyful and sorrowful, wholesome with laughter and fruitful of tears, as life itself. In one word, it is a common novel, as *Amelia* is and *Vanity Fair*. It ends as happily as the feeblest and flimsiest of visions in three volumes, and is only distinguished from the ruck of its contemporaries in being the work of a man of genius and a great artist.

The story (which we do not purpose to anticipate) is of the simplest. It tells how Diana Merion becomes Diana Warwick, and then, after a certain necessary ordeal, is led to change her name for the second time and last. The ordinary novelist is always, it would seem, a great deal more inventive; the most savage 'realist' at least as unadventurous and plain. And yet it is not so. The book is instinct with imagination, is quick with interest as life itself, is full of matter and movement as a corner of the actual world. Not since *The Egoist* has there appeared an essay in fiction at once so novel and so true, so personal and peculiar and, at the same time, so pregnant and convincing. It is only the story of a woman's heart and the record of her spiritual growth. There are no more violent incidents than an elopement which is planned and does not come off, and the revelation from very ordinary motives of a secret which is thrust into the intrigue from without, and is essentially of consequence to nobody; and though the heroine is deceived, and comes near to dying of the deception, the means by which this crisis is brought about are commonplace, and its effect is simply natural. But there is meaning in every word of it. Every touch is to the purpose, every sentence packed with significance and luminous with insight. Diana's experiences are so much life taken in the fact. She speaks, and it is from her very heart; she suffers and rejoices, and it is in her own flesh and her own soul; she thinks, aspires, labours, wins, loses, and wins again with an intensity of perception, an emotional directness and completeness, that, so cunning is the author's hand and so unerring his principle of selection, affect the reader more powerfully than the spectacle of nature itself: as a great portrait is more persuasive and imposing than its original, as a perfect tragedy is more appalling than the circumstance, however dreadful, on which it is based. This is indeed the merit and distinction of art: to be more real than reality, to be not nature, but nature's essence. It is the artist's function not to copy, but to synthesize; to eliminate from that gross confusion of actuality which is his raw material whatever is accidental, idle, irrelevant, and select for perpetuation that only which is appropriate and immortal. This is what Mr Meredith has done in *Diana of the Crossways*. He has considered his material with 'that eye of steady flame' which he discerns in his Shakspeare, and the outcome of his contemplation is Diana Merion—that is to say, such a sublimation of character and life as suggests the kindred achievements of Rosalind among women and Lovelace among men.

It is said that she is studied from Mrs Norton. Indeed, in Mr Meredith's first chapter—the most characteristic piece of writing (in other words, the only sustained piece of literary egoism) in the book—it is confessed that she lived once, and was famous in her day, and queened it in society, and was the bright particular star of diarists and the dealers in anecdote. Here, with a noble plea for philosophic fiction, and more wit and wisdom than most men contrive to put off in three whole volumes, there are quotations from the lady's works; also a most subtle and authoritative analysis of her intelligence and the quality of her wit; and passages, descriptive and historical, from the diaries of 'Henry Wilmers' and 'Perry Wilkinson', and other distinguished creatures *ejusdem farinæ*. Moreover, in the novel itself Diana is Dan Merion's daughter—Dan Merion, the wit, the humourist, the Irishman; she marries a certain Mr Warwick, who is made a magistrate by her interest; she suffers impeachment in her fair fame in connection with an elderly but enchanting Premier; she wins her case in the courts, repudiates her husband, writes novels for her bread, and plays such a part in society as was played by Caroline Norton; so that the lady who was Sheridan's grandchild and Lord Melbourne's Egeria may well be her prototype. Whether this be or be not the case is absolutely immaterial. As we know her Diana Merion is an original creation, and one of the loveliest in fiction. She suggests Mrs Norton, it is true, but she suggests Mr George Meredith still more, and Rosalind most of all. The comparison is no doubt startling, but, we take it, it is legitimate. For such a union as she presents of capacity of heart and capacity of brain, of generous nature and fine intelligence, of natural womanhood and more than womanly wit and apprehensiveness, we know not where to look save among Shakspeare's ladies, nor with whom to equal her save the genius of Arden. Like Rosalind, she is pure woman; and like Rosalind (and her sisters) she has in her enough of her spiritual sire to proclaim her birthright and affirm the illustrious kinship. Mr Meredith has wrought from within, and behind his Diana you feel the presence of her maker, as you are aware of your Shakspeare when you consort with Rosalind and Hermione. Now and then her wit is, like

Rosalind's, her father's own, her intelligence and expression are touched with a familiar attribute—when her empire totters, and her influence is for a second in peril of wavering. But this is only now and then. Throughout, as with Rosalind, her royal origin is patent otherwise; like Orlando's mistress, she betrays her parentage in a hundred gallant and inspiring qualities—the quickness and brilliance of her blood, her exquisite and abounding spirit, her delicate vigour of temperament, her swiftness of perception, her generous intensity of emotion. In love, in war, in friendship, in ambition and sorrow, in thought and deed and feeling, she is ever her noble self. She is admirable even in her delusions; you visit her errors with unfailing respect. She is a woman, she has a woman's needs; and she betrays them in terms so quick and warm, yet so chaste and sweet, they make the reader think a certain episode in *The Mill on the Floss* as grosser and more offensive than perhaps it really is. And the fate of Percy Dacier—'mated with a devious filmy sentimentalist, likely *"to fiddle harmonies on the sensual strings"* for him at a mad rate in the years to come'—appears, albeit thoroughly deserved on his part, and on hers the earnest of salvation, a punishment almost savagely inhumane.

Having said thus much—and only readers of Mr Meredith's three volumes can know how little it is—of the heroine herself, we have but small space in which to treat of the brilliant crowd of characters with which she is environed. Some are in Mr Meredith's finest manner—are firm in outline, radiant with sympathy emotional and intellectual, touched with the true fire of being; and these are fully worthy of their companionship with our latter-day Rosalind and of their place in her history. Such is the recreant Percy Dacier—as fine a study of ambition and the political heart and intelligence as exists in fiction. Such, in a less degree perhaps, is the loyal Redworth, in whom Mr Meredith has depicted with much freshness and force a particular sort of English gentleman. Such, above all, are Sir Lukin and Lady Dunstane: he a babbler, a society ass, a gallant and accomplished soldier, a husband fixed in adoration and incapable of fidelity, an embodiment of 'the simply sensational man'; she a perfect friend, a perfect wife, a perfect sufferer, high in mind and holy of heart, a woman of the most exquisite nature. Chief in effect among the lesser lights of this new galaxy are Constance Asper and Lady Wathin, types of the British virgin and the British matron, two species that our author does not love. They are cruelly and splendidly successful; they would go far to make him unpopular were he as widely read as Ouida. To reflect that he is not, and thereafter turn to certain scenes in this new masterpiece of his, is to give way to wonderment and a sense of the infinitely inexplicable. Here is fiction of the freshest, the rarest, the most vigorous and wholesome type; it is all compact of wit, passion, character, humour, sex, of living speech and consummate portraiture; it is stamped in every word the achievement of a philosophic artist—

> Ein wechselnd Weben,
> Ein glühend Leben;[1]

and it may be said to have been written, as *Don Juan* was composed, for the author and 'two or three friends'! That it is not a book to be read 'with the eyelids only' is undeniable; undeniable, too, that it deals not with dolls, but men and women, and that 'in Lebensfluthen, im Thatensturm'—at the crises of existence, at the highest of the press of action and emotion. But what then? Are these great qualities but great defects? In this over-educated and avowedly æsthetic age—this age of doubt and inquiry and art and 'spiritual unrest'—shall nothing prevail that is not base, common, and popular? is our civilization so far a failure, and have we less taste of literature than our thickwitted and unlettered forefathers?

When we have satisfied English sentiment, our task is done, in every branch of art, I hear: and it will account to posterity for the condition of the branches.

Thus, with some bitterness, our author is moved to deliver himself. It is a shrewd thrust, and true; but fortunately for work of this sort—'the celestial refreshment of having a pure decency in the place of sham; real flesh; a soul born active, windbeaten, but ascending'—there is no decay. 'Us, too', says Mr Meredith of a certain 'intolerant enemy' whose features we seem to recognize—'us, too, he holds for the day, to punish us if we have temporal cravings. He scatters his gifts to the abject, tossing to us rebels bare dog-biscuit. But the life of the spirit is beyond his region; we have our morrow in his day, when we crave nought of him'. This also is a truth, and more acceptable, take it how we will, than the one that went before.

In *Diana of the Crossways* the style, quick as it is with imagination, pure brainwork even as the matter it contains, is singularly luminous and clear. Here and there we are confronted with a metaphor in four dimensions (as it were), whose conquest appears to demand the instant and active exercise of all the five senses at once, and which even then emerges from the fight unvanquished. To say that is to say that the

---

[1] Untraced; literally, 'Oh change and weaving,/Oh glowing life'.

book is by the author of *The Tragic Comedians*. But such defects are rare. Mr Meredith writes such English as is within the capacity of no other living man; and in epigram as in landscape, in dialogue as in analysis, in description as in comment and reflection, he is an artist in words of whom his country may be proud.

71. C. Monkhouse, *Saturday Review*

lx, 21 March 1885

William Cosmoe Monkhouse (1840–1901) produced several volumes of poems between 1865 and 1902, and published one novel and numerous biographies and criticisms.

In *Diana of the Crossways* Mr George Meredith, not for the first time, has the authority of history for the main incidents in the career of his principal character. He fully appreciates the truth that fact is stranger than fiction, and the value of an impregnable base for his inventive campaigns. Such a career as that of his Diana might well bring down upon his head the charge of extravagance if he could not point to well-known facts in support of its most startling incidents. Diana's beauty and wit; her social, literary, and political power; her unfortunate early marriage; her dangerous intimacy with a distinguished statesman, and the consequent scandal; her betrayal of an important Cabinet secret; the failure of her husband's attempt to obtain a divorce—all these are facts, and quite sufficient to form the basis of a very 'sensational' novel. It need scarcely be said that in Mr Meredith's hands the materials are turned to greater advantage. The book is nevertheless full of striking situations, described with great power and animated by vivid dialogue; it has no lack of excitement or romance, and one of its most eminent qualities is the realistic force with which both scenes and characters are presented. Diana is the chief and most vital figure of all; 'never did woman carry her head more grandly, more thrillingly make her presence felt'; but, as with her, so it is in a less degree with several others of the *dramatis personæ*; and, whether we accompany Redforth on his chivalrous embassy to the Crossways, or listen to Dacier's wooing, or Sir Lukin's self-reproaches, the world is alive about us. Nevertheless, although the author has not neglected the dramatic opportunities suggested by the career of a once celebrated Queen of Beauty, the problems, social, intellectual, psychological, which it starts, seem to have had the greater fascination for his genius. To construct a character which would fit the known facts; to create a woman dazzling by the brilliancy of her personality, and liable by the very force of the qualities which raised her above the crowd to commit indiscretions unpardonable by the world, was a congenial exercise to his inventive faculty, and the result is a singularly vivid conception, worked out with great literary power. It is to be doubted whether even a poet is a more difficult character for fiction than a witty woman of the world; and amongst all his intellectual and literary feats Mr Meredith has perhaps never accomplished one more striking than in making us feel that his Diana justified her reputation. He has made her move and speak before us as a living woman, dowered with exceptional gifts of 'blood and brains'. Of the two the brains 'have it' decidedly. She is too much like Charles II in the contrast between her sayings and doings. The latter are almost invariably foolish. Though not without precedent, she is none the less difficult to credit or to sympathize with in this particular. Her first folly, her marriage with a fool and a brute, is explained, but scarcely justified, by circumstances; the 'queenly comrade', with 'a spirit leaping and shining like a mountain water', should not have been at a loss for a nobler mate. To be 'the crystal spring of wisdom' to a potent old Minister was more worthy of her, and palliates much indiscretion, but to take up with and fall fatally in love with his inelastic and commonplace prig of a nephew, even though he also were a politician of some mark, was almost as silly as her marriage. She was young and impulsive, and love is blind, and the rest of it, no doubt, and that might be an excuse for her in real life; but in fiction the heroine has no right to go so very near wrecking herself on a character for whom the reader has not an atom of regard or admiration. Allowing also as historic the fact that a lady sold her friend's political secret to the *Times*, it yet seems incredible that Diana should do so; and it is still more improbable that this woman, so full of knowledge of the political world, should plead that she 'had not a suspicion of mischief' in doing so. But of the reality of her brains there is no doubt; she is intellectually the same woman throughout. If she cannot manage her conduct wisely, she can reason about it. Her reviews of her various situations of difficulty, her analysis of her own motives, her arguments for and against herself and the world, are at once clear and subtle, and stirring with vitality. Joyful or joyless, sweet or bitter, they are animated by the same rich intellect, the same noble and passionate soul. They are nearly always witty also; and, in saying this, we do not allude to those laboured 'sayings' of hers with which the book is somewhat overcrowded. Some are excellent, as this: 'Oratory is always the more impressive for the spice of temper which renders it untrustworthy'; others are far too 'difficult' to have any chance of success in conversation. Such a *mot* as the following would fall hopelessly flat: 'The talk fell upon our being creatures of habit and how far it was good. She said:— "It is there that we see ourselves crutched between love grown old and indifference ageing to love"'. Here there is too much of Mr George Meredith, and especially of that tendency of his to suppose that a thought is the more profound the more deeply it is buried in words. What he calls the 'literary covering' of his ideas makes his books hard reading even to the hard-headed, and the swiftness and agility of his thought requires more intellectual exercise than most readers are able or willing to take. Those who take it will be rewarded not only mentally, but morally; they will experience that pleasant fatigue which follows unusual exertion, and reach that Christian condition which enables them to 'suffer fools gladly' for a time.

72. Unsigned review, *Pall Mall Gazette*

xli, 28 March 1885

At the time that this article appeared the *Pall Mall Gazette* was in the hands of W. T. Stead (1849–1912), powerful journalist, founder of the *Review of Reviews*, spiritualist and pacifist and one of Meredith's personal friends.

In reading Mr George Meredith one is perpetually divided between admiration for his genius and irritation at his perversity. The genius was always there, but the perversity increases. Mr Meredith has a theory of his own about style, and the more evident it becomes that consistent adherence to that theory makes him unreadable to ordinary mortals, the more pertinaciously, defiantly, he develops it. It is a matter of conscience with him, and truly he has made great sacrifices for conscience' sake. Perhaps the very fact that he, who towers head and shoulders above contemporary novelists, an intellectual giant, has never attained the vogue of a dozen milk-and-water romancers, that he remains, despite the warm admiration of the esoteric few, almost an unknown name to the 'reading public'—perhaps this very want of vulgar success confirms him in his proud contempt for directness of thought and plainness of speech. To make concessions to the banal preference for intelligibility would be a desertion of principle. Ought genius to bow the knee to the shallow criticism which frets at a novel if the perusal involves hard intellectual exercise, and longs to dash through its three volumes at an easy hand gallop, without being pulled up by philosophic quagmires or five-barred gates of overloaded aphorism? The more piteously sloth cries out at the severity of the steeplechase, the more industriously does Mr Meredith add fence to fence and pile obstacle on obstacle. To read him in his most characteristic mood is like construing a stiff chapter of Thucydides. Of course Mr Meredith may be right in his theory. Profundity of thought may involve obscurity of language. The subtle changes and nuances of human feeling and designing may demand for their adequate portraiture, the Cretan mazes and Gordian knots of phrase which he takes such pleasure in devising. At any rate, this is not the place, nor is a humble newspaper critic the person, to engage in a controversy on the subject with a philosopher like Mr Meredith. Suffice it to observe that the best argument against Mr Meredith's theories is afforded by Mr Meredith's practice when he is not engaged in living up to them. He is always most admirable when he is least involved, least elaborate, least, we were going to say, affected. His best thoughts are as intelligible as A B C . His finest touches are laid on with the lightest hand. His keenest shafts of epigram go as straight to the mark, and with as easy a flight, as arrow from the bow. He drops gems of wit, so to speak, into his waistcoat pocket as he goes along, and hardly seems to be aware of them. But when he sits down to elaborate a Feast of Wit, when he gathers all his clever characters round a table, and makes them fire epigrams at one another through eight or ten successive pages, he is excruciatingly tiresome. All the intricacies, the obscurities, the contortions of expression, which frighten away the commonplace reader, add nothing to the real force or originality of his work. They are like the prickles of the pineapple, lending no additional flavour to the fruit which they make so difficult of access.

That *Diana of the Crossways* should be thus repellent to the world at large is all the more to be regretted because the work is by no means a falling off all round, like *The Tragic Comedians* There are situations in the story as strong and true as any that Mr Meredith has ever conceived, and the characters, especially the minor ones, are drawn as no other living writer could draw them. The figure of the heroine is a poetical and sympathetic portrait of one of the most famous wits and beauties of this century, and she and some of the other leading characters will be easily recognizable by every one who is well acquainted with the political society of the Thirties and Forties. The story begins a little heavily, but increases in interest as it goes on. It is somewhat hard to realize why the brilliant and beautiful Diana Merion should have married a stick like Warwick, simply to escape from the solicitations of an unchivalrous world, against which so many worthier men were ready to protect her. In this as in another critical act of her life, the betrayal of Dacier's secret, her motive is inadequate to explain the fateful act. That Warwick, however, the selfish, dense, and unsympathetic, should have grown madly jealous of his dazzling wife, especially in her intimacy with so dangerous a cavalier to a woman of talent and political interests as the old statesman-gallant Lord Dannisburgh, and should even have gone the length of suspecting and accusing her of infidelity, was only to be expected. Very natural, too, under the circumstances, and very powerfully described, is Diana's bearing in this ordeal—her first ill-considered impulse to fly, then her successful stand against her accuser, and afterwards the long wrestle of the wrongly aspersed woman against the great polite, scandalous world, with her very charms fighting at once for and against her. It is in the course of this struggle, heightened in intensity by her want of means—for our heroine is of a reckless hospitality, which even the ample earnings of her brilliant pen cannot long sustain—that Diana, in fact a widow though still by law a wife, the cause of love in so many others, hitherto herself unscathed, at length falls a victim to the tender passion. Percy Dacier, the favoured lover, a rising young statesman, is one of the most unpleasing and perhaps the only unreal character in the book. Handsome and rich, able and ambitious, with the highest prizes before him and the world of women at his feet, he is yet entirely carried away, surprised for a moment into genuine warmth and uncalculating devotion, by the overflowing vivacity and grand nature of Diana. Her influence stimulates, inspires, guides him, ennobles his aims, quickens his insight; while she on her side worships the exalted being, partly of her creation, partly of her imagination, until she is willing, in a moment of impulse, to sacrifice everything, virtue, reputation, social pre-eminence, to his pleading. An accident saves her, and the impulse does not return. Yet her love for Dacier increases, and her eyes are only opened to the real poverty of this imposing character when for a single fault (grave, no doubt, but committed in unconsciousness of its gravity and under a great temptation) he remorselessly turns his back upon her for ever. Her lover's cruelty, joined to an overwhelming sense of her own guilt, nearly crush the erring but noble-spirited woman, yet they lead in the end to a happy consummation, indicated from the beginning of the story, but which during the moving accidents of its later stages had come to seem quite hopeless. This is Diana's union with her old and faithful but long disregarded lover, Tom Redworth. Redworth is intended to be a typical John Bull, as Diana is a typical Irishwoman, and certainly the sober prose of his character—with its sturdy loyalty and almost unendurable perfection of common sense—forms an effective contrast to the poetical figure of the heroine. But the greatest triumphs of figure painting are in the minor characters: Emma Dunstane, Diana's wise and loving friend; a beautiful picture of a thoughtful yet thoroughly womanly woman; her husband, Sir Lukin, the empty-headed, warm-hearted, weak-willed man of pleasure; Lady Wathin, the fussy representative of sour upper-middle-class morality. Both the latter are perfect types and yet of a convincing individuality. And these are only some of the most prominent in a very striking gallery of living human faces. There is a healthy, vigorous realism about Mr Meredith's representation of character which is infinitely refreshing. To feel that fresh breeze of original creative fiction blowing in your face, in these sultry late summer days of namby-pamby imitation—for that and for the enjoyment of his abundant humour, for the thousand fresh jets of thought with which he is for ever surprising and refreshing his reader—one can afford to endure a great deal from Mr Meredith—and we have endured a great deal.

73. Unsigned review, *Illustrated London News*

lxxxvi, 28 March 1885

Seldom is it the privilege of the reader of modern novels to take up one so fresh, so vivid, so strong in its incidents as is *Diana of the Cross-ways*, by George Meredith. Writing of the early part of this century, the author makes his heroine—Diana—a moving, living, breathing being; with a rare beauty, a rare wit, so alive to the reader that time passes on and he feels that she also is living her life, with all its storms, its passing currents, its amusements, its interest. And this Diana is not an entire creation, but she was a social reality, mentioned often in the diaries of the day; and the incident of the publication of the Cabinet secret (although, with permissible license, it is stated to have been intrusted to a personal confidant by Mr Meredith) is a matter of history, and refers to the premature disclosure of Sir Robert Peel's intended repeal of the Corn Laws by one of the Cabinet to the empress of his heart, and so—to the editor. But all is brocaded with gems of thought and harmonized by the skill of an artistic hand. The poetical friendship between two women—so poetical, so ideal, and so possible—is very powerfully described. Emma's love has the worshipping fibre in it which there must be on one side, coupled with talent, intellectual gifts to a certain extent, and the nobility of faith; with Diana, it is the feeling of being thoroughly understood, even to every vibration of voice, every shade of word, and, stronger still, the certainty that here there will always be found rest, trust, and love till the world's end, that binds her soul to that other. Excitement and sensationalism of the best there are, surely, for those to whom such sensations are a necessity in their reading: in the ride of Redworth through the burning sunset 'with junipers behind him'; the curious sensation stealing over his frame when he fancies he sees two figures vanishing through the churchyard, where in the moonlight the gravestones were legible; the amusing and characteristic episode of the man Hedger (a true Hampshire and Sussex name), and the dissection of the 'fair white pig'; the night-watch of Diana, so well drawn that it is not over-drawn; and the thrilling scenes between the passionate lovers. Then, how clever is the dissection of Lady Wathin and her particular world, and how she is visible in the description 'a lady of incisive features bound in stale parchment'; how true to her nature the supposition and earnest conviction that Diana would, on hearing of Mr Warwick's death, try to detach Percy Dacier from Constance Asper. The difference between the heroine's nature and Lady Wathin's is contained so succinctly in a sentence that we quote it, 'The intrusion of the spontaneous on the stereotyped would have clashed'. That this vein (the stereotyped), strongly developed, runs through the English as a people is well known, and the condemnation of originality is sweeping amongst mortals brought up on the usual lines of the commonplace. How accurately Diana's phases of thought and surging dreams are read, shows what a thorough grasp of her character the author has. To be noted, besides, are Percy's wakeful night with the Bell at Rovio, a little village below the Generoso, and his parting scene with Diana—on her part the awful maddening rising of the thought that by her deed she had betrayed the man she loved, her acceptation of the punishment, and the powerful ending of the scene, which is not too long, not too short, but word for word what it should artistically be, each parting from each as those two would have parted. Mr Meredith can perfectly describe the passionate woman controlled by her immense self-respect; and he profoundly appreciates the little inflections of voice, the little finenesses of manner, the choice of ordinary words put in such a way that they are commonplace no longer; and the voice is heard, the manner felt; and the reader is conscious that it is the instinct of great talent, the shrewdness of wit, the discrimination of tact, which can divine and essentially balance. The English is expressive and unique; sometimes the phrases and joint words are a little brusque, a little over-strained, and give the impression of affectation; but this only occasionally; and the splendid originality, coupled with the absolute truthfulness of the feelings described in many passages, fascinate the reader. Can anything be better told than the scene of Lady Dunstane's visit to her heartbroken friend, and her soothing ministrations? The characters are all well drawn and lifelike; but the heroine is the key-note to the book—the presiding central figure round which all the others revolve, not as round an exaggerated deity, but round what is assuredly more attractive, as it is certainly more difficult of description —a perfectly natural woman. The interest heightens as the story and life grow older—no flagging attention for the reader—on he is impelled —the beauty of some soft saying, the lure of some passionate love scene, the lament of the woman that, by the confession of her love, she is humiliated—all bear him on, on resistless wings.

74. F. V. Dickins, *Spectator*

lviii, 18 April 1885

Frederick Victor Dickins (1838–1915) wrote a number of books on Japanese art and culture.

In the preface to this latest, and, perhaps, most characteristic, of Mr Meredith's philosopho-sociological novels, the leading motive of the book is stated in language so striking that it were unfair not to quote the description. The object is not, it must be premised, to retell the story of the gifted woman whose talents and misfortunes made her one of the most prominent figures of the earlier years of the century's middle-third. 'Very little of it', says the author, 'shall trouble the reader'.

It is the position that is faced (that of an innocent, if unwise, heroine of a great scandal), and this:

[Quotes i, from 'Is one of the battles' to 'and add no yapping to the spectacle'.]

Dianas, however, who are neither wroth with, nor shy of, Actæons, must bear as best they may comments which the goddess never heard on Olympus. No woman can be wife to one man and Egeria to another without risk of a storm. She cannot both profit by and offend the arrangements of society. The outer accidents of her vagaries are alone visible to spectators; the case for the defence is known only to herself. The world cannot avoid coming to some judgment, and comes naturally, without being malevolent, to the judgment the materials at its command and common experience justify upon the probabilities. The story of Diana Warwick, née Merrion [sic], hardly enlists the reader's sympathy on her side. Mr Meredith claims that even in the teeth of foul rumour it were well not to believe a woman 'mentally active up to the point of spiritual charity, and also fleshly vile; a guide to life and a biter at the fruits of death; both open-minded and a hypocrite', though the records of mankind furnish not a few instances of natures compounded of such apparently incompatible ingredients. Diana had all the advantages of person and mind entitling her to the description given of her prototype, 'a queen of the period fit for homage'. So endowed, well-friended, and fair-fortuned, she was under no need to come to hasty resolutions or tread perilous paths. But she did both, and walking on the edge of the slough could not wonder that from a distance she might seem to be walking in it. At the outset she steers straight for the commonest of the rocks a woman makes shipwreck of her career upon—an ill-assorted marriage. Possessed of the rarest beauty and the finest wit, she links herself to a man whom she describes as 'a gentlemanly official', a sort of personification, according to her biographer, of the 'Monsieur Anglais' of a French theatre who 'inside his boundary . . . had neat phrases, opinions in packets. Beyond it . . . the world was void of any particular interest'. His one positive virtue was the possession of a 'fine taste in wine'. The marriage is shortly followed by the Egeriaship. The dearest of Diana's many friends of either sex, some one or other of whom never fails to appear in the hour of need, Lady Dunstane, the invalid wife of a very disagreeable personage in the story, a rollicking retired general with a turn for being 'fast', ventures a mild remonstrance. The answer is briefly that whatever Lord

Dannisburgh, the Numa of the story, may have been in his younger days, he is all that is admirable now; and the Egeriaship and all its incidents will be continued, let the world wag its tongue as it will. And, of course, the world does wag its tongue; what else could it do? Why should Platonicism be especially probable between the powerful Minister and the lady who was clever, and in many ways, perhaps, useful, but also very fair? The crisis ensues, the dull prose of Law threatens, and the lady meditates flight. From this she is saved by Lady Dunstance and a male friend, who is the chorus of common-sense in this soul's tragi-comedy; but only after a sore conflict, described with great power, the struggle lying between her desire for freedom and her sense of deference to her friends, who see with horror the evil tongues justified by a flight. Diana, satisfied with the verdict of her own set, felt able to defy the world, and yielded, as she supposed, against her reason; yet she had qualms, memories of handholdings too long by half a minute—and half a minute is a long time in these matters—of over-friendly looks and letters; but, she writes, 'these were trifles, things that women of the world have to combat'.

The reversion of the Egeriaship fell to Lord Dannisburgh's nephew, Percy Dacier, also a 'gentlemanly official', but of the statesman class—a coldly enthusiastic politician, with a hot vein in his nature that cropped out on the surface in a manner that was felt at times to be inconvenient. With him Diana gradually glides into love; whether he is ever really in love is somewhat uncertain. At all events, both when his suit is rejected, and when, after being accepted, it is rendered fruit-less by one of those cross-chances that embarrass the paths of all lovers, he congratulates himself upon what he takes to be evident escapes. Dacier is a most skilful portraiture, by far the most life-like of the men-kind who come under the heroine's spell, and save a lay-figure or two, there are no men in the book who do not. But he has another string to his bow in the shape of a Miss Asper, as fair a blonde as Diana is a rich-complexioned brunette, as wealthy as her rival is poor, as correct and cold as the half-Irish damsel is Bohemian and warm-blooded. To her Dacier runs the moment Diana's extraordinary conduct sets him finally free. He had told the latter an important Cabinet secret—nothing less, indeed, than the resolve of the Premier to break with his party, and carry the total Repeal of the Corn Laws. Her powers of authorship, upon which she depended for bread, had failed her; and under pressing need of money, she sold the secret the same night to the great editor, Mr Tonans, who, of course, made it the theme of a leader the next morning. It is difficult to regard this episode otherwise than as a blot in the story. Egeria's excuse that she did not know the secret was a secret at all, or, at any rate, an important one, is an absurdity. Nor is the treachery necessary to the action of the narrative, while it is too violently out of keeping with the heroine's whole character. Dacier's love could surely have been slain in some less inartistic manner. Diana's ultimate fate, too, which we refrain from disclosing, is open to the objection that it is a somewhat commonplace *terminus ad quem* in the career of so magnificent a creature.

Whether Mr Meredith's *apologia* for witty and beautiful ladies who love to skate upon thin ice is a successful one, may be doubted. But, as a literary display, the novel is unequalled. It is written with a cleverness that is almost painful; epigrammatic sentences, phrases stuffed to bursting with meaning, make up, with the least possible matrix of padding, a literary mosaic, as perplexing often to the ordinary novel-reader as an Aristophanic chorus to a schoolboy, or Mr Browning to an exoteric public. But, with some patience, these difficulties may be overcome, and the reward is not small. The novel is decidedly the best Mr Meredith has given to the world. The diner-out will find it a very storehouse of pungent and pregnant texts; the social philosopher will be dazzled and delighted by the flashes of electric light thrown upon various aspects of his subject; and the literary expert will be no less charmed by the knowledge, fertility, and dexterity apparent in every page—it might well be said in every sentence, for in truth there is no padding at all in the book.

In the preface the author, in his trenchant way, tells his fellow-workers 'that if we do not speedily embrace philosophy in fiction the art is doomed to extinction, under the shining multitude of its professors'. Let the art, however, be so fortified, and 'rose-pink and dirty-drab will alike have passed away. Philosophy is the foe of both, and their silly, cancelling contest, perpetually renewed in a shuffle of extremes . . . will no longer baffle the contemplation of natural flesh, smother no longer the soul issuing out of our incessant strife'. And philosophy means 'hatred of the sham-decent . . . derision of sentimentalism', which is but 'the fine flower of sensualism'—in a word, truth, which is divine as charity, because it embraces all things and all aspects of things. The view is a lofty one. The art that shall produce real pictures of human life in its environment—neither photographs, unfaithful in their very accuracy, nor daubs, unfaithful through lack of knowledge, experience, or power—will be among the noblest of arts.

273

But the novelist's art gains nothing by obscurity, which is a very different thing from mystery; and an elliptic, compressed, and pregnant style is the reverse of artistic when the primary intention of the writer can only be arrived at by a painful effort on the part of his readers, and the wit, humour, and suggestiveness of his work can only be extricated by a difficult process of mental decipherment.

75. Arthur Symons, *Time*

N.S., i, May 1885

Arthur Symons (1865–1945), poet, translator, critic and editor, author of several books which remain current, was one of Meredith's most eager supporters during his early years as a writer, though he cannot be said always to have understood his subject. See below, No. 122.

Mr Meredith's latest novel is the event of the day to a small, but very select and very devoted, circle of admirers. That it should be this, and little more than this, is a practical satire on contemporary taste more convincingly bitter than the sharpest of Mr Meredith's purposed epigrams. Is the general public then truly given over to its 'rose-pink' and 'dirty drab', its rose-pink of sentimentalism, its dirty drab of so-called realism? Certainly when Charlotte M. Yonge is openly adored, and Emile Zola sneakingly relished, it looks like it. To read, without the trouble of a thought, to read with lazy acquiescence, with agreeable sensations of relish, softly charmed by the mild radiance of the rose-pink, shrewdly appealed to by the strong savour of the dirty drab; that seems to be the ideal of the novel reader. And of course he gets what he wants. Union is strength, and the novel readers are a strong band, firmly formed against the foe, shoulder to shoulder. 'Everybody knows', says Mark Pattison, 'that we go to a novel in order that we may occupy a vacant mind without giving attention'; and he remarks it in explanation

of Mr Meredith's unpopularity. 'Mr Meredith's prose requires attention
—an impertinent requirement on the part of a novelist'. As a consequence—I still quote Pattison—his name is a label warning novel
readers not to touch.[1]

To reflect on it makes one feel sermonic. Here is a man who for a
quarter of a century has been producing a series of the most brilliant
novels, written in English, since the death of Thackeray; a man whom
Swinburne and Myers[2] name in the same breath with George Eliot;
and for the general public, for the public that buys up editions and
makes what is called a 'success', he is still only a name, and a name of
terror. We have recently seen the success of a piece of puppet-work like
Called Back; a success to be only reverently spoken of in the hundred
thousands.[3] It is a singular picture of our public, breathless gentlemen
running to the railway bookstalls for copies of Called Back. After all,
honestly, this is what we admire, if we would only confess it; which we
unconsciously do once in a while. A villain with blood-stained hands;
a faultless heroine suffering the woes of good women in a wicked world;
some sort of a space-devouring hero, Apollo among the herdsmen; that
is the programme, in rough, of the truly popular novel, the novel quite
to our minds and tastes. Now, taking this as a standard, is Mr Meredith
even likely to be popular beyond the small circle of persons who think?

I fear to hope it. Let us look at a few of his leading characteristics, and
see if they seem very likely to harmonize with the public taste. In the
first place, Mr Meredith conceives that the novelist's prime study is
human nature, his first duty to be true to it. Moreover, being an artist,
he is not content with simple observations; there must be creation, the
imaginative fusion of the mass of observed fact. And it should be
noticed that to Mr Meredith, human nature does not begin and end in
those surface traits which we carelessly seem to know our friends by,
and which can be cunningly selected and joined together without
difficulty by any clever story-teller. It is needful to say it, because this
operation is often considered very profound, and the result a wonderful
triumph of psychology, human nature in photograph almost. To Mr
Meredith the conditions of truth seem harder; and I suppose they seem
very hard indeed to the reader.

Philosophy in fiction; that is Mr Meredith's demand in the introduction to Diana of the Crossways, and it is for philosophy in fiction

[1] See above, No. 67.
[2] Frederick William Henry Myers (1843–1901), poet and critic.
[3] Called Back (1884) was by Hugh Conway.

that he has been battling all his days. Do not ask if this is the road to popularity; the very word is ominous to the reader of novels. Philosophy in fiction! Double notes of exclamation cannot convey the emphasis with which I hear it shrilled in chorus. Yet perhaps these deriders would require a certain amount of 'truth to nature'? 'To demand of us truth to nature, excluding philosophy', says Mr Meredith, 'is really to bid a pumpkin caper. As much as legs are wanted for the dance, philosophy is required to make our human nature creditable and acceptable'. Nowhere, more than anywhere, writer and public are at the poles. An obtuse public requires a revelation of human nature in a series of explosions, galvanically directed acts, with little expressed connection, cause, or likelihood; only startling. Above all, there must be those 'set scenes of catching pathos and humour', which Mr Meredith declines to supply. Why? He declines to supply them, he consciously, purposely loses what are called 'good points', because it is not in nature to run to a crisis at every action. When they come, in the course of things, he rises to them, and treats them grandly, as he alone can; but he does not strain for them, nor break the right development of events for a sensation's sake. With a reliance profoundly true and artistic he subordinates incident and character, working everywhere under the lead of philosophy in fiction.

This philosophy of his seeking is only another name for intuition, analysis, imaginative insight. It can subsist, I suppose, without creation. It should presuppose this, as in Mr Meredith it does. He has comprehension of a character from height to depth through that 'eye of steady flame', which he attributes to Shakespeare, and which may be defined in every great artist. He sees it, he beholds a complete nature, at once and in entirety. His task is to make others see what he sees. But this cannot be done at a stroke. It must be done little by little, touch upon touch, light upon shade, shade upon light. The completeness, as seen by the seer or creator—the term is the same—must be microscopically investigated, divided into its component parts, produced piece by piece, and connected visibly. It is this that is meant when we talk of analysis; and the antithesis between analysis and creation is hardly so sheer as it seems. Partly through a selection of appropriate action, partly through the revealing casual speech, the imagined character takes palpable form; finally it does, or it should, live and breathe before the reader with some likeness of the hue and breath of actual life. Here it would seem we must stop, to judge by the conduct of most of our esteemed writers. But there is a step farther, and it is this step that Mr Meredith is strenuous to take. You have the flesh, animate it with spirit, with soul. Here is the task for the creator. If his eye be not of steady flame, if it falter here, he is lost. But seeing with the perfect completeness of that vision, it is possible, step by step, with a trained multitude of the keenest words of our speech, to make plain, though in our groping twilight, the incredible acts of the soul. If this is an unworthy aim, contemn Shakespeare. This is Mr Meredith's, and it is this and no other consummation that he prays for in demanding philosophy in fiction. As to the chances of popularity with our public, I have not observed that our present 'favourite novelists' aspire to philosophy in fiction.

Then again, Mr Meredith's style is a singular one. His swift-glancing wit is very trying to the general reader, his irony is terrible in its subtle unexpectedness. The public loves an easy style; a style that it considers direct, not trifling. Mr Meredith's style is confessedly not easy; but the difficulty in it is due very much to a careful attempt at that very directness and veracity which men ignorantly worship. An ordinary style of the flowing sort, such as we are educated into acquiescence with, may be said to be the legitimate ideal of the journalist, and very rightly fitted for the purposes of journalism. The purposes of journalism, and of such writing as resembles it, are obvious. Journalism is a means of conveying the opinions of the average man to the average man in a manner between the sermonic and the conversational. There is neither pretence nor attempt at a very deep insight or a very profound view. No doubt this is quite as it should be. It is of the essence of the game of politics, and must subsist; but the consequence in the direction of style is a general lowering, or rather extending, of the value of words, a general regularity of construction, according to tacitly accepted patterns, which leaves us in danger of forgetting that 'fossil poetry' is poetry as well as fossil. The main peculiarity of Mr Meredith's style is this: he thinks, to begin with, before writing—a singular thing, one may observe, in the present day. Then, having certain definite thoughts to express, and thoughts frequently of a difficult remoteness, he is careful to employ words of a rich and fruitful significance, made richer and more fruitful by a studied and uncommon arrangement. His sentences are architectural, and every word is a plain or an adorned piece of masonry fitting into the general structure. It is natural that in reading him you are inclined to cry out at the strangeness; perhaps you will add, the affectation. It is not affectation, but a rarely-revealed nature, such as we usually expect in poets, but are not thankful for in prose writers. The poet's cunning use of words in another than the common way; his art in surcharging them with a wealth of spiritual meaning. This is a commonplace of our criticism, and is accepted in the poet. Why not then in the man of prose? Mr Meredith, who is likewise so fine a poet in the actual metre, is, in this sense, as well as in others, a poet in prose.

But I have mentioned his wit. Everybody acknowledges the wit. Wit surely is popular! Then why not Mr Meredith's? It is not popular, in the first place, because it is too dazzling for weak eyes; because it is too fantastical, too learned, remote, allusive; very much because it is subtly ironical; perhaps most of all because it is shrewdly stinging to our prejudices. What is known as 'social satire' is very taking; the more rabid the better. But it is so by compromise. The satirist must chuckle behind the sneer, must wink in token of concealed amity behind the mask of the professional Diogenes, and the public will be ready in return to smile a pleasant enjoyment. But if the satirist is very much in earnest, and terribly bitter, and terribly true, it is another matter. Like the greatest of his fellows, Mr Meredith is not a story-teller merely, he is a spiritual fighter. His shafts are deadly to the dull, the sham, the conventional; the cruelty of the world, its folly, tyranny, and panics, its ancestral treatment of women—a pet topic, and a dangerous. A good critic, and a competent observer and chronicler of current society, has said of two portraits in Mr Meredith's latest novel—Constance Asper and Lady Watkin, 'types of the British virgin and the British matron; two species that our author does not love'—that they are 'cruelly and splendidly successful. They would go far to make him unpopular were he as widely read as Ouida'.[1] This satire is too quiet, too clinging, too pervasive and incontestable, to be taking. The *sauce piquante* to the British palate is a lighter condiment than this, which is prepared from a recipe not in its cookery books.

Thus much for Mr Meredith's present chances of popularity beyond that small circle to which I referred; the circle of persons who think. How very small this is it is not pleasant, but may be profitable to reflect. I had recently the pleasure of perusing a list of our chief novelists, as given in a book of stately proportions and voluminous matter. Seventy or eighty names were mentioned; they ranged from Walter Scott to Hawley Smart—a long interval, in time and much else. The name of George Meredith was indeed 'conspicuous' by its absence in so comprehensive a catalogue. Again, I have been gravely asked by bookish people if I do not mean *Owen* Meredith by *George* Meredith. It is easy

[1] See above, No. 70.

to say, *Non ragionam di lor, una guarda e passa*,[1] but the cheap contempt is ineffectual. These people insist on being talked of, for it is owing to them, and such as they are, that Mr Meredith's books are a prize to bibliophiles and a problem to would-be readers. For a few shillings you can get almost any novel of any living novelist, small or great. Mr Meredith is, I think, the one exception. I believe the majority of his books have never even trod the well-worn round from the three volumes to the one. Not more than one or two are now accessible (save to a patience and a purse not given to all) in any shape or form.

For this we have to thank the good people who do not know the difference between George Meredith and Owen Meredith. One cannot suppose the publishers to be blind to their own interests, and it is presumable that if even a moderate section of the reading public cared to read Mr Meredith's novels, the publishers would see the wisdom of occasionally allowing one to buy a copy at a reasonable rate. When we may expect this privilege I do not know. As it is a question of supply and demand I suppose we are foolish to dream of it. Meanwhile, one is curious to know how long *Diana of the Crossways*, for the present Mr Meredith's latest novel, will remain accessible to the ordinary buyer. It is a practical question, perhaps seemingly too practical for a refined criticism; but it is significant of much. It means simply this: how much less than the consideration we show to a thousand-and-one tales of sentiment and sensation, shall we show to a novel that is purely a work of genius, and in which almost the exactness of science is wedded to all the charm of art?

76. Unsigned review, *The Times*

1 June 1885

To pass a verdict upon this novel of Mr George Meredith is a difficult task, for it cannot be judged by the tests applied to ordinary novels. The author's style and matter are like no others. Mr Meredith might

[1] Dante, *Inferno*, I, iii, 51: 'Do not let us reason of these, but look and pass on.'

pose for the Carlyle of fiction, so rugged is his style, so uncouth his ellipses, so powerful the collocations of his words. Such a mannered style does not sit well on a novelist, especially in dialogue, where the speakers are made to appear uniformly *bizarre* of speech. His conception of a novel, as he hints in his preface, is philosophy sweetened by romance—a sufficiently high ideal, were we to hold that in *Diana of the Crossways* it has been attained. Honestly speaking, his Diana enshrines much wisdom of the serpent, and much epigrammatic wit to which, by a little straining of language, we may allow the title of philosophy. But the inappositeness of Mr Meredith's philosophy is too often veiled under a spasmodic style of writing. In a writer less clever, less gifted with the power of compelling attention, such interpolations would be called by another name. The story is of a beautiful and witty woman, the victim of an unhappy marriage, who, living separated from her husband and supporting herself by her pen, attempts, by indifference to social usage, to defy the opinion of a world which interprets *tête-à-tête* with admirers in only one way. Diana Warwick, it will be surmised, is a wrong-headed woman; but, despite her imprudences, she has our sympathy until the main incident of the story, when she betrays her chief admirer in the most base and heartless manner, by selling for money the Cabinet secret which he has intrusted to her only. Strangely, Mr Meredith views the offence as venial. The Hon. Percy Dacier thinks differently; he leaves Diana abruptly and for ever. Perhaps he goes too far when he engages himself the same day to Constance Asper in marriage. He can, at any rate, be excused for ceasing to love where he could no longer respect. Yet he is stigmatized, apparently with the author's sanction, as exhibiting 'a type of the externally soft and polished, internally hard and relentless, who are equal to the trials of love only as long as favouring circumstances and seemings nurse the fair object of their courtship'. Lack of space prevents us from giving specimens of the many wise sayings that are to be found in this book, which, if for them alone, well repays reading. If we may be censorious we would object that the tone is distinctly modern, although the period is dated some 50 years back, when there ought to have been no society papers, and when it would not have been easy for a married woman to sell her landed property without the concurrence of her husband. And even 50 years ago we do not know that in cricket the fielder at 'long-off' was called 'long hit off'.

77. W. L. Courtney on Meredith's claims to eminence

1886

W. L. Courtney (1850–1928) was an influential journalist, editor of the *Daily Telegraph* and *the Fortnightly*. The article appeared in the *Fortnightly Review*, xxxix, June 1886, entitled 'George Meredith's novels'.

Is it true that since the death of George Eliot we have no novelist of the first rank? Will the future historian of the novelistic literature of the nineteenth century cease his study with a review of the author of *Romola* and *Middlemarch*, and class the numerous writers of the present day under the head of what Mr Stedman calls, in poetry, the 'General Choir'?[1] It is clear at all events that the peculiar literary condition of the modern novelist's craft has been unalterably fixed by Thackeray and George Eliot, and that no author can now claim the highest rank unless he possesses that analytical gift which turns some novels into psychological treatises and others into studies in pessimism. And it is also clear that no one understands better the conditions under which he writes than the clever author whose works, from the *Shaving of Shagpat* in 1855, down to *Diana of the Crossways* in 1885, have filled the latter half of the present era. Only in such an age as ours could a novelist like Mr George Meredith be acceptable, for only in such an age could his peculiar gifts win for themselves recognition or even tolerance. That they have not failed to make their mark is sufficiently witnessed by the handsome edition of his works which is now being issued from the press by Messrs Chapman and Hall. In the presence, however, of so far-reaching a question as that with which we began, we instinctively find ourselves trying to reckon the gifts which distinguish the supreme novelist. Is it too much to insist that the primary one is the capacity for telling a story, and that the conscious and wilful neglect of this apparently obvious fact is the cause why so many novels are such hard

[1] This phrase is used as title to ch. vii of E. C. Stedman's *Victorian Poets* (1875).

reading? Only in the second place must come the psychological instinct which analyses the various forms in which the subtlety of human feeling disguises itself, and reduces the unity of existence into a diversity of conflicting motives. For the first is creative, spontaneous, original, while the second is introverted and critical. When the scalpel of the anatomist makes mock at the wonder of life, as though it were something so ordinary that it can be divided upon the dissecting board, there is usually the attendant spirit of cynicism, if not of scepticism. What analysis has destroyed, that synthesis must restore; and if the creative gift be absent all the ideal elements disappear. Many other traits may be ascribed to the character of the novelist, such as a sense of humour, a vivid imagination, and a power of vigorous expression; but these clearly rank below the level of the two that have been singled out as his especial gifts.

The relative importance of the creative and the critical faculty has been differently estimated in past ages of our literary history. The present age is clearly that which attributes most importance to the critical gift. If we take the supreme works of our modern novelists, the *Esmond* and *Vanity Fair* of Thackeray, the *Adam Bede* and *Romola* of George Eliot, while their chief merit is that they have added to the inevitable analysis the synthetic elements of a new creation of characters, their chief value for us is their keenness of insight into the springs and levers of human action. Directly a novelist lifts himself from the common herd it is in virtue of a certain psychological power which works not so much by intuition as by ratiocination. Hence it is that nothing pleases the fastidious taste of a public that has grown too wise to enjoy and too refined to admire, except the patient unweaving of that complex web of sentiment and thought and volition which makes up the whole of human existence.

Mr Meredith is so much the child of his age that he exhibits at once its characteristic strength and weakness. The fatal gift which appears to have been bequeathed to thoughtful novelists by the influence of Thackeray is a positive incapacity for enjoyment. Thackeray, as is well known, attempted to construct a picture of society and of human nature in which the heart was conspicuously omitted. Those who have felt the fascination of his artistic power have imitated him also in his treatment of humanity. No one, it would appear, ever acts with spontaneous simplicity except silly girls and little children. For the rest, humanity has to bear the burden of its reasonableness, and to give up with complacent resignation the faculty of being ingenuous or single-hearted. For there is no action in which analysis cannot discover the confluence of discordant motives; it is forgotten that at the time when the action was performed there was no consciousness of discord, but only the singleness of some predominant purpose. Hence the touch of cynical bitterness with which the panorama of human activity is surveyed. For, clearly, if we look deep enough there is nothing we say or do which does not bear the suspicion of some low and crawling motive. The fault, however, lies with those who insist on looking with such microscopic severity, the upper levels of feeling being untouched by the baseness of our composite nature. It is one of the tendencies of psychological analysis to breed cynicism and to belittle the dignity of energetic action. Meanwhile the joy of living expires in the sustained effort to disclose the springs on which it depends.

We must add, as an especial characteristic of Mr Meredith, a certain desperate cleverness, which is undoubtedly a source of fascination, but at the same time as often fills the reader with a profound despondency. Nothing is so disintegrating as cleverness. Genius is inspiring, because it is full of a collective sympathy, but cleverness is always isolated, repellent, obstructive. The clever man is never otherwise than self-conscious, and self-consciousness is a constant source of irritation. Never does Mr Meredith lose himself in some generous overflow; over all his creations perches the inevitable shadow of the author, as though it were some ill-omened bird adding its hoarse chorus at the end of each paragraph. The cleverness is not always of malice prepense; it may readily be allowed to be the natural gift of a man who has also made its exhibition the chief solicitude of his literary life. But cleverness it is and ends in being; rarely enough does it ascend into genius, just as it equally rarely descends into the homeliness of commonplace. And though it is welcome enough to certain moods—when the mind is weary, for instance, of the daily newspaper or the Sabbath sermon—it is chilling to the mood of receptivity or intuition. It tickles the lower levels of intelligence, and never awakens the sudden glow of a higher thought. The form in which Mr Meredith's cleverness is especially exhibited is the style of his composition. He is above all the artist of epigrams—a meaner sort of artistic work, which exhibits all the defects of conscious purpose. The style consequently is never easy or flowing; ever and anon we are brought up short by some arresting phrase, which keeps us painfully on the alert for the next challenge. Of all introductory chapters to an interesting novel, surely that which prefaces the history of *Diana of the Crossways* is the most irritating. It may be presumed that many a reader brought face to face with such a bristling rampart of phrases has sadly gone back and walked no more with an author of so appalling a cleverness.

Many illustrations of such characteristics can be gained from a perusal of Mr Meredith's works. If, for instance, we desired to describe the author's view of life by a significant phrase, we should call it essentially the view of the middle-aged spectator. Long ago have the rosy illusions of youth been got rid of; the prevalent colouring of experience is the middle point between black and white. There is some of the benevolence also of middle age, a benevolence which is not wholly sympathetic, but largely motived by cynicism, the benevolence, let us say, of Montaigne rather than of Herodotus. A good-natured tolerance of follies, combined with a merciless exposure of frailty; a humorous smile at delinquency with the corners of the mouth turned down at the shifts and evasions of hypocrisy; laughter and tears, not indeed spontaneously welling from a full heart, but of that gentlemanly sort which conserves the rule of μηδὲν ἄγαν;[1] a shrewd, self-controlled attitude throughout, with a remarkable discernment of all the various shades of grey—such are the endowments of the middle-aged spectator. In one of the earliest and one of the best of Mr Meredith's novels, *The Ordeal of Richard Feverel*, there is a character which admirably represents the habitual posture of the author. It is that of Adrian Harley, 'the wise youth' as he is always called, a character over which considerable trouble is expended, and which deserves all the careful exposition which it receives, for assuredly it is that which comes nearest to being the author's own. Adrian Harley, for instance, might easily have been described as writing *The Egoist*, or spoiling the story of Ferdinand Lassalle, by the curiously cumbrous title of the *Tragic Comedians*. A critical age is always preternaturally old, and the wise youth has also a sagacity beyond his years. He has indeed his own pleasures, but they never amount to positive happiness, because they are too clear-eyed and precocious. Once or twice, when he or his creator writes about the innocent loves of two young people in a hopeless state of calf-affection, his style gets lighter and sweeter. Almost, there is the true lyric touch in the chapters of *Richard Feverel* which deal with the hero's love-making with Lucy Desborough. 'The sweet heaven-bird shivered out his song above him. The gracious glory of heaven fell upon his soul. He touched her hand, not moving his eyes from her nor speaking, and she with a soft word of farewell passed across the stile, and up the pathway through the dewy shades of the

[1] 'Nothing too much.'

copse, and out of the arch of the light away from his eyes'. But listen to the irony of the description of such a scene—'a diversion on a penny whistle'; and hear the wholly unnecessary apologies—'Hail the occasion propitious, O British young! and laugh and treat love as an honest god, and dabble not with the sentimental rouge'. 'They have outflown philosophy. Their instinct has shot beyond the ken of science. They were made for their Eden'. Yes, the lovers may have outflown it. The critical eyes of Adrian Harley look down upon the innocent fair with just that touch of tolerant pity and condescending kindness which mars the simplicity of the picture. The very insistence upon the innocency proves that it is too conscious to be true. If it were not too unkind a thing to say, it might be plausibly asserted that through such spectacles one feels more at home with the illicit love of Feverel and Bella Mount. At all events, no author is more capable of giving such sudden shocks of coarseness as we have to endure in these novels. Sometimes, though perhaps rarely, the gorge rises at sentences of an almost incredible indelicacy, at other times we have a whole chapter filled with such offensive rubbish as the 'Dinner Party at Richmond' in *Richard Feverel*. Are such interludes surprising? Psychologically, no, though we have a right from an artistic standpoint to expect otherwise. The revulsions from a strained pitch of critical analysis are often found to reach lower and more shameful levels than are possible to contented commonplace.

Perhaps in no novel do we find the absence of joy more conspicuous than in *Harry Richmond*. Here is a young man who goes through a series of surprising adventures quite removed from the sphere of probability. He is fallen in love with by a German princess, and finds a lost father attitudinizing as a bronze image on the top of a hill. The only literary excuse for such extravagances would be the rollicking character of the hero, such a one, for instance, as was endeared to our childhood by Captain Marryat or Kingston.[1] But Harry Richmond does not rollick; he is never young, but talks about himself with the *maladie de la pensée* of a modern age. 'Books and dreams, like the two rivers cited by my father, flowed side by side in me without mixing: and which the bright Rhone was, which the brown Arve, needs not to be told to those who know anything of youth; they were destined to intermingle soon enough. I read well, for I felt ground and had mounting views;

---

[1] Frederick Marryat (1792–1848), author of *Mr Midshipman Easy* (1836) and *Masterman Ready* (1841). William Henry Giles Kingston (1814–80) produced a series of novels and romances. He also translated Jules Verne and edited *Kingston's Annual for Boys, Kingston's Magazine for Boys*, and the *Union Jack*.

the real world, and the mind and passions of the world, grew visible to me'. Poor youth! or rather, poor wise youth, preternaturally middle-aged, to whom the real world and the mind and the passions of the world grew visible! 'The foregoing conversations with Ottilia and her teacher, hard as they were for passion to digest, grew luminous on a relapsing heart'. Is this the boy who can fight a duel with Otto and be the ideal of the romantic Ottilia—a youth who has mounting views and a relapsing heart? '"One gets so addle-pated thinkin' many things," said Mrs Berry simply. "That's why we see wonder clever people al'ays goin' wrong—to my mind. I think it's al'ays the plan in a dielemmer to pray God and walk forward"'. If only Mr Meredith had sometimes followed the advice of his admirable Mrs Berry! What a comfort it would be if he would allow us sometimes to picture him as praying God and walking forward!

But Mr Meredith is in these matters only paying the penalty for being an analyst and a psychologist. He cannot well help himself; he must be the child of his age. The problem, it would seem, of the future novelist is to combine the most searching analytical power with the gift of narrative, and the combination appears undoubtedly a formidable one to accomplish, if we choose to compare all those contemporary writers who can tell a story without being able to draw a character on the one side, with those on the other who can analyse motives and yet are unable to compose an interesting fiction. In Mr Meredith's own case we have works which represent different stages in this effort to combine the obstinate elements. If we wish to see an instance where analysis seems to end with itself, we have but to take up *The Egoist*, or, better still, the *Tragic Comedians*. The latter book was indeed in some ways a literary mistake. Here was a well known story of how a thoughtful Socialist suddenly and unaccountably fell in love with a more or less mundane young lady, fought a duel with another and more military lover, and came by a tragic end. It was a piquant study for a psychologist; but the obvious difficulty was to understand the woman for whom the political philosopher was ready to make such a sacrifice. Unfortunately, the lady herself had told her own story, and though it was a curiously uninstructive apology or self-vindication, yet after all it possessed much more vital interest than any philosophical reconstruction of her motives could inspire. Mr Meredith's analysis hardly tells us anything that was not known before, and it sadly lacks the flesh and blood which might animate the logical skeleton. We turn to *Diana of the Crossways*, and we seem to breathe a new atmosphere.

There is the same analytical power, the same liking to probe and expound, to unweave and explicate the throbbing nerves of human life. There is as much and more cleverness exhibited, and heaven fore-fend that all our acquaintances should express their thoughts in the same scintillating phrases. But there is the life we feel and know—the same warm and palpitating flesh, the same human, throbbing, inconsistent heart of which we are conscious. Diana is a real living and breathing woman, gracious in all her divine impulse and her mortal errors. The philosophy has taken to itself wings and soars; the analysis has clothed its clanking skeleton ribs with comfortable tissue. It is not only in the principal character who gives her name to the book that this transformation has taken place, but many of the other and sub-ordinate personages have caught the infection and begin to be vital. Sir Lukin is an admirable sketch, so is Lady Wathin, so is Mr Redworth, so too is the youthful poet, Mr Rhodes. It may perhaps be a disadvantage that so many of the incidents and so much of the character-drawing are taken out of actual modern history; and there are of course those who can point to the actual Diana, and pierce beneath the transparent disguise of Mr Redworth. But novels are not written only for those who are *au courant* with the phrases of London Society. *Nous autres* may enjoy and admire, and the author has given us much for common thankfulness. Leaving aside the introductory chapter, which all may safely do without injury to the tale, and with positive advantage to themselves, there are the charming episodes of Diana's re-awakening and of Dacier's wooing, the two contrasted interviews of Diana and Dacier, of which the first is all sunshine and the second the gloom of Erebus, and the fresh play of feeling with which the relations between Tony and Emmy are touched over and over again by the author's facile hand. With the one exception of *Richard Feverel*, *Diana of the Crossways* contains Mr Mere-dith's most clever and successful work.

It is indeed not easy to over-estimate some of the elements which form Mr Meredith's character as a novelist. If one or two of the obvious drawbacks strike one most at the first reading, many of the solid advantages are more conspicuous on a second view. The novels may require diligent study, and it may be difficult to defend some of them on the hypothesis that the primary task of a novelist is to amuse. But Mr Mere-dith, though sometimes obscure owing to the sudden transitions of his thought, is never really dull. He may not be interesting in the ordinary sense of the term, but he is eminently stimulating and suggestive. He possesses a wonderful gift of fancy, and is not devoid of the saving grace of humour. The reader may catch himself wondering what position in the cricket-field is signified by 'a long-hit off' (*Diana*, p. 360); and marvel at clouds which 'threaten the shower they retain, and teach gloom to rouse a songful nest in the bosom of the viewer'. But though the imagination may sometimes be perversely irritating, it is often brilliant, and at times felicitously illustrative. It is never quite the imagination of the poet, despite the author's ingenious volumes of verse; for it is never instinctive, enthralling, inevitable. But there is the acute penetrative insight of the philosopher and the imagination of a matured and inventive critic.

Philosophic novelist Mr Meredith claims to be, and with considerable justice. He has a theory on the subject which he puts in the forefront of his latest novel in explicit and definite form, though, unconsciously perhaps, it had guided his practice all along. The passage is worth quoting, for it expresses one of the most characteristic ideas which distinguishes the novelistic art in its modern acceptation. Formerly perhaps, when the novel was in its early youth, it might claim to be mainly narrative and romantic. Now it must vindicate its position by being a disguised treatise on mental philosophy, 'The forecast may be hazarded that if we do not speedily embrace philosophy in fiction, the art is doomed to extinction. Instead, therefore, of objurgating the timid intrusions of philosophy, invoke her presence, I pray you. History without her is the skeleton-map of events: Fiction, a picture of figures modelled on no skeleton-anatomy. But each, with philosophy in aid, blooms, and is humanly shapely. To demand of us truth to nature, excluding philosophy, is really to bid a pumpkin caper. As much as legs are wanted for the dance, philosophy is required to make our human nature credible and acceptable. Fiction implores you to heave a bigger breast and take her in with this heavenly preservative helpmate, her inspiration and her essence'. All of which means, though it is written in Mr Meredith's habitually jerky style, that the highest culture is necessarily philosophic, and that as civilization progresses each art must have its roots deep within the soil which is cultivated by psychologists and metaphysicians. For what is the alternative? So far as fiction is concerned, it is that we must for ever be in one-sided extremes, and either accept the namby-pamby optimism of clerics or the realistic pessimism of the democratic vulgar. Assuredly we have a right to exclaim, 'Ni talons rouges, ni bonnets rouges'. Think of a national fiction which was divided between Mrs Henry Wood on the one hand, and Zola on the other! Yet to such issues is art driven when it either knows nothing

about or cares nothing for psychology. It is Mr Meredith's merit that
he sees this clearly enough, and that he traces it to its right cause. As
he puts it in his enigmatically graphic style, 'Philosophy is the foe of
both rose-pink and dirty drab, and their silly cancelling contrast.
Philosophy bids us to see that we are not so pretty as rose-pink, not so
repulsive as dirty drab; and that instead of everlastingly shifting those
barren aspects, the sight of ourselves is wholesome, bearable, fructifying,
finally a delight'. Whether Mr Meredith has thoroughly learnt his
own lesson, is of course another matter. Certainly he has here and there
a truly psychologic insight, but as often as not his philosophy seems to
consist in aphorisms such as were extensively popular in the time of
the Seven Wise Men, before the true era of Greek philosophy began.
He has a strange fondness for these aphoristic utterances, which at their
worst are assuredly better than Mr Tupper's proverbs,[1] and at their
best have some of the concentrated wisdom of Baconian maxims. In
Richard Feverel, for instance, there is the recurring burden of the
'Pilgrim's Scrip', a series of sagacious apophthegms which is supposed
to be composed by the hero's father; and in *Diana of the Crossways* we
have the quotations from the diaries and the brilliant sayings of the
gifted Mrs Warwick. It is, however, true to add that *The Ordeal of
Richard Feverel* is itself a truly philosophic study, being in its essence a
treatise on methods of education.

Of the more properly artistic elements, it is impossible to attribute
to our author the gift of style, except in a very special sense. He has
indeed the faculty for many a suggestive and piquant phrase, and on
every page there is found the rich deposit of a singularly wide and
far-reaching culture. But style is something different from this—that
fine literary spirit and impalpable charm which George Eliot possessed
only rarely, which makes Thackeray's *Esmond* so supreme a novel,
which in a simple form breathes through Jane Austen's works and for
ever lifts them from the commonplace, and of which among living
writers only Mr Froude seems to possess the veritable secret.[2] Once
under the influence of this magic we instinctively feel the artist, and
when it is absent we only coldly admire the writer. Yet it would be in
the highest sense unjust not to recognize the true artistic feeling with
which Mr Meredith places his characters in an atmospheric background
of nature. Nature he knows and loves, and when he speaks of her it is in

[1] Martin Farquhar Tupper (1810–89) was famous for his *Proverbial Philosophy* (1838–42).
[2] James Anthony Froude (1818–94), novelist, historian, Editor of *Fraser's Magazine*
from 1860–74, and Thomas Carlyle's literary executor.

the true spirit of a devotee. 'The sun is coming down to earth, and the fields and the waters shout to him golden shouts. He comes, and his heralds run before him, and touch the leaves of oaks and planes and beeches lucid green, and the pine-stems redder gold; leaving brightest foot-prints upon thickly-weeded banks, where the foxglove's last upper-bells incline, and bramble-shoots wander amid moist, rich herbage. The plumes of the woodland are alight: and beyond them, over the open, 'tis a race with the long-thrown shadows; a race across the heaths and up the hills, till at the farthest bourne of mounted eastern cloud, the heralds of the sun lay rosy fingers and rest'. The curious thing is that when Mr Meredith allows himself these poetic interludes he is much more of the poet of nature than when he sets himself to write *Poems and Lyrics of the Joy of Earth*. Perhaps the conscious effort begets a certain frigid brilliancy instead of native warmth. Who would exchange the hints of natural beauty in his novels for 'The Woods of Westermain' or the 'Lark Ascending'? In these as elsewhere there is the taint of an introspective personality, the conscious cleverness of Adrian Harley. We feel uneasy under the strain, as though the tension of living up to an epigrammatic level was not only too much for the reader's nerves, but might possibly prove fatal to the author. There is much comfort in a writer who neither strives nor cries, but is the serene master of his own wit and genius.

Thus the question with which we opened remains unanswered, or only answered in part. How much of Mr Meredith will our children read? Perhaps two or three novels at most—*Evan Harrington, Richard Feverel*, and *Diana of the Crossways*. Even these we can hardly imagine entering into their life, as *Romola* and *Adam Bede* have into ours. For towards Mr Meredith we always must have a certain reserve; he does not come into the heart, we are still out of doors. Yet his is a powerful mind, full of philosophic culture. Some of his sayings will not leave us, even though the total impression be forgotten. This is just what might be expected in the case of a clever student of life, whose analytic power has been fostered at the expense of constructive art.

78. Unsigned review, *Pall Mall Gazette*

xlv, 26 May 1887

'Unhappy poets of a sunken prime'! sang Mr Meredith in a former volume. 'You to reviewers are as ball to bat'. Accepting the image (not a very luminous one) we must confess that Mr Meredith's new volume is a ticklish ball to play. It is delivered with prodigious energy and with a cunning twist; but in our opinion it twists away from the wicket. We even fear that the great umpire, Time, may pronounce it a 'wide'.

Mr Meredith has written a good deal of verse that ought to live, most of it being contained in that now 'seld-seen' volume 'Modern Love'. One or two of the misnamed *Poems and Lyrics of the Joy of Earth* may also pass to posterity, but we question whether many, or any, of the ballads in the new volume are likely to sing in the ears of coming generations. For Mr Meredith, like many other poets of this 'sunken prime', seems to misconceive the function and end of poetic expression. Poetry, according to him, should surprise rather than charm, should aim at quaintness in the first place, loveliness only in the second place, if at all. He is certainly not one of the singers who sacrifice meaning to music, but he shows one symptom of their disease in postponing reason to rhyme. He treats rhyme as an independent beauty, a thing to be desired for its own sake and to be achieved at whatever loss of perspicuity, dignity, style, or sense. In French poetics, as we understand it, this theory is strictly orthodox. It would seem that to the French ear the mere chiming of two syllables, or still better of two pairs of syllables, is in itself a positive pleasure. Our English ears are differently constructed. A forced rhyme, however sonorous, is to us either irritating or grotesque. What we primarily and peremptorily demand in poetry, as in prose, is that the words in which any given thought is expressed shall be apt and beautiful in themselves, and in their collocation clear and forcible. To neglect this condition is to sin against the fundamental law of style. But when we find that these well-chosen and well-arranged words fall naturally into musical cadences, and rhyme, to all seeming, of their own accord, we receive from this coincidence of all possible graces and excellences of expression that highest of pleasures which it is the peculiar gift of poetry to confer. Every one who has ever attempted verse knows that, as a matter of fact, the rhyme suggests the thought at least as often as the thought the rhyme; but this is one of those trade secrets which should be studiously concealed from the uninitiated. Any verse in which it is allowed to leak out is, for that reason, bad poetry. It may be vastly ingenious, surprising, even admirable, but it belongs essentially to the *Ingoldsby* or Gilbert school of art.[1] An English rhyme should never surprise us, unless by the fact that there is nothing surprising about it. We are aware that this theory conflicts with the practice of many modern poets, Mr Meredith among the rest; but we state it with none the less confidence. Take the very first stanza in Mr Meredith's new book:

[Quotes 'The Two Masks', st. i.]

This seems to be Mr Meredith's way of stating the familiar fact that it is but a step from the sublime to the ridiculous, and it surely cannot be said that his ornate utterance adds either force or clearness to the observation. Is, then, the loss of force and clearness compensated by a gain in absolute beauty? There may be persons to whom the imperfect jingle of 'people' (pipple) with 'ripple' gives satisfaction, and who so delight in the chiming of 'Athos' with 'pathos' as to overlook or excuse, perhaps even to admire, the titanic effort whereby the mountainous metaphor is lugged into the verse. Even these persons, however, must surely wonder what is meant by a 'museful ripple', and ask themselves whether the 'tendril hooks' of Thalia's lips do not exist simply and solely for the purpose of hanging on to the 'looks' in the second line. We do not argue that there is no meaning at all in the 'tendril hooks'. With a little good will one can force a meaning into the veriest gibberish. What we do maintain is that the sense is so painfully farfetched as to make it obvious that the rhyme suggested the image, and so to vitiate any possible gratification which the ear might receive from the concord

[1] A reference to Richard Harris Barham's *Ingoldsby Legends* (1840) and William Schwenk Gilbert's *Bab Ballads* (1866–71).

of 'looks' with 'hooks'. Again, what a contorted and cumbrous line is this:

> Perchance may change of masks midway demand.

The idea expressed is obscure (who is to change masks?); the arrangement of words is feeble and unnatural; and the measure is heavy and halting. Altogether, this is a good example of the stanzas, too frequent in Mr Meredith's work, wherein the artifice of verse neither conceals nor justifies itself, but rather tempts us to wonder why anyone should be at such pains to express himself so badly. Take again these stanzas from 'King Harald's Trance':

[Quotes st. v–viii.]

Surely this is a case for Thalia to bring her 'tendril hooks' into action. It is characteristic of Mr Meredith as a narrator that he should omit to mention the central fact of his poem. Having informed us that 'the toasts hurrahed' until 'awink' King Harald bade his wife retire, he proceeds to describe the phenomena of the King's trance without a word as to how he fell into it. The lines:

> Mountain on his trunk,
> Ocean on his head.

we do not profess to interpret; they are a dark saying. Then, when the poet designs to tell us that the king lay speechless, he remarks that 'This Thor failed a weak lamb's baa'. We purposely write the phrase as though it were prose, in order to show what execrable prose it would be. Mr Meredith may urge that the best of verse, because of its rhythmic quality, would make bad prose; but this prose is bad, not because it is rhythmic, but because it is not rational human speech. We are here at the kernel of the matter. Though a whole generation of poets should testify against us, it is our firm conviction that poetry, no less than prose, is subject to the laws of rational human speech. Against this thraldom Mr Meredith's proud spirit is too apt to rebel.

'The Nuptials of Attila', the longest poem in this collection, is to our mind the finest. Its movement is magnificent. Next to it stands 'France, December, 1870', an ode with many noble passages. 'Aneurin's Harp' is quaint and spirited, and there is a breath of warm life in 'The Young Princess'. 'Archduchess Anne' and 'A Preaching from a Spanish Ballad', on the other hand, are in Mr Meredith's crabbedest manner, while 'The Song of Theodolinda' and 'The Last Contention' are enigmatic to a degree. The following versicles, headed 'Hernani', have a haunting trip in them:

[Quotes 'Hernani'.]

Mr Meredith excels in these odd little gargoyles upon the fabric of his fantasy. If only he would keep contortion and grotesqueness in their right places, and not have them cropping out irrelevantly, here, there, and everywhere.

79. W. E. Henley, *Athenaeum*

No. 3111, 11 June 1887

For W. E. Henley see above, No. 57, headnote. Lionel Stevenson records that this review gave Meredith 'peculiar annoyance', and that the phrase 'a harlequin, a performer of antics' is repeated in his letter to G. P. Baker (see below, No. 81) (*The Ordeal of George Meredith*, 1954, 275). It is perhaps significant that, after this article, Meredith refused Henley's offer of a presentation copy of his reprinted reviews.

Mr Meredith rarely says anything not worth hearing. He has too much ability for that; and, besides, he is strenuously in earnest about his work. He has a noble sense of the dignity of art and the responsibilities of the artist; he will set down nothing that is, to his mind, unworthy to be recorded; his treatment of his material is distinguished by the presence of an intellectual passion (as it were) that makes whatever he does considerable and deserving of attention and respect. Unhappily for us, however, the will is not seldom unequal to the deed; the achievement is often leagues in rear of the inspiration; the attempt at completeness is too laboured and too manifest—the feat is done, but by a painful and ungraceful process. There *is* genius, but there is *not* felicity. That, one is inclined to say, is the distinguishing note of Mr Meredith's work, in prose and verse alike. There are magnificent exceptions, of course, but they prove the rule, and broken though it may be, there is no gainsaying its existence. To be concentrated in form, to be suggestive in material, to say nothing that is not of permanent value, and only to say it in such terms as are charged to the fullest with significance—this would seem to be the aim and end of Mr Meredith's ambition. Of simplicity in his own person he seems incapable. The texture of his expression must be stiff with allusion, or he deems it ill spun; there must be something of antic in his speech, or he cannot believe he is addressing himself to the Immortals; he has praised with perfect understanding the lucidity, the elegance, the ease of Molière, and yet his aim in art (it would appear) is to be Molière's antipodes, and to vanquish by congestion, clottedness, an anxious and determined dandyism of form and style. There is something *bourgeois* in his intolerance of the commonplace, something fanatical in the intemperance of his regard for artifice. 'Le dandy', says Baudelaire, 'doit aspirer à être sublime sans interruption. Il doit vivre et dormir devant un miroir'.[1] That, one is tempted to believe, is Mr Meredith's theory of expression. 'Ce qu'il y a dans le mauvais goût', is elsewhere the opinion of the same unamiable artist in paradox, 'c'est le plaisir aristocratique de déplair'.[2] Is that, one asks oneself, the reason why Mr Meredith is so contemptuous of the general public—why he will stoop to no sort of concession, nor permit himself so much as a mite of patience with the herd whose intellect is content with such poor fodder as Scott and Dickens and Dumas? Be it as it may, the effect is the same. Mr Meredith is bent upon being 'uninterruptedly sublime'; and we must take him as he wills and as we find him. He loses, of course; and we suffer. But none the less do we cherish his society, and none the less are we interested in his processes, and delighted (when we are clever enough) with his results. He lacks felicity, as has been said; but he has charm as well as power, and, once his rule is accepted, there is no means of shaking him off. The position is that of the antique tyrant in a commonwealth once republican and free. We resent the domination, but we enjoy it too, and, with or against our will, we admire the author of our slavery.

In the present volume there is—one need hardly note it—an abundance of matter for dispute. It is hard, for instance, to follow the poet through the tortuosities of 'Archduchess Anne'; it is a ballad, and to break the secret of a ballad one should not need a dark lantern and a set

[1] 'Mon coeur mis à nu', iii.
[2] 'Fusées', xii.

of jemmies. There is good matter in 'A Preaching from a Spanish Ballad'; and though the verse is somewhat obvious in movement, and the phrase is often a trifle dark with excess of brightness, it claims and commands more readings than one. In 'Aneurin's Horn' we find a notable warning to the England of today set forth with admirable energy and directness, and in 'The Song of Theodolinda' the expression of a vexed and troubled soul in terms of singular intensity. The effect of 'Bellerophon' is that of one of Rembrandt's most tragic portraits; that of 'Periander'—which in two verses of its opening stanza,

> A woman who is wife despotic lords
> Count faggot at the question, Shall she live,

contains an enigma which would break the heart of a Shakspearean commentator—one rather of heroic intention than complete achievement; that of 'The Young Princess', one romantic, lyrical, and dramatic in a breath; that of 'The Nuptials of Attila', the impression that this is Mr Meredith's right work, and that if he always wrote as here, and were always as here sustained in inspiration, rapid of march, nervous of phrase, apt of metaphor, and intoxicating in effect, he would be delightful to the general, and that without sacrificing on the vile and filthy altar of popularity. In this last, indeed, he is successfully himself. C'est tout dire. We clap for Harlequin, and we kneel to Apollo. Mr Meredith doubles the parts, and is irresistible in both. Such fire, such vision, such energy on the one hand, and on the other such agility and athletic grace, are not often found in combination.

A higher level is reached in 'France, December, 1871', [sic] an ode— irregular in form, lofty in inspiration, in symmetry a little broken, somewhat excessive in length—in which the poet laments the ruin wrought on

> Her that sunlike stood
> Upon the forehead of our day,
> An orb of nations, radiating food
> For body and for mind alway.

Here the issues are human and tragic; and, as is usual with Mr Meredith when this is so, the antic vein is stopped, the style is strong and simple, the inspiration masculine, the effect immediate and profound. We have marked more passages than one for quotation, but the thing should be read as a whole; the eloquence is too vigorous, the poetry too constant and sustained, to be shown in samples. That, too, is the case of 'Phaéthôn', an achievement in the galliambic measure, which, as we read it, contains but one line too many (we shall not quote it), and which, if less elegant and correct than the Laureate's 'Boadicea', is touched with a quality of imagination that is almost epic, and should be read, not as galliambics, but as poetry pure and simple, while English poetry endures. But we have quoted nothing from Mr Meredith as yet; and one passage of the 'Phaéthôn' is so striking and so complete that to refrain from citing it is impossible:—

[Quotes 'Phaéthôn', ll. 98–120.]

To the ear that lingers with ecstasy upon the 'Atys' the music of this passage may sound rough and arbitrary enough. Attempts of the kind Mr Meredith has made are seldom successful. It is doubtful, however, if the peculiar genius of the metre could be recalled in alien material with greater daring or a finer prodigality of diction; and it is certain that if the passage be nothing else it is poetry at least, and poetry of a good type and high quality.

80. Unsigned review, *Westminster Review*

cxxviii, September 1887

We have little doubt that Mr Meredith's reputation as a poet would be greater if his reputation as a novelist were less. The world is suspicious, not always without reason, of a man with two strings to his bow. One of the two strings, it is apt to think, must be a mere makeshift. And very often it is so. It was so with George Eliot. But Mr. Meredith, even in his prose, is a good deal of a poet; and when he writes in verse he is simply obeying a natural instinct. This is not saying that his verse is by any means equal to his prose; we do not think it is; we do not think even 'Modern Love' can be compared with *Richard Feverel*, and we are sure the 'Woods of Westermain' would not be an equivalent for the twentieth chapter of *Sandra Belloni*. But his poetry is poetry; it is essentially the work of a poet; it is native, unborrowed, a thing apart in the poetry of the period, and, though very unequal, it has merits of the most solid, as well as of the most startling, character.

Mr Meredith, as every one is aware, began his career by publishing a volume of poems, at what is generally called an early age. We have not been fortunate enough to see that very rare volume; but we have been told by those who have seen it that the book as a whole is original without being eccentric. This was in 1851; in 1862 (after *The Shaving of Shagpat*, *Farina*, *Richard Feverel*, and *Evan Harrington*) appeared a second volume of verse, entitled *Modern Love, and Poems of the English Roadside, with Poems and Ballads*. From 1862 to 1881 Mr Meredith published nothing but prose; occasionally a poem would be found in a number of the *Fortnightly*, the *New Quarterly*, or *Macmillan*; but save in these momentary glimpses the poet was hidden away out of all sight or thought in the astonishing and incomparably brilliant novelist. In 1883 appeared the *Poems and Lyrics of the Joy of Earth*; and now, in 1887, we have the *Ballads and Poems of Tragic Life*. Three small volumes form a slight equipment for a poet in these prolific days, and it is on three small volumes that Mr Meredith's claims must for the present rest. What qualities do we observe, what characteristics can we discover, in these three volumes of Mr Meredith's poetry?

Roughly speaking, all Mr Meredith's poems might be classed under the titles of his last two books, *Poems of the Joy of Earth* and *Poems of Tragic Life*. Between these two classes there is a sharp and sheer division. How it comes about that the same poet's outlook on Nature should be so serene and on life so sombre, we do not profess to be able to explain. These two elements, Nature a source of joy and healing, Life a tragic tangle, form between them the substance or the basis of Mr Meredith's poetry. View him from this side, and he is the singer of simple, natural delights, of the ecstasy of mere living, of the infinite contentment of nature. View him from that side, and the reed-pipe has given place to an iron harp. It is only the style that remains much the same. The style, it is true, has changed considerably since 1862, but the change is little more than a development of principles implicit from the first. Its chief characteristic is a defiant avoidance of the commonplace, a determined effort to think and to say everything in a new, an unexpected and an exceptionally significant and exact way. A trite image, a stereotyped mode of expression, is scarcely to be found in the whole range of poetry. Mr Meredith's hatred of the commonplace is indeed carried to a regrettable excess; for it leads him, only too often, to reject a good but obvious expression for one which is original certainly, but, in Landor's words, 'as original as sin'. All the same, these excesses are the defects of a noble quality. To be content with no idea until it is thoroughly his own; to be content with nothing short of the most exact rendering in words of that idea: this is Mr Meredith's stand against the facility of conventional thought and diction. Whether thought or imagery is to be rendered in the Pre-Raphaelite manner which Mr Meredith has adopted, may admit of question. But it is a gallant onslaught on the possibilities of language, and it has unquestionably stormed many redoubts. With regard to 'the accomplishment of verse', in the more limited sense of the term, Mr Meredith is curiously and exasperatingly unequal. We can scarcely remember anyone capable of writing such good verse who is capable also of writing such bad verse. Mr Meredith has written lines which any poet who ever wrote in English would be proud to admit among his work; he has also written lines as tuneless as a deal table and as rasping as a file. He has written in several exceptionally difficult metres with great success; he has footed the tight-rope of the Galliambic measure and the swaying planks of various trochaic experiments; and every now and then, without warning, in the midst of a simple easy-going tune, he will break the time, drop out of step, and presently pick up again without apparent consciousness of the interruption. We have again to confess that we cannot explain the cause of this singular contradiction.

Mr Meredith's Nature-poetry—that which he has himself called poetry of the Joy of Earth—is unlike, so far as we are aware, any other Nature-poetry in the world. It has an almost pagan sense of the abiding life, the veiled nearness and intimacy, of the great mother of us all— Earth, the awful and benignant powers of Nature. We scarcely know after all whether to call this pagan and primitive or modern and scientific. Perhaps the new and the old view, however different their terminology, are really at bottom not so very different. But if Mr Meredith sings Evolution, he sings it in a lyrical rapture, and with a thrill of personal ecstasy. It is the ecstasy of Melampus, not of the Mænads. His vision of Earth is not so much of 'the *wild* joy of living', as of the joy of living in perfect accordance with Nature, in collectedness, in simplicity, in sanity. It is almost possible to gather a creed, at least a philosophy of life, from the lyrics and sonnets of the volume of 1883; that philosophy or creed would be contained within the walls of the garden of Epicurus. Every reader of Mr Meredith's novels will remember the exquisite flashes of description which light up ever and again the pages of narrative and dialogue; flashes of description which only Mr Ruskin has equalled, and even Mr Ruskin not often surpassed. In such poems as 'The Woods of Westermain', 'The Day of the Daughter of Hades', and the blithe and matchless 'Love in the Valley', we have passages and touches of similar closeness and charm. Indeed, the closeness, the exactitude of loving knowledge, is even greater, if the charm is somewhat less. Of the separate poems, besides those we have mentioned, none perhaps is quite the equal of 'Phœbus with Admetus', classic in every sense of the term, a masterly handling of a very peculiar and really noble rhythm, never elsewhere attempted in English, we believe, save in a tentative experiment of Sir Philip Sidney. 'The Lark Ascending' challenges an incomparable model; it is the highest possible praise to say of it that it may be enjoyed even after Shelley.

The *Poems of the Joy of Earth* are comprised in a single class, and may be dealt with in a single handling. But the *Poems of Tragic Life* comprise a much greater variety of tone and treatment. 'Modern Love', by far the greatest of them all, stands almost by itself as an analytical study of contemporary life and manners; the 'Roadside' poems deal synthetically with country humours and country pathos; there is a number of romantic poems and ballads, and these have at least two remarkable divisions among themselves. 'Modern Love', Mr Meredith's longest poem—it is written in fifty sonnet-like stanzas of sixteen lines—is also, beyond a shadow of doubt (so it seems to us), by far his best work in verse. It is a most remarkable poem, and it has never received anything like due recognition at the hands of critics or public. We trace to it, perhaps wrongly, but we think not, the origin or suggestion of at least the manner of two subsequent poems of considerable importance and merit, James Thomson's *Story of Weddah and Om-el-Bonain* and Mr W. S. Blunt's *Love Sonnets of Proteus*.[1] We have no authority but internal evidence for this supposition, though we know that James Thomson had a very great admiration for 'Modern Love', and used often to speak of it. In certain qualities both *Weddah and Om-el-Bonain* and the *Love Sonnets of Proteus* are superior to Mr Meredith's poem; but besides the extremely important fact that Mr Meredith was first in the field, his poem as a whole is to our mind decidedly superior to either of those with which we have classed it. We have never been able to tell quite what it is that gives to these sonnet-like stanzas (with all their obscurities

---

[1] James Thomson's *Weddah and Om-el-Bonain* was published in 1881. Wilfred Scawen Blunt (1840–1922), had his *Love Lyrics and Songs of Proteus* published by the Kelmscott Press in 1892 from two earlier volumes, *Sonnets and Songs by Proteus* (1875) and *The Love Songs of Proteus* (1880).

of allusion and their occasional faults in versification) a certain charm
and power which fascinate and fasten upon mind and memory at once.
Mr Meredith has never done anything else like it; this wonderful style,
acid, stinging, bittersweet, poignant, as if fashioned of the very moods
of these 'modern lovers', reappears in no other poem (except faintly
in the 'Ballad of Fair Ladies in Revolt'). The poem stands alone, not
merely in Mr Meredith's work, but in all antecedent literature. It is
altogether a new thing; we venture to call it the most 'modern' poem
we have.

'Modern Love' is a poem of the drawing-rooms; it is tinged throughout with irony; it moves by 'tragic hints'. In the same volume we have
a group of 'Poems of the English Roadside', studies, as they are also
termed, of 'Roadside Philosophers'. Here we are in a new atmosphere
altogether, an atmosphere in which we can breathe more freely, under
the open sky, upon the road and the heath. This little group of homely
poems, to which should be added 'Martin's Puzzle', a poem of the same
period, seems to us, after 'Modern Love', perhaps the most original
and satisfying contribution made by Mr Meredith to the poetry of his
time. One poem at least is an absolute masterpiece, and of its kind it
is almost without a rival. There is a sly and kindly humour in 'The
Beggar's Soliloquy', a quaint wit in 'The Old Chartist', a humorous
wisdom tinged with pathos in 'Martin's Puzzle'; each of these poems is
a greater or less success in a line of work which is much more difficult
than it looks; but 'Juggling Jerry', notwithstanding a flaw here and
there in the rhythm, quickens our blood and strikes straight from the
heart to the heart as only a few poems here and there can do. We said
that of its kind it is almost without a rival; we may say, indeed, quite
without a rival, outside Burns.

Allied to both 'Modern Love' and the 'Poems of the English Roadside' by the intensity of their emotion, but in tone and manner and
subject removed equally from either, four or five poems, wonderfully
powerful and original, from another distinct group. These are 'Cassandra', in the volume of 1862, and 'The Nuptials of Attila', 'The Song
of Theodolinda', 'King Harald's Trance', and 'Aneurin's Harp', in the
new volume. There is something fierce, savage, convulsive almost, in
the passion which informs these poems; a note sounded in our days by
no other poet, not even by M. Leconte de Lisle in the *Poèmes Barbares*.[1]
The words rush rattling on one another like the clashing of spears or
the ring of iron on iron in a day of old-world battle. The lines are

[1] Charles-Marie-René Leconte de Lisle (1818–94), *Poèmes barbares* (1862).

javelins, consonanted lines full of savage power and fury, as if sung or played by a Northern Skald harping on a field of slain. And this is the poet of the joy of Earth! Romantic ballads such as 'The Young Princess', even narrative ballads like 'Archduchess Anne', two notable new poems, we can reconcile to some extent with the singer of Earth; but 'The Nuptials of Attila!' Somewhat in the same category, midway between 'The Young Princess' and 'The Song of Theodolinda', stands a single poem, one of Mr Meredith's most wonderful achievements only just falling short of the very highest excellence, 'the powerful and pathetic ballad', as Mr Swinburne has justly termed it, of 'Margaret's Bridal-Eve'. Mr Swinburne, in the passage from which we quote, places it second only to Rossetti's 'Sister Helen'[1] (that was before the publication of 'The King's Tragedy') among the ballads of our time; second only, we quite concur with him in placing it; but how real and unmistakable the difference in workmanship between the two poems! 'Margaret's Bridal-Eve' is imagined with little less intensity than 'Sister Helen' itself; it has flashes of almost elemental inspiration scarcely excelled by anything even in 'Sister Helen'; but compared with the flawless art, the entire command of himself and his material shown by Rossetti in the shaping and perfecting of his conception, the art of Mr Meredith appears ineffective and uncertain.

Uncertain we cannot but hold Mr Meredith's art to be; and it is this, and this alone, that can at all render doubtful his claim to a very high place among contemporary poets. He has imagination, passion, real and rare harmony, varied gifts—gifts utterly wanting to several poets we might name, whose possession of just the one gift in which he is lacking has allowed them to far outstrip him in the popular estimation, and may do much to foist them permanently into a place above him. How sure his art *can* be we need go no further than the poem entitled 'France, December 1870', to discover; a noble poem, printed many years ago in the *Fortnightly*, and only now published—the most sustained, we think, as it is one of the loftiest, of Mr Meredith's compositions in verse. But over too much of his harvest-field an enemy, an enemy within, has sowed tares. As in the parable, wheat and tares grow together; there is no plucking out the weeds without carrying the good corn with them; and we must leave it to Time the careful reaper, the reaper who never errs though he is long in reaping, to gather together first the tares, and bind them in bundles to burn them; but to gather the wheat into his barn.

[1] A. Swinburne, *Essays and Studies* (1875), 87.

81. G. P. Baker, Jnr, on Meredith as a Philosophical Novelist

Harvard Monthly, June 1887

George Pierce Baker (1866–1935), a student at Harvard when this article was written, later became a critic and student of rhetoric and drama.

People have been slow in recognizing the merit of the novels of George Meredith. He has been writing for over thirty years, yet only recently have signs of a general interest in his work appeared. This lack of popularity is not, however, strange for the novels of Mr Meredith are in no sense mere works of fiction. They are immensely expanded statements of a philosophical theory of their author, which is rendered extremely forcible by the striking pictures and the telling examples of the form in which he embodies it. The books do not tell us merely the fragmentary chance thoughts of one man about his fellows; each has a message to convey, a principle to maintain. They are ten brilliant, skillfully arranged expositions of a philosophy of life. Since the novels are of this nature, it is not strange, certainly, that they have won readers slowly.

To read the stories and sayings of George Meredith is to come upon a nineteenth-century version of the doctrines of Socrates. 'Intellect', Mr Meredith is quoted as saying 'should be our aim. It can be developed in training. The morbid and sentimental tendencies in the ordinary healthy individual can be corrected by it. Starting wrongly, a man can be brought right by it. . . . Truth seeks truth, and we find truth by the understanding. Let the understanding only be fervent enough, and conduct will follow naturally. . . . Perceive things intellectually. Keep the mind open and supple. Then, as new circumstances arise, man is fit to deal with them and to discover right and wrong'.[1] Certainly here is a trust in the guiding power of reason and intellect, as

---

[1] 'George Meredith', F. L. Shaw, *New Princeton Review*, April 1887.*

strong as that of the old Greek philosophers! But these words are no mere theorizing. They form a doctrine on which Mr Meredith acts. The idea that our purely reasoning power is the guide to keep us out of the difficulties of life underlies all his writings. The mentor, the support of men is, according to George Meredith:

> High Philosophy, less friend than foe,
> Whom self-caged Passion from her prison-bars
> Is always watching with a wondering hate.[1]

The eternally existing contest between these two forces is most real to this author. For him life is but the battle-field of these powers. Men and women are like the suffering, laboring soldiery of the field of strife —some falling early in the fight; some living on, though wounded; some passing through danger and struggle to victory at the end. But to Mr Meredith these striving creatures are interesting primarily not so much in themselves as from the fact that in each, however unimportant, some phase of the great contest can be studied. Mr Meredith believes that he sees the road along which victory lies. He feels, too, that only by study of the efforts of their fellows can men learn the way. Through the portrayal, therefore, of typical struggling men and women he endeavors to inculcate his ethical doctrine.

It is, then, as a philosopher that George Meredith writes his novels. His figures are but as models with which he illustrates his ideas, though they are lovingly and tenderly drawn. Each novel by its ingenious construction and masterly workmanship leads the wondering reader on till the old precept under its new guise is stamped upon the memory.

But, someone may say, it is not a startlingly new position for a man to take, to say that Reason is our guide and to strive to make other men see it—you yourself admit that Socrates rather antedates Mr Meredith. True it certainly is that this Englishman is not the first to recognize the everlasting struggle between passion and intellect and to deify the latter. Nor is it new for a novel to turn on this contest; the freshness comes in the point of view. We have had philosophy in English fiction; but it has been almost always first the story, then the philosophy. With Mr Meredith the importance of the order is directly changed about. The souls of men have often been laid open for us by authors, but too often the operation has been performed simply for the amusement it gives the reader. In such work the struggling itself of the tried soul may interest, or it may be only the clever analysis which is attractive.

---

[1] 'Modern Love', Sonnet iv.*

Whichever is the case, the philosophical import of the situation is often entirely lost, or is considered as of only secondary importance. But in these life-histories of George Meredith the particular man and his fate are as nothing compared with the lesson in ethics which his career illustrates. The characters do not come into existence to act a play, but to elucidate, as clearly as possible, certain ideas. His novels are all tales of mental and moral growth, and the development of individuals is the momentous question. The evolution is viewed in all possible lights. If it is necessary, a character is traced in its growth from boyhood. We see it shaped and formed as it passes through strong sensations and marked experiences, but our attention is asked not for the various episodes themselves, but rather for the effect which they have upon the moral and mental development of the person in question. I am tempted to compare the methods of these books with experiments in biology, and to say that in them George Meredith studies the development of men and women in the struggle between passion and the intellect with much the patient enthusiasm of him who is watching the growth into being of some life-germ. In the past too much attention has been paid to striking dramatic episodes in the evolution, too little to the entire set of circumstances which made the change possible, and to the ideas which the metamorphosis exemplifies.

The point of view of Mr Meredith is unusual in this, too, that he is not strictly either a Realist or an Idealist. He believes sincerely that 'the mistake of the world is to think happiness possible to the senses' and he will not 'fiddle harmonics on the strings of sensualism'. He never portrays sinning men and women with the tender touch that makes them doubly winning in their evil-doing. He is not a sentimental looker-on at life, ready to laugh or weep as occasion calls. Rather his spirit is that of the strictly impartial judge. All the mitigating circumstances of natural disposition, of training, and of environment, are given their proper share of responsibility, but the fact that wrong has been done, sin committed, is not palliated or made insidiously fascinating.

This failure to gloss over the evil existing in the world has brought Mr Meredith much unfavorable criticism. To see ourselves as we are, neither better nor worse, is always an unpleasant revelation, but none the less beneficial. 'This looking at the roots of yourself', Mr Meredith has said, 'if you are possessed of a nobler half that will do it, is a sound corrective of an excessive ambition'. Readers, however, seem to be roughly divisible into two classes, those who desire to see themselves painted as better than they are, and those who wish to see themselves as they might be when partially bestialized. Mr Meredith will not entirely please one party or the other. The Realist can find little in these novels to suit his jaded taste. George Meredith never depraves mankind. Scenes of passion, of intensity, there are at times in his books, it is true. Some scenes of *Richard Feverel* read without reference to the rest of the story, may seem questionable, but when the purpose of the book is remembered it is at once plain that without them the terrible impressiveness of the tale would be lost. Reading *Diana of the Crossways* merely as a novel, many a reader may question its propriety, but consider it as an ethical study and it must be admitted that there is ample justification for all that is in the book.

On the other hand, the Idealists, the sensitive readers, complain that George Meredith is cynical, because he does not paint his men and women as heroes and heroines. He paints them as they are, creatures of sensations and feelings, yet with god-like powers within them, to be developed, according as the men and women strive or not. What more are any of us, idealize us as you will?

The so-called cynicism of George Meredith is but the cynicism which comes with all knowledge. It were doubtless pleasant if we could still look at the changes in nature with the wondering, imaginative eyes of childhood, but does it remove the beauty from the fringing out of the elms to know that a hard and fast law lies back of it? As the man who knows one friend even as himself, loving him for his very weaknesses, can not honestly join in the wildly enthusiastic praises of some person whom his friend has momentarily pleased, so it seems to be with Mr Meredith and his fellow-men. He sees and knows them as they are, and he refuses to deprave or idealize them. Does it necessarily deprive a lofty and sweet character of fiction of its charm to know that it, too, is human, tempted by a lower nature, but striving, and successfully, toward the intellectual freedom which will loose its bonds? The tone of Mr Meredith is not that of a cynic—far from it. His satire, powerful and shattering as it is in its blows, is never aimed at honest endeavor or eager effort for what is noble. It is hurled at the shams and sentimentalities of life. There is no hatred for mankind in these books; on the contrary, every man who reads them rightly must gain a strengthening lesson for the battle of life. Each novel is a plea for more living intellectually, less sentimentally, passionately. Even as the blocks of the kindergarten teach, so these creations of the brain of George Meredith instruct. Each book is an object-lesson in morality.

Even as the child, too, must think to understand what is before him, so the reader must bring his brain to bear on these novels, if he is to appreciate their real meaning. They are, plainly, far different from general fiction in trend. They are not stories for an idle hour, but rather, as I have said, life-histories worthy of thoughtful study. They offer few attractions to the undiscriminating reader of novels. They are not sensational; they are long; they have, on the whole, few dramatic scenes—indeed, they lack all the elements of the strictly 'popular' work of fiction. Mr Meredith evidently, however, makes no effort to please the average reader, if the following can be trusted: 'Narrative is nothing. It is the mere vehicle of philosophy. The interest is in the idea which the action serves to illustrate. Without action the mind fails in grasping the idea; therefore action becomes necessary, but the understanding must be fixed upon what lies behind'.[1]

We are not then to have mere pictures, entertaining dialogues, and stylistic neatness, there must be thought in what is put before us—'brain-stuff' as Mr Meredith calls it. 'The brain-stuff of fiction is internal history, and to suppose it dull is the profoundest of errors'. Philosophical thought must lie at the basis of all that you write, if your work is to have real force and value. Without it fiction is 'a picture of figures modelled on no skeleton-anatomy'.

If then, these books are read as novels simply, their real essence is missed entirely. When judged by the common standard for a work of fiction, that it must interest and amuse in the briefest, brightest possible way, they may even be thought to be faulty, to show tendencies which should hardly be encouraged in novels. But read them as pleas for less sentimentality in life, for greater scope for reason and for intellectuality, as the earnest endeavor of a sober thinker to make his lessons effective by powerful examples, vivid similes, brilliant pictures, and then the power and success of the books must be admitted.

One reason for the diversity of opinion which we hear about the work of George Meredith is doubtless due to his many-sidedness. It is well-nigh impossible to make any critical statements about this author till all of his novels have been read. Finishing one book, you may feel that Mr Meredith is not strong in dramatic force, but this idea is destroyed if you turn to *Richard Feverel*, *Rhoda Fleming* or *Vittoria*. You may feel that he can not draw clearly pure, strong men; that he can only shadow them forth; then 'Merthyr Powys' and 'Redworth' will shake your conclusions. Or you may say that women can never like the

---

[1] 'George Meredith', F. L. Shaw, *New Princeton Review*, April 1887.*

female characters of these books, but unless you demand that they should be only a little lower than the angels, 'Lady Dunstan' and 'Vittoria' must make you waver. Your belief as to the humor, the pathos, the satire—as to all the characteristics of this author, must change constantly as you reed his books. 'Mrs Mel' and 'Tim Cogglesby' prove that Mr Meredith has a humor almost as genial as that of Dickens; parts of *Richard Feverel* and of *Rhoda Fleming* that his pathos is of the saddest kind, not that which brings tears, but that which makes the heart ache long after the pages have been read. Indeed a reader must vacillate constantly in his opinions as he turns from one to another of the books of this author, and it is only when he has closed the tenth volume that he can really reach definite conclusions. It is not with George Meredith as with many authors, he does not show the full extent of his powers in one book, and thereafter only masquerade before us, playing the old tricks in a new environment and with new accompaniments. Some similarity there may be in his books in so far as each works out the underlying problem of the struggle between intellect and passion, between sentimentality and reason, but the characters and the plots are different.

It is pleasant if we find a rare gem in a perfect setting. To the Purist who reads and admires these novels it would be a satisfaction if the style were at times more fluent and correct. Mr Meredith sometimes uses expressions which jar on a sensitive ear and writes sentences which are strangely loose and involved in their reference of part to part. Yet the more one reads these books the more one feels that the thought was the absorbing idea of the writer as he composed, and that even as Carlyle rushed out his ideas in a style often uncouth, but always emphatic and forcible, so this author in striving to express his exact meaning, sometimes makes a sacrifice of elegance and force. Indeed, I can not but believe that Mr Meredith has felt strongly in style and thought the influence of Thomas Carlyle.[1] At times he writes in the half-allegorical, abrupt, metaphorical phrases of the author of *Sartor Resartus*. Indeed, I can not better criticize the style of George Meredith than by applying to it the words which Carlyle wrote of the work of Herr Teufelsdröck:

> Occasionally we find consummate vigor, a true inspiration; his burning thoughts step forth in fit burning words, . . . a rich idiomatic diction, picturesque allusions, fiery poetic emphasis, or quaint tricksy turns; all the graces and

[1] See the character of Dr Shrapnel in *Beauchamp's Career*, which is evidently modelled after that of Carlyle, page 328.*

terrors of a wild imagination, wedded to the clearest intellect, alternate in beautiful vicissitude.[1]

Nor do the two men seem to me very unlike as thinkers. Both recognize the omnipresent struggle in the universe; with both the cry is for more light, for more free intellectual play. Both hate sham and sentimentality. Both paint without idealization, yet both look for ultimate growth and success, in spite of the faults and failings of mankind. May not George Meredith be called the Carlyle of fiction?

That Mr Meredith will ever be, in the strict sense of the word, a 'popular' novelist seems hardly probable. He does not wish to be. As one of his critics has pointed out, too, the reader is an essential part of his books. He who comes to them must think. His novels are not companions to turn to at all times, and in all moods, for entertainment and sympathy, as we go to those of Thackeray. They are too full of their purpose, too solid for that. Rather, they are an intellectual storehouse to which we can always go, feeling that we shall come away with new strength and ardor for the contest of life.

As I have said, George Meredith hardly suits the taste of either the Realist or the Idealist, and accordingly his popularity suffers. Taste, however, appears to be changing. We seem now to be at the beginning of a transition. As a character says in Sandra Belloni: 'We are still fighting against the Puritan element in literature as elsewhere'. Yet a new way seems to be opening. Last year Vernon Lee pleaded in Baldwin for something in fiction between French Realism and English prudery.[2] Lately Rider Haggard has written in The Contemporary calling for more manliness in literature, for a more straightforward treatment of the difficulties of the world, one which will neither heighten them in color, nor lower them in tone.[3] We have had sentimentality in literature long enough. May not this agitation bring something which will be neither strictly Realistic nor strictly Idealistic —something Non-sentimental shall I say—which, avoiding the extravagances, will have the good points of both the old schools? 'Imagine the celestial refreshment of having a pure decency in the place of sham; real flesh; a soul active, wind-beaten, but ascending. Honorable will fiction then appear; honorable, a fount of life, an aid to life, quick with our blood'. 'Then, ah then, moreover, will the novelist's art, now neither blushless infant nor executive man, have attained its majority. He can

---

[1] Sartor Resartus (1833–4), I, iv.
[2] Vernon Lee was the pseudonym of Violet Paget (1856–1935), whose Baldwin: being Dialogues on Views and Aspirations was published in 1886.
[3] Contemporary Review, li, February 1887, 172–80.

then be veraciously historical, honestly transcriptive. Rose-pink and dirty-drab will alike have passed away. Philosophy is the foe of both, and their silly cancelling contest, perpetually renewed in a shuffle of extremes, as it always is where a phantasmal falseness reigns, will no longer baffle the contemplation of natural flesh, smother no longer the soul rising out of our incessant strife. Philosophy bids us see that we are not so pretty as rose-pink, not so repulsive as dirty-drab, and that, instead of everlastingly shifting those barren aspects, the sight of ourselves is wholesome, bearable, fructifying, finally a delight'.[1] If this condition of which Mr Meredith writes so enthusiastically comes, it will be greatly due to his work. Whether it comes or not, the popularity of George Meredith is evidently just beginning. Though he may say proudly:

> Of me and of my theme think what you will
> ★ ★ ★ ★ ★ ★ ★ ★ ★ ★ ★ ★ ★ ★
> But I have never stood at Fortune's beck,

still it is to just these men who, with something to say, bide their time for popular recognition that fame most surely comes at last.

[1] *Diana of the Crossways*, ch. 1.★

82. Meredith's reply to G. P. Baker

22 July 1887

Baker seems to have sent Meredith a copy of his article (see above, No. 81). The text of the following reply is taken from *Letters* (1970). It was printed by Baker in *Harvard Monthly*, xxvi, 127–8, under the title 'The Attitude of George Meredith Toward His Novels'. See D. D. Baily, *American Literary Criticisms of George Meredith, 1860–1917*, (1950), 71–5.

Box Hill, Dorking,
England, *July* 22, 1887.

MY DEAR SIR—When at the conclusion of your article on my works, you say that a certain change in public taste, should it come about, will be to some extent due to me, you hand me the flowering wreath I covet. For I think that all right use of life, and the one secret of life, is to pave ways for the firmer footing of those who succeed us; as to my works, I know them faulty, think them of worth only when they point and aid to that end. Close knowledge of our fellows, discernment of the laws of existence, these lead to great civilization. I have supposed that the novel, exposing and illustrating the natural history of man, may help us to such sustaining roadside gifts. But I have never started on a novel to pursue the theory it developed. The dominant idea in my mind took up the characters and the story midway.

You say that there are few scenes. Is it so throughout? My method has been to prepare my readers for a crucial exhibition of the personae, and give the scene in the fullest of their blood and brain under stress of a fiery situation.

Concerning style, thought is tough, and dealing with thought produces toughness. Or when strong emotion is in tide against the active mind, there is perforce confusion. Have you found that scenes of simple emotion or plain narrative were hard to view? When their author revised for the new edition, his critical judgment approved these passages. Yet you are not to imagine that he holds his opinion combatively against his critics. The verdict is with the observer.

In the Comedies, and here and there where a concentrated present-ment is in design, you will find a 'pitch' considerably above our common human; and purposely, for only in such a manner could so much be shown. Those high notes and condensings are abandoned when the strong human call is heard—I beg you to understand merely that such was my intention.

Again, when you tell me that Harvard has the works, and that Young Harvard reads them, the news is of a kind to prompt me to fresh productiveness and higher. In England I am encouraged but by a few enthusiasts. I read in a critical review of some verses of mine the other day that I was 'a harlequin and a performer of antics'.[1] I am accustomed to that kind of writing, as our hustings orator is to the dead cat and the brickbat flung in his face—at which he smiles politely; and I too; but after many years of it my mind looks elsewhere. Adieu to you.—Most faithfully yours,

GEORGE MEREDITH.

83. George Moore on Meredith in *Confessions of a Young Man*

1888

My fat landlady lent me a novel by George Meredith—*Tragic Comedians*; I was glad to receive it, for my admiration of his poetry, with which I was slightly acquainted, was very genuine indeed. 'Love in a Valley' is a beautiful poem, and the 'Nuptials of Attila', I read it in the *New Quarterly Review* years ago,[2] is very pleasant in my mind, and it is a pleasure to recall its chanting rhythm, and lordly and sombre refrain —'Make the bed for Attila'. I expected, therefore, one of my old passionate delights from his novels. I was disappointed, painfully

[1] See above, No. 79.
[2] *New Quarterly Magazine* (not *Review*), l, January 1879, 47.

disappointed. But before I say more concerning Mr Meredith, I will admit at once frankly and fearlessly, that I am not a competent critic, because emotionally I do not understand him, and all except an emotional understanding is worthless in art. I do not make this admission because I am intimidated by the weight and height of the critical authority with which I am overshadowed, but from a certain sense, of which I am as distinctly conscious, viz., that the author is, how shall I put it? the French would say 'quelqu'un', that expresses what I would say in English. I remember, too, that although a man may be able to understand anything, there must some modes of thoughts and attitudes of mind which we are so naturally antagonistic to, so entirely out of sympathy with, that we are in no true sense critics of them. Such are the thoughts that come to me when I read Mr George Meredith. I try to console myself with such reflections, and then I break out and cry passionately: jerks, wire, splintered wood. In Balzac, which I know by heart, in Shakespeare, which I have just begun to love, I find words deeply impregnated with the savour of life; but in George Meredith there is nothing but crackjaw sentences, empty and unpleasant in the mouth as sterile nuts. I could select hundreds of phrases which Mr Meredith would probably call epigrams, and I would defy anyone to say they were wise, graceful or witty. I do not know any book more tedious than *The Tragic Comedians*, more pretentious, more blatant; it struts and screams, stupid in all its gaud and absurdity as a cockatoo. More than fifty pages I could not read. How, I asked myself, could the man who wrote the 'Nuptials of Attila' write this? but my soul returned no answer, and I listened as one in a hollow mountain side. My opinion of George Meredith never ceases to puzzle me. He is of the north, I am of the south. Carlyle, Mr Robert Browning, and George Meredith are the three essentially northern writers; in them there is nothing of Latin sensuality and subtlety.

I took up *Rhoda Fleming*. I found some exquisite bits of description in it, but I heartily wished them in verse, they were motives for poems; and there was some wit. I remember a passage very racy indeed, of middle-class England. Antony, I think, is the man's name, describes how he is interrupted at his tea; a paragraph of seven or ten lines with 'I am having my tea, I am at my tea', running through it for refrain. Then a description of a lodging-house dinner: 'a block of bread on a lonely place, and potatoes that looked as if they had committed suicide in their own steam'. A little ponderous and stilted, but undoubtedly witty. I read on until I came to a young man who fell from his horse,

or had been thrown from his horse, I never knew which, nor did I feel
enough interest in the matter to make research; the young man was
put to bed by his mother, and once in bed he began to talk! . . . four,
five, six, ten pages of talk, and such talk! I can offer no opinion why
Mr Meredith committed them to paper; it is not narrative, it is not
witty, nor is it sentimental, nor is it profound. I read it once; my mind,
astonished at receiving no sensation, cried out like a child at a milkless
breast. I read the pages again . . . did I understand? Yes, I understood
every sentence, but they conveyed no idea, they awoke no emotion in
me; it was like sand, arid and uncomfortable. The story is surprisingly
commonplace—the people in it are as lacking in subtlety as those of
a Drury Lane melodrama.

Diana of the Crossways I liked better, and had I had absolutely nothing
to do I might have read it to the end. I remember a scene with a rustic—
a rustic who could eat hog a solid hour—that amused me. I remember
the sloppy road in the Weald, and the vague outlines of the South
Downs seen in starlight and mist. But to come to the great question,
the test by which Time will judge us all—the creation of a human being,
of a live thing that we have met with in life before, and meet for the
first time in print, and who abides with us ever after. Into what shadow
has not Diana floated? Where are the magical glimpses of the soul?
Do you remember in *Pères et Enfants*, when Tourgueneff is unveiling
the woman's, shall I say, affection, for Bazaroff, or the interest she feels
in him? and exposing at the same time the reasons why she will never
marry him. . . . I wish I had the book by me, I have not seen it for ten
years.

After striving through many pages to put Lucien, whom you would
have loved, whom I would have loved, that divine representation of all
that is young and desirable in man, before the reader, Balzac puts these
words in his mouth in reply to an impatient question by Vautrin, who
asks him what he wants, what he is sighing for, '*D'être célèbre et d'être
aimé*'—these are soul-waking words, these are Shakespearean words.[1]

Where in *Diana of the Crossways* do we find soul-evoking words like
these? With tiresome repetition we are told that she is beautiful, divine;
but I see her not at all, I don't know if she is dark, tall, or fair; with tiresome reiteration we are told that she is brilliant, that her conversation is
like a display of fireworks, that the company is dazzled and overcome;
but when she speaks the utterances are grotesque, and I say that if anyone spoke to me in real life as she does in the novel, I should not doubt

[1] *La Dernière Incarnation de Vautrin*, in *Splendeurs et misères des courtisanes* (1839–47).

314

for an instant that I was in the company of a lunatic. The epigrams are never good, they never come within measurable distance of La Roche-foucauld, Balzac, or even Goncourt. The admirers of Mr Meredith constantly deplore their existence, admitting that they destroy all illusion of life. 'When we have translated half of Mr Meredith's utterances into possible human speech, then we can enjoy him,' says the *Pall Mall Gazette*. We take our pleasures differently; mine are spontaneous, and I know nothing about translating the rank smell of a nettle into the fragrance of a rose, and then enjoying it.

Mr Meredith's conception of life is crooked, ill-balanced, and out of tune. What remains?—a certain lustiness. You have seen a big man with square shoulders and a small head, pushing about in a crowd, he shouts and works his arms, he seems to be doing a great deal, in reality he is doing nothing; so Mr Meredith appears to me, and yet I can only think of him as an artist; his habit is not slatternly, like those of such literary hodmen as Mr David Christie Murray, Mr Besant, Mr Buchanan.[1] There is no trace of the crowd about him. I do not question his right of place, I am out of sympathy with him, that is all; and I regret that it should be so, for he is one whose love of art is pure and untainted with commercialism, and if I may praise it for nought else, I can praise it for this. . . .

84. Oscar Wilde on Meredith

1888–91

From 'The Decay of Lying: a Dialogue', *Nineteenth Century*, January 1888:

Vivian. Ah! Meredith! Who can define him? His style is chaos illumined by flashes of lightning. As a writer he has mastered everything except language: as a novelist he can do everything, except tell a story: as an artist he is everything, except articulate. Somebody in Shakes-

[1] Robert Williams Buchanan (1841–1901), novelist, poet, and critic. Sir Walter Besant (1836–1901), founder member of the Society of Authors, novelist and critic. David Christie Murray (1847–1907), novelist, dramatist, and essayist.

peare—Touchstone, I think—talks about a man who is always breaking his shins over his own wit, and it seems to me that this might serve as the basis for a criticism of Meredith's method. But whatever he is, he is not a realist. Or rather I would say that he is a child of realism who is not on speaking terms with his father. By deliberate choice he has made himself a romanticist. He has refused to bow the knee to Baal, and after all, even if the man's fine spirit did not revolt against the noisy assertions of realism, his style would be quite sufficient of itself to keep life at a respectful distance. By its means he has planted round his garden a hedge full of thorns, and red with wonderful roses. . . .'

From 'The True Function and Value of Criticism; A Dialogue', *Nineteenth Century*, July 1890:

'Yes, Browning was great. And as what will he be remembered. As a poet? Ah, not as a poet! He will be remembered as a writer of fiction. . . . The only one who can touch the hem of his garment is George Meredith. Meredith is a prose Browning, and so is Browning.'

From 'The Soul of Man under Socialism', *Fortnightly Review*, February 1891:

'One incomparable novelist we have now in England, Mr George Meredith. There are better artists in France, but France has no one whose view of life is so large, so varied, so imaginatively true. There are tellers of stories in Russia who have a more vivid sense of what pain in fiction may be. But to him belongs philosophy in fiction. His people not merely live, but they live in thought. One can see them from myriad points of view. They are suggestive. There is soul in them and around them. They are interpretative and symbolic. And he who made them, those wonderful, quickly moving figures, made them for his own pleasure, and has never asked the public what they wanted, has never cared to know what they wanted, has never allowed the public to dictate to him or influence him in any way, but has gone on intensifying his own personality, and producing his own individual work. At first none came to him. That did not matter. Then the few came to him. That did not change him. The many have come now. He is still the same. He is an incomparable novelist.'

85. William Watson, an attack on Meredith

1889

William Watson (1858–1935) was a poet who combined in his own person both the vices he attacked in this article. Between 1880 and 1923 he produced some twenty-seven volumes of poems and two of essays. W. Robertson Nicoll records that after this article was published Meredith went out of his way to invite Watson to dinner and took frequent occasion to praise his poems (*A Bookman's Letters*, 1913). The article was entitled 'Fiction—Plethoric and Anaemic', and was published in *National Review*, xiv, October 1889. Meredith was only accused of being plethoric. The charge of anaemia was directed at Robert Williams Buchanan (1841–1901), a minor poet, novelist and essayist.

Mr George Meredith was in the field long before Mr Howells or Mr James, but although he has been writing for upwards of a quarter of a century, the credit of discovering his transcendent greatness has apparently been reserved for the crescent generation. On the whole, the lateness of the discovery may well give us pause in our acceptance of it as a genuine 'find'. A poet may have, and frequently has, his due recognition by the public unjustly and cruelly retarded, but such a fate is hardly possible to the novelist, and it may be questioned whether a single decisive instance of it can be pointed to in the whole record of English literature. Although there are always persons ready to appreciate good poetry when they find it, they are comparatively a small sect, and, besides, it is doubtful if even they can be said to be in a state of positive eagerness and impatience to welcome everything in the shape of meritorious verse that is offered. But there is a novel-reading public which is not only large but may really be said to be always on tiptoe to see and applaud everything first-rate in fiction—a public actively bent upon allowing nothing good in that kind to escape it. It is a vigilant public, a hungry public, a public of gourmands, ever avid for some new dish, and interested even in a new sauce. It has read all the best novels long ago, and never thinks of going back to them, or if by chance any unit of this public does so, he finds himself curiously out of touch with his early favourites; something in the tone and atmosphere of them seems foreign and distant; in a word, the books have grown old-fashioned, which poetry, however old, never can become. Consequently, this class is perpetually on the look-out for new talent in fiction, and has a pretty keen scent for its discovery. Still it is quite conceivable that a really great novel by an unknown man might, from some conjuncture of inauspicious accidents, find simply no readers; but once let it find any at all, though but a dozen, and the report of its greatness will spread infallibly, and the immediate success of that novel is assured. Now Mr George Meredith always had *some* readers, at least enough to form the requisite nucleus for a novelist's public. How comes it that this public held off so long? Why, until the other day, was this all-capacious epicure so loth to be feasted?

One can hear an admirer replying that although Mr Meredith is one of the master minds of the age, who has chosen the novel as the medium through which to utter his burden, this selection of a vehicle has been in a sense accidental, and the so-called novel-reading public are not precisely the people at whom he aims, or whose intellectual jurisdiction he acknowledges. This is much as if one should write stage-plays, and use means to get them acted, at the same time disclaiming any ambition of pleasing a theatrical audience. If a man has a burden to utter, why select for his expressional medium the one form in favour with that one class whose ears and whose suffrages he neither expects nor desires to gain? Shakespeare is commonly thought to have been one of the master minds of *his* age, and though it probably never occurred to him that he had a burden to utter, he nevertheless uttered it through the medium of stage-plays, and there is no reason to believe that he considered the audiences at the Globe and the Blackfriars the one section of the community peculiarly disqualified to pass judgment upon his productions. Dickens, Thackeray, George Eliot—surely Mr Meredith's peers—had confidence that a fair verdict could be obtained from a representative jury of novel-readers; and if a novelist carries his appeal to some other court, even though a higher court—denying the authority of the one tribunal which his fellows submit to as decisive—it is because he is not essentially and primarily a novelist at all. Yet the claim which Mr Meredith's admirers put forward on his behalf is that he is the greatest novelist of the age.

Now it is easy, and it is also unfair, to quarrel with anything because it is not something else. We have no right to anathematise a still wine because it does not sparkle, or a white one because it is not red. Besides, real greatness can afford to have plenty of very real faults. It is easy to say that Scott's women are mostly failures—at least those of them who are respectable, and they unfortunately form the majority. Has he not plenty of men, respectable and otherwise, who are incomparable successes? It is easy to say that his history is shaky in places; may not unsound history, made attractive, be about as good in a novel as sound history carefully made dull? It is easy to say that his mediævalism is spurious; and of whose mediævalism can we moderns feel quite sure that it is genuine? But when greatness is claimed for a novelist, there are certain broad and obvious tests which it is both pertinent and natural to apply, and by which he must submit to stand or fall. Is he great at construction? Is he great as a master of narrative? Is he great as an artist in dialogue? Is he great as a creator of character? It is perhaps conceivable that a novelist may be found wanting in one or more of these cardinal virtues, and yet be able to make good his claim to a somewhat unbalanced and maimed greatness; but this much at least is certain, that if he staggers equally under the application of all these tests, the validity of his title to greatness is irreversibly disproved.

Criticism in superlatives is so much the habit of the day that no one perhaps attaches much importance, or even meaning, to announcements like Mr Louis Stevenson's that *Rhoda Fleming* is 'the strongest thing in English letters since Shakespeare died'.[1] Such utterances are scarcely taken seriously, and it is hard to believe that they are even meant seriously. As a matter of fact, *Rhoda Fleming* is not even Mr Meredith's own 'strongest thing'. Like most of his books, it is an ill-constructed and very unequally written story, having some fine scenes and clever, if unattractive, character studies. If only an author could live by virtue of sporadic good things! But a novelist, at all events, cannot. The nominal and official heroine is a farmer's daughter, beloved by Bob Eccles, *alias* Robert Armstrong, and eventually married to him. She does not give evidence of caring very much for him, and therein she certainly has our sympathies, since we do not care for him either. A more thoroughly uncompanionable and unmagnetic young man the writer does not remember to have met, even in real life. For some mysterious reason, however, he wins the affectionate regard of the gentle and chivalrous Major Waring; and the friendship, as of equals,

[1] See Introduction.

319

between these two men, in whom disparity of social rank forms perhaps the least incongruous feature of their comradeship, is one of those aggressively unintelligible things with which Mr Meredith's novels abound, and which he seems almost to make a parade of declining to account for. The reader expostulates: 'Surely, Mr Meredith, one never sees a friendship like that between two such persons in real life?' to which we seem to hear Mr Meredith replying, in victorious epigram, 'Perhaps not; but fiction, you see, is so much truer than reality', and the contumacious reader is crushed. The tragedy of the story is the fate of Rhoda's beautiful sister Dahlia, who has been led astray by a well-born young London lover, Edward Blancove. He is perhaps the most realizable person in the book, and as such its most satisfactory piece of portraiture. A young man of the world, not without ambition and some thin hard intellectuality; entirely incapable of heroism, yet not deliberately a scoundrel, he wins Dahlia's trust, and betrays it. Circumstances, he subsequently explains, have been against him. For a while he seems to have deserted her utterly, but in the end he returns to her, truly penitent, and filled with an ardour of atonement. One does not see what motive impels him to this course, which might not be presumed to have been equally operative all along, but anyhow he turns up at the eleventh hour, for the purpose of righting Dahlia's wrongs so far as he may. At this point Rhoda for the first time emerges into positive action. She has hitherto been pictured as a young woman of great and rather stubborn moral force, but playing a very passive part in the story. She now displays an amount of cruel wrong-headedness that goes far to place her outside the reader's sympathy. She thinks it her duty to frustrate the union of the lovers, from hatred and contempt of the man who has wronged her sister, but whose present conduct argues, if not heroism, at least reclamation. The scene where Dahlia discovers how Rhoda has blindly injured her, and barred the way against returning happiness, is very moving and powerful. It has a convulsive, paroxysmal kind of strength which recalls the fine things in some of the more spasmodic of our old dramatists. Unfortunately, like many another of Mr Meredith's strong scenes, it is led up to by a sequence of moral incredibilities which admit of no intellectual defence. Dahlia and Edward are now irrecoverably lost to each other, but one sees no earthly reason why this should be so. Rhoda has stubbornly refused him admittance to the house, where her sister passionately prays for his return, and such a trivial obstacle as Rhoda's foolish obstinacy turns the scale against him. Dahlia has meanwhile been persuaded by her well-meaning sister and father into an incredible marriage with a low brute and ruffian, whose villainy is apparent to all the rest of mankind in his hideous countenance, but whom these good people, on no grounds that Mr Meredith condescends to indicate, believe in as an admirable young man. Dahlia and this miscreant are married, and he then immediately casts her off at the church porch. He had already, it transpires, another wife, and he has been bribed with a thousand pounds (why, or by whom, the reader will need to make profound researches in order to discover) either to marry her, or, having married her, to renounce her immediately—I really do not know which. It may be much to a reader's discredit that he is forced to confess ignorance or uncertainty on such vital points, but the incidents are so confused, the story in places is such a jungle, and the task of 'thridding the sombre boskage' of this thicket of narrative is so laborious and cheerless, that even a fairly vigilant reader is often finding himself at fault in this way. And the obscurity which frequently hangs about Mr Meredith's narrative has no such excuse as a canvas crowded with figures, or an elaborately complex structure of incidents might supply. In the way of story he has not very much to tell, and he is obscure simply because he has not an aptitude for telling it. There is literally no construction, but a certain not too great abundance of material lying loose about in various stages of disorder.

In such a book as *Diana of the Crossways*, the thinness of the subject-matter may be forgiven in consideration of the frequently glittering dialogue, and the brilliance of the author's asides. But in *Rhoda Fleming* we have nothing of that; the people are mostly humble country-folk, or are supposed to be, for to tell the truth Mr Meredith is not at home with them, and makes them talk neither like country-folk nor any other well-defined class of whom one has experience. Rhoda herself, it must be owned, says extremely little throughout the whole story, and is to be congratulated on her attainments in silence, seeing that her father, whom the author depicts as a plain, rough, bluff, matter-of-fact, every-day English yeoman, is made to talk in this imaginative fashion—'That letter sticks to my skull as though it meant to say, "You've not understood me yet." . . . In any case, Robert, you'll feel for me as a father. I'm shut in a dark room, with a candle blown out. I've heard of a sort of fear you have in that dilemmer, lest you should lay your fingers on edges of sharp knives, and if I think a step—if I go thinking a step, and feel my way, I do cut myself, and I bleed, I do.'

In this book, Edward Blancove's brother, Algernon, is a clever and faithful, but uninteresting and profitless study of the heartless and brainless young man of the upper classes. What impels Mr Meredith to produce such careful photographs of this dreary type of humanity it is not easy to see. The limited truth of photography is there certainly, together with its unlimited hardness; but that is all.

Mr Meredith's real powers are much better shown in such a book as *Diana of the Crossways*. He is essentially an artificial writer, and when he tries to move freely and look at his ease among simple folk he fails. If one may so put it, naturalness is not natural to him; but when he is frankly artificial, he is then himself, and may be expected, at least intermittently, to coruscate. In *Diana* he is frankly artificial, and produces a clever and entertaining book. Twice, indeed, the interest in the mere story rises high, making us regret all the more that the author usually thinks it good form to have so little to tell. Elsewhere the story is attenuated enough, and the interest mostly centres in the brilliancy of the casual comment on society. This is often sparkling and keen. The account of Diana Warwick's peculiar position and social arts is about as good as anything of the kind could be.

Wherever Mrs Warwick went, her arts of charming were addressed to the women. Men may be counted on for falling, bowled over by a handsome face and pointed tongue; women require some wooing from their insphered and charioted sister, particularly if she is clouded. Now, to woo the swimming matron and court the settled dowager, she had to win forgiveness for her beauty; and this was done by forbearing to angle with it in the press of nibblers. They ranged about her individually unnoticed. Seeming unaware of its effect when kindled, she smote a number of musical female chords, compassion among them. A general grave affability of her eyes and smiles was taken for quiet pleasure in the scene. . . . Nature taught her these arts, through which her wit became extolled entirely on the strength of her reputation, and her beauty did her service by never taking aim abroad.

Or take the following:

The witty Mrs Warwick, of whom wit was expected, had many incitements to be guilty of cheap wit; and the beautiful Mrs Warwick, being able to pass anything she uttered, gave good and bad alike, under the impulsion to give out something. . . . She discovered the social uses of cheap wit; she laid ambushes for anecdotes, a telling form of it among a people of no conversational interlocution. . . . Irish anecdotes are always popular in England, as promoting, besides the wholesome shake of the sides, a kindly sense of superiority. Anecdotes also are portable, unlike the lightning-flash, which will not go into the pocket.

Passages like these show Mr Meredith at his brightest; and how felicitous is this bit of commentary upon the ridicule of things English: 'If the English do it themselves, it is in a professionally robust, a jocose, kindly way, always with a glance at the other things, great things, they excel in; and it is done to have the credit of doing it.' Occasionally an aphorism as concise as true falls from his pen, as when he finely says, 'Observation is the most enduring of the pleasures of life.' But, speaking generally, Mr Meredith's admirers exaggerate his epigrammatic talent, real and considerable as it is, and overlook the fact that the epigrams, even when good, are often in the way. The hard staccato movement, and brittle snip-snap of conversations literally carried on in epigrams, tires the reader. It is not dialogue, but a series of mental percussions. Mr J. M. Barrie, in the *Contemporary Review* for last October, calls Mr Meredith 'the most brilliant of living writers.' He is also 'the greatest wit this country has produced', and 'Sheridan is not visible beside him'. Poor Sheridan! Mr Barrie tells us that he could, an if he would, 'tattoo the *Contemporary* with Mr Meredith's triumphs of phraseology'. With admirable self-control, he forbears to do so, and I shall follow in his footsteps, and refrain from tattooing the *National*. I take this opportunity of saying, however, that critical extravagances like Mr Barrie's are just the sort of thing which deters sensible people from approaching an idol enveloped in such 'thick, strong, stupefying incense-smoke'. Mr Meredith is a wit: thus much may be conceded. But a great wit he is not, and his *esprit*, such as it is, exhibited in season and out of season, plays him an ill turn almost as often as it does him real service. It is a fine keen rapier blade, but you cannot plough a field with it. Or it is an amusing companion in whose society Mr Meredith neglects his business. And this liability to be diverted from the main matter in hand is too apt to infect his whole method of work. With conscientious art and with a vigorous hand he sketches some minor and unimportant figure, while he leaves his chief personages half-defined. Sir Griffin [*sic*] Dunstane, in *Diana of the Crossways*, is drawn with bold firm strokes, and stands out real and living from the canvas. Redworth and Dacier, characters of prime moment to the story, move pale and vague before the reader's mind.

The book, however, which, of all Mr Meredith's books, gives the greatest pleasure to the greatest number of readers is unquestionably *The Ordeal of Richard Feverel*. To call it clever would be to underrate, almost to libel it, for it contains much that is better than any cleverness. Over and above its other merits it is even, in many parts, a well-told story, and that is the first requisite in a book professing to be a novel. A man may be a keen observer of life, a brilliant wit, a suggestive social essayist, and many other admirable things; but can he tell a story clearly and well? If not, do not let us call him a great novelist—he is not even a good one. Sir Austin Feverel, a 'scientific humanist', otherwise a unique prig, pedant, and *doctrinaire*, has two great objects in life: the one to leave posterity a legacy of aphorisms embodying that gnomic wisdom which is his peculiar attainment, the other to see much wisdom monumentalized in the person of an only son, who is to grow up a theory made flesh. To keep the youth absolutely unspotted from the world, a system of semi-seclusion and espionage is enforced, and especially he is to be guarded from all possibility of sexual influence, whether gross or pure. On the whole, a history of an ideal experiment of this kind would perhaps be more interesting if the material to be experimented upon were an average rough-and-tumble English lad with commonplace human failings and the visible germs of ordinary human vices. The problem of how to keep a typically young male biped absolutely clean, spiritually and carnally, is one which many a father might like to see worked out, if only on paper. But Richard Feverel, in many respects an ideal youth, lends himself to an ideal experiment somewhat too naturally and easily for the solution of the problem to be in a high degree exciting, or even instructive. Not that he is by any means universally acquiescent or ductile. Occasionally he is disaffected, as when, on his fourteenth birthday, he rises in revolt against the indignity of submitting to medical examination; but, on the whole, the subjection of his individuality to his father's 'scientific humanism' provokes less friction than would be observable in the case of most youths similarly operated upon by rigid theoretic machinery. Ultimately the story resolves itself into a chronicle of how Richard did at last break his bonds, and finally emerge from his 'Ordeal', in some respects manifestly the stronger and wiser for it, in others as manifestly the weaker and more foolish. Somehow, one would like to know what is Mr Meredith's own private verdict upon the whole matter. It seems a case in which, without pedantry, an author may be asked to be more explicit as to his own drift and intention. Was Sir Austin's 'system' altogether a tragic blunder? Then let us see calamitous consequences naturally flowing from its operation. Calamitous consequences do indeed flow, but not *naturally*, so far as the reader can see, from anything; certainly not from 'the system'. They are directly chargeable, not upon Sir Austin's *doctrinaire* perversities, but upon his son's utterly inconceivable and inexplicable conduct after his marriage with a delightful girl-wife, whom, with a callous cruelty wholly at variance with his own previous record, he almost immediately deserts for the space of three months, and for no earthly reason that the reader can discover. Even the reverential Mr Barrie admits that he cannot fathom this mystery of the master's art, and doubtless he has brooded upon it, and perhaps even dared to seek light from the master himself, after the manner of Eckermann when he asked Goethe to explain 'the mothers', and Goethe either would not or could not.[1] To put it mildly, this is one of the cases (an unusually flagrant one perhaps) in which Mr Meredith really pays scant courtesy to an average reader's intelligence. To pass off such an episode upon us is almost an affront. But, in truth, orderly and natural evolution of incident is one of the things Mr Meredith hardly ever has at his command; and such a deficiency, needless to say, is more than a mere surface-flaw in a novelist; it is a vital and radical defect, and inevitably relegates him to an inferior rank among imaginative creators. Nay, more, it proves his essential unfitness for the novelist's task—an unfitness which may, of course, co-exist, as in him it undoubtedly does co-exist, with many extraneous gifts and graces. Is it extravagant to surmise that Mr Meredith's early adventure in a quite different field, that of arabesque romance—has left a fatal mark upon all his subsequent and quite dissimilar work? Absence of logical progression, of natural outgrowth and sequence—a glaring want of organic evolution in narrative—this is what vitiates his stories, destroying them as works of art. In profuse but disorderly brilliance he can heap together blocks of porphyry and chalcedony and jasper: he cannot build. In that astonishing feat of unbridled fancy *The Shaving of Shagpat*, such a defect is scarce distinguishable from a virtue. There we are delighted with the mere reign of lawlessness, the riot and anarchy of invention, the magnificent irresponsibility and libertinism of a dream. There we are content to wander through gorgeous palaces of enchantment, without requiring that they shall have any foundation more solid than a cloud or a sunbow. But something of this unchecked, self-chartered freedom seems to appertain to Mr Meredith's literary methods in departments of imagination where it is wholly out of place, with the result that his leading incidents often lack not only moral inevitableness but artistic cohesion. It is not thus that the masters of fiction weave their web of human lives and fates. No thread of it is purposeless or casual. No flight

---

[1] J. P. Eckermann, *Conversations with Goethe* (1848), Sunday 10 January 1830. The phrase refers to an incident in *Faust*.

of the shuttle across their loom but is reminiscent of all that has gone before, and secretly ominous of all that is to come.

But serious as are the blemishes referred to, they are redeemed in *Richard Feverel* by real and great beauties. I think there is nothing in fiction more charming than the early love-scenes between Richard and Lucy. The account of their first meeting, when Richard, rowing on the lake, sees the maiden sitting beside an old weir, engaged in the pretty pastime of eating dewberries, is deliciously sweet and fresh and pure.

[Quotes xiv, from 'Above green-flashing plunges' to 'two electric clouds'.]

Mr Meredith has nothing else that is comparable to these scenes. They are touched with a delicate bloom and roselight, and all about them one feels the breath of nature, the mystery of the earth, the seriousness of the sky.

Then she sang to him one of those majestic old Gregorian chants that, wherever you may hear them, seem to build up cathedral-walls about you. . . .
The strange solemn note gave a religious tone to his love, and wafted him into the knightly ages and the reverential Heart of Chivalry.

Richard Feverel himself reminds one a good deal of the youthful Shelley, as pictured in the masterly pages of Mr Dowden[1]—a sort of youthful Shelley minus Shelley's intellectual greatness. The somewhat impracticable youth is also accompanied by a matter of fact foil in the person of Ripton Thompson, a sort of Jefferson Hogg, minus Hogg's perfidy and ability. Nothing in the book is more spirited and vivid than the sketch of Mrs Mount, 'a superior priestess of Paphos', an audacious but powerful study, with more of pathos in it than Mr Meredith ever attains when he is deliberately on the track of that quality. Clare's diary, in this story, shows pathos of the determined sort with which we are all too familiar. Some of the remaining persons of the story are laborious and dreary failures. The uncles, Adrian [sic] and Hippias, tend to become mere tedious personifications of qualities. Adrian is cynicism and selfish intellectuality. Hippias is little more than gluttony and indigestion. Both are prodigies of boredom to the reader, who wishes them sunk deeper than did ever plummet sound.

'But *The Egoist*,' one hears some disciple of Mr Meredith asking; 'what of that unique masterpiece, *The Egoist*?' For that is the novel which seems to call forth more unlimited enthusiasm among the

[1] *Life of Shelley* (1886).

members of a certain esoteric cult than any other of our author's works. That is pre-eminently the sacred book by which the faithful swear. And here let me quote Mr Louis Stevenson, whose tone is certainly very impressive:

[Quotes 'Books Which Have Influenced Me', from 'I should never forgive myself' to 'serviceable exposure of myself'. See below, Appendix I.]

Well, it is only fair to avow that I distrust myself to speak of *The Egoist*. A critic can only record his own impressions, always taking care to test and revise them by such light as his own private study of the principles of literary art may lend him; and speaking in sober literalness, with due attention to the force and value of words, my impression of *The Egoist* is that it is the most entirely wearisome book purporting to be a novel that I ever toiled through in my life. At the same time here is a writer of Mr Stevenson's eminence whose delight in the book is manifestly real, and who, moreover, is able to give a lucid and telling account of the faith that is in him concerning it. In the face of such evidence an unbeliever does well to pause. Opinions and tastes may be questioned; delight in a thing cannot be argued with. Although Sir Willoughby Patterne, his insufferable selfishness, his colossal puppyism, his stilted phraseology, and his endless triflings with the hearts of the very unrealizable women who revolve around him, are to me simply soporific in their monotony and inanity, it is none the less clear that the book has qualities which fascinate some superior minds, and a reader who cannot enjoy them will do best to recognize the fact that he is not one of Mr Meredith's elect, acknowledge his own limitedness, and say no more about it. On the subject, however, of literary style, even a person not preordained from the beginning of things to appreciate Mr Meredith's peculiar intellectuality, may venture to say a word. In all this author's books one is apt to be irritated by occasional verbal extravagances usually taking the form of a perverse reluctance to say a plain thing in a plain way. 'Hippias perspired conviction.' Somebody 'infrigidated a congenial atmosphere by an overflow of exclamatory wonderment'. 'Her head performed the negative.' 'His novel assimilation to the rat-rabble of amatory intriguers tapped him on the shoulder unpleasantly,' and so forth. But what is at worst a rather too frequent indulgence elsewhere, becomes in *The Egoist* a habitual vice. Hardly a page but is disfigured by some fantastic foppery of expression. 'He tried to say in jest, that it was not always a passionate admiration that held the rogue fast; but he muddled it in the thick of his conscious

thunder.' 'The accidental blossoming of his ideal, with Mrs Mountstuart, on the heels of Clara's offence, restored him to full command of
his art of detachment, and he threw her out, quite apart from himself,
to contemplate her disgraceful revolutions.' 'His mouth shut rigidly,
and there was a springing increase of the luminous wavering of his
eyes.' 'A strong smell of something left out struck Dr Corney.' (This
gentleman says to a boy, 'You are worthy of a gratuitous breakfast in
the front parlour of the best hotel of the place they call Arcadia.')
'Clara swam to meet them.' 'The celestial irony suffused her, and she
bathed and swam on it.' 'She swam for a brilliant instant on tears.'
'Mrs Mountstuart swam upon Willoughby.' (All the people in Mr
Meredith's novels swim a great deal in conversation, besides frequently
'pouncing' and 'plumping' upon one another.) 'De Craye shadowed a
deep droop on the bend of his head before Clara.' (This means he
bowed to her.) 'Willoughby expected no. In his expectation of it he
hung inflated.' 'He was taken with galvanic jumpings of the spirit
within him.' 'She squeezed herself shadowily.' 'She saw young Crossjay, springing with pots of jam in him, join his patron at a bound, and
taking a lift of arms, fly aloft, clapping heels.' Somebody describes a
girl as 'just a whiff of an idea of a daughter of a piccadillo-goddess
[sic].' Sofa cushions are 'redolent of ladies' hands'. Threatening to kiss a
girl is 'shadowing forth a salute'. 'The gulf of a caress hove in view like
an enormous billow hollowing under the curled ridge'. What kind of
English is the following—'This petrifaction of egoism would from
amazedly to austerely refuse the petition'—or this—'The father of the
little maid's appreciation of his volatility'? A young lady had a nose
that was 'not acutely interrogatory or inviting to gambols', and we
learn that 'the build of her winter-beechwood hair lost the touch of
nymph-like and whimsical, and strangely, by mere outline, added to
her appearance of studious concentration'.

No milder word than detestable can be applied to the preposterous
style of which the foregoing sentences are examples, and vile as it is, it
is surpassed in extremity of insufferableness by the—what shall we call
it? Intellectual coxcombry seems a blunt phrase, but is any courteous
phrase available that will adequately describe the airs of superiority, the
affectations of originality, the sham profundities, the counterfeit subtleties, the pseudo-oracularisms of this book? 'The poet is at once the
spectre of the kitchen-midden and our ripest issue.' 'The Egoist is the
Son of Himself: he is also the Father.' Pretentious verbiage like this,
spread over three volumes, which contain no more solid substance in

the shape of actual story than might have been fitly compressed into three chapters, becomes, to a common-sense reader, simply nauseating. As for the meagre and bloodless puppets that jibber and posture before us in lieu of credible human figures, Mr Meredith himself has unintentionally described them by anticipation long ago in *The Ordeal of Richard Feverel.* Honest Farmer Blaize is looking at the coloured prints in a book of feminine fashions, and is requested to admire the attitudes. 'Attitoods!' he exclaims. 'Why, they're all attitood! They're nothing but attitood!'[1]

To be the idol of the æsthetes, the darling of the superior people, is perhaps a hard fate, but no one can be held accountable for the antics of his own admirers. Rather is he to be condoled with on the folly of his friends, the friends from whom, perhaps, he deserves to be saved. Severe criticism will not necessarily kill even the worst and most meretricious writer, but such a one cannot long survive deification. We see hurry, strain, fatigue, written even upon Mr Meredith's best work; what true service is rendered him by pitting him against the easeful, victorious masters? The one blunder of Marsyas was challenging the god.[2] Happily there is much in literature which, though it falls far short of greatness, we could yet ill spare. The age of the giants may possibly be past, but

the feet
Of fabled fairies, when the sun goes down,
Trip o'er the grass where wrestlers strove by day.[3]

We have many delightful novelists still amongst us, and their charm is usually strongest when they seem freest from any supposed obligation to be great, from any tendency to assume that greatness is expected of them. They are the men—and women—who have gauged their own powers, recognized their own limits; who know what they can do, and do it quietly. Mr Meredith is not one of them. He tries to do something more, and a look of defeat, of frustration, of perplexity, hangs about his partial achievement. It is painfully reflected in his style, which suggests a perpetual craning forward to snatch something that swings out of reach. Now, mere ease of style often gets more credit than is its due. It is ease with power, or ease with splendour, that is the valuable thing. Anybody can be at ease in a shooting-jacket and knickerbockers.

[1] This is a slight misquotation of a passage left out of editions after the first. See *Works of George Meredith*, xxxvi (1911), *Bibliography and Various Readings*, 84.
[2] Marsyas challenged Apollo's skill as a musician and was flayed alive after his defeat.
[3] Untraced.

To look comfortable in court-dress is distinction. Either costume has its recommendations; but Mr Meredith seems to fancy himself in a combination of the two, and the effect is not happy. It is not a sartorial triumph. A style that seems at once stiff without dignity and lax without ease; a style that attempts rapidity, to achieve fuss; a style aggressively marked and mannered, an intractable style that takes the initiative, leads the way, dominates the situation, when it should be (as style should always be in prose fiction) simply an obedient instrument, a blade to carve with, not to be flashed in our eyes; the possession of such a style may not seem to argue a high degree of fitness for any line of literary effort, but it does assuredly indicate a special degree of unfitness for the task of telling a story. And in truth Mr Meredith can at all events do anything else better than he can tell a story. Without constructive ability, without power to conceive and fashion forth realizable human creatures, without aptitude for natural evolution of incident, without the *raconteur's* instinct for knowing what will keep his company awake, he has yet many endowments. He is an epigrammatist, with scintillations of steely-cold wit; he is a poet, with glimpses of beauty; he is a social essayist, with acute observation and suggestive criticism of human conditions and conventions. He is all these excellent things, and more; and the fault is nature's rather than his, that he is not a novelist.

86. Sir Arthur Conan Doyle on Meredith's 'audacious genius'

1890

This passage is taken from an article on 'Mr Stevenson's Methods in Fiction', *National Review*, xiv, January 1890.

Meredith was made to be imitated. His mission is not so much to tell stories himself, as to initiate a completely new method in the art of fiction, to infuse fresh spirit into a branch of literature which was in much need of regeneration. His impatient and audacious genius has refused to be fettered by conventionalities. He has turned away from the beaten and well-trod track, and has cleared a path for himself through thorny and doubtful ways. Such a power would have worked in vain were there not younger men who were ready to follow closely in his steps, to hold what he has gained, and to strike off from it to right and to left. It is a safe prophecy to say that for many generations to come his influence will be strongly felt in fiction. His works might be compared to one of those vast inchoate pyramids, out of which new comers have found materials wherewith to build many a dainty little temple or symmetrical portico. To say that Stevenson was under the influence of Meredith is no more than to say that he wrote in the last quarter of the nineteenth century, and was familiar with the literature of his day. All good work, especially all early good work of a man, shows the influence of some model upon which he has fashioned his style of work. Meredith, himself in his loquacious and motherly Mrs Berry, shows the influence of Dickens. . . .

87. Richard Le Gallienne's reply to Watson

1890

Richard Thomas Le Gallienne (1866–1947), one of the younger generation of critics, was one of Meredith's most enthusiastic readers. His volume, *George Meredith; Some Characteristics* (1890) was the first book-length study of Meredith. Stray papers on the same subject were published in his *Retrospective Reviews* (1896). This article originally appeared in *Time*, N.S., xi, March 1890, under the title 'The Meredithyramb and Its Critics'.

By this time that exemplary person who is always deferentially anxious about what he *should* read and what he *ought* to think, that person for whom Sir John Lubbock and Mr Alexander Ireland sift and winnow

literature,[1] and for whom the philanthropists of Fleet Street and Pater-
noster Row proclaim a catch-penny bookish salvation; that exemplary
person has by this time become aware that there is a new literary god
whom men ought to worship. He has bought the 'Camelot' Ibsen, the
Newcastle Tolstoi, and he is now 'taking in' the neat cheap edition of
Mr George Meredith 'in monthly volumes'.

Mr Robert Louis Stevenson, in *The British Weekly*, is mainly responsible for that investment, no doubt, though the anonymous writer of
'Letters to Living Authors' in *Wit and Wisdom*,[2] will have led some
souls into the way of grace, and Mr Barrie, in *The Contemporary*, has
probably a small claim for commission. It is just possible that this 'young
man in a cheap literary suit' has come across Mr Courtney's *Fortnightly*
article in the old magazine box at Mrs Bennett's,[3] though James
Thomson's reviews in *The Tobacco Plant* will probably have escaped
him.

So far, saving a few qualms from Mr Courtney's pages, he has had
no cause to fear for his investment: he has, poor soul, been tossed on
many winds of criticism as to which of the master's works is *l'œuvre*,
but not till a month or so ago had he to bear the shock of a heresy,
which if it were as potent as it is provincial, would speedily send his
stock far away below par.

It is too true that October's *National Review*, 'with its wild reverberations as of thunder in the mountains,' may not even yet have reached
him; we will pray that it never will, so that he may still cherish his new
possession free of a fear which reassurances of mine can scarcely hope to
comfort. How horrific, too, is the title of Mr William Watson's article.
He calls Mr George Meredith's work 'anæmic', and if 'anæmic' will
not frighten his admirers, are they not bold indeed? It is ill disturbing
the happily-buried, and I but resurrect Mr Watson's article on 'Fiction
—Plethoric and Anæmic'—of which three pages deal with Mr Robert
Buchanan, and fourteen with Mr George Meredith—that it may serve
as a text. For it is interesting, not so much as serious criticism, but as the
British Public's long insensitive disregard of Mr Meredith finding
voice, and endeavouring to justify itself, graceless and unrepentant. It is
also curious as being one more proof of that futility of criticism which
we all hold as a creed—and follow as a creed. Indeed, Meredith 'litera-

[1] Sir John Lubbock, Baron Avesbury (1834–1913), scientist and political essayist, author
of *The Pleasures of Life* (1887–9), *The Beauties of Nature* (1892), and *The Uses of Life* (1894).
Alexander Ireland (1810–94), journalist and Editor of *Manchester Examiner*.
[2] J. A. Steuart, *Wit and Wisdom*, 11 May 1889, 9–10.
[3] Untraced.

ture', even within the camp, has already most abundantly illustrated that. For example—almost every novel of Mr Meredith's in succession has by one or another critic been declared his masterpiece. With James Thomson it was *Emilia in England* (then so named) with its sequel *Vittoria*; for Mr Stevenson it is *The Egoist*; give Mr Barrie *Harry Richmond*. Mr Watson would seem to find it in 'that astonishing feat of unbridled fancy, *The Shaving of Shagpat*'. (*The Egoist* is to him 'the most entirely wearisome book purporting to be a novel that I ever toiled through in my life'.) Mr Courtney has with him so much of 'the world' as is Mr Meredith's (not a hemisphere, one fears) in his unhesitating choice of *Richard Feverel*, while it is by far the most 'superior' thing to cry 'Great is *Diana*'.

'Mr Meredith writes such English as is within the reach of no other living man,' says a critic, in *The Daily News*. 'His style,' says James Thomson, 'is very various and flexible, flowing freely in whatever measures the subject and mood may dictate. At its best it is so beautiful in simple Saxon, so majestic in rhythm, so noble with noble imagery, so pregnant with meaning, so vital and intense, that it must be ranked among the supreme achievements of our literature. A dear friend said well when reading *Vittoria:* here truly are words, that if you pricked them, would bleed.' Yet Mr Courtney says that Mr Meredith's style is 'never easy and flowing', and that 'it is impossible to attribute to our author the gift of style' at all, 'except in a very special sense'; while Mr Watson (though not wishing to be thought rude), holds that 'no milder word than detestable can be applied to' (that 'supreme achievement of our literature'), 'the preposterous style of which' certain quoted 'foregoing sentences are examples'. To James Thomson, Mr Meredith's dialogue is 'not only the best of our age, but unsurpassed, if equalled, in our whole literature: it is so spontaneous, unexpected, involuntary, diversified by the moods, the blood, the nerves, the ever-varying circumstances and relations of the interlocutors; differing thus in kind from the dialogue of ordinary novels and plays, just as the actual interview between any two or more persons differs from the suppositious interviews which each has mapped out beforehand'. Yet for Mr Watson 'it is not dialogue, but a series of mental percussions', its 'hard staccato movement, and brittle snip-snap tries the reader'. The introduction to *Diana* again is a famous *crux*. 'Of all introductory chapters to an interesting novel', Mr Courtney deems it 'the most irritating'; and yet for the accomplished critic of *The Manchester Examiner*, it is the one thing in the book. And so on *ad infinitum*, till the brain fairly reels with

333

contradiction, and in agony of soul, one calls again, 'what, indeed, *is* the use of criticism?' Is it any use? Waiting for a clearer mood wherein to answer the question, when our eyes have grown a little accustomed to these mists of confusion, we may come to see some solid ground whereon to stand. After all, these contradictory figures have a common denominator, and by that may be illustrated what is to my mind the one yet very notable service of criticism. Whatever else is to be proven, one thing is certain, that George Meredith is a centre of power, of whatever nature, in whatever degree, no matter. So much have we learnt by being thus sent, as we say, 'from pillar to post'.

And that, indeed, is all that criticism should say with any tone of finality—here is a notable figure, consider him! If he does more things than one, it cannot presume to say which he does best, or in doing which he has most value. That each individual must decide for himself so long as light is coloured by the glass it shines through. Of course, if the ideal critic were possible it might be different, but the ideal critic is like the ideal king—if we could all agree about his wisdom, his power and so on, there would be no need of politics, government would be solved. So if we could all agree on the man who had the finest culture with the subtlest temperament, his *dicta* might take the place of our *contradicta*. But really and truly such dreams are hollow things, for they are based on a forgetfulness of so essential a fact of our nature as our inequality and the relativity of all impressions to that. It is not impossible that after all this wrangling about Mr Meredith's novels, posterity in its quiet way will go up to the shelf and lay its hand on *Modern Love*. Who knows?

And yet one may see individual systems applied daily with a confidence as though each were generally accepted as long measure, writers weighed one against another with the certitude of an accredited troy or avoirdupois, and various heights of inspiration calculated as though they were church steeples, and criticism trigonometry. If criticism must be dubbed a science, its place is rather among the 'occult', and the divining-rod no bad symbol of its function. We may trust it to find out where gold is hid, and then, if we like, we may proclaim the discovery for gold, sky-high; but, measuring and weighing are uses impertinent to it, except purely for any satisfaction that may accrue to the measurer or the weigher himself, and those who chance to be of his mind. There is only one quality of good work (as they say of that dreadful Swiss milk)—'The Best'.

Yet some critics have a loose way of talking about *true* poets and *true* poetry, of bad art and good art, as if poetry and art can be appraised like butter into best, second quality, and common; a thing is either poetry or it is not, it is kind, not degree, about which criticism should busy itself. Perfection is equal, and all art stands on the equality of perfection.

All which seems simple enough, yet why do we so often forget it in fruitless comparative criticism of things on planes between which no comparison is really possible? What conceivable ground of comparison can there be between Scott and Mr Meredith? and yet Mr Barrie, talking wildly of Mr Meredith's pre-eminence, gives him a giddy place, 'without dethroning Scott'. Because they were both novelists, Mr Watson as well as Mr Barrie would cry—you might as well compare their works because they were men. And here we see the mistake of so much criticism.

Instead of going to their man to find out 'the virtue, the active principle' in his work, and noting it 'as a chemist notes some natural element' (to quote the helpful words of Mr Pater),[1] many critics go to him with abstract definitions of what he ought to be, and by that pattern (should he disagree) condemn him. If he cannot be made to fit the ready-made court-suit they bring him, well, he must stand shivering in the nakedness of unpopularity, and—do they really think?—of oblivion.

The suit into which Mr Watson and others of his persuasion would try to force Mr Meredith, is a narrow and shallow interpretation of the term novelist. 'Is he great at construction? Is he great as a master of narrative? Is he great as an artist in dialogue? Is he great as a creator of character?' asks Mr Watson, all in a breath; to which questions he immediately sets to work to attach vivacious negatives, with the alacrity of one filling up No! No! to the 'Are you married?' 'Have you any children?' of certain application forms. No! he cannot weave twopence halfpenny mysteries. No! he doesn't tell us the old, old stories over and over again. No! 'he tires the reader'. No! Adrian Harley is a mere 'tedious personification, a prodigy of boredom to the reader'!!! Are not the types eternally fixed, who shall increase them?

Of course, as Mr Courtney writes, 'it may be difficult to defend some of' Mr Meredith's novels, 'on the hypothesis that the primary task of the novelist is to amuse', and such, indeed, despite Mr Watson's contempt for the ordinary novel-glutton, would seem to be his hypothesis. 'Does he keep awake? will he while away an idle hour? are the only questions which he really seems to have had in his mind.

Is the novel, of all forms of Art, to be allowed no expansion? Is it for

[1] *Renaissance* (1873), Preface.

ever to coincide with a dictionary definition and be as old Noah Webster has it, 'a fictitious tale or narrative in prose, intended to exhibit the operation of the passions, and particularly of love'?[1]

If so, it had logically no right to outgrow its first form of the *novella*, and as the nineteenth century has no *Arcadias*, it should, therefore, have no novelists. Most will agree that the great elemental passions are the proper, indeed the only themes for Art, but as the work of race-breeding goes on surely these are continually becoming 'touched to finer issues'.

> Change is on the wing to bud
> Rose in brain from rose in blood.

Less and less do our lives express themselves in the extremes of action. We are learning to be merciful to the superlative, to know something of self-control and the sense of proportion. So there is more meaning in our little finger nowadays than in the whole strong right arm of the men of old time. We lift an eyebrow where our ancestors had committed manslaughter. Is picturesque sentiment to be for ever the only language of love, and Union Jack heroism the only garb of courage? Has selfishness no other form than cannibalism and cruelty, no subtler than foolish violence or a coarse malignity? Why, therein is the limitation of the stage, which must always be more or less restricted to the presentation of such life as is expressed in outward and visible sign—and does all, does the finest life always find such expression? Is there no drama but that of labelled 'act and deed'? Surely thought is the most dramatic of all things, and yet can the French stage (on which Mr Barrie well says Mr Meredith would have some chance of justice) give us that? Of course, Mr Watson knows all this, for he is one of George Eliot's disciples, with the most ardent of whom the present writer too would fain be counted.

She knew the drama of thought and gave it us for some types, but must 'victorious analysis' stop with her or them? There are subtler individualities than Tito, and shall we not welcome their drama? Sir Willoughby Patterne of Patterne Hall is a subtler, and Mr Meredith has given us his drama of nerves. By and bye there will be a subtler than he, and then may be we shall need a stronger lens. Wherever there is life there is a story (as wherever there is criticism there must be platitudes); all are equally well worth telling, the old as well as the new, the new as well as the old. Mr Watson and the British public would seem to dis-

[1] Noah Webster (1758–1843), *Dictionary of the English Language* (1828).

THE CRITICAL HERITAGE

agree with Mr Meredith, not because he cannot tell a story, but because he will not tell the particular stories they are alone interested in. The disagreement is natural, we can but applaud what appeals to us, like the squire at Vauxhall in Mr Dobson's poem:

> He praised the thing he understood,
> 'Twere well if every critic would.[1]

If the 'various shades of grey' are invisible to us, how can we be expected to be interested in them?

With regard to character, is the word to bear no other than the 'professional' stage significance of 'character parts', and to be applied only to the whimsical, the eccentric or the provincial?

Again, is dialogue a *sine quâ non* of the novelist's art? Do all characters, do all stories reveal themselves in talk? The drama postulates that they do, and is an arbitrary form to that extent; but on what compulsion must the novelist? Certainly not from exigency—like the drama—for truer methods lie to his hand. And as to the objection against Mr Meredith's dialogue, that all his characters talk Meredith, that never man spake like this man, and so on, does not the same apply to Shakspere and Mr Browning? Yet I don't think Hamlet or Lippo Lippi are less alive to us for that. Literalness is not the essential of dialogue, truth to the spirit of the speaker is. There are many instances when the letter would distort the whole significance of a character—indeed, it is oftener so than not. If the novelist *is* to use dialogue, why should he be refused the same freedom with it as the dramatist or the poet? But, indeed, only one of Mr Watson's provisions is fundamental—that the novelist should be able to tell a story. What story and how he tells it is his business, not ours. Dialogue or disquisition matters not, so that the end is reached; the end of presenting to us a living thing, for in Art the end does justify the means. Character-drawing is really included in that fundamental power, for unless we have a living sense of the *dramatis personæ*, the story is not really told at all. A chronicle of what happened to lay-figure M or N may be interesting, but till we know who or what either was it is not a story. Events have no significance of themselves—except to schoolboys, who get over the difficulty by appropriating them, through their imaginations, to themselves. It would really be as true to say that the power of creating character is the *sine quâ non*, for no character can really be drawn apart from the lights and shades of its various relations with other characters and things, to set forth which involves a story.

[1] 'The Squire at Vauxhall' (1884), Austin Dobson.

337

To show how any being or fact is alive is the end of all Art, and especially of the novelist's. If he can do that for half-a-dozen he has succeeded. Why should 'the million' or the average intelligence be the test of Art? Fame, either present or posthumous, is no test. It may be (as it would seem to be in Mr Meredith's case) that the novelist's methods of presentation are eccentric and difficult, that his particular story needs a new technology, like science. He may speak in the language of an outlandish or forgotten people, he may write in Norwegian or in Latin. If so, he must not expect to be as lucky as Ibsen or grumble if he shares the oblivion of 'Vinny Bourne'.[1]

There is no reason why he should do his work in the British vernacular. It is time the superstition of 'good plain Saxon' was exploded. To do much with little is a fine quality, but to *do* is the essential, and once done, neither number and variety of tools nor prodigality of material can depreciate perfection.

That Mr Meredith does not write the vernacular, at least in that of his work which is most really his own, that which we can find nowhere else, does not really so much matter as may at first sight appear; for, supposing it imaginable as having been written in any other style, in their own Saxon, would *The Egoist* have had any stronger appeal to 'the general' than it has at present? I think not, for though to some of us, there is there an unmistakably living man (and the greatest masters cannot do more than make his creations alive), and a story as much tragedy as 'a comedy in narrative'; he is a man who, if they could be made to understand him, could not possibly interest them, and it is a tragedy which they could not appreciate, for there are not four deaths in the fifth act—only the marriage of a girl whose soul has been slowly atrophied with a man who has come to be but the corpse of her god. You cannot really appeal to the heart (by which one means the elemental centre within us) without first appealing to the brain, and the average brain is still busy with the obvious. In this respect Mr Meredith is really in the position of a poet's poet—one might call him the novelist's novelist. Indeed, it is a question for thought, it seems to me, if that is not always the position of every great artist. It is a commonplace to say that he is always in advance of his age, but does posterity ever catch up with him? There is a great deal more cant than truth in the chatter about the universal appeal of Shakspere, and who is it that reads Dante? The fact is, that posterity is as much in the dark as their own age was,

[1] Evelyn Bourne or Burne, the name under which Ethel Bourne published *Storm-beaten and Weary. A Novel* (1887).

but a few dead critics have made a noise about them, so it tries to get over the difficulty by unintelligently making a superstition of them. Was it Thoreau who said that the great artists have really been taken by the world on the faith of a few critics? That was certainly a fine saying of his—'The great poets have never yet been read by mankind, for only great poets can read them. 'And yet, at the same time, there are at least two of Mr Meredith's books that should make that 'universal appeal', one thinks, dealing with interests near home, and written mainly in the vernacular. Surely there is plenty of 'human interest' and ruddy enough humour in *Evan Harrington*, and I cannot imagine a public taking *Adam Bede*, and finding nothing in *Rhoda Fleming*. *Richard Feverel* is largely on another plane and makes a subtler appeal, but if it gave one critic (I forget where I read his words) the idea that Mr Meredith should be able to write a good boys' book, there must be much in it to suit the public, for, after all, 'boy's books' are really what the public want. 'Plenty of blood and brawn, never mind brain', is their demand, and that of a certain so-called masculine school of critics. Do they ever reflect that the craving for that so-called masculine comes of the feminine side of our nature?

But while it is really Mr Meredith's stories for which his critics have no taste, it is about his style that they make the great fuss—it is even a stumbling-block to the wise, at times. We glanced at some diversity of opinion regarding it above. Everybody agrees in quoting the Ferdinand and Miranda passage in *Richard Feverel* as perfection, everybody quotes it in small type; fewer seem to have come across the 'Wilming Weir' chapter in *Sandra Belloni*. But his phrase-making! It seems hopeless to expect agreement upon that. With Mr Watson it stands for nothing but 'intellectual coxcombry', and yet who will agree with Mr Barrie, when, though he feels Mr Meredith to be the most brilliant of living writers, yet, making the strangest choice of pet phrases, he says of others, probably one's own, 'these are misses'?

Many of the greatest artists among the painters have ground their own materials. To that, I believe, we owe much of their individuality of colouring; and what they have done with colour the literary artist must nearly always do with language. Every artistic message needs a new medium for its expression peculiar to itself, as surely as each new soul finds a new body; and to me it seems impossible to imagine, vain to hope for, a style more adapted for the work which it is called on to do than Mr Meredith's.

¹ H. D. Thoreau, *Walden or Life in the Woods* (1854), 'Reading'.

His power of metaphor is certainly unequalled by any English contemporary known to me, and to me it seems that not since Shakspere has there been a handling of imaginative phrase more truly masculine. The manner in which continually a vivid word comes like a flash of lightning and lights up some hidden track of thought, some inaccessible lair of sensation, fairly takes one's breath at times. It hardly seems to be metaphor at all, but the very process of thought and feeling literally described.

The distinction between objective and subjective is overleaped, and we seem to see matters of spirit and nerve with our very physical eyes. Indeed, that is just what such art as Mr Meredith's must do; for in proportion as it is art, will the relevancy of that distinction diminish, if it is true, as surely it is, that the subjective once embodied in art really becomes objective. It is this very realistic closeness to the fact, I am persuaded, that has misled many, unfamiliar with the *nuances* of experience with which it deals, to charge Mr Meredith with fantasticality. His fancy is prolific and delightful indeed, or we must have missed *Shagpat* from our shelves, but the metaphor I speak of comes of a higher power with which Mr Meredith is no less richly endowed—imagination. His images have roots, they are there for another service than fancies. Moreover, he has apparently discovered the secret of a mental process which operates more or less with us all, but of which we are only occasionally, some perhaps never, conscious; for, is it not true that all impressions come to the most unimaginative through a medium of imagination more or less fantastic in its influence, and that thus the most commonplace occurrence often assumes the quaintest guise? Through the subtlety of his imagination Mr Meredith has come into possession of this distorting glass, and it is either because we have never realized the process in ourselves, or are unable to recognize it again in his characters that he may sometimes seem puzzling or overstrained. In short, Mr Meredith's imagination is subtle enough to embody the workings of imagination. An example will best illustrate my meaning, and I will take one that is a favourite with unsympathetic critics, from *The Egoist*.

' "You are cold, my love? you shivered," said Sir Willoughby Patterne, as he walked across his park one morning with his betrothed, Clara Middleton, then in the throes of her first effort to break off her engagement.

' "I am not cold," said Clara; "someone, I suppose, was walking over my grave." The gulf of a caress hove in view like an enormous billow hollowing under the curled ridge. She stooped to a buttercup; the monster swept by.'

This image has more than once been selected for scorn, from the impression, I suppose, that it is merely a piece of extravagant fancy, a wilful euphuism, whereas, it is surely an example of a most subtle realism. To a sensitive girl such as Clara, in such an attitude as hers to her betrothed, already beginning to dread his loathsome attentions, it would really be in some such large image of fright that a threatened caress would menace her, especially as her fear had already set her imagination in a state of ferment: and to have simply said that she shrank from his caress and escaped it would have been merely the statement of an onlooker, and have given us little idea of her internal tumult as she did so. We should only have seen her shrink, whereas now we feel her do so. I am convinced that the majority of Mr Meredith's so-called fantasticalities have such true imaginative basis, and that if the reader cannot realize it, the fault is certainly his own. Not that I would say that Mr Meredith never misses. Like everyone else, he has 'the defects of his qualities', and it would not be difficult to place one's finger on images that seem the result of his employing his method in uninspired moments—a certain bewildering and unbeautiful personification of old Time, for instance, on an early page of The Tragic Comedians—but such are quite inconsiderable set against page after page of brilliant success.

I am not about to make the mistake of quoting phrases in support of my opinion. That just referred to was but introduced to justify it against those who have already quoted it profanely. If our normal prose has not homogeneity, Mr Meredith's has. Quotation of single lines and phrases from The Egoist is especially futile. Some critics may be able to apply the methods of palæontology to Art and judge of the fabric and its design by one strange thread—if they can, it is well, but in Art it is as dangerous as it is unnecessary, and I will make no such attempt. Indeed some of the phrases I might quote have already been quoted by Mr Barrie as 'misses' and Mr Watson as 'coxcombry'. To me, and many more, I am glad to believe, they are neither. But cui bono? It is all in 'the point of view' as Mr Robert Louis Stevenson has said.[1] Criticism is perhaps the one thing in which we must live to ourselves. At most, the critic is but the tribune of a temperament, the representative of a certain intellectual interest. All we should try to express, is (as Mr Pater has taught us), what a certain piece of work, or a certain personality is to

[1] Familiar Studies of Men and Books (1882), 'Preface by Way of Criticism'.

us;[1] but in doing so do let us be careful of other people's feelings. It is in Art as in religion, we all worship the same thing under different forms; there is but one Spirit of Beauty, and whatever artistic fetish—be it 'masculine' or what you please—our neighbour is kneeling at, we can tell by his face and his voice, whether he sees that spirit there. I am quite willing, for my part, to believe that of those to whom Mr Meredith is little more than Shibboleth, and yet at the same time, I do not feel the superior person that Mr William Watson says the admirer of Mr Meredith always does feel. Moreover, though I know a great many admirers of Mr Meredith, as yet I have not found in them either that peculiar conceit. Really, I think Mr Watson must have made a mistake, or maybe he has been amongst some of those people who turn every new faith into a cant before it is a week old. There are such in town. If so, I sincerely sympathize with him.

The great danger to other people's feelings lies in comparisons. Why we make them, I do not know; they are constantly growing out of date, and while current they are futile. Nothing so much as criticisms impress one how truly odious they are. It is well to admire Mr Meredith's skill with boys in *Richard Feverel*, indeed we would not lose that splendid fight for much; but why need Mr Barrie be so positive that Thackeray's boys are not so genuine, why dethrone Traddles, why say that there are no boys like them in contemporary fiction—even if we have been so industrious as to have reaped bare so large a field? There are boys in *A Daughter of Heth* surely. Criticism should not need to be dated, and such, to have any value at all, would need to be. Richard Feverel and Ripton Thompson are *boys*, typical boys, real and living. Is not that enough to say?

Let us too avoid the superlative. It is a vulgar form. It is not half so dignifying as the simple positive. It is a poor civic tinsel of a word. We can only wear it in our little town, and that only in our little day. For it is but a relative term, its value must be for ever fluctuating, but plain 'good' endures, and no contingency can ever set to it a limitation.

The parable of the Talents is suggestive here. The man with the four was called 'good and faithful', but the man with the ten was called nothing more. So Art considers her children. In the house of Fame there are many mansions.

For me, maybe for you, Sandra and Diana are a part of Art's own dream of great women; Lucy and Richard by the riverside are with the great lovers; for a while, indeed, they are in the starry air of the Vita

---

[1] W. Pater, *loc. cit.*

Nuova; Roy Richmond holds you by the heart, Adrian Harley by the brain—and somehow by the heart too, for the more one knows him, the less one fears his cynic pose, one begins to suspect him of a heart. Sir Willoughby takes a place in your moral mythology; he is your wholesome *bête noir*, every day you cry him 'Retro'. Maybe you love not Thackeray's inns better than the Aurora; you often think of Evan Harrington and the postilion, of that delicious ride of his with Polly, and who shall forget the great Countess! Dr Middleton and that aged and great wine have perhaps made your cheap port seem the richer at your occasional symposia. You know a good part of the 'leg' passage in *The Egoist* by heart, I daresay, and often find Meredithese floating on your talk. You have quoted 'the vomit' as you poured with the stream from the theatre; maybe you have known a dear face *swim* up to you 'for a brilliant instant on tears', and been grateful to Mr Meredith for that so offensive phrase, and thoughts *have* rung little silver bells through your brain in the midnight. When your blood runs a little thick, have you never taken down *Vittoria* and lived over again that great fight in the Stelvio pass, or harrowed yourself once more with old Squire Beltham's slaughter of poor Roy Richmond, by his merciless, shuddering invective?

You have felt you had beauty, comedy, tragedy, in all these, and in how many other characters and scenes? So have I. But *he* has not. Let us pray.

ONE OF OUR CONQUERORS

1891

88. Unsigned review, *Anti-Jacobin*

i, 25 April 1891

There is many a living man whose new books we expect in pleasure, and read with no disappointment: pretty iterations of the old times, genial repetitions of the old sentiments, we read them at leisure with an indolent relish. Of this kind consists modern literature; and the writers to whom the statement does not apply are but some four or five in number. Mr Meredith is foremost amongst them.

Reading any book by Mr Meredith, we read with our whole powers and faculties in harmony: the brain thinks, the senses feel, the imagination sees, the heart understands. To think of Mr Meredith's old books, fifteen or so in number, is to remember whole troops of friends known to us by heart. But to read a new book by the same master is exhilaration of both mind and body.

But a cry of delight, though natural, is not altogether explanatory, and the source of our delight in Mr Meredith is very simple. It is, that he can be read and accepted without concessions; his work, as is true of all good work, satisfies with the satisfaction which is given by a perfect building or by perfect music. Mr Meredith reconciles so many tiresome quarrels: real and ideal, optimist and pessimist, romance and analysis, adventure and psychology. We do not say of his books that they are admirable in a certain manner, as we say of Flaubert or of Fielding. They demand for their comprehension our entire service, and at first the unusual demand is irksome; but once tuned to willing obedience we have our reward. For Mr Meredith, taking men and women and their life on earth as his material, omits nothing and intrudes nothing; he is faithful to the truth at all heights and in all depths, and upon the plain levels of human life. The play of forces, from within and without,

344

upon men and women; the ensuing complexity of sensation and ideas; the sure laws of nature, steadily at work; the comedy and the tragedy of those who protest and revolt; the strength of those who in the light of reason follow nature; these are the elements with which Mr Meredith constructs and animates his work.

But here comes in the difficulty of criticizing any one book by Mr Meredith taken alone. Each book deals with one great conception, and each conception is treated with equal power. You may prefer the problems of *Richard Feverel*, and I those of *The Egoist*: it is a matter of temperament. But between the artistic excellence of the two books, the mere writer's ability and success, there is little or no distinction. We can but fall back upon Mr Pater's canon, if a book have certain fine qualities of beautiful construction and spiritual distinction, it is good art; but, 'if it be devoted further to the increase of men's happiness, or the enlargement of our sympathies with each other, or to such present-ment of new or old truth about ourselves and our relation to the world as may ennoble and fortify us in our sojourn here, or immediately, as with Dante, to the glory of God, it will be great art'; for then, 'it has something of the soul of humanity in it, and finds its logical, its archi-tectural place, in the great structure of human life'.[1] Mr Meredith's new book, then, is not only good art, but great art also; it is filled and alive with this intimate concern for human nature in that battle of circum-stance which is the condition of social life. Victor Radnor, in early youth, constrained and fascinated half unconsciously by the prospect of wealth, married a woman greatly his senior: a marriage with which nature had nothing to do. This he more clearly understands when he meets Natalia Dreighton, his wife's young companion. Taking their fortune into their own hands, they face the world as husband and wife. Victor, a man of ardent energies and hopes, attains commercial success, a society of loyal friends, and all his desires. Now and then, malicious gossip and what is called the prejudice of society cause trouble; but upon the whole, he lives well with his worldly enterprise and his devoted friends of wit, and music, and cordial sympathy. Nataly, a woman of that strong and winning nature loved by Mr Meredith, swept away by Victor's impetuous confidence and prosperity, stifles her anxiety and her longing for seclusion and for rest. Their trial in the sight of nature and of reason comes upon them through their one child, Nesta; of whom we can but say that she ranks with Clara Middleton and Lucy Desborough. The father, always expecting his first wife's

[1] *Appreciations* (1889), 'Essay on Style'.

death, plans and labours for the social establishment of his child; not condemning his own action, but half conquered by social circumstances on her behalf. The mother, not condemning her own action, is also half conquered by the knowledge of Nesta's practical compassion towards 'a low woman'; Nesta being ignorant of her parents' position. Her mother, worn out with a long continued strain of anxiety, bitterly misunderstands her. If Nesta so looks upon such a woman, it is because she inherits from her birth the lawless defiance of social obligation; or because, hearing at last her mother's history, she sees no difference between it and the history of any 'low woman'. In all this Mr Meredith shows great courage, great insight, great power. He here confronts two main questions: England and Mammon, and England and Women. Under these two heads are included nearly all other 'social questions', and in no previous book has Mr Meredith's command of language served his purpose better. 'Obscure', one man may say, 'exaggerated', another; and the obscurity is not to be denied. But if they will only take the trouble to examine the thoughts and to 'learn the great language' of Mr Meredith, they must confess with admiration that he is himself, in the best of senses and in an enduring fashion, 'One of our Conquerors'.

89. H. S. Wilson, *Athenaeum*

No. 3314, 2 May 1891

Henry Schütz Wilson (1824–1902), a critic, essayist and novelist, was a regular contributor to the literary journals.

'The Burman, and her Notions', to plagiarize the title recently adopted by the ingenuous Mr Shway Yoe,[1] might fittingly serve as a sub-heading for Mr Meredith's latest novel. All through the book, though she is studiously kept in the background and her utterances are limited

[1] *The Burman, His Life and Notions* (1910), was by Sir James George Scott (1851–1935).

to a dozen lines, the grim figure of this much-wronged lady haunts her victims like a veritable Erinnys, whether she is sitting 'with her fashionable no-bonnet striding the contribution chignon on the crown, and a huge green shade over her forehead', ghoulishly sampling new mixtures in the chemist's shop at Charing Cross, or crazily imagining herself 'the wife of the ex-Premier, widow of Prince Le Boo, and engaged to the Chinese Ambassador', or (as in the final reconciliation scene at her own house near the Regent's Park) gazing with 'wide orbits for sunken eyes', a wasted ghost, 'from a pale blue silk veiling'. Her interminable existence, the unconscionable time she takes a-dying, 'a limpet of vitality with drugs for blood', constitute the key to the whole tragedy, the *dignus vindice nodus* which defies the cheery optimism of Victor Radnor and the patient sufference of his Nataly. When young and foolish—'an innocent, a positive innocent', as he describes himself —he married the old woman for her money—'a small boy tempted by a varnished widow, with pounds of barley-sugar in her pocket'—and, speedily finding the situation intolerable, ran off with her charming companion, the gentle contralto Natalia Dreighton. His awe-inspiring spouse devised and executed a terrible revenge. Desertion without reasonable excuse, when coupled with adultery, is, as we may all know, a cause for which a wife may obtain a decree of divorce; but Mrs Burman Radnor has no intention of putting the law in motion against her husband. Wherever the hapless couple elect to take up their abode, this ill-omened creature or her spectral butler-emissary Jarniman stirs up prejudice against them, and, like the harpies at the Virgilian banquet,

Diripiuntque dapes, contactu que omnia fœdant Inmundo. [1]

driving the unwedded lovers from pillar to post—from Craye to Creckholt—with remorseless persistence. The case is complicated for them, poor souls, by the fact that their daughter Nesta knows nothing of the bend sinister that blots her scutcheon, and as she grows up the difficulty of explaining these constant changes of residence becomes greater. People fall in love with her, too, and then explanations are necessary. Lakelands, the great house in the country, the magnificence of which is to compel recognition on the part of Mrs Grundy, never receives its inmates for permanent occupation. The big speech which is to establish Victor's position as candidate for a South London constituency remains unspoken. For just as Mrs Burman, on her long-deferred

[1] *Aeneid*, III, 227–8: 'And they tear apart the banquet and with foul touch befoul everything.'

deathbed, proclaims a tardy forgiveness, and all is being prepared for
the ceremony which will right the wrongdoers in the eyes of a censorious world, comes the crushing blow of Nataly's own decease, but five
hours and a half before that of her aged rival. And so, with Victor's
lunacy, the edifice of his aims and ambitions falls crashing to the ground,
and the lifelong tragedy of this irregular union finds burial in his grave.

We must not, however, ignore the relief afforded by the underplot
that deals with Nesta's love affairs. The Rev. Septimus Barmby, the
Hon. Dudley Sowerby, and Capt. Dartrey Fenellan are a trio of characters whose working-out is accomplished in Mr Meredith's happiest
manner; and Nesta herself is an exquisite creation, fit to rank beside
Lucy Feverel and Clara Middleton. The scenes in which the Rev. Septimus takes part are full of rich humour, as witness the following, where
he ponderously urges his unwelcome suit:

[Quotes xxxiii, from 'Mr Barmby headed to the pier' to 'on its dull
green back'.]

If Mr Barmby's solemnity inspires mirth, the mental limitations of
the second aspirant, Dudley (good fellow though he be), render him an
equally unattractive wooer. He plays the flute with considerable skill,
and is 'tall, straight-featured, correct in costume, appearance, deport-
ment, second son of a religious earl and no scandal to the parentage'.
But one can see at a glance that he will never suit the quick-witted,
warm-blooded Nesta; and his advances and retreats, his qualms and
questionings, as depicted in a masterly chapter which exhibits 'a conventional gentleman endeavouring to examine a spectre of himself',
deprive him, once for all, despite subsequent accesses of 'generosity', of
the reader's esteem. He has learnt, be it said, from her own mother's
lips the story of the girl's illegitimacy:

[Quotes xxvi, from 'Venerating purity as he did' to 'at the commission
of the act'.]

No, Dudley will not do, emphatically. But what of Dartrey Fenellan? Let Mr Meredith describe him:

Not two minutes had passed before she was at home with him. His words,
his looks, revived her spirit of romance, gave her the very landscapes, and new
ones. Yes, he was her hero. But his manner made him also an adored big
brother, stamped splendid by the perils of life. He sat square, as if alert to rise,
with an elbow on a knee, and the readiest turn of head to speakers, the promptest
of answers, eyes that were a brighter accent to the mouth, so vividly did look
accompany tone.

This is the beginning of their intercourse—friendship, big-brother-hood on his part, dawning love on hers. But events move swiftly between a pair like these, both so high-couraged and so free from commonplace trammels. A few pages further on we find them discoursing after this fashion, on the subject of Nesta's innocent indiscretion in visiting the unhappy Mrs Marsett:

[Quotes xxxviii, from ' "So, my own mother, and loving me" ' to 'Never did girl so give her soul'.]

There is only one man alive in England who could have written that passage, and he is Mr Meredith. Its subtlety and strength are alike astonishing, and it reveals him at his very best.

The minor characters of the novel are no less original than the bulk of their author's personages. Little Skepsey, the confidential clerk, with his scheme for the regeneration of England by means of the resuscitation of the noble art of self-defence, and his repeated collisions with the authorities, is a droll and lovable figure; and the Duvidney ladies, especially in that immortal 'night piece' which deals with the malodorous irruption of their lapdog Tasso and its important consequences, evoke hearty laughter. The Priscilla Graveses and Peter Yatts, and the rest of the strange crew who 'could meet and mix in Victor's concert-room with an easy homely recognition of one another's musical qualities, at times enthusiastic', are not very clearly defined, and do not rouse more than a passing interest. But Colney Durance and Simeon Fenellan, the embodiments respectively of a gloomy and a gay cynicism, are not without their attraction for the discriminating reader; while there is much skill in the flesh-and-blood portraits of Mrs Blachenoy [sic] and Lady Grace Halley.

To say that the book is by Mr Meredith is to say that it is full to the brim of brilliant things. The hand that dispensed the treasures of the 'Pilgrim's Scrip' is still prodigal of epigram. The best specimens of his workmanship in this kind are fathered (with somewhat tedious iteration) upon the saturnine Colney Durance, who 'crushes a class to extract a drop of scathing acid'. Surely never was a man so quoted by his acquaintance. 'As Colney says', 'As old Colney would remark', 'That is like Colney's', 'That reminds me of Mr Durance's'—such are the too obtrusive pegs on which Mr Meredith loves to hang the dazzling garments of his wit. Yet critics must be thankful, after yawning over the inanities which pass for conversation in the ordinary novel, for the display of a wardrobe so resplendent.

349

There is incidentally a good deal of fine description of natural objects. The following sketch of the change from night to day as seen from a Channel steamer is remarkably happy:

> Now was the cloak of night worn threadbare, and grey astir for the heralding of gold, day visibly ready to show its warmer throbs. The gentle waves were just a stronger grey than the sky, perforce of an interfusion that shifted gradations; they were silken, in places oily grey; cold to drive the sight across their playful monotonousness for refuge on any far fisher-sail.

Till a few lines later one reads of the

> splendour of the low full sunlight on the waters, the skimming and dancing of the thousands of golden shells away from under the globe of fire.

Or take this passage conjuring up, as in a glass, the whole charm of the scenery of Tyrol:

> He had in memory prominently now the many glorious pictures of that mountain-land beckoning to him, waving him to fly forth from the London oven:—lo, the Tyrolese limestone crags with livid peaks and snow lining shelves and veins of the crevices; and folds of pinewood undulations closed by a shoulder of snow large on the blue; and a dazzling pinnacle rising over green pasture-Alps, the head of it shooting aloft as the blown billow, high off a broken ridge, and wide-armed in its pure white shroud beneath; tranced, but all motion in immobility, to the heart in the eye; a splendid image of striving, up to crowned victory.

But Mr Meredith is not always so fortunate in his phraseology. He will occasionally be striking at whatever cost, and the result is, not unnaturally, pure 'caviare to the general'. The vagaries of genius are visible both in grammar and spelling, to say nothing of the daring with which this prose Pindar

> per audaces nova dithyrambos
> Verba devolvit[1]

to be the stumbling-blocks of simple souls. We have 'toneing' in one line, but 'changing' in the next. 'Defense' meets us in its American guise, and a dress-maker's block becomes a 'dumby'. The verbs 'spring' and 'jump' are used strangely: Nesta's words 'sprang a stinging tear to the mother's eyelids', and of an episode in Colney Durance's satiric serial it is said that 'it jumped me to bravo the cleverness'. On one occasion 'Mademoiselle rippled her shoulders', on another 'Victor jerked a dead

[1] Horace, *Carmina*, IV, ii, II: 'he rolls new words through daring dithryambs'.

laugh'; while Dr Gannius 'crashes cachinnation', and M. Falarique 'damascenes his sharpest smile'. People are continually 'crapeing' and 'drapeing' all sorts of queer things. Mr Meredith has also some fearful and wonderful adjectives, or collocations of words doing duty for epithets. The 'stern-ajerk empty barges' which occur in a capital description of the Thames as seen from London Bridge, and 'the bank of blueish smack-o'-cheek red [cloud] above Whitechapel', may serve as illustrations. 'Busy antish congregates' and 'hypocritical judex air' are other adjectival essays, to our mind not over-felicitous. 'The stormy square of the first of seamen', 'the Riverina green field on the rock', 'Afric's blue mud of the glittering teeth', 'the hallowing squire of the stables' (= a riding master), 'the raised orchestral flooring' (=a platform), and 'the brown-paper envelope of the wires' (= a telegram) are other odd flowers of speech. Mr Meredith shows a liking for the termination '-ly'—'Quakerly' and 'martyrly' are both to be found in these pages. Gulls (as we have already seen) are 'briny', like the element they soar over, and a baboon is 'branchy'.

The proper names selected for the characters are often successful, but in naming his creations the author does not show the unerring instinct of Thackeray, who could people a dinner-table with appropriately christened guests at a moment's notice. 'Septimus Barmby' is good, and so is 'Groseman Buttermore'; 'Colney Durance' is artfully suggestive; but we cannot away with 'Stuart Rem' or 'Mancate Semhians', and 'Julinks' and 'Beaves Urmsing' strain our powers of belief to breaking-point.

Is it too late to beg of Mr Meredith that he will have some compassion on his weaker brethren in these and such like matters? They are but the mint and cummin of literature, but they provoke an irritation which does something to prevent the growth of his popularity. Without acknowledging ourselves to be of the number of those who cannot stomach his tougher utterances, we are sure that we voice the feelings of many would-be admirers when we ask him to allow the stream of his genius to flow a little less turbidly. That it can do so, much of his earlier work, and many pages of his new novel, conclusively prove. As he is strong, let him be merciful.

90. Unsigned review, *The Times*

18 May 1891

Mr Meredith's new novel, which succeeds *Diana of the Crossways* after an interval of six years, will revive an admiration and a regret. With most people, we fancy, the regret will exceed the admiration. Mr Meredith, like Mr Browning, has his special circle of worshippers, who appear to adore his eccentricities as part of his genius. Is it too unkind to suggest that intellectual pride has something to do with this enthusiasm? Delighted with themselves for being able to distinguish magnificent shapes in it, they are pleased to imagine their admiration of the intricate pattern is a mark of superior understanding. But we may fully apprehend the lightnings which—to adopt Mr Oscar Wilde's metaphor—play through the Meredithian chaos without admitting the scene lit up by their zigzags to be beautiful in any sense of the word. Could Mr Meredith's ideas but be reduced into lucid English! But his is one of those cases in which form and matter seem inseparable. He is, apparently, incapable of sending the most profound truth or the most obvious truism into the world until he has worked it up laboriously into epigram or anagram. A philosopher above all things, Mr Meredith appears to think that the character cannot be kept up without a philosophic contempt for plain language. It may be so; but the multitude, upon which the philosopher must depend for fame and influence, naturally asks itself, Is it worth while? The main object of a novel is to amuse—to appeal to heart or understanding through the sense of pleasure. Mr Meredith's novels make the appeal through the sense of pain; but until an era of asceticism in amusement arrives, the penitential exercise of reading his works will never be really attractive to the generality of cultivated minds. In the meantime it is well to recognize that, if Mr Meredith has won his way into the ranks of authors of genius, he has done so, not in consequence of his peculiar mode of expression, but in spite of it.

In a novelist who chose his model in the days of the Crimean war, and has kept to it ever since, it is too late to expect any unbending now. *One of Our Conquerors* is, if possible, more Meredithian than ever in style. It will hardly be ranked, even by the novelist's admirers, as equal to *Diana of the Crossways*, *The Ordeal of Richard Feverel*, or *Evan Harrington*. Still, it exhibits that unity of purpose without which no novel can be great, but which, taken alone, is not greatness. *One of Our Conquerors* is Victor Radnor, the City man, the sanguine, the compeller of fortune, at whose feet all that has not fallen already is, in his optimist expectation, about to fall. The very magnificence of Lakelands, the country mansion built as a surprise to his family by this irresistible man, whispers of some pursuing Nemesis. Daring, indeed, is he who can throw down such a challenge to fortune, when the fabric of his domestic happiness is built upon the violation of the marriage tie. Legally, Victor is the husband of an old woman whom he married while yet a boy, intoxicated with the glamour of wealth. In the eyes of the world, or all of it excepting a handful of friends and enemies, he is the affectionate partner of a beautiful, accomplished, and devoted lady, and the adoring father of a lovely girl. It is out of these materials that the tragedy is constructed. All Mr Meredith's psychological penetration is devoted to analyzing and developing the relations between father, mother, and daughter; the obtuse optimism of the man, the painfully keen consciousness of the loving woman whom he will have brave the humiliation of a possible unmasking, and the heroism of the girl when the time comes for her to slowly realize the truth. For Nesta is the heroine of the tale; and her character, like that of Diana, must be cited as an example that men are able to seize the highest attributes of the other sex better than women can create the heroic man. Her father's schemes have been rewarded by her engagement—more obedient than spontaneous on her part—to the Hon. Dudley Sowerby, the quintescence of conventional propriety. This Mrs Grundy in a frock coat is, however, not beyond the reach of impulse. When Nesta's mother takes the first independent step of her life, and tells him the real situation, he is shocked into withdrawal. Love works on him, and he prefers his suit again. But Nesta, while riding at Brighton, has, in the innocence of her heart, become the friend and confidante of a lady who is only ostensibly married; and her name is blown upon in places where men do congregate. Another shock for the Hon. Dudley; but again he advances, with the condition that Nesta should sever the compromising tie. But Nesta believes that she can save this woman, and she refuses the condition. Nesta's influence over Mrs Marsett—gained, apparently, by nothing but innocent eyes—and the facility with which Captain Marsett yields to solicitations that Judith should be made an honest woman, are among the weak places in the scheme of events. Nor are these the only incidents which show that, however much of a philosopher Mr Meredith may be in analyzing the feelings of his favourites, he can disregard facts and probabilities when it suits his purpose. Victor Radnor's temperament, for example, is just that of a man who does not usually take the world of finance by storm. This, however, is by the way. It will be seen that the position in which Victor and Nataly are placed towards their daughter is not without its irony. Nataly especially is destined to assert against her innocent daughter, with a vague dread of taint in the blood, an exaggerated regard for those conventions to the violation of which the girl owes her being. The author forbids the parents to enter the promised land towards which they are always straining their eyes, but entrance to which is for their daughter alone.

That all this is finely conceived we think no one who has the patience to study it will doubt. It is the execution that repels. The most brilliant epigrams do not atone for a failure to touch the emotions. Even the enjoyment of these would be more sincere were they launched as an integral part of dialogue or reflections. This time it is one Colney Durance who is First Satirist, with Simeon Fenellan for Second. Here is the latter's paraphrase of Depression in the City, which shows Mr Meredith in his ultra-Carlylean vein:

Business hangs to swing at every City door, like a ragshop Doll, on the gallows of over-production. Stocks and shares are hollow nuts, not a squirrel of the lot would stop to crack for sight of the milky kernel mouldered to beard. Percentage, like a cabman without a fare, has gone to sleep inside his vehicle. Dividend may just be seen by tip-toe stockholders, twinkling heels over the far horizon.

Here is a squib of a different kind:

Mr Beames Urmsing turned square-breasted on Fenellan, 'Fellow's a born donkey.'
'And the mother lived?' said Fenellan.

This is very well; but in general Colney and Fenellan are quoted at us. Whenever an epigram is on its way it is 'as Colney says', or 'Fenellan would say'. Whatever is humorous in our soliloquies is furnished for us by one of these two gentlemen, whose sayings everybody has by heart.

Skepsey's head dropped lower, he went as a ram. The sayings of Mr Durance about his dear England—that 'her remainder of life is in the activity of her diseases;' that 'she has so fed upon Pap of Compromise as to be unable any longer to conceive a muscular resolution;' that 'she is animated only as the carcase to the blow-fly,' and so forth—charged on him during his wrestle with his problem.

This reporting of *bons mots*, which is one mode of underlining good points, brings nausea after a time, none the less that the author accompanies the report sometimes with disparagement of the jest. The device is carried to the greatest pitch in Colney's great satire of 'The Rival Tongues', which, doled out in instalments in *oratio recta* or *obliqua*, seems to be productive of great amusement to the satirist's friends, but may possibly have a more soporific effect upon the reader. Indeed, whatever the dramatic merit of the central incidents of the tale, there is a fatal want of variety and lightness about their setting. The most frivolous incident and the most humorously-intended character are run into the same heavy mould, and bear the impress of the cynical philosopher. Skepsey, for example, whose citation of Colney Durance is given above, might have been expected to lighten the story as a middle-aged City clerk with a mania for pugilism. What a hearty laugh Dickens would have made out of such a man! But this Skepsey is a philosopher with theories about the regeneration of England through the medium of boxing; his sparring is not spontaneous; he too obviously comes out of the philosopher's workshop.

91. Unsigned review, *Saturday Review*

lxxi, 23 May 1891

'Puzzles,' says Mr George Meredith (vol. i. p. 6), 'are presented to us now and then in the course of our days; and the smaller they are the better for the purpose, it would seem; and they come in rattle-boxes, they are actually children's toys, for what they contain, but not the less do they buzz at our understandings, and insist that they break or we, and in either case, to show a mere foolish idle rattle in hollowness.' This sentence is not only a fair sample of Mr Meredith's style, but admirably describes the state of mind of the person who attempts to read through *One of Our Conquerors*. The author's usual faults of incoherence, prolixity, straining after epigram, seeking after the uncommon, lack of firmness in character-drawing, and allusiveness, are intensified in his latest work, and few indeed of even his most fervent admirers will be able to boast that 'they have read every line'. He *has* a story, and one that of itself contains the elements both of dramatic incident and pathos; but it will not let itself be told. Chapters of extraneous matter are interposed; lengthy descriptions of a flock of perfectly uninteresting and useless people, each with a catchword of his own; the reflections of a clerk while running to the station; disquisitions on nationality, temperance, boxing, even the long past conversation of the clerk with a pork-butcher, on his favourite subject of the 'gloves', anything and everything but the tale that the reader is wishing to hear. And this habit of Mr Meredith's is the more provoking as his story is simplicity itself, and could be told in three lines. Mr Victor Radnor (the 'Conqueror' of the title, and one of the most blatant cads we have ever come across) marries at the age of twenty-one, a very rich woman of 'more than middle age', and marries her confessedly for her money. This is the sort of action that damns a man as hopelessly as cheating at cards. It is use-less for him to say that 'he has nothing on his conscience with regard to the woman'; and to refuse to admit the truth of a friend's accusation that he had 'entered into bonds with somebody's grandmother for the sake of browsing on her thousands'. The fact speaks for itself, and bears no discussion. Well, having once married this lady, Mrs Burman by name, he falls in love with a beautiful girl of good family, who comes to live in the house, and finally they depart together to do what the French describe as *vivre maritalement*. When the novel opens, this state of things has lasted for twenty years. Radnor has become colossally rich, and has one daughter, who is always spoken of in the most irritating fashion as 'our girl', never once as 'our daughter'. This young lady is intended to be the incarnation of nobility and charm, but like all the other characters she is a mere name with no more individuality than one of the dancers in a *corps de ballet*. The burning—or rather the smouldering—question throughout the whole book is, whether Mrs Burman, who is a great invalid, will be good enough to die and let 'Mrs Radnor', or, strictly speaking, Miss Deighton, be made an honest woman. The subject is meant to be one of the deepest interest to both the Radnors; yet his devotion to his 'mate', as she is generally called, which is sometimes insisted on in an unpleasant and somewhat material manner, does not prevent his affectionately kissing a charming widow of his acquaintance, and keeping up a secret flirtation with her. After many false alarms Mrs Burman at length does die; but not until 'Mrs

Radnor', undermined by the long waiting and anxiety, is dead, and Radnor, whose fortune we are led to infer has disappeared, dies too, after a brief period of madness. Of course Nesta, the 'girl', has many lovers; but the reader is but languidly stirred by any of her love affairs. She gets herself into a terrible scrape by mixing herself up with a lady of no reputation at Brighton whose lover is so much inspired by Nesta's heroism in standing by his mistress, that he consents to take the lady to the altar. Nothing is more curious in the whole novel than the unpleasant relations between husbands and wives. In no single instance do they live together happily or even tolerably. There are Mrs Burman and Radnor, Captain Dartrey Finellan [sic] and his wife, who at the time of his introduction to the reader has died in Africa, after behaving abominably; there is Lady Grace Halley, whose husband 'out of the saddle is asleep. She called on bell-motion of the head to toll forth the utter night-cap negative.' But the moment he is in his grave she makes love to Radnor. There are Captain Marsett and the lady who goes illegally by his name, and Mrs Blathenoy, who proposes to Dartrey Finellan [sic] to elope with her, and failing that to kiss her. In his former books Mr Meredith did often succeed in writing clever passages and smart epigrams; but there are few specimens of either in One of Our Conquerors, while phrases that are perfectly meaningless abound. Who can follow, for instance, the first paragraph of the novel?—'A gentleman, noteworthy for a lively countenance and a waistcoat to match it, crossing London Bridge at noon on a gusty April day, was almost magically detached from his conflict with the gale by some sly strip of slipperiness, abounding in that conduit of the markets, which had more or less adroitly performed the trick upon preceding passengers, and now laid this one flat amid the shuffle of feet; peaceful for the moment as the uncomplaining who have gone to Sabrina beneath the tides' (vol. i. p. 1). This surely is not the way to write.

92. J. A. Noble, in *Spectator*

lxvi, 30 May 1891

James Ashcroft Noble (1844–96) produced a volume of poems (1887), published his memoirs and wrote regularly for the *Spectator* and the *New Age*.

As a general rule, no sensible person attempts to find a reason for a fashion in literature, any more than he would think of attempting to find a reason for a fashion in dress. The vogue of each concrete novelty is sufficiently explained by the existence of an insatiable craving for novelty in the abstract. Women wear plain gowns one season simply because they are tired of the elaborate trimmings of the season before; and the books which last year were never 'in' at Mudies, now gather dust peacefully on shelves from which they are never taken down. Sometimes, however, one comes across a fashion-puzzle that must excite to some amount of intelligent curiosity, and one of these puzzles is the rise of Mr George Meredith. He has been writing for considerably more than a quarter of a century, and during the greater part of that time his audience was scanty, and to all appearances tepid in admiration; but within the past five years, the enthusiasm of a little band of critics has been communicated to a section of the reading public, and it is becoming a common experience to meet cultivated persons who gravely assure us that Mr Meredith is our greatest living novelist. As Mr Meredith is not a new novelist, his present vogue is not susceptible of the usual explanation; and we must frankly admit that to us it is altogether inexplicable. His books are by no means deficient in imagination; some of them contain passages of considerable power and beauty, and all of them abound in a too generally misdirected cleverness; but so far from being a great novelist, he does not seem to us to possess the qualifications which go to the making of a capable novelist of even the second rank; and even if those qualifications were his, their effect would be ruined by a literary manner which even in these days of affectation and strain is of unique perversity. It must, however, in fairness be admitted that his latest novel, *One of Our Conquerors*, does him less than justice; for while his characteristic merits are in abeyance, his characteristic defects are in evidence on every page. The mere narrative is so clumsily managed that the most acute reader will nearly reach the end of the first volume before grasping the nature of the slight, shapeless, and very unattractive story which Mr Meredith has chosen to tell; and the outlines of his characters reveal themselves vaguely and indeterminately through the mist of utterly impossible conversation which provides the atmosphere in which they live and move. The hero in his youth has married for money a woman considerably older than himself, the deed being, to quote his own refined description of the transaction, that of 'a small boy tempted by a varnished widow, with pounds of barley-sugar in her pocket'. The high-minded young man elopes with his wife's companion, who is, of course, young and beautiful, and the couple have a daughter, from whom the secret of her birth has been kept—a reticence which, when suitors begin to present themselves, is the cause of awkward complications. As, moreover, the deserted wife is supposed to be bent upon a vengeance which she has certainly power to inflict, the illicitly united pair, who are supposed by the world to be married people, live an increasingly uncomfortable life, until the story is brought to a sudden and violent conclusion by the death of both women and the madness of the man. We are quite ready to agree with any sensible interpretation of the critical dictum that the telling of a story is of more importance than the story itself; but of the telling of this particular story praise is impossible—indeed, it is more by good luck than good management that it is told at all. Mr Meredith disdains straightforward narrative, and his disdain for straightforward description and characterization is still more intense. He would not call a spade an agricultural implement, but 'the earth-cutting knife ungraspable by peculating stewardship'. A city statue of a deceased King is 'the figure of royalty worshipful in its marbled redundancy'. Instead of saying that Lady Grace Halley was a little, talkative woman, Mr Meredith writes, 'her stature was rather short, all of it conversational'; and as might have been expected of a lady of conversational stature, she 'gesticulated ecstasies'. Another lady on a trying occasion 'seemed to be hugging herself up to the tingling scalp'. When Mr Meredith *means* that Sowerby looked sympathetic when Durance was predicting national misfortune, what he *says* is, that 'the Honourable Dudley's expressing lineaments showed print of the heaving word, alas! as when a target is penetrated centrally'. Nor are these exceptional lapses from sane and lucid expression which have to be laboriously sought for: the thing which is hard to

find is a simple, natural, unstrained phrase or sentence. So affectedly
grotesque a style would ruin even a good novel, and to describe *One of
Our Conquerors* as a good novel is impossible.

93. Lionel Johnson, in the *Academy*

xxxix, 13 June 1891

Lionel Pigot Johnson (1867–1902), journalist, critic and poet,
became familiar with Meredith in his later years.

The works of a writer past the prime of life are apt to display a certain
excess or extravagance: what was once his strength has now become his
weakness, and his virtue has changed into his vice. This is most often
seen in the case of very strong and masterful writers; those whose good
work is all done in some one *annus mirabilis*, or flowering season, fall
into mere decay, as Coleridge or as Wordsworth. It is in writers whose
whole life has been full of successful toil and untiring effort, that manner
degenerates into mannerism. Such writers, and, indeed, all artists of
such a kind, are often men who have discovered some new way in art,
and who possess a secret and a power proper to themselves; the world,
used to the old and familiar ways, will not at once take notice of them.
In proportion to their faith in themselves and their fidelity to their art,
these artists, unshaken and undeterred, continue upon their way, rather
increasing than relaxing their unappreciated labours. Slowly and gradually the world comes round to their side, is converted to their faith,
welcomes them with applause. But what of the artists, all this long
time? Is there no danger that, in a kind of unconscious defiance and
challenge, they will have gone too far, and grown enamoured of that in
their work which the world did well to blame? If the world cried out
upon their obscurity, where there was some obscurity but not much,
was it not natural in them to have replied with worse obscurities, out of
an impatient contempt and exasperation? It is permissible to think that
Browning had a little of this feeling, when he filled his later books with
so much more argument than imagination. Landor dared to think that

Milton, in *Paradise Regained*, was 'subject to strange hallucinations of the ear'.[1] Now, Milton held, although the world does not, that *Paradise Regained* is superior to *Paradise Lost*. It is as though, foreseeing the 'revel of rhyme' that was to supersede his greater harmonies, he gathered himself together, and went nigh to straining the resources of his rhythm beyond its just capacity.

It has been said of late that Mr Meredith, in his new book, has likewise exhibited 'the defects of his qualities', that his former work reached the farthest limits of successful audacity, and that *One of Our Conquerors* has passed beyond them. Cordial and enthusiastic admirers of Mr Meredith are ringing the changes upon 'wilful eccentricity' and 'wanton obscurity' and 'lack of proportion in design'. Since the present writer is unable to share these opinions, it is incumbent upon him to acknowledge that, upon reading the book for the first time, he did not reckon it a masterpiece. Read three or four times, the book grows upon the reader, the apparent confusion disappears, the intricacies of design become intelligible, and the whole greatness of design is evident. Hasty impression yields to careful meditation.

Let us take, first, a question of style: is *One of Our Conquerors* written in a style of grotesque and perverted eccentricity, while *Richard Feverel* or *The Egoist* is full of true force and beauty? That can be maintained only by one who has not read Mr Meredith's earlier books for a year at least; one who retains a sense of their greatness, forgetting all but their final and permanent effect. Again, he who maintains that view must have ignored this fact: that with Mr Meredith style and subject change or grow together. In proportion as the subject is simple, or idyllic, or tragic, or humorous, or rapid, so does the style assume those qualities. If the chief influences brought to bear upon the chief characters be influences of the great and busy world, of crowded and complicated life, then the style reflects the nature of those influences. All Mr Meredith's books are full of stir and animation; but three of them, in especial, are full of this general or social life, this business and animation felt in the very atmosphere. In *Beauchamp's Career*, and *Diana of the Crossways*, and *One of Our Conquerors*, it is not too much to say that 'the world', or 'society', or 'the public', or 'the nation', seems to rank among the *dramatis personae*. Now, most English writers who wish to make an effect of this kind, to suffuse their work with this breath of the general life, attempt it by pages of reflection and description, in which the words are abstract and the sentences are sentiments. Unless the

---

[1] *Foreign Quarterly Review*, xxix (1842), 337.

writer be very skilful, his writing will be very dull; at the best, it will too often be mere rhetoric. But Mr Meredith differs in this from almost every other novelist of eminence: that he sees thoughts as things, emotions as images, the abstract as the concrete. He has eyes for the form and colour of an idea; he presents it to us full of life. It is now a truism to say that a cause is identical with its effects; but the illustration may help us out. When an ordinary writer gives us an idea, he gives it us in a dull and sparing way; the implicit truth is there, but it remains implicit: he states, as it were, a cause. Mr Meredith states the effects, the explicit operations of the cause, the thought is expressed in concrete terms. His lively phrases are not metaphorical, but logical; the ideas are translated into their equivalent expressions in actual life. Those readers are surely wrong who regard Mr Meredith's characteristic phrases as so many attempts at epigram and wit. Critics have published lists of Mr Meredith's 'failures' in epigram. They might as well be called his failures in epic. All such characteristic phrases are rather faithful translations of general and abstract ideas into expressions of their concrete contents of meaning: translations by a humourist, whose humour need not relish the phrase, which may be ludicrous, but the act of making it, the discovery that, do but examine such and such an idea, and the phrase will be found to express it. So that when Mr Meredith is accused of straining after wit, he is in reality but keeping close to facts, which is apt to be a grimly serious form of humour. It may not be amiss to compare with Mr Meredith's manner of expressing ideas, his manner of expressing nature. His poems, for keenness of sight, for close contact with the most precise details, have few rivals: and here he reverses his process, and from an expression of the visible or the audible in nature, he passes to its meaning for man in thought. In this way he keeps touch with both sides of life: real and ideal, analytic and synthetic; he cannot understand one without the other.

As is always the case with all true writers, the consideration of Mr Meredith's style passes insensibly into that of his subject. It may be assumed that most readers of the ACADEMY are now acquainted with *One of Our Conquerors*; so that, instead of a lame description of the book, we may consider one or two points, which are of the greatest interest. To begin with Victor Radnor, and his position. When a young man, he, to put it with all possible crudity, married an old woman for her money. Certain critics have cried 'Cad!' and refused to consider the possibility of his ever afterwards redeeming that dishonourable act of youthful folly. Such a criticism shows the inadequacy of petrified moral codes. Victor's act was not merely an offence against conventional laws of honour, which change with time, but against immutable laws of nature; and his next act was in defiance of conventional law, but in harmony with reason and with nature. He took for his true wife, in all but legal rights, a woman prepared to obey her nature and his. The first wrong to nature is redressed by a disregard of convention. Now, all this talk about nature and conventionality might, in the case of a weak writer, have been no more than a some-what nauseous cant, in the least desirable style of Rousseau. But Mr Meredith—need it be said?—ignores nothing. With a conception of tragic art and of moral law, which is among his greatest achievements, he shows us the failure of both father and mother, Victor and Nataly. Victor is too enamoured of the world which he has defied and coaxed, and Nataly too afraid of it. But he also shows us their triumph, in their child, in Nesta. We agree with Colney Durance when

he considered the shallowness of the abstract Optimist exposed enough in Victor's history. He was reconciled to it when, looking on their child, he discerned that, for a cancelling of the errors chargeable to them, the father and mother had kept faith with Nature.

Nesta—neither cherishing a prosperous superstition about the world based upon worldly success, nor a shrinking fear and deference bred of one noble disloyalty to convention—can face the world upon fair terms. She neither accepts its stupid prose, nor dreams over its false poetry; but, interpreting the reason in nature, she has every true power upon her side. Mr Meredith has drawn more portraits and characters of true women than any other Englishman, but Shakspere and Browning; Nesta is, it may be thought, the truest of them all:

> Thou hast left behind
> Powers that will work for thee—air, earth, and skies;
> There's not a breathing of the common wind
> That will forget thee; thou hast great allies;
> Thy friends are exultations, agonies,
> And love, and man's unconquerable mind.[1]

The lines came into our mind, when reading the last pages of the book, as applicable to the woman who, with all her zeal upon unpopular sides and for bold causes, never lost tolerance for the world of folly and of intolerance, except only 'when she thought of it as the world con-demning her mother'.

[1] W. Wordsworth, sonnet to Toussaint L'Ouverture.

THE EMPTY PURSE

1892

94. Unsigned review, *Saturday Review*

lxxiv, 17 December 1892

The reviewer who happens to know Latin, and therefore understands the meaning of *Cui bono*, must always be rather tempted to apply that venerable but ill-treated phrase in reviewing a volume of Mr Meredith's poems, supplying not *fuit* but *erit*. Whom will such a review profit? But to enter into such inquiries only leads to madness. It is better to cultivate the garden simply and *sans phrase*. In the present volume there are a dozen or fourteen poems—four of which occupy some five-sixths of the total space. Supposing that someone—a competent someone—opened it without having ever read any of the author's verse before, he would, like a well-conducted person, read the first poem first. It runs thus:

[Quotes 'Wind on the Lyre'.]

He would then (always supposing him of competence) experience a great delight and an almost greater puzzlement. He would say, 'Those last two lines are perfect; allow for a little mannerism, and they cannot be improved. You can't beat them: it is only too probable that you can't equal them. The mood of *ivresse* with beautiful objects, natural or artistic, is described there once for all as it has not been described before, as it will not be described again. This is the kind of man you can recommend to a friend to delight him or to an enemy to confound him. I shall have no small joy of this book'. And then he will put the said book down and begin to doubt and shiver. 'Yes,' he will say, '9 and 10 are superb; 1 and 2 are all right, so are 7 and 8. But how about 3–6? Of course I know what they mean; of course they mean the right thing; but is there not something wrong about the expression? Is not the

364

phrase of 3 clumsy, the imagery of 4 *outré*, the grammar of 5 awkward, the matter of 6 doubtful and irrelevant? Why these conundrums? Is the poet unable to express himself simply and greatly? Is he able, but chooses out of mere wilfulness to hide and distort his expression? Is he doing it of malice prepense to puzzle one kind of fool? Is he doing it of weakness to please another kind?' And so our competent innocent is left in shallows and in miseries of doubt till the last couplet comes once more to his relief, and assures him that this Todgers's can certainly do it when it chooses. There is no possible mistake about that.

We half envy and half do not envy the successive sensations of the hypothetical reader as he proceeds with the somewhat short gross of pages which make up the book. We do not think that he will have much doubt about Mr Meredith's meaning anywhere. Just as we never succeeded in discovering that obscurity of Mr Browning which was so much vaunted and decried by turns, seeing that every person of brains could understand Mr Browning well enough, and that the fools did not matter, so we are unable to blame this new cryptographic style for concealment of meaning, much less for meaninglessness. The meaning is there all right enough. 'The Empty Purse', for instance, itself, the title poem, the longest and the most Meredithian in superfluity of verbal gymnastics, is a straightforward, and, on the whole, a sound criticism of life enough, if you must have criticisms of life in poetry. It is led up to and its meaning is helped by a second partly exquisite lyric, 'The Youthful Quest'. We would undertake to paraphrase it all in prose which the wayfaring man might read, without missing a point, and at no very exorbitant length. Even the wayfaring man cannot mistake 'Jump to Glory Jane', and he must be a very chuckleheaded wayfaring man if he cannot understand 'Youth in Memory', for all its mannerism. 'The Comic Spirit' may puzzle him a little more; but we can assure him that it also is not *plus raide que ça.* You have got but to unhusk and unshell it, and there it is.

'But,' says our innocent (and really we do not know what to answer), 'why this unconscionable allowance of shell and husk? Why give me my poetry like this; why, when my breast is a shell that tingles for sounding, my blood a dew that is ready to burst into light, apply your plectrum and your torch in this fashion of all others?':

[Quotes 'The Empty Purse', ll. 246–63.]

'O Mr Meredith!' *innocens loquitur,* 'you remark yourself,
    Does it knock too hard at thy head if I say

something? I reply: No, it does not knock too hard. But why are we to be on these knocking terms? Why, instead of comfortably feeding me with the beef of which you have such good store, chuck it at me, bones and all, as if you were a Dane in a byrnie and I were Archbishop Alphege? You have celebrated generously the virtues of good wine. Would you be grateful to any one who took a bottle of '51 port, of '70 claret, and whirled it, bottle and all, about your brains? Let us in the name, not of Mars, but of Bacchus, Apollo, and virorum, have our wine decanted and our poetry served ready to sip!'

Sic innocens. We have no doubt Mr Meredith knows what to reply to him; we very frankly admit that we do not. We can only say that he may be, on the whole, thankful that he gets him. For ourselves we would, even if the kernel were worse than it is, read ten 'Empty Purses' for the sake of one 'Wind on the Lyre', and a dozen odes to the 'Comic Spirit', even if they contained less fine things than this, for the 'Night of Frost in May'. Let anybody find fault who will with the following passage; but let him know at the same time that his fault-finding is due to wretchlessness of most unclean desperation in him at never having felt what Mr Meredith describes:

[Quotes 'Night of Frost in May', st. ii–iv.]

But can we possibly rebuke in terms as harsh him who should object to more than one passage, or one score of passages elsewhere? We really do not think we can. The sense, as was said above, is sound enough. But the cookery of the sense—the expression—is all wrong. It is as either done too much or not done enough.

We are very glad to see in this book two military-political pieces—'To Colonel Charles' and 'England before the Storm'—which have the root of the matter in them, and are frankly and forcibly put, the second especially. 'Tardy Spring' is only inferior to the 'Night of Frost in May'. In short, there is nothing bad in the book; there is only good *per se*, and good in masquerade.

It is, probably, quite hopeless to ask Mr Meredith why he chooses to masquerade at all. It may be a just punishment for the fools who long ago would neither understand or admire him. It may be an ungodly private satisfaction to him, as to many, to say 'Pape Satan' and 'Rafel Mai', and other things not understanded of the people. It is, no doubt, a great joy to the other fools—the old fools turned inside out—who gape after everything that Mr Meredith chooses to say, and are all the more convinced of the blessedness of Mesopotamia the more absolutely unbathed they are either in Tigris or in Euphrates. But is it not rather a pity, even from these points of view, as well as a much greater one, and a great injustice to boot, from a point of view much better worth taking? What did the fools who erst (and, partly, now) would not buy or read Mr Meredith matter? They punished themselves; not him. What do the fools who now go into ecstasies over his weakest points matter? Their admiration does him considerably more harm than the others' contempt; and, besides, even if he were intelligible with ease, it would make very little difference to them; they would not understand him any the more. Lastly, it has been observed of the ancients that it is not good perpetually to say 'Pape Satan', and so forth, for there comes a time when you find a difficulty in saying anything else.

On the other hand, there is now, we believe, a not inconsiderable body of tolerably elect persons who have the highest appreciation of what Mr Meredith chooses to give them, as he can give it when he chooses; and who, while perfectly able to understand what he chooses to give them when he is in the other mood, are sincerely vexed to see an Englishman, with a faculty for letters not often excelled in our time, play tricks with his genius instead of putting it to the worthy work which it can do so well. If Mr Meredith really thinks that he cannot speak well, except when he makes 'surprise packets' of his speech, he is the most unfortunate, and the most signal, instance of misplaced modesty that we ever met, nay, that we ever heard of. We have known people who would persist in doing what they could not do, but it is very seldom that one finds a man who deliberately abstains from doing what he can do, or prefers to make a *chef d'œuvre inconnu* of it when he has done it.

95. Meredith as a story-teller

1893

This article appeared unsigned in *Temple Bar*, xcvii, April 1893, entitled 'George Meredith'.

To anyone concerned to trace the growth of an opinion, the general estimate of the novels of Mr George Meredith might be selected as a fruitful example. Some fifteen years ago Mr Meredith had already produced much of his finest work—although *The Egoist* and *Diana of the Crossways* had still to appear, the lovers of *Rhoda Fleming, Beauchamp's Career*, and *The Ordeal of Richard Feverel*, might perhaps be disposed to say his very finest—but his name, except to a small circle of admirers, was practically unknown. Since then he has come upon the public with all the prestige of a discovery. The appearance of a new work from his pen is hailed by every journal that occupies itself with literature as the great literary event of the day; his books pass into cheap editions that mark the growing demand for them; in America, where not a few English writers find a fuller and warmer appreciation than in their own country, he has an audience more ardent and more enthusiastic possibly than even among ourselves. Popular, in the sense in which Dickens and Walter Scott on the one hand were popular, or on the other in which Miss Braddon and Mr Rider Haggard are popular, he is not and never will be. For good, or for the reverse of good, he has not the vulgar ear. But it is impossible to imagine Mr Meredith ever bending for a moment to catch the vulgar ear. He sits among the gods, who sup off the nectar of high imaginations, the ambrosia of philosophic musings. In so far as he cares for applause at all, that which he receives and continues to receive in increasing measure, may probably be as much to his mind as any other kind that could be offered him.

It would be manifestly unfair not to attribute this growing popularity of Mr Meredith's work chiefly to an adequate appreciation of its great qualities. It has, in fact, qualities that ought to command the largest success. A splendid and restless imagination, a treatment of character at once profound and original, a magnificent glow of colour, a vision of life largely and purely human on one side, if on another too obviously and too obtrusively ironical—the praise of an author equipped with virtues such as these should need, one would think, no explanation beyond their mere enumeration. But we are perhaps doing human nature no injustice in assuming that a certain intellectual difficulty in reading Mr Meredith, a certain tortured obscurity of phraseology that occasionally makes a strong pull upon the intelligence and the patience of the reader, counts for not a little in the worship of the increasing band of disciples eager to hail him master. Something, not only of perseverance but of faith, is demanded on the part of the neophyte; to be rewarded presently by an enormous dose of self-complacency. Mr Meredith (to use a well-worn comparison) is like those various admirable things that begin by exciting a wry face perhaps, but that presently tickle the persevering consumer with the sense of a palate of superior discrimination to that of the rest of the world. To be examined by one of these thorough-going followers of Mr Meredith, on the subject of fiction, is calculated to make a nervous person shiver: Do we like this or that novelist? do we care for this or that story? And then with bated breath: Are we an admirer of Mr George Meredith's novels? All is well; we may pass; but the tension for the moment has been extreme. We feel that we have escaped with our life; that we were within an ace of being branded and flung with contumely among the vulgar herd.

For the rest, an excess of admiration is no bad thing in itself, and the only quarrel one ought to have with it is, that it is apt to provoke a reaction and array the world on the other side. Mr Meredith's place as a great novelist, however, is too assured, it rests upon foundations too solid to be affected by the follies of a *clique* or the airs of the initiated. And even they perhaps, in more sober moments, would admit that Mr Meredith's occasional obscurity is not absolutely his chief excellence; that it is rather through other and more admirable qualities (such as those at which we have hinted above) that he has gained a foremost place among the chief novelists of the day.

I

Perhaps the first, the predominant impression made by a study of Mr Meredith's work is that of an immense grasp. He may or may not rouse in us something of antagonism; we may, or we may not, dispute his accuracy of vision, his mode of thought, his method of representation, the atmosphere he creates for us; but he, at least, never swerves. He has his vision of things, and he never shrinks from developing it. One of the most sophisticated of writers, there is yet something primitive, something Titanic in the force with which he hurls aside the rocks of difficulty, disperses the mists, seizes and controls the whirlwinds he has raised. The reader may seem to himself to have lost his way in a somewhat bewildering confusion of digressions, philosophizings, unfamiliar phraseology; but he may have faith in his author. The unswerving grasp is always there; and he finds presently that the scene, the character, the incident to be conjured up, have shaped themselves out of chaos, and stand complete before him. If the power strikes one occasionally as a trifle perverse, it is always amazing.

This suggestion of something primitive and elemental at work recalls the name of another writer with whom, we venture to think, Mr Meredith has more than one point in common. It is a little in the fashion of the moment to endow every man of letters with a literary ancestry. 'Heredity', without which we seem unable to get on in these days, has its place here also; and not a French novelist of eminence, for example, but has his spiritual pedigree made out with the precision and detail of a genealogical tree. It is a custom that lies well within the particular genius of the nation; but in English literature, as in English art, there have always been a certain number of free lances; and in respect of a writer so individual, so personal to himself as Mr Meredith, we should feel disposed to limit both the number of his ancestors and the influence of any school whatsoever. If, in short, we assign him a literary parent at all, we should be inclined to date that parent some ninety years back, and name him Jean Paul Richter. We are mistaken, indeed, if at one period of his life Mr Meredith did not give a particular attention to Jean Paul's writings. His habit of philosophizing, a little in season and out of season, the splendour and poetic glow of his descriptions, his somewhat laboured and far-fetched metaphors, all seem to connect him not remotely—they may of course be mere coincidences—with the great German romancer. The influence may be less open than in the case of Carlyle; but it is, nevertheless, we believe, to be very distinctly traced through several of Mr Meredith's books. Two passages, among a hundred, may be quoted in illustration of the point:

In her half sleep that night, she heard the mighty thunder of the city, crashing tumults of disordered harmonies, and the splendour of the lamp-lighted city appeared to hang up under a dark-blue heaven, removed from earth, like a fresh planet to which she was being beckoned.

'Over claret,' was to have been the time for asking; and Algernon waited dinnerless until the healthy-going minutes distended and swelled monstrous and horrible as viper-bitten bodies, and the venerable Signior Time became of unhealthy hue.

For better or worse, these passages have in them much of the ring of Jean Paul's phraseology. Mr Meredith has not, perhaps, the vast and dominant imagination of his great predecessor; his humour is grimmer and less human; he has not, or only rarely, the intimate pathos that distinguishes the creator of Siebenkäs and Lenette; on the other hand, he has a wider outlook on life, he is less extravagant, he has none of the complicated machinery that Jean Paul borrowed from the romantic furniture of his time; with a finer analysis, he is more guarded, he is less simple in his relation of emotions and sentiment. He is an Englishman of today, in short, instead of a German of a century back.

The intention, however, is not to institute any detailed comparison between Mr Meredith's work and that of Jean Paul, a kind of comparison that is never very fruitful of results. Whatever tradition, moreover, may have helped at any time to influence Mr Meredith, tradition has very little to say to his writings; he is no one if not Mr Meredith. Nevertheless, to refer once more to Jean Paul, though our English author has no use for that romantic machinery that did some service to the German novelist, we are mistaken if a genuine love of romance is not common to both; there are times even when one may be tempted to believe that the earliest affections of the author of *The Egoist*—that extraordinary work of subtle analysis without an incident to speak of from beginning to end—were placed not on the novel of character and analysis, but on the novel of romantic incident and adventure. We are led to this supposition partly, no doubt, by the fact that one of the most charming of Mr Meredith's novels, the one written apparently with the greatest ease and directness, is a story of adventure, of adventure pure and simple, no less than of character; we allude, of course, to *The Adventures of Harry Richmond*. This book, which, to begin with, is a *tour de force* in its power of translating the reader into a child's strange, dim, dislocated yet acute vision of the life going on around it, leads us through a series of delightful incidents by land and by sea, worthy of Mr Louis Stevenson, to the fairyland atmosphere of a petty German court, and that most exquisite of small heroines, the little Princess Ottilie [sic]. The grown-up adventures of the hero who relates his own history from the age of four, if somewhat less engaging (Mr Meredith is never happier than when treating of the young life of boys), are hardly less thrilling; while the characters—his delineation of Harry Richmond's father strikes one as a triumph of portraiture—are marked throughout by much of that fine discrimination which may be held, perhaps, to constitute Mr Meredith's pre-eminent claim on the admiration of the world.

Harry Richmond is, in fact, almost the only novel of its kind that he has given us; and in seeking the reason that there has been no repetition of that happy venture, we can only suppose that the author has an intellectual impulse apart from that natural bent, and stronger; that the imagination of psychology is much more to him finally than the imagination of incident. The supposition is confirmed by the fact that a second (though earlier) story of adventure, in spite of some scenes and passages of great beauty, is, to our mind, the least readable of his novels. *Vittoria* is almost entirely a novel of incident, as the phrase goes; character, that is to say, is subordinate to a given series of events; but although the period to which those events refer, the North Italian insurrection of 1848, should be, one would suppose, of irresistible inspiration to an imagination on which it has taken hold at all, Mr Meredith makes much less of it than might have been expected. The plot is too loose, the interest of the story too scattered; the reader follows with a comparatively languid attention the intricate thread of the heroine's adventures—we have greatly loved her as Emilia in that novel of inequal merit of which *Vittoria* is the sequel—and with somewhat languid indifference assists at her final appearance on the scene. In these two novels, *Harry Richmond* and *Vittoria*, of which the first-named followed the other at an interval of four years, Mr Meredith seems to have exhausted his love of adventure pure and simple—unless that brilliant and entertaining *jeu d'esprit*, *The Shaving of Shagpat*, ought to be included in the category. We arrive, not indeed chronologically, but through similarity of method, at what, out of the dozen novels our author has given us, we venture to regard as his masterpieces: *The Ordeal of Richard Feverel*, *Beauchamp's Career*, *The Egoist*, and *Diana of the Crossways*.

II

In thus roughly dividing Mr Meredith's novels into those inspired by the romantic impulse, and those more directly due to the observation of life and character, it must be immediately added that the division is to a great extent arbitrary. It must be taken to indicate chiefly the disappearance of the element of romantic incident from his pages; the element of romance remains, an inalienable quality in the writer's work; he is not unfrequently content, that is to say, to let his imaginative vision of things take the place of the actuality of life. Nothing, indeed, can be more unlike the clear impartial daylight, which may be held to characterize the novel of observation and manners properly so called, and the atmosphere charged and permeated with personal colouring which Mr Meredith presents to us in certain of his books. There are moments when, in reading him, we feel that he has less in common with the modern novelist than with the Elizabethan dramatist; that his particular genius lies less in a general picture of life than in a passionate power, that burns and glows and quivers through his pages, of representing and embodying human passion and emotion.

Let us turn, for instance, to *Rhoda Fleming*, a novel that must always hold a foremost place with the lovers of Mr Meredith's work. That passionate power of which we speak pervades the book from end to end; in the betrayed girl, in the stern old father, in the strong and devoted sister, we seem to be gazing at human beings stripped of all conventions and disguises, left to the conflict of fierce and elemental flames of love and pride and consuming despair. But as we close the volume we feel less that we have been assisting at a tragedy of actual life, than that we have been watching a drama of absorbing interest, in which the veracious and masterly presentation by two or three great actors of the shock of passions has made us indifferent to the want of reality in their surroundings. There is, in fact, something extremely notable in the contrasts that meet us now and again throughout Mr Meredith's work. On one page we may have the most moving, the most pathetic picture given with profound insight, with absolute veracity; on the next, perhaps, we find ourselves contemplating a scene in which we feel as though every outline had been slightly distorted and discoloured by some perverse trick of the medium through which we gaze. It reminds one of those ingeniously-contrived rooms in which at one moment we look through clear glass at a landscape glowing in natural colours, and the next see it suffused with strange and alien tints through some green or crimson pane. Mr Meredith, who can give us glass of crystal clearness when he wills it, chooses, we would submit, to interpose the coloured pane too often.

The matter, we readily admit, is, in part, one of personal predilection.

There are many of Mr Meredith's admirers to whom his unevenness of surface, if we may so term it, gives his books their greatest charm; who find in his personal expression the most valuable quality of his work. To value individuality rather than impersonality in an artist is, of course, in one sense, a perfectly legitimate point of view, especially when the individuality is so commanding and so original as that of Mr Meredith; but it may, on the other hand, be permitted every one to prefer those moments in which the individuality—or rather the voluntary expression of it, since the most impersonal writer must still remain individual—falls into the background, leaving us free to contemplate the play of emotions and character, undisturbed by comment spoken or implied. It may be permitted the more readily, that Mr Meredith, whose outlook on life is of the widest, shows himself, at his best, singularly disinterested; his range of observation and selection giving him an air of large impartiality that sets his puppets extremely free, and obliterates every trace of the showman and the wire. We venture to say at his best; for altogether apart from that question of personal colouring and atmosphere we spoke of above, there are times when we feel that the showman comes very much to the front. That this is constantly done with intention, no student of Mr Meredith's books can doubt; the opening chapter of *The Egoist*, with its appeal to the Comic Muse as the fittest interpreter of life, may be held to illustrate his attitude in general with some completeness. On the other hand, the fact seems to be so intimately connected with another side of his theory of work, with that well-known and characteristic eccentricity of phraseology even, now brilliant and now obscure, to which we have more than once referred, that it may be worth while to pause for a moment and consider the matter.

Every writer attentive to style in the present day must be alive to the inconvenience (to say the least of it) lamented over by more than one contemporary French man of letters, of coming so late in the day, of arriving at a date when the resources of the language have been used and re-used, till phrases, originally expressive and pregnant, have become nearly effaced, as it were, through much handling, and convey no more salient meaning than the effigy on a worn-out coin. They have a certain value, as stating a definite fact; but their particular beauty and suggestiveness are gone. More than one method is adopted by the modern writer anxious to clothe thought with some distinction of words; one, perhaps, sets his faith on a studied simplicity; another searches the best periods of English prose for words somewhat fallen into disuse, but still capable of happy service in giving freshness of colouring to familiar thought; a third may find his account in epigrams and the particular construction of sentences and paragraphs. Mr Meredith seeks salvation in that strangeness of style, that rather far-fetched phraseology that seems, as we have hinted, to have been not unsuggested by an early study of Jean Paul, but which he has ended by making completely his own. It is a style which, however inspiring to the disciple, has presented so many stumbling-blocks to the uninitiated reader, that it is impossible (speaking as such) not to feel some concern that Mr Meredith should have adopted it, and lost the opportunity of edifying and instructing the public in that art of novel-writing of which he is so great a master. The applause of the general reader may not, indeed, be of such value as to demand any sacrifice of principle; nevertheless, the first aim of a story-teller being, it may be plausibly maintained, to tell stories to an audience, that aim becomes a little obscured when the stories are told in a language difficult of interpretation by the greater part of the audience to whom they are addressed.

We suspect Mr Meredith himself, however, of being tolerably indifferent in the matter; and should he reply that it is his business to tell stories in the best way he can, leaving his audience to apply their own intelligence to his interpretation, it would be impossible to dispute the matter with him seriously. An artist is no doubt bound to work according to his own ideas of the best method of producing his work; and Mr Meredith has certainly succeeded in what we presume to be, at least in part, his aim, that of arresting attention upon his phrases; they have little hooks to them, as it were, that catch the mind and oblige it to pause, instead of slipping over them with easy indifference. We are compelled, notwithstanding, to think that Mr Meredith somewhat exaggerates this horror of the simple and the commonplace, since we discover it, to return to the point from which we originally started, not only in his style but in certain of his characters, to the injury, one cannot help thinking, of his work as an artistic whole. We are the more disposed to think so, that nothing can be broader, more admirable, more simply human than his treatment of some of his principal characters—of Richard Feverel, of Nevil Beauchamp, or Vernon Whitford, of Lucy Desborough and Clara Wentworth. It is when we come to the minor personages that the strain begins; that the showman, as we have hinted, peeps out, and invention seems to take the place of imaginative observation and insight. It is as though Mr Meredith had said: A thousand novels have been written, crowded with the insignificant and the commonplace; in my novels the commonplace shall not only become significant [the most legitimate of aims], it shall become salient through an eccentricity that nature has denied it, but which it shall receive from me. Hence that singular ticketing, that obtrusive nomenclature—the Wise Youths, the Lady Blandishes, the Dr Shrapnels, the Pilgrim's Scrips, the Fine Shades—that curious air of reducing life to an allegory, that, to our mind, disfigures rather than adorns some of Mr Meredith's finest efforts. He cannot consent to be simple when he thinks there is a danger that simplicity may be confounded with the ordinary. His stories occasionally excite in one the sensation that might be afforded by a picture of which the principal figures should be painted in the finest style of the Italian Renaissance and the attendant crowds as mediæval grotesques. The grotesque has its place in life, but a crowd of masks simply confuses our sense of the proportion of things, and finally defeats its own ends. It leaves us, not discriminating, but confounding the individuals of whom the crowd is composed in one common glare of unreality. More than this, it even gives at times a sense of thinness; a strange defect, indeed, to discover in a writer of Mr Meredith's profound insight. But it is the inevitable penalty paid for removing a personage in any measure from the immediate contact of humanity; the slight touch of caricature gives an impression of surface only; the character at once rings, not human, but hard and metallic.

We need, as has been said, have no serious quarrel with Mr Meredith on this account. We should be too grateful for the splendid work he has produced; and if on one page the Pilgrim's Scrip and the incredible Mrs Caroline Grandison, for example, tend to rouse in us something of irritation, we have only to turn the leaf to find ourselves on the Enchanted Island in that famous scene where Richard Feverel and Lucy Desborough meet to fall in love—a scene one might feel disposed to designate the most exquisite in English fiction, but for that other, no less famous and no less exquisite, in the same romance, where the two sit by the border of the lake and listen to love's piping and the cry of the night-jar. By no one indeed has love been depicted with at once a profounder passion, a more absolute purity of touch than by our author. Mr Meredith has the gift of the poets; he can contemplate, he can present love with a total blindness to its base, its trivial, its commonplace side. There is more than one novelist of eminence who stiffens, as it were, into self-consciousness at the mere approach of love-making. He has the sense of intrusion, perhaps, the sense of absurdity; or in the effort to overcome his shyness, he strains his effects and touches a false note. This self-consciousness, either of diffidence or audacity, is apt to communicate itself to the reader. He feels intrusive in his turn; he finds an indiscretion in assisting at a scene where he is made to feel himself an unwelcome third. Hence, the novels in which the love-scenes, when they are given, can be read with pleasure, might almost be counted on the fingers of one hand. But Mr Meredith has the higher gift. His vision of the moment is too sure for self-consciousness, his conception of it too pure and exquisite, too removed from common things to raise any emotion in the reader commoner than itself. He no more feels intrusive than he would feel it intrusive to walk in a garden among flowers glowing at each other in the evening light. Familiar though it may be, let us listen again for one moment to this duet between Richard and Lucy.

[Quotes xix, from 'For this is the home' to 'from her you may hear it'.]

To turn from a scene like this, to the chapter in *Rhoda Fleming*, where the stubborn old farmer insists that his ruined and heart-broken daughter shall rejoin her supposed husband, is to measure Mr Meredith's range upon the scale of passion. Sublime too, in point of description, is the thunderstorm in the forest, when Richard wanders for a night through the Rhineland and a tempest of remorse, to be reconciled with himself in the breaking dawn.

[Quotes xlii, from 'An oppressive slumber' to 'All at once the thunder spoke'.]

The whole passage, which is too long to quote in its entirety, might be recommended to anyone careful to study Mr Meredith's fashion of dealing with what are called natural effects. In descriptions such as these he is unsurpassed, it might almost be said, unapproached. The word, the sentiment, the intimate feeling never fail him; he has the gift of inform-ing the elements with vitality, with the very essence of nature and of the humanity that looks on nature. The fact may be dwelt on with the more enthusiasm, that he is too good an artist (it need not be said) ever to introduce descriptions for the mere sake of description. Whatever their intrinsic beauty, they never stand alone; they are invariably interwoven with, they are there to illustrate that movement of passion, that subtle and admirable psychology that constitute finally, as we have said, the author's foremost claim on our admiration.

377

III

There are many things in Mr Meredith's novels, but one thing there is not, or in scant measure only; there is very little 'modernity', to use a term that has nothing but its convenience to recommend it. By this we do not mean to imply that he is not of his day, or that he could have written just as he does at any other epoch than the present. He is, on the contrary, extremely modern; he illustrates his generation in a hundred ways; and in no way more forcibly perhaps than by an occasional grimly humorous pessimism, almost Nihilism, a capacity for turning the world inside out, and exhibiting it as an old and empty sack, woefully in want of repair. It is a feat to which one may be permitted to attach more or less value; but such as it is, Mr Meredith knows how to perform it with a great completeness and sense of humour. But however it may represent a prevailing mood of the time, the feat, it need hardly be said, is less characteristic of the present age, than of a temper common to all ages since the world was young; and in naming 'modernity', we intend rather that exhibition of the newest theories, the newest crotchets, the newest manners, fashions, modes of thought, mingled with a somewhat indescribable quality, an implied sense that the newness of these things means not youth, but age, not hopefulness, but decay, which gives its distinctive note to so much of the literature of the day. From all these matters Mr Meredith stands a little aloof, or introduces them as side-lights only. We may turn page after page of his novels and find hardly a trace of heredity or neurosity or indifferentism or half a dozen other burning subjects that so incessantly preoccupy some of our French contemporaries. His characters, to put it briefly, have less the value of special 'documents', than that of the perennial quality of humanity.

This is nowhere more apparent than in the author's treatment of his heroines. Their value to the reader, like that of Shakespeare's women (with which they are very commonly compared), lies in their constant womanhood, and not in any passing mood borrowed from the fashion of the hour; in the essential qualities which, under one or another influence, bloom from century to century into one and another transient form, and not in the transient form itself. It is quite possible to unite the two, to give the permanent root and the flower of the moment; but with such ephemeral blossom our author concerns himself but little. A good deal has been written about Mr Meredith's women, and there is undoubtedly much that may be said. No writer, perhaps, not of their own sex, has treated them with a comprehension so sensitive to the complex mingling of their better and their weaker impulses; and this combined with what may be termed the outside view, the man's particular appreciation of the feminine charm, a point of view that no woman-writer can absolutely adopt—she is apt to fall into terrible blunders when she attempts it—gives Mr Meredith's delineation of women an extreme fascination. It is true that he has a theory concerning them that he propounds from time to time, and which is the only approximation to a purpose, as distinct from a philosophy, that appears throughout his work. The theory, crudely and briefly stated, is, that men require too much of women; that so long as their own lives are not irreproachable, they have no right to demand a flawless perfection in their fellow-creatures of the opposite sex. This is the theory put nudely; but it is naturally capable of much amplification, and more broadly it may be said that it is a protest against the sentimental conception of woman as an ethereal and bloodless being, with only just so much flesh as will suffice to make a decent garment for her soul. Nothing, Mr Meredith's readers do not need to be told, can be further removed from his conception of the ideal woman than such a woman as this; we have only to glance at the contrast between Diana and her rival, in *Diana of the Crossways*, to see how far removed. To quote from an ingenious and enthusiastic 'Appreciation' lately published under the title of *George Meredith—Some Characteristics*: 'If asked what is the quality that especially distinguishes Mr Meredith's women, it would be no bad answer to say that they eat well and are not ashamed'.[1] The formula is a trifle meagre, but it expresses not amiss that glow of youth and vitality and rounded symmetry that characterize our author's most attractive heroines. It must be immediately added that he makes no effort to press home the theory hinted at above, or to set it in motion in the person of those heroines. There is never a trace of coarseness in the admirable young creatures whom he sets before us with their glance half divine and wholly feminine. In honour, purity, sweetness and tenderness, Lucy Desborough, Cecilia Halkett, Princess Ottilie [*sic*], and the exquisite Clara Wentworth [*sic*], again belong to the category of Shakespeare's women. Even Diana of the Crossways, one of the most fascinating, but also one of the most imperfect of Mr Meredith's creations, is guilty of nothing worse than an excess of imprudence—for we refuse to believe that Diana, being what she was, would ever have sold her lover's secret for a sum of money.

[1] By Richard Le Gallienne (1890).

In considering Mr Meredith's heroines, then, it is unnecessary to lay much stress on a theory that he himself is content to leave very much in the background. It is more profitable to dwell on the extreme insight and sympathy with which he knows how to depict the young girls and women who sway the fortunes of his heroes, the particular grace of feminine impulse and charm with which he endows them. Mr Meredith has also that conception of simple goodness in good women, the goodness without guile, to which Balzac, for example, hardly ever attained, and the want or neglect of which led him now and again to present such singular monstrosities. Mr Meredith's appreciation of this quality is at once artistic and sympathetic. He leaves it in its right place; he allows it to be duly modified by caprice, by passion, by gaiety, by wilfulness or ignorance; it is never obtrusive and never mawkish; but in his best characters it is always there, an indestructible core of crystal, the inalienable quality that in its turn modified every other; the result is seen in the heroine he presents to our admiration.

In his presentation of older women (and occasionally of older men) Mr Meredith strikes us as less constantly happy. His sympathies, we feel, are largely with youth, its rashness, its inconsequence, its fine flow of animal spirits. He may be congratulated, indeed, on having vanquished a difficulty over which Thackeray, and Scott, and Dickens, and another novelists of greater or less note have stumbled and fallen; he has succeeded in making his young heroes interesting. His treatment of boys is invariably fresh and delightful; their ingenuousness, their deceptions, their enthusiasms, their indifference, are presented with a genial and humorous observation attempted by no other master of fiction but Mr Louis Stevenson; and no other that we can remember has so concerned himself with the awakening of youthful and crude emotions. *The Ordeal of Richard Feverel* is, in fact, as all Mr Meredith's readers know, the history of an education. Sir Austin Feverel, having an only and infant son left on his hands by a wife who basely deserts him, determines to bring him up on a System. The System, as might be expected, breaks down in much grief and anguish to the hero, though Sir Austin is represented as convinced to the end of its particular merits. The moral each reader may infer for himself; the interest of the book indeed lies, apart from any moral, in the novel skill with which the boy's character is unfolded and developed from youth to manhood. The same may be said of *Beauchamp's Career*, which in some respects we should feel disposed to rank even higher than *Richard Feverel*. It contains, indeed, no single passages of such consummate beauty, no such sweep of

passion and pathos as we find in the incomparable scenes that close the
earlier romance; but there is on the whole less of that fantastic nomenclature, that touch of caricature that seem to us to mar some of Mr
Meredith's finest work; the range of life and scene is wider; we feel
more distant horizons and larger issues. Mr Meredith, moreover, has
no happier creation than Rosamund Culling, in all her delicate and
difficult relations with the stormy old Lord Romney [sic], and with the
enthusiastic and impracticable young hero of the story; no more gallant
and charming portrait of a young English girl than Cecilia Halkett,
whom we seem to see always bounding over the waves with the white
wings of her yacht outspread, or flying on horseback across the Sussex
downs. We find it hard to forgive the hero his neglect of this enchanting
creature, full of the purest health and life and gaiety, for the somewhat
bloodless and unsympathetic Jenny Denham. His marriage with this
latter is the one thing that reconciles us to that tragic ending which
makes so magnificent a close to the novel, but leaves the reader
penetrated with sadness.

It will be perceived that we have treated Mr Meredith almost entirely
in his primary character of a story-teller. There is, of course, another
aspect under which he may be regarded, that of a philosopher; and we
believe that it is in that light that many of his admirers prefer to
contemplate him. It is only the accident, they would have us believe, of
his having been born in a century of novel-writing, that has made him
a novelist; it is as a great philosophy of life that they choose to regard
his tales; and in fact a complete system of many things might be
deduced from a careful and comparative study of the witty, or humorous, or brilliant aphorisms that enrich, or as we may think, occasionally
retard the action of his story. No other novelist offers so wide a field for
research and comment; no other perhaps, in equal degree, gives us at
times the sense of being set at the root of things and presented with an
ironical, a satirical, or a purely human view of life. Nevertheless, not
only do we differ from the above theory in believing Mr Meredith to
be a born romancer; but holding that the chief glory of a novelist is to
tell a story well, we prefer still to consider him, as before and above all,
a story-teller. A profound moral (and the opening chapter might seem
to justify the hypothesis), a profound philosophy may be the groundwork and crown of that singularly powerful piece of workmanship,
The Egoist; but it is in the admirable conduct of the story, the development of the characters, the gradual ensnaring of the Egoist in his own
conceits, until he is left stripped at last of all pretensions, shivering under

his abandonment by the woman whom he has courted, his rejection by the other women whom he has neglected, that the capital merit of that masterpiece of psychology lies.

Even from this point of view, however, there is a legitimate mode of regarding Mr Meredith as a philosopher—and one, we may imagine, that a great novelist enamoured of his art would most willingly accept —the illustration by his characters, that is, of the wisdom gained through a large and penetrating observation of humanity. Much more; impatient, too impatient, perhaps, of the simpler texture of life, he has a power, unequalled by any other writer of the day, of conveying a magnificent movement of passion, a certain illusion of splendour, an abounding, an overflowing life and warmth and vigour to the action and personages of his dramas. As we began, so we leave him, with the sense that he has an immense grasp.

LORD ORMONT AND HIS AMINTA

1894

---

96. Unsigned review, *Saturday Review*

lxxviii, 7 July 1894

The taste for Mr George Meredith's later novels is a sentiment personal, freakish, tiptoeing an impertinent superiority of glance. From a pinnacle of the supercilious it twinkles a cavalier stare:—below, the swinish; above—the stars. *Georgium sidus*!

You see the trick on't, and could scrawl yourself if bitten by the asp of metaphor, loving the wrong word in the improper place, a wide critique as difficult to read as any novel in this manner done.

To return to the English language; Mr Meredith occupies in fiction a place very like that which Mr Browning held in prose. It is a high place, and was won long ago by dint of romance much more to our private taste than *Lord Ormont and His Aminta*. But Mr Meredith, like Mr Browning, is master of a *ducdame*—a spell to lead persons of no conspicuous taste or sense into a circle. The faults of both authors, the tormented style, the volunteered obscurities, have become an attraction to many students ambitious of posing as *raffinés*. Yet the faults are so conspicuous, and, to the lovers of the English language and of lucidity, so vexatious, that unambitious readers are compelled to be protesting when they would far liefer be admiring.

What does mankind want from a novel? It wants a plain and an alluring tale; characters vivid, well discriminated, and easily to be remembered; Claverhouse or Captain Costigan, Beatrix Esmond or Diana Vernon. A varied discourse, expressive of themselves, ought to be in the mouths of these personages. Now, we cannot honestly call Mr Meredith's new tale interesting, nor his characters sympathetic as people, nor so drawn and posed as to persuade us of their reality. This lack of reality, again, seems partly to come from the uniform Mere-dithian manner of their conversation. Thackeray had a very marked style of his own, but Mr Harry Foker does not discourse in it; nor does Captain Dobbin, nor does Captain Costigan, or Harry Warrington. Thackeray's characters all talk each in his or her own voices. In this novel almost all of Mr Meredith's people talk in Mr Meredith's voice. There is hardly more difference of accent among them than we listen to from the mouths of the *dramatis personæ* in the tragedy of *Punch and Judy*. The one voice, here, is high pitched and not in the natural manner of life. Mr Meredith himself, as Chorus, talks a great deal, and his voice is also the voice of his personages. We cannot sincerely affirm that the result is, to our taste, dramatic, or even entertaining. The constant chase of metaphors prompts the reader to skip. Man cannot live on squibs and catherine-wheels alone, and he turns for relief to the plain and varied prose, to the life and colour and vicissitude and friendly charm of Mr Du Maurier's *Trilby*. We are urged by Nature herself to skip. Yet skip we may not, for fear of losing the word of the enigma. 'Wherefore do they so'? Why do Mr Meredith's people behave as they do behave? Mystery! but we must labour to elucidate.

Lord Ormont was a distinguished cavalry officer, much admired as a hero by the boys at Mr Cruder's [*sic*] private academy. One of these boys, the chief of them, Weyburn, also admired a Miss Aminta, a dark young lady, whom he met on his Sunday walks, she, too, marching with the girls of a female seminary. They corresponded, we fear not by the time-honoured method of notes inserted in triangular jam puffs. Lord Ormont got into trouble for some salutary high-handed act in India; he conceived rancour against an ungrateful country. 'This, all this, was in the olden time long ago', before duelling went out, and railways came in. Now, Lord Ormont was one of those candles at which the feminine moth scorches her wings. He, sulking in his tent, was attended by a Briseis, a beautiful dark lady, whom some persons called 'Lady Ormont', while others doubted of her status. Why Lord Ormont left his wife (if she was his wife, as we make little or no doubt) in this penumbra, and in society something shady, is just the problem; but, to be sure, the story could not get on without this behaviour. With sub-mission we take it that the peer's conduct was part of his general sulkiness; and, again, part of his elderly dislike to being actually married and done for. At all events, Aminta (for she, as the acute reader will have divined, was Lady Ormont) became very dissatisfied and gunpowdery. A wicked Mr Morsfield wrote love letters to her, which she kept in her jewel-box. He was aided by her idiotic aunt. However, Aminta did not encourage Mr Morsfield, nor did she complain to Lord Ormont, as not desiring a duel. To them enter Weyburn, the schoolboy lover, now, of all things in the world, a youth who wants to found a kind of international school for boys in Switzerland. He becomes Lord Ormont's secretary; and, when we have added a free-spoken, fierce sister of Lord Ormont—a Lady Charlotte— we have the elements of the romance. It were unfair to go more deeply into the fable, including the duel with foils of which the duellists knocked off the steel buttons. This is a feat so hopeless to perform that it exists only in novels, though it is said to be forbidden in the French army. We leave Aminta and Weyburn apparently keeping the international school together; whereto Lord Ormont sends his grand-nephew, as thinking the school a good school.

This, of course, is the merest skeleton of a plot. The reader must make up his own mind as to whether he likes the company of the courageous and beautiful Aminta, of the earnest Weyburn, of the patriotic but sulky Lord Ormont, of the infatuated Morsfield, and of the rest, or not. It has not been given to us to interest ourselves greatly in their fortunes. Weyburn is like one of Scott's young men—brave, honest, muscular, not too clever, except in discourse. But Henry Morton would never have run away with a married Aminta. As to the style—wherein we read of 'pinaforing a jigging eagerness', and so forth—it often leaves us uninstructed; but that may well be the result of mere stupidity on our side. In vol. i., p. 205 the mystery in the first sentence of the second paragraph is probably caused by a slip of the pen, 'Lady Ormont' being written for 'Lord Ormont'. 'She flushed her dark, brown-red late-sunset'. This is a hard saying, and there are many like it. Mrs Lawrence says, 'Matthew Weyburn! We both like the name. I've seen it on certain evenings—crimson over an olive sky'. Perhaps people talk like this; but one is unconvinced. 'The tip-toe sparkle of a happy mind did not leap from her at wayside scenes'. 'Tip-toe sparkle'—is it a good phrase, a desirable conceit, or is it not? As for the moral problem, the unacknowledged, or half-acknowledged, wife running away with the schoolmaster, the schoolmaster himself thinks that he offends 'good citizenship', but not that he offends 'Divine law'. 'Advantage seldom comes of it', says the poet, sardonically, and it is certainly a drawback in the profession of education. As a mere matter of creeping fact, we conceive that the boys would have been taken away from the international academy. However, some persons may steal a horse, while others may not look over a hedge, and in this instance the hero and heroine were of the privileged class. On the whole, we agree with Lord Ormont, 'if a story had to be told he liked it plain, without jerks and evolutions'. From evolution we can in no wise escape, but it is possible to dispense with jerks. 'The ball *must* be bowled, not thrown or jerked', says the law. Mr Meredith jerks it, and many persons revel in results which, we are certain, will gratify them, as ensuing from *Lord Ormont and His Aminta*. 'And the rest they must live and learn'.

Among these still uninitiated readers, not yet confirmed devotees, the verdict on Mr Meredith's novel will probably be that he has imagined a good and puzzling moral situation. The early lovers meet and renew their affection, when the woman can hardly be called the wife of another man, so vague is her legal position. Of course, if ever our sympathies are to be with Tristram and Iseult, if ever we are to excuse their troth-plight (renewed as they swim together), it is in such a very unusual situation as theirs. Here, then, is the 'problem' so dear to all who have given up the notion that the game of life must be played according to the laws of the game, whether we call them human laws or divine. But, granting the situation, the characters are not winning. The young dominie is out of place in such a galley as this. And as to the style, we have said enough, or too much, yet the style is the novel.

97. Lionel Johnson, in *Academy*

xlv, 7 July 1894

The story which bears this fascinating title, so suggestive of a certain gallantry and romance, is Mr Meredith's twelfth novel—exclusive, that is, of *Shagpat* and *Farina*. It will not rank with *The Egoist* and *Richard Feverel* and *Rhoda Fleming*. It has not their airs of greatness, their splendour and enchantment, their prodigality of power. It gives us no character of supreme charm. Aminta herself is not upon the level of her elder sister, Nesta, the last of Mr Meredith's heroines. Beside

Aminta, there are three chief characters: Lord Ormont, Lady Charlotte, Matthew Weyburn. Contrary to the writer's common habit, there is no crowd of minor characters surrounding the great actors: no professed wits, or butts, or comedians of any kind, to carry off their creator's sometimes superfluous flow of the comic spirit. The very style is less characteristic than usual. The places where the reader is blinded with a 'coruscation', to use Johnson's word, or breathless from the speed of his author's imagination, are in this book but few. There is no one magnificent chapter, for ever memorable: one scene or incident wrought out in words that burn with beauty. Not one of Mr Meredith's books is more characteristic in tone, intention, spirit, theme: none less so in the execution. For strength of thought, for imaginative vision, for intensity of purpose and appeal, it has all the writer's most distinctive excellences; but there is a reticence or restraint of manner which will make the story a favourite with some readers, something of a surprise and disappointment to others. The story would be spoiled past recognition by any summary; let the following passage tell in part the conclusion of the whole matter. 'Matey' Weyburn speaks to Aminta, when she is resolved no longer to endure and do the wrong of her loveless marriage with Lord Ormont: when the lovers, hitherto honourably separate, conclude that they can come together for life with no sacrifice of honour.

[Quotes xxviii, from 'I shall not consider' to 'on the stream of the blood'.]

It is possible and, for certain readers, necessary to refuse assent to this answer of a great question; but what honesty and wisdom, fruits of rational humour, are plain here to see, contrasting with the shriek of the precipitate reformer! Marriage, sex, love; these are terrible words in modern novels. Mr Meredith has always treated them with a world of genius and of sanity.

> Quanti dolci pensier, quanto disio
> Menò costoro al[1]

we will not say 'doloroso passo' must be left untold, so elaborate are the subtilties of the story. It is a story of conflicting hero-worships. Lord Ormont, England's greatest soldier, a modern paladin, her saviour in the East, a man of active chivalry and infelicitous speech, the

[1] Dante, *Inferno*, v, 113: 'How many sweet thoughts and how much delight led them to the . . .'.

scorn of able journalists, the delight of patriotic enthusiasts, was
cashiered and ignored by his country. To 'Matey' and 'Browny',
otherwise Matthew and Araminta, boy and girl lovers at neighbouring
schools, he was a kind of English archangel in arms, radiant and
irresistible, the natural prey of pursy citizens, the true embodiment of
national glory. Stung and stabbed by English ingratitude, he came
home to proud and resolute retirement. Wandering the world, he met
Aminta, she adoring the hero, he finding solace in her devotion. He
married her, but still kept to his determined obscurity. Brought back
to England by her desire, he maintained there the same attitude, to such
a degree that the 'world' of his family and his equals, knowing him
to have many resemblances to Caesar, and resenting the notion of his
marriage with a girl of unequal station, refused to believe in the
marriage; so adding to his own instinct of seclusion the further bar
of deliberate exclusion from society, for the wounding of Aminta's
pride. Matthew Weyburn enters the scene again as Lord Ormont's
secretary: she finds him, with certain pangs of disappointment and
disillusion, fallen, as she thinks, from the heights upon which the early
prophecies of her heart had set him. He is to be no soldier: young,
brilliant, something of a paragon, his ideal is to promote the comity
of nations by an international school, where the various virtues of blood
and brain are to blend, in one new common spirit, the youth of many
races. Lady Charlotte, the Earl's sister and his feminine counterpart,
lady of strength and insight, leads the protesting disbelievers in his
marriage, despite the advocacy of her protégé, young Weyburn.
Aminta's aunt, a person of delicious vulgarity, with social theories
about the better pronunciation of her name, lives in Lord Ormont's
household, a thorn in the flesh. Without are a few friends and acquaintance, some with no character and some with no reputation, whom
Aminta or her aunt have made, Lord Ormont being half indifferent
and half pleased. And in due time the leading performers discover
their respective mistakes: Aminta, that she married her hero without
loving him, in a mixture of sympathetic worship and ambition; Lord
Ormont, that his personal pride had made him unjust to the rights and
claims of his wife. Matthew, with no reproach, found himself possessed
again of Aminta's heart; she recognizes in him one not only to reverence
but to love. And when Aminta, fully awakened, through a series of
experiences, to the impossibility of her life with her husband, has left
him, he discovers too late the strength and meaning of his love for her;
and yet not too late, for with a foregoing of pride, very much at variance

with the world's common code, he believes in the truth and justice of
Aminta and of Matthew in their action. Lady Charlotte also, after long
fighting against her brother, nobly comes to his side in his sorrow with
a generous inconsistency. He entrusts to Matthew and Aminta, in their
school, his own grand-nephew. In brief, after a prolonged conflict of
pride, endurance, and misconception on all sides, we are left with a
sense that the currents of these lives are following their true courses.
There is infinite comedy in all this, lamentable as is the confusion of the
actors, their falsity of position for so long and perplexed a time. And
false as even the disentanglement may seem to some, it is at least
courageous: the note of exhilarating faith is sounded.

A great charm in this book is its soldierly spirit: as in *One of Our
Conquerors*, national patriotism prompts many a wise saying and strong
warning. It is the spirit of Mr Meredith's poems, 'Aneurin's Harp', 'To
Colonel Charles', 'England before the Storm'. There is a satisfactory
laughter in the sentence: 'They passed an English defensive fort, and
spared its walls in obedience to Matthew Shale's good counsel that
they should forbear from sneezing'. There is a deal of sword-play and
of bugle-call flashing and pealing in the talk of Lord Ormont, Matthew,
Lady Charlotte, Aminta also. And Matthew's realized dream, the
international school, is a heartening conception, full of valiant energy
and goodwill. The hatred of lazy folly is a staunch sentiment in all the
writings of Mr Meredith. A decorous illiberality is also the target of
his arrows. Says Lady Charlotte:

[Quotes xvii, from ' "I've met men in high places" ' to ' "Now explain
it, if you can" '.]

And Weyburn does explain it: he has studied the matter among 'the
people we call common, men and women, old wayside men especially'.
He found them 'at the bottom of wisdom, for they had in their heads
the delicate sense of justice, upon which wisdom is founded'. Whereas
(and the phrase 'flashed a light' into Lady Charlotte) 'the men called
great, who have risen to distinction, are not men of brains, but the men
of aptitudes'. Weyburn, as the young Englishman of an healthy brain
and wits well at command, if a little too admirable, even in his self-
restraint, is a very bright and blithe example of a Young England
pioneer, his face set straight to the light: as Lady Charlotte, whilst
essentially 'of her own order', is an excellent aristocrat with a working
mind. Lord Ormont is perhaps less persuasive a character: for the
reticent man of deeds, whose writing is a model of indiscretion and

impatience, he talks too well and too much. Yet the great soldier, the fighter of England's battles, self-sentenced to a struggle with woman-kind and their obstinacies, has no slight attractiveness and strength.

The book abounds in beauty, in those brilliant simplicities of happy phrase, which are more delightful than the best of epigrams. In certain qualities of narrative, Mr Meredith stands alone, or with Charlotte Brontë for sole English companion. He excels in the description of movement: there are two perfect passages, one a country journey, the other a swim in the sea, which have much of his richest art. His style in such places has the brilliance of rippling and sparkling waves, laughing and dancing shoreward, with a kind of delighted waywardness, a grace upon their strength. It is joyous writing, cordial and entrancing; it clears the air to an exulting serenity. There is much of this brave humour in these pages, winning their reader to an admiration and an enjoy-ment, in which he cannot but feel it an ingratitude, or a misappre-hension, to question the spiritual and rational truth of certain issues of the story. After all, these difficult matters of conduct must be decided right, straight reason, ὡς ἂν ὁ φρόνιμος ὁρίσειεν.[1] The decision is always difficult also, but Mr Meredith is eminent among οἱ φρόνιμοι. Mr Mere-dith, who in this book once again fascinates us, from his opening pages, devoted to the humours of the English schoolboy, to the concluding letter from that mistress of admirable speech, Lady Charlotte Eglett.

98. J. Stuart, in *Athenaeum*

No. 3481, 14 July 1894

James Stuart (1843–1913) was a regular contributor to the *Athenaeum* and other journals. He edited the *Courier* and the *Star* (1892–7) and published a volume of *Reviews and Essays* (1884).

The desire to criticize Mr Meredith is not the one that takes possession of the reader after a first perusal of one of his novels, and a disposition

[1] 'As the reasonable man would judge it.'

for acquiescence, be it vague or be it intelligent, is even further away. After one has been stung with a whip, or battered on the brain with a quarterstaff, it is not the pretty wrist-play nor the artful bludgeoning that gets the praise; before praise is mentioned there is something to say of the smarting wales, of the aching bumps on the skull. Mr Meredith provokes a thousand issues whose relation to the story is not easy of detection; his arguments clamour for debate or answer; the search light is turned upon the principles that have worked upon his characters, and less upon their actions than upon the motive which he saw in their actions. He has been compared to Zeus—a rather flippant Zeus, hurling thunderbolts with his right hand and letting off squibs with the left.[1] It is not flowers and not *confetti* that he hurls the while his car rolls on majestically; fireworks suit his purpose better. At the end of it one seems to have lived and tried to think in a whirling atmosphere of catherine-wheels and Chinese crackers, not walking 'with the tender and growing night', but beneath a heaven of shooting stars. It is for this reason that there is something to be said for the method of serial publication Mr Meredith so often adopts. He is not difficult of piecemeal digestion, but he makes you difficult mouthfuls to gulp whole. Let the minor arguments be settled every four weeks; let his phrasing and his imagery be a matter of monthly reflection, and the ground is thus cleared of its tanglewood and undergrowth, the mind can turn to a whole and steady vision of the novel. The only other possible means of appreciation (which is more than comprehension) is in repeated reading, whereby new beauties are seen and still increasing light. But our preference inclines to the more gradual method of assimilation.

Having assimilated, one is entitled to ask if the novel be a good novel, and if it be a novel good enough for Mr Meredith to have signed. After *The Tragic Comedians* we should never say that Mr Meredith cannot write a bad novel; but nowadays he is more likely to fail, if he is to fail, as he failed in *One of our Conquerors*. That is, a quaint, perverse vocabulary may unite with a cryptic system of metaphor to produce confusion where the intellect should be illuminated. Stimulants (and Mr Meredith is a perpetual stimulant) are well enough when they clarify the brain, but they fail of their end by too much potency. In *Lord Ormont and His Aminta* Mr Meredith is less of a puzzle than his last novel made us fear that he might be. Certain chapters of *The Egoist* —notably the discussion of 'a great and an ancient wine' and the storm scene—show a more concise significance of language, but the remainder

[1] That is, by Henley; see above, No. 57.

of *The Egoist* and all that Mr Meredith has since written are mere fogginess beside *Lord Ormont*, a fact which goes to show that increasing years and frequent service have not dulled the edge of the weapon he has fashioned for himself. You may see an ungraceful stroke frequently, and a clumsy stroke now and again. For instance, here is a sentence whose analysis we can leave to the reader, and confidently wish him joy of it:

The looking forward turned them to the looking back at the point they had flown from, and yielded a momentary pleasure, enough to stamp some section of a picture on their memories, which was not the burning *now* Love lives for, in the clasp, if but hands.

It has a meaning, a dimly descried meaning. But why would plain English not have done as well? Mr Meredith has restrained his largesse of epigrams, also. His conclusiveness is less instant than it used to be, and its expression is the surer without the help of the treasuries of earth and heaven. Nothing could be better than this, in its way:

Whether a woman loves a man or not, he is her lover if he dare tell her he loves her, and is heard with attention.

Or this:

In dealing with a woman, a man commonly prudent—put aside chivalry, justice, and the rest—should bind himself to disbelieve what he can't prove. Otherwise let him expect his whipping, with or without ornament.

In defence of our view that this novel is 'good Meredith', and before we examine it as a piece of fiction, let us quote a passage of sane philosophy, a passage which possesses dignity of thought and sound expression that can hardly be matched, even from 'Lord Ormont's' greatest predecessors:

[Quotes ii, from 'Tender is not a word' to 'Some do'.]

On Lady Charlotte Eglett and her views of the proper way to do things the fortunes of the heroine and of the two heroes of this story depended, in so far as human fortunes can depend on any one person. She was sister to Lord Ormont, and Lord Ormont had been a very famous general of cavalry in India, who had made the mistake of doing his duty in a fashion that did not commend itself to the English middle classes. He had ridden

at the head of two hundred horsemen across a stretch of country, including hill and forest, to fall like a bolt from the blue on the suspected Prince in the midst

of his gathering warriors . . . and the high-handed treatment of the Prince **was**
held by his admirers to be justified by the provocation and the result.

But the popular mind was sorely divided. 'These are the deeds that
win empires! the argument in his favour ran. Are they of a character to
maintain empires? the counter-question was urged'. In the end Lord
Ormont was left by the graceless ingratitude of his country to kick
his heels in sullen discontent. But he had fervent, faithful admirers.
Among these were 'Matey' Weyburn, a schoolboy, and Aminta Farrell,
a schoolgirl, whose 'crocodiles', if we may use the slang word for a
two-by-two procession, used to pass one another every Sunday. Here
is the portrait of Aminta—or Browny, as the schoolboys called her:—

[Quotes i, from 'She had a nice mouth' to 'she could not much help
herself'.]

It was not for years that Aminta could go over the world with
Matey. We regret to say that there was the natural and reprehensible
clandestine correspondence; but soon the boy and girl went on alien
ways. They met again when Matey had become tutor to Lady Charlotte
Eglett's son, at a time when she was alarmed at Lord Ormont's writing
testy, truculent letters to the press, and at a rumour that he had married
some young woman in Spain. That Lord Ormont should 'form an
attachment' was possible, but Lady Charlotte could not bring herself
to believe that he would drag the family name so low in the dust as to
marry a person whom she could not receive. The further report that
the hero was writing his memoirs—and perhaps to please 'that woman'
—made her send Matey to play the private secretary. And 'the woman
—lady—calling herself Lady Ormont—poor woman, I should do the
same in her place'—is of course Aminta, who was legally married to
the idol of her youth. But he refused to recognize her, to take her to
the family seat, or to have her presented at Court. Thus you have two
stories on convergent lines. For while Aminta was doing her utmost to
fortify herself as Lord Ormont's wife, she was also falling in love with
the real idol of her youth. She would have won her way with her
husband, but an accident gave the victory to Lady Charlotte, who had
been in silent, ceaseless opposition to her. The last scenes are conceived
and written in Mr Meredith's gayest and most romantic style. They are
'probable, but not possible', radiant with humour—at moments with
ironical humour—and of a gallant, persuasive vitality. The swim
seawards, when the lovers become for moments the boy and girl they
had known at school, is an audacity that is audacious even from him;

but it comes well out of the hardest criticism—except, perhaps, that criticism which observes how wet and weedy the sea must have made Aminta's hair, unless she had covered it with an ugly india-rubber cap, and how Matey's sodden duck trousers must have been void of comeliness and form. We feel as Lady Charlotte felt, and as Lord Ormont felt in the end, that this twain was for one another from the first, and came to one another at the last by an inevitable law.

Matey Weyburn is the least interesting of the chief characters, and Aminta—sister as she is, and as she shows that she is, to so many heroines of untold charm—sometimes lacks colour. Lord Ormont could not have been bettered, nor could Lady Charlotte. They are drawn in Mr Meredith's finest and most dignified manner; they ring true at every touch, and the luck of their lives, the changes and chances of their fates, hold the reader. Indeed, the story leaves one feeling that, despite Aminta's natural nobility, she was never quite good enough for Lord Ormont: possibly because it was after she knew him that she was stretched on the rack of this tough world. One cannot help taking sides in reading the book, because all the characters are bristling with life and the humours of life. In fact, the story reconstructs the masques and triumphs and pageantries of the world's show, in this world's atmosphere, to the tune that the world's pulse beats. We know no better commendation of a novel than that it should thus own the essentials of romantic sanity and health.

99. Unsigned review, *Pall Mall Gazette*

lix, 20 July 1894

Though much may be achieved by the attention of devoted imitators, by the mimicry of rancorous enemies, a man's best parodist is himself. He understands involuntarily the kicks and antics of his own expression; he has but to force an effect, and straightaway he commits that form of literary suicide, caricature of self. When the brain is tired, style slips insensibly into manner, and what else is manner than style parodied? No writer has been more industrious in the exaggerated mimicry of himself than Mr George Meredith. *The Tragi-Comedians* [*sic*] might already have been the invention of a malicious humour, and *The Egoist*, despite the eulogy of Mr Stevenson, remains for us a *tour de force* and the memory of a headache. But in *Lord Ormont and his Aminta* Mr Meredith has surpassed all previous efforts in the art of caricature. From beginning to end the book is a tirade; the jaded reader gets not an instant's respite. The characters declaim, and declaim, and declaim, ever in the same tone, and ever with the same phrase. There is no attempt to suit the style to the character. Men and women, ladies and hoydens speak all the same language, which is not English but Meredith. The many dialogues between Lord Ormont and his sister, Lady Charlotte, are always puzzling, sometimes unintelligible, because Mr Meredith, speaking through each mask, makes no attempt to differentiate the spirit and temper of his puppets. The style is so tortured and elaborated that scarcely for half-a-page are you unconscious of the means; and though we are all for artifice, we recognize that variety of tone and occasional relief are the essentials of art. But Mr Meredith allows you no rest; he bids you dance to his staccato measure, until you are compelled to cry him mercy from sheer exhaustion.

And as is inevitable when the phrase is sought and sought for a weary seven hundred pages, the phrase is not always found, or is often discovered a phrase with no corresponding idea. 'A heavy trifle of suspicion'—could there be a more hapless 'derangement of epithets'? Who can endure in patience this jumble of nouns and adjectives: 'his parasitic thrasyieon apeing coxcomb'? The passage here following might be set in a general paper along with a verse of Browning's, to test the limits of undergraduate understanding. 'He boasted it to a sister sharing the pride—exultant in the cry of a hawk, scornful of ambitious poultry; a passed finger-post to the plucked, and really regretful that no woman had been created fit for him'. Thus it is that everywhere you encounter words too large for their effect, and fumble at obscurities which, when pierced, are found to conceal platitudes. The images, moreover, wherein Mr Meredith delights, are too seldom characteristic, they too seldom have that simplicity and rightness which distinguish the great masters of simile. 'He was as fond', says Mr Meredith of the usher at Cuper's, 'of giving out the name of Murat as you see in old engravings of tobacco-shops men enjoying the emission of their whiff of smoke'. The simile is completely inapposite, or rather, it would seem just as apposite to any other conceivable utterance. Yet now and again we delight in Mr Meredith's ancient habit of eloquent expression, his dainty use of the right word and the convincing image. This description of Amy May, the wife of the famous fighting captain, could not be bettered: 'Her hair was radiant in a shady street; her eyelids tenderly closed round the almond enclosure of blue pebbles bright as if shining from the seawash'. Do you not henceforth know her for a beautiful woman? But these jewels of speech glitter rarely in the book, and you wish that Mr Meredith had taken counsel with his own Lord Ormont. 'It's like what you call good writing', said my lord of fencing, 'the simple way does the business, and that's the most difficult to learn, because you must give your head to it'. How far is the novelist's practice divorced from this excellent theory!

This much for the manner; and what of the matter of the book? Here also you mark a decline. In vain you seek the lyrical quality of *Richard Feverel*, the tempered merriment of *Evan Harrington*, the bubbling champagne of *Harry Richmond*, the fierce conviction of *Rhoda Fleming*, the middle-class romance of *Sandro* [sic] *Belloni*. Instead you have a set of characters, who are never held in hand. Up and down the book they wander, aimless and indistinct, and the reader can hardly hope to understand what the author himself has imperfectly grasped. Lord Ormont himself appears a monument of inconsequence. In one sense he is a negation of Steadism, a living outrage upon the Non-conformist conscience.[1] But you feel that the suppression of Aminta, the masquerading of his wife as a mistress, are entirely without motive. Aminta, in spite of Lady Charlotte's denunciation, is pictured a lady, and can you conceive an ancient *roué* putting a slight upon the woman he loves out of pique to an ungrateful country? This contrariety is a hopeless impoverishment of Lord Ormont, whose action should have been either less logical or more precise. But Lady Charlotte, who stands for the honour of the family, is an admirable invention. If only she had spoken with an accent of her own, she would have been a masterpiece: even as it is, Mr Meredith says a hundred good things through her mask. Her zealous championship of her brother, the sound brutality of her views, her contempt for the neighbours and the parish priest are excellently set forth, and so long as she is on the stage you catch a breath of the old Meredith. The fight for the family jewels (for example) is rendered with amazing vigour and rapidity, while the

[1] William Thomas Stead (1849–1912) used his influence as a powerful journalist and newspaper proprietor in favour of the peace movement started by Tsar Nicholas II in 1898.

quarrel over the family pew compels you to sympathy. But my lady is not always before the audience, and Aminta's aunt is a poor substitute— though once upon a time Mr Meredith had a rare genius for the portraiture of aunts. The others are neither very real nor very amusing. Matthew Weyburn, being a bundle of excellencies, is a sorry prig, and the career of a schoolmaster is the best that could have been offered him. How well we know the type! The muscular undergraduate, bent upon the regeneration of his college and hungry for the golden opinion of his tutors! Most often he grows into a healthy, athletic don, and remains to the end of his days the overgrown, intelligent schoolboy he was at the beginning. Now, Mr Meredith does not send his Matthew to college, but he seems to have studied the type, and neither the schoolmaster's international aspiration nor his attachment for Aminta is sufficient to humanize him. Far better understood is Lord Ormont's Aminta. And if generally she be but a shadowy outline, there are moments when she appears a living and a courageous woman. The villains are of the approved Adelphi type, and the bully Cumnock has been kept so long in the novelist's stock of puppets that we are aston-ished that Mr Meredith should have trotted him upon the scene again. As is ever the case, the small irrelevancies of the picture are suggested with a light and pretty touch, which reinforces the opinion that elaboration was the death of Lord Ormont. Once or twice also you think yourself on the brink of a great situation, as when the characters, all at loggerheads, meet at Steignton. Here might have been an occasion for a flood of epigram and repartee, but no sooner are the ill-matched personages confronted than they slink away, leaving Lady Charlotte triumphant, and you with a bitter sense of disappointment. However, the 'marine duet' is brilliant in the ancient manner. Who, save Mr Meredith, would have permitted Matthew Weyburn, with no other covering than a pair of white ducks, to encounter his Aminta in the rolling billows? And who, save Mr Meredith, having set his characters in so unexpected a situation, would have gifted them with so keen an enjoyment of life and fun, and have brought them to land so happily uncompromised? That, in truth, is the one great passage of the book. For the rest, once more let us quote the General against his Creator: 'If a story had to be told, Lord Ormont liked it plain, without jerks and evolutions'. And Lord Ormont could not, with a clear conscience, have smiled approval upon his biographer.

100. J. A. Noble, in *Spectator*

lxxiii, 4 August 1894

For J. A. Noble see above, No. 92, headnote.

We do not think that we are afraid of superlatives in criticism and we certainly do not wish to reduce eulogistic appraisement to the level of damnation by faint praise. It is, however, our deliberate opinion that we have barely a dozen works of imagination in the English language which would justify the piled-up epithets of panegyric applied during the past five or six years to the novels of Mr George Meredith, and that among such dozen no single work from Mr Meredith's pen can justly be numbered. No candid or right-feeling critic can find it pleasant to speak in terms which might seem depreciatory of books written by a man of unquestionable ability, who in an age of self-advertisement has never raised a finger to advance his just claims; who through years of comparative neglect worked on in quiet dignity; and who has abandoned nothing of that dignity while the late chorus of excited, undiscriminating laudation has been ringing in his ears. It is nevertheless the fact that, so far as Mr Meredith is concerned, English critical opinion has passed from one extreme to the other; and as the sudden push of the pendulum has, at any rate, rectified an injustice, we should not regret the swing, were it not for the thought of the inevitable return. Readers of discriminating judgment and sane temper may, in their irritation at extravagance, ignore the measure of truth which the extravagance holds in solution; and even those who are now held in bondage by an artificially imposed vogue may, as the fetters gradually fall away, indulge in insolent licence of revolt. In both alternatives Mr Meredith's reputation is, in the long-run, bound to suffer.

Our own impression of him—the impression which we believe will finally survive—is of a poet, a phrase-maker, and an intuitive rather than consecutive thinker, who has been made by accident a novelist. His novels abound in imagination and in wit, and they are rich in gleams of a certain kind of insight; but, on the other hand, they lack that organic integrity, that complete command of a series of vitally related incidents or situations, which is the *sine quâ non* not merely of great, but of really competent fiction. It may have been noticed that Mr Meredith's most extravagant eulogists are wont to justify their eulogy almost exclusively by reference to certain admired passages— the beautiful 'Ferdinand and Miranda' chapter in *Richard Feverel* being perhaps the one most recently cited: it hardly ever occurs to them to dwell upon the entire conception of a novel, except indeed in the case of such a book as *The Egoist*, where that conception is exhausted by the presentation of a single individuality. It seems to us that Mr Meredith has just missed his true work in literature. He is deficient in some of the essential qualifications of a novelist; he has many of the essential qualities of a poet, and his poetical reputation—save with the elect—has been damaged not by defect, but by a fine bewildering excess. As an essayist, we believe he would have been all but wholly successful; and as a delineator of 'characters' after the fashion of Theophrastus, La Bruyère, and William Law (whose fine work in this kind should never be ignored),[1] his triumph would have been indubitable; it would not have been a triumph to be profaned by an 'all but'. This judgment is certainly supported by *Lord Ormont and his Aminta*, a fairly representative book. It is less good than *Richard Feverel* and *Diana of the Crossways*; it is indefinitely better than that dreary, unreadable *One of Our Conquerors*. It exhibits with a fine impartiality all that we can possibly wish to see of the author's weakness, and enough to delight us of his peculiar strength. His style in various passages has that exasperating quality, which if not affectation must be an almost unique natural perversity; the mere story is so unnatural and incredible that we should do injustice to it by a summary; the moral—that love may ignore marriage, and in ignoring it, look the world in the face with no glance of apology—will be regarded by the best readers as not a moral but the reverse. On the other hand, when Mr Meredith is at his best, his literary manner has a wonderful charm of word and phrase and image and general form. The sentences sparkle oftener than they glow, but when they glow—as in the chapter in the third volume, 'Lovers Mated'—we can warm ourselves in the radiance. In single ingenuities of metaphor, Mr Meredith is as happy as ever; witness the sentence in which he remarks that 'passionate devotion to an object strikes a vein through circumstances, as a travelling run of flame darts the

[1] William Law belongs in this list by virtue of the character sketches scattered through his *A Serious Call to a Devout and Holy Life* (1729).

seeming haphazard zigzags to catch at the dry of dead wood amid
the damp', or the beautiful simile, 'absent or present, she was round him,
like the hills of a valley'. It is, however, in two or three of his men and
women, seen in simple prose rather than in dramatic activity, that Mr
Meredith shows his power. He is not a master of *character*, exhibiting
itself in action, and therefore he is not a novelist to the manner born;
but Lord Ormont, as the disappointed soldier, Aminta, as the dis-
illusionised woman, and Lady Charlotte Eglett all through, are admirable 'characters', in the sense of that word familiar to the three masters
already mentioned. Mr Meredith has, in short, a singularly fine literary
instinct, but more than this is needed for the production of permanently
satisfying fiction; and the 'more' is what he lacks. . . .

101. Review, *Bookman*

vii, August 1894; signed 'G–Y'

Has Mr Meredith ever been adequately studied as a Briton? I think
not; though one of his most recent critics has insisted on his patriotism,
and seems to have no doubt about his brains as well as his limbs being
made in England. It is true one has only to read from *The Ordeal of
Richard Feverel* and *Harry Richmond* onwards, to feel convinced of his
intense enjoyment of many phases of English life and manners, an
enjoyment quite as great as Fielding's, but differing as much in kind as
in expression; and what more can one say? The attitude of Mr Meredith to things English has never been a simple one, but it partly explains
itself in his newest novel. It is the attitude of admiration, but the admiration, of an outsider, with a far better understanding of the game than
all save a very few of the insiders. *Lord Ormont and His Aminta* compels an inquiry into the nationality of Mr Meredith's mind—though it
gives no very definite answer. Read in one light, the book is a glorification of English boys, English schoolboy honour, English pluck
and daring, an eloquent tolerance of, an artistic esteem for, English
defects. This kind of sentiment used to be embodied in stories by

Mr Thomas Hughes. Nowadays an excellent interpreter of the Anglo-Saxon temper in its tougher moods has been found in Mr Rudyard Kipling. (Was Mr Meredith ever brought into such incongruous company?—but the incongruity is just the point). They take English superiority for granted calmly, or hoist the flag aggressively, ignore the faults they do not wish to see, or berate their country for others, and mainly for not being English enough. Mr Meredith's lyrical enthusiasm for his country, and his intellectual enjoyment of her limitations, are something entirely different. With his cosmopolitan sympathies, his personal freedom from insular prejudices, he is exactly the type of man whom you expect to look on John Bull as a barbarian, and hold all Philistines in horror as unclean, or not conversible-with fellow-citizens. But he does nothing of the kind. In the first place, perhaps, he has too much humour, but, secondly, he comes with such fresh, untired eyes to look at the Philistines that he finds them most amusing fellows, and thereupon sits down, not to laugh at them, but to describe their points of view till you are persuaded he is bringing you into a company of distinction. He is like a foreigner turned Anglophile, and there is nothing sincerer and heartier than the admiration of such. Just as the descendants of the English of the pale became more Irish than the Irish, so Mr Meredith, with a mind that one does not at all recognize as native, is in certain moods more British than the British. I am not going to try and put a label on the nationality of his mind; perhaps there is no nationality ready to admit it on the score of very near kinship. But it is something swifter than English, and not only more agile, but more delighting in agility; not more emotional or imaginative, but with a keener intellectual sense of the value of emotions and of the part imagination plays in ordinary life. What reconciles his style to those who are not admirers of it *per se*, is that it is convincingly the sign of a difference of vision between him and the world that uses a different English; and the difference lies mainly in rate of speed. Speech is too slow and sluggish and unwieldy a thing for the gait of his thought; he wrestles with it, rushes through it, makes unheard of demands on it, passes half of it by, setting at nought all its habits in making it serve his hurried purposes.

With his agility he sees most of the game. More than there is to see, say breathless readers, who cannot run with him. And it is not only a swift but a double vision he would have those employ who follow his guidance, one that shall mark the motive and final meaning in the imperfect act that was their sorry manifestation. Thackeray made his men talk and walk as we see men talk and walk in Piccadilly and Fleet Street, as an Englishman sees them, taking many things about them for granted, lumping their contents often. They are distinctive figures, and fairly easy of classification as fools, or knaves, or heroes. Richmond Roy is perhaps as real as Barry Lyndon and Richard Feverel as Pendennis, but your attitude towards the Meredith characters is quite different. They force you out of the rôle of mere passer-by, or outright approver or condemner, into a kind of excited student of them as well, and if you cannot take quick notes of the throbbings, and eye-glances, and thrills noted in the professor's demonstration, you are apt not to learn as much as you would have done from a lay figure.

Now *Lord Ormont and His Aminta* does not present more points than any of the other books for a study of English minds and manners, but it does present Mr Meredith's attitudes to these more distinctly. *Harry Richmond*, *Richard Feverel*, and *Sandra Belloni*, are far better stories. Rhoda and Lucy and Diana are greater women than Aminta. Aminta has great moments, nevertheless; but we see her mainly through the eyes of those that loved her. 'Her look was like the fall of light on the hills from the first of the morning'. 'Absent or present, she was round him, like the hills of a valley'. 'She was that fire in the night which lights the night and draws the night to look at it'. There are a few memorable pictures where we look at her directly and not through her lovers' eyes. One is the swimming scene, which is either very comic, or magnificent, according to one's humour. Mr Swinburne should set it to verse. Another is as she lies waiting for lightning, 'her black hair scattered on the pillow like shadow of twigs and sprays on moonlit grass, illuminated intermittently; smiling to him, but her heart out and abroad, wild as any witch's'. Great or small, she is very picturesque, and we feel a resentment, whether false romanticism breed it or not, that Aminta of the radiant sunset face, should be dedicated to the service of schoolboys. Matey Weyburn, most decorous of young heroes and schoolmasters, decorous even in his defiance of the world's conventions, is a manly young fellow. But if he hadn't been made by Mr Meredith, he would have been made by a woman; he has that quality of preter-natural solemnity which in women's heroes answers, in frequency, to the love of being mastered in men's heroines. The book, if not among the best, takes us back, nevertheless, to Mr Meredith's best time. It is full of things that are clear sighted, just, and beautiful. Here are some picked at random:— 'Muscular principles are sown only out in the world; and, on the whole, with all their errors, the wordly men are the

truest as well as the bravest of men'. 'The men called great, who have
risen to distinction, are not men of brains, but the men of aptitudes. . . .
They are not the men of brains, the men of insight and outlook. Often
enough they are foes of the men of brains'. 'We do not get to any
heaven by renouncing the Mother we spring from; and when there is
an eternal secret for us, it is best to believe that Earth knows, to keep
near her, even in our utmost aspirations'.

But there is an interest in it apart from its spots of excellence and
beauty. In all the principal characters, save only Aminta, you see
British qualities sublimated—in the schoolboys, in Lord Ormont, in
Lady Charlotte, that magnificent combination of aristocratic insolence
and generosity, tempered by a sense of abstract justice, and a capability
for welcoming ideas, both rather alien qualities. Not that the patriotism
is fulsome. The book is loud with the hard knocks at England's faults,
many of them rapped out by the great Briton himself, Lord Ormont,
the real personage of the story, notwithstanding Lady Charlotte and
her picturesque vagaries. And you see the appreciative outsider continually pricking the Britons to outstrip themselves, to be their best,
their most spirited selves.

Mr Meredith, in his more individual humours, has to be translated—
this is not, by the way, one more weary reference to his style—and his
conceptions do not always tally with their rendering by ordinary minds.
His Lord Ormont is a daring, military genius, sage in council, mighty
in the field, but neglected by his country because he had used the
sword too promptly in an Indian difficulty, in contempt of civil
authority. 'Counting the cries, Lord Ormont won his case. Festival
aldermen, smoking clubmen, buckskin squires, obsequious yet privately
excitable tradesmen, sedentary coachmen, and cabmen of Viking descent, were set to think like boys about him; and the boys, the women,
and the poets formed a tipsy chorus'. This sounds like laughing; but if
so, it is only for a moment. Gallant and duellist—it is not a story of
today—his reputation other than military is romantic and dangerous.
He is far down in burgess estimation. His temper is high, and his letters
to the press make friends and foes alike jeer and laugh. No longer a
young man, he marries the beautiful, youthful Aminta, somewhat in
Oriental fashion. He is not in favour; therefore it is right she should
feel it, and she is caged up in a luxurious prison, leaving the world in
doubt whether she is Lady Ormont at all. He is a most respectful jailer,
and the coldest of husbands. But when the time comes, appointed by
his wisdom, he prepares her entrance into the world, in grand style,

and regardless of trouble. Her presentation would have been something worth beholding. Indeed, his dignity and cocksuredness are such that we join the 'tipsy chorus' at once—if we don't read him in translation. Only, he miscalculated, forgot he was not dealing with a perfectly trained and valuable horse. Aminta unwittingly surprised him in his preparations for her reception in the home of his boyhood. She appeared before him in ambiguous company, but he was too magnanimous to doubt her innocence. He only dismissed her loftily, with no scandal, just as if he were giving field orders, or rather as if he were a calm Providence, a little surprised that its children should not trust implicitly through years of beneficent, if totally unexplained, designs.

Translated, he is a brave, blundering Briton of tyrannical manners and narrow mind, who sulks when he is neglected, and looks on his wife as a chattel, and who is not even jealous of others not at all inclined to be cold to her, disbelieving even the possibility of her preference for anyone else. Never were conceit and unimaginativeness more perfectly combined.

But is it not better to read the original, and catch the glamour from his adventurous life, from his dignified assurance bred of his courage and his inability to see the petty, instead of gibing at the 'injured veteran, who compressed, almost repressed, the roar of Achilles, though his military bright name was to him his Briseis'? The mere fact that one understands a man enough to detest him with good reason, is no proof that one understands him finally; and it is liberalizing to have a sublimated vision of the possibilities of anything, or any one, no matter how imperfect. The British officer, brave, impatient of ideas other than military ones, limited, a bully, though not a petty bully, is seen in such a vision in Lord Ormont. This is the use of Mr Meredith's point of view. His enjoyment and appreciations stretch so far beyond his personal sympathies. One less alien to the actors in his plays would miss half from thinking he knew all about them already. A real foreigner would miss the fine shades, and would blunder over names, for all his interest. Mr Meredith's interest is as keen as if he had just landed in our midst, but he never blunders with shades or names. He needs running after, and keeping difficult pace with to an extent that makes expostulatory criticism legitimate; otherwise he would have hardly a rival for giving, sympathetically, the innermost hearts of men and women. His is not merely the dramatic instinct of clothing his characters in their rightful appearance and conduct, but an enthusiastic endeavour to understand them perfectly—which overshoots itself occasionally, it must be confessed, and presents only a confused impression. It is in some degree a feminine quality, this glow of interest in his personages, his hot partisanship for their point of view, for the moment. The plain Briton thinks he is fooled by Mr Meredith: a novelist who can make a compact, understandable figure like Pickwick is the novelist for him. But the plain Briton should know his friends, and he has never had so near a chance of being understood and explained in that wider and final way he puts off hoping for till he reaches a better world, than by the pen of this writer whom he feels to be an alien, but who nevertheless admires English character with the impartiality of a disinterested looker-on, and loves it not in sections, but in its fulness.

102. Henry James on *Lord Ormont*, from a letter to Edmund Gosse,

22 August 1894

The passage reproduced here is a spontaneous outburst reflecting James's opposition to Meredith's approach to novel-writing. In fact, James had more respect for Meredith than this comment would imply. It was an early reading of *Evan Harrington* which first stimulated James to be a writer. Later, when he came to know Meredith, an affectionate though not intimate relationship grew up, and when Meredith died James remarked: 'He did the best things best'. A later comment of his on reading Meredith's letters represents his attitude more fully: 'Still it abides with us, I think, that Meredith was an admirable spirit even if not an *entire* mind; he throws out, to my sense, splendid great moral and ethical, what he himself would call "spiritual" lights, and has again and again long strong whiffs of manly tone and clear judgment. The fantastic and the mannered in him were nothing, I think, to the intimately sane and straight; just as the artist was nothing to the good citizen and the liberated bourgeois' (letter to E. Gosse, 15 October 1912).

Moreover I have vowed not to open *Lourdes* till I shall have closed with a final furious bang the unspeakable *Lord Ormont*, which I have been reading at the maximum rate of ten pages—ten insufferable and unprofitable pages, a day. It fills me with a critical rage, an artistic fury, utterly blighting in me the indispensable principle of *respect*. I have finished, at this rate, but the first volume—whereof I am moved to declare that I doubt if any equal quantity of extravagant verbiage, of airs and graces, of phrases and attitudes, of obscurities and alembications, ever *started* less their subject, ever contributed less of a statement—told the reader less of what the reader needs to know. All elaborate predicates of exposition without the ghost of a nominative to hook themselves to; and not a difficulty met, not a figure presented, not a scene constituted—not a dim shadow condensing once either into audible or into visible reality—making you hear for an instant the tap of its feet on the earth. Of course there are pretty things, but for what they are they come so much too dear, and so many of the profundities and tortuosities prove when threshed out to be only pretentious statements of the very simplest propositions. Enough, and forgive me. Above all don't send this to the P.M.G. [*Pall Mall Gazette*]. There is another side, of course, which one will utter another day.

103. Unsigned review, *Cosmopolitan* (New York)

October 1894

The most 'important' book in belles-lettres of the month is, doubtless, Mr Meredith's *Lord Ormont and His Aminta*. Mr Meredith may be called the doyen of English novelists. He has wit, almost too much wit; he has passion, and poetry: the defects of his qualities we all know. The qualities in his new book are less apparent than the defects. To myself, unfashionable critic as I am, it really is a drawback that all the characters talk in the same jerky, and mannered, and metaphorical style as Mr Meredith himself employs, when he comes, as he often does, to the front of the stage, and plays the part of Chorus. The novel has a moral problem. Two young people, who had been lovers at private schools, and had adored a common hero, Lord Ormont, a cavalry officer, meet later. The girl is the wife of Lord Ormont; the man is a secretary, or private tutor, and his object is to found an international academy in Switzerland. Now Lord Ormont, ungratefully treated by his country, is a sulky veteran. All his life he has been a free lance in love: at sixty, or so, he has married Aminta, in Madrid. He does not introduce her to the world as his wife; he lets her associate with dubious women of the three-quarters monde. In a man of honor and of pride this behaviour seems very incredible. His sister, a noisily outspoken woman, a great favorite of the author's, disbelieves in Lady Ormont. That poor lady is besieged by a lover who, to myself, seems a very shadowy character. So Aminta and Weyburn, the young tutor, fall to their old love again; Aminta leaves her lord; she and Weyburn have a brilliant love-scene as they swim together; they depart, and set up an international academy.

Entertaining Sir Walter Scott's notions about schoolmasters, I confess that I am out of sympathy with Weyburn. That the pair should get pupils appears to me as improbable as anything in *She*.[1] I believe in the seventh commandment, and dislike the new example, but that, of course, is an ethical objection. Why not, if a book turns on an ethical situation? The whole to me seems thoroughly artificial. Nothing is less congenial than fault-finding with the work of a great and distinguished genius. But criticism is nothing if not honest. There is, in Mr Meredith's novel, no sign of the decadence caused by advancing time; it is not a case of *Count Robert of Paris*.[2] He has merely permitted his less excellent to dominate his more natural and central genius: or, at least, so it appears, to one reader, who must sadly confess that he has not been entertained as he was by *Richard Feverel*, *Rhoda Fleming*, *Evan Harrington*, and *Harry Richmond*. And, perhaps, advancing time has told on the reader.

104. Unsigned review, *Literary World* (Boston)

8 September 1895

After the publication of *One of Our Conquerors* there was little said about Mr Meredith's greatness as a novelist. That novel was a grievous disappointment to even his best friends. It was loudly heralded and much talked about before it appeared. After its publication there was a great deal of ridicule from the author's critics and a discreet silence on the part of his friends. It was dreary and unprofitable, and clever people said that no man or woman actually survived its perusal. After

---

[1] Henry Rider Haggard's *She* was published in 1887.
[2] Scott's penultimate novel (1831).

this bitter disappointment the Meredith cult was ridiculed by unsympathetic critics more than ever, and many meaningless passages culled from his works found their way into print and were made the subject of much sarcasm.

It is therefore with great pleasure that Mr Meredith's admirers proclaim that *Lord Ormont and His Aminta* ranks among his very best novels; perhaps it is destined to be the most popular of all. We will not say that it is wholly free from its author's peculiar and exasperating faults of style, and we will not promise any beginners on his novels that the first chapters of the book are easy reading; but certainly the writer has a story to tell and tells it with the novelist's skill, the essayist's wit, and the poet's beauty of style. There is no overcrowding of the canvas with characters, there is no overburdening of the plot with incidents, and Mr Meredith does not allow himself to be drawn aside from his main lines by any side issues. The book has not the philosophic purpose or the wide range of character which made *The Ordeal of Richard Feverel* so tremendous, nor has it the sparkling brilliancy which dazzled us in *Diana of the Crossways*, but, after we once get hold of the threads and learn to know the characters, it is wonderfully interesting.

The novel begins with a description of a boys' school, and the hero appears first in the light of a schoolboy lover. We see him in the youthful hero-worshiping stage. Lord Ormont is his hero and Aminta is his first love. In the early chapters, bewildering and irritating as they are in point of style, Mr Meredith accomplishes his purpose and brings his chief actors quickly before us. Those who forgive the few puzzling passages in these first chapters will have a feast of rare enjoyment before the book closes. A passage such as we find on the fifth page, differentiating the dark girl from her fair sister, is, we confess, hard to bear patiently, unless we are content to admire the writer as a verbal acrobat:

Some of the boys regretted her not being fair. But, as they felt and sought to explain, in the manner of the wag of a tail, with elbows and eyebrows, to one another's understanding, fair girls could never have let fly such a look; fair girls are softer, woolier, and when they mean to look serious overdo it by craping solemn; or they pinafore a jigging eagerness, or hoist propriety on a chubby flaxen grin, or else they dart an eye, or they mince and prim and pout, and are sigh-away and dying-ducky, given to girls' tricks.

The character of Lord Ormont, the military hero on whom the enthusiastic schoolboy and his adored Aminta lavished all the wealth of admiration which their young hearts held, is strongly drawn; he is unlike any other of Mr Meredith's creations; and as an English nobleman, with all the strength and all the weakness of his class, he is an admirable type. 'A chivalrous gentleman up to the bounds of his intelligence', Lord Ormont was stronger in will and muscle than in brain. He had a great sense of honor, but not a fine sense of what was honorable. His views of women and of politics were old-fashioned, and his intense class feeling colored all his opinions and limited his horizon in every direction; yet he had a kind of instinctive nobility which made him a representative Englishman of the old school—one that his countrymen need not be ashamed of.

Lady Charlotte, Lord Ormont's sister, is another original addition to Mr Meredith's gallery of women portraits, and her strong, proud nature, warped on many sides, is drawn with rare skill. Aminta is a less complete character. The author purposely lets us see her possibilities and watch her in the process of evolution. She has not quite the brilliancy of Diana, but she has a certain consistent earnestness behind her varying moods which Diana lacked.

The plot of the story and its morals may raise almost as great a hue and cry as Mr Hardy's *Tess*. Much of it is unnatural, and the end is almost abnormal. Aminta, Lord Ormont's young wife, neglected by him and refused recognition by society, runs away with her old schoolboy lover, who comes by chance to be her husband's private secretary. So far there is nothing unusual, but the daring unconventionality of the writer appears when the two illegal lovers go to Switzerland and there start a model school for boys. To this school, some years later, the deserted husband sends his grandson [*sic*]. Now, for the sake of society, the marriage tie cannot be lightly broken, and in any country these two lovers would be social outcasts. In setting them up as instructors of youth Mr Meredith will rightly call down the disapproval of all right-minded people on his head; but the disapproval of the whole world will not affect him, however; he has chosen to go his own way and to stand apart from the rules and regulations of society, and the most impossible and abnormal part of his book is, we must confess, the most interesting. Mr Meredith's conception of the world is a poet's conception, far away from the realist's of today. In his poet's world Lord Ormont would have been generous towards his young wife and seen her conduct from the standpoint of ideal justice perhaps; but in the world of today these things cannot be—all these socialistic dreams of free love must do harm to society. We doubt, however, if this book will do much injury, for Mr Meredith's audience is an intellectual, not an emotional, one.

No one can read 'A Marine Duet' without a thrill of pleasure, and the whole chapter called 'Lovers Mated' is a poem. The passage that ends, 'He had gone, and the day lived again for both of them—a day of sheer gold in the translation from troubled earth to the mind', is as exquisite as any Mr Meredith has ever written. The pictorial imagery, the ingenious metaphors, and the brilliant epigrams scattered all through *Lord Ormont* unquestionably prove the author a man of genius. Indeed, the greatness of the writer, rather than the greatness of any one of his books, must impress the student of all his novels.

Let critics battle as they will over the question which troubles the editor of the London *Spectator* greatly, whether Mr Meredith is a good story-teller or not, one point all will agree upon—in almost all his novels, surely in *Lord Ormont and His Aminta*, the reader is brought into close contact with a man of genius. This of itself makes the reading of his last book an experience not often to be repeated. Every one criticizes *Les Miserables* as a novel, but every one enjoys the intimacy with Hugo's rich, luxuriant, poetic mind. Never has Mr Meredith's genius been more evident than in this latest novel. It is artistic, it is dramatic, it is absolutely original, and it makes an ineffaceable impression on the mind. By its side *Marcella*[1] seems commonplace. No novel has been published for years which will bear closer scrutiny and more careful reading. Mr Meredith is to be felicitated; so is the reader who has the perusal of *Diana of the Crossways*, *The Ordeal of Richard Feverel*, and *Lord Ormont and His Aminta* before him.

[1] *Marcella* (1894) was by Mrs Humphrey Ward.

105. H. M. Cecil on Meredith at his best and worst

1894

Hugh Mortimer Cecil was also author of *Pseudo-philosophy at the end of the Nineteenth Century* (1897). This article, entitled 'George Meredith', was published in *Free Review*, ii, August 1894, over Cecil's pseudonym, 'Ernest Newman'.

There are certain kinds of art and literature that seem to win the good opinion at once of the humbler sort of uncritical minds, and of those higher beings who claim to approach literary and artistic questions with a conscious and reliable power of criticism. Gounod's *Faust* and Bizet's *Carmen* hold unquestioned sway over the minds not only of those who go to opera for the enjoyment of an evening, but of cultivated musicians who know good work from bad, and who would not commend music of the simply ear-tickling order, without deeper and more permanent qualities. And the artist who can do work that seems to appeal impartially to high and low and mediocre intelligences, an artist like Mascagni, who can write an Intermezzo that lifts men above all distinctions of intellect, is surely one of the happiest of mortals in his art.[1] Round him will rage little of the conflict of critics; his reputation and his income, in these days, are both assured. But on the other hand there are men whom public and critics alike have come to look upon as tortuous problems, incurable spirits of perversity; men who, like Wagner and Browning, are anathema to certain worthy souls, and heaven's own inspiration to other souls, equally worthy. Some frankly confess them to be incomprehensible; others claim to comprehend them, but half-heartedly admit that the comprehension is scarcely worth the trouble of attaining it; while others again hug the mysterious and the esoteric, and laud the Master as the evangelist of a new dispensation. One can pardon the enthusiastic disciples who have done what the rest of the world has not brains or temper enough to do: the

[1] Pietro Mascagni (1863–1945), Italian composer.

man who has read Browning from *Pauline* to *Asolando*, who knows Ibsen from first to last, who comprehends Wagner the politician, Wagner the philosopher, Wagner the aesthetician, as well as Wagner the musician: the man who—crowning achievement of all—has got honestly through the Second Part of *Faust* without skipping, has certainly something to be proud of. It may be that disciples like these are really the salt of the earth; there is certainly nothing in their writings or their attitude towards opponents to contradict that opinion. But a perverse public refuses to be either bullied or cajoled; it steadfastly resists the process of enrolment in the ranks of students of this or that great artist. Browning will never be popular; Wagner is tending more and more to be known through excerpts on the concert platform rather than by full performances of his operas on the stage. There is only one mode of consolation left open to enthusiastic admirers—to found a Browning or a Wagner Society, wherein, snugly cocooned from a clod-pated world, superior intelligence may create a little Eden for itself, and eat perpetually of the tree of knowledge.

From this last maltreatment Mr Meredith has been happily spared. The prose Browning, as he has been called, has literary sins enough to answer for; but criticism of him can be fairly temperate and unsatiric so long as his frenzied admirers have not formed a Meredith Society for the discovery of the new Secret Doctrine. And the fact that the public knows so little of his private life, while it hinders the critic in some ways from tracing causes and effects, helps in another way to lessen his responsibility, by making the study of the author one solely of a literary presentment. He has been the subject of frenzied eulogies and of no less frenzied objurgations. It may be possible, by looking at him from the standpoint neither of discipleship nor of antagonism, to come to a fairly accurate reading of his mind and art.

I

Looking back at Mr Meredith's first volume—*The Shaving of Shagpat*, published in 1856—we can see fairly foreshadowed the Meredith of the later works. We notice in the early volume an intense feeling for beauty, great imaginative power, strong sensuousness, delight in form and color for their own sakes, an exquisite sense of the values of words as factors of style, an extreme felicity of phrase, a humor original, kindly, and penetrating; on the other hand, too little power of concentration, an imagination too exuberant for the mind's constructive power, a frequent failure of the sense of proportion, an occasional oddity of language, a disposition to write simply for the pleasure of writing, regardless of the need for reserve, and to make the characters talk for the mere sake of talking. Mr Meredith's development has proceeded consistently along both these lines. The one has led him to the exquisitely delicate character-drawing and phrase-making of *The Egoist*, and the swift dithyrambic passion of *The Tragic Comedians*; the other has landed him in the Serbonian bog of conversational triviality in parts of *Diana*, and the chaos of the first half of *One of Our Conquerors*.

Mr Meredith's mind seems to be a blend of the poet's and the philosopher's. There is no reason why a novelist should not be both poet and philosopher, provided his duality of temperament be not so pronounced as to make his work fluctuate uneasily between fictive realism on the one side and poetic idealism on the other. Now Mr Meredith, it may seem paradoxical to say, is more a poet than a novelist; that is, his main concern is with the flux and reflux of human sentiment and emotion, regarded in their most ideal aspects. Thus it comes about that while professing as his aim philosophy in fiction, and declaiming against realistic fiction as being essentially unphilosophical, he is betrayed into the very error that is always attributed to the realist—the unphilosophical error of taking a part of human life for the whole. For idealism like Mr Meredith's is really just as little a philosophic viewing of the whole of life as is the realism so energetically censured. Perhaps the truth may be found in the suggestion that the so-called realist is in point of fact an idealist, almost as idealistic as the idealist proper; seeing that he also has to choose his material, select what he will display, reject what he will not, and give to his selected material the color of his own mind and temperament. The main difference between idealist and realist is not that the one is imaginative and the other is not, but that they are both imaginative on different planes; the one consciously seeking to actualize the fictitious, the other unconsciously casting the glamor of the imagination over what he conceives to be a close reproduction of the actual. Mr Meredith might perhaps repudiate the title of idealist, pointing out that he is against the rose-pink equally with the dirty-drab view of human life; but in the sense in which I here use the word—in that he chooses to deal rather with the isolated ideal emotions of men than with the physical or external materials that give birth to and sway these emotions—he may fitly accept the name of idealist. If he chooses to claim, as he has practically done in the preface to *Diana*, that fiction in this style is a veritable philosophy of life; that these creations of the poet-philosopher are more real than the creations of the realist, what Shelley calls:

> Forms more real than living man,
> Nurslings of immortality,[1]

he will no doubt find many students of æsthetics to agree with him. Platonism is not yet dead in art.

A glance here and there at his method of handling his characters will justify this classification of them. It is noticeable that where he has to deal with characters and emotions that may be treated from two points of view—the more idealistic and the less idealistic—he invariably chooses the former. Take, as an example, the political ground-work of *Beauchamp's Career*. Here Mr Meredith has, besides his usual ideal love-interest, the choice of the actual interest of politics. Characteristically, throughout the greater part of the book he hovers irresolutely between these two interests; but in the end, as might have been expected, the political interest becomes purely subordinate, and, read in the light of the final chapter, might have been almost dispensed with. Mr Meredith has been all along intent on the solution of the emotional problem. This is spun out to an inordinate length; and while the small motive of love and marriage is made one of elaborate psychologizing, what might have been the larger motive of the political interest—the reflexion in the mind of an individual of the great mind of the nation—is handled in a merely perfunctory manner, and only made to serve as one of the factors in determining the course of the love-interest. Would any other of our great modern dramatic or fictive artists have been so lacking in the sense of psychological proportion as to contrast so imprudently matters of such vastly different degrees of importance, and finally to make the smaller motive bulk most largely?

Or again, to take a still better instance. What other writer could have so dealt with the character of Lassalle as to have almost omitted the bare mention of the vast social movement of which Lassalle was the head? It is not that Mr Meredith is incapable of reading political and social movements accurately—for *The Tragic Comedians* and *Beauchamp's Career* contain the shrewdest political sense—but that he instinctively prefers the more ideal color. What he is concerned with is not Lassalle as he really was, not Lassalle's mind as a whole, but that mind solely on the erotic side; and *The Tragic Comedians* becomes nothing but a superb description of a man's bearing under the stress of the emotion

[1] *Prometheus Unbound*, i, 737.

kindled by a woman. The main human interest vanishes, and we are left with merely one man and one woman; the ideal aspect of the situation is chosen, rather than the real.

All his life, indeed, Mr Meredith has hovered uncertainly between heaven and earth. He began with the purely imaginative writing of *The Shaving of Shagpat*, dealing with characters and situations and emotions utterly divorced from any practical human interest. Then, in *Richard Feverel*, he seems to have desired to turn his artistic vision upon the actual lives of men. Yet even here the choice of subject was characteristic of his poetical temperament. Artist as he was, quick with emotion, quiveringly alive to every suggestion of sensuous beauty, and finding in the emotion of the sexes such scope for passionate and pictorial treatment, it was natural that his first incursion into reality should have been through the portals of youthful love. At once sensuous and intellectual himself, the problem that suggested itself to him was one of the psychology of the sexes—the conduct and career of a young man who had been brought up with especial and systematized care in order to fit him to take his place among women. Now nothing could be more illustrative of Mr Meredith's temperament and intellect than his choice of such a subject and his manner of treating it. He was impelled to it by the ardor of his emotional imagination; but having once looked at the problem, his treatment of it amounts to little more than an illogical evasion. As a psychological study of sexual evolution along certain lines it is inconclusive and aberrant; for the tragedy, which should follow inexorably from the method of training adopted by Richard's father, has little logical connection with this. The tragedy, which, to be artistically convincing, should be attributable to this cause alone, is one that might reasonably be attributed to other causes. The psychological line of evolution is a broken one, and the conclusion reached is one that does not necessarily follow from the premises that have been laid down so elaborately and with such show of inevitableness. But while *Richard Feverel* fails in this way, it carries on to higher planes all the unique beauties of the earlier volume. The humor is as refined and as exquisite —the delightful humor of the philosopher demurely smiling; the feeling for beauty is a passion—more than a passion, a religion; and he is seen in his unequalled power in such a thoroughly artistic chapter as the fifteenth, where prose seems to be gifted with all the ravishment of the highest poetry.

II

The weakness of his hold upon plain, broad reality becomes still more apparent when we review the characters he has created. It is noticeable that he has rarely attempted to depict the life of men in circles lower than the aristocratic, and that where he has attempted to pourtray a commoner, he invariably drifts back again into the silken circle in which he feels more at home. Lucy Feverel, though living with her uncle, a rough old farmer, cannot be made a daughter of the fields herself. Mr Meredith is careful to inform us that she is the daughter of a naval officer; and the final reconciliation of Richard with his father depends upon this very fact. Mr Meredith was unable to treat the complications that would have arisen had the girl whom Richard clandestinely married been of anything but gentle birth. In *Rhoda Fleming*, again, the story deals with two girls who are professedly a farmer's daughters. To all intents and purposes, they are no more a farmer's daughters than Mrs Lovell or Clara Middleton. The making of them country born and bred is purely factitious. Bob Eccles is indeed a commoner in some ways, and the most successful commoner Mr Meredith has drawn; but even he is unconvincing. In his relations with Major Waring he is as little a son of the soil as that gentleman himself. Again, Mr Meredith is careful to suggest that Emilia's parents are of humble origin, and equally careful not only to keep them almost entirely out of sight, but to depict Emilia herself in such a way that the making her of humble birth is pure waste of energy.

It might be urged against this view of the novelist that his keeping the commoner out of his novels is not because he is out of sympathy with the democracy, but is rather a merely accidental omission. That this excuse is invalid may readily be seen by a perusal of *Evan Harrington*, the worst-constructed and lamest of all Mr Meredith's works as a whole, yet containing some of his finest writing and happiest character-drawing. Here he sets out with a young man, the son of a tailor, having the *entrée* to refined and wealthy society. His father has left some thousands of pounds of debts behind him, and his mother urges with reasonableness that he can only hope to pay off these debts and redeem his father's honor by carrying on his father's business. The situation is complicated by the young man's aristocratic instincts rebelling against the business of a tailor, and by his being in love with the daughter of a country gentleman. Now, this is as pregnant a situation as a novelist of thews and sinews could desire; one can easily imagine what Balzac would have made of it. Mr Meredith's treatment of it is so utterly lacking, not only in the constructive power of the artist, but in common dignity and manhood, that one can only account for it by supposing him to have been at that time passing through his phase of social green-sickness. As a matter of fact, neither Evan nor his father is a tailor in anything more than name; they are gentlemen as much as Melville Jocelyn or Ferdinand Laxley, just as Rhoda and Dahlia Fleming are on the same plane as Mrs Lovell. But even this might be passed over, were it not for the utter lack of social stamina in the story. Evan Harrington finds salvation, not in paying off his father's debts by working, as his mother would have him do, but by the old, old snobbish expedient of marrying an heiress. The whole problem is obscured; we rise from the perusal of the novel with the sense that we have been artistically cheated and morally insulted. If the novelist of our time is to see life steadily and see it whole, it were well for him to realize that ethical and social codes, with which, after all, he has to deal, are constantly changing, and that a democratic age like this looks with scant favor on so essentially vulgar and commonplace a motive in fiction as the pursuit of an heiress. If virtue is to have a reward in these days, it must be a reward somewhat nobler and more rational than this; and the novelist who thus retains one of the worst ideals of the commonplace generation that preceded us shows himself to have imperfectly understood, in this respect at all events, the world of men in which he actually lives.

That this was not altogether a passing phase with Mr Meredith, that it is a congenital defect of his nature, is shown by his treatment of the commoner in all his novels since *Evan Harrington*. He will not take anyone seriously who is not an aristocrat. He missed a magnificent opportunity in *Beauchamp's Career* by treating Dr Shrapnel in a spirit of absurd caricature; and in his latest novel the commoners—Skepsey and Matilda Pridden—are still treated in the old tone of indulgent irony and grotesque. Mr Meredith apparently does not think life has any seriousness except for those who are clothed in purple and fine linen, and fare sumptuously every day.

III

Taine, in his essay on Balzac, pictures the astonishment and perplexity of a 'man of taste', coming to read Balzac for the first time, at the novelist's extraordinary linguistic abortions.[1] The academic 'man of taste' is rather a French product than an English; nevertheless English critics can reasonably object, and have objected, to some of Mr Meredith's freaks and perversities of style. What is important to remember is that his defects are the almost inevitable correlatives of his qualities; the peculiarly vivid imagination that has empowered him to write pages of the most virile and suggestive prose in the language, is the same imagination that has decoyed him into some of his deplorable experiments with our tongue.

One of the defects of the personifying habit of the eighteenth century was that it frequently failed through its maladroit handling of the personification—dragged the image, as it were, into bad company. The defect of the soaring imagination of the nineteenth century is that in the effort to heap up suggestion upon suggestion and to give a complex idea in a flash of verbal lighting, it is apt to disorganize the system of word-values, trying to obtain from one turbulent amalgam of words an effect that can only be legitimately obtained by a much more roundabout process. Keats was a notable offender in this way. In his early poems, at least, he was perpetually striving after the maximum of pictorial effect by the device of turning one of his substantives into an adjective of description. He speaks of a 'lawny crest', of 'moon-beamy air', of a 'broidered floating vest', of 'swelling leafiness', of 'pillowy silkiness', of 'liney marble', of 'sphery strains'—with an effect almost invariabley grotesque. The quickly-concentrative imagination of Keats is possessed by Mr Meredith, and is answerable for some of his woeful distortions of language. Mannerisms he displays in abundance. His ladies never walk; they swim. Mrs Doria swims to meet Richard Feverel; Mrs Mount swims 'wave-like to the sofa'; Lady Rosely swims 'sweetly' into the room; Mrs Lovell swims 'into the general conversation'; Madame d'Auffray swims to meet Beauchamp; Diana is always swimming—on one occasion she swims 'to the tea-tray'. Still more extraordinary are some of his other expressions. There is a 'combustible silence' in *Farina*; when Hippias Feverel is asleep, his door is a 'somnolent door'; a hooked fish comes, we are told, to 'the gasping surface'; Adrian 'opens his mouth to shake out a coil of laughter'; when Mrs Berry weeps, we hear that 'the black-satin bunch careened to a renewed deluge'; the Countess de Saldar 'rambles concentrically'; Caroline sits down 'within her hands joined in pale

[1] Hippolyte Taine (1828–93); his essay on Balzac was first published in *Journal de Débats* (1858) and later included in *Nouveaux essais de critique et d'histoire* (1865).

dejection'; Cornelia's eyelids 'shed a queenly smile'; Dahlia 'eyes' Edward 'a faint sweetness'; Robert Eccles 'flings a lightning at him'. As time went on, this tendency in Mr Meredith became almost irresistible. When he wishes to convey to us an idea of a woman in the days before she became man-like, he tells us, 'Yet was there an opening day when nothing of us moustached her'. When she does become somewhat masculine, we are 'amazed by the flowering up of that hard rough jaw from the tender blooming promise of a petticoat'. Sometimes the very artificiality of the style is not without a charm, as in the description of Sir Willoughby about to embrace Clara: 'The gulf of a caress hove in view like an enormous billow hollowing under the curled ridge. She stooped to a buttercup, the monster swept by'. But gradually we come to the thoroughly distorted style that dominates the works. It begins on the opening page of *The Egoist*, although that novel as a whole is of remarkable purity of phrase: 'Who, says the notable humorist, in allusion to this book, who can studiously travel through sheets of leaves now capable of a stretch from the Lizard to the last few poor pulmonary snips and shreds of leagues dancing on their toes for cold, explorers tell us, and catching breath by good luck, like dogs at bones about a table, on the edge of the Pole'. In *One of Our Conquerors* the degeneration is complete. Not to mention the celebrated phrase of Dr Peter Yatt about 'feeling a rotifer astir in the curative compartment of a homæopathic globule', we have expressions of such elegance as this: 'The word "Impostor" had smacked her on both cheeks from her own mouth'; and this: 'She called on bell-motion of the head to toll forth the utter night-cap negative'. In the face of so much perversity and affectation, can we sum Mr Meredith up better than in his own chastened and elegant sentence: 'a fantastical planguncula enlivened by the wanton tempers of a nursery chit'!

On the other hand, his excellencies and beauties of style are so great and so many that quotation is almost a work of supererogation. Perhaps he has never surpassed some of the writing in *Shagpat* for color and luminosity. The description of Bhanavar and the serpents is a forerunner of the exquisite description of Clara's curls: 'Then she arose, and her arms and neck and lips were glazed with the slime of the serpents, and she flung off her robes to the close-fitting silken innervest looped across her bosom with pearls, and whirled in a mazy dance-measure among them, and sang melancholy melodies, making them delirious, fascinating them: and they followed her round and round, in twines and twists and curves, with arched heads and stiffened tails; and the chamber swam like an undulating sea of shifting sapphire lit by the moon of midnight'. And there is the beautiful picture of the enchanted sea, alive with ravishing color: with 'glimpses of enthralled vessels, and mariners bewitched on board; long paths of starlight rippled into the distant gloom, and the reflection of the moon opposite was as a wide nuptial sheet of silver on the waters; islands, green and white, and with soft music floating from their foliage, sailed slowly to and fro'. Sometimes he has an unexampled felicity of phrase and imagery: 'So, she clenched her hands an instant with that feeling which knocketh a nail in the coffin of a desire not dead'. 'She ran ahead of his thoughts like nimble fire'. He says of Cecilia in one of her troubled moments: 'her heart had entered on a course of heavy thumping, like a sapper in a mine'. One of his most admirable phrases is that in *One of Our Conquerors*: 'Skepsey toned his assent to the diminishing thinness where a suspicion of the negative begins to wind upon a distant horn'. The glorious dithyramb of the lover's meeting in *Richard Feverel* is well known. He is seen at his best on his lighter side in the beautiful passage in *The Egoist*: 'He placed himself at a corner of the doorway for her to pass him into the house, and doated on her cheek, her ear, and the softly dusky nape of her neck, where this way and that the little lighter-colored irreclaimable curls running truant from the comb and the knot—curls, half-curls, root-curls, vine-ringlets, wedding-rings, fledgling feathers, tufts of down, blown wisps—waved or fell, waved over or up or involutedly, or strayed, loose and downward, in the form of small silken paws, hardly any of them much thicker than a crayon shading, cunninger than long round locks of gold to trick the heart'; and on his serious side in the passage in *The Tragic Comedians* where Alvan speaks to Clotilde of the other face of the moon: 'But no! the handsome face of the orb that lights us would be well enough were it only a gallop between us two. Dearest, the orb that lights us two for a lifetime must be taken all round, and I have been on the wrong side of the moon. I have seen the other face of it—a visage scored with regrets, dark dreams, burnt passions, bald illusions, and the like, the like!—sunless, waterless, without a flower! It is the old volcano land: it grows one bitter herb: if ever you see my mouth distorted you will know I am revolving a taste of it; and as I need the antidote you give, I will not be the centaur to win you, for that is the land where he stables himself! yes, there he ends his course, and that is the herb he finishes by pasturing on'. And for pure pathos nothing could surpass the description of the meeting of Richard Feverel and his mother: 'The blood of her son had been running so long alien from her that the sense of her motherhood smote her now with strangeness, and Richard's stern gentleness seemed like dreadful justice come upon her. Her heart had almost forgotten its maternal functions. She called him Sir, till he bade her remember he was her son. Her voice sounded to him like that of a broken-throated lamb, so painful and weak it was, with the plaintive stop in the utterance'.

IV

Mr Meredith's mind is one of such consistency throughout that it is easy to see how the faults of the earlier volumes have developed into those of the later. The exuberant, unchecked imagination that made *The Shaving of Shagpat* so admirable in parts and so wearisome as a whole, the tendency to write for writing's sake that made that work and *Farina* so unsatisfying by their disconnectedness, the inability to see when the right moment has come for laying down his pen, have been the sources of all his many faults of construction as a novelist. It is hardly too much to say that not one of his novels is well and firmly and convincingly put together, with the exception of *The Egoist*, which, by paradox, is well constructed simply because from its nature and scenery it requires no construction. Not a novel of his but is marred by the invertebrate structure and the unconvincing handling.

His excellencies are mainly excellencies of detail; the novels would come under the Voltairean characterization of 'some fine moments, but some bad quarters of an hour'. In *The Shaving of Shagpat*, the 'Story of Bhanavar the Beautiful' and the 'Punishment of Khipil' are admirable in themselves, but the work as a whole grows wearisome through sheer longinquity. In *Farina* the combat on the Drachenfels is so entirely independent of the rest of the story that for a generation, readers have been asking the meaning of its inclusion. The only possible answer, apparently, is that it appears because Mr Meredith had written it, and thought it so good that is must see the light of day somewhere or other. In *Beauchamp's Career* anti-climax after anti-climax weakens the interest of the novel, and the ending is lamentably feeble. It reminds us of the sudden descent to bathos in the old Scotch popular legend of 'The Shifty Youth', who, after many admirable adventures, one day died accidentally, without any apparent reason for such an abrupt proceeding. *Richard Feverel*, though not a well-constructed novel, is not a noticeably ill-constructed one; but *Evan Harrington* is truly deplorable.

It shows Mr Meredith at his worst in everything that is worst in him—his bad social sentiment, his feeble construction, his dummy characters, and an evident attempt to rival Dickens on his own ground in the characters of Mr Raikes and the Cogglesby brothers. But the entire work is a mass of bad articulation. The whole handling of the two brothers, the fictitious devices by which Evan is maintained in ease and idleness, the sudden and inexplicable elevation of Mr Raikes to fortune, the intercepting of a letter from Evan to Rose, the contents of which are communicated to her by Evan himself a few pages after, thus rendering the whole episode futile; the fictitious bankruptcy of the brothers, the inconceivably clumsy scheming to have the Harrington family under the one roof in Lymport, in order that the final scenes may be brought about—are only some of the worst faults of the work.

The jerkiness and inarticulation of the novels as a whole reappear in the individual characters. Setting aside the obviously dummy characters, whom not even Mr Meredith's brilliant writing can galvanize into life, it is evident at times that his hold on his main personages is by no means certain. A careful tracing of their springs of action shows that they change inexplicably; sometimes, like the caterpillar, they commence as one being and end as another. This weakness is undoubtedly due to Mr Meredith's small power of organic construction. His novel grows together from many peripheral points, so that having developed one set of characters with fair consistency, he finds that the exigencies of construction at this point compel him to make certain other characters act in a way for which there is no warrant from their previous conduct. Yet so skilful is he in psychologizing that he can frequently almost persuade us against our better judgment that the character is compact and consistent. To see the process of change clearly, however, and the preparatory psychologizing by which Mr Meredith paves the way for the change, an excellent example may be had in the episode of the robbery of the gold by Anthony Hackbut in *Rhoda Fleming*. It is utterly inconceivable that the Anthony of the previous chapters should act in such a way; he only does it because Mr Meredith wants him to do it for the sake of his story. And, conscious that the change of character is wholly unjustifiable, Mr Meredith tries to cover his retreat by writing a preparatory dissertation on 'A Freak of the Money-Demon', and does it so dexterously that only on second thoughts do we detect the device, and the purpose it is meant to serve.

But Mr Meredith's characters are always doing inconceivable things, and doing them for no other reason than to bring about the catastrophe or the happy solution. If one asks why Diana should betray the secret of state in so inexplicable a manner, the only answer is that she does so because Mr Meredith has to bring about her estrangement from Dacier. If you ask why Victor Radnor should not tell Nataly that Dartrey Fenellan has lost his wife, the answer is that Mr Meredith was scheming to marry Dartrey to Nesta, but that in the meanwhile the usual process had to be gone through in the shape of the preliminary courtship of Dudley Sowerby, and that Nataly could not have permitted Dudley to supplant Dartrey had she known that the latter's wife was dead, and he an eligible suitor for the hand of her daughter. Mr Meredith is always weak in the jineing of his flats.

Hardly less noticeable than his weakness in construction is his frequent inability to animate his characters, or to create them in perfect and necessary relations with their surroundings. In almost every one of his novels there are personages on whom he has spent infinite pains, yet without being able to convince us that they are actual breathing men and women. Dr Shrapnel, Ottilia, Major Waring, Mr Raikes, the two Cogglesbys, Vernon Whitford, Purcell Barrett, Agostino, Dacier, Colney Durance, are cleverly-jerked puppets, but puppets for all that, and not actual human beings. And almost all his novels run on pretty much the same lines. There is generally either the man hovering between two or three women, or the woman hovering between two or three men. There is the wit who is always saying brilliant things, or things that are fondly supposed to be brilliant; the wit who is Mr Meredith in one or other of his diverse moods of irony or sarcasm or humor —Adrian Harley, or Stukeley Culbrett, or Jorian de Witt, or Agostino, or Diana, or Horace de Craye, or Colney Durance, or Simeon Fenellan, or Tracy Runningbrook. And there is reduplication everywhere in the novels; characters reappearing in the later ones that are merely variations on some in the earlier works. His women, though as a rule more accurately drawn than his men, are curiously alike, as the men are. Victor Radnor is a reincarnation of Richmond Roy in another sphere; Vernon Whitford is Purcell Barrett with Mr Meredith on his side instead of against him.

V

The problem of Mr Meredith's personality is almost a baffling one. His novels show curiously little of himself either as moralist or propagandist. It is only here and there that we get face to face with the actual man, in his prefaces or his soliloquies. By one set of critics, not too robust in themselves, he is lauded as the exposer of sentimentalism, against which modern vice he has raised the banner in *Sandra Belloni* and in the preface to *Diana*. It is hardly profitable to follow him into his analysis of sentimentalism; all the more so as the very books in which he wars against it are those in which he has inflicted upon us something almost worse than sentimentalism. One asks, after reading *Sandra Belloni*, wherein the sentimental ladies, Arabella, Adela, and Cornelia, and the sentimental gentlemen, Barrett and Wilfrid, are worse than the heroic Merthyr and the heroinic Georgiana. Certainly it would be hard to find two more insufferable incarnations of the prig than these. Mr Meredith's complacent declaration that he is on the side of the angels creates in us, when we see the company he keeps, an insatiable longing to be on the side of the other immortals. His declamation against the sentimentalist would be something really valuable if he could convince us that the men and women he sets up in opposition to the sentimentalist were even slightly better types. But they are, if anything, worse. His pattern-hero, Merthyr, is funereal; his very excellencies are, as O'Connell said of Peel's smile, like the silver plate on a coffin. And his women with brains are sometimes so intolerable as to make men even long again for the old ideal of woman—the 'veiled virginal doll' of the sentimentalists. Diana's conversation at times is an affliction of the understanding. If Mr Meredith's idea of women with brains is that of women who talk as he makes them talk in the drawing-room encounters of chapters twenty-eight and thirty of *Diana*, a frenzied male can only say that he would prefer women of the other sort.

Mr Meredith, however, is always on the woman's side. A lady once told Amiel that he was 'superlatively feminine'[1]; the characterization would apply very accurately to the Meredith of the later novels. *The Egoist* is so exquisitely delicate an analysis of a woman's feelings in relation to a man who offends, not through over-grossness, but through over-refinement, that one might be reasonably pardoned for supposing the author of it to be a woman. It is noticeable that his last three novels—*The Egoist*, *Diana*, and *One of Our Conquerors*—have been mainly a statement of the woman's side of the case, a pleading that could hardly be equalled for force, delicacy, insight, and pathos. If you consider the extremely tenuous nature of the interest in *The Egoist*, you will be all the more astonished at the rare psychological ability with

1 Henri-Frédéric Amiel (1821–81), diarist and critic.

which that interest is maintained throughout. We unconsciously become feminine in sensation and emotion in the reading of the novel; we feel something of Clara's subtle, feminine shrinking of the flesh at the approach of Sir Willoughby's caress. In *Diana*, not all the abortive attempts at wit can make us do anything but love and sympathize with the noble woman who has the courage to stand against the masculine grossness of the world; while *One of Our Conquerors*, which, perverse as it is, contains some of the finest of Mr Meredith's writing, is planned on large motives and is supremely pathetic in interest. In all these books he achieves his wonderful success because he is 'superlatively feminine'. And reading him in this light, one smiles at Diana's story of the girl in her service who had a 'follower'. 'She was a good girl; I was anxious about her, and asked her if she could trust him. "Oh, yes, ma'am", she replied, "I can; he's quite like a female"'. It is sad to think that Mr Meredith himself, possessing as he does this desirable virtue of being quite like a female, has not yet become a favorite of the sex in England. It may be that the feminine reader is more perplexed at him than the masculine in this respect. There is something in the saying of the wise woman Mrs Berry: 'That's where everybody's deceived by him. . . . It's because he keeps his face, and makes ye think you're dealin' with a man of iron, and all the while there's a woman underneath. And a man that's like a woman he's the puzzle o' life! We can see through ourselves, my lady, and we can see through men, but one o' that sort, he's like somethin' out o' nature'.

VI

Imitating a phrase of somebody about somebody else, we may see that Mr Meredith has written many good books and scarcely one good novel. His defects of construction are too many to permit of him taking rank as a great novelist. It would seem as if he would be remembered and admired for other qualities and achievements; for a fine if sometimes unruly style, for his delicate, poetic sense of beauty, his charm and variety of manner, his clever character-drawing here and there, and a general sense in reading him that we are in the company of one of the sweetest and sanest spirits of any time. His virtues show themselves mainly in detachments. His humor, when he is really humorous, is something to thank the gods for. He can range from the choice and deliberate Oriental gravity of 'The Punishment of Khipil' to the redolent earthy humor of the conversation of the tramp and the tinker under the hedge; from Adrian Harley to Horace de Craye; from Mr Raikes to Mrs Chump; from Skepsey to Master Gammon; a humor always kindly, always illuminative, free from bitterness or cynicism, full of the distillation of the best of human experience, a brightener of the dusty road of life. In consideration of what he has given us in this regard, we can even pardon him the embassy to the Court of Japan.

Weak too, as his constructive ability is, he can yet hold on to a complicated interest with rare tenacity. He is always at his best in tracing the mazy threads of feminine diplomacy and intrigue. The many shifts and endless resources of the Countess in *Evan Harrington* make that story, whenever she appears in it, social comedy of the finest kind. The delicate feminine element in his nature always serves him in good stead when he has to carry his women through a crisis, or when they have to rise in towering supremacy of soul. His Clara and Diana are rare creations; the scene in *Sandra Belloni* in which Lady Charlotte twists Wilfrid round her finger, is as fine in one way as the inditing of Mrs Chump's letter or the purloining of Mrs Berry's ring is in another. If his 'great ladies', his Mrs Mountstuart and Lady Gosstre and the rest of them, are generally intolerable nuisances, we can place to his credit on the other hand such an entirely original and successful creation as Sandra, the singer wholly wrapped up in her art, to whom the world is something born of music, and everything in it translateable into music —a finer study of the musical temperament than anything since Balzac's Gambara.[1]

And threading our way here and there through the novels, admiration at their strength and fineness gets the upper hand of annoyance at their perversity and their shortcomings. Who else, we then ask, could have put together such scenes as those that fill the canvas of *Richard Feverel*? Who else could have carried the Countess de Saldar or Richard Roy through their extraordinary involutions and evolutions to conquer a society, scarcely ever letting the narrative grow dull or the intrigue lose its interest? And who else could have painted so wholly admirable a picture of the relations of Italians and Austrians in Italy's struggle for freedom; a picture so perfectly balanced in its coloring? It is pretty safe to assert that in the description of such a struggle the sympathies of nine novelists out of ten would have been entirely with Italy. Read Mr Meredith's account of it, especially the account of the combat of Angelo and Weisspriess, and you will appreciate the broad,

[1] In the novel of that name (1837).

healthy humanity of the writer who could treat such a subject without the heroics or the sentiment of the partisan. When he rises to the occasion, too, he can be Olympian in his serenity. One knows nothing since Shakspere so thoroughly Shaksperian as that final scene of *Harry Richmond*, where the tragic comedian dies in the ashes of his last mad scheme—the ending of that career of mingled tears and laughter, the career of the jester who takes himself with such sad seriousness: or that superb chapter in *Beauchamp's Career* (the nineteenth), the scene between Everard and Rosamund, that has the high solemnity of elemental nature. In face of the vast amount of excellent work he has done, we can readily condone his faults and perversities; nay, we can almost come to like them. Few would willingly give up the first two hundred pages of *One of Our Conquerors*, though their bearing on the story is so slight; and no one would wish to part from Skepsey, though he has practically no connection whatever with the march of the story.

To blame Mr Meredith for his perversities, indeed, would be sometimes to blame the innocent. The guilt for much of it must lie on the shoulders of the public. Cordial recognition of his work in the beginning would have made him less secretive, less inclined to retire inward upon himself, and would have spared him and us that conviction that he is writing for a select few, whose contempt for the long and hairy-eared public is as great as his own. This isolation and want of recognition have made him take up the part of the smiling philosopher regarding the foibles and follies of men; a part that can only be played by a posing that sometimes becomes painfully apparent. That he can still write vigorous prose and draw living characters is amply shown in the latter half of *One of Our Conquerors*, where he drops the part of satirist and ceases to pose. Few have perceived the personal note of sadness in that passage in *Beauchamp's Career* in which he confesses his estrangement from an inappreciative world:

[Quotes xlviii, from 'We will make no mystery about it' to 'my own voice more than is good'.]

When we consider how much of his weakness is due to this constant feeling that he is acting to vacant benches, we can realize that perhaps he has been more sinned against than sinning. And as there can be no doubt that the habit of listening for years to his own voice more than is good is answerable for many things the capricious public blames him for, it may reasonably be suggested that the public has the simple remedy for that in its own hands.

THE AMAZING MARRIAGE

1895

106. Edmund Gosse, in *St. James's Gazette*

xxxi, November 1895

Edmund William Gosse (1845–1928), novelist, critic and scholar, knew Meredith and concerted with Leslie Stephen and Thomas Hardy to collect signatures for the 1898 testimonial to him.

There is an unfailing law in literature which determines that if a writer of strong individuality has indulged a mannerism in early life, that wilful peculiarity of style shall grow upon him and shall render his latest productions a vexation to his critics. Mr George Meredith is a novelist to whom in no small degree has been given the quality of genius. But when he was young he was not content to shine: he desired to dazzle also, and he soon adopted the deplorable habit of saying nothing simply or easily, but always in the oddest language possible, with the maximum of effort. When he was at the height of his power the images which flooded his mind were so brilliant, the flow of them so copious, that he constantly overruled this tendency and wrote—never, it is true, simply—yet often vehemently and nobly. But with the increasing and inevitable languor of years his imagination has grown less active, and he has allowed it—without conscious affectation, we are sure—to take refuge beneath the increasing extravagance of his artificial diction. We hardly know how to say it without seeming to pay less than respect to a very distinguished and original writer, but it must be said—the Alexandrian extravagance of Mr Meredith's style has now reached such a pitch that it is difficult to enjoy and sometimes impossible to understand what he writes. In the *Amazing Marriage* we seem to be listening without a break to a rhapsody of Sir Piercie Shafton's.[1]

[1] A Euphuist in Scott's *Monastery* (1820).

We are not so unreasonable as to wish Mr Meredith to be other than his nature makes him. He has always had an extraordinary gift in the construction of illustrative phrases; he belongs to the same class as Jeremy Taylor and Fuller. Every object, every idea, that crosses his consciousness suggests to his flashing fancy some other idea, some other subject. In his present book he says of a certain lady that when she entered a room 'language became a flushed Bacchanal in a ring of dancing similes'. This is a charming phrase, and exactly describes Mr Meredith's style at its best. But when the dancers never are still for a page, and the Bacchanal flings and tosses without a pause through two long bewildering volumes, he must be an enthusiast indeed who does not shut his aching eyes and hold his throbbing brows. If the dance could be stopped here and there, if the language were ever calm, lucid, and natural, we should forgive everything. We should admit gladly that a joint of mutton is 'the vertiginous roast haunch', and that no rural phenomenon is more common than for 'a shaving north-easter to tear the scream from hedges and the roar from copses'. We would willingly give Mr Meredith his lapful of metaphors; he should fling them at us with both hands, and we would never wince at the *confetti*. But to have nothing else: to surmise dimly that a really noble and stately scene is rendered invisible to us by these hurtling confectioneries, is really too much. We are suffocated with all this sweetness; we need not confess to a more than common stupidity, for instance, in not being able, in such a passage as the following, to catch the eminent novelist's meaning without fatigue. A simple young man sees gambling-tables for the first time, and this is the result:

Philosophy withdrew him from his temporary interest in the tricks of a circling white marble ball. The chuck-farthing of street urchins has quite as much dignity. He compared the creatures dabbling over the board to summer flies on butcher's meat, periodically scared by a cloth. More in the abstract, they were snatching at a snap-dragon bowl. It struck him that the gamblers had thronged on an invitation to drink the round of seed-time and harvest in a gulp. Again, they were desperate gleaners, hoping, skipping, bleeding, amid a whizz of scythe-blades, for small wisps of booty. Nor was it long before the presidency of an ancient, hoary Goat-Satan might be perceived, with skew-eyes and pucker-mouth, nursing a hoof on a knee.

How clever—how deplorably clever and distressing! And this is what, to a crowd of gaping young men and women just beginning to 'take up literature', is proffered as a model of sober and beautiful style!

This is a matter of taste, and opinions here may differ. But honest criticism will hardly question that under its brocades and its embroideries there walks in *The Amazing Marriage* a very fine story. And this fact has always distinguished Mr Meredith from the mere Gongorist or Marinist that, whatever his ornament may be, there is solid flesh beneath it. He has always something excellent to say; and this it is, indeed, which increases our annoyance that he will not say it lucidly. Here, amid a crowd of more shadowy personages, some of them too obviously ticketed with mere tricks of manner, he conducts for us, through singularly trying conditions, two thoroughly human, consistent, interesting beings. The fortunes of the Earl and Countess of Fleetwood, whose 'amazing marriage' electrified society, are strange and strangely moving: they themselves are faulty, natural, creatures; each with a fine tempestuous individuality which clashes with that of the other. The Earl marries his mountain bride in a fit of pique, and leaves her at once: when, conquered by her dignity and wholesome sweetness, he would undo the past, it is too late; he has outstayed the period for forgiveness, and she is now as stubborn as he was. In Carinthia, Lady Fleetwood, Mr Meredith has conceived one of those sturdy amazonic women whom he loves to portray—half Roman matron, half Elizabeth Fry—with a glowing heart beneath a broad marmoreal bosom. The development of her instincts, in the slow change of her sentiments towards her capricious and unreasonable husband, is worked out with a happy mastery, and no oddity of phraseology can ever conceal that chivalrous attitude in face of all the problems of life which has always been Mr Meredith's high distinction.

107. B. Williams, from a review in the
Athenaeum

No. 3553, 30 November 1895

Basil Williams (1867–1950) was active as a historian and produced a number of books on a variety of historical topics.

Among the few really exciting events in literature is a new novel by Mr Meredith. Other living novel-writers, even taking the very best, have an appearance of tentativeness, of working from a theory, by which they sometimes produce charming and even great results, but still results which leave something incomplete, something to be desired. But Mr Meredith knows. After reading a novel by him one usually feels that there is nothing more needed; there is no other way of looking at the subject he takes up, for he lives in his characters and a hint from him expresses more than pages of laborious description. The truth is, little as it may appear so at first sight, Mr Meredith belongs to that great school of writers of whom Aristophanes, Rabelais, Montaigne, Fielding are some of the most splendid names—writers who are filled with the glory of human life, pagans who love a good eater and a good hater, one who can give hard knocks and receive them, whose soul is untroubled with sentimentality, but who holds to whatsoever things are lovely and whatsoever things are of good repute, and can laugh a fine bass laugh at the puny miseries and absurdities of the world. Mr Meredith loves with an exceeding great love the rich brown earth, the mother of men, and all her stalwart sons and daughters: even the sham, the sentimentalist 'who fiddles harmonies on the sensual strings', he does not hate; he sees him as he is, a false and darkling son of his frank and joyous mother, to be pitied and even sympathized with. Like all great writers, he has a philosophy of life; without it life is an aimless game and fiction impossible, for there would be no more reason for one action than another; and it is a brave and strong philosophy, a philosophy of self-reliance and self-repression, but not for that of joylessness. Man is responsible for his own fate is the constant burden of his theory.

Life said, As thou hast carved me, such am I,

comes in one of his poems, in words curiously recalling one of Montaigne's *obiter dicta*, 'La vie n'est de soi ny bien ny mal, c'est la place du bien et du mal, selon que vous la leur faites';[1] and, again, in the novel before us now:

But the man alive, if but an inch alive, can so take his life in his clutch, that he does alter, cleanse, recast his deeds:—it is known: priests proclaim it, philosophers admit it.

But strongly marked and prominent as is this theory of life in all the novels, it is not misused. It is impossible to feel that any of them is written for the sake of expounding the theory—in other words, that Mr Meredith is ever guilty of writing a tract or a pamphlet in disguise. It is one of the rarest and most essential marks of literary greatness for a man with clearly defined and importunate beliefs to be able to avoid writing up to his theory instead of using his theory as the handmaid of his art; for, after all, theories and philosophies of life are merely the spectacles through which the great writer looks to test his characters. To Mr Meredith the story, the living acts of his characters, are everything, and it is just because of this that his philosophy, which supplies him with a reasoned method of explaining them, is so important. He uses his philosophy to explain his story; smaller writers invent their stories to expound their theories. It is interesting in this connection to notice how frequently he takes some actual character or some historical event as the subject of his novels: Mrs Norton, Ferdinand Lassalle, the Earl of Peterborough, are well-known examples; in *The Amazing Marriage*, too, the industry of journalists has already discovered several prototypes of the characters. But he is never content to relate their histories simply as they appeared to the world, interesting even superficially as many of them are; he explains seemingly incongruous events and apparently irrational people by making them live, and shows how, as interpreted by his philosophy of life, they enter into a rational and orderly scheme of human emotion and human intelligence. He is never content with Dame Gossip's 'endless ejaculations over the mystery of life, the inscrutability of character'. This is the method of the Greek dramatists: they chose subjects—hackneyed indeed to them and their audiences—about heroes who had done or had suffered more than falls to the share of common humanity, and interpreted them by the light of their philosophy, so that men could feel, not that they were no longer wonderful but that they were probable and real.

[1] *Essais* (1580), I, xx.

In almost all Mr Meredith's novels, but especially in the later ones, the first and most lasting impression is of the women. There is no other among English novelists who has created such a glorious company of beautiful, noble, and fearless women. They are a joy to think upon as they pass through the mind in their full-blooded strength and pride of body and of soul. They are no weaklings these, with Clara at their head, bending her proud neck to escape Sir Willoughby's kiss; and Rose, gentle and quiet, but strong enough to bear the beloved's shame; and Ottilia, grave and wise and beautiful; and even poor Lucy, most beautiful of all, with her fair ringlets framing her face on the river's bank. And great, too, is Carinthia Jane, the wife wedded in mockery, who bears bravely with the shame, and learns to live by suffering. She lives and breathes and looks wistfully beautiful from the very first, when she gives her heart to the brilliant young lord, full of ill-digested enthusiasms and vague aspirations, who takes her by storm in the riot of his first disappointed ambition. She loves him quietly, doggedly, trustfully, at first believing in him as in herself, and unable to conceive that he is unstable: with the simplicity of noble minds she thinks that there is some mistake which only wants explaining to restore the heat of his love to her. She squanders herself on 'my husband' only to be spurned by him. Almost by these two words and by the way Carinthia uses them, Mr Meredith suggests the whole extent of her splendid abandonment and half the tragedy contained in her betrayal. Then gradually, like a child, she awakens astonished at the world: she learns to forgive her husband, but forgiveness is the knell of love; and when he has at last forced her to carve out her life for herself, he finds there is no place in it for his petty desires and wastrel, half-begotten schemes. But strong as Carinthia becomes, and unyielding to the husband she at last sees through, she never grows hard and unwomanly; indeed, there is no one but Mr Meredith who could maintain as he does our sympathies for Carinthia in the final development of her character.

But hardly less remarkable than the character of Carinthia is that of her husband the Earl of Fleetwood. Pitilessly as he forces himself on to his own doom by his obstinacy and his fear of personal humiliation, the charm of the man is never lost sight of. He is always meaning well, and he has a soul above his destiny, but he has not the strength of mind to recall his errors; he is a delightful companion, generous if not prodigal, eager to hear the thoughts of thinkers and quick to seize them—nay, not unequipped with wise thoughts of his own. He is a true nobleman in manner, and only loses his nobility in the savagery of disappointed passion; and he can do a fine act unostentatiously and well. But he has no plan, and so he fails; his actions are all in jerks and impulses, so he is always seeking rest, and never finds it till his 'living suicide' in the monastery. Thus some of the finest thoughts in the book are his, even though, unstable as water, he does not pursue them.

If there were space, one might dwell on the beauty of the characters of Madge, Carinthia's faithful maid, and of Gower Woodseer, the itinerant philosopher of nature; but a word must be spared for the art with which Mr Meredith introduces a tributary character in the story, and with a word or two paints her whole life and influence. Rebecca Wythain, the first wife of the man whom Carinthia afterwards marries, thus describes herself to Carinthia:

[Quotes xxix, from ' "Let me say in my turn" ' to 'You abound in power to give'.]

It were, however, to be wished that the strong, earnest men of whom Mr Meredith is so fond—like Vernon Whitford, Mr Redworth (who kept 'a dungeon-vault for feelings that should not be suffered to cry abroad, and into this oubliette he cast them, letting them feed as they might or perish'), and Owain Wythain [sic] in this book—were not quite so inarticulate in their strength. They win admiration, it is true, but they give the impression of being hard, which they are not meant to be, and leave the reader cold. However, in this case Mr Wythain [sic] has a very slight effect on the story.

As to style, The Amazing Marriage contains none of that too obvious pirouetting on the point of an epigram which mars some of the other novels. Mr Meredith's style is not, as a rule, so obscure as it is often represented to be: it is undoubtedly over elaborate, but it is with the elaboration of one who refuses to clothe great thoughts in slipshod language, and it is a notable fact that, although all his characters certainly talk with more subtlety of phrase and thought than is common in real life, there is never any possibility of mistaking them for one another or of imagining the author to be talking through them. The artificiality of style never interferes with the dramatization of the characters. On the other hand, though there are some beautiful passages in this book, especially in the wonderful description of Carinthia and her brother's first walk, such exquisite bits of writing as are common in Richard Feverel and Harry Richmond are not to be found here.

108. Alice Meynell, *Illustrated London News*

cvii, 14 December 1895

For Alice Meynell see above, No. 68, headnote.

This brilliant and painful book has such a vitality as nothing can hinder, or, rather, such a vitality as all things serve. It is a flame to which all that might have hindered does but minister. There is no intricacy, there is no labour, there is no accumulation that does not pass up into that flame of life and make it more swift and erect. Artificial words—and Mr Meredith's are full of extreme artifice—must needs have made a lesser life than the life of his work to languish and pause. This vitality is the chief thing. Intellect, beauty, drama, hesitating narrative, turns and returns of thought—all pass into the springing and beating flame. As for the dramatic mental action of the story, readers of *The Egoist* are aware of the way in which a single sentence is made in this author's pages to reflect, to face itself, to reply; and the words at the same time are full of images. You might liken the phrase to a stream flowing westward and taking the colours of the westward aspect, while the innumerable little waves beat backwards and reflect the spaces of the upper sky, the chill blue of the east, the shadows of the forest, and the needles of the early stars; all flies one way, but with a score of aspects as it flies. Or, again, the thought of the thinker and the speaker in his drama of passions seems to reflect itself like a mirror that faces a mirror. You look and know not whether you see a certain thing reflected directly or for the third time; nor how many times, visibly, the shuttlecock of thought is returned by opposing shocks. The men and women of the book stand so, considering; and the author's record has the same kind of multiplicity. The reflection of mirrors takes no time, the reflection of motives little, the narrative more; but the suggestion, at least, of instantaneousness is given in the long phrase that includes so many actions of the mind.

Seldom has a more poignant story been told, for the pathos is the deliberations between life and death by the social laughter of the ignoble, but Mr Meredith himself distresses us by the importunate injustice of this perpetual commentary. Was London, indeed, in the years between Byron and the first railway, so intent upon one story, and so foolishly unkind? And was it so impossible for anyone to be unconscious of the clamour, but that a passionate novelist must pause to catch its echoes continually? He hurts us effectually enough.

Carinthia, who is one of the greatest women of Mr Meredith's invention, is the daughter of a Beauty whose story is told with the levity of retrospection in the Prologue. For love of an Old Buccaneer, that Beauty had thrown her word of honour to the winds and had fled from her husband, who was a fool, to make, in time, a pious wife to a wise man. She and her mate die broken-hearted—the one for grief at her son's shame of her story, the other for the loss of her. Their daughter is a mountain maid, who is nothing at the outset but loyal and simple, with all the divine promises, closed in those two qualities in an implicit state, to be kept in time. To her in her first ball-room the amazing marriage is proposed by Lord Fleetwood, the richest nobleman of a day when nobleman was a word in use—a young tyrant, with England, philosophy, the ring, the racecourse, a company of gamblers, all circling round his purse and his patronage. One thing he cannot have—the hand of Henrietta, who has given her rather corruptible heart to Carinthia's brother. In the extravagance of his disappointment Lord Fleetwood asks Carinthia, as an incident of the dance, to be his wife. It is nothing incredible to her, and she accepts him. He lets time pass, absents himself, and finally asks her, by a message intended to win him his freedom, whether she means to bind him to his engagement. The question is passed on to her, but not the insult; and she simply replies 'Yes', and marries him. Lord Fleetwood thinks himself authorized to avenge himself—to avenge men, women, liberty, poetry, romance, and love—upon a creature so insensitive.

And never was anything devised more over-whelmingly painful than the young bride's wedding day on the box seat of her lord's coach. He takes her to a prize-fight (a fine passage of the author's work, but the fine passages are continuous), drives away to a ball, and leaves her at an inn. There is a secret heart of love in the bitter story, but it is only by degrees that the last grief of the gentle and indignant bride is told. He leaves her again—for ever, as it proves. She lies forsaken at the country inn, then flies to her maid's little home in a Whitechapel street. And the Whitechapel Countess's pursuit of her husband becomes the theme of the not quite credible, not quite important gossip in the

West, and of broad-sheet ballads in the East. Carinthia is wise, warlike, good, selfless, simple when her ignorance is gone, and loyal after her illusions. Through all the slow changes of her fate she holds on, grave after her agony, until it is her lord who would give much more than life for leave to woo her whom he had once won. But it is too late. And Mr Meredith uses accident cruelly, as fate does, to make the lateness fatal. It is not by a true refusal that Carinthia finally rejects her husband. He had done two half-hearted evil things, and never was able to tell her that he was half innocent; and she sails away when he is hurrying to the shore and returns when he is a Carthusian—an impossible Carthusian. It is an amazing book; and yet the word amazing is wrong enough. In order to express surprise we use a word which would mean that we are stupefied; whereas Mr Meredith's work almost confers genius.

109. Unsigned review, *Saturday Review*

lxxx, 21 December 1895

Lord Ormont and His Aminta had, to the sense of some of us, a touch of autumn. There were whispers that Mr George Meredith was growing old. But here is the dispelling of such doubts, a book fit to stand beside anything that he has ever written. Of his previous work it is most like the *Egoist*. Lord Fleetwood, the central figure, is a wealthy young nobleman, a monster of aristocratic self-respect, 'the slave of his word', surrounded by a group of toadies, yet anxious to do his duty by the country so far as a busy and somewhat preoccupied country will permit, encourager of field sports, and especially of the noble art. But he has far finer possibilities in him than the Egoist, and carries us at last altogether out of comedy. He begins magnificently with a fine ambition to be the idol of his countrymen and countrywomen and perishes at last 'of his austerities', Brother Russett in a mountain monastery. The other party to the marriage is another of Mr Meredith's triumphant androgynes, a wonderful girl with a man's heart, born and bred in the remoteness of the Carinthian mountains, flung suddenly thence to be nursed, married, hated, discarded, insulted, and finally (too late) loved by the imperial Fleetwood. And set about these two are the *eyes*, the wonderful chorus of characters which Mr Meredith uses so persistently and with such amazing effect. The difficulty and peculiar individuality of his style lie not so much in his phrasing, distinctive though it is, as in his method of telling his story indirectly, through the means of puppet proxies. It is in her failure to understand this, in her endeavour to suggest Meredith by mere verbal inversions and obscurities that 'John Oliver Hobbes' shows the insufficiency of her study of her master.[1] Take, for instance, the fight upon the Haslemere Punch Bowl in the vivid short story of three chapters which forms the introduction to the narrative. 'Dame Gossip' asks: 'Who then was the gentleman who stopped the chariot with his three mounted attendants, on the road to the sea, on the heath by the Great Punch Bowl'? 'Countess Fanny must have known him, and not once did she open her mouth to breathe his name. Yet she had no objection to talk of the adventure, and tell how. . . .' And so on for a vivid paragraph. Then, 'Simon Fettle was a plain, kindly creature, without a thought of malice, who kept his master's accounts. He fired the first shot at the foremost man, he relates, . . .' and so we go on for a space, hearing more of the business from Simon Fettle. Then comes a wonderful miniature of Charles Dumps, the postillion, who made a little fortune talking about the business, but contradicted himself sadly. 'Yet we have the doctor of the village of Ipley, Dr Cawthorne, a noted botanist, assuring us . . .'

It is this perpetual shifting of the standpoint that limits Mr Meredith's public. As a method of narrating pure incident, as in this case, it is certainly not a little tiresome to many a well-meaning reader. But where it comes in with a superlative success is in such an employment as the analysis of the effect of Carinthia, who is by common standards a plain girl, upon Fleetwood. We have among the chorus one Woodseer, a character remarkably suggestive of the Stevenson of the Overland Voyage, a phrase-maker with a note-book. It is he calls her, 'A beautiful Gorgon—a haggard Venus'. He writes again, 'a painting look, a look of beaten flame; a look of one who has run, and at last beholds'. Woodseer himself, we see—to the black finger nails—through the unfriendly comments of Sir Meeson Corby. He follows us through the book, to marry at last the girl Madge, who is there as exponent of all the feminine sympathy, the activity and usefulness of Carinthia. Besides

[1] The pseudonym of Pearl Mary Teresa Craigie (1867–1906), author of fifteen volumes of novels and tales between 1891 and 1906.

Woodseer's memoranda we have fluttering on the edge of the tale, the pages of the book Carinthia's father wrote long ago (only a few copies extant) of 'Maxims for Men'. Out of it all, out of her effect on Dame Gossip, on Woodseer, on Madge, on Fleetwood, and on Lady Arpington, one conceives the woman, and how living she is! So blurred at the outline she has atmosphere, perspective—you turn to some explicit impersonal writer, and behold sheet-tin as men walking! Plausible and well coloured perhaps from the one right point of view, but even from that, harsh of contour, and from elsewhere, *showing the edge*.

There is no one right method of telling a story—only the preposterous Unknown of *How to Write Fiction* believes that. But for the presentation of a human being, at least, this artifice of seeing through the eyes of characters is supremely effective. Otherwise you can have only the author's view. The theory of a scientific, an impersonal standpoint, is fallacious. The really logical scientific method would be to deal with Carinthia as so many pounds of bone, muscle, blood, and flesh, and state her velocity, orientation, latitude and longitude, from moment to moment. But a soul is determined by its surfaces of contact with other souls. It may be Mr Meredith sometimes carries his indirect method to excess, and puzzles a decent public, nourished on good healthy, straightforward marionettes. But we can find it in us to return thanks even for his excesses. And assuredly this book is as fine, and vigorous, and subtle as anything he has ever written.

110. Unsigned review, *Pall Mall Gazette*

lxi, 23 December 1895

This is perhaps not a book that whoso runs may read, but at least you can read it sitting. We have sat ourselves down to it each time with fresher satisfaction, and risen with greater reluctance. It takes us back to the day of Mr Meredith's early and greatest books, a pleasant stride into a past whose fleeting we had feared irrevocable; for it can stand side by side with the best of them, and not be ashamed. Throughout the whole there is strength of colour and movement, rich as a concert of changing hues; a whirl, a haze, a maze of moving form and influence, that the eye and brain strive half in vain to follow. And yet with love and a trifle of patience that following can be done, and most rewardingly. It is like a battle or procession picture of some old Uccello with intricate, inextricable warriors and horses and trappings and pomegranates, all woven into a patterned confusion with such infinite care and unerring precision of perspective, that no matter where you take your stand, the very feet of the fallen horsemen seem to face and follow you with an almost unearthly persistence.

The first part of the book is perhaps the most entirely satisfactory. The prologue is lit with charm and delicacy. Countess Fanny flashes dancingly into view, and dies away with a pathetic grace; the Old Buccaneer draws and keeps an affectionate fellow-feeling to the end, in spite of his preposterous age, despite too his 'Maxims for Men', perpetually propounded, but seldom to the point. Our short friendship with them leaves us warmed and ready for the welcoming of their offspring, Carinthia, 'saint and martyr', and Chillon Switzer Kirby Levellier (the name!), her adored, but wholly not adorable brother. The opening chapters. 'Farewell to an old home' and 'Mountain walk in mist and sunshine', in which these two make their first appearance are beyond praise. The gentleness, the mastery, and the perfect beauty of expression are a gift and a possession for ever, for which we would do homage on our knees; and they make it the more impossible to tolerate Mr Smalley's unworthy attack in an American newspaper on Mr Meredith's obscurities.[1] The occasional ruggedness, obscurity, even distortion of his style, are indeed undoubted, and we should be the last to deny, or to do other than deplore it; but, like Browning as he is in this, so also like Browning does he seem at times to rise superlatively master of both style and self and of the whole great seething world. As some great forest bird winging through branches into sunlight, he bursts upon us moment by moment, with a wonder, a splendour of flight and sometimes song, that are unapproachable except by God's greatest. And to him that loveth much shall much be forgiven.

We confess, indeed, that with his own darling Dame Gossip, whose talent for embroidery and for irrelevant criticism is charming, we occasionally work ourselves up 'to a grey squall in detestation of

---

[1] 'George Meredith's Bad English', a rather tasteless attack by George Washington Smalley (1833–1916), appeared in *New York Herald*, 1 September 1895, section 4, page 7.

imagerial epigrams'; and sometimes also draw a laboured breath at the coining of such adjectives as 'freshish', 'strung-wire'. But this occurs with comparative infrequency; never have his words been so instant to their meaning, so compelling or so pregnant. That which on the whole is most to be regretted is an increasing tendency to shirk the crucial scenes and episodes of the story, and to vouchsafe but the vaguest of allusions and sketchiest of accounts, introduced into the casual talk or letters of outsiders. We like a little mystery, and, notably in these days of reeking realism, we are grateful for a little reticence; but both these virtues may be carried too far. Take, for example, the scene of the Earl of Fleetwood's proposal to Carinthia—the pivot upon which turn all the whirlings of 'this funny whirly world'. Nothing of it transpires, except in the most roundabout and fleeting way, in a letter from Henrietta to her 'plighted' Chillon. It therefore remains throughout the whole story unconvincing and unreal, a canopy of doubtfulness from which the heroine never quite succeeds in emerging. While as to the appearance of the infant heir—a 'miracle baby', a wonder child indeed —it must, if we are to judge from all accorded lights, have been a deeply interesting case of spontaneous generation; and the likeness to the erring earl, who had to the best of our knowledge parted from his bride at the coach wheel on the wedding day, a very striking instance not of throw-back but of throw-forward, that should at once arrest the attention of every scientific inquirer. There is, indeed, an elusive reference to ladders, intended presumably to assist the jibbing intellect, but it is a feeble and a mocking aid.

We will but indicate the plot. The Earl of Fleetwood (Mr Meredith is the only writer of this generation who can be thus redolent of titles without vulgarity) meets in a German ball-room Carinthia Kirby, an innocent Amazonian maid, with a simplicity born of the mountains. He succumbs, we gather, or rather, perhaps, proposes without succumbing, and is accepted on the spot; retires then to Wales in a longing to forget the untoward incident, but is held to his word by the all-trusting ignorance of the girl, and the, perhaps, mercenary firmness of her friends. So the marriage takes place with the amazing results that form the ground tone of the book—results that seem to us to shed about equal blame on all concerned, and so to present a more life-like reading of earth's stories than we are accustomed to expect.

If we take the characters of the book separately to consider and analyze, Carinthia naturally comes first; but too much time must not be wasted upon her, as our readers will already have learnt their duty

towards this 'Shakspearian' woman in the recent glowing column of
our beloved Autolycus.[1] We think, indeed, that his well-known
partiality for ladies has a little affected his estimate of her personality, in
opposition to that of her wrong-headed but surely retrievable husband.
We ourselves are not wholly in love with her, not as much perhaps
as with some of the older Meredithian heroines. Still, she is undoubtedly
full of power and picturesqueness and pathos—a very present personage;
and at that first portraying of her, standing among the 'slim and
straight-grown flocks of naked purple crocuses in bud and blow', with
'her look of beaten flame: a look of one who has run and at last beholds',
we catch our breath with a new joy. What spoils our sympathy and
loses our love is the tactlessness that she shows—the heavy hand and
unsensitive eye—on the coach and after, especially in her reiterated
parrot cry of 'It is my husband'; and still more the hardness that she so
fatally keeps up to the end towards the sinning but sorry father of her
child. Her relations with Owain are also tiresome and a shade unworthy;
for his greatest merit was admittedly that of being a 'hearty simpleton',
and this preference of him seems too severe a straining of the supremacy
of models over intellect.

In the Earl himself we find an enigmatic, inconsequent personality
that irritates while attracting us. His hasty, unconsidered leap towards
a new-found poetic realization awakens our sympathies; and they are
with him still in his equally hasty backward leap of dawning distrust.
At his subsequent behaviour they do indeed falter and fall behind, but
the last scenes whip them up again, and they die only with his death.
Henrietta, sister-in-law and rival, is in some ways the most alluring of
all the portraits; to be on letter-writing terms with her would add a
new pleasure to life. Countess Livia, too, demands admiration: 'a most
heavenly lady, composed of day and night in her colouring', and in her
character also, we fear. Madge the maid and Gower Woodseer are the
two actors of the piece that we cannot away with. Madge indeed is in
herself a delicious woman, but it is impossible to believe that after so
long a period of devotion and self-sacrifice to the splendidly drunk and
human prize-fighter Kit Ines, she would ever have sunk to marriage
with a prig and bore so consummate as the Earl's friend and protégé
turns out to be. For a prig and a bore Gower Woodseer undoubtedly
is; and not the less must this be said, but rather the more, that he might
be intended as a presentment of a great erratic lovable genius, who has
of late gone down into silence.

[1] That is, Alice Meynell, whose column in *Pall Mall Gazette* bore this signature.

For a last word, this book is undoubtedly a masterpiece by a master hand. Mr Meredith is easily first of our living English authors, and among the highest of all time his rank is high. He stands towering above his contemporaries, distinguished by an especial power of delicate, intricate analysis; of a passionate energy of imagination; of a style that grips and holds the mind; of a subtle sense of humour; of a lightly-poising mockery; and of a romantic rare refinement of attitude towards the world that is his and ours alike, truly, but in how different and humbling a degree of possession!

111. Unsigned review, *Bookman*

x, January 1896

Mr Meredith's latest story does not lose, gains rather, if read in bits. This is not all dispraise, for it means the book is good all through, that each portion will somehow reward you. Except for one man's character, and even that is so complex and contradictory that its understanding can best be reached by stages, with pauses between, there is nothing that needs to be viewed as a whole. The first chapters are magnificent, and we are not alone, possibly, in feeling disappointment that the marriage of the Old Buccaneer and Countess Fanny was not the amazing one chosen for the serious story. There you have a quick, dashing romance. After it you settle down to one that needs much explanation. The plan, however, is excellent. You hear the curious tale now from Fleetwood's side, now from his wife's, now as amusingly travestied by Dame Gossip. Then, in no other story has Mr Meredith let loose more of his lyrical faculty. His spirits, too, are high; his humour, save where his heroine is concerned, alert. His sketches of the parasites that flocked round Fleetwood are inimitable. And his narrative powers are here and there at their liveliest. But these powers do not wait on our sentimentalities, for unquestionably the strongest portion of the book is that ghastly marriage scene, the furious drive of the wrathful bridegroom and his abject bride, and his fiendish entertainment of her at a prize-fight.

Fleetwood draws away our best attention from the other characters. The curious mixture of brains and brutality, of superfine instincts and caddishness, of black moods and conventional elegance, in the young spoiled millionaire nobleman, is treated by a master hand. He is only not so perfectly successful as the Egoist, because he is infinitely more complex and difficult for us to take in. Readers, it should ever be remembered, make one of the conditions of a writer's success. With the wandering scholar of Nature who fascinates us in the beginning, he is in imperfect sympathy. Woodseer settles down to domesticity prematurely; there were further developments in his history, for certain. Perhaps we seldom accept Mr Meredith's characters as inevitably what he makes them. Harry Richmond's father and Sir Willoughby, of course, are exceptions. Is this a lack in them, or a proof of strong human interest, prompting us to interfere with their opinions and careers as we like to do with those of our flesh and blood neighbours? Something of both. For instance, when our sympathies are being tossed to and fro between Fleetwood and his wife, we do not say, at one black point, Yes here he was a brute; Mr Meredith was creating a brute. On the contrary, we grow indignant, and say it is against nature, which means against our desires. So with Carinthia—which brings us to an interesting point.

Mr Meredith has perhaps his warmest admirers among women. Some of them hold him to be their best interpreter. Well, he cherishes a wealth of kindly feeling towards them, and he has a rare sense of justice, and of chivalry. But his observations of them are not very wide. Only one or two types does he deeply understand. And then there is that crying offence of his—his forgiveness of Diana's meanness. He may go on multiplying his types of men. Long ago he came to the end of his women. We like his Amazons as a rule. They are excellent comrades. And at the verbal description of this one, Carinthia, we kindle. 'Living faces, if they're to show the soul, which is the star on the peak of beauty, must lend themselves to commotion. Nature does it in a breezy tree or over ruffled waters. Repose has never such splendid reach as animation—I mean in the living face. Artists prefer repose. Only nature can express the uttermost beauty with her gathering and tuning of discords. Well, your mistress has that beauty'. Again, from Woodseer's notebook, 'From minute to minute she is the rock that loses the sun at night and reddens in the morning'. But the Carinthia that plays an active part is a bore. In Fleetwood's most brutal moments we have a sneaking sympathy for him; she had the worst fault to a quick spirit like his—obtuseness. Life had to bore holes with a pickaxe to let understanding into her. She goes about, in the beginning at least, with muffled hands and veiled eyes, and cannot see how her weary quotations of her father, and her clawing, abject manners, rile the man she has bestowed her affection on. The spirit of humour does not breathe in her or on her. But she might be excellent, we own, as Mademoiselle de Levellier, fighting in Spain with the Carlists.

The book makes one bristle here and there, but it is the best work Mr Meredith has given us since *Diana of the Crossways*, and if without the charm of that it is also without its alienating feature. And it reveals Mr Meredith's sympathies more openly than almost anything else in his prose. He is the Welshman here, and Wales may be proud to claim *The Amazing Marriage*. Great nonsense is often talked in connection with the Celtic Renascence. But Mr Meredith has much of interest to say concerning face characteristics, and one truth, which is almost a discovery, finely uttered:

Now, to the Cymry and to the pure Kelt, the past is at their elbows, continually. The past of their lives has lost neither face nor voice behind the shroud; nor are the passions of the flesh, nor is the animate soul, wanting to it. Other races forfeit infancy, forfeit youth and manhood with their progression to the wisdom age may bestow. These have each stage always alive, quick at a word, a scent, a sound, to conjure up scenes in spirit and in flame. Historically, they still march with Cadwallader, with Llewellyn, with Glendower; sing with Aneurin, Talliesin, old Llywarch; individually, they are in the heart of the injury done them thirty years back, or thrilling to the glorious deed which strikes an empty buckler for most of the sons of Time. An old sea rises in them, rolling no phantom billows to break to spray against existing rocks of the shore.

112. W. E. Garrett Fisher, from a review in the *Academy*

xlix, 11 January 1896

William Edward Garrett Fisher (d. unknown) also wrote *The Transvaal and the Boers* (1896).

There are certain books which are independent of contemporary criticism, because they are above it. Most of the works that come in the way of the reviewer, while they may move his admiration, his wrath, or his weariness, are yet obviously enough the production of men of like passions with himself, and so fair game for the young, light-hearted masters of the pen. It is only in a rare volume here and there that one has the chance to encounter the large utterance of the early gods, and to approach a book of such transcendent power, sympathy, and insight that in its presence criticism seems to be an impertinence, while the mere reading of it is a liberal education in the art of life. And when one has that happiness in the present generation, it is a safe wager that twice out of three times the name on the title-page will be that of Mr George Meredith.

The Amazing Marriage affords no exception to this rule. There is only one man living who could criticize it adequately, and he, as it happens, wrote it. The ordinary critic has to turn 'descriptive reporter' for the nonce. Then he finds that it is, like almost all Mr Meredith's books, devoted to the narration of an episode

> In that great duel of Sex, that ancient strife,
> Which is the very central fact of life.[1]

The episode in question reminds one in certain respects of *Diana of the Crossways* and of *Lord Ormont and His Aminta*. The 'central fact' of it is the development of a woman's character by reason of the ill-usage that she experiences from the man who should have loved her. Like

[1] Untraced.

447

Browning, Mr Meredith is chiefly interested, here as in almost all his works, in 'the development of a soul'. He might say, with Keats, to his reader, 'Call the world, if you please, 'the Vale of Soul-making'. Then you will find out the use of the world'.[1] So we are invited by his incomparable art to consider the progress in soul of a man and woman, Lord Fleetwood and Carinthia Jane Kirby, under the burning sunshine and heavy showers of life. Carinthia herself, the heroine of 'the amazing marriage', is one more of those noble pieces of portraiture such as no English novelist before Mr Meredith has ever achieved. 'She was a warrior woman, Life her sword, Death her target, never to be put to shame, unconquerable'. This sense of seriousness and strength, her hereditary right, is the keynote of her story. It fell to her lot, as most readers now know, to be mated with one of the young men who have not learnt 'that life is no longer a game when they have a woman for partner in the match'. Lord Fleetwood 'was born with suspicion of the sex. Poetry decorated women, he said, to lime and drag men in the foulest ruts of prose'. He cast eye on Carinthia out of spite at the insensibility of 'the golden Riette', and married her but to 'fling the world at her', as Lord Ormont in a different spirit had done with Aminta. But Carinthia was no meek-spirited Griselda to play at patience, nor yet one of 'the inexplicable sex' whose action under insult can never be predicted. She is a daughter of the mountains as well as of the Old Buccaneer, dowered with the freshness, sincerity, and courage that come from such a double parentage. Hence arises a noble opportunity for the treatment, in Mr Meredith's best style, of Carinthia's growth from curious, impressionable girlhood into noble, steel-fibred womanhood. Carinthia's figure must be placed loftily among the many portraits of 'fair and desirable women' that Mr Meredith's creative brain and subtly shaping hand have already given to a grateful world.

The other striking creation in the book is the character of Lord Fleetwood. This gentleman is compact of those nice shades and subtle elements that Mr Meredith mingles in so masterly a fashion. Like Sir Willoughby and Wilfred Pole, with both of whom he has a touch in common, Lord Fleetwood is a captivating though by no means a great man. His true nature may be easily guessed from his two conflicting, but equally genuine, friendships, for the Catholic Lord Feltre, and the humanist Gower Woodseer. He is, you are told repeatedly, 'the wealthiest nobleman in all England'. 'He is accustomed to buy men and

---

[1] Letter to George and Georgiana Keats, 14 February–3 May 1819.

women', urges Riette, in her fine 'lyrical cry' at the end of the book. *There* is the weak spot—the touch of the 'beast of prey'. You see that he has noble instincts by his sincere affection for Woodseer, who brings him into contact with the work-a-day world of the brown earth; by his no less sincere leaning to Feltre, Woodseer's antipathetic opposite, who points an ascetic finger to the Church. But the training in luxury, the flattering of Sir Pandarus, have spoilt it all; and he comes in contact with the noblest of women only to fulfil his and her destiny by dashing her aside and learning her worthiness too late. Feltre and Woodseer, his foils, are comparatively simple. The complexity of Lord Fleetwood's character is fascinating in the extreme.

The style of the book is beyond all praise. Mr Meredith at one time (for it is permitted to see spots even on the sun) showed a tendency to develop certain of those mannerisms which come almost inevitably with the years to a great master of language. In his two latest books he has achieved the feat that proved too much for Browning or Mr Ruskin, Carlyle or Thackeray, and has returned to the simplicity of his earlier manner, touched with a depth of thought and a mellowness of sympathy that only the ripening years can be supposed to bring. There is nothing here quite in the glorious poetic style of *Ferdinand and Miranda* or *By Wilming Weir*, but there is at least one chapter that will linger as fondly in the mind's ear as either of those perfect idylls of youth. One quotation from it must be made for affection, if not to give an idea of the whole. Carinthia and her brother have just left their Tyrol home for the last time.

[Quotes v, from 'She did not look back' to 'out of the chamber of death'.]

This 'intervolving' of the landscape with the mind of a person is peculiarly charactersitic of Mr Meredith, as it is of serious life.

The background in which the main plot is set argues an opulence of fancy and a ripe knowledge of humanity to which only the very greatest of our writers ever rise. One especially recalls the figures of 'the golden Riette', the laughing, light-hearted beauty whose love for Chillon is the only element of gravity in her nature; of the Countess Livia, who took excitement 'as the nymph of the stream her native wave, and swam on the flood with expansive languor, happy to have the master passions about her'; of the girl Madge, who 'could be twisted to laugh at herself, just a little. Now the young woman who can do that has already jumped the hedge into the high road of philosophy, and may

449

become a philosopher's mate in its by-ways, where the minute dis-coveries are the notable treasures'. All the Fleetwood circle are sketched with the hand of a master. But perhaps the most remarkable of all the minor characters is that of the roving philosopher, Gower Woodseer, who shares the taste of Vernon Whitford for country walks and plain speaking, but has a fund of wit and philosophy that are all his own, though some have curiously taken for granted that they must be copied from a real human being whose similar possessions are now known to all of us. Woodseer's social creed, indeed, is happily expressed in a song of Mr Stevenson's that has just been published:

> Give to me the life I love,
>   Let the lave go by me,
> Give the jolly heaven above,
>   And the by-way nigh me.
> Bed in the bush with stars to see,
> Bread I dip in the river—
> There's the life for a man like me,
>   There's the life for ever![1]

The spirit of *An Apology for Idlers* and *Travels with a Donkey*, too, is strong in Woodseer.

'I put on my hat one day,' he says, 'and walked into the country. My college fellows were hawkers, tinkers, tramps and ploughmen, choughs and crows. A volume of our poets and a history of philosophy composed my library. I had hardly any money, so I learnt how to idle inexpensively—a good first lesson. We're at the bottom of the world when we take to the road; we see men as they were in the beginning—not so eager for harness till they get acquainted with hunger, as I did, and studied to myself the old animal having his head pushed into the collar to earn a feed of corn.'

Mr Stevenson has more than once put on record his immense and laudable admiration for the author of *The Egoist*; and this sketch is a new proof, if one were needed, of the essential sympathy that existed between the minds of the greater writer and the lesser. Mr Meredith might have been our earlier Stevenson, if he had not been our later Shakspere. I use the phrase advisedly. Exaggeration, either of praise or blame, is a hateful thing, although it is far too common nowadays. But when one casts back through our literature for a parallel to the author of *Richard Feverel* and *The Egoist*, *Rhoda Fleming* and *Sandra Belloni*, where is one to find it save in the author of *As You Like It* and *Hamlet* and *King*

---

[1] 'The Vagabond', st. 1; *Songs of Travel* (1896), i.

Lear? At any rate, without pushing the parallel askew, one may safely assert that no man since Shakspere has created such fair, human, and red-blooded women as Mr Meredith. Warm-hearted Sandra, brave Rose Jocelyn, lively Diana, enchanting Peggy Waring, [*sic*] peerless Clara Middleton, grave-eyed Aminta—do not the very names hold out a promise of delight never to be unfulfilled for the wise reader? So, too, Bessy Berry, the Countess, that Irishwoman, Mrs Chump, and Mrs Pagnell, who rhymed with spaniel, testify to the possession of that kindly and lambent humour which makes a perennial joy out of the most common-place of things. Carinthia herself is fully worthy to take place beside the finest of these 'Shaksperian women', as someone has happily called them. And the two worthy volumes in which her sober and simple, yet powerful, story is unfolded with such admirable skill are a fresh and most welcome contribution to that great Handbook of Humanity which is Mr Meredith's supremely valuable gift to the literature of the world.

113. J. A. Noble, *Spectator*

lxxvi, January 1896

For J. A. Noble see above, No. 92, headnote.

It is always with a sense of mental confusion and trepidation, not allayed by gleams of faint disturbing hope, that we open a new book by Mr George Meredith. We have of late years been often assured—not only by irresponsible young critics, but by various men who speak with authority—that Mr Meredith is a great novelist; and from our consciousness of a personal conviction that he is simply a novelist whose books contain a few isolated great things, is born two discordant temptations—the temptation to shout in a voice of shrill dogmatism, or to whisper in accents of quavering self-distrust. Our only encouragement to rely upon our own instincts is provided by the fact that where we are today there were all the critics some ten years ago. Mr Meredith's warmest eulogists will allow that the novels on which his claim to greatness must be based had been published prior to 1885, but up to that year no suspicion of his supremacy had visited either the public or the critics. Indeed, the public, naturally but unwisely, ignored Mr Meredith altogether, and his critics agreed that he was a writer of considerable intellectual grip, with very remarkable literary gifts, but that as a novelist he was so very unequal and at times so laboriously ineffective that it was all but impossible to place him. This is certainly the view that is suggested by his recent performances, and especially by *The Amazing Marriage*. It is rich in shrewd observation, in wise reflection, in witty epigram—indeed Mr Meredith's wit is his most distinctive endowment—and there are just a few scenes which have a certain dramatic flavour; but in the qualities which make a great work of fiction recognizable as a creative organism, it is even conspicuously deficient. The story—if story it can be called—has just three landmarks, the marriage itself, which is 'amazing' only in virtue of the fact that Lord Fleetwood deserts his wife almost immediately after the ceremony, the birth of a mysterious and unaccountable baby, and the final retirement of the incredible husband into a monastery. In the intervals a number of people pop in and out, or hold the stage for a time, with the apparent purpose of providing material for Mr Meredith's Meredithisms of epigram or paradox; for they are bodiless phantoms which give us no feeling of flesh and blood. Of course there are passages in the novel which arrest and startle, which make the intellect tingle with a prickly tingling as of a galvanic current; there are even passages which charm —witness that early chapter, 'A Mountain Walk in Mist and Sunshine' —but the book as a whole is terribly hard reading for the natural man. Of course it will be haughtily said by the Meredithians that Mr Meredith does not write for the natural man, that his caviare is not intended to appeal to the palate of 'the general'; but in this case, what of the claim to greatness? Homer, Dante, Shakespeare, and Cervantes appealed to a world, not to a côterie; but the mention of such names as these is cruel to Mr Meredith, so we will simply note the fact that his contemporary, Thackeray—a novelist of genius if ever there was one—made himself heard with delight by the ratepayer in Suburbia, as well as by the lounger at the literary clubs. Mr Meredith might have had a place beside Thackeray; he has chosen a place beside Lyly, and only the intellectual vigour of much of his work will prevent the new Euphuism—a great literary nuisance it is!—from being as short-lived as the old.

114. J. M. Robertson on Meredith's 'preciosity'

1897

John Mackinnon Robertson (1856–1933), critic and biographer, whose works included *Walt Whitman, Poet and Democrat* (1884), *Criticism* (1902–3), *Browning and Tennyson as Teachers* (1903). In the first part of his article, not reproduced here, Robertson establishes his definition of 'preciosity', describes the conditions under which it is found and briefly discusses the work of Carlyle, Browning, Pater and Swinburne. The article appeared in *Yellow Book*, xiii, April 1897.

VII

Whatever dispute there may be over the foregoing criticisms, there can be none, I think, over the judgment that Mr Meredith's style is the most pronounced outbreak of preciosity in modern English literature. There, if ever, we may allow ourselves a quasi-Pantagruelian protest. It is indeed impossible for a reader who respects Mr Meredith's genius to read him—or at least his later works—without irritation at his extraordinary ill-usage of language. Old admirers, going back to his earlier works, never free from the sin of preciosity, recognise that there has been an almost continuous deterioration—the fatal law of all purposive preciosity. In the earlier novels there were at times signal beauties of phrase, sentences in which the strain towards utterance was transmuted into fire and radiance, sentences of the fine poet who underlay and even now underlies that ever-thickening crust of preciosity and verbal affectation. Even in *One of Our Conquerors* there seemed, to the tolerant sense, to be still some gleams of the old flame, flashing at long intervals through the scoriæ of unsmelted speech. But in *Lord Ormont and His Aminta* neither patience nor despair can discover in whole chapters aught but the lava and cinders of language. In mere tortuosity the

453

writing is not worse; it could not well be; but now, after the first few chapters, one has given up hope, and instead of desperately construing endless paragraphs of gritty perversity one lightly skips every mound in the path, content to follow the movement of a striking story behind a style that in itself has become a mere affliction. With the exception of Zola's *La Terre*—hard reading for a different reason—*One of Our Conquerors* was the hardest novel to read that I ever met with; but I have found *Lord Ormont and His Aminta* easy enough. After a few chapters I no longer sought to read Mr Meredith. I made a hand-to-mouth *précis* of nearly every page, and soon got over the ground, only pausing at times to reassure myself that all was ill.

Hardly once, so far as I have read, do we find an important sentence really well written; never a paragraph; for the perpetual grimace of expression, twisting the face of speech into every shape but those of beauty and repose, is in no sense admirable. Simple statements, normal reflections, are packed into the semblance of inspired and brilliant aphorisms. As thus:

That great couchant dragon of the devouring jaws and the withering breath, known as our London world, was in expectation of an excitement above yawns on the subject of a beautiful Lady Doubtful proposing herself, through a group of infatuated influential friends, to a decorous Court, as one among the ladies acceptable. The popular version of it sharpened the sauce by mingling romance and cynicism very happily; for the numerous cooks, when out of the kitchen, will furnish a piquant dish.

The violent metaphor, thrust into the fore-front of the sentence to impress us in advance, remains a grinning mask which moves no more; the dragon becomes 'the numerous cooks'. And the satire baulks no less than the poetry; for when society's problems are thus admittedly contemptible, what becomes of the satirist's story based upon one of them? A few paragraphs further on we set out similarly with 'the livid cloud-bank over a flowery field', which at once lapses to 'the terrible aggregate social woman . . . *a mark of civilisation on to which our society must hold*'. It is after a grievous tirade of this sort that we have the avowal: 'The vexatious thing in speaking of her is, that she compels to the use of the rhetorician's brass instrument'. Well, we have really heard no note concerning her that does not belong to Mr Meredith's own orchestra; and yet when we attempt, as we are so often moved to do, a translation of the passage into sane English, it is hardly possible to save it from the air of platitude. So little security does strangeness of style give for freshness of thought.

The case is past arguing. Short of the systematic counterfeiting of the Limousin student,[1] nearly every element that men have agreed to vituperate in preciosity is found in this insupportable idiom. And all the while we recognise it as the writing of an artist of unusual insight and originality; a novelist, if not of the very first rank, yet so powerful and so independent that to apply to him the term second-rate is not allowable. He must be classed by himself, as a master with not worse limitary prejudices than those of Balzac; with more poetic elevation than any novelist of his day; a true modern in many things, despite a fundamental unrealism in his characters and an almost puerile proclivity to old-world devices of circumstantial plot. How, then, is the egregious vice of style to be accounted for?

Why, by one or other of the antecedents which we have seen to be involved in all preciosity; and as there is and can be no Meredithian school or clique, we go at once to the solution of individual self-will, defiance of censure, persistence in eccentricity, and self-absorption in isolation. It is all sequent. His first novels, with their already eccentric style, were given to a generation unable in the main to appreciate the originality and importance of their problems and the subtlety of their treatment; and the denunciations of dull critics nettled him. In a letter to the late James Thomson, published some years ago, he spoke with due causticity of the usual spectacle of the author haled up, with his hands tied behind his back, before the self-elected and enthroned critic, who tries and scourges him for the offence of writing his own book in his own way. Contemning those who contemned him, Mr Meredith persisted in being cryptic, eccentric, fantastic, elliptic. As if it were not enough to be artistically too subtle for his generation, he must needs persist in being gratuitously difficult and repellent as a writer, perverting a fine faculty to the bad ambition of being extraordinary, nay, to that of seeming superior. The prompt appreciation of the few good readers did not teach him to look on the reading-public as what it is, a loose mass of ever-varying units, in which even the dullards have no solidarity: he entrenched himself in the Carlylean and Browningesque manner, personifying the multitude as one lumpish hostile entity, or organized body of similar entities. Thus when, after an interval of silence, he produced *The Egoist*, and the accumulating units of the new generation, the newer minds, appreciated the novelty of the problem and the solution so generally as to make the book the success of its year, he was understood to be cynical over the praise given to a work

[1] Rabelais, ii, 6.

which was in his opinion inferior to its predecessors. The new generation has since proceeded to read those earlier works; but Mr Meredith had fixed his psychological habits, and no sense of community with his generation could now avail to make him treat language as a common possession, which anyone may rightly improve, but which no one may fitly seek to turn into impenetrable jungle for his own pleasure. Ill health may have had something to do with Mr Meredith's æsthetic deviation from 'the general deed of man'; and his contemporaries have their share of responsibility; but we must recognize in him what we have recognized behind all forms of preciosity—a specific limitation or one-sidedness, a failure to develop equably and in healthy relation to all the forces of the intellectual life. It cannot indeed be said of him that he has not grown. In his last book, despite the visible survival, in part, of the commonplace Jingoism of which he gave such surprising evidence in some violent verses eight or ten years ago, he has touched a position that is much better; and he has ventured on one solution of a sex problem which in former years he shunned. But the very lateness of these advances is a proof that he lost much by his isolation. Lesser people had got as far long ago. It has been recently told of him that he now reads in few books save the Bible and a few Greek classics—a regimen which would ill nourish even smaller minds. What he long ago confessed of himself in *Beauchamp's Career*—that he had acquired the habit of listening too much to his own voice—is now too obvious to need confessing. It all goes to produce, not only that defect of relation to current life which we see in his unhappy style, but that further defect which consists in his lapses into unreality as a novelist. For many of us there is such unreality in those devices of plot complication to which he so inveterately clings, and which so vexatiously trip up at once our illusion and our sense of his insight into the dynamic forces of character. A recent illustration is the episode of the concealment of Weyburn and Aminta in the wayside inn while their pursuers ride past—an episode which belongs to the art of Fielding and Smollett. While, however, some readers may still see no harm in these venerable expedients, every reader who knows enough to be entitled to form a judgment must be startled by the amazing episode of the swimming-encounter of Weyburn and Aminta when the former is on his way to the Continent. That is the imagination of a man who either never knew what swimming is or has forgotten what he knew. The occurence, as related in the novel, is an impossible dream. Mr Meredith may be in touch with the developments of fencing—an old hobby of his—but his conception of what people do or can do in the water is pure fantasy. In this, indeed, there is pathos; and perhaps the ideal reader would see only pathos—or literary picturesque—in the kindred aberration of the novelist's prose. But when writers are still so imperfect, there can be few perfect readers. We end by deploring, as contemporary criticism always must, a particular case of excessive preciosity, after setting out to find the soul of goodness in the thing in general. As it was in bygone instances that we could best see the element of compensation, the saving grace, it may be that the difficulty in seeing it in contemporary cases, and above all in Mr Meredith's, is one which will lessen for posterity; though it is hard to believe that posterity, with its ever enlarging library, will have the time to ponder all of that tormented prose, supposing it to have the patience. A misgiving arises as to whether much of Mr Meredith must not inevitably go the way of Donne. But whether or not, his case clinches for us the lesson that is to be learned from more ancient instances; and that lesson may be summed up as consisting or ending in a new view of the meaning of democracy. It is in the democratic age that we seem to find, after all, at once the freest scope for individual literary idiosyncrasy and the least amount of harmful contagion from it—the maximum of the individual freedom compatible with a minimum of the harm. It would thus seem that language, at least, is becoming effectively socialized. And here, let us hope, lies the security against that mild form of the malady of preciosity which is apt to follow the wide diffusion of an imperfect culture. The preciosity of democratic half-culture, in an age of knowledge, is at the worst a much less extravagant thing than the preciosities of the upper-class culture of ages in which all culture was narrow. So that the so-called process of 'levelling-down', here as in other matter, turns out to give the best securities for a general levelling-up.

115. Arthur Symons on Meredith as a decadent

1897

This essay was originally published as 'A Note on George Meredith', *Fortnightly Review*, lxii, November 1897. A year later Henri Davray used it as a Preface to his translation of the *Essay on the Idea of Comedy* (1898) and Meredith wrote to Davray asking him not to include it in further editions. Meredith thought it 'entirely misleading' and 'ludicrously childish' to call him a decadent. For Symons see above, No. 75, headnote.

A volume of *Selected Poems*, recently published, will perhaps remind some readers that Mr George Meredith, though he has written novels, is essentially a poet, not a novelist. It will also remind them that he is a poet who is not in the English tradition; a seeker after some strange, obscure, perhaps impossible, intellectual beauty, austere and fantastic. If he goes along ways that have never been travelled in, that is because he is seeking what no one before him has ever sought; and, more absolutely than most less-absorbed travellers, he carries the world behind his eyes, seeing, wherever he goes, only his own world, a creation less recognizable by people in general than the creation of most image-making brains. That is why he is so difficult to follow, and why you will be told that his writing is unnatural, or artificial. Certainly it is artificial. 'Let writers find time to write English more as a learned language', said Pater;[1] but Mr Meredith has always written English as if it were a learned language. Aiming, as he has done in verse, at something which is the poetry of pure idea, in prose, at something which is another kind of intellectual poetry, he has invented a whole vocabulary which has no resemblance with the spoken language, and whose merit is that it gives sharp, sudden expression to the aspects under which he sees things. So infused is vision in him with intellect, that he might be

[1] 'English Literature', *Guardian*, 17 February 1886.

said to see things in words; the unusual, restless, nervous words being a part of that world which he has made for himself out of the tangle of the universe.

The problem of Meredith is the problem of why a poet has spent most of his life in writing novels, novels which are the most intellectual in the language, but not great novels; while the comparatively small amount of verse which he has written is even further from being great poetry. Probably for the reason which made Gautier, a born painter, put down the brushes and paint in words; a mere question of technique, as people say; or, as they should say, that fundamental question. To so deliberate an artificer as Mr Meredith, technique must always have been valued at by no means less than its true worth. Having written a lovely poem in 'Love in the Valley', and a fascinating, strangely exciting, not quite satisfying poem in 'Modern Love', he must have realized that such achievements with him were too much of the nature of happy accidents to be very many times repeated. It was the period, and he was the friend, of Rossetti, of Morris, of Mr Swinburne, each a born poet, and each, in his own way, an instinctively perfect craftsman. Conscious that he had something new to say, and knowing that he could never say it in verse as these poets had said what they had to say, he turned to prose, and began by inventing *The Shaving of Shagpat*, which is like nothing that anyone, least of all an Arabian story-teller, had ever said before. English literature has not a more vividly entertaining book; nor has the soul of a style been lost more spectacularly.

It is only by realizing that Mr Meredith began by a volume of poems, continued in the Arabian entertainment of *The Shaving of Shagpat*, and the Teutonic fantasy of *Farina*, and only then, at the age of thirty-one, published his first novel, *The Ordeal of Richard Feverel*, that we can hope in any measure to understand the characteristics of so disconcerting a mind, so apparently inexplicable a career. Remember that he has the elliptical brain of the poet, not the slow, cautious, logical brain of the novelist; that he has his own vision of a world in which probable things do not always happen; and that words are to him as visual as mental images. Then consider the effect on such a brain, from the first impatient, intolerant, indefatigable, of a training in consciously artificial writing, on subjects which are a kind of sublime farce, without relation to any known or supposed realities in the universe. Writing prose, then, as if it were poetry, with an endeavour to pack every phrase with imaginative meaning, every sentence, you realize, will be an epigram. And as every sentence is to be an epigram, so every chapter is to be a crisis. And every book is to be at once a novel, realistic, a romance, a comedy of manners; it is to exist for its story, its characters, its philosophy, and every interest is to be equally prominent. And all the characters in it are to live at full speed, without a moment's repose; their very languors are to be fevers. And they will live (can you doubt?) in a fantastic world in which only the unexpected happens; their most trivial moments being turned, by the manner of their telling, into a fairy story.

All this may be equally refreshing or exhausting, but it is not the modesty of nature; and as certainly as it is not the duty of the poet, so certainly is it the duty of the novelist to respect the modesty of nature. Every novel of Mr Meredith is a series of situations, rendered for the most part in conversation, as if it were a play. Each situation is grouped, and shown to us as if the light of footlights were cast upon it; between each situation is darkness, and the drop-curtain. And his characters have the same inconsequent vividness. They are never types, but always individuals, in whom a capricious intellectual life burns with a bright but wavering flame. They are like people whom we meet in drawing-rooms, today in London, next month in Rome, and the month after in Paris. They fascinate us by their brilliance, their energy, their experience, their conversation; they have in their faces the distinction of birth, of thought, of culture; they are always a little ambiguous to us, and by so much the more attractive; they move us to a singular sympathy, with which is mingled not a little curiosity; we seem to become their friends; and it is only when we think of them in absence that we realize how little we really know them. Of their inner life we know nothing; their eloquent lips have always been closed on all the great issues of things. Of their characters we know only what they have told us; and they have told us for the most part anecdotes, showing their bearing under trying circumstances, which have proved them triumphantly to be English gentlemen and ladies, without, it would seem, always settling those obscurer judgments in which the soul is its own accuser and judge. We remember certain extraordinarily vivid looks, words, attitudes, which they have had in our company; and we remember them by these, rather than remember that these had once been a momentary part of them.

Not such wandering friends, coming and going about us as if we had made them, are Lear, Don Quixote, Alceste, Manon Lescaut, Grandet, Madame Bovary, Anna Karenina. These seem to flow into the great rhythms of nature, as if their life was of the same immortal substance as the life of the plants and stars. These are organic, a part of the universe; the others are enchanting exceptions, breaking the rhythm, though they may, with a new music.

And the books in which they live are at once too narrow and too wide for them. Their histories are allowed to develop as they will, or as the situations in them become interesting to their creator. Yet, like almost every English novelist, Mr Meredith is the bond-slave of 'plot'. Plot must be an intricate web, and this web must never be broken; and the stage must be crowded with figures, each with his own life to be accounted for, and not one of them will Mr Meredith neglect, however long his hero or heroine may be kept waiting on the way. But, to be quite frank, what English novelist, from Fielding onwards, has ever been able to resist the temptation of loitering, especially if it is over a humorous scene? Humour is the curse of the English novelist. Certainly he possesses it; he has always possessed it; but his humour is not the wise laughter of Rabelais, in whom laughter is a symbol; and it is always a digression. Dickens, in particular, from the very brilliance of what is distressing in him, has left his fatal mark on the English novel. And it is often Dickens, bespangled with all the gems of Arabia, that I find in Mr Meredith's comic scenes; never, certainly, when he is writing good comedy. Then, as we might infer from that *Essay on Comedy*, which is his most brilliant piece of sustained writing, he is intellect itself, a Congreve who is also a poet.

The Tragic Comedians, which is the title of one of Mr Meredith's novels, might well be applied to the whole series. So picturesquely, under the light of so sharp a paradox, does he conceive of human existence. But he is too impatient, too forgetful of the limits of prose and the novel, to work out a philosophy in that indirect, circumambient way in which alone it can minister to fiction. Life may indeed be a tragic comedy at every moment, but it is not visibly and audibly at every moment a tragic comedy. In spite of the fact that action, in Mr Meredith's novels, seems often to linger on the way, his novels are always in action. To him and his people,

> To do nought
> Is in itself almost an act;[1]

every conversation is a hurry of mental action; the impressiveness with which nothing happens, when nothing is happening, is itself a strain on the energy. And the almost German romance which tempers in

---

[1] D. G. Rossetti, 'Soothsay'.

him the French wit, adding a new whirl of colours to the kaleidoscope, helps to withdraw this world of his creating further and further from the daylight in which men labour without energy, and are content without happiness, and dream only vague dreams, and achieve only probable ends. He conceives his characters as pure intelligences, and then sets them to play at hide-and-seek with life, as if England were a treasure island in the Pacific.

Again, it is the question of technique which comes to enlighten us. We have seen, I think, that with Mr Meredith the question of how to write must have arisen before the question of what to write; certainly before the choice of the novel. A style conceived in verse, and brought up on Arabian extravaganzas and German fantasies, could scarcely be expected to adapt itself to the narration of the little, colourless facts of modern English society. With such a style, above all things literary, life recorded becomes, not a new life, but literature about life; and it is of the essence of the novel that life should be reborn in it, in the express image of its first shape. Where poetry, which must keep very close to the earth, is condemned, even, to avoid the soiling of the dust of the streets, the novel must not, at its peril, wander far from those streets. Before the novelist, human life is on its trial; he must see it with cold, learned eyes; he must hear it with undisturbed attention; he must be neither kind nor cruel, but merely just, in his judgment. Now Mr Meredith's is not a style which can render facts, much less seem to allow facts to render themselves. Like Carlyle, but even more than Carlyle, Mr Meredith is in the true, wide sense, as no other English writer of the present time can be said to be, a Decadent. The word Decadent has been narrowed, in France and in England, to a mere label upon a particular school of very recent writers. What Decadence, in literature, really means is that learned corruption of language by which style ceases to be organic, and becomes, in the pursuit of some new expressiveness or beauty, deliberately abnormal. Mr Meredith's style is as self-conscious as M. Mallarmé's. But, unlike many self-conscious styles, it is alive in every fibre. Not since the Elizabethans have we had so flame-like a life possessing the wanton body of a style. And with this fantastic, poetic, learned, passionate, intellectual style, a style which might have lent itself so well to the making of Elizabethan drama, Mr Meredith has set himself to the task of writing novels of contemporary life, in which the English society of today is to be shown to us in the habit and manners of our time.

It is, then, to be wondered at that every novel of Mr Meredith breaks every rule which could possibly be laid down for the writing of a novel? I think it follows; but the strange thing which does not follow is that the work thus produced should have that irresistible fascination which for many of us it certainly has. I find Mr Meredith breaking every canon of what are to me the laws of the novel; and yet I read him in preference to any other novelist. I say to myself: This pleasure, which I undoubtedly get from these novels, must surely be an irrational kind of pleasure; for it is against my judgment on those principles on which my mind is made up. Here am I, who cannot read without the approval of an unconscious, if not of a definitely conscious, criticism; I find myself reading these novels with the tacit approval of this very difficult literary conscience of mine: certainly it approves me in admiring them; and yet, when I set myself to think coldly over what I have been reading, I am forced to disapprove. How can these two views exist side by side in the same mind? How is it that that side of me which approves does not condemn that side of me which disapproves, nor that which disapproves condemn that which approves? There are some secrets which will never be told: the secret of why beauty is beauty, of why love is love, of why poetry is poetry. This woman, this book, this writer, attracts me: you they do not attract. Yet I may admit every imperfection which you can point out to me, and at the end of your logic meet you with perhaps but a woman's reason. I shall never believe that such an instinct can be false: inexplicable it may be.

The fascination of Mr Meredith is not, I think, quite inexplicable. It is the unrecognized, incalculable attraction of those qualities which go to make great poetry, coming to us in the disguise of prose and the novel, affecting us in spite of ourselves, as if a strange and beautiful woman suddenly took her seat among the judges in a court of law, where they were deciding some dusty case. Try to recall to yourself what has most impressed you in Mr Meredith's novels, and you will think first, after a vague consciousness of their unusual atmosphere, of some lyric scene, such as the scene in *Richard Feverel*, where Richard and Lucy meet in the wood; and that, you will see, is properly not prose at all, but a poem about first love. Then you will think of some passionate love-scene, one of Emilia's in *Sandra Belloni*; or the Venetian episode in *Beauchamp's Career*; or the fiery race of events, where dawn and darkness meet, in *Rhoda Fleming*; and all of them, you will see, have more of the qualities of poetry than of prose. The poet, struggling against the bondage of prose, flings himself upon every opportunity of evading his bondage. Even if he fails, he has made us thrillingly conscious of his presence. It is thus by the very quality that has been his distraction that Mr Meredith holds us, by the intensity of his vision of a world which is not our world, by the living imagination of a language which is not our language, by the energy of genius which has done so much to achieve the impossible.

ODES IN CONTRIBUTION TO THE SONG OF FRENCH HISTORY

1898

116. Francis Thompson, *Academy*

liii, 12 March 1898

Francis Thompson (1859–1907), Catholic poet, wrote regularly for *Academy*. He made the acquaintance of Meredith through the Meynells. It is the first of Meredith's three new odes on French history, 'The Revolution', published in the March issue of *Cosmopolis*, that Thompson is reviewing.

I have read Mr Meredith's Ode in the current *Cosmopolis* with an amazement passing words. Amazement for its power, amazement for its sins, its flagrancies, its defiant pitching to the devil of all law recognized even by the boldest, the most scornful of merely conventional tradition; amazement—for it fulfils its title, it is itself an anarchy, a turbulence, tumultuously eruptive as the Revolution in its first unchaining. To say it is not a perfect poem would be mild. It challenges all order; it has every fault within a poet's compass, except the tame faults, except lack of inspiration. On the plenitude, the undeniable plenitude, of its aggressive force, it seems to stake everything. No one can complain that Mr Meredith fears his fate too much. I am in tune with most audacity, but Mr Meredith leaves me gasping.

You must read the poem once, as you play a difficult fantasia once, merely to see how it goes; a second time, to begin to read it; a third time, to begin to realize it. All the arduous power and all the more repellent vices of Mr Meredith's poetic style are here at grips, exalted by mutual antiposition and counteraction. Never has he been more intermittently careless of grammatical construction, obscuring what is

465

already inherently difficult. He storms onward like his own France, crashing and contorting in his path the astonishing sentences, now volcanic and irresistibly thundering, now twisted and writhing or furiously splintered. The metre is likewise; lines blocked, immobile, inflexible, with needless rubble of words, or whirring all ways like snapped and disintegrated machinery; yet at times forcing their way to rightness through sheer inward heat, and leaping like a geyser-spout —magnificently impressive.

For the Ode is wonderful, though an unlawful wonder. The first nine stanzas, with all their perverse difficulties and disfeatures, are full of astonishing imagery, passages like the loosing of pent fires. The poem has a devil in it. By no other word can we describe the magnetic intensity of its repellentness and arrestingness. Those who overcome their first recoil must end in submission—if protesting submission—to its potency. No youth could rival the nether furnaces of this production of age, no young imagination conceive these images which outpour by troops and battalia. Mr Meredith's own language can alone figure the poem:

> Ravishing as red wine in woman's form,
> A splendid Maenad, she of the delirious laugh,
> Her body twisted flames with the smoke-cap crowned,
> . . . who sang, who sang
> Intoxication to her swarm,
> Revolved them, hair, voice, feet, in her carmagnole.

That splendid outburst is all for which I have room. If this Ode be not a success (as I wish I might persuade myself it is), more power has gone to such a failure than would make a score of reputations. And assuredly much, very much, it were blind to call anything but success.

117. Unsigned review, *Saturday Review*

lxxxvi, 12 November 1898

In his later poetry Mr George Meredith taxes the fidelity of his loyal admirers rather severely. We can honestly say that few things would give us greater pleasure than to offer a tribute of cordial and unstinted praise to these odes on the history of France. Their author is, today, of living English writers still militant and active, the one around whom most of sympathy and admiration centres. We are proud of him; we delight in the fine attitude of his mind; he relinquishes nothing in his fight with what is poor and commonplace. But even in his prose, and even in the best of his prose, there are elements of confusion and extravagance that bring a cloud across our satisfaction, while in his verse, and especially in the worst of his verse, these chaotic qualities take a prominence which destroys the greater part of our pleasure. When we have read the volume before us with bewilderment and acute mental distress, we feel inclined to make a despairing appeal to the eminent author himself, to ask him, with all respect and humility, whether he can really defend the system on which these odes are composed, and what he would think of them if they were presented to him as the work of another person. If they showed signs of weakness or decay we should be very careful to avoid, so far as possible, any disrespectful reference to the fact; but they do not. The voice is as triumphant as ever, the intellectual force as rapid and authoritative; it is the scheme of poetics which seems to us so arrogantly false. Even Mr Meredith must not write like this and expect nothing but commendation from his critics.

The 'Odes' are four in number, and they deal with the Revolution, with Napoleon, with the Invasion of 1870, and with the problem of Alsace-Lorraine. The third of these has long been known to us, for it was published twenty-eight years ago; the other three, but especially the first and fourth, bear internal evidence of having been recently composed. Comparison between, let us say, the third and the first, shows in how striking a degree Mr Meredith has permitted the peculiarities of his style to grow upon him since 1870. The Invasion ode does not rank very high among Mr Meredith's poems of the same general date, but it is astonishingly lucid and intelligible when compared with the odes of 1898. What we discover, by this convenient parallel, to have grown upon Mr Meredith is the desire to dazzle and deafen the reader. The phrases are now more gorgeous than they were, the illustrations more astonishing, the rhetorical vocabulary more emphatic. It has always been Mr George Meredith's snare that in the almost pathetic desire to escape anything that savours of the commonplace, he has been led to adopt a key of language too high for the theme in hand. As he has grown older, and especially in his verse, he has carried this emphasis to such an extreme that what began as a merit has become a distressing and even a perilous fault.

Mr Meredith's horror of the banal has led him to a more and more violent search for extraordinary words, images, and turns of fancy. Triviality is so hateful to him that he has become insensible to the fact that in order to address his fellows at all, certain familiar locutions must be permitted. Mr Meredith defies intelligibility by clothing not only rare and splendid conceptions with magnificent verbiage, but by lavishing it everywhere, so that his very scavenger-boys run about in cloth-of-gold. He is full of defiances. He evidently does not write verse with ease, a peculiarity which we are far from upbraiding him with. But he is nervously anxious to destroy the traces of his difficulties, and he does this, or thinks to do it, by curious stratagems. When he has been drawn into the use of a particularly extravagant or inapt image, he tries to enforce our admiration by repeating it again and again. The amazing simile of the 'cherubim' and the 'mastodons' is one example of this, and the unfortunate but reiterated phrase about 'Earth's fluttering little lyre' another.

Surely, the aim of poetry should be to give enthusiastic pleasure. But, for this purpose, it must offer us the passion of great music, great thoughts, or great illustrations. In extended poems, however, this excitement cannot and should not be sustained uninterruptedly, and the intermediate passages, in which the intensity is subdued, must at least be lucid and graceful. To prove the truth of this we have but to examine any lengthy and successful composition of Dryden, or Wordsworth, or Spenser. But here is one of Mr Meredith's intermediate passages:

> For the belted Overshadower hard the course,
> On whom devolves the spirit's touchstone, Force;
> Which is the strenuous arm, to strike inclined,
> That too much adamantine makes the mind;

468

Forgets its coin of Nature's rich Exchange;
Contracts horizons within present sight;
Amalekite today, across its range
Indisputable, tomorrow Simeonite.

We will not awaken controversy by saying that this has no meaning; but we will be bold enough to say that it has no beauty, that it fails to produce any one of the effects upon which poetry bases its claim to human attention.

Disapproving, as we must have the candour to do, the whole system on which these odes are composed, and denying to them, in spite of their eloquence and force, any pretension to be called successful as poems, we hasten to speak of what we can enjoy in compositions so wilful and grotesque. First of all, even in the precipitous jumble of their imagery, they frequently bear witness to their author's extraordinary observation of natural objects. If we free ourselves from the bondage of Mr Meredith's intolerable emphasis by taking one of his thundering tirades to pieces, we shall often be rewarded by a line or a phrase of concentrated vision. Such verses as 'sack-like droop bronze pears on the railed branch-frontage', and such a couplet as:

Forth from her bearded tube of lacquey brass
Reverberant notes and long blew volent France,

show what a magician Mr Meredith can be. A group of words, such as:

the robber wasp
That in the hanging apple makes a nest,
And *carves* a *face of abscess* where was fruit
Ripe ruddy,

shows how he can abuse his magic, because the image here, although marvellously seen, is so preposterously over-emphatic in the context that we forget all about the historical aspect of which Mr Meredith is speaking, and think of nothing but the intolerably vivid image. So that fancy here defeats its own object, and, while professing to illuminate its theme, merely drowns it in a momentary glare of blinding lime-light.

The 'Napoleon' ode is certainly the best, and offers us a somewhat vague but large and elevated portrait of a great man with whom Mr Meredith's sympathy is not of yesterday. The strophe beginning 'Ah! what a dawn of splendour' is less turbid than usual, and offers us some

magnificent rhetoric of the order of Shelley's 'Ode to Naples' and
Mr Swinburne's 'Eve of Revolution'. It is sustained, too, in a pure flow
of reverberating pomp, and not spoiled, as is so frequently the case, by
such sudden intolerable interpolations as

> The friable and the grumous, dizzards both,

certainly, one of the most extraordinary lines in the English language.
The character of Napoleon is analyzed in the earlier strophes of this
ode with great penetration and with a directness and clearness which is
like that of some serious passage in Boileau or Pope, very acute and just,
although essentially unimaginative. On the whole, however, the most
delightful passage in the volume, and that which torments us least with
over-emphasis or a restless search after oddity, after the unusual, is the
temperate and generous praise of France in the tenth strophe of 'Alsace-
Lorraine'. Had all, or much, been like this, we should not have had to
record, with genuine grief, our conviction that this ambitious cycle of
odes had better have been left unattempted.

118. Unsigned review, *Literature*

ii, 26 November 1898

More than a quarter of a century ago, while France was lying prostrate
under the heel of the German invader, Mr Meredith published in the
Fortnightly Review what many people regarded, and still regard, as one
of the noblest of his poems. It was great, not only in pure poetic quality,
but in dignity of attitude and wisdom of counsel. Full of passionate
sympathy with the conquered nation, with that

> Bellona and Bacchante, rushing forth
> On yon stout marching schoolmen of the North,

the poet was yet able to look with the calm gaze of justice upon the
conqueror—able, too, to see the Nemesis in her fate, and to tell the
truth to her even while her misery wrung his heart. 'France, December,

1870'; was a real contribution to the 'Song of French History'—a genuine anticipation of the epic of the future. Mr Meredith has dealt many a shrewd satirical blow at the Teutonic stock, both before and since, and delivered himself of not a few lyrical extravagances in praise of the Celt; but one felt that in this poem his genius had lifted him into a serener atmosphere and to heights of a broader outlook, and that he had managed to view that Titanic world-struggle of contending races as much with the impersonal and impartial eye of the historian as with the all-embracing sympathy of the poet.

The years that have elapsed since the first publication of this magnificent ode and its reappearance in the volume before us as one of four lyrical pieces, in which he recites the stormy song of French history from 1789 to the present day, have in nowise altered Mr. Meredith's attitude towards his great theme. Throughout 'The Revolution' and 'Napoleon', the two pieces which precede the republished 'France', there runs the same consciousness of the essential unity of this mighty, agelong drama, with the splendid madness of its opening scenes and the terrible retribution of its climax; while the closing piece, 'Alsace-Lorraine', a prophetic vision of a France victorious over herself, and accepting her bereavement with dignity and fortitude, is set to the same lofty strain of consolation that made itself heard in the concluding lines of the poem of 1870. On France, sings Mr Meredith:

[Quotes 'Alsace-Lorraine', st. x, ll. 23-32.]

A cruel political critic might say that he sees little signs of the fulfilment of this aspiration; but poets are entitled and indeed bound to have a more distant horizon than political critics, and after all even the politician may remember that five and twenty years ago he would with equal scorn have scouted the suggestion that France would prove capable of the self control in international matters which she has maintained for more than a quarter of a century.

But if Mr Meredith's political philosophy has remained unchanged by time, the same thing cannot, we fear, be said of the quality of his poetry. A comparison of 'France' with 'Napoleon', or, more significant still, with 'Alsace-Lorraine', affords painful evidence of the extent to which the parasite of intellectual subtlety has overgrown and disfigured, where it has not, as is too often the case, actually hidden, the parent stem of Mr Meredith's genius. Even in 1870 he was not an easy poet, and 'France' is not an easy poem; but to pass from it to any one of its companions is like exchanging ordinary language for cryptogram.

There are passages in it which do yield up their meaning at a first reading, but they are the comparatively rare exceptions, not the rule. We do not have, as we have in 'Alsace-Lorraine', to 'construe' painfully line by line, page after page, and in many cases to give it up at last. Throughout 'France' we have no such puzzles of classification as the division of the French people of the Napoleonic era into

> The friable and the grumous, dizzards both;

no such enigmatic mataphors as

> him her young
> In whirled imagination mastodonized;

no such mysterious questionings as

> Does nought so loosen our sight from the
>   despot heart, to receive
> Balm of a sound Earth's primary heart at
>   its active beat;

no such cryptic references to the processes of Nature as

[Quotes 'Alsace-Lorraine', ll. 41–6.]

no such syntactic *cruces* as

> We see a Paris burn
> Or France Napoleon.

In the whole three hundred lines or so of the earlier poem, though it has its occasional obscurities, there is nothing to compare with the above extracts, which belong, in truth, to a later period of Mr Meredith's art—to a period when the purely intellectual part of him has mastered the emotional part and the foaming torrent of his vocabulary has submerged both. In this cataclysm it is not only simplicity which has been swept away, but beauty also, even the mere form of poetry itself. In the long-lined metres, of which the last two extracts afford examples, this is especially noticeable. Except for the tag of the rhyme at the end they might often be mistaken for mere Whitmanese, their metrical regularity, such as it is, being almost lost in their dissonance.

And yet, as if to show that this unbridled revel of words, this persistent pursuing of a fanciful thought through the tangled under-wood of a too luxuriant diction, is but the result of a habit which has grown upon Mr Meredith, we find him at the outset of the finest of the three new poems still able, when he chooses, or, at any rate, for as long as this inveterate habit will let him, to strike as grandly resonant a note as ever.

[Quotes 'Napoleon', st. i, ll. 1–8 and 14–19.]

This is a stirring prelude, and every here and there the same note occurs. And, of course, in the series of dashing strokes in which the poet has limned Napoleon's character there are frequent felicities of touch. How could it be otherwise with Mr Meredith? The mixture in the great Emperor's composition of broad-minded ruler and legislator and unscrupulous tyrant always ready to smite on the least suspicion that he was in danger of being smitten is described throughout with astonishing vigour, and, indeed, is admirably summed up in two lines:

> The statesman steered the despot to large tasks,
> The despot drove the statesman on short roads.

This again of his downfall is not unworthy of its tremendous theme:

[Quotes 'Napoleon', st. xiii, ll. 102–8.]

It is not till we enter on the final poem that the densely-rolling vapours of Mr Meredith's imagery settle down upon the page, a veil rarely penetrated by the reader, and only at still more infrequent intervals rent asunder by a flash of the poetic intelligence from within. Even, too, when the drift of the passage is plain enough, as in the description of the shade of Napoleon looking on the battle-field of Sedan, the opportunities of a greatly conceived situation are frittered away in sesquipedalian lines abounding in such stumbling-blocks of phrase as 'his underworld eyeballs grip the cast of the land for a fray, expugnant'; 'a timed artillery speaks full-mouthed on a stuttering feeble reduced to naught'; and (of the Germans, whose wits Napoleon had himself quickened by his warlike aggressions) 'he is there in the midst of the pupils he harried to brain-awake'.

The close of the poem can be read with less effort and greater pleasure, but we would give it all for that magnificent strophe in 'France', beginning 'Ah! what a dawn of splendour when her sowers Went forth and bent the necks of populations'. Never has Mr Meredith been more loftily inspired than in this dithyramb of the Revolutionary armies in their whirlwind course:

[Quotes 'France', st. v, ll. 9–end.]

What has become of the restraint and measure which do so much to enhance the effect of these impassioned lines? Surely posterity will believe that there has been a mistake in dates. 'France', it will be said, is the work of the poet's maturity, while the other contents of the volume show all the unchastened exuberance, all the uncritical flamboyancy of 'green unknowing youth'.

119. Owen Seaman, *Athenaeum*

No. 3713, 24 December 1898

Sir Owen Seaman (1861–1936) was a poet and essayist and author of *War-time Verses* (1916).

It is well to possess the intellectual strength of a giant; but to use it like a giant is to be a source of unrest to the devout. When Mr Meredith evolved the preface to *Diana of the Crossways*, it was admitted to contain some of the darkest sayings in English prose. But in the present volume he has summoned to his aid the resources of a form of art which offers even greater possibilities for the darkening of counsel. Browning, in one of his letters, says: 'I never designedly tried to puzzle people, as some of my critics have supposed'. And indeed the fact that he liked, as in *Sordello*, to deal allusively with names and episodes drawn from the less-known chapters of history may sometimes account for his alleged obscurity. Mr Meredith has no such excuse in the volume before us. He has chosen themes of which the historical details are familiar to every moderately educated man. The arbitrary caprice of his manner—for one hesitates to describe it more emphatically—can only commend itself to those with whom the master's name justifies him of all his works, however wanton. It is true that the obscurity does not here arise from defective vision in the author; but neither this reflection nor the splendid beauty of his intervals of lucidity can adequately console the reader for the unnecessary pains to which he is put.

Nor have we here the kind of rugged strength which Time is supposed to mellow to sweetness:

> Sweet for the future, strong for the nonce.

Unless this is indeed the language of the future, one can hardly hope for posterity to unravel what the writer's contemporaries, if they are honest, confess to be at times beyond them. And the title of it is a *Contribution to the Song of French History*. Yet, if we except the fine sweeping measure of the second movement in 'Alsace-Lorraine', that tells of the restorative power of Nature and the Hours, with their

> Balm of a sound Earth's primary heart at its active beat,

there is scarcely a note of pure 'song' in all these odes. Imaginative force there is, without rival in modern poetry; fertility, too, of language such as Mr Swinburne or Mr Francis Thompson alone could compass, but involved and weighted with a pregnancy of meaning which the author of *Songs before Sunrise* would contentedly have resigned for greater beauty of sound.

But in this volume Mr Meredith stands revealed as his own best critic. What is at once the most convincing testimony to his earlier power in this kind of writing and the sternest comment on certain characteristics of his later achievements is to be found in the ode to 'France', written in December, 1870, and now republished from his *Ballads and Poems*. Here is the same imaginative force, the same fertility of language, the same pregnancy of meaning; but clear, but ordered, but noble in its rhythmic dignity. Let a typical passage be taken from this earlier ode:—

[Quotes st. iv, ll. 22–end.]

Or, again, the trenchant lines from the same earlier ode:

[Quotes st. v, ll. 25–end.]

Compare with these a later passage from 'Revolution', where the 'young Angelical'—presumably the Spirit of Liberty—looks down upon the dreadful ending of the work that France had begun for love of him:

[Quotes st. xiii, ll. 55–68.]

Compare also with his younger work these lines from 'Alsace-Lorraine', that have the air of Carlyle turned metrist. The 'Purgatorial Saint' seems to be Napoleon, with whom the 'credible ghost' is also, apparently, identical:

[Quotes st. vii, ll. 1–3 and 11–16.]

And once again, from the same ode:

[Quotes st. viii, ll. 15–20.]

To turn for relief and in conclusion to those admirable qualities of subtle perception and keen incisiveness which we have learnt to look for in all Mr Meredith's work, the passages in which they are most effectively illustrated are perhaps those that treat of the resilient energy with which France recovered from her fall, and those that sum up the character of Napoleon in relation to his country:

[Quotes st. ix, ll. 11–22.]

Can this last word conceivably be a mis-print for *meal*?

Here, in this ode to 'Napoléon', for all its profusion of imagery, Mr Meredith often concentrates his strength in memorably pungent phrases:

[Quotes st. ix, ll. 102–12.]

There is a touch of Lewis Carroll here.

A READING OF LIFE

1901

120. Unsigned review, *Academy*

lx, 29 June 1901

A new volume of poems by George Meredith! It warms one's antici-
pations; we know we cannot be entirely defrauded of matter for
delight, whether or not it be on a level with the work we loved of yore.
That quick and vigorous brain can never work to mere futility; some
matter will come from it. Meredith, the poet, we bear fresh in memory
(for there are two George Merediths—a duality in unity, poet and
novelist). Convoluted thought; rapid force, zig-zagging with lightning
swiftness and abruptness; magnetic and quivering to the finger-tips
with that super-subtilized emotional vitality we call poetry; spinning
images into the air like coin, with an audacious joy in watching how
they will come down—such is Meredith the poet. Withal, a certain
Browningesque obscurity, arising partly from a Browningesque carelessness as to connections. William Morris, in Manchester, once accused
his 'cursed Celtic love of fine language', which had obscured the plain
meaning he would fain have driven to the head in his audience. Mr
Meredith has no small portion in this 'cursed Celtic love of fine
language'—Apollo Delphicus be thanked for it, amid the present
cursed Saxon love of corrugated iron language! But more overmaster-
ing than this, for good or for evil, is his Celtic impetuosity. It sweeps
him into the avalanchine precipitance of 'Attila' (Attila, *our* Attila!);
and into the most exasperating insolences of grammar—nay, too heedless for so conscious a word as 'insolence'. They are not absent in this
book:

[Quotes 'The Vital Choice', st. i.]

Aided by the sequent line, we discern 'Each can torture if divided' to
mean 'if worship be divided between them'. But grammatically the

477

line cannot mean this; and it might be a puzzling matter to decide what it did mean, were it not for that illuminating sequent line. Nevertheless, this volume is notably freer from grammatical puzzles, ambiguous ellipses, docked connective particles or pronouns, and lapsed intersticial words in general, than has been the case with Mr Meredith's previous poems. It certainly gains in clearness.

One cannot say that any poem rises to the height of the author's foregone achievement. Yet of all it can be said that no other man could have written them; and there are poems where the old Meredithian fire flames forth in welcome fashion. With 'The Huntress' he darts forth impetuous of movement, and with daring lance-flings of expression, remarkable in such a veteran of the poetic chase. Hear him:

[Quotes ll. 9–10 and 19–47.]

That catches the blood in its vivid vision, the racing bound of the verse, the phrase cast like a pebble from the sinewy hand. The image, 'legs like plaited lyre-chords', may strike at first like the sudden surge of chill water to the chest, making you catch your breath with a scarce-welcome surprise, and doubt whether you like it. But it is most apt to the thing imaged, when you come to grasp the idea. It indicates the tensity of the lyre-chord, strung to pitch; and compares this to the tensity of the limbs out-stretched, new-lighted from their leap. So it is with other phrases in the poem, and throughout Mr Meredith's work: after their first brusque novelty, you grow to relish them.

Yet of the poems as a whole, we have suggested that they are not the complete Meredith; though they do not fail in those new and significant facets of thought which we expect this writer to startle us with wherever we glance at him. Thought; apt image, often bold, even audacious, as is the way with Mr Meredith; expression drawn tense to the arrow-head; all these things are there. What, then, is lacking? Well, all these we have in Mr Meredith's prose: but the indescribable, unnameable lift, the swift or subtle wing-sweep of emotion preter-human—in our staled word, divine—which sends through a verse the electric current, or air from heaven, we call poetry; this incommunicable thing is somehow felt wanting, save by flashes. Mr Meredith's prose is often half-poetry: but to make it absolute poetry something more is needed than to fling it into verse. Yet of such nature, it seems to us, is the bulk of these verses; which (by who shall say what elusive degree?) are just not *vinum merum* of song—the unallayed wine of poetry. We miss that last refinement and white light of emotion which severs Mr Meredith's subtlest prose from his authentic poetry. It is difficult to find a poem of quotable length which will example our meaning. Perhaps 'The Hueless Love' is the nearest:

[Quotes 'The Hueless Love'.]

Here, as it appears to us, in the first two stanzas and the last we feel the touch of poetry. But the main portion of the poem is a piece of subtle and imaginatively couched analysis such as occurs constantly in Mr Meredith's novels, just as close in the gateways of poetry, but no further. Really to understand our criticism, however, it is necessary to read the longer poems as wholes. None of the shorter pieces effectually bears out what we have been saying, for these do not exhibit the higher flashes in which we meet again the Meredith of former poems. Yet it is in the dangerous comparison with himself that this present volume falls short: for any new writer it would be the beginning of a reputation. That the fire and eagerness as of twenty should still animate many of the poems is a remarkable tribute to the green vigour of the elder race, which few of the rising generation can hope to emulate.

121. Unsigned review, *Saturday Review*

xcii, 13 July 1901

Mr Meredith has always suffered from the curse of too much ability. He has both genius and talent, but the talent, instead of acting as a counterpoise to the genius, blows it yet more windily about the air. He has almost all the qualities of a great writer, but some perverse spirit in his blood has mixed them to their mutual undoing. When he writes prose, the prose seems always about to burst into poetry; when he writes verse, the verse seems always about to sink into prose. He thinks in flashes, and writes in shorthand. He has an intellectual passion for words, but he has never been able to accustom his mind to the slowness of their service; he tosses them about the page in his anger, tearing them open and gutting them with a savage pleasure. He has so fastidious a fear of dirtying his hands with what other hands have touched that he makes the language over again, so as to avoid writing a sentence or a line as anyone else could have written it. His hatred of the commonplace becomes a mania, and it is by his headlong hunt after the best that he has lost by the way its useful enemy, good. In prose he would have every sentence shine, in verse he would have every line sparkle; like a lady who puts on all her jewellery at once, immediately after breakfast. As his own brain never rests, he does not realize that there are other brains which feel fatigue; and as his own taste is for what is hard, ringing, showy, drenched with light, he does not leave any cool shadows to be a home for gentle sounds, in the whole of his work. His books are like picture galleries, in which every inch of wall is covered, and picture screams at picture across its narrow division of frame. Almost every picture is good, but each suffers from its context. As time goes on, Mr Meredith's mannerisms have grown rigid, like old bones. Exceptions have become rules, experiments have been accepted for solutions.

In Mr Meredith's earliest verse there is a certain harshness, which seems to come from a too urgent desire to be at once concise and explicit. 'Modern Love', published in 1862, remains Mr Meredith's masterpiece in poetry, and it will always remain, beside certain things of Donne and of Browning, an astonishing feat in the vivisection of the heart in verse. It is packed with imagination, but with imagination of so nakedly human a kind that there is hardly an ornament, hardly an image, in the verse: it is like scraps of broken, of heart-broken, talk, overheard and jotted down at random, hardly suggesting a story, but burning into one like the touch of a corroding acid. These cruel and self-torturing lovers have no illusions, and their 'tragic hints' are like a fine, pained mockery of love itself, as they struggle open-eyed against the blindness of passion. The poem laughs while it cries, with a double-mindedness more constant than that of Heine; with, at times, an acuteness of sensation carried to the point of agony at which Othello sweats words like these:

> O thou weed,
> Who art so lovely fair, and smell'st so sweet
> That the sense aches at thee, would thou hadst ne'er been born![1]

Mr Meredith has written nothing more like 'Modern Love', and for twenty years after the publication of the volume containing it he published no other volume of verse. In 1883 appeared *Poems and Lyrics of*

[1] *Othello*, iv, 2.

the Joy of Earth, in 1887 *Poems and Ballads of Tragic Life*; and, in 1888, *A Reading of Earth*, to which *A Reading of Life* is a sort of companion volume. The main part of this work is a kind of nature-poetry unlike any other nature-poetry; but there are several groups which must be distinguished from it. One group contains 'Cassandra', from the volume of 1862, 'The Nuptials of Attila', 'The Song of Theodolinda', 'King Harald's Trance', and 'Aneurin's Harp', from the volume of 1887. There is something fierce, savage, convulsive, in the passion which informs these poems; a note sounded in our days by no other poet, not even by Leconte de Lisle in the *Poèmes Barbares*. The words rush rattling on one another, like the clashing of spears or the ring of iron on iron in a day of old-world battle. The lines are javelins, consonanted lines full of force and fury, as if sung or played by a northern skald harping on a field of slain. There is another group of romantic ballads, containing the early 'Margaret's Bridal Eve', and the later 'Archduchess Anne' and 'The Young Princess'. There are also the humorous and pathetic studies in 'Roadside Philosophers' and the like, in which, forty years ago, Mr Meredith anticipated, with the dignity of a poet, the vernacular studies of Mr Kipling and others. And, finally, there is a section containing poems of impassioned meditation, beginning with the lofty and sustained ode to 'France, December 1870', and ending with the volcanic volume of *Odes in Contribution to the Song of French History*, published last year.

But it is in the poems of nature that Mr Meredith is most consistent to an attitude, most himself as he would have himself. There is in them an almost pagan sense of the nearness and intimacy of the awful and benignant powers of nature; but this sense, once sufficient for the making of poetry, is interpenetrated, in this modern poet, by an almost scientific consciousness of the processes of evolution. Earth seen through a brain, not a temperament, it might be defined; and it would be possible to gather a complete philosophy of life from these poems, in which, though 'joy of earth' is sung, it is sung with the wise, collected ecstasy of Melampus, not with the irresponsible ecstasy of the Mænads. It is not what Browning calls 'the wild joy of living', but the strenuous joy of living in perfect accordance with nature, with the sanity of animals who have climbed to reason, and are content to be guided by it. It is a philosophy which may well be contrasted with the transcendental theories of a poet with whom Mr Meredith may otherwise be compared, Emerson. Both, in different ways, have tried to make poetry out of the brain, forgetting that poetry draws nourishment from other soil, and dies in the brain as in a vacuum. Both have taken the abstract, not the concrete, for their province; both have tortured words in the cause of ideas, both have had so much to say that they have had little time left over for singing.

Mr Meredith has never been a clear writer in verse; 'Modern Love' requires reading and re-reading; but at one time he had a somewhat exasperating semblance of lucidity, which still lurks mockingly about his work. A freshman who heard Mallarmé lecture at Oxford said when he came away: 'I understood every word, but not a single sentence'. Mr Meredith is sometimes equally tantalizing. The meaning seems to be there, just beyond one, clearly visible on the other side of some hard transparency through which there is no passage. Have you ever seen a cat pawing at the glass from the other side of a window? It paws and paws, turns its head to the right, turns its head to the left, walks to and fro, sniffing at the corner of every pane; its claws screech on the glass, in a helpless endeavour to get through to what it sees before it; it gives up at last, in an evident bewilderment. That is how one figures the reader of Mr Meredith's later verse. In the new book there is a poem called 'A Garden Idyl'; it is meant to be a simple tale, with the suggestion of an allegory in it; but all one's wits are needed, with the closest attention, to find out so much as exactly what happened. The first lines which we chanced to read, on opening the book, were these:

> Bands of her limpid primitives,
> Or patterned in the curious braid,
> Are the blest man's.

Turn a few pages, and you will read:

[Quotes 'The Test of Manhood', ll. 222–30.]

Now it is not merely that Mr Meredith's meaning is not obvious at a glance, it is, in such passages, ugly in its obscurity, not beautiful. There is not an uglier line in the English language than:

> Or is't the widowed's dream of her new mate.

It is almost impossible to say it at all. Often Mr Meredith wishes to be concise, and squeezes his thoughts together like this:

> and the totterer Earth detests,
> Love shuns, grim logic screws in grasp, is he.

482

In his desire to cram a separate sentence into every line, he writes such lines as:

Look I once back, a broken pinion I.

He thinks differently from other people, and not only more quickly; and his mind works in a kind of double process. Take, for instance, this phrase:

Ravenous all the line for speed.

An image occurs to him, the image of a runner, who, as we say, 'devours' the ground. Thereupon he translates this image into his own dialect, where it becomes intensely vivid if it can be caught in passing; only, to catch it in passing, you must go through two mental processes at once. That is why he cannot be read aloud. In a poem where every line is on the pattern of the line we have quoted, every line has to be unriddled; and no brain works fast enough to catch so many separate meanings, and to translate as it goes.

How fine Mr Meredith can still be when at his best, and how much we lose by losing one of his meanings, may be seen from this sonnet, called 'At the Close', in which a noble thought is rendered with splendid and reticent dignity:

[Quotes 'At the Close'.]

The thought, in Mr Meredith's work, is always noble; he is always careful to

Give to imagination some pure light;

his air is always bracing, when once we have climbed through the clouds which coil about his feet. No writer of our time has been loftier-minded, subtler in intelligence, or more instinctive in feeling. 'More brain, O Lord, more brain'! he cries, on behalf of women, in 'Modern Love', and it is to the brain that he has always addressed himself, with a consistent disregard of the easier appeal of the emotions.

Assured of worthiness we do not dread
Competitors,

he has said, proudly conscious that, in spite of some weaknesses and more excesses, he has little to dread from most of the 'rivals, tightly belted for the race' whom he has seen straining towards the same goal.

122. Arthur Symons, *Athenaeum*

No. 3847, 20 July 1901

For Symons see above, No. 75, headnote.

Mr Meredith has half the making of a great artist in verse. He has harmony without melody; he invents and executes marvellous variations upon verse; he has footed the tight-rope of the galliambic measure and the swaying planks of various trochaic experiments; but his resolve to astonish is stronger than his desire to charm, and he lets technical skill carry him into such excesses of ugliness in verse as technical skill carried Liszt, and sometimes Berlioz, in music. Mr Meredith has written lines which any poet who ever wrote in English would be proud of; he has also written lines as tuneless as a deal table and as rasping as a file. His ear for the sweep and texture of harmonies, for the building up of rhythmical structure, is not seconded by an ear for the delicacies of sound in words or in tunes. In one of the finest of his poems, the 'Hymn to Colour', he can begin one stanza with this ample magnificence:

> Look now where Colour, the soul's bridegroom, makes
> The house of heaven splendid for the bride;

and can end another stanza thus lumpishly:

> With thee, O fount of the Untimed! to lead,
> Drink they of thee, thee eyeing, they unaged
> Shall on through brave wars waged.

In the new volume he can flood the eye with splendour and delight the ear with vivid sweetness, as in these lines:

[Quotes 'With the Persuader'. ll. 1–14.]

On another page he sets the teeth on edge by

> Combustibles on hot combustibles
> Run piling,

484

outrages ear and distracts intelligence by

> But your fierce Yes and No of butting heads,
> Now rages to outdo a horny Past,

and descends to the trivial and contorted awkwardness of

> Midway the vast round-raying beard
> A desiccated midge appeared;
> Whose body pricked the name of meal,
> Whose hair had growth in earth's unreal.

Mr Meredith is not satisfied with English verse as it is; he persists in trying to make it into something wholly different, and these eccentricities come partly from certain theories. He speaks in one place of

> A soft compulsion on terrene
> By heavenly,

which is not English, but a misapplication of the jargon of science. In another place he speaks of

> The posts that named the swallowed mile,

which is a kind of pedantry. He chooses harsh words by preference, liking unusual or insoluble rhymes, like 'haps' and 'yaps', 'thick' and 'sick', 'skin' and 'kin', 'banks' and 'thanks', 'skims' and 'limbs'. Two lines from 'The Woods of Westermain', published in 1883 in the *Poems and Lyrics of the Joy of Earth*, sum up in themselves the whole theory:

> Life, the small self-dragon ramped,
> Thrill for service to be stamped.

Here every word is harsh, prickly, hard of sense; the rhymes come like buffets in the face. It is possible that Mr Meredith has more or less consciously imitated the French practice in the matter of rhymes, for in France rarity of rhyme is sought as eagerly as in England it is avoided. Rhyme in French poetry is an important part of the art of verse; in English poetry, except to some extent at the time of Pope, it has been accepted as a thing rather to be disguised than accentuated. There is something a little barbarous in rhyme itself, with its mnemonic click of emphasis, and the skill of the most skilful English poets has always been shown in the softening of that click, in reducing it to the inarticulate answer of an echo. Mr Meredith hammers out his rhymes on the anvil on which he has forged his clanging and rigid-jointed words. His verse moves in plate-armour, 'terrible as an army with banners'.

It is characteristic of Mr Meredith's method that he writes for the most part in single lines, without *enjambement*, each line being almost a separate sentence. In his early work—in 'Modern Love' particularly—he broke up his page by an infinity of full stops; now he more often uses colons and semicolons, often in the place of mere commas. Take, for instance, this passage in 'The Test of Manhood':

[Quotes ll. 131–42.]

The aim is at emphasis, at detached yet cumulative force, at a kind of vivid monotony; and the same method is used in the fine and interesting experiment in blank verse, 'The Cageing of Ares', especially interesting as being, we believe, the only blank verse which Mr Meredith has published since the volume of 1851. Here are some lines torn from it, a little roughly, for the passage is too long to quote in full:

[Quotes ll. 133–46.]

The blank verse suggests rhyme, and has in it something of Marlowe's first attempts to do without rhyme, before he had mastered his great new instrument. It is full of uncouth force, and is not the only experiment which Mr Meredith has made in his new volume. At the end of the book there are some interesting essays in translation: eight fragments from the *Iliad* in English hexameters, and some stanzas from the *Mirèio* of Frédéric Mistral.[1] If hexameters are to be accepted at all as an English metre, those of Mr Meredith are certainly among the most successful ever attempted. They have weight and speed, and they rarely suggest effort in the adjustment of syllables. The lines from the Provençal are almost word for word, occasionally, as in the last lines, better than the original; but it is a pity that the first stanza is written in a different metre from the others, which almost exactly copy the curious stanza which Mistral invented for his modern epic.

To Mr Meredith poetry has come to be a kind of imaginative logic, and almost the whole of his last book is a reasoning in verse. There are a few exceptions, as in this delicate lyric called 'Song in the Songless':

[Quotes 'Song in the Songless'.]

He reasons, not always clearly to the eye, and never satisfyingly to the ear, but with a fiery intelligence which has more passion than most other poets put into frankly emotional verse. He reasons in pictures,

[1] Frédéric Mistral (1830–1914), Provençal poet, author of *Mirèio* (1859). Meredith knew Mistral through his friend, Bonaparte Wyse.

every line having its imagery, and he uses pictorial words to express abstract ideas:

> But not ere he upheld a forehead lamp,
> And viewed an army, once the seeming doomed,
> All choral in its fruitful garden camp,
> The spiritual the palpable illumed.

By such precise imagery does he render his doctrine, sometimes with words of a lusty lusciousness, as here:

> As peaches that have caught the sun's uprise
> And kissed warm gold till noonday, even as vines.

Disdaining the common subjects of poetry, as he disdains common rhythms, common rhymes, and common language, he does much by his enormous vitality to give human warmth to arguments concerning humanity. He does much, though he attempts the impossible. His poetry is always what Rossetti called 'amusing'; it has, in other words, what Baudelaire called 'the supreme literary grace, energy';[1] but with what relief does one not lay down this *Reading of Life* and take up the 'Modern Love' of forty years ago, in which life speaks! Mr Meredith has always been in wholesome revolt against convention, against every deadening limitation of art, but he sometimes carries revolt to the point of anarchy. In finding new subjects and new forms for verse he is often throwing away the gold and gathering up the ore. In taking for his foundation the stone which the builders rejected he is sometimes only giving a proof of their wisdom in rejecting it.

[1] This reference is untraced.

123. S. P. Sherman on Meredith's historical importance

Stuart Pratt Sherman (1881–1926) also published an essay on Meredith in his book, *On Contemporary Literature* (1917). This essay was published in *Nation*, lxxxviii, 3 June 1909.

I

The refusal of the authorities of Westminster Abbey to allow George Meredith to sleep among the dead whom England delights to honor was by no means surprising. In spite of the endorsement of the Society of Authors and the Prime Minister, the future of his reputation still remains in a high degree problematic. If he had died twenty-five years ago, though the work on which his fame must rest had then been accomplished, it is doubtful whether the general voice would have decreed him this solemn tribute. Indeed, from his first appearance in literature down to the time of his death no writer of his power had received less recognition for his virtues or more persistent praise for his faults. George Eliot, Swinburne, Watts-Dunton, and a following of enthusiasts felt his might, and for the most part tried to persuade the world that he was a great literary artist. Others asserted with equal vehemence that he was an incoherent thinker, making his artificial, choked, and stuttering novels the vehicle for a mass of epigram. The so-called man in the street, if he chanced to overhear the discussion, promptly decided that it did not concern him, either way. If Meredith attended to the early notices of his books, he must often have sighed as one who watches for the morning. Even so late as 1880 the *Westminster Review*, traditionally favorable to his reputation, commented upon the recently published *Egoist*—now often considered his weightiest contribution to fiction—as follows:

> Mr Meredith is, perhaps, our most artistic novelist, and, for that very reason, by no means popular with mere subscribers to Mudie's. His audience is few, but

488

fit. . . . He is, in a word, what the world would vulgarly call too clever. . . . This is Mr Meredith's great fault—he overdoes his cleverness. If he was more simple, he would be far more effective. *The Egoist* is full of poetry, subtle observation, and sparkling epigram.[1]

This review, with its emphasis upon the literary artist, is typical, and, unless I am mistaken, is about the quintessence of bad criticism. For it has yet to be demonstrated that perfection of art has interfered with the success of any matter whatsoever, even among the subscribers to Mudie's. And those who value Meredith's work most wisely will not extol him for his artistry, but rather deplore his lack of it as one of many obstacles that have stood in the way of his popularity. Furthermore, to say that he 'overdoes his cleverness' is to suggest that he consciously strains for effect. If this critic had really been one of that piteous fit audience though few, he would rather have suggested how insuperably difficult it was for Meredith not to be clever, how utterly impossible it was for him to be simple, how entirely regrettable that he did not receive an English academic training. How might not the Oxford culture have disciplined his Celtic lawlessness and subdued his turn for 'natural magic'! Welsh and Irish in ancestry, Meredith was educated at a Moravian school in Germany. In the plastic time of his youth, he, like Browning and Carlyle, was his own master of rhetoric. Like Carlyle, he wrote prose as if Dryden had never shown the superiority of Charles the Second's English to the flowered and conceited exuberance of the Elizabethans. Like Browning, he wrote verse as if Pope had not died to save us from the sins of the metaphysical school. If Donne, as honest Ben declared, for not keeping of accents deserved hanging, so did Meredith. He wanted art. He was not wanting in a perception of the supreme beauty of style—perfect identity of thought and expression. In his essay on the 'Idea of Comedy' he showed the keenest critical appreciation of the style of Menander and Terence, writing almost with rapture of their 'Elysian speech, equable and ever gracious'. But two years later, in the prelude of *The Egoist*, he was guilty of such sentences as this:

Who, says the notable humorist, in allusion to this book [Book of Earth], who can studiously travel through sheets of leaves, now capable of a stretch from the Lizard to the last few pulmonary snips and shreds of leagues dancing on their toes for cold, explorers tell us, and catching breath by good luck, like dogs about a table, on the edge of the Pole?

1 *Westminster Review*, lvii, January 1880.

II

He wanted art no less as a story-teller than as a stylist. It is true that he undertook a very difficult task. He desired to represent men and women dramatically, revealing the secret springs of their characters in their speech and acts. But for fatally long periods in many of his novels he would allow them neither to speak nor to act. Sometimes, like the messenger of the Senecan tragedy, he reported the great things that were going on behind the scenes. Sometimes with a kind of choric fury he drowned the voices of the actors and assaulted the ears of the audience with a prolonged and often partly enigmatic commentary. Sometimes he translated whole conversations into telegraphic Meredithese. These methods of telling a story are inartistic, because they deprive the auditor of the legitimate and expected pleasure of hearing the *ipsissima verba* in the critical moment, and the spectator of seeing the decisive gesture with his own eyes. Defenders of Meredith will say that he was bent on our perceiving the finer meanings of act and speech, and that he could be sure of his purpose by no other method. That is to confess again that he wanted the skill of the supreme literary artist, that his intention was greater than his power. He had himself a subtle sense of the deeper implications of speech, but he did not possess steadily that master instinct which finds a single word to tell all . . .

III

But if Meredith was not a first-rate literary artist, is it possible that he was a first-rate literary genius; or are the two things inseparable? It would be gratifying to find some substantial ground for the apparently extravagant claims of his friends. One of them, Robert Louis Stevenson, has been convicted before a just judge of uncritically juxtaposing Meredith and Shakespeare in the enthusiasm of his admiration for *Rhoda Fleming*. Looking through Stevenson's letters, however, I have been pleased to observe that he says very little about Meredith as a literary artist. . . . Stevenson mightly fairly call the man a genius who had taught him his literary gospel and shown him a reasonable way of envisaging life.

There are numerous indications, some of doubtful value, that the followers of Meredith are shifting to this more stable ground. The select literary clubs, which in the old days used to read the riddle of the Sphinx in *Childe Roland*, discovered some time ago that Meredith's *Read-*

ings of Earth [*sic*] were less trite and equally difficult. Some of the novels, too, have attracted those curious persons who find their chief pleasure in perusing what their friends declare impossible. Within four or five years as many books have been devoted to the exposition of Meredith's art and ideas, not all of which are harder to read than the works which they explain. But chiefly we must reckon in the decisive tribute of the younger generation of writers who by imitation and open avowal declare their deep indebtedness to him. 'At the present moment', says Mrs Craigie, 'all the most worthy English novelists, with the exception of Thomas Hardy, are distinguished disciples of George Meredith'.[1] The heterogeneous character of the alleged Meredithians—Stevenson, Du Maurier, Henley, Sara Grand, Anthony Hope, Maurice Hewlett, W. G. Locke, George Bernard Shaw, G. K. Chesterton, and many others—is extremely suggestive. It means that to young authors he has not been primarily a literary model—those who have caught most of his spirit have least imitated his style. It means that if Meredith is 'built for immortality', he will survive not merely as an epigrammatist, or as a subtle poet, or as a psychologizing novelist, but as a man with a mine of vital ideas, a constructive critic of life, if not an artist, at any rate a genius, one of the spokesmen and master spirits of his time.

IV

Herein lies one of his most indubitable claims to genius—he solved the problems of our contemporary literature half a century before it existed. Though his exposition was unequal to his insight, and his own coevals missed his points, such of our authors today as face the future smiling have found him out. The problems of contemporary literature are manifold in appearance, but in essence single: How to present a view of life both wise and brave, answering to experience as well as to desire, serviceable in art or the daily walk? Single in essence, in appearance they are manifold: How to give pleasure without corrupting the heart, and how to give wisdom without chilling it? How to bring into play the great passions of men without unchaining the beast? How to believe in Darwin and the dignity of man? How to believe in the nerves without paralyzing the nerve of action? How to recognize the weakness of man, and not forget his heroism? How to see his acts, and believe in his intentions? How to renounce his superstitions, and retain his faith? How to rebuke without despising him? How to reform society

[1] This reference is untraced.

without rebelling against it? How to smile at its follies without contempt? How to believe that pain is invincible, and that joy is invincible,
too? How to believe that evil is fleeing forever before good, but will
never be overtaken and slain? How to look back upon a thousand
defeats, and yet cling to the fighting hope? If you go through this list of
questions, you will not find one which Meredith did not answer. Long
before Mr Shaw broke into mock Mephistophelean laughter, and Mr
Chesterton discovered his loyalty to the universe, when they—if one
can conceive such a thing—were quietly sleeping in their cradles,
George Meredith had already bottled their thunder.

Richard Feverel, published in 1859 with The Virginians, Adam Bede,
The Tale of Two Cities, and The Origin of Species, was a repudiation and
a prophecy, but was recognized as neither. The Westminster Review,
though perceiving in it observation, humor, passion, and tenderness,
declared that the 'book offers no solution of any of the difficulties it
lays open to us; the nineteenth century struggles through it with but
faint glimpses of its goal'. With interspersed hints in subsequent novels,
with critical prefaces, and with poems Meredith tried to amend the
reviewer's error, but not till 1877 when, Aristotle to his own dramatic
cycle, he published the 'Idea of Comedy', did he finally make clear his
message. From that time it began slowly to be evident that he had
made his novels, after all, but the vehicles of an impassioned conviction.
He, like so many earnest men of his century, had sought a way of
salvation from skepticism, melancholy, ennui, and despair; and he had
found a way. Other men had other remedies. For Newman the 'one
thing needful' was to submit to authority and enter the Roman fold.
Carlyle thought the best that could be done for a man was to find him
a master, and set him to work. For Mill the key to happiness was free
logical discussion in the interests of humanity. For the men of science it
was the following of truth wherever it leads. Arnold held that none of
these things was of importance in comparison with the ability to recognize the grand style wherever one found it. To those who have read
intelligently Meredith's 'Idea of Comedy' I do not think it will seem an
anticlimax to say that he believed the one thing needful, synthesis of
all needs, was to instruct men in the proper uses of the comic spirit that
they might laugh and be laughed at unto their souls' salvation. For to
him the comic spirit is a fine celestial sunlight in the mind, answering
to the theological grace of God in the heart, which preserves those into
whom it passes from a very evil thing. It is not hostile to prayer, nor to
labor, nor to logic, nor to truth, nor to grandeur, but very friendly to

them all. It keeps prayer sweet, labor cheerful, logic sane, truth service-able, and grandeur human. But over every form of animalism, egotism, sentimentalism, cowardice, and unreason, 'it will look humanely malign, and cast an oblique light on them, followed by showers of silvery laughter'. For, to quote from the ode to the same beneficent spirit, it is the

> Sword of Common Sense!
> Our surest gift: the sacred chain
> Of man to man.

V

Once grasp that idea of comedy and you suddenly find yourself at the centre of a coherent critical system. You open his works anywhere and you find yourself at home in an ordered world. You perceive why the younger generation is turning toward him, and you see the relation in which he stood to his fellows in fiction fifty years ago. The definitions by which in the essay the comic spirit is isolated furnish a complete critical arsenal. 'The sense of the Comic is much blunted by habits of punning and of using humoristic phrase; the trick of employing John-sonian polysyllables to treat of the infinitely little'—that does not by any means dispose of Dickens, but it casts an 'oblique light' upon him. Much more penetrating is this: 'Comedy justly treated . . . throws no infamous reflection upon life'. How that judges the all too frequent passages in the novels of Thackeray like the following:

Oh, Mr Pendennis! (although this remark does not apply to such a smart fellow as you) if Nature had not made that provision for each sex in the credulity of the other, which sees good qualities where none exist, good looks in donkeys' ears, wit in their numskulls, and music in their bray, there would not have been near so much marrying and giving in marriage as obtains, and is necessary for the due propagation of the noble race to which we belong.

That principle is far reaching; it condemns in a single breath the whole miasmic marsh-land of naturalism. 'It is unwholesome for men and women to see themselves as they are, if they are no better than they should be'—there is the ethical, or, if one prefers, the sanitary, plank in the platform of the new idealism. 'The same of an immoral may be said of realistic exhibitions of a vulgar society'—there is the repudiation of wide wastes of the dryasdust realistic fiction, a much-needed denial of the democratic notion that all subjects are fit for art.

In some of the poems the Comic Spirit becomes almost truculent in its glee. It is clearly so in pitching upon any theatrical rebel against society; for example, in the verses called 'Manfred':

> Projected from the bilious Childe,
> This clatterjaw his foot could set
> On Alps, without a breast beguiled
> To glow in shedding rascal sweat.
> Somewhere about his grinder teeth,
> He mouthed of thoughts that grilled beneath,
> And summoned Nature to her feud
> With bile and buskin Attitude.

Meredith arrived a little too late to play Childe Harold or Don Juan; but if he had not been protected by his guardian spirit, he might easily have taken a part in that more plaintive and dismal literature of despair represented by numerous poems of Matthew Arnold. In the crushed and crabbed verse of Meredith's jibe at Arnold's *Empedocles*, I confess to finding something very tonic, something that Arnold as critic would have himself called tonic:

[Quotes 'Empedocles', st. i and st. ii, ll. 8–10.]

VI

But what has comedy to do with tragedy, and how do they become tragi-comedy? Well, in the luminous intoxication of the morning following the symposium, Socrates forced Agathon and Aristophanes, who alone had stayed it out with him till cock-crow, to confess not only that tragedy and comedy may be composed by the same person, but also that 'the foundations of the tragic and comic arts were essentially the same'.[1] Aristodemus, who reported the conclusion of the dispute, was unfortunately asleep during the discussion. With this, for that reason, unexplained opinion of Socrates, Meredith was obviously in accord. To his view, life is neither wholly comedy nor wholly tragedy, but both at once. In order to distinguish either element one must be able to distinguish both; the comic spirit, one may almost say, is that which perceives the tragic fault. In order to represent life bravely and wisely, one must see it steadily, and see it whole. Such sight is given only to deep and grave heads. Those endowed with this vision discern that the great girders which bear up the world of man are the

[1] *Symposium*, 223.

discipline of the passions by the mind, loyalty to reason, and faith in civilization. Whatever forces attempt to weaken these girders—the cynicism of Don Juan, the despair of Empedocles—the Comic Spirit holds them, to adopt the Cæsarian euphemism, *in numero hostium*—puts them to the sword of common sense. The discernment that these great girders are essential to civilization, and the loyalty which in grave men springs with the discernment, underlie every true comedy and every true tragedy. But the struggle which most men undergo in disciplining their passions, learning to walk in the light of reason, and preserving their faith in civilization, is a strange series of ups and downs. Comedy attends to their foolish falls; tragedy to their painful failures; to re-present the whole course of the struggle is to write tragi-comedy.

Tragi-comedy as the position of equipoise in life and art—that, in Meredith's time, was a notable discovery. When we attempt to measure his achievement we should not lose sight of the originality, the scope, and the difficulty of his design. He planned to produce thoughtful laughter, an aim which demanded that the characters in his novels, as well as in his audience, should possess some of the culture of the drawing-room. But he planned at the same time to move the great passions which are generally attenuated under intensive cultivation. Since the Restoration they had almost disappeared from the fiction of high life. Wordsworth had been obliged to seek out the great universal impulses in the cottages of Cumberland peasants. The Brontës studied them in mad country squires. George Eliot found them among the yeomen of Warwickshire. Even Thomas Hardy has had to resort to shepherds and dairy-maids—so fugitive is our sense of solemn splendor from the roar of cities and civilized men. But what pitiful antagonists of destiny these rural people of Mr Hardy's make. The intelligence of mortals is wholly inactive in the combat. In condemning the ways of God to man this grim artist seems obsessed by the idea that all nature is conspiring to bring a helpless humanity to degradation and shame. That is hardly to see life whole. Meredith sought his splendor in another place. His problem was how to make tragedy and comedy meet to-gether in the drawing-room. Comedy was there to stay; but as for tragedy, Thackeray, for example, avoided it. Dickens and his public really preferred murder. To his fellows in fiction Meredith owed very little. On his serious side nearest akin to George Eliot, he preceded her into the field. Carlyle and Browning and Wordsworth were all his natural allies, but his master was Shakespeare. From him he learned to choose out for the favorite theatre of his play a country-house, where, as in a court, were assembled enough actors of civilized life to be visible against the scenery. From him he learned to let poor clowns play humble parts, and if anyone had to be sent out on a barren heath to send a king who even in madness was a match for the storm. From him he learned to line the back and sides of his stage with the gray and middle ages of wisdom, pedantry, sanctity, craft, and cynicism; and then to release in the foreground young Romeo and Juliet, or Perdita and Florizel, or Ferdinand and Miranda to discover the brave new world under a stinging rain of comment from prudent or disillusioned antiquity; and then, at last, whether to youth and beauty the vista of days opened smiling, or whether some dire mischance closed their fond eyes forever, to intimate that to youth belong the untrodden ways.

VII

Meredith's life began and closed on that note. In an age when a general disintegration of ideas was taking place, he showed an extremely keen sense of what was permanent and what transitory. He woke early to the necessity and the possibility of a new organic synthesis. Though his creative power and craftsmanship were inferior to his critical faculty, they worked harmoniously, and, therefore, effectively. Several of his contemporaries possessed separately in a higher degree the intellectual or emotional powers with which he was gifted; but no one of them fused within himself so many and so diverse powers. In close touch with distinguished utilitarian and positivist leaders, though he did not subscribe to all their philosophical and political doctrines he heartily partook in their sense of stern responsibility to society and in their resolution to make war without truce against the confederated lusts and egotisms of the unredeemed animal man. His sonnet to 'J. M.' is almost Miltonic in its note of militant resolution:

[Quotes 'To J.M.'.]

124. Meredith in perspective

1909

This attempt at a balanced appreciation of Meredith's career was by the Rev. James Moffatt (1870–1944), a writer on theological and Biblical subjects and author of *A Primer to the Novels of George Meredith* (1909). The article appeared in *Bookman*, xxxvi, July 1909, under the title 'George Meredith'.

'Poetry we have none and but little philosophy', Mark Pattison wrote bluntly in 1830.[1] When Meredith published his first volume of poems twenty-one years later, it was recognized that a poet of promise had arisen, but no one then could foretell that the author would produce prose as well as poetry which embodied a definite and original philosophy of life. Meredith ended, as he had begun, with verse. *A Reading of Life* appeared exactly half a century after the *Poems* of 1851, but the difference of tone and style, which appeared as early as the second volume of poetry in 1862 and became increasingly patent in the intervening novels, recalls the change felt in passing from *Pauline* to the subsequent poems of Robert Browning. Meredith has acquired a philosophy in the interval; it is a philosophy of Nature, and it has been responsible in large measure for the vital and the ephemeral qualities of his output.

From first to last he showed a remarkable power of delicate realism in his treatment of natural sights and sounds. This gift of sensuous charm, almost Keatsian in its quality, was what struck Kingsley and Rossetti and Hort[2] in his early poems. Other interests absorbed his later mind, but never to the entire exclusion of this direct sensitiveness to Nature. One of his earliest pastorals, echoed in a famous chapter of

---

[1] Not in 1830, but in 1845; 'Gregory of Tours', *Christian Remembrancer*, IX, 1845: 'Poetry we have almost none and but little philosophy; but history has attracted great attention among us.'

[2] Fenton John Anthony Hort (1828–92), Biblical critic and scholar, perhaps responsible for one of the reviews of the 1851 *Poems*.

Lord Ormont and His Aminta, includes this exquisite glimpse of a summer day beside the Thames:

[Quotes 'Pastorals', vii, ll. 41–7.]

Over and over again, in prose and verse, he shows this power of reproducing a natural scene in its detail and charm. Thus, in his last volume, we get the following lyric, a vignette of autumn:

[Quotes 'Song in the Songless'.]

But Nature came to mean far more than this to Meredith. Thomas Love Peacock, his father-in-law, to whom the volume of 1851 was dedicated, had cited in his *Misfortunes of Elphin* a Welsh triad upon 'the three primary requisites of poetical genius: an eye that can see Nature; a heart that can feel Nature; and a resolution that dares follow Nature'.[1] The first two requisites never abandoned Meredith. His sensitiveness to Nature enabled him to round the inward vision by lyric, lucid transcripts of what he saw and felt, from blackbirds to larks and nightingales, from the Thames to the Alps, from the crocus to the wild cherry-tree. His prose and verse repeatedly vibrate with such passages—sometimes a sentence or stanza, sometimes a paragraph or chapter—of direct intuition and unaffected charm. But another spirit of affectation and complexity struggled for his soul as a literary artist. Its hold upon him was due to the prominence assigned to his peculiar conception of the third requisite in the Welsh triad. Nature to him meant the cosmos of modern evolutionary science, and loyalty to Nature involved an ethical idealism which sought the ethical standards as well as the physical origin of man in his relationship to the facts and forces of this living organism. This frank recognition of human nature as part of Nature produced Meredith's characteristic attack on sentimentalism and his buoyant, grave message of courage and joy. But it was responsible for serious defects in his literary method. Into its philosophic merits or demerits we need not enter here. The point is that his propaganda led not only to an ultra-subtle handling of motives, which investigated human nature with a lens and a scalpel, but to a disproportionate and unseasonable intrusion of philosophic analysis upon the course of his novels and the movement of his larger poems. To read some of the latter is like listening to a canary in a room full of typewriters at work: you catch occasional notes of song amid the metallic and staccato click of the machines. As for the romances, they are studded with half-

[1] *Misfortunes of Elphin* (1829).

defiant, half-contrite apologies for the intrusions of the Philosopher, but the latter is too much in evidence. He takes you behind the booth to let you see the strings by means of which the showman works his puppets. The result is that the characters are not always kept at blow-heat, while the reader's attention is apt to flag. It is as if Marcus Aurelius had embodied his philosophy in tales of the Romans and the Quadi.

This pre-occupation springs from the correct perception that human motives are to be sought in the ideas rather than in the appetites, but Meredith pays too little attention to the facts and incidents which give rise to the ideas in question, and in which his characters ought to have been allowed to reveal themselves more fully than they do. What interests him is the effect produced upon his characters by certain events in the chain of circumstance, and, in his eagerness to analyze the former, he often commits the inartistic blunder of merely hinting at the latter. He allows his antipathy to the reporting columns of sensational fiction to carry him too far. When he chooses, he can give his readers Stevenson's luxury of laying aside the judgment and being submerged by the tale as by a billow. But the trouble is that he often chooses the worst part. Instead of letting himself go, he will prefer to keep your head prosaically safe above the water, or even to drag you ashore, while he expounds in diverting and ingenious words the sequence of the tides. Thus the duels are never described directly in *The Tragic Comedians* or in *Beauchamp's Career*, while the horse-whipping in the latter book is only alluded to. The divorce-case in *Diana*, and Lord Fleetwood's nocturnal visit to Carinthia are similarly ignored, except by way of allusion. Things happen, of vital moment to the story. We only hear of them incidentally. The Greek dramatists employed a Messenger to tell the audience such incidents, but while Meredith creates an equivalent to the Greek chorus, he forgets to include in his *dramatis personæ* any Messenger, the result being that his method of telling a story frequently suggests a forgetfulness of the distinctions between the psychological essay and the romance. Thus, in the searching and poignant sequence of poems entitled 'Modern Love', it is not easy, even after a second or third reading, to make out the precise facts which underlie the actions and emotions of the husband and the wife as they blunder against one another in the snare of their own devising. But this perverse habit of allusiveness became more irritating than ever in the prose romances, when the author had less excuse for his failure to be explicit and definite.

Style is ultimately a matter of temperament, and it is the same passion for suggesting a multiplicity of more or less obvious ideas which is largely responsible for the elliptic discords and the conceits in Meredith's brilliant and energetic phrasing. After Rosamund Culling had listened to Dr Shrapnel, 'it was perceptible to her that a species of mad metaphor had been wriggling and tearing its passage through a thorn-bush in his discourse, with the furious urgency of a sheep in a panic; but where the ostensible subject ended and the metaphor commenced, and which was which at the conclusion, she found it difficult to discern'. De te fabula, the exasperated reader of Meredith is often tempted to exclaim. No one can go quite so far wrong as a clever man, when he sets his mind to it, or rather as a genius who is also a clever man and who, as Henley grumbled, sometimes prefers his cleverness to his genius.[1] But the genius is there, and it reasserts itself before long, even in the most ornate and grotesque chapters of the novels. Yes, 'genius' is the word for him, intellectual and imaginative genius. The Times reviewer singled out his first great romance as 'penetrative in its depth of insight and rich in its variety of experience',[2] while George Eliot had already hailed The Shaving of Shagpat as 'a work of genius' in its own way.[3] The subsequent novels bore out the promise of these initial works. The four most characteristic of the series—The Ordeal of Richard Feverel, The Egoist, Beauchamp's Career, and Diana of the Crossways—rank among the contributions of the Victorian age to the great literature of English fiction. They possess the line and colour of master-pieces, stamped with the individuality of a profound intellect. And they are flanked by poems such as the 'Hymn to Colour', 'The Nuptials of Attila', 'Earth and a Wedded Woman', 'The Thrush in February', 'Juggling Jerry', 'The Woods of Westermain', 'Love in a Valley', and 'Melampus'—to name only representative specimens of the author's versatile talent. These all testify to the essentially 'great' note of his mind, to the extraordinary penetration and wide grasp which inform the luxuriant fancy and terse energy of the style upon the higher levels of his prose or verse.

For Meredith's eccentricity is of expression rather than of ideas. Like his own 'later Alexandrian', 'mystic wrynesses he chased'—and caught and fondled. The style is often as condensed and enigmatic as the digressions are prolix. But his thought, or rather his penetrating outlook upon life, has an equipoise and unity of its own. His ideal of life according to Nature saves him, even in his most daring and radical moments, from falling into the extravagances of the crude theorist, who

[1] See above, No. 59.   [2] See above, No. 23.   [3] See above, No. 7.

would either flout Nature or worship natural instincts or fall into raptures before the 'green thought in the green shade'. One of the best illustrations of this balance occurs in his stringent criticism of pluto-cratic society in 'The Empty Purse' and in *Beauchamp's Career*, where his denunciations are carefully accompanied by a frank recognition of the place due to tradition and of the risks run by the extreme reformer. But perhaps a comparison of his treatment of the lark with the similar poems of Shelley and Wordsworth will serve to bring out what is meant by the equilibrium of his judgment. To Shelley the lark rep-resented an 'unbodied joy', which scorns and surpasses the earthly measures of men. Wordsworth saw in its mounting and dropping an emblem of 'the wise who soar, but never roam' from their appointed lot on earth. Meredith combines the joy and the link with earth in a higher synthesis. His lines upon 'The Lark Ascending' begin with a passage of genuine poetry describing the bird's song:

[Quotes 'The Lark Ascending', ll. 1–8.]

But Meredith finds in the lark a truth of his own philosophy. The lark's song thrills with that simple and rich joy of earth which comes from a life in harmony with Nature. The bird's song expresses the rapture of its natural existence, whereas, he contends, men are prone to fall out of touch with their surroundings and conditions.

[Quotes 'The Lark Ascending', ll. 89–94.]

The inward, spiritual interpretation of the bird's song, as it mounts alive and aglow with the joy of the earth below it, is that the true love of earth means self-forgetfulness. What spoils the happiness and strength of men, the poet argues, is their rampant egoism; they exaggerate their personal likes and dislikes until they lose touch with the great, sane, wise order of Nature, and fall into the extravagance either of passion or of melancholy. Real eccentricity, according to Meredith, lay in egoism, and it was against this error in every phase of life that he shot his sharpest arrows. False pride, in its variety of forms, represented to him the really abnormal thing in human life. If his analysis of it became frequently hyper-subtle, the reason is that he felt its ramifications rayed out from a central error and were in many cases undetected alike by the sinner and the spectators, simply because they failed to grasp the con-stituent relation of human life to the natural order. He enjoyed splitting psychological seeds. He enjoyed the display of his own dexterity in handling them. But, at his best, when the method ceased to be over-intellectual, and the materials were other than some wilful derangement or aberration, he made his readers feel that he was taking a survey of human life from its centre, and not merely cataloguing with caustic insight the delicate traceries and gossamer filaments upon fantastic orchids in some garden of modern civilization.

When a criticism of life is passed through the creative imagination of a novelist and poet, its effectiveness largely depends upon the particular form assumed by his analysis. Meredith did not choose an easy form. He abjured satire and irony, which anyone could have understood, little as they might have liked them. He chose a subtle, intellectual form of humour which he dubbed the Comic Spirit, and the main difficulty of appreciating his treatment of life arises from this idiosyncrasy. It is often so delicate, and makes such heavy demands upon the wit of the reader, as to suggest an eccentricity, a wilfulness, a perversity, which is unfairly attributed to the original and stimulating philosophy which it embodies. Fortunately, the 'Essay on Comedy' supplies the necessary clue to the poems and the novels alike, especially to the latter. 'Comedy is the fountain of sound sense; not the less perfectly sound on account of the sparkle'. 'Philosopher and comic poet are of a cousinship in the eye they cast on life: and they are equally unpopular with our wilful English of the hazy region and the ideal that is not to be disturbed'. Meredith's humour is exactly defined in the last of these sentences. It is the humour of a serious thinker who, for all the fun and farce in him, wants to disturb conventional ideas and ideals. For an appreciation of his method he had to create his public, and the comparatively slow recognition of his genius has been due in part to his own mischievous delight in puzzling his audience, in part to the difficulty which people felt about taking grave criticisms of society from a writer of gaiety and romance. Still, the philosophy of his laughter has won its way at last. Its success has been and will be hindered by the handicap which he imposed on himself, but its impact is now recognized, and recognized as a factor in the increase of sanity and sincerity throughout modern life. 'He did stout service in his day. If the bad manners he scourged are now lessened to some degree, we pay a debt in remembering that we owe much to him; and if what appears incurable remains with us, a continued reading of his works will at least help to combat it'.[1] Meredith wrote these words about one of his great predecessors in English fiction, and we are justified today in applying to himself what he said gratefully of Thackeray.

[1] Introduction to W. M. Thackeray's *The Four Georges* (Red Letter Library ed. 1903).

125. A Final Appreciation

This excellent article was by Percy Lubbock (b. 1879), a proponent of Jamesian principles, author of *The Craft of Fiction* (1921), and one of the most influential of twentieth-century critics. The article appeared in *Quarterly Review*, ccxii, April 1910, as a review of the *Collected Works*.

The art of fiction, in all its innumerable divagations of the last hundred and fifty years, must truly by now have provided material enough for a generalized criticism of its nature, its scope, its limiting conditions; but criticism can hardly be said to have yet made any calculated attempt to survey the whole parti-coloured field and to define the principles which seem to be implied. In the early and bravely irresponsible days of the novel there could be no possibility of such a definition. So long as the art was still purely experimental, so long as it could spread in all directions over virgin soil, criticism could merely watch discreetly and take provisional note of failures and successes. But fiction must follow, and is already following, the line of development which carries it from its first expansive thoughtlessness to self-conscious deliberation. It must run its course, like other forms of art; it must lose certain qualities and assume others; it must submit to maturity and make the best of it without trying to reproduce the essentially youthful graces of its past. It continues so unmistakably to hold its own as the most characteristic form of our time that a distinguished future, it is impossible to doubt, still lies before it. But it must pay the penalty of its prolonged predominance by learning to 'know itself' and to realize its principles. Such a process implies loss in a hundred ways, loss perhaps of the very qualities for which we most incline to value the art; but if the sacrifice is inevitable it is only the sharper challenge to the novelist to develope new values in their place. An artist is of his time, and if he inherits a form which has already yielded its first freshness he has to find the base of his work in the qualities that remain. Criticism steps in at this stage and tries to express the results that have been established, patiently hoping, be it confessed, to avoid its usual mistake of making the art square with its formula instead of moulding its formula on the art.

No attempt can of course be made here to co-ordinate the scattered achievements of fiction in the manner suggested; but the single illustrious case to be considered will be approached as far as possible from this point of view. The work of George Meredith, so sumptuous and so varied, has for its admirers intellectual, moral, philosophical appeals which have perhaps to some extent obscured the question of its strictly artistic characterization. Much has been written upon the strong consistent view of the world, of nature and society, which lies alike behind his novels and his poetry; but the art which went to its expression has usually been treated as a detachable matter, something to be estimated side by side, even if in the same prominence, with the personal doctrines of the great writer. Meredith cut so deep into his material and laid open such new sources that the fruition of his thought has occupied his critics before the form in which it was embodied. If it is attempted to reverse the process there can be little danger of over-looking the matter for the sake of the manner, for from this side the two things cannot be separated. The personality of an artist can be disentangled from his art, but never his art from his personality.

True, surely, of all writers, this is trebly true of Meredith, so sharply stamped with the mark of his brain and spirit was everything he touched. The most obviously Shakespearean in a certain sense of modern authors, he was nevertheless the least so if the word is used of that aspect of Shakespeare's work which gives us the most striking example in all literature of an apparent exception to our rule, the aspect in which the writer is merged, almost beyond possibility of recovery, in his creations. Meredith is never for an instant in this sense dramatic. His own presence dominates every page of his books; and often enough, both in his prose and his poetry, we seem less to be handling a fashioned and self-complete work of art than to be actually present in his studio, watching while he flies impetuously at the marble which hides the statue, and perhaps at times more conscious of the process, of the crackle of blows and the hail of white chips, than of the lurking goddess. Yet even so, though the din and the effort may interfere with one kind of enjoyment, the display of power, the determination and the onslaught, joined with the sense that the possible prize is worth the struggle and that the unconquered block does in fact conceal the divine—all this makes of such an experience an exhilarating memory for craftsman or critic. It fires the athletic quality which is part of the mind of every artist, and shows in the perfected work, when at other times it is given us rounded and flawless, the temper which the highest beauty receives from brain alone.

Meredith's art, indeed, as we follow it from book to book, reflects one long conflict with stubborn and recalcitrant material. It is as though he could never be content until he should make language do a little more that it ever will. Most writers by middle life have acquiesced in the limitations of their medium, and their submission is dignified, rightly enough, by the style of mastery of their craft. There is, then, in the typical case, a moment at which hand and brain work in harmony and produce their best work, before the time arrives when the hand, now completely controlled, is found to be closing upon a gradually weakening substance. That is, on the whole, the evolution more or less clearly to be traced in most cases. But Meredith's record is utterly different. The compromise between intention and result, between thought and word, is struck with extraordinary precocity in his earliest work and with ever increasing difficulty in his later. Not of course necessarily on this account is *The Ordeal of Richard Feverel* a better book than *One of Our Conquerors*, when the scope, the significance, the final product of the balance is considered, as well as its nicety. But while it is solely a question of the command of the medium in which he worked, it is easy to see that the Meredith of 1859 was far surer of poised and sustained effect than the Meredith of thirty years later. The rocky utterance with which his stories tended more and more to be wrenched into being was the exaggeration no doubt of an inherent mannerism; but to name it thus does not carry us far. With the living force which Meredith throughout poured into his work, the history of its style becomes the history of its substance; and the growing sense of effort merely implies that he charged his art with ever more complicated burdens. No other imaginative writer of our time has had to reckon with a brain so perennially insurgent and insistent. Meredith's intellect touched life at an immense number of points and could rest at none of them. He was only incidentally a painter of nature and society; essentially he was an interpreter of one and a critic of the other. The distinction places him nearer Carlyle than Browning; for Browning, though in his case also intellectual curiosity never relaxed its strain upon his art, was far less a critic than a portrait-painter, and was more interested in character, for its own sake, than Meredith ever was.

We thus arrive at what must be called a fundamental weakness in Meredith's attitude as a novelist pure and simple. Character is the corner-stone of fiction, and the variation of an inch in its position must more or less insidiously affect the whole fabric. It is perfectly true of course that a novel is in one sense necessarily a criticism of life, for the simple reason that nothing a human being may say or do can imaginably be anything else. Nor must it be suggested that good fiction cannot be produced except upon the most strictly impersonal lines. All this may be admitted without touching the assertion that fiction is the master-art of representation, and is more than this only at its own risk and on its own responsibility. So far from resenting the limitation, fiction should glory in it and be ever ready to look jealously on the tendency to infringe it. It is, or it should be, the especial pride of this beautiful art that it can *represent* more fully and freely, with greater subtlety and greater precision, than any other; and it ought not to forget that, however often it may do it with impunity, to allow other considerations to cloud the issue is really by just so much to compromise its unique power. To be interested first and foremost in character as such is the novelist's safeguard and justification. Meredith's interest in character was ultimately relative; it was closely modelled, that is to say, upon his philosophy, and it was in their bearing upon his philosophy that men and women appealed to him. The desire to show their value or their uselessness was the larger part of his desire to portray them; and, often as he might portray them magnificently, this constant preoccupation must be taken into account if we try to speculate as to the verdict which will eventually be passed upon his work. It must also be distinguished from the obvious truth that for the strictest novelist human beings have a varying range of values, the difference being that judgment depends for him upon the æsthetic and not upon the ethical elements of the case.

We are here promptly confronted with the question whether the novel was really the form best fitted for this masterful imagination, or whether it might not have expressed itself with less hindrance in some more confessedly personal shape. But it will not do, we must be firmly reminded, to be tempted at this point by a question so completely in the air; the plain fact being that when Meredith began to write, as indeed when he ceased, no other form was possible for creative work on a scale so extended. Art, it would seem, insists on claiming that at least its greatest followers should, at any given epoch, keep to the main lines of its evolution. They must accept the forms which lie to their hand, wilfulness in such a matter being allowed only to those whose force is intense rather than broad. Meredith's power was too varied for any but the central stream, whatever its disadvantages; he was a novelist by predestination. Nor should it be forgotten that this very clash between the claim of art on one hand and individual impulse on the other may actually discover compensating sources of strength; as indeed conflict in some shape or other, with consequent sacrifice, seems ever necessary for the engendering of the best. It is surely, for example, not fanciful to trace to what we have called Meredith's initial weakness as a novelist one of the most characteristic and important qualities of his work. With an outlook on life so little detached, with an interest so speculative and constructive, with a range of opinion so positive in its operations, Meredith's grasp of actuality was far-reaching in proportion to his want of impartial serenity. This may seem a paradox in view of the inevitable objection that 'actual' is the last word one would apply to the world of his novels; and it is of course true that in the sense of a photographic transcript nothing could well be further from daily fact. And yet it must be felt that Meredith's novels, for all their curiously alien atmosphere, are somehow or other deeply embedded in life. Other writers may draw more recognizable scenes; Meredith contrives to place us in company which, in spite of seeming at times like a mad dream, never allows us to question that something living and genuine is going forward.

Yet, vivid as was Meredith's sense of life, his rendering of it was always in indirect terms. He was as entirely in and of the Victorian age as man could be, and his types were for the most part of the essence of the nineteenth century; but the air he set them in and the light he shed upon them have the effect of carrying the whole action back to the most spacious days of the *ancien régime*. Horse-whippings, duels, abductions, heroic conviviality, high-handed rollicks of all kinds— Meredith's drama, whatever the scene or the period, was ever charged with epic reverberations of such matters. It is needless to say that this whole-hearted delight in the romantic stock-in-trade had nothing about it either vulgar or obvious. It was not the commonplace desire of the man of letters hungering to take a hand in great enterprises for which he has been born too late. It was something much more fundamental than this, much more entwined in his artistic aims. If real life enacts itself in Meredith's novels upon a plane of unreality, it must be remembered that a peculiarly heightened and concentrated effect was thereby obtainable. Meredith singled out certain qualities—courage, spirit, pride, sentimentalism—and threw them into the strongest possible relief. He did much more than record them; he blazed light upon them, he raised their power, so to say, by intensifying their setting. The

19‑>‑

level of ordinary life was much to low for the strongly symbolic parts his heroes and heroines had to play. 'My people are actual, yet uncommon', he himself pointed out. 'It is the clockwork of the brain that they are directed to set in motion'. High comedy cannot be rendered in terms of our daily intercourse; it requires isolation, a swept stage, an artful disposition of lights. The framework which for Meredith gave the required relief was florid and artificial; in it his characters could not merely be themselves, they could be strikingly and exceptionally themselves.

All novelists are, of course, confronted with this problem, which is simply the all-embracing problem of turning life into art, the discovery of the right artistic notation for the theme selected. Of this part of the business Meredith was a past-master. His presentation of life is everywhere homogeneous; it bears to actuality a uniform and consistent relation. To choose one method of presentation, and not to be reduced (within the same work) to appealing for help from another, is perhaps less recognized as the plainest demand of art in fiction than in any other form. Perfect examples of this admirable economy are plentiful through the length and breadth of Meredith's novels. To single one out, we may point to two scenes from *Sandra Belloni*—the moonlight expedition, with its characteristic interweaving of irony and lyrical rapture, in search of the unknown singer in the wood, and the delirious farce of Mrs Chump's capture of Braintop to help her in concocting her letter to the Miss Poles. Remote from each other, the two scenes are yet translations from life into one and the same language. Mrs Chump's voluble indignation and despair are no more 'realistic' in treatment than Emilia's liquid melody ringing through the night. Both are equally true, both are at the same angle to literal fact. There is no descent from one to the other; they are wrought up to the same pitch and by the same broad, sweeping strokes.

As marked as Meredith's care for consistency of tone was his curious indifference to background. This again may seem for the moment a paradox if we think of his superb power of brushing in a whole landscape in half a sentence, or if we remember only certain scenes in which outbursting emotion melts into sea or sky or land, transfusing and transfiguring them, absorbing their very essence into its own mood. But chapters like 'Morning at Sea under the Alps', or 'By Wilming Weir', are exceptional invocations of the beauty of day and night to surround and envelop human passion. Such exquisite visions of poetry are only for moments of great exaltation. For the most part we ask in vain for any sufficient means of realizing pictorially the action which is passing. The defect is particularly noticeable in the uncomfortable sterility with which so many of them open. *Vittoria*, with its rapturous initial ascent into the crystal mountain air of Italy, is an exception; *Harry Richmond* very notably another, with its picture of the sleeping house suddenly roused, the door opening to the soft February night. But in most of them we are allowed no chance of feeling *placed* at the start. We are plunged straight into the moral atmosphere of the action; but the absence of suggested form is a little bewildering to the most steady-headed reader. In the whirl of distant talk and laughter which opens the story proper of *Diana of the Crossways* it is as though the play had begun before the raising of the curtain; and indeed throughout that wonderful book a full square view of the scene is seldom permitted. In *The Egoist*, with its entirely simple scheme of time and place, the disadvantages of the spectator's position are still more obvious, for the scene never shifts after the first few chapters, and yet Patterne Hall remains to the end more or less of an abstraction. Quite as much as any toughness of phrasing, this defect is no doubt responsible for the obscurity which must in candour be allowed, even by the expert, to be a reasonable charge against many or most of the novels. It is essential to clarity that the sense of *where* the characters are should be plainly given; and we ask the question, in reading Meredith, a great deal oftener then we receive an answer.

But here again it is important to be reminded that a defect so obvious demands, in a writer like Meredith, something more than simple indication. Its origin and its reason need to be further traced in the texture of his art, and this demands a closer examination of his method of handling a story. The later novels differ very considerably in structure from the earlier; and it is in the later that the featurelessness of the background, whilst it is also more pronounced, is by the nature of the case more explicable. That extraordinary maze of poetry and fantasy, *The Shaving of Shagpat*, stands apart; but from *The Ordeal of Richard Feverel* to *Beauchamp's Career* the treatment is that of a chronicle rather than of a study. There is no sharply marked break; the change is gradual, and *Beauchamp's Career* itself has almost as much affinity with the later books as with its predecessors. But, broadly speaking, if we compare (say) *Evan Harrington* with *Diana of the Crossways*, the difference is clear enough for an attempt to define it. Each deals with a particular figure and a particular case; but the first is felt as something to be recorded and described, the latter as something to be interpreted and explained. The first therefore has the greater externality and should naturally take the more pictorial form. So to some extent it does; and *Harry Richmond*, with its wider sweep, has more than the rest a certain panoramic quality. But even in these simpler histories the pre-occupation of the critic, noted a few pages back, affects the method of the chronicler. Meredith's exuberant brain was always driving his perception of his characters into opinions about them, and to the same extent leaving him neither time nor patience to give his *mise-en-scène* its full value for the eye. He felt the relation of his figures to the social picture, English or international, more acutely than he felt their relation to the background of the moment. He could not 'curb the liberal hand, subservient proudly', in Browning's phrase.[1] At the same time he did, in his earlier work, on the whole handle the story as a sequence of events, to be approached from without and carried through at a more or less even pace.

In the later books the treatment is less biographic and more discursive; 'what did they do'? gives place to 'how did they come to do it'? The change of structure may be expressed by saying that the movement spreads outwards from within, surging from side to side into the recesses of the character to be examined. In *The Egoist* and *Diana of the Crossways* the centre lies in a single figure whose actions are but the point of departure for a searching exploration of the groundwork of the mind underneath them. In *The Tragic Comedians* as in the three latest novels (*One of our Conquerors, Lord Ormont and his Aminta, The Amazing Marriage*), the centre is found in a particular situation, in at least two cases based upon actual record, the problem being to reason back from the facts, objectively stated, to their inner history. Such, says Meredith in effect, is the story of Alvan and Clotilde; the facts are these; now what are we to make of them? Thus Lord Ormont treated his wife: why? and what motives, scrutinizing the case as closely as we may, can we find underlying her rejoinder? Evenness of pace is now of small account. The story lingers and broadens, leaps an interval, lingers again. It is as though the whole action lay spread out before the writer at the start; he surveys it, comments on it, disposes of it point by point; he does not *tell* it. Artistically speaking, these packed overflowing studies of character and dilemma are open to the destructive objection that their density is governed by no definite design. Vital aspects become huddled and fore-shortened, sometimes even almost overlooked, in the exposition. How insufficiently, for example, is the amazing

[1] 'One Word More.'

marriage itself prepared for in advance; we have to swallow it, an indigestible fact, while still imperfectly seeing how it arises out of the character of the pair. Again, the position, when their history opens, of Victor Radnor and Nataly, the legacy of twenty years of difficulty which is already behind them—how shadowily this past is realized before we are plunged into the development of the situation. Many examples could be given of this impatience of preparation, which, added to the increased scenic bareness, makes the reader's task ever less straightforward. Yet to the end, though the gathering force of the directing intellect seemed more and more to be baffled by the difficulties of clarity, these later books are full as ever of the torrential imagination which expressed itself in so many living and memorable shapes.

In Meredith's gallery of creations there can be no doubt which series stands out most bravely and takes the eye with the freshest beauty and originality. In Shakespeare only can we find anything to set beside his long series of portraits of women. Since Shakespeare no one but Meredith has painted women with the same full and romantic sureness. He drew them—his especial strength was that he did so—from a securely masculine point of view. It is this that, even when he most boldly tracks their inner thought, always prevents the picture from becoming a mawkish or sentimental abstraction. He never lost sight of the sane relations of man and woman to each other; and, highly as he might idealize his heroines, this ever-present consciousness was the charm which kept every most subtle touch perfectly sound and robust. The heroine of romance sprang with his first book straight to the position which she had never occupied since the days of Rosalind and Portia. She became a woman in a more complete sense than a woman drawn by a feminine hand can ever be. Only where strong imaginative sympathy is grounded upon a firmly balanced virility, a sufficiently rare conjunction, are such portraits possible as those of Lucy Desborough or of Emilia, of Clara Middleton or Carinthia. The heroes who are mated with these peerless creatures fall into two main groups, one typified by Richard Feverel and Harry Richmond, the other by Vernon Whitford and Redworth. The admirable vividness of the former and the colourless tenuity of the latter proves curiously how necessary for a successful portrait it is that sympathy should be stoutened by a certain detachment. Meredith had imaged Richard and Harry from without, had watched and noted them, before he pictured them from within; and for the latter part of the process imagination had to make a definite effort and readjustment of itself. But Vernon and Redworth, Merthyr Powys and Owain Wythan, were too closely akin to the writer's mind to be surveyed as images before being described as characters, with the result that they do not crystallise sharply enough to form recognizable figures. For a true comprehension of Meredith himself they need close examination; but as actors in their own dramas it must be admitted that they utterly fail to stand out.

Their inconclusiveness, however, is the less felt that none of them occupies or is designed to occupy a place in the front plane of the books in which they appear. They do not therefore contradict the judgment that Meredith had an unrivalled power of consistently giving his principal figures their full emphasis. The latter hold the stage and predominate; the most strongly marked of the subsidiary characters never dispute it with them. Even the matchless and irrepressible Countess de Saldar gets no more than her due. *Evan Harrington*, moreover, illustrates another delicacy which shows the cunning of Meredith's hand in this matter of relative prominence. It is necessary to the story that the presence of the great Mel should make an effect at the start out of all proportion to our actual glimpses of him; and Meredith manages with extraordinary art that he shall unforgettably pervade the atmosphere. An analogous case is that of Richmond Roy, the irresistible *bravura* of whose personality is felt as much in his absence as when he is brought before us. Where, as in *Lord Ormont and His Aminta*, several characters have to be kept simultaneously to the fore, the handling is no less masterly. Indeed the one comparative failure in this respect is *The Amazing Marriage*, where the different figures do no doubt tend to jostle and obscure each other unduly.

It is impossible here to examine in detail the army of minor creations which crowd to the mind in the wake of the foremost. Their variety, the wide range of station and type from which they are culled, expresses Meredith's great comprehensive reach over the social structure and the multiplicity of his affinities with life. He is as familiar in *Rhoda Fleming* and *Harry Richmond* with the atmosphere of the wallflower-coloured farmhouses in which he so delights, as elsewhere with the highly artificialized aspirations of the Poles or with the alert restlessness of Diana and her circle. Mrs Berry, Mrs Chump, Mrs Waddy, form a chapter by themselves; Ottilia's Professor, Shrapnel, Dr Middleton, another. All of them, it must again be emphasized, receive the figurative treatment, the deliberate translation from literal fact, which was indicated above. It is no criticism to say they are 'exaggerated'; though it may be confessed that occasionally, as with the terrible Ladies Busshe and Culmer of *The Egoist*, and with the Peridons and Pemptons of the Radnors' music-making circle, they approach mere formulæ, impossible of recognition. But we must pass over the tempting opportunities for insight into Meredith's art which are afforded even by failures of this kind, and be content with selecting two aspects of character peculiarly illustrative of his power.

The first is one familiar enough in life to make its unfamiliarity in fiction a proof of the extreme difficulty of portraying it. The warmth, the freshness, the fragrant charm so often worn by middle age are qualities that only the most sensitive art can catch in their likeness and unlikeness to the same qualities as worn by youth. Their representation is a matter of half-tones and veiled lights which elude any but the lightest hand. Many a practised novelist can draw the sympathetic elements of character which belong essentially to middle life and are born of it; but Meredith, in such sketches as Dorothy Beltham and Rosamund Culling does much more than this. He draws youthfulness that remains young and desirable though shadowed and softened by time. Our modern idea of the point reasonably to be called the *mezzo del cammin*,[1] is of course a great deal more generous than that of our grandfathers; and Dorothy, at any rate, may perhaps be regarded as middle-aged only in the same sense as Anne Elliot, who, as we know, had resigned all pretensions to youth long before she was thirty. But the actual number of ascribed years do not affect the question. Anne is middle-aged because Jane Austen so conceived her; and we may place not only Dorothy but the beautiful heroine of the *Tale of Chloe*, that fine picture of tragic passion in a setting of the most fantastic rococo, in the same category. But Meredith's supreme triumph in this connection is the figure of Nataly in *One of Our Conquerors*. Here we have a portrait, full and complete, which probably could not be paralleled in our literature. In her Meredith achieved the feat of describing one of his own young heroines—for Nataly in her youth would have been unmistakably a subject for him—leaving her all her buoyant beauty, yet enriching it with difficult experience. Thackeray no doubt did something of the same kind in drawing Lady Castlewood, but his task was an easier one by the extent to which his view of femininity was narrower. By the time he imagined Nataly, Meredith had long ago emancipated the heroine of fiction from her obligation to square with the earlier view of her as incurably, charmingly unjust and capricious

---

[1] Dante, *Inferno*, ix, 1: 'middle of the way'.

and jealous. She was built upon finer lines by now and demanded a more comprehensive insight.

The other aspect of Meredith's command of character which we will single out shall be his unique grasp of international contrast. No one else has ventured to bring men and women of other languages so freely to the front of the picture as did the creator of Ottilia and Vittoria and Renée, of Dr Julius von Karsteg and Mr Pericles and Carlo Ammiani. Meredith's keen sense for what is English was sharpened by his strong appreciation of complementary qualities to be looked for elsewhere. He carried his discriminations too far, perhaps, in his insistence on the somewhat arbitrary antithesis between Celt and Saxon; his fondness for tracing certain sterling qualities to a Welsh strain was possibly a little more loyal than critical. But in the wider field his perception was that of a man who dealt directly with life and accepted no conventional figments. The individual charm of their different countries is expressed in Ottilia, Vittoria, Renée, as ripely as is the English spirit in Lucy and Rose Jocelyn and Janet Ilchester. And for vigorous criticism, digging to the roots of character, the questioning to which Harry Richmond is subjected in his midnight colloquy with Dr Julius shows Meredith at his full strength. This scene in particular is so indicative of Meredith's personal point of view that a few sentences may be quoted:

[Quotes *Harry Richmond*, xxix, from 'He sent out quick spirts' to 'all in a rut" '.]

The whole of this admirably expressive chapter reveals the rich and trenchant mind of the author himself. It yields a clue to the recognition of the embracing plan to which all Meredith's work was ever related. 'Yes, yes, I comprehend', says Dr Julius a little later; 'your country breeds honourable men, chivalrous youngsters. . . . It's not enough—not enough. I want to see a mental force, energy of brain'. There we have it. All gifts of character, good dispositions and good intentions, vigour and perseverance, love and pride and chivalry—there is nothing that may not crumble to calamity, the best to the worst, where the initial impulse is not started by a clear and candid brain. It is brain only that can point the way, brain only that can utilize aright all the conflicting elements received by us from nature, none of which can man afford to suppress and to none altogether to trust himself. Life is not so simple a matter as the rejection of one-half of nature and a blind faith in the other; our task is nothing so simple as a flat discrimination between good and evil, each bearing an unqualified title. Blood, brain, and spirit—so Meredith figured the great triad on the harmonization of which our lives have to be built; and if the discerning principle of brain is not incessantly active and vigilant the true chord will never be struck. All the tragedy and comedy of Meredith's creative work revolves round this central doctrine. It is present in his wit and in his irony, in his fierce exposure of sentimentalism, in his insistence on the rottenness of pride that is grounded in egoism; it is present in his glorification of freedom and sanity, and in the imperishable beauty of his lovers' idylls. 'Trace these spirited actions and these fine raptures to their roots', he seems to say. 'If they spring from the sound understanding that is ready to give each side of our nature its due, and no more than its due, all will be well. But if character has been stunted or warped by any failure to see life in its true proportions, then expect disaster'.

The doctrine is expanded and reiterated to the last fullness in his poetry. It is here that we find, varied in a hundred different moods and strains, and in a form so elaborately symbolised that it is possible perhaps to read too much into it, his view of earth as the beginning and end of man, the universal origin to which humanity must be ever attuned. It is easy to lay a too mystical interpretation on Meredith's magnificent homage to earth the mother of man. His personification of her is his recognition of the example to man in the undeviating sanity of nature. The reckless waste and cruelty of nature does not disturb him. The grandeur of the life outside ourselves is for him its poised deliberation, its self-centred completeness, its univeral g rasp.

> Never in woods
> Runs white insanity fleeing itself: all sane
> The woods revolve: as the tree its shadowing limns
> To some resemblance in motion, the rooted life
> Restrains disorder: you hear the primitive hymns
> Of earth in woods issue wild of the web of strife.
> ('Melampus.')

To this great example then let man conform himself, remembering ever that the intellectual and spiritual in him is drawn from earth as surely as the physical. The animality in man readily confesses its parentage; and the mistake of the ascetic, a mistake as abhorrent to the mind of Meredith as that of the sensualist, is to set up an antagonism between the material and the immaterial, to assert that one must be destroyed as base-born and the other enthroned as of diviner origin.

Spirit is as sour and thin in divorce from the body as the body is gross and ugly in divorce from spirit. Body and spirit are divine by the same divinity; and the test of manhood is to think and act, above all else to love, with a just understanding of both. Through all Meredith's 'nature poems' this theme is the under-current; its final expression is to be found in the grave and stately measure of 'A Reading of Life'.

The same theme is touched at a different point by the 'Hymn to Colour'. Reason about it, test it, disprove it as we may, the spirituality of earthly things remains for the human mind an abiding fact. Language may lay hold of it and riddle it through and show that it has no true substance; and yet it is known to all of us at moments that something not to be netted by language survives and escapes. As magnetism transfuses dead metal, so in beauty there is an essence and an influence which eludes our closest definition of beauty itself. It is for this, the intangible aura which hangs round beauty, that poetry exists; and poetry can render it only by symbols and imagery. And so in the 'Hymn to Colour' it is pictured as the transient moment of dawn, seen through the eyes that are the most poignantly quickened to seize it, the eyes of Love:

> Love eyed his rosy memories: he sang:
> O bloom of dawn, breathed up from the gold sheaf
> Held springing beneath Orient! that dost hang
> The space of dewdrops running over leaf;
> Thy fleetingness is bigger in the ghost
>   Than Time with all his host!
> Of thee to say behold, has said adieu:
> But love remembers how the sky was green,
> And how the grasses glimmered lightest blue;
> How saint-like grey took fervour: how the screen
> Of cloud grew violet; how thy moment came
>   Between a blush and flame.

As colour in the world of nature, the shafts of rose and gold which bring day out of night, so is the spirit in man's life, the spirit without which life itself is dead. And love being the highest and widest and greatest of man's capacities, it is in love that the absence of the spirit is most a disaster and its presence an enchantment.

Finally, brushing through our modern tangle of doubts and hesitations, salting the labours of heart and brain, comes the health-giving force which Meredith invoked as the spirit of comedy. 'Sword of common sense', he apostrophized it; he was never tired of insisting that the best of things are the better for liberal seasonings of laughter. He was no doubt, in the strict sense, an optimist, if we care, indeed, to use so exhausted a title; but the word as trivially used, to denote the temperament that slides lightly over sin and sorrow, denying the power of either, has no application for him. He perfectly saw that the simple central life which he upheld grows harder with the growth of the world and that the duty of brain to carve a shapely existence out of our huge legacy of advancing knowledge and increasing bewilderment becomes the heavier as we drive, 'shell and spirit', the further into the void. The more need therefore that brain itself should be purged and fortified by that power of laughter which reminds us that, though self-consciousness is our pride and our distinction, it is also our ineluctable curse. We have learnt to survey ourselves, and there is no fear that we shall not find the sight absorbing. But there is the fear that we may dwell on it with such loving interest as to forget how relative is our importance; and equally in these days there is the fear of obsession by the horrors of the spectacle, till we magnify out of all proportion the strange disabilities which undermine our strength. Laughter purifies the air and corrects the dangerous refraction of our vision. Even in that sombre and difficult tragedy, to which Meredith gave the bitter name of 'Modern Love', the irony that watches the death and burial of passion has the securely anchored sanity which we owe to the same great gift. And if it has virtue in tragedy, how much more certainly will it sweeten the beauty of hope and joy, where these have found their fulfilment. Its final and perfect effect is in the clear ring and flawless brilliance of 'Love in the valley'.

Such, in summary outline, was the work and temper of a high and many-sided genius. His death we may readily see as the close of a great period of literature. His long career started in the days when romance was still supreme in art, and romance, with all its powers and all its limitations, was the material in which he wrought. Art has put on since those days so new a panoply that an artist, as we now understand the word, Meredith undoubtedly was not. That there is much splendid art scattered through his books the preceding pages have tried to show; but the restraining hand, the deliberate design, the critical sense of perfection, these are not to be found. More comprehensive still, the single-minded attitude of the artist before his work, his unqualified homage to it and it alone—this too was wanting. Yet with the literature of the past before us we must admit that romance did in its eagerness plunge its fingers more generously into life than art nowadays seems to have the secret of doing. Meredith's profusion, his exuberance, his ever-shaping imagination, his pomp of poetry, survived into a generation to whom such qualities as these have all the heroic fascination of a past more spacious and more intensely coloured than the present. Those who are gone are always greater than those who remain—this we may recognize and concede. But in a more special sense we may realize that with Meredith died the last of his race. In art his aims are no longer ours, nor in life perhaps his creed; yet the further we may diverge from either, the more clearly we must perceive the strength and beauty which crowned so widely based and so living a work.

126. H. G. Wells on *One of Our Conquerors* in *The New Machiavelli*

1911; 'Adolescence', 7

H. G. Wells (1866–1946) seems to have preserved a high opinion of Meredith throughout his life. In his early days as a reviewer for *Saturday Review* he frequently referred to Meredith's work with respect. This passage from *The New Machiavelli* shows an unusual understanding of some aspects of *One of Our Conquerors* and describes its effect on Wells's contemporaries.

A book that stands out among these memories, that stimulated me immensely so that I forced it upon my companions, half in the spirit of propaganda and half to test it by their comments, was Meredith's *One of Our Conquerors*. It is one of the books that have made me. In that I got a supplement and corrective of Kipling. It was the first detached and adverse criticism of the Englishman I had ever encountered. It must have been published already nine or ten years when I read it. The country had paid no heed to it, had gone on to the expensive lessons of the War because of the dull aversion our people feel for all such intimations, and so I could read it as a book justified. The war endorsed its every word for me, underlined each warning indication of the gigantic dangers that gathered against our system across the narrow seas. It discovered Europe to me, as watching and critical.

But while I could respond to all its criticisms of my country's intellectual indolence, of my country's want of training and discipline and moral courage, I remember that the idea that on the continent there were other peoples going ahead of us, mentally alert while we fumbled, disciplined while we slouched, aggressive and preparing to bring our Imperial pride to a reckoning, was extremely novel and distasteful to me. It set me worrying of nights. It put all my projects for social and political reconstruction upon a new uncomfortable footing. It made them no longer merely desirable but urgent. Instead of pride and the love of making one might own to a baser motive. Under Kipling's sway I had a little forgotten the continent of Europe, treated it as a mere envious echo to our own world-wide displays. I began now to have a disturbing sense as it were of busy searchlights over the horizon. . . .

One consequence of the patriotic chagrin Meredith produced in me was an attempt to belittle his merit. 'It isn't a good novel, anyhow', I said.

The charge I brought against it was, I remember, a lack of unity. It professed to be a study of the English situation in the early nineties, but it was all deflected, I said, and all the interest was confused by the story of Victor Radnor's fight with society to vindicate the woman he had loved and never married. Now in the retrospect and with a mind full of bitter enlightenment, I can do Meredith justice, and admit the conflict was not only essential but cardinal in his picture, that the terrible inflexibility of the rich aunts and the still more terrible claim of Mrs Burman Radnor, the 'infernal punctilio', and Dudley Sowerby's limitations, were the central substance of that inalertness the book set itself to assail. So many things have been brought together in my mind that were once remotely separated. A people that will not valiantly face and understand and admit love and passion can understand nothing whatever. But in those days what is now just obvious truth to me was altogether outside my range of comprehension. . . .

APPENDIX I

Robert Louis Stevenson on Meredith

1882–94

Robert Louis Stevenson (1850–94) was one of those most influential in spreading the name of Meredith among the public. His own reputation made his published comments important. Stevenson's first meeting with Meredith (reported by Alice Brandreth (Lady Butcher, *Memories of George Meredith*, 1919)), took place in April 1878. The relationship which followed was warm, involving passionate admiration on Stevenson's part. His manner of thought coincided with Meredith's in several ways and he was deeply influenced by the older writer. (See also Introduction for Stevenson's comment on Meredith to a San Francisco journalist.)

From a letter to W. E. Henley, April 1882:

Talking of Meredith, I have just re-read for the third and fourth time *The Egoist*. When I shall have read it the sixth or seventh, I begin to see I shall know about it. You will be astonished when you come to re-read it; I had no idea of the matter—human, red matter he has contrived to plug and pack into that strange and admirable book. Willoughby is, of course, a pure discovery; a complete set of nerves, not heretofore examined, and yet running all over the human body—a suit of nerves. Clara is the best girl ever I saw anywhere. Vernon is almost as good. The manner and the faults of the book greatly justify themselves on further study. Only Dr Middleton does not hang together; and Ladies Busshe and Culmer *sont des monstruosités*. Vernon's conduct makes a wonderful odd contrast with Daniel Deronda's. I see more and more that Meredith is built for immortality.

From 'Books Which Have Influenced Me', *British Weekly*, 13 May 1887:

I should never forgive myself if I forgot *The Egoist*. It is art, if you like, but it belongs purely to didactic art, and from all the novels I have read (and I have read thousands) stands in a place by itself. Here is a Nathan for the modern David; here is a book to send the blood into men's faces. Satire, the angry picture of human faults, is not great art; we can all be angry with our neighbour; what we want is to be shown, not his defects, of which we are too conscious, but his merits, to which we are too blind. And *The Egoist* is a satire; so much must be allowed; but it is a satire of a singular quality, which tells you nothing of that obvious mote, which is engaged from first to last with that invisible beam. It is yourself that is hunted down; these are your own faults that are dragged into the day and numbered, with lingering relish, with cruel cunning and precision. A young friend of Mr Meredith's (as I have the story) came to him in an agony. 'This is too bad of you', he cried. 'Willoughby is me'! 'No, my dear fellow', said the author; 'he is all of us'. I have read *The Egoist* five or six times myself, and I mean to read it again; for I am like the young friend of the anecdote—I think Willoughby an unmanly but a very serviceable exposure of myself.

From 'A Gossip on Romance', *Memories and Portraits* (1887):

The last interview between Lucy and Richard Feverel is pure drama; more than that, it is the strongest scene, since Shakespeare, in the English tongue. Their first meeting by the river, on the other hand, is pure romance; it has nothing to do with character; it might happen to any other boy and maiden, and be none the less delightful for the change. And yet I think he would be a bold man who should choose between these passages. Thus, in the same book, we may have two scenes, each capital in its order: in the one, human passion, deep calling unto deep, shall utter its genuine voice; in the second, according circumstances, like instruments in tune, shall build up a trivial but desirable incident, such as we love to prefigure for ourselves; and in the end, in spite of the critics, we may hesitate to give the preference to either. The one may ask more genius—I do not say it does; but at least the other dwells as clearly in the memory.

From a Letter to Henry James, March 1888:

I was vexed at your account of my admired Meredith: I wish I could
go and see him; as it is I will try to write; and yet (do you understand
me?) there is something in that potent, *genialisch* affectation that puts
one on the strain even to address him with a letter. He is not an easy
man to be your self with; there is so much of him, and the veracity and
the high athletic intellectual humbug are so intermixed.

From a letter to W. B. Yeats, 14 April 1894:

Some ten years ago, a . . . spell was cast upon me by Meredith's 'Love
in the Valley'; the stanzas beginning 'When her mother tends her'
haunted me and made me drunk like wine; and I remember waking
with them all the echoes of the hills about Hyères.

APPENDIX II

George Gissing on Meredith

1885–95

Gissing's first contact with Meredith was when the latter acted as publisher's reader for the Ms. of *The Unclassed* in 1883. At that time Gissing did not identify the reader as Meredith, but got to know him shortly afterwards and remained friendly with him till the end of his life.

From a letter to his brother, 14 March 1885:

You have seen the review of Meredith's new novel in the *Athenaeum*. Is it not amazing that the man is so little known or read? He is great, there is no doubt of it, but too difficult for the British public.

From a letter to his brother, 29 April 1885:

By hook or crook get hold of *Diana of the Crossways*. The book is right glorious. Shakespeare in modern English; but, mind you, to be read twice, if need be, thrice. There is a preface, which is a plea for philosophic fiction, an admirable piece of writing, the English alone rendering it worthy of the carefullest pondering. More 'brain stuff' in the book, than many I have read for long.

From a letter to his brother, October 1885:

It is incomprehensible that Meredith is so neglected. George Eliot never did such work, and Thackeray is shallow in comparison.

From a letter to his brother, 9 October 1885:

I have in hand George Meredith's *Evan Harrington*. Chapman is publishing a new one-volume edition of Meredith's works. I have read most of them and shall now go through them again. It is amazing that such a man is so neglected. For the last thirty years he has been producing work unspeakably above the best of any living writer and yet no one reads him outside a small circle of highly cultured people. Perhaps that is better than being popular, a hateful word. You must read him someday, but not till you have prepared yourself by much other study.

From a letter to Edward Bertz, 2 December 1892:

I suppose that Meredith is the strongest literary man, all things considered, at present among us. I do not feel enthusiastic about his novels, but I recognize his great power of characterization, and the profoundness of his intellectual glance. He has done fine things in poetry, too; but his latest verse is more obscure than the worst of Browning. Obscurity in poetry is a contradiction in terms.

From a letter to Edward Bertz, 22 September 1895:

He is a man of high culture, and most liberal mind. His philosophy is wonderfully bright and hopeful. A scholar, he yet thinks the best of Democracy, and believes that emancipated human-kind will do greater things than the old civilization permitted. There is a fine dignity about him, and I feel proud to sit in his room.

Select Bibliography

The following is a chronological list of items relating to the history of Meredith's reception in Europe and America.

1890   Richard Le Gallienne's *George Meredith: Some Characteristics*, with notes on Meredith's reception in America by W. M. Fullerton and a Bibliography by John Lane.

1909   M. B. Forman, *George Meredith: Some Early Appreciations*. Sir J. A. Hammerton, *George Meredith in Anecdote and Criticism.*

1910   E. J. Bailey, *Meredith in America: a Comment and a Bibliography*, in *Studies in Language and Literature in Celebration of the Seventieth Birthday of James Morgan Hart.*

1918   S. M. Ellis, *George Meredith: His Life and Friends.*

1923   R. Galland, *George Meredith and British Criticism.*

1950   D. D. Bailey, 'American Literary Criticism of George Meredith' (unpublished doctoral thesis for the University of Wisconsin).

1954   H. B. Staples, 'English Literary Criticism of George Meredith's Works, 1886–1951' (unpublished doctoral thesis for the University of California).

1960   L. T. Hergenham, 'A Critical Consideration of the Reviews of the Novels of George Meredith . . .' (unpublished doctoral thesis for the University of London).

M. B. Forman's *Meredithiana, being a Supplement to the Bibliography of George Meredith* (1924), though incomplete and sometimes innacurate, is indispensable. In view of the date at which it was composed, it is an admirable work of scholarship.

Index

II. PERIODICALS AND NEWSPAPERS

III. NAMES AND TITLES

Barham, R. A., 292
Barrie, J. M., 13, 14, 323, 325, 332, 333, 335, 336, 339, 341, 342
Barry, W., 15
Baudelaire, C., 295, 487
Beddoes, T. L., 35, 36
Bell, Currer, *see* Brontë, C.
Bentley, G., 176
Béranger, P.-J., 99
Berlioz, L.-H., 484
Besant, Sir Walter, 315
Bizet, A.-C.-L., 412
Boileau, Despréaux, N., 470
Boudoir Cabal, The, 177
Bourne, E., 338
Bourne, Vinney, *see* Bourne, E.
Braddon, M., 4, 124
Bradshaw, G., 150
Brontë, C., 47, 390
Brooke, H., 84
Broughton, R., 177
Browning, E. B., 29, 38
Browning, R., 9, 10, 13 , 28, 29, 60, 92, 103, 171, 177, 187–8, 192–3, 225, 233, 245, 273, 313, 316, 337, 352, 363, 365, 383, 395, 412–13, 449, 453, 455, 474, 477, 480, 481, 489, 495, 497, 505, 510, 524
Buchanan, R. W., 315, 317, 332
Butler, A. J., 7, 155, 167
Byron, G. G., Lord, 92, 176, 437, 494

Call, W. M. W., 37
Called Back, 275
Canterbury Tales, 176
Carlyle, T., 125, 176, 179, 202, 212, 233, 243, 279, 308, 309, 313, 354, 370, 449, 453, 455, 462, 475, 489, 492, 495, 505
Carr, W. C., 9, 182
Carroll, Lewis, 17, 476
Cataline, 176
Cecil, H. M., 16, 412

Cervantes, M. de, 207, 226, 452
Chapman and Hall, 12, 281
Chesterton, G. K., 491, 492
Childe Roland, 490
Chorley, H. F., 59
Clough, A. H., 28
Coleridge, S. T., 360
Collins, W., 4, 7, 134
Confessions of a Young Man, 312
Congreve, W., 109
Conway, H., 275
Correggio, A. A., 37
Count of Monte Cristo, The, 134
Count Robert of Paris, 408
Courtney, W. L., 12, 281, 332, 333, 335
Cousine Bette, La, 204
Cousin Pons, Le, 204
Craigie, P. M. T., 439, 491
Crotchet Castle, 230

Daniel Deronda, 234
Dante, 135, 155, 253, 278, 338, 345, 387, 452, 513
Darwin, C., 491
Daughter of Heth, A, 342
Davray, H., 21, 458
Deckar, *see* Dekker, T.
Defoe, D., 53
Dekker, T., 28
Dickens, C., 2, 13, 47, 83, 188, 295, 308, 318, 331, 355, 368, 380, 422, 461, 492, 495
Dickins, F. V., 270
Disraeli, B., Earl of Beaconsfield, 145
Dobson, A., 337
Don Juan, 92, 106, 261
Donne, J., 457, 480, 489
Dowden, E., 326
Doyle, Sir A. Conan, 330
Dryden, J., 468, 489
Du Maurier, G., 384, 491
Dumas, A., 134, 295

THE CRITICAL HERITAGE SERIES

GENERAL EDITOR: B. C. SOUTHAM

Volumes published and forthcoming